INDIA'S WARS I

Praise for *India's Wars I*

'Arjun Subramaniam is a remarkable soldier-scholar who combines an avid interest in history with keen strategic insights. He writes with great clarity and balance on India's modern conflicts. His sound history fills a major lacuna in the field of contemporary Indian history and could contribute to a more informed formulation of policy and strategy in the future.'

– Sugata Bose, Member of Parliament and Gardiner Professor of Oceanic History and Affairs at Harvard University

'Military history is a seriously under-researched field in India. This outstanding book on India's military conflicts since Independence is, therefore, very welcome. As a scholar-practitioner, Air Vice Marshal Arjun Subramaniam is uniquely qualified, and both aspects of his background are revealed to good effect in his book. The close attention to the technical and organizational aspects of the armed forces, combined with a rich and nuanced analysis of the conflicts themselves, makes for compelling as well as instructive reading.'

– Ramachandra Guha, historian and author

'Deftly telescoping six decades of India's conflicts in a single volume, Arjun Subramaniam presents an objective and compelling tri-service narrative which I found hard to put down. He joins a select band of service officers who have, in the tradition of Thucydides, shown the intellectual acumen as well as courage and perseverance to put pen to paper while still in uniform.'

– Admiral Arun Prakash (retd), former Chief of Naval Staff and Chairman, Chiefs of Staff Committee

'Air Vice Marshal Arjun Subramaniam's deep insights into the first twenty-five years of independent India's military history fill a big gap in our understanding of modern India's political evolution. As Delhi rises to be one of the world's leading economic and military powers,

Subramaniam's narrative contributes to the construction of a more productive discourse on India's strategic future.'

– C. Raja Mohan, foreign affairs columnist and director, Carnegie India

'Considering the scope and nature of conflicts that the Indian armed forces have engaged in since Independence, presenting a narrative within a tri-service perspective is a daunting task by any measure. Air Vice Marshal Arjun Subramaniam has rendered yeoman service to the profession of arms and to the idea of 'jointmanship' that will need to be the bedrock of military operations in the future. Very well researched and authenticated with exhaustive interviews, striking photographs and detailed maps, the narrative meets the rigour of academic discourse. It certainly has the potential to form part of the curriculum for study of contemporary Indian military history at war colleges and universities. It is what many of us would call a "labour of love", by a person who has enjoyed being in the profession of arms, and has therefore tried to place its achievements, and, I dare say, inadequacies, in the public domain for the greater benefit of society in general, and the Indian armed forces in particular.'

– Lieutenant General Satish Nambiar (retd)

'A well-researched, well-written, very readable account of the development of the Indian armed forces over the last 300-plus years and, particularly, their performance during the wars fought in independent India up to 1971. The book is a saga of the spirit and commitment of the Indian armed forces in spite of being consistently surprised by our adversaries and forever low on resources. The author has often trodden virgin ground and produced what can only be termed as a "special work", peppered with his personal views, that will intrigue and interest the lay reader and the professional. Any such work has to rely on books and interviews, and history is a many sided study. Some disagreements on details are likely, but that does not detract from the quality of the essential narrative. The author deserves kudos and accolades.'

– Air Marshal Vinod Patney (retd)

'For too long, the military contribution to India's post-Independence development has been underplayed in standard histories. Arjun Subramaniam provides a detailed, thoughtful and compelling view of this missing factor in understanding the turbulent years after 1947. A valuable and innovative work of history.'

– Rana Mitter, professor and director of the China Centre at Oxford University

'Arjun Subramaniam deserves praise for diligence and resolve in delivering his maiden opus in the midst of a busy military career.'

– *Asian Age*

'The author has maintained a detached, scholarly approach, devoid of service and regimental loyalties or even patriotic emotions. To that extent, the book is a benchmark.'

– *Indian Express*

'This latest book on the military history of post-Independence Indian Armed Forces is special because of the passion with which the author has woven a well-researched and factual account of the wars with what he calls the DNA of each wing of the armed forces.'

– *Hindu*

'The book communicates well as it is written in a style that makes the complex subject of India's wars easy to read and understand and hence accessible to the common man even as it draws a delicate line between the popular narrative and academic research.'

– *Tribune*

INDIA'S WARS I

A MILITARY HISTORY

1947–1971

ARJUN SUBRAMANIAM

HarperCollins *Publishers* India

First published by HarperCollins *Publishers* in 2016
4th Floor, Tower A, Building No. 10, DLF Cyber City,
DLF Phase II, Gurugram, Haryana – 122002
www.harpercollins.co.in

This edition published 2025

2 4 6 8 10 9 7 5 3 1

P-ISBN: 978-93-5177-749-6
E-ISBN: 978-93-5177-750-2

Typeset in 10.5/13.5 Adobe Caslon Pro
By Saanvi Graphics Noida

Printed and bound at
Replika Press Pvt. Ltd.

Khudadad Khan | Indra Lal Roy
Prem Bhagat | N. Krishnan
D. Shanker | Jumbo Majumdar
Arjan Singh | P.C. Lal | Moolgavkar
Sam Manekshaw | Thimayya
Inder Gill | Somnath Sharma
Mohd Usman | Mehar Singh
Hari Chand | Joginder Singh
Shaitan Singh | Harbaksh Singh

Dedicated to
India's Soldiers, Sailors and Air Warriors

Tarapore | Abdul Hamid
Devayya | Johnny Greene
Ranjit Singh Dayal | Sartaj Singh
Sagat Singh | Nirmaljit Sekhon
Chandan Singh | Arun Khetarpal
Albert Ekka | Bharat Kavina
Mahendra Nath Mulla
Hoshiar Singh | Vinod Patney
Arun Prakash | W.A.G. Pinto
and many more...

CONTENTS

Part V: Conclusion

PART I

OPENING PERSPECTIVES

Major
Hoshiar Singh

Flying Officer Nirmaljit
Singh Sekhon *(posthumous)*

Lance Naik Albert Ekka
(posthumous)

Second Lieutenant
Arun Khetarpal *(posthumous)*

The four Param Vir Chakra winners from the 1971 war

1

SIGHTER BURST

In the old days when fighter pilots had the luxury of making multiple passes over the target areas during ground attack missions, they let loose what was called a sighter burst in their first pass to check whether their guns were firing properly or not. This burst also allowed them to size up the enemy, assess ranges and impose themselves psychologically on the enemy. As the first chapter in Part I ('Opening Perspectives') of the book, 'Sighter Burst' aims at none of the above. Instead, it attempts to give you, the reader, an overview of what to expect in the pages ahead. Old habits die hard, they say, and I could not but help looking at this project as a mission with four primary objectives.

The first is to showcase the legacy of modern India's military pioneers along with the exploits and sacrifices of its armed forces in protecting India's sovereignty and democracy to both an international readership and a bulging youthful segment of the country's population. My second objective is to chronicle the largely fragmented contemporary military history of India in the form of an easily readable joint narrative devoid of too many statistics, tables, graphs, or emphasis on casualties, claims and counter-claims. My third objective is to convince policymakers at all levels of the need to adopt a progressive approach towards declassifying material about national security and learning from the mistakes of previous wars, campaigns and conflicts, both external and internal. This would then, I sincerely hope, create a missing link between the study of military history and its impact on contemporary Indian strategic culture. My last objective is to urge not only India's men and women in uniform but also the growing number of informed and literate youth to read more about war and conflict in the subcontinent after Independence as part of India's overall historical discourse and draw inspiration from some of the brilliant military commanders of independent India.

Along the way, I hope to bring out some of the central themes of the book. Among these are the strong historical legacies, ethos and professionalism of the Indian armed forces; their slowness in shaking off colonial attitudes and legacies; their sustained contribution and sacrifice to maintain India's chaotic democracy; how they have coped with the changing contours of modern conflict; and why India's armed forces have emerged as a critical element of nation building – one which the nation at large can ill afford to ignore.

'A Personal Quest' is an honest attempt to share my personal experiences of soldiering over thirty-three years, and why I feel that not enough has been done to chronicle India's conflicts after Independence from a joint war-fighting perspective. The chapter is a tribute to my fellow warriors in olive green, white and blue. Their sacrifices on the battlefield so that their fellow countrymen may live in peace have no parallel in human endeavour. 'Whither Military History' briefly examines the multiple reasons for the absence of modern Indian military history from the larger historical discourse in the country.

Part II of the book looks at the 'DNA of India's Armed Forces'. It sets the pace for an introductory and evolutionary overview of the growth of the armed forces, and attempts to provide the reader with a snapshot of the Indian Army, Indian Air Force and Indian Navy from the early years of the modern era till India gained Independence from the British in 1947. Rather than attribute the entire DNA to a colonial legacy, an attempt has also been made to highlight the influence of late-medieval Indian military thought on military ethos.

Part III of the book comprises 'Teething Years'. It covers three principal conflicts during the early years after Independence – the first India–Pakistan war of 1947–48; the liberation of Hyderabad and Junagadh; and the short campaign to evict the Portuguese from Goa in December 1961. India's baptism as a nation state was by waging war against state-sponsored tribals and regular Pakistani forces, which attempted to exploit the rather precarious political situation in the state of Jammu and Kashmir and sever it from the Indian Union. Thousands of tribals from the North-West Frontier Province (NWFP), complemented by regulars of the newly formed Pakistan Army, united under the flag of Islam and raided Kashmir in October 1947. In a three-pronged attack aimed at capturing the whole of Kashmir and forcing the Maharaja of Kashmir to cede to Pakistan, the raiders surprised both the maharaja and the Indian government with the timing and audacity of their attack. In response to an SOS from the Maharaja of Kashmir to the Government of India, the conflict, which began as a rearguard action by the Indian Army and the Royal Indian Air Force to save the state capital, Srinagar, expanded into a full-blown conflict between India and Pakistan across three distinct geographical sectors that lasted over a year. The conflict only ended when a UN-brokered agreement was signed by India and Pakistan in late 1948 to peacefully resolve the Kashmir issue.

While the war was raging in Kashmir, the government had to launch a small but coercive military action against the princely state of Junagadh to force it to abandon its secessionist aspirations and join the Union of India. In September 1948 a larger military action involving an army division backed by air power was launched against the Nizam of Hyderabad to compel him to abandon his grandiose plans of ruling over an independent state that was surrounded by the Union of India. While the Hyderabad military campaign was later termed a 'police action', from a strategic perspective it merits attention as India's first successful attempt at coercion orchestrated by an assertive home minister, Sardar Vallabhbhai Patel.

After almost thirteen years of relative peace and failed attempts by India to reach a negotiated settlement with the Portuguese over the colonies of Goa, Daman and Diu, a multi-pronged, tri-service operation code-named Operation Vijay was launched in December 1961 to evict the Portuguese from India and bring an end to centuries of colonial rule in India. Though the operation was a success and resulted in some chest-thumping by the Indian military, it deflected some amount of national attention from a more pressing security problem that was brewing on India's northern and eastern frontiers with China.

Part IV of the book is titled 'Across Borders' and deals with India's experiences with full-blown conventional conflict in diverse terrain along borders with hostile neighbours. It begins with the India–China war of 1962, which was fought over vast expanses of mountainous and jungle terrain. The narrative then shifts focus to the two large-scale wars with Pakistan in 1965 and 1971, which were fought over mountainous terrain in Jammu and Kashmir; across the plains of Punjab; in the riverine areas of East Pakistan; and, finally, southwards across the deserts of Rajasthan and swamps of Kutch.

India's inability to gauge China's grand strategy in the 1950s and understand its key determinants of securing historically unsettled frontiers, resolving border disputes from a position of strength, and building capabilities for pan-Asian hegemony resulted in the ill-fated conflict of 1962. An objective analysis of the entire conflict from a politico-intelligence and military viewpoint with key input from diverse stakeholders could put the conflict in the right perspective and offer some lessons for the future.

Still smarting from the inability to force the secession of Kashmir in 1947–48, Pakistan's aggressive politico-military leadership led by their young and aggressive foreign minister, Zulfiqar Ali Bhutto, and a fading military dictator, Ayub Khan, took the opportunity to surprise India in the western swamps of Kutch and the state of Jammu and Kashmir during April and August 1965. The September 1965 conflict with Pakistan across three battlefronts was actually 'a baptism by fire' for India's almost non-existent joint war-fighting capability. Though many tactical and operational assessments over the years pointed at a stalemate, the inability of Pakistan to achieve any of its strategic objectives may well be considered a 'victory' for India and helped it regain much of its confidence in terms of the battleworthiness of its armed forces.

The 1970s began with a decisive strategic and military success for India in the two-front 1971 war against Pakistan. The Indian armed forces not only resoundingly defeated the Pakistani armed forces in the eastern sector with a clinical display of joint war-fighting prowess and paved the way for the formation of Bangladesh, they also notched up limited successes in the western sector with armoured thrusts, effective employment of air power and telling maritime attacks against critical infrastructure in West Pakistan. The 1971 conflict is also India's best documented conflict, which only re-emphasizes a stark reality that India's strategic and military establishment is largely comfortable with recording military victories and strategic game plans that have worked.

The narrative then attempts to look at how Kautilya, ancient India's foremost strategist, would have assessed India's modern conflicts till 1971. Revered in India much as Sun Tzu is in China, or Machiavelli and Clausewitz are in Europe, bringing Kautilya into the discourse is a tribute to his foresight and strategic acumen.

This book is not a definitive compilation of individual service, regimental, fleet or squadron histories and accomplishments; nor is it an attempt to highlight the achievements of a select set of regiments or individuals. I have the greatest respect for the regimental, fleet and squadron ethos of the Indian Army, the Indian Navy and the Indian Air Force. If any regiment or squadron has been highlighted more than the others, it is without any motive or malice. I take full responsibility for all omissions as the challenge was to put together a concise volume. While there are a reasonable number of primary sources, the book is drawn mostly from secondary sources, and I have used them to create a new synthesis of India's military history during the early years after Independence. I have offered enough references and suggested further reading for those who wish to dig deeper for I have just scratched the surface of what has actually been a fascinating period of evolving military history. I claim no new revelations based on archival or documentary research, or access to any classified information; and rather than sources, I believe that the core of the book revolves around the innovative nature of my argument and a conviction that as a scholar, I have the freedom to dissect and analyse issues of diplomacy and higher strategy and challenge status quo when it comes to sticking to academic rigidity that often limits a practitioner-scholar's horizons. Weaving in myriad issues of statecraft into military history is essential if one is to get a holistic perspective of wars and conflict. Writing in his latest book on broad-spectrum strategy titled *Strategy: A History*, Sir Lawrence Freedman argues:

> Research for this book has taken me into unfamiliar territory. Part of the enjoyment of writing this book has come from my exposure to

> some wonderful scholarship in social science and fields supposedly distant from my own. Despite the best efforts of colleagues I have undoubtedly over-reached in a number of areas. Nonetheless, the exercise has reinforced my conviction that academics worry too much about making a good impression within their own disciplinary boundaries while not paying enough attention to what is going on beyond them.[1]

I can take heart from Sir Freedman's thoughts on crossing 'domain boundaries'.

The thrust, throughout the book, has been to discuss in a layered manner, much like peeling an orange, numerous facets of higher strategy, operational art and tactical joint operations through the lens of the major participants. The flavour of the book revolves around people and not just events. As these stories unfold, they will, I hope, reinvigorate the spirit of soldiering and 'Jointmanship'. For a first-time reader of modern Indian military history, 'Jointmanship' is a term exclusively used within the Indian armed forces to highlight synergy and interoperability between the three services. It is said to have been clearly articulated some time in 2001 at the Defence Services Staff College, Wellington, in the salubrious Nilgiris district of Tamil Nadu – the first truly joint Staff College in the world – as 'Integrated planning and application of military power at the strategic, operational and tactical levels, with proper sequencing of combat power of the three services in time and space.'[2] Finally, I wish I could loiter over the target area for longer, but that would be inviting danger. I guess it is time for the 'first pass' after leaving you to ponder in an age of multi-skilling and multitasking over one of Vivekananda's[3] quotes that inspired me throughout the period I was researching and writing this volume: 'Take up one idea. Make that idea your life – think of it, dream of it, live on that idea. Let the brain, muscles, nerves, every part of the body be full of that idea, and leave every other idea alone. This is the way to success.'

2

A PERSONAL QUEST

I grew up on a staple diet of the great Indian epic Mahabharata, the Iliad, and *Readers Digest Illustrated Story of World War II*. Arjuna, the principal protagonist warrior of the Mahabharata, Achilles, Alexander, Shivaji – the defiant Maratha king of the seventeenth century – Napoleon, Rommel, Patton, Montgomery, Subhas Chandra Bose, Wingate and Douglas Bader were my heroes. The small and highly popular *Commando* comic series allowed me to wade through the Battles of Britain, Monte Casino (where an Indian division performed admirably), Alamein, Normandy, Coral Sea, Guadalcanal, Imphal and Kohima. I was a ten-year-old when India fought the 1971 war with Pakistan and Major Hoshiar Singh, Second Lieutenant Arun Khetarpal, Flying Officer Nirmaljit Singh Sekhon and Captain Mahendra Nath Mulla, India's heroes in that war, caught the attention of a grateful nation after their exploits in battle.

As a teenager at the Rashtriya Indian Military College (RIMC), a highly pedigreed military school with illustrious alumni that not only included four army chiefs and one air chief from independent India, but also two air chiefs from the Pakistan Air Force (PAF), history and geography were my favourite subjects. Even today when I read a military history campaign, I like having a map around; it gives you a sense of proportionality. Toynbee, Churchill and Nehru were my favourite historians, though I found them a little hard to digest. I found Romila Thapar, the noted Indian historian, easier to digest. I was dismayed, however, that she hardly referred to the exploits of independent India's military in her chapters on contemporary Indian history. However, I read all of them mainly because my father insisted I do so in his many long letters to me. He argued that if I really wanted to study the military dimension of history, I must arm myself well. Our history teacher introduced me to John Keegan when I complained to him that I could not lay my hands on any worthwhile book on Indian military history. Though he hardly wrote on Indian military history, I tracked the growth of John Keegan as a military historian of international repute and marvelled at his passion for the profession of arms despite not being in uniform. I would rediscover Keegan a few years before he passed away in 2012.

In a preface to one of his last books, he emotionally shared the various reasons that motivated him to devote a lifetime of endeavour to the study of modern British military history. As he narrates in the 'Introduction' to his superb book, *A History of Warfare*: 'I was not fated to be a warrior. A childhood illness had left me lame for life in 1948 and I have limped now for forty-five years.' He goes on to add: 'Fate nevertheless cast my life among warriors ... It aroused an interest in military affairs that took root, so that when I went up to Oxford in 1953 I chose military history as my special subject.' The end to his introduction makes for riveting reading and it is this paragraph that got me deeply thinking about our attitudes to warriors and warfare in the modern era. He writes: 'Soldiers are not as other men – that is the lesson I have learned from a life cast among warriors ... War undoubtedly connects, as the theorists demonstrate with economics and diplomacy and politics. Connection does not amount to identity or even similarity. War is wholly unlike diplomacy or politics because it must be fought by men whose values and skills are not those of politicians and diplomats ...' Though these views, expressed by him during an era of large conventional conflicts, are at variance with the Clausewitzian school of warfare, they nevertheless merit serious attention. The only difference I could detect now was that modern warfare demands that warriors acquire multiple skill sets including the ability to engage in diplomacy and provide governance when called on to do so, particularly in stability operations. The bottom line with John Keegan, of course, was a fascination and a deep respect for the profession of arms.

Despite the many wars and constant skirmishes and face-offs along its troubled northern and western borders, it was quite clear to me that the overwhelmingly dominant narrative of contemporary India's history since 1947 is of a country that operated internationally and domestically through deft diplomacy and peaceful democratic politics. Military history has mainly been a sideshow to the main political and diplomatic narrative.[1] This, to me, was a half-baked narrative even in school, and for years I have felt that the issue demanded closer scrutiny by India's historical community.

My personal tryst with India's recent military history began as a pilot officer in a MiG-21 training squadron in Tezpur in 1982; not as a participant, but as a distant observer. The 4 Corps headquarters was located in Tezpur and I not only had the opportunity to interact with officers who were involved in the ongoing counter-insurgency operations in the north-east, but also with a few civilians who had fled from Tawang and Bomdila and settled down in Tezpur following the 1962 conflict with China. The archives at Tezpur University had a small collection of memoirs and recollections of prominent citizens, which were collected after the 1962 war. I did manage to visit the university when I commanded a squadron at the same base in the late 1990s and browsed through some of the translations.

I was next posted at Adampur airbase near Jalandhar in the heart of Punjab during Operation Blue Star in 1984, the operation against Sant Bhindranwale, the separatist Sikh preacher, and his fierce militia. Many of my army course mates from the corps at Jalandhar were involved in operations which culminated in the storming of the Golden Temple in Amritsar, the holy shrine of the Sikhs where Bhindranwale had sought sanctuary, unmindful of the collateral danger he was subjecting thousands of innocent devotees to. The year 1985 saw me moving to another MiG-21 squadron, which participated in Operation Brass Tacks, the massive joint exercise on the western front with Pakistan and the brainchild of the mercurial chief of the army staff (COAS), General Sundarji. My squadron was at the time the only electronic warfare squadron in the IAF. We escorted Jaguar strike aircraft on simulated strikes along the international border (IB) with Pakistan and I will never forget the rush of adrenalin whenever our radar warning receivers (RWR) picked up F-16 radar signals, or when an excited fighter controller would give us a call 'Rapier formation to turn around, bogey at 12'o clock and closing in fast'.

I still remember the sheer audacity of the whole exercise, orchestrated as a show of force by General Sundarji, arguably one of the most visionary and brilliant soldiers of our time, though many whom I spoke to over the course of writing this book would not agree as they felt that he failed to understand or anticipate the changing nature of warfare.

Four of my fighter pilot contemporaries were selected in the mid-1980s to switch to the newly inducted Mi-25 attack helicopters. Little did they realize that they would hone their skills in the cauldron of Sri Lanka with the Indian Peacekeeping Force (IPKF). Fighting the LTTE (Liberation Tigers of Tamil Eelam) in the jungles of Jaffna, Vavuniya and Trincomalee changed their perspectives on modern warfare. Their experiences formed part of my PhD thesis on fourth-generation warfare. The 1990s were grim years for the Indian Army, particularly in Jammu and Kashmir (J&K). As part of a Mirage-2000 squadron we used to conduct patrols in the extreme northern portions of J&K whenever the proxy war with Pakistan escalated, attempting to draw out Pakistan F-16s from Chaklala, the closest Pakistani airbase in the area. As the political establishment sporadically debated 'hot pursuit' as a strategy to deter the proxy war strategy of Pakistan, we happily honed our operational procedures. One clear day, I remember being able to see Skardu from almost 30,000 feet as we approached the northernmost limit of our patrols, and wondered how we let go of it in 1948. I can also clearly recall in the early 1990s that while most Indian military commanders supported the idea of 'hot pursuit' as a strategy to counter Pakistan's proxy war in J&K and debated the issue extensively, very little was done on ground to operationally support such a strategy in terms of realigning joint force employment strategies with respect to rapid response; particularly in terms of exploiting the various Indian Air Force capabilities. This, arguably, made the political and strategic leadership uncomfortable about articulating 'hot pursuit' as a state policy of coercing Pakistan and making the price of supporting a proxy war in India too high to sustain.

When I moved on as the flight commander of a MiG-21 squadron in the mid 1990s, we often moved to the Kashmir Valley on summer detachments for valley-flying practice to the Avantipur airbase situated in the beautiful but troubled Pulwama district of the Kashmir Valley (it was earlier in the Anantnag district), which at the time was the epicentre of Pak-sponsored terrorism in the southern areas of the Valley. The airbase was located close to the headquarters of an Indian Army formation, which was engaged in counter-insurgency and counter-terrorism operations. I spent many free evenings at the army officers' mess, listening to friends talk about their numerous fierce encounters with foreign terrorists of Afghan and Pashtun stock in the Kashmir Valley, and along the Pir Panjal and Kishtwar ranges. Many of these foreign terrorist had operational experience in Afghanistan against the Russians in the 1980s; the officers grudgingly said that the foreign terrorists fought like tigers. I even sat as an observer during an interrogation session with one of them, chilled to the bone hearing his rationale for waging jihad against India. It was also during one of these detachments that I lost a course mate from the National Defence Academy (NDA) and a dear friend, Lieutenant Colonel Ajit Bhandarkar, in one of the fierce encounters that often raged in the Valley between army patrols and terrorists.

I will also never forget one crisp September morning when one of our young pilots sauntered across to me and literally demanded that I allow him to fly a sortie that I was slated to fly. Impressed with the lad's enthusiasm, I said, 'Go ahead, take my aircraft and have a ball!' The lad ejected in terrorist-infested terrain after his aircraft experienced severe technical glitches while recovering after a routine valley-flying mission. The speed with which the Indian Army launched the recovery operation with their best team set me deeply thinking about terrorism and the proxy war. I closely followed India's war on terror thereafter. I would do my dissertation entitled 'Protecting India against Terrorism' at the National Defence College twenty years later and publish a version of it in an international journal soon after.

My experiences with the Indian Navy were pretty exhilarating too. For many years in the 1990s, Western Naval Command used to play host to Mirage-2000s from Gwalior during annual fleet exercises off the Mumbai coast. I was posted to 1 Squadron flying Mirages and we used to operate from Goa, escorting Jaguars from Pune as they attempted to penetrate the solid air defence and electronic cordon around the aircraft carrier INS *Viraat*. While the Jaguars from 6 Squadron were comfortable flying at 100 feet above the sea, it took us a while to get used to the idea of having the salt spray spot your windshield from time to time. Skimming the waves was exhilarating, but the moment our radar warning receivers (RWRs) would start flashing and beeping, the good times over the sea would end and the business end of the mission would commence. While the cat-and-mouse game between us and the ring of screen ships protecting the carrier was always a challenge, the experience for me was more about getting to know the navy, its ethos and work ethics. The icing on the cake of course was a sortie I got to fly from the carrier on a Sea Harrier. Even though it was in the trainer and I hardly got to touch controls on the approach for landing on a bobbing and swaying deck in swirly conditions, I realized that flight deck operations from a carrier is probably the most exciting and hazardous experience in military aviation.

Like most active-duty fighter pilots who did not see action during the Kargil conflict with Pakistan, I was deeply disappointed. I envied my fellow 'Mirage boys', Nambi, Tiwi and the others who dropped laser-guided bombs (LGBs) on Tiger Hill and decimated a large logistics hub, Muntho Dalo, with unguided or 'iron bombs'; marvelled at the bravery of some of the Mi-17 aircrew who flew in hostile air space without much self-protection; and admired the doggedness of 17 Squadron, a MiG-21 reconnaissance squadron that took great risks in photographing the occupied heights around Kargil, Dras and Mushkoh, and then went on to fly risky bombing missions. I followed the Kargil air–land campaign closely – as an aviator during the conflict, and later as a military historian. A moderately critical piece on air–land operations was refreshingly published by a well-respected army journal without any cuts,[2] indicating changing mindsets within India's army-dominated military culture about air power's ability to influence warfare across the spectrum of conflict.

I must mention here that my renewed interest in chronicling India's modern wars was also influenced by the seriousness and solidity with which a Western air power historian, Dr Benjamin Lambeth, went about researching the Kargil war from an air power perspective. His monograph on the Kargil air war is by far the most authoritative and objective writing so far on the use of air power and joint operations in Kargil.[3]

After the barrage of criticism that followed the Kargil war regarding suboptimal inter-service cooperation, I discerned only superficial improvements in synergy. There were very few proactive and innovative approaches to joint war fighting in varied terrain. However, a limited offensive aerial action in mid-2002 by IAF Mirage fighter-bombers during Operation Parakram, the year-long face-off between India and Pakistan following the terrorist attack on the Indian parliament in December 2001, demonstrated some synergistic coercive capabilities, albeit against an intrusion into Indian territory. The fact that there is still not enough debate in India's institutions of professional education on whether the Kargil war could have been fought differently is worrisome, to say the least. By now questions should have been asked: Was it right to commit such a large force upfront without softening the targets adequately with artillery and aerial bombardment? Or, were our troops adequately prepared for a frontal assault? Or, why did the IAF need to evolve high-altitude bombing tactics only when confronted with a Kargil-like situation when they had operational high-altitude ranges available in Ladakh from 1986 onwards? I was a squadron commander in the north-east from 1999 to 2001 and I remember being tasked after the Kargil conflict to explore the operational feasibility of opening a high-altitude air-to-ground weapons range in Arunachal Pradesh. My flight commander and I flew sorties over that area in MiG-21s and found it fit for firing during the winter months when the range was snowbound. There was only one problem – the proximity to Tibet made it an uncomfortable geopolitical proposition even though it was a perfectly legitimate training requirement for the IAF.

As we entered the twenty-first century, classical definitions of war as it was experienced in the previous century started blurring across the world; so was it in India. I was commanding a large station in 2008 when the IAF got involved in the fight against left-wing extremism in a purely supporting and non-kinetic role despite some of its helicopters being shot at and damaged. This only reiterated India's restraint and willingness to look at minimal and calibrated force application against its own citizens. The debate on the use of air power in full-spectrum operations has reached new levels, as has the discourse on the declining role of force in statecraft.

By conventional yardsticks, the years 2012 to 2014 were intellectually productive for me and I benefitted from a period of glasnost which gave me the freedom to expand my intellectual and academic horizons.

Apart from my responsibilities at Air Headquarters (HQ), New Delhi, as the assistant chief of air staff looking after space, concepts, doctrine, media and public relations amongst other things, I also started writing extensively in the open media on larger issues of military history, statecraft, diplomacy and the need to build intellectual capital within India's armed forces. In mid-2012 I moved to Pune as air officer commanding, Advance Headquarters, an Indian Air Force interface with the Southern Army Command as I had all the QRs that were required for this assignment, and I was told that there was a fresh impetus being given to strengthening joint service structures. It was in Pune that I started reading, researching and writing furiously on India's modern wars. When my elder daughter left for boarding school in mid-2013, followed soon after by my wife and younger daughter, who returned to Delhi for the latter's schooling, I had enough time at my disposal. After finishing off routine office work, I would read, write and interview veterans with combat experience. So in a way, I have to thank the IAF for unwittingly enabling me to have an intense period of intellectual awakening. Though I was a fairly conspicuous social recluse, my time in Pune opened new academic and publishing horizons, which till then had seemed a distant dream.

This book attempts to showcase the exploits of the Indian armed forces from a 'joint perspective' as objectively and analytically as is possible by someone who has served in the same organization for over thirty-three years. The book is not meant to be a critique or a detailed analysis of India's modern conflicts; it does not claim to be an 'official history'; nor is it a PR effort to glorify the exploits of India's armed forces. It has to be merely seen as an honest and 'hybrid' piece of work, which seeks to amalgamate a simple and easy-flowing 'people-centric' historical narrative with operational and strategic overtones, and a fair element of academic rigour.

3

WHITHER MILITARY HISTORY AND UNDERSTANDING THE MILITARY

Military history from a political context is the structured study of force application in furtherance of statecraft and state policy.[1]

Opening Salvo

India's armed forces occupy a unique position in modern Indian society, and yet there is an uneven and lopsided perception and acknowledgement of their contribution to the growth, development and stability of the Indian nation state. In February 2013, I wrote a mail to Ramachandra Guha, arguably India's most accomplished contemporary historian, complimenting him for his collection of liberal essays on politics, religion and other issues in *Patriots and Partisans* which he felt were important to chronicle as part of the diminishing liberal discourse in India. However, I expressed my anguish that in this large collection of essays, he did not find it fit to include even one essay on anything even remotely connected with the Indian armed forces. I argued that one of the reasons for the survival of modern Indian democracy was the politically detached countenance of all elements of the armed forces – in particular its leadership. He very graciously accepted the omission by writing: 'You are completely right about the unacknowledged role of the armed forces in sustaining a secular and democratic India, especially given the importance of the army of the political systems of Pakistan, China, Bangladesh, etc.

It is striking that no war hero has stood for elections in India.' Ram Guha was close enough as one of the few decorated war heroes who attempted to make a mark in politics as a parliamentarian was Major General Rajinder Singh 'Sparrow', a two-time winner of the Maha Vir Chakra, India's second highest gallantry award. However, apart from him there have been a number of officers and men who have entered the hurly-burly world of Indian politics, the most recent ones being General V.K. Singh, a former chief of army staff, and Lieutenant Colonel Rajyvardhan Singh Rathore, an accomplished soldier sportsman, joining active politics after winning parliamentary seats in India's 2014 general elections. Others like Major General Khanduri and Jaswant Singh, both of whom were ministers of great distinction in Prime Minister Atal Bihari Vajpayee's government, have contributed greatly to nation building. Another remarkable transition that reflects the egalitarian nature of India's military has been that it has not only been the officer cadre that has contributed to politics, but in recent times, there have been non-commissioned officers like Naik Surender Singh, a decorated soldier from the Kargil conflict and an NSG (National Security Guards) commando who took part in the anti-terrorist operation following the Mumbai attacks of 2008, who have successfully contested elections at the state level.[2]

At the National Defence Academy (NDA) at Khadakvasla near Pune, our head of the department in the faculty of military history and international relations, Prof. Rajan, urged us to look closely at military history, not as an isolated discipline, but always as an adjunct of political strategy and diplomacy. This contextual relationship, he said, was imperative for a clearer understanding of military history, failing which the study of military history would remain only a description of battles and campaigns. I have never forgotten that advice. Since then I have always looked at military campaigns through multiple processes of statecraft, but always remained in touch with the 'heat of battle' as the brilliant American military historian, Russell Weigley, emphatically argued in one of his most widely read books on WW II, *Eisenhower's Lieutenants.*

Neglect of Military History

I have always wondered why the discipline of military history, particularly in the post-Independence era, was a laggard in India's contemporary historical discourse. I also wondered whether it had anything to do with the 'pacifist' tag which was attached to modern Indian strategic thinking and the reluctance to showcase the exploits of a military that still carried a perceived colonial legacy. My gut feeling was that the numerous social, political and intellectual historians who have dominated the modern Indian historical discourse were more comfortable in writing and teaching history that was socially relevant, politically engaging, and showcased India's rich civilizational heritage and multiculturally vibrant democracy. Making matters difficult for a minuscule number of military historians has been the archival carelessness and opaqueness when it came to periodic declassification of matters military. Many Western universities look at military history as a clear subset of history that focuses on strategy, operational art, campaign studies and tactical battles. I guess it just did not make sense for Indian universities to devote time to this genre of history when other topics were attracting attention.

While India's military and wars since Independence have been well chronicled within the country and abroad as part of a larger strategic landscape by scholars like Sumit Ganguly, Stephen Cohen, Steven Wilkinson, Jaswant Singh, Srinath Raghavan and Neville Maxwell, it is only a handful of civilian writers like Ravi Rikhye, Samir Chopra and P.V.S. Jagan Mohan who have written extensively about specific campaigns and battles. However, conflicts of all genres have only been covered in totality as part of India's current historical landscape, albeit briefly, in the most critically acclaimed book on contemporary Indian history, *India after Gandhi*, by Ramachandra Guha. I must also acknowledge the seminal contribution by a number of soldier scholars like Air Chief Marshal P.C. Lal, Major General D.K. Palit, Major K.C. Praval, Air Commodore Jasjit Singh, Air Marshal Bharat Kumar, Vice Admiral Mihir Roy and Rear Admiral Satyendra Singh to name but a few, who have taken pains to chronicle various wars, battles and campaigns.

Having taught extensively at two of India's flagship institutions of professional military education, I remain unhappy at the manner in which India's military history after Independence from colonial rule is being holistically studied at our military academies, war colleges and universities. None of our universities have a dedicated department of military history. Why blame the universities when the armed forces themselves have not seen value in scaling up dedicated departments of military history at the Indian Military Academy (1932), National Defence Academy (1954) and Defence Services Staff College (1948)?

What about writing dedicated military history? Because the study of military history stagnated after Independence, only a handful of modern historians like S.N. Prasad, U.P. Thapliyal and P.N. Khera have written exhaustive operational narratives on India's recent conflicts with research assistance from a few soldier scholars. These are laudable efforts no doubt, but are seen as works that have remained mainly as research references and not books that are easy-reading. Another worrying thought is that despite all the talk of inter-service cooperation and bonhomie, no scholar after Air Chief Marshal P.C. Lal has concurrently attempted to understand the three services to the extent required to chronicle and narrate an academically acceptable work on post-Independence military history of India.

With that as a backdrop, I have often wondered how we are going to sensitize India's huge youth bulge in the years ahead on the exploits of India's armed forces and the role they have played in nurturing and protecting its vibrant, secular, multi-ethnic and multicultural democracy. I have also wondered whether the absence of a focused military history discourse in our university and education system would lead to a decline in the attractiveness of the armed forces as a career option. Military matters in a large and inclusive democracy like India are not the exclusive preserve of a handful of generals, bureaucrats, politicians and strategists. War is serious business and when the citizenry is largely ignorant about the circumstances under which a nation goes to war, the chances that a nation pays heavily for the mistakes made by a few decision makers looms large on the horizon. The widespread study of military history is one way to avoid such aberrations.

Western Perspective

The use of force as a tool of statecraft is as old as civilization itself and after the evolution of monarchies and nation states it has primarily been exercised as an instrument of policy by the sovereign or the state through the military. Military history from a political context therefore is the structured study of application of force in furtherance of statecraft and state policy – and that is how I suppose Clausewitz or for that matter Kautilya would have liked it to be known as.

Western democracies have emerged and reinvented themselves around armed conflict and wars. Monarchies and autocratic forms of rule have been replaced with myriad forms of democracy by waging war. Modern theories of international relations, which look at balance of power and national interest, or universalism and collective security as a final objective of state policy, invariably have had war as a tool to achieve it, although it was always articulated as a least preferred option. The West has for long considered the study of war as being vital for survival of the state in the face of periodic threats from totalitarian forms of invasive and disruptive political philosophies. Nations like the US, Great Britain, France – all flourishing democracies – have government-backed institutions that take great pride in chronicling wars and saving the lessons for posterity. Writers and scholars like William Dalrymple and Christopher Bayly have wonderfully chronicled the military exploits of the British Raj even when it was in its death throes. Academics like Sir Michael Howard, John Keegan, Russell Weigley and Williamson Murray have made a name for themselves as military historians of rare pedigree, while journalist scholars like Rick Atkinson continue to tell the story of the exploits of American soldiers in World War II through masterfully written narratives.

The Way Ahead

Unfortunately, India has no such system in place where scholars who aspire to showcase the operational exploits of free India's military campaigns in easily digestible narratives are encouraged by mainstream academia. In 2012, I was exploring opportunities to take a sabbatical and write a comprehensive joint narrative of India's modern conflicts, but, to my horror, not one Indian university or think tank was willing to take me under their umbrella without my own funding. One distinguished professor even told me, 'We are not really interested in the past – we want to look ahead and prognosticate about the future!'

War in the current century will be waged not only to meet political objectives but also to express cultural, ethnic and civilizational aspirations. The military history of the twenty-first century may be distinctly different from previous centuries; politically motivated wars in the twenty-first century may be better calibrated and controlled, and may result in fewer casualties as compared to the horrific wars of the previous centuries; the savagery of war may not be as widespread as it was earlier, but ethnic and religious bigotry will continue to throw up horrific acts of barbarism and brutality reminiscent of medieval times.

The objectives of structured interstate wars and insurgencies, however, will be the same if one were to look at them as Clausewitz did – as merely an extension of politics and a means of forcing your adversary to do what you want him to do, should diplomacy or other benign forms of negotiating tools fail. Ethnic, religious and civilizational wars would continue to be driven as they were in the past by emotions like hatred and fear. However, the bottom line would remain that wars would continue to be significant markers in geopolitics as long as greed, fear, honour and interest continue to drive relationships between countries and people.

It is understandable that India does not want to abandon its overarching principles of non-violence and peaceful coexistence as key determinants of its political philosophy. However, considering the realities of modern geostrategic compulsions and expanding national interests, it is high time that it institutes radical changes in the way it records, analyses and disseminates its military history and record of wars that it has fought after Independence. I have disliked the tags of 'pacifist' and 'soft state' being attached to modern India whenever India's internal and external wars are discussed in international seminars and academic circles. Honest chronicling of India's recent wars and conflicts by a soldier scholar with both operational and academic competencies in the form of a flowing narrative, will, I hope, not only contribute to showcasing the country's military exploits as an intrinsic part of its modern history, but also help in the wider mission of helping the new generation understand the perils of going to war. Reinforcing my mission is a wonderfully researched book by a Yale academic, Prof. Steven Wilkinson, titled *Army and Democracy: The Military and Indian Democracy.* Published in early 2015, he writes:

> New data I have collected for this book show that immediately after independence in 1947 around three quarters of India's officers and men were from a small number of provinces and 'classes'... Half of all India's most senior officers came from one single province, Punjab, with only 5 per cent of the new state's population. This kind of narrowly recruited and cohesive army is dangerous ... Yet despite these challenges India has managed to keep the army out of politics and preserving its democracy unlike its neighbor Pakistan, which has had three long periods of military rule and a lot of indirect army control and interference besides.[3]

Reading Prof. Wilkinson's book, which largely attributes the apolitical nature of independent India's armed forces to structural and deft manoeuvring in the form of coup-proofing by its political masters,[4] only steeled my resolve to tell the story of modern India's soldiers, sailors and airmen who have not only 'stayed clear of politicizing the armed forces but, more importantly, have protected India's democracy for almost seven decades.

At the purely academic level, I cannot but help share a few perspectives from a paper written recently by Dr Tami Davis Biddle, a faculty member in the Department of National Security and Strategy at the US Army War College. Co-authored with Robert M. Citino from the University of North Texas and titled 'The Role of Military History in the Contemporary Academy', the paper is a powerful plea for the widespread examination and analysis of why societies go to war and its various consequences.[5] The authors go on to argue that military history not only enriches traditional historical discourse, but also influences work in political science, sociology and public policy and plays an important role in developing thoughtful and informed citizens.[6] Hence, its importance transcends traditional academic boundaries. My understanding of military history blends perfectly with what the two learned academics pitch for when they write:

> Several decades ago the phrase 'new military history' arose to highlight a shift away from traditional narratives that focused on generalship and troop movements on the battlefield. The 'new military history' is simply what military history is today: broad based, inclusive and written from a wide range of perspectives.[7]

The duo emphatically argue that 'to avoid the study of war is to undermine our opportunity to fully comprehend ourselves – and our evolution over time – in social, political, psychological, scientific and technological realms.'[8]

It is only right that I commence my narrative in Part II by highlighting the DNA and ethos of India's 1.5-million-strong armed forces as its military exploits over the last five decades are not only largely unknown in most parts of the world, but in many parts of India too. Large portions of southern India are still untouched by the influence of the armed forces; fast-developing Gujarat has amongst the lowest intake into the armed forces despite sharing a long desert and swamp border with Pakistan. The eastern states of Odisha and West Bengal, and portions of the large central state of Madhya Pradesh fare no better. It was time, I felt, that profiling the DNA of one of the finest and most professional armed forces in the world was the first step to ensure that the country at large consistently acknowledged its contribution, both in peace and war.

Another reason to reiterate the importance of studying India's armed forces and their performance in wars is that if prescriptive theories of modern warfare turn out to be right, and if conventional wars are largely going to be consigned to the pages of history, it is highly possible that the rich ethos, war-fighting traditions and exploits of India's soldiers, sailors and airmen could fade away into oblivion in the midst of spectacular economic growth, development and prosperity. However, that said, the retention of large volunteer armed forces in the years ahead will remain an inescapable necessity. While this large force may not engage in widespread military action, continued regional instability across multiple fronts and internal fissures and cracks will make it impossible for India to downsize its armed forces.

Indian tales of courage, valour and bravery in the face of insurmountable odds are not an exclusive preserve of the warrior princes of ancient and medieval India, or those of a colonial force in the dust and grime of WW I and WW II, but also of soldiers, sailors and airmen of a secular, democratic and modern India. One of the ways of upholding the pride of India's armed forces in a largely peaceful world and understanding their role in maintaining peace and stability is by telling its story to people at large in a manner that is neither celebratory or self-adulatory; nor derogatory or overly critical; but in a way that allows us to learn from our mistakes and take pride in our past. It is only right that the senior service, the Indian Army, occupies pride of place in any discourse on the DNA of India's armed forces.

PART II

The DNA of India's Armed Forces

4

THE INDIAN ARMY: INDIAN OR COLONIAL?

My packs are full and ready; my rifle is oiled and loaded. As I walk the road of death, I fear no one. I am an Indian soldier born to fight. Sleep peacefully in your homes, we are guarding the frontiers – Jai Hind.[1]

SHOWCASING THE INDIAN ARMY

Ayo Gorkhali! Har Har Mahadev, Jwala Mata ki Jai, Bole So Nihal Sat Sri Akal and many more war cries represent the astounding diversity of the Indian Army; a diversity, which is the key DNA of a force that has fought in the alien lands of Afghanistan, Mesopotamia, Egypt, Abyssinia, Italy, France and Burma in the two great wars. In its modern avatar, it has done the nation proud in battles fought on varied terrain – from the icy heights of the Siachen glacier to the dense jungles of Congo as part of UN peacekeeping missions; and from the sun-baked deserts of Rajasthan to the pristine valleys and lofty mountains of Jammu and Kashmir. It has fought adversaries ranging from clear-cut enemies on conventional battlefields, to jihadis and misguided fellow countrymen of similar stock – embedded within the local population in ill-defined battle spaces – in what is commonly known as counter-insurgency and counter-terrorism operations.

Even though I joined the Indian Air Force and engaged in many bruising academic and intellectual battles with my colleagues from the army and navy on myriad issues of joint operations at the Defence Services Staff College, where I spent some of the best years of my service career, my emotional connect with the Indian Army runs deeper than I could imagine. This was because of my interest in military history and the fact that my grandfather was seconded from the Nizam of Hyderabad's army as a sepoy to fight alongside the Indian Army in Iraq in WW I. Though I have not been able to dig up much about his experiences in Iraq, I was motivated to get to know the Indian Army better.

Late Medieval Indian Ethos

Popular Western discourse on the origins and ethos of the Indian Army repeatedly emphasizes that the colonial era from the middle of the eighteenth century to the period when India gained Independence from British rule marks the period in which the Indian Army emerged as a cohesive fighting arm. However, it is only fair to acknowledge that the DNA of the Indian Army goes beyond that to a period when two martial communities, the Marathas and the Sikhs, were contesting the Mughals for control over vast tracts of the country.

The Marathas and Sikhs

First was the purely home-bred guerrilla force under Shivaji. The courageous and wily Maratha chieftain along with his successors and, subsequently, the Peshwas, defied the Mughals and other Muslim invaders for almost a century from the latter half of the seventeenth century[2] and expanded the Maratha Empire till it covered much of the Indian heartland. Next were the hardy and proud Sikhs and Dogras under Maharaja Ranjit Singh, who kept the East India Company at bay for over four decades in the early part of the nineteenth century with a modern and well-trained hybrid army of multi-ethnic and multi-religious troops and generals comprising Sikhs, Dogras, Muslims and even French advisors.[3] The armies of Shivaji, his Maratha successors, the Peshwas, and Ranjit Singh revolved around a highly organized structure, disciplined cadres and focused leadership that quickly assimilated new military ideas and technologies brought in from warring Europe.

The Maratha Empire at the peak of Shivaji's reign extended across large swathes of the Deccan Plateau and included large portions of what are currently the Indian states of Gujarat, Maharashtra, Karnataka and Andhra Pradesh. The robustness, expansiveness, self-belief and longevity of Shivaji's military legacy translated into Maratha military power, which dominated most of the Deccan Plateau and the Indian heartland up to the River Indus for almost a century after Shivaji's death till Ahmed Shah Abdali, the Afghan general, comprehensively defeated the Maratha general Sadashivrao Bhau at the Third Battle of Panipat in 1761. This defeat, accompanied by the fragmentation of the Maratha Empire into a confederacy of five states, accelerated the decline of the Marathas till the British East India Company finally wore them down in the early part of the nineteenth century. The Marathas under Shivaji can, therefore, rightly lay claim to being amongst the pioneers of the modern Indian Army in terms of providing a totally indigenous flavour to soldiering.[4] In real terms, the prolonged struggle of the Marathas to contest Mughal domination of India could well be considered as India's first war of independence from foreign rule. No praise for Shivaji is better than the one bestowed on him by James Grant Duff, a captain in the First Regiment of the Bombay Grenadiers and later the political resident at Satara. Writing effusively in his three-volume book *The History of The Mahrattas* in 1863, he says:

> Sivajee was patient and deliberate in his plans, ardent, resolute and persevering in his execution. But to sum up all, let us contrast his craft, pliancy and humility with his boldness, firmness and ambition; his power of inspiring enthusiasm; the dash of a partisan adventurer, with the order and economy of a statesman; and lastly, the wisdom of his plans which raised the despised Hindoos to sovereignty.[5]

Notwithstanding the rather disparaging remarks made about Maratha troops by Lord Roberts[6] which led to their exclusion as a martial race during the period when the reorganization of the Indian Army was being done in the aftermath of the First War of Independence, or the Indian Mutiny as the English liked to call it, the legacy of the Marathas provides adequate indigenous inspiration for the Indian Army even today. Mason writes very perceptively about Mughal inefficiency and Maratha nationalism and this is one of the reasons why I chose to ignore the Mughal legacy. Of course, as far as I was concerned, the Mughals were invaders, and notwithstanding Emperor Akbar's attempts at integrating the Rajputs and creating a pan-Indian ethos, I am inclined to look at the Mughals as foreigners who ravaged India. Mason writes with great clarity:

> Thus the Mughal armies combined almost every military vice. They were without discipline, they could not move swiftly or manoeuvre in the face of an enemy, their supply arrangements were rapacious and inadequate, and above all there was neither the spirit nor organization to hold them together. In a few generations, they had lost the hardiness, the simplicity and the mobility of the invaders under Babur … The Maratha Army at its best suggested the beginning of the kind of nation state that grew up in England from Tudor times onward. The idea of a nation was still hardly understood in India. But had Sivaji lived longer and had his principles been followed by his successors, the Maratha spirit would have surely grown into nationalism.[7]

However, Bipin Chandra, a reputed Indian historian is scathing in his criticism of the Marathas after they promised so much. He writes:

> Unlike the Mughals, they failed to give sound administration to the people outside Maharashtra. They could not inspire the Indian people with any higher degree of loyalty than the Mughals had succeeded in doing. Their dominion, too, depended on force and force alone. The only way in which the Marathas could have stood up to the rising British power was to have transformed their state into a modern state. This they failed to do.[8]

Though they started off as hardy fighters with good fighting skills and frugal habits, it is possible that they mellowed over the years after acquiring static and empire characteristics. The Marathas still are hardy, courageous, disciplined and frugal in their approach to both life and soldiering; traits that live on with the Maratha Light Infantry and the Mahar Regiment, two regiments that continue to draw most of their

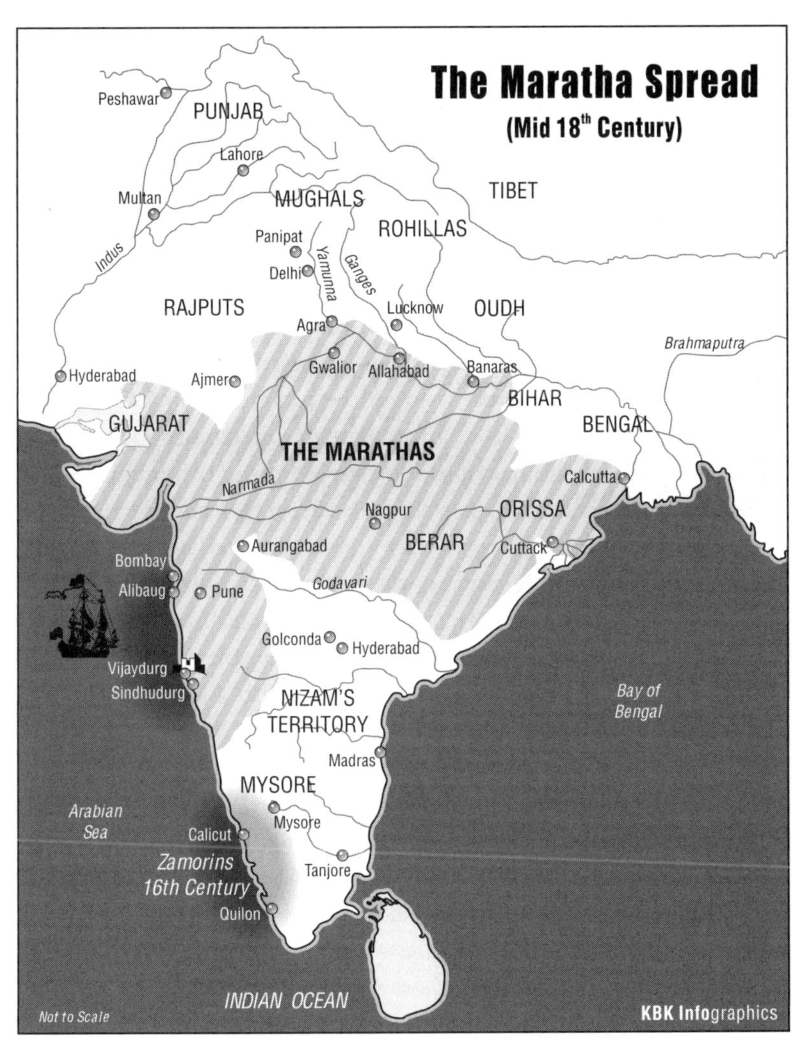
The Maratha Spread
(Mid 18th Century)
Peshawar
PUNJAB
Lahore
Multan
MUGHALS
TIBET
Indus
Panipat
ROHILLAS
Delhi
Yamunna
Ganges
RAJPUTS
Lucknow
OUDH
Agra
Brahmaputra
Gwalior
Allahabad
Hyderabad
Ajmer
Banaras
BIHAR
GUJARAT
BENGAL
THE MARATHAS
Narmada
Calcutta
Nagpur
ORISSA
Aurangabad
BERAR
Cuttack
Bombay
Alibaug
Pune
Godavari
Golconda
Hyderabad
Vijaydurg
Sindhudurg
NIZAM'S
TERRITORY
Bay of
Bengal
Madras
MYSORE
Arabian
Sea
Mysore
Calicut
Zamorins
16th Century
Tanjore
Quilon
INDIAN OCEAN
Not to Scale
KBK Infographics

soldiers from the warrior and peasant communities of the Deccan Plateau.

Some military historians may contest the exclusion of Haider Ali, Tipu Sultan and the Mysore Army from a modern Indian military discourse – not without good reason as they were amongst the first to contest the East India Company's expansion into the Indian hinterland in the late eighteenth century.[9] However, the main reasons for doing so are the relatively short duration of this contest as compared to the Maratha and the Sikh experience, the fragmented demographic profile of the soldiers who comprised the Mysore Army, and poor strategic vision on the part of Tipu Sultan, which saw him fight multiple adversaries (Nizam of Hyderabad, the British and the Marathas) at the same time.[10]

After the Marathas, the longest-serving martial community to have left an indelible impact on the ethos of the contemporary Indian Army has been the Sikh warrior clan. The remarkable metamorphosis of these peace-loving and agrarian people into a fierce warrior community can be attributed primarily to the persistent persecution by Mughal emperors.[11] Successive leaders, or gurus, as they were called, resisted persecution by taking up arms and organizing the community into twelve *misl*s or confederacies based on equality.[12] This, they soon realized, was the only way that the clan would survive. Sandwiched on the plains of Punjab as they were by the Mughal Empire to the south and south-east and persistent Persian and Afghan invaders to the north-west, the Sikhs emerged as a warrior clan during the time of Guru Gobind Singh, the tenth and last Sikh guru.[13] From then on, armed as they were with a powerful set of personal beliefs that were symbolized by the five Ks – Kesh or long hair, Kanga or comb, Kara or a steel wrist band, Kachh or short breeches and Kirpan or a short sword[14] – they were a changed clan, bound by a powerfully secular scripture called the Guru Granth Sahib. However, like the Marathas, the military prowess of the Sikhs can be largely attributed to one leader, the enigmatic and dynamic Maharaja Ranjit Singh. Amongst his numerous achievements were the modernization of the Sikh armies and the introduction of a 'combined arms' strategy that saw the concurrent expansion of the infantry and artillery along with the traditional Sikh cavalry.[15]

Endowed with exceptional tactical acumen and a truly strategic mindset, Ranjit Singh realized that the only way to survive in that region was by expanding outwards and minimizing the spaces from where invaders could descend on the fertile and rich alluvial plains of Punjab. Pitted against this powerful regional satrap, the British, after initially attempting to take him head-on militarily, realized that it would be more appropriate to appease him while they fought the Marathas and bide their time before annexing the Sikh Empire.

Acknowledging his suzerainty over large tracts of Punjab, North-West Frontier Province and portions of Kashmir and Ladakh in the Lahore Treaty of 1809, the British felt reasonably certain that north-west India was secure from Russian encroachment.[16] They even ignored his forays into eastern Afghanistan against a weakening Durrani kingdom.[17] This allowed them to concentrate on consolidating their hold on the Indian hinterland. Ranjit Singh's death in 1839 created a vacuum in the Sikh leadership which the British exploited. The two Anglo-Sikh wars during 1848–49 severely denuded the fighting potential of the Sikhs despite a large British army almost being defeated by an alliance of Sikh chieftains in the Battle of Chilianwalla on 13 January 1849.[18] The persistent British, however, broke the back of Sikh military capability a month later in the Battle of Gujarat, which marked the end of organized Sikh military resistance to British expansion.[19] Ranjit Singh's prophetic words to a cartographer a few months before his death would come true:

> 'What does the red colour stand for?' asked Maharaja Ranjit Singh when he was shown a map of India. 'Your Majesty,' replied the cartographer, 'red marks the extent of British possessions.' The maharaja scanned the map with his single eye and saw nearly the whole of Hindustan except the Punjab marked red. He turned to his courtiers and remarked, 'ek roz sab lal ho jaiga – one day it will all be red.'[20]

To the credit of the British, instead of alienating the Sikhs by engaging them in constant conflict, the British won them over with a combination of deft diplomacy and devious manipulation.[21] As a result, they were able to call upon the Sikh leaders to assist them in defeating the Marathas in the last Maratha war, quelling stray expressions of military opposition

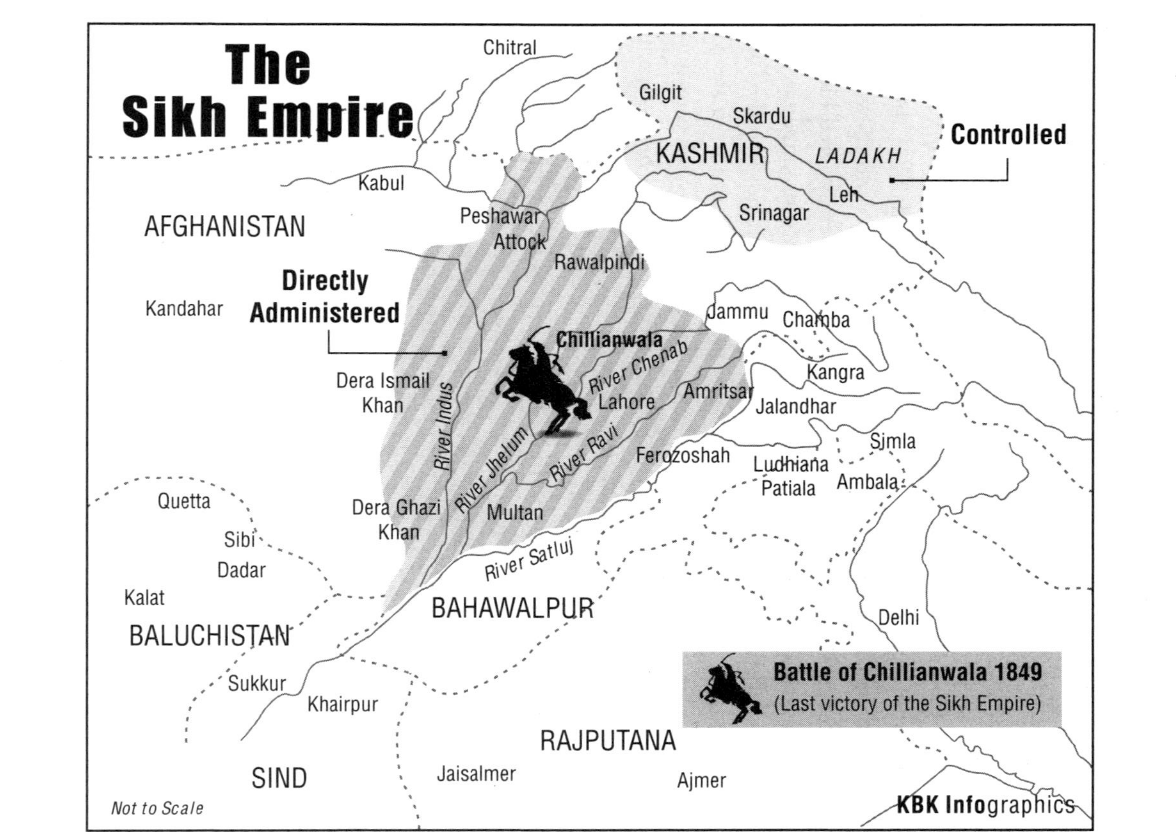
The Sikh Empire
Chitral
Gilgit
Skardu
KASHMIR
LADAKH
Controlled
Kabul
Leh
Srinagar
AFGHANISTAN
Peshawar
Attock
Rawalpindi
Directly Administered
Kandahar
Jammu
Chamba
Chillianwala
River Chenab
Kangra
Dera Ismail Khan
River Indus
Lahore
Amritsar
Jalandhar
River Jhelum
River Ravi
Sjmla
Ferozoshah
Ludhiana
Patiala
Ambala
Quetta
Dera Ghazi Khan
Multan
Sibi
Dadar
River Satluj
Kalat
BAHAWALPUR
Delhi
BALUCHISTAN
Battle of Chillianwala 1849
(Last victory of the Sikh Empire)
Sukkur
Khairpur
RAJPUTANA
SIND
Jaisalmer
Ajmer
Not to Scale
KBK Infographics

from the Rajputs and the Jats, before using them to put down the Indian Mutiny of 1857. The gradual and peaceful assimilation of the army of the Sikh Empire into the colonial British Indian Army is one of the great success stories of the British 'divide and rule' policy wherein they were able to convince Sikh warriors that their martial legacy would be better protected by the British. The Sikh Regiment is one of the oldest regiments of the Indian Army and it was only befitting that the first military action taken by India after Independence had 1 Sikh Regiment leading the way.[22] Part III of the book will address the exploits of this regiment in greater detail.

The Rajputs and the Jats

Hailing from parts of the plains of northern India, the Rajputs and the Jats, the former being an acknowledged martial community and the latter of hardy peasant stock, can also rightly claim to be stakeholders and participants in the creation of India's modern army. While the Rajputs occupy centre stage in any military discourse on medieval India and were at the forefront of the initial opposition to the Mughals till the late sixteenth century,[23] their proximity to the Mughal Empire ensured that their warrior potential was systematically degraded by the Mughals. As the fighting potential of most Rajput rulers ebbed, they amalgamated themselves into the Mughal Empire and ceased to be an independent fighting entity like the Sikhs or Marathas. However, the British were keen to exploit their martial prowess while restructuring the Indian Army later. The Jats are a community of hardy peasants hailing from what is today the Indian state of Haryana, part of western Uttar Pradesh and eastern Rajasthan. They too met with the same fate as the Rajputs, and were either defeated in battle or amalgamated into the Mughal army. Like the Rajputs, they too would be included in the future restructuring of the Indian Army. It is about time to move on and study the impact of India's colonial masters on the Indian Army as it moved into turbulent times of the mid-eighteenth century.

British Legacy

Restructuring and Professionalism

Considering the huge volume of both primary and secondary sources of literature that is available on the indelible imprint of British colonial legacy on the shaping of India's modern army, it is impossible not to acknowledge their important role in this process. The influence of the British East India Company can be traced to the operational ethos of the three provincial armies of Madras, Bombay and Bengal. However, the fragmented and personality-oriented leadership, along with deteriorating officer–men relationship, was considered by the British Indian Army as being responsible for the revolt of 1857, also called by many Indian historians as India's First War of Independence.[24] The ensuing slow response by the armies of the East India Company to put down the rising precipitated the rapid restructuring of the British Indian Army in India as the Company was replaced by the Crown as the direct ruler of the colony of India. Shocked by the rebellion of large sections of the Bengal army and a sprinkling of Muslim, Maratha and Jat warriors, who constituted the bulk of the rebel Indian force that aspired to defeat the East India Company, the Crown took over the reins of governance of its colonies in India from the Company. It ordered a sweeping restructuring of the British Indian Army, placing it under a single commander-in-chief (C-in-C). Steered by battle-hardened C-in-Cs like Lord Roberts and Lord Kitchener, the transformation of the British army in India from a set of regional armies to a single army that was capable of furthering the colonial and strategic objectives of the Crown was complete by the end of the first decade of the twentieth century.

A change in recruitment pattern was accompanied by professionalism and officer training. This was then put to test in various operational campaigns in Afghanistan and NWFP and validated in the cauldron of WW I. These times also brought with it the first signs of conflict between the viceroy and the C-in-C over who would exercise control over the military. The clash between Lord Curzon, the imperious viceroy, and Lord Kitchener, a battle-hardened C-in-C with experience during the Boer War and the Battle of Omdurman in the late nineteenth century, is well documented and quite fascinating.[25]

Despite the recommendations of a few committees like the Peel Commission in 1859 and the Eden Commission in 1879, which recommended an inclusive approach to recruitment,[26] one of the first steps that Lord Kitchener initiated – influenced in no small measure by the analysis of Lord Roberts, his illustrious predecessor a few years earlier – was a recruitment drive which identified martial races from different parts of the subcontinent. These were chosen carefully from amongst races that had displayed loyalty to the Crown during the First War of Independence and possessed singular fighting skills. Stephen Cohen has liberally quoted from the writing of Lord Roberts in his book and I will follow suit:

> Each cold season I made long tours in order to acquaint myself with the needs and capabilities of the Madras Army. I tried hard to discover in them those fighting qualities which had distinguished their forefathers during the wars of the last and beginning of the present century. But long years of peace, and the security of prosperity attending it, had evidently had upon them, as they always seemed to have on Asiatics, a softening and deteriorating effect; and I was forced to the conclusion that the ancient military spirit had died in them, as it had died in the ordinary Hindustani of Bengal and the Maratha of Bombay, and that they could no longer with safety be pitted against warlike races and employed outside the limits of Southern India.[27]

From these races were created battalions and regiments that would form the bulk of fighting troops for the British Indian Army. These troops would be trained to fight as professional soldiers with loyalty to the regimental flag and their community, and not get swayed and distracted by nationalistic aspirations that were expected to emerge in the years following the First War of Independence. Great pains were taken to map demographic trends and identify those races in the three Presidency armies of the East India Company (Bengal, Bombay and Madras) that either did not display adequate martial characteristics or had displayed anti-British sentiment during the revolt of 1857.[28] It is for these reasons that the Bengalis, Madrasis, Marathas and Mahars (lower-caste Maratha soldiers who served in large numbers in Shivaji's army) were excluded from the list of martial races and retained only as sapper or engineer regiments. The exclusion of Maharashtrians and Bengalis in part explains the key roles they played in catalysing opposition to colonial rule in late nineteenth and twentieth centuries. Interestingly, most major leaders of the Congress as also of armed revolutionary groups were, before 1920, from either Bengal or Maharashtra.[29]

The British rightly identified the fighting capabilities of both the Rajputs and the Jats along with the Sikhs, Gorkhas, Dogras and select Muslim communities from Punjab and Baluchistan, and included them as key martial communities in their reorganization plan.[30] They did this also because the recruiting areas of these races were closer to the North-West Frontier Province, which was deemed to be the main area from where a security threat to the British Empire was envisaged from the expanding Russian Empire.[31]

A word about the indomitable and courageous Gorkhas is in order. The Gorkhas are a martial clan from the area encompassing modern- day Nepal with fierce fighting skills that belie their short stature. Relatively insulated from the Indian masses and having no links with the nationalist movement, they were defeated by the British in the last Gorkha War in 1816 after having defied the East India Company for almost two decades.[32] Promised regular employment by the Crown after being rightly identified as ideal material for recruitment as soldiers, the Gorkhas were initially insulated from the rest of the martial races, and moulded and trained to be loyal to the regiment and the Crown. Ten Gorkha regiments of two battalions each emerged from this drive and proved to be a master stroke by the British as the Gorkhas were to repeatedly prove themselves in battle.

From a nationalistic perspective, the shrewdness and deviousness of the British was clearly evident as they played the communal, caste and race cards in an attempt to polarize the Indian Army so that it would never rise as one body again. Charles Wood, secretary of state for India, in a letter to the viceroy wrote:

> I never wish to see again a great army, very much the same in its feelings and prejudices and connections, confident in its strength, and so disposed to rise in rebellion together. If one regiment mutinies, I should like to have the next regiment so alien that it would be ready to fire into it.[33]

Changed recruitment patterns were concurrently accompanied by a concerted drive at improving the quality of leadership by replacing officers of the East India Company with regular officers of the Crown and introducing compulsory professional military education. Many of these officers, with battle experience from the Napoleonic and the two Afghan Wars between 1839 and 1880, were able to infuse a sense of professionalism, discipline and regimental loyalty, and offer security to the troops and their families with the promise of a regular income. Thus, by the end of the nineteenth century, the British Indian Army had transformed from a ragtag army to a professional force that moulded the raw fighting abilities of India's martial races into excellent military capability with Western professionalism and leadership, exposure to technology and latest armaments, and, most importantly, a sense of regimental belonging and ownership that transcended nationalistic feelings. Finally, though the decision to restructure the Indian Army commenced in 1880, it finally saw fruition only in 1902 when Lord Kitchener renumbered the various units and created a unified army.[34] What Kitchener initially did was to merge the three Presidency armies and the Punjab Frontier Force into one army with its cavalry and infantry regiments numbered consecutively.[35] Apart from one more regimental restructuring in the inter-war years, the preceding paragraphs encapsulate in short the British legacy of the Indian Army – something that lives on today.

Analysing the recovery of the British Indian Army from the shock of the revolt of 1857, Stephen Rosen, a Harvard professor, identified four distinct reasons why the army of the East India Company and the British Indian Army were able to prevail over the Mughal, Mysore, Maratha and Sikh armies despite their significant numerical disadvantage. In his sweeping and significantly incisive book on the evolution of the Indian Army entitled *India and Its Armies*, he goes on to identify professionalism, unity, organizational cohesiveness and a relative detachment from society as being the main reasons for the spread of the British Empire in India through military conquest.[36] While drill, discipline and careful attention to logistics allowed the army of the Company to prevail over their Indian opponents in the eighteenth century,[37] rapid assimilation of modern technologies from the battlefields of Europe led to a significant asymmetry between the Company's armies and, later, the British Indian Army and the various indigenous armies like those of the Marathas and Sikhs.[38] Significant amongst these were improved field and siege artillery with superior firepower created out of systematic improvements in gunpowder at laboratories and ordnance factories.[39]

The ability of the East India Company to assimilate and learn from their opponents was also a key factor in the continuous improvement in the military capabilities of the Company's army. Taking a leaf out of Mughal tactics and Tipu Sultan's weaponry, the Company used elephants to drag artillery and blast open Maratha forts in hilly terrain, and assimilated rockets into their firepower after having seen their effectiveness when used by Tipu against them in the Third Mysore War (1790–92).[40] The powerful Sikhs had their own set of cultural problems that hampered their tactical acumen. Obsessed with the predominance of lightly armed cavalry and hampered by hostility towards French advisors, the Sikhs, after the death of Maharaja Ranjit Singh, were no match in the long run against a combination of heavy cavalry and well-trained infantry that made up the Company's army. Finally, had the Marathas and the Sikhs shown adequate strategic vision and combined to take on the Company, sandwiching them from the south and north respectively, we may well have seen a different India at the turn of the nineteenth century.

Entering the Twentieth Century

As the Indian Army entered the twentieth century, hardened by its experience in the First and Second Afghan Wars and increasingly patronized and supported by the Crown, it started being seen through different lens by both the larger Indian populace and nationalist leaders. Since large sections of the rural population of India of those times were oppressed by landlords and zamindars, they searched for a livelihood other than agriculture. Apart from government service, which required some degree of literacy, the Indian Army represented an attractive employment option for the semi-literate and unskilled masses. Nationalist leaders also saw this as an opportunity to push for a greater 'Indianization' of the British Army in India including the recruitment of Indian officers. This, they hoped, would one day lead to a ground swell of popular support against the British leading to swaraj or independence for India from British rule. The British resisted this move for some time and it was only when the clouds of WW I loomed on the horizon did the British scurry to scale up recruitment and include what was called the King's Commission for selected Indian officers and the Viceroy's Commission for non-commissioned officers (also called jemadars, risaldars, risaldar major, subedar and subedar major). Realizing that they had to address the rising aspirations of diverse classes, some older regiments were revived; and others were recruited into supporting arms like the engineer regiments. Some castes, which had been dropped from the army list,[41] were recruited into separate regiments like the Mahar Regiment that were created, and even the recruiting base from among the Sikhs was expanded. Interestingly, many of these recruitment patterns continue till today.

As a result of this massive recruitment drive, the strength of the Indian Army just prior to WW I rose to approximately 2,50,000 troops comprising old-fashioned cavalry, infantry and limited artillery. John Gaylor puts the fighting strength as closer to 1,50,000 in his book *Sons of John Company: The Indian and Pakistan Armies.*[42] The army was unwieldy and broadly comprised thirty-nine cavalry regiments, 135 infantry battalions, three engineer or sapper regiments and a mere twelve mountain artillery batteries. Its primary role was to tackle insurgencies in the North-West Frontier Province and beat back any likely expansionist incursions into the region by Russia in the 'Great Game' that was unfolding in the region. The strength of the Indian Army continued to rise as the war progressed to a final figure of approximately 15,00,000 with over one million deployed overseas to support the war effort during WW I.[43]

5

THE INDIAN ARMY: COMING OF AGE

The safety, honour and welfare of your country comes first, always and every time; the honour, welfare and comfort of the men you command come next; your own ease, comfort and safety come last, always and every time.[1]

The story of India at war from 1939 to 1945 has been pushed to the margins by the telling and retelling of the story of independence and the partition of British India into the republics of India and Pakistan.[2]

– Christopher Bayly and Tim Harper

The Great War

Though hastily deployed initially in large numbers as an Indian expeditionary force with little or no acclimatization after the initial reverses faced by the Allies in Europe, the Indian Army performed gallantly during WW I, particularly in the early battles of France and the deserts of Egypt, Palestine and Mesopotamia. In a scathing indictment of the callous manner in which the Crown inducted the Indian Army into the European theatre of battle, David Omissi writes: 'As they arrived, these underequipped troops were fed piecemeal into the frontline in an attempt to stem the German rush between Ypres and La Bassee.'[3]

Operating as an integrated corps-sized force with approximately two infantry and two cavalry divisions, Indian troops soon won the respect of their German adversaries for their tenacity and courage under extreme fire. During the first Battle of Ypres in October 1914, Sepoy Khudadad Khan of the 129 Baluch Regiment was left as the last man standing and won the Indian Army's first Victoria Cross (VC).[4] Naik Darwan Singh Negi of the Garhwal Rifles was the second Indian soldier to win the VC in the Battle of Neuve Chapelle in November 1914 [5] as units of the Sikh Regiment, Bhopal Infantry and Garhwal Rifles did the Indian Army proud both in offensive and holding operations. Indian sappers (military engineers) too would prove their mettle with Havildar Maruti Jadhav being among the few Indian soldiers to be awarded the French Legion of Honour for displaying courage and initiative of the highest order at Neuve Chappelle in France on 28 October 1914.[6] Fighting in cold and alien weather conditions till March 1915 in brutal trench warfare and hand-to-hand combat operations, the Indian Army can be proud of taking part in the first offensive operations launched by the Allies.

Indian cavalry units too acquitted themselves with distinction as units like the Poona Horse, Hodson's Horse,[7] 2nd Lancers and Skinners Horse rode across the wet plains of Europe fighting for a cause they did not really understand. Lance Daffadar Gobind Singh of 2nd Lancers was among the few Indian cavalrymen to win a Victoria Cross as he carried messages across the battlefield under withering fire during the Battle of Cambrai in December 1917.[8] Gallipoli and Mesopotamia were also witness to the courage and bravery of Indian troops who suffered heavy casualties in the various battles fought in that sector. Similarly, the Allied campaign in Egypt and Palestine too relied heavily on the Indian Army.[9] By the end of the war the Indian Army had lost 74,000 men and won eleven Victoria Crosses (Indian soldiers) and ninety-nine Military Crosses.[10] More importantly, it had won the respect of the British Army and the gratitude of the Crown, albeit with tremendous loss of life.

Philip Mason writes poignantly about the sacrifices made by Indian troops during WW 1:

> No one can think of the carnage of this war without horror. But in the case of the Indian deaths there is a special question to be asked,

> grim but wry. In every English village, there, survivors thought they knew why these men had died. It was to defend their homes. For Indian soldiers, though, there was no village memorial.[11]

Mason goes on to try and understand how the British Indian Army commemorated their dead at the end of the Great War:

> To die for one's country or to save the life of a leader or comrade is a noble end. To die for the regiment is not very different if that regiment is part of the national tradition. But in India's case the regiment was not part of the national tradition and the time was not far off when the allegiance of the regiment would be transferred from the King Emperor to the President of India.[12]

While the British officers of the Indian Army propagated the idea that the men had died for the regiment, deep down the men knew that their comrades had really died for izzat or honour – for their clan, their villages and their individual honour. Many colonial historians believe that the core ethos of the Indian Army emerged from the bloody battlefields of WW I. They believe that the creed of Naam, Namak, aur Nishan (individual honour, integrity and loyalty to the regimental flag) emerged from the bloody trenches of the Great War and still remain as defining benchmarks for service in the Indian Army. While that was true to some extent in colonial India, I will argue later in the book that there were other drivers that shaped the DNA of independent India's army. The valour of the British Indian Army during WW I is enshrined on the walls and pillars of the magnificent memorial at India Gate in the national capital of Delhi. It is a moving memorial and took ten years to build. Designed by Edwin Lutyens, who designed what is modern New Delhi, it was completed in 1931. It signified awakening of the conscience of India's colonial masters and a realization of the need to honour their dead soldiers and the role they played in building and sustaining their empire. Eighty-five years old now, India Gate remains the most magnificent war memorial in India; ironically built by India's colonial masters in honour of the 'natives' who laid down their lives for 'the empire'. After years of procrastination by successive governments on the need for independent India to have a central war memorial, the Modi government recently approved the construction of a National War Memorial very close to India Gate. India commemorated 100 years of WW I in 2014 with a series of wreath-laying ceremonies at all WW I cemeteries at cantonments like Kirkee (near Pune) and other Indian cities that had large army presence during those days.

Inter-War Years

The post–WW I era saw the tired Indian Army emerge victorious in a one-sided campaign in Afghanistan called the Third Anglo-Afghan War of 1919 against Amanullah Khan, the jihad-declaring emir. The same force, comprising mainly Gorkha battalions, was also involved in stray skirmishes against Afridi and Mahsud tribes in Waziristan[13] before the soldiers returned to their barracks in the various cantonments to recoup after the war. This phase was one of rapid demobilization, development of the 'cantonment culture' and the relative alienation of the army from the masses. As a result of the introduction of the regimental system many pairs of cavalry units were merged to form one unit, five to six infantry battalions were regrouped into regiments, and officer affiliation with fixed tenures for troops ensured that there was a greater degree of integration, commitment and loyalty of the troops not only towards the Crown, but also towards the regiment. In response to growing nationalist aspirations, a few promising young Indian youth with officer potential were educated at public schools like Daly College, Indore, and the Prince of Wales Royal Indian Military College, Dehradun,[14] as a precursor to officer training at the Royal Military Academy at Sandhurst. Illustrious soldiers like Field Marshals Cariappa and Ayub Khan, General Thimayya and Lieutenant General L.P. Sen were amongst those from the first few batches of Kings Commissioned Indian Officers or KCIOs about whom you would read more as we go along.

Unable to cope with the increased requirement of Indian officers, the Indian Military Academy was opened at Dehradun in 1932. While this saw an increased number of Indians as KCIOs and the commencement of formal professional military education, it also brought into the open the discrimination between officers commissioned in England and those commissioned in India. While the former could serve in any regiment of His Majesty's Land Forces, the latter could only serve in regiments of His Majesty's Indian Land Forces.[15] In essence, while the former could also command British troops, the latter could only command Indian troops.

The year 1919 was surely a 'black year' for the Indian Army as it saw the blind obedience of Indian troops at Jallianwala Bagh in Amritsar where Brigadier General Dyer asked Indian troops of the Gorkha regiment to open fire on innocent and unarmed civilians who had gathered for a meeting on the auspicious occasion of Baisakhi[16] inside a walled compound. In the ensuing massacre it is estimated that there were approximately 1,500 casualties including 379 dead. This incensed India's nationalist leaders and was the beginning of a growing divide between Indian soldiers and officers of the British Army and the growing band of nationalist leaders led by Jawaharlal Nehru. This suspicion was to linger on after Independence and could be considered as the beginning of the civil–military divide in modern India. Despite championing the cause for increased indigenous officer representation in the Indian Army, leaders of India's peaceful freedom movement had little empathy for the growing band of Kings Commissioned officers.

Coming of Age: World War II

If WW I was the testing ground for the British Indian Army, WW II would be a sterner challenge and a 'coming of age' for the men and officers of the Indian Army. They would go on to prove that they had transformed themselves into a truly professional army under senior British leadership and a large number of junior and middle-ranking KCIOs at the battalion and brigade levels. Troops were exposed to armoured warfare in the deserts of Africa, mountain warfare at Casino and jungle warfare in the Burma theatre. Celebrated field commanders like Viscount Slim and Field Marshal Auchinleck mentored Indian officers under them in actual battle conditions and assiduously prepared them for higher command. Auchinleck in particular was perceptive enough to realize that Indian aspirations for command and leadership could not be subdued for long and ensured that Indian officers were gradually given command responsibilities whenever British officers were on leave.[17] Officers like

Cariappa served as a company commander with the 10th Division in Iraq; fought in Iran and Syria; saw action with the celebrated 8th Army in North Africa and then came back to India to become the first KCIO to command an infantry battalion, the 17th battalion of the Rajput Regiment. He then headed to Burma to serve with the 26th Indian Division till almost the end of the war under the legendary Lieutenant General William 'Bill' Slim.[18]

It is believed that the downsizing of the Indian Army after WW I led to widespread unemployment with a large proportion of retrenched soldiers returning home to rural areas to engage in subsistence farming. Therefore, when the call to arms was sounded across rural India in 1939, the number of volunteers was overwhelming and the Indian Army, which was considered by the Crown as a strategic reserve, turned out to be one of the key factors in the initial success of the Allies in North Africa in 1941, and later on in Burma in 1944–45. From an army of 2,00,000 at the beginning of 1939, which primarily comprised ninety-six infantry battalions and eighteen cavalry regiments,[19] the Indian Army grew to 15,00,000 by 1941 and more than 25,00,000 by the end of the war in 1945.[20] As in WW I, the Indian Army faced severe equipment shortages with most of the logistics and equipment being diverted to the regular British Army. Yet, they trained hard in anticipation of being inducted sooner than later into the desert theatre of Iraq, Persia and North Africa.[21] This training paid rich dividends and under commanders like Wavell and Auchinleck, Indian divisions like the 4th and 5th played a pivotal role in the defeat of the Italians in East Africa before they were moved north in early 1941 to support Wavell's holding action and Auchinlecks's counter-attacks against Field Marshal Erwin Rommel's Afrika Korps offensive.

The Indian Army's first Victoria Cross in WW II was won by Second Lieutenant Premindra Singh Bhagat, a sapper officer in Abyssinia (modern-day Ethiopia) of the 4th Indian Division. Excerpts from his citation from the War Office in London dated 10 June 1941 reads:

> During the pursuit of the enemy following the capture of Metemma on the night of 31 Jan/01 Feb, 1941, 2 Lt Bhagat was in command of a section of a 21 Fd Coy, Sappers and Miners, detailed to accompany

> the leading mobile troops (Bren Carriers) to clear the road and adjacent areas of mines. For a period of four days and over a distance of 55 miles this officer in the leading carrier led the column. He detected and supervised the clearing of fifteen minefields. Speed being essential, he worked at high pressure from dawn to dusk each day. On two occasions when his carrier was blown up with casualties to others and on third occasion when ambushed and under close enemy fire, he himself carried straight on with his task. He refused relief when worn out with strain and fatigue and with one eardrum punctured by an explosion, on the ground that he was now better qualified to continue his task to the end. His coolness, persistence over a period of 96 hours and gallantry, not only in battle, but throughout the long period when the safety of the column and the speed at which it could advance were dependent on his personal efforts, were of the highest order.[22]

Wilting under relentless pressure, the British and Indian 4th and 5th Divisions fought a series of bruising rearguard battles at Benghazi and Tobruk in Libya before falling back to Egypt in late 1942 and holding a defensive line; waiting for Rommel to tire himself out and stretch his logistics line. That, however, is the story of the 8th Army with the 4th Indian Division remaining the only Indian formation to remain in the deserts of North Africa and taste victory under Montgomery a year later.[23]

A Sapper's Tale

Lieutenant Colonel Chanan Singh Dhillon from the Bengal Sappers passed away in 2011 at the ripe old age of ninety-four. A WW II veteran with combat experience with 41 Field Park Company of the 8th Army in North Africa as a non-commissioned officer, he was two days away from sailing back to India to accept an officer's commission when he was captured by Rommel's Afrika Korps during the Battle of Mersa Matruh in June 1942 as the 8th Army retreated into Egypt towards El Alamein. His remarkable and fascinating story was narrated to me one night in one of the narrow lanes of South Extension, a popular residential neighbourhood of south Delhi, by his son, Gurbinder Dhillon.[24]

Following his capture between Mersa Matruh and El Alamein on 29 June 1942, Dhillon and over 300 other Indian prisoners were bundled onto an old freighter, *Loreto,* on 9 October and shipped to Italy across the Mediterranean to be interned at one of the POW camps there. Fate, though, had ensured that the freighter would be tracked and sunk by the British U-class submarine, HMS *Unruffled.* Dhillon was among the survivors who lived to tell his tale. Transported from an Italian POW camp to a *Stalag* (camp) near Frankfurt in Germany after a series of escapes and recaptures, he was repatriated after the war and served the Bengal Sappers as a junior commissioned officer till he was granted a commission in the Indian Army in 1960, eighteen long years after he was originally slated to wear his pips. After hanging up his uniform in 1975, Lieutenant Colonel Dhillon meticulously recorded his life and there is a wonderful story waiting to be written. Till that happens, readers will have to be satisfied with this small snippet – a story that epitomizes the grit and determination of the ordinary Indian soldier of yesteryears.

Into Italy

The reputation of the Indian Army during the invasion of Italy in 1943 was only enhanced with the conduct of the 8th Indian Division of the 8th Army. Comprising mainly Sikh, Punjabi and Gorkha troops and commanded with distinction by Major General Dudley Russell, the division landed at Taranto, a port on the southern coast of Italy, on 24 September after the town had been captured by a British Para Division. Almost seventy years later a distinguished retired captain of the Indian Navy had this to narrate in an email on one of the history Yahoo Groups after his ship docked at Taranto in 1967:

> The expression of regret by the Mayor of Taranto (Italy) some time ago for the killing of two Indian fishermen by Italian marines from the Enrica Lexie, and his offer to take up the responsibility of educating the bereaved children gains significance from the city's historical association with India. I discovered that association quite by chance in 1967 when I was an officer on board INS *Brahmaputra.* My ship was diverted to Taranto owing to a coup against King

Constantine in Greece, our original destination. The ship berthed in Taranto in the early hours of a Sunday. There was no one there apart from the shore berthing party of a few men. As time went by, a large number of Taranto's residents, including several senior citizens, started congregating near the ship. They carried placards welcoming the Indians to Taranto. It was a mystery to us as to why such a crowd was building up. We were told that the news of the Indian ship's arrival was announced on the local radio. By the evening, the crowd had swelled. Several residents held placards inviting us to dinners, lunches and picnics.

I was invited to dinner by the family of the late Ms. Ines Ghosh, the Italian wife of the late Surgeon Rear Admiral J.N. Ghosh, Indian Navy. Ghosh met Ines in Taranto where he was a prisoner of war.

There I heard heart-rending stories of World War II. They narrated how when the British 8th Army comprising British, Australian, Canadian, Indian and troops of other nationalities invaded southern Italy in July 1943, soldiers from all armies except the Indian Army indulged in rape, molestation and plunder. One of the elderly ladies present told us how she was being chased by two Allied soldiers when an Indian soldier intervened and protected her. He told the chasing soldiers not to harm her because she was his sister! In another instance a posse of Indian soldiers voluntarily guarded an apartment building and prevented soldiers of the other Allied armies from entering it. There were numerous stories of heroism like this. These marvellous episodes bear testimony to the ethical standards and professionalism of the Indian Army.

The following day there was a special reception in honour of the personnel of our warship INS *Brahmaputra* at the town hall. When the ship left port finally after four days, virtually the entire town was on the jetty with several bands in attendance to bid adieu. It was a very moving and emotional experience. The ethics of the magnificent Indian Army and its gentlemanly officers and men is still etched in the memory of the citizens of Taranto.[25]

Burma

It is now time to shift focus to the steamy jungles of South-East Asia and Burma where the British Empire was under grave threat from the advancing Japanese. Stunned by the rapid advance of the Japanese Army along the twin fronts of Malaya and Burma in late 1941, the British Empire tottered as never before with the surrender of almost 85,000 troops as they fell back to the fortress of Singapore, which finally capitulated in February 1942. Of these, almost 60,000 were Indian troops – their confidence in the military might of Britain shaken badly.[26] As the remnants of General Alexander's Burma Corps retreated into India in April 1942, Lieutenant General William Slim (he would be promoted to Field Marshal as the war progressed), the commander of the newly formed 14th Army, set about reorganizing and preparing his army for an offensive while the Japanese were kept busy through multiple attempts by Allied forces to retake the Arakans. The composition of the 14th Army was a telling comment on the impact of colonial troops on the final outcome of the Burma campaign and the downward trajectory of British power in Asia: almost 70 per cent of the troops were Indian, Gorkhas, Burmese and Africans.[27] Six Indian divisions with another three in reserve comprised the main punch of Slim's force.[28]

In an audacious move to outflank and cut off Slim's army in Burma and make inroads into India, the Japanese attacked the thinly held garrisons of Imphal and Kohima in March 1944. The defence and lifting of sieges of Kohima and Imphal proved to be the finest hour of the Indian Army in Burma and saw the emergence of significant synergy between the Indian Army and the Indian Air Force, which played a stellar role in not only sustaining the garrisons, but also in providing close air support under trying conditions. The ultimate honour for the Indian Army was to come almost seventy years later in April 2013 when a nationwide survey and public debate in Britain sponsored by the National Army War Museum chose the Battle of Imphal and Kohima as the *Greatest Battle fought by Britain.*[29] In a prize-winning essay titled 'Everybody's Friend' in the British newspaper, *The Financial Times*, Raghu Karnad, a young Indian military historian, calls the Battle for Kohima 'as desperate as any in the war, and although seldom remembered, it was as fateful as Tobruk or Normandy'.[30] By the time the Japanese retreated from the frontiers of India in early 1945, they had stretched themselves to the limit both in South-East Asia and the Pacific, and were on the back foot against a rejuvenated Allied army that was seeking redemption for all the humiliating losses in the preceding years.

A unique experiment was tried out during the recapture of Burma in 1944–45 to validate the military prowess of a *pure* Indian brigade. The 51st 'All Indian Brigade' was formed in 25 Infantry Division to allow the Indians to either 'leap high or drown'. The three battalions in the brigade were commanded by three accomplished Kings Commissioned Officers (KCOs), Lieutenant Colonels L.P. Sen, S.P. Thorat and K.C. Thimayya.[31] The brigade distinguished itself in the Battle of Kangaw in early 1945, which none other than Field Marshal Slim called 'the fiercest battle fought in Burma'. All the three Indian battalion commanders were decorated with Distinguished Service Orders (DSOs) for their outstanding leadership during the Kangaw operations.[32] The exploits of one of the battalions, 8 Kumaon Regiment (then 8/19 Baluch Regiment), reflects the courage of the entire brigade and is well chronicled in the archives of the Kumaon Regimental Centre at Ranikhet, excerpts from which are highlighted below:

> During the winter of 1944/45 the allied offensive to recapture Burma was in full swing and the Japanese were on the retreat. Kangaw, a small village was held by the Japanese on the coastal road, about 50 miles south of Myobaung, the ancient capital of Arakan. Kangaw was to be taken with utmost speed and for that purpose a wide flanking surprise approach through the sea was the only answer. On 23 Jan, 8 Kumaon under Lt Col (later Gen.) KS Thimayya was inducted into the beachhead with orders to capture Kangaw. On 29 Jan, after a fierce battle the regiment captured the village Kangaw and also a small hill feature close by to effectively deny the use of the road to the Japanese. The Japanese left 25 dead against own loss of three killed and six wounded. The Kangaw village and nearby hills were then held doggedly by the regiment as the Japanese counter attack on night of 06/07 Feb 1945 was beaten back. This marked the defeat of Japanese and victory of 51 Inf Bde in Kangaw.[33]

In his inimitable and racy style, D.R. Mankekar, a war correspondent during the Burma campaign, described the three Indian commanding officers:

> Thimayya struck me as a hail-fellow-well-met, tall athletic personality. His uninhibited laughter chased out the blues and put cheer in your soul. He was adored by his men as well as officers, who included three Britishers. Thorat, commanding 2/2 Punjabs, was a typically rugged Maratha, who with his clipped moustache looked every inch a soldier and talked of his men and their deeds like a proud and loving father. L.P. Sen, commanding 16/10 Baluch, only thirty-four, was the youngest of the three C.O.s and one of the youngest to command a battalion. He struck me as very handsome and very shy and had to be coaxed to speak about himself and the exploits of his battalion.[34]

By the end of the war, Thimayya had been promoted to the rank of brigadier and taken over the Indian brigade at Rangoon. He also became the first Indian to command a brigade as part of the peacekeeping force that was sent to Japan during the post-war reconstruction period.[35]

The exploits of the Indian Army during WW II will not be complete without heading back to Europe, this time to Sicily and Italy, where for the first time during WW II, three Indian army divisions (4th, 8th and 10th)[36] of the 8th Army fought alongside US troops of the 7th Army as part of an expeditionary force that was to capture Italy. Of all the battles fought in Italy the battle for the monastery at Monte Casino and its surrounding heights was the bloodiest and involved a number of Indian battalions from the 4th and 8th Indian divisions. Indian troops won five Victoria Crosses in Italy and the respect of the American commander of the 15th Army Group, Lieutenant General Mark W. Clark, who commented in the foreword of a book *The Tiger Triumphs*:

> I have had the distinction of having under my command a trio of great Indian divisions – the Fourth, Eighth and Tenth – whose fighting record in Italy has been a splendid one. No obstacle has succeeded in delaying these Indian troops for long or in lowering their high morale or fighting spirit.[37]

The Indian Army of WW II with approximately 2.5 million men was the largest volunteer army of all times. Nearly 50,000 Indian troops and officers lost their lives in the war.[38] Of the nearly 6,300 awards won by the Indian Army for gallantry during WW II were thirty-one Victoria Crosses, four George Crosses, 252 Distinguished Service Orders (DSOs) and 1,311 Military Crosses.

The Indian National Army

No analysis of the Indian Army during WW II is complete without looking at the Indian National Army (INA) and its impact on the consciousness of the Indian Army and the Indian nation at large. Inspired in part by the revolutionary Bengali leader Rash Behari Bose and led by the intensely nationalistic and militant Congressman, Netaji Subhas Chandra Bose, who attempted to seek help from the Axis powers to evict Britain from India, the core of the INA was called the Azad Hind Fauj. Comprising over 20,000 troops of the 60,000 Indian troops who surrendered at Singapore in February 1942, it was mainly manned by Sikhs and Muslims.[39] Literally abandoned by their British officers, many young Indian officers who had joined the Indian Army because of their interest in soldiering felt cheated by the abominable collapse, and gravitated towards the idea of a 'liberation army'. The INA also included a motley bunch of Indian lawyers, businessmen and plantation workers from across Malaya and Burma who felt that the ongoing non-violent struggle for independence was largely ineffective.[40] Stirred by intensely nationalistic and militant indoctrination by Netaji and his band of freedom fighters, they dedicated themselves to waging war to evict the British from India.

How did other Indian officers react to what the British called a 'betrayal'? Lieutenant General W.A.G. Pinto, an emergency commissioned officer during WW II, remarked in an interview with the author in 2014 that most of the Indian officers kept quiet and hardly discussed the issue as they were not privy to what actually happened in Singapore. But, he added, personally he felt that what his colleagues did by joining the INA was against basic tenets of soldiering like loyalty and allegiance. He added that the existing ethos and military programming of the time made most Indian officers uncomfortable with the idea of a uniformed person revolting against the authority he had voluntarily sworn to follow.[41] Harbaksh Singh, one of India's most distinguished commanders with combat experience in WW II, the India–Pakistan wars of 1947–48 and 1965; the India–China war of 1962, and a Japanese POW after the fall of Malaya, is one of the few officers who turned down the call by Netaji to join the INA. He did so not because he was any less of a patriot, but because he was not convinced of the INA's mission and its ability to execute a successful military campaign against a tested British Army.[42]

Netaji's core group of military leaders included the likes of J.K. Bhonsale, Captain Mohan Singh (later a general in the INA), Captain Shahnawaz Khan and Mohd Zaman Kiani, all of whom clearly justified the use of violence as a means to achieve political aims.[43] However, this force did not have the anticipated operational impact on the war as it attempted to enter India by fighting alongside Japanese formations as they advanced through Burma into India. Comprising three divisions by mid-1943, including guerrilla units, which infiltrated Burma before the main Japanese advance, the INA deployed one division (approximately 12,000 men) to lead the advance into Burma alongside approximately 84,000 troops from front-line Japanese divisions.[44] Less known is that Subhas Bose was adept at covert operations too. Before his forces advanced alongside the Japanese into Burma, four teams were landed on the Kathiawar coast by a Japanese submarine and melted away into the countryside in different directions. One of the teams operated from Calcutta from early 1944 onwards and remained in radio contact with Netaji for most of the remaining period of the war.[45]

After significant initial success that saw the force rapidly advancing through Burma in 1943–44, and knocking on the doors of India by mid-1944, they were outmanoeuvred and outfought by a numerically and tactically superior Allied force that numbered close to 1,55,000 troops.[46] After having said to have raised the Indian flag at Moirang,[47] about 45 kilometres south of Imphal in what is today the state of Manipur, their last frontal battle was fought further north at Kohima and Imphal in 1944 where thousands were killed and many surrendered when faced with the ferocious resistance from well-trained defenders and highly experienced Allied field leadership.[48] Led by Bose himself, remnants of the INA retreated over 2,000 km to Bangkok without food or equipment – a feat that was acknowledged by the British as a masterpiece of military tactics and strategy.[49] One of the INA's last stands during this southbound retreat in early 1945 was at the Buddhist shrine of Mount Popa near Meiktila in Mandalay district of central Burma where the INA 2nd Division attempted to hold the rampaging 14th Army at bay.[50] By May 1945 it was all over for Bose as he reached Bangkok. Of the number of INA's Viceroy's commissioned officers (VCOs), non-commissioned officers (NCOs) and sepoys who were captured before the end of the war, a few were tried for espionage and sabotage and executed.[51]

The British classified the INA personnel after the war as 'white', 'grey' and 'black'. While the 'whites' were reinstated because they assisted the British, 'greys' were those who expressed regret for their action and were merely dismissed. The 'blacks', however, were put in detention camps to await trial for sedition and treason amongst other charges.[52]

Unfortunately, the reported demise of Bose in a mysterious plane crash in August 1945, which is still shrouded in secrecy, and the largely liberal historical discourse in independent India do not give him and the INA sufficient credit in the struggle for independence. The largely secular and egalitarian profile of the INA was also to play a significant role in influencing the demographic profile of independent India's armed forces. While the trial of high-profile INA prisoners including three officers in the Red Fort was an event of national importance and all of them were acquitted of the charges of sedition and treason, none of the officers, men and women of the INA were allowed to join the Indian armed forces even after Independence.

Though not much archival material is available on the actual reasons for this, it is possible that a quid pro quo agreement was reached between the British and the future leaders of India prior to the trial at Red Fort. In response to repeated requests from Nehru to acquit the numerous INA prisoners still held in prisons all over the country in 1946, Lord Mountbatten wrote to Nehru saying:

> When you get your independence and have your own army, the people you want are those who remain loyal to their oath and will stay with you and not those who just change according to political opportunism.[53]

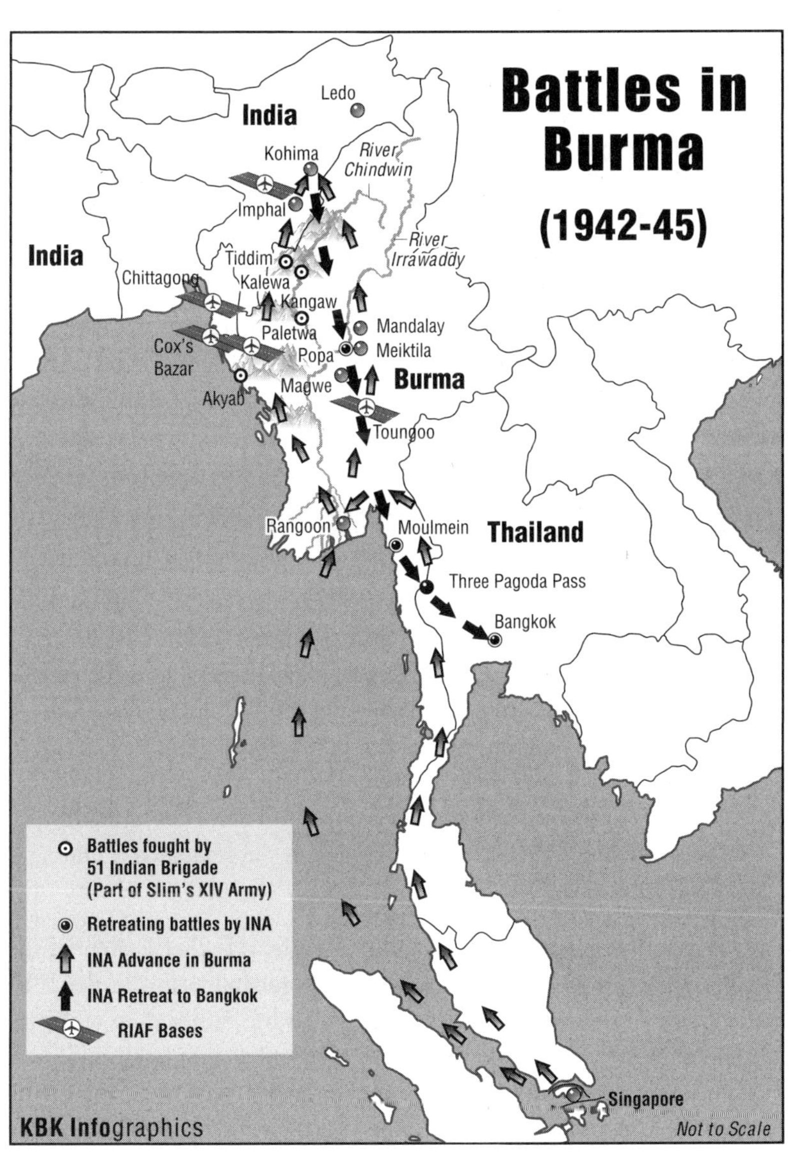

Battles in Burma
(1942-45)
India
India
Ledo
Kohima
River Chindwin
Imphal
River Irrawaddy
Tiddim
Kalewa
Chittagong
Kangaw
Paletwa
Cox's Bazar
Akyab
Popa
Mandalay
Meiktila
Magwe
Burma
Toungoo
Rangoon
Moulmein
Thailand
Three Pagoda Pass
Bangkok
Singapore
Battles fought by 51 Indian Brigade (Part of Slim's XIV Army)
Retreating battles by INA
INA Advance in Burma
INA Retreat to Bangkok
RIAF Bases
KBK Infographics
Not to Scale

From November 1945 to April 1946, a number of high-profile INA prisoners were tried by military court martial for offences ranging from murder to waging war against the king. Many were harshly sentenced to transportation for life, cashiered, or made to forfeit their pay and allowances. Only after the trials were completed did Auchinleck, the C-in-C, remit the sentences to mere cashiering[54] and thereafter agree to drop all charges against INA soldiers except that of physical torture of other Indians.[55]

Of all the British generals who commanded Indian officers and troops during WW II, it was Auchinleck who understood them best, be it on the battlefield or after the war as they struggled to make sense of the ongoing freedom struggle. Not only did he contribute immensely to raising the self-esteem of Indian officers and men as military professionals in an overtly racial British Indian Army, it is his sagacity which paved the way for an INA trial that combined military propriety with the recognition of a growing countrywide unrest. Writing to the viceroy and a fellow WW II field commander, Field Marshal Wavell, he argued:

> I know from my long experience of Indian troops how hard it is for even the best and most sympathetic British officer to gauge the inner feelings of the Indian soldier, and history supports me in this view. I do not think any senior British officer today knows what is the real feeling among Indian ranks regarding the I.N.A. I myself feel, from my own instincts largely, but also from the information I have from various sources that there is a growing feeling of sympathy for the I.N.A and an increasing disregard for the brutalities committed by some its members ... It is impossible to apply our standards of ethics to this problem ...[56]

It is also likely that though Gandhi, Nehru and other leaders of the Congress party were highly vocal about the rehabilitation of the INA soldiers, they preferred that they join civilian life rather than return to the Indian Army. This, they felt, would ensure the completely apolitical nature of free India's armed forces as they feared that the entry of the former INA personnel into the armed forces would bring with it the aggressive political legacy of Subhas Chandra Bose. They, however, reaped enormous political mileage from the trial as Nehru very eloquently and publicly urged Field Marshal Auchinleck and Lord Wavell to reconsider their initial tough stand and drop charges of sedition and treason.[57] The acquittal of Shahnawaz Khan, Prem Kumar Sehgal and Dhillon in January 1946 was seen as a triumphant moment for nationalism though large numbers of INA prisoners continued to languish without benefits till years later. Many of the Muslim commanders of the INA chose to shift their allegiance to Pakistan after Independence and were rehabilitated, though they faced some resistance from the Pakistan Army when it came to amalgamating them into the mainstream. Some like Kiani even participated in the covert war against India in Poonch during the 1947–48 conflict and then faded away into oblivion.[58]

However, to be fair and objective about its overall impact on the British psyche, the INA put a serious doubt in the minds of Britain's post–WW II leaders that such a force had the potential to lead another internal war of independence. My own analysis and the intensely passionate and incisive biography of Subhas Chandra Bose by his grand-nephew, Prof. Sugata Bose, a history professor at Harvard and a current member of parliament, points at the coercive impact of the INA on the British decision to leave India before it was too late. Speaking in Thailand on 21 May 1945, Bose urged Indians to fight on for freedom saying, 'It may be that we shall not go to Delhi via Imphal, but the roads to Delhi are many like the roads to Rome.'[59] As Bipin Chandra, an eminent Indian historian, reflects in his analysis of Subhas Bose and the INA:

> Even though his strategy of winning freedom in cooperation with the fascist powers was criticised at the time by most nationalists, by organising the INA he set an inspiring example of patriotism before the Indian people and the Indian army.[60]

Writing on the impact of the INA on the British Indian Army despite its defeat in a chapter titled 'We Fight On' in *Chalo Delhi*, a compilation of his works, Netaji Bose argued:

> There is, however, one silver lining in the cloud that has overtaken us, and that is, the British Indian Army of today is not the British Indian Army of the last war ... There is no doubt that at heart large sections of the British Indian Army sympathize with the Azad Hind Fauj and its fight for freedom. But the British Indian Army is not yet ready to

> take the risk and line up with the revolutionaries. After coming into Burma, the eyes of the British Indian Army will be opened. They will see for themselves what the Provisional Government of Azad Hind and Azad Hind Fauj have done and how they have fought for India's freedom. The effect of this experience on the British Indian Army, and all other Indians who have come into Burma alongside the British, is bound to be great in the days to come.[61]

In a prize-winning essay written for an Indian defence journal in 2013, Brigadier R.R. Palsokar (retd), one of the Indian Army's committed scholars and a brigade commander during India's turbulent intervention in Sri Lanka during 1984–87, writes with a detached objectivity about the British Indian Army and the INA trials:

> There is a tendency to romanticise the deeds of the soldiers of the British Indian Army and the relations between the British officers and their Indian troops, particularly during the two world wars. But in a nationalistic context one has to take a more detached view. Two incidents prior to independence affected the Indian armed forces greatly. One was the affair of the Indian National Army led by Subhas Chandra Bose. Of particular interest is how the British dealt with the matter even as independence was round the corner. The Commander-in-Chief, Field Marshal Claude Auchinleck insisted that he would hold a symbolic trial of one Hindu, one Muslim and one Sikh, in the Red Fort for 'waging war against the King Emperor'. His purpose, as described later, was different and showed great sagacity. His main aim was 'to maintain the reliability, stability and efficiency of the Indian Army whatever the government be. He also believed that every Indian officer (at the end of the war there were 15,000 of them) and soldier was or should be a nationalist who wanted independence for his country. So he decided 'to confirm the findings of the guilt, confirm the sentence of cashiering, but to show clemency in respect of the sentence of transportation for life, which he remitted'. Knowing that the country was to become independent shortly, the temptation not to do anything and let matters drift must have been very great. But by this one action, Auchinleck left behind a legacy which was rightly upheld and continued by the first

Indian C-in-C, General K.M. Cariappa that the army's creed was, 'I will obey.' If the Indian Army and the armed forces have remained apolitical, great credit must go to these two.[62]

The legacy of the INA was rightfully recognized by General Shankar Roy Chowdhury, the chief of the army staff between 1994 and 1997, when he ensured that the stirring marching song of the INA became the official song of the Indian Army. Composed by Mumtaz Hussain and set to music by Ram Singh Thakur in March 1943,[63] the song is titled '*Qadam Qadam Badhaye Ja*'. Literally translated, it means Forward March – Step by Step. Considering the turbulence of the moment, feeling of abandonment by a traditionally 'suppressed' community and the stirrings of freedom, the INA had a significantly greater impact on the British decision to leave India than what the existing historical discourse in both the countries is willing to acknowledge.

Transition, Adjustment and Freedom

How did the Indian army cope with the post–WW II period and the adjustments it had to make in the run-up to the Partition of India in 1947? Like the period after WW I, large-scale demobilization took place as the Crown struggled with the financial challenges of post-war reconstruction in Britain and Europe. Economist John Maynard Keynes pegged the cost of maintaining the Empire at 2,000 million pounds, with revenues declining alarmingly because of the drop in exports.[64] Within a year of the end of WW II, the strength of the Indian Army was reduced to less than half from 20,00,000 to 8,00,000 with plans to reduce it further to around 4,00,000 by 1947.[65] This caused some amount of heartburn amongst sections of India's martial communities like the Jat Sikhs[66] and caught the attention of people like Field Marshal Auchinleck who were engaged in restructuring the Indian Army with independence looming on the horizon. The aftereffects of demobilization were also factored into the whole process of timing the grant of Independence to ensure minimum loss of face for the Crown.

Sir Michael Howard, one of Britain's greatest military historians of the modern era, writes poignantly in his book *War in European*

History about the decline of British military power in the aftermath of WW II[67]:

> The British, economically exhausted and chastened after a humiliation at the hands of the Japanese that not even their successful reconquest of Burma could redress, quickly accepted the impossibility of retaining the Indian subcontinent and abandoned it to its own devices, relinquishing thereby the Indian Army that had alone given them the status of a global military power.[68]

The other major fallout of the mass mobilization phase prior to the two wars was that the Indian Army at Independence was no longer an elitist force dominated by martial races or upper castes but an inclusive force that represented the diversity of India – something that has also ensured the survival of the fledgling democracy. For example, four new regiments were raised by the British in 1941, which reflected this approach. These were Sikh Light Infantry, Mahar (one battalion of this regiment was raised in 1917, only to be disbanded after WW I), Bihar and Assam regiments.[69] One has to look no further than Pakistan to realize that one of the main reasons for repeated martial rule in Pakistan is because the Pakistan Army has been dominated over the years by one major martial community, the Punjabi Muslim community.[70] Stephen Cohen, an accomplished US academic and arguably the most incisive western analyst on military matters in the subcontinent, has tracked the Indian and Pakistani armies closely for the last five decades and no study of the DNA of these two armies, particularly from a demographic and attitudinal perspective, is complete without a reading of his works.[71]

As the Indian Army came out of WW II with its head held high, one cannot but help detect a weakening of British attitude towards the demand for independence. While traditional historians would argue that that the Quit India civil disobedience movement had reached a high point and significantly impeded the Crown's attempts to hang on to the Empire, astute British generals like Wavell and Auchinleck, who had had fought alongside Indian troops in various campaigns, played a prominent role in convincing the post-war British government that it would be hard to hold on to India. This, they argued, was not only because of the surging countrywide aspirations for Independence, but also because the Indian

Army along with its large band of Indian officers had matured to a point where the British would not be able to handle another military revolt, a sample of which had already taken place at Jabalpur where 1,700 men of the Signals Training Centre (STC) revolted on 26 February 1946 in the aftermath of the naval revolt. More of that will be highlighted in the next chapter. Eighty men behind the revolt were court-martialled and dismissed without pay and pension. Forty-one others were sent to prison. But the incident was quickly hushed up. The Jabalpur revolt had the British worried about what they took for granted – the British Indian Army's loyalty. Added to all this was the lingering impact of the INA and the legacy of Subhas Bose, which accelerated the British exit from India. Auchinleck in particular had reported back to the chiefs of staff in London that five divisions of completely loyal troops would be required to put down any widespread uprising this time around.[72]

Christopher Bayly and Tim Harper in their eminently readable military history narrative of the last years of British Asia, *Forgotten Armies,* corroborate the military catalyst that accelerated the demise of the British Raj by writing:

> Above all it was Indian soldiers, civilian labourers and businessmen who made possible the victory of 1945. Their price was the rapid independence of India.[73]
>
> The VCOs and Kings commissioned Officers, loyal and increasingly well trained were not only the last soldiers of the British Raj, they were the advance guard of the new nation.[74]

On the eve of Independence, the Indian Army was divided proportionately between India and Pakistan, with India retaining a strength of approximately 2,80,000 troops with less than 1,50,000 going to Pakistan. The Indian Army's share comprised fourteen cavalry and eleven infantry regiments from the erstwhile formations along with six of the ten Gorkha regiments. Speaking on the Gorkhas and their legendary bravery, Field Marshal Manekshaw is said to have once remarked: 'If a man says he is not afraid of dying, he is either lying or is a Gorkha.'

These forces were supplemented by the four new regiments that were raised in 1941and alluded to earlier in the chapter.[75] Regiments were still segregated into single-class, fixed-class, mixed-class or all-class entities[76] and attempts to do away with this system partially failed due to the fragile class and caste system that prevailed at the time of Independence. The system would continue for decades to come. However, to be fair to the Indian Army, a genuine attempt to move towards an egalitarian and a broad-based regimental system commenced in 1949 with the formation of the Brigade of the Guards. Now comprising nineteen battalions, the four initial battalions of the brigade were drawn from among the oldest battalions in the Indian Army. These were 2 Punjab Regiment, 1 Grenadier Regiment, 1 Rajputana Rifles and 1 Rajput Regiment. These were followed by the 5th battalion, which comprised troops from all the hill districts of India (Garhwal, Kumaon and the north-eastern hill districts among others). Soon after, the 6th battalion was formed with troops from all the south Indian states. A perceptive group captain once asked me whether the Indian Army's inability to completely do away with racial regiments after Independence meant that in part it acknowledged the foundational correctness of the policy. I explained to him that while to some the myth of the superiority of the so-called 'martial races' was a hangover from the colonial era, contemporary Indian military leaders looked at this merely as a method to ensure greater cohesion and homogeneity, rather than an exercise in keeping races separate. Actions in later years would prove the correctness of the latter argument as the Indian Army gradually moved towards a multi-class composition in most raisings, most significant being the raising of the Rashtriya Rifles to counter the insurgency in J&K.

Not entirely confident of passing on the leadership of the Indian Army to its own young generals like Cariappa, Rajendra Sinhji and Thimayya, and influenced in no small measure by Lord Mountbatten, Nehru and his cabinet chose to continue with General Lockhart and General Roy Bucher as the first two C-in-Cs of independent India's army. As the specially formed Punjab Force grappled with the horrors of the Partition, free India's army would be involved in a major military operation across three sectors in the princely state of Jammu and Kashmir within three months of Independence.

Officers and Men

A last word in this chapter about the officers and men who formed the immediate core of the Indian Army after Independence is important to understand civil–military relations as they unfolded in the years ahead. Endowed with a typically British flavour of soldiering in terms of operational orientation, but demonstrating an integrity and commitment to the new nation that they were now part of, despite not being active in the freedom struggle, most officers took time to absorb the idea of India, the contradictory nature of the INA struggle and the vision of their political masters. The experience of the Indian officers' relationship with their British counterparts was a mixed bag. While some were treated as equals in every way, many others like Major Generals U.C. Dube and 'Monty' Palit were scathing in their indictment of British racial overtones. Dube recollects that in the Gorkha regiment he was posted to, Indian officers were asked to dine in a separate room during guest nights when ladies would join the officers for a community meal in the officers' mess.[77] Palit is equally caustic when he says: 'I was never asked by my commanding officer, second-in-command or my company commander for a meal or a cup of tea in his (sic) house.'[78]

The emerging political class too grappled with the complexities of understanding that the integrity and training of these officers would ensure that they would do whatever it took to protect the fragile democracy that India was nurturing. To make matters difficult, the inclusiveness that had permeated troop recruitment had not seeped down to the officer class which came mainly from the upper classes and martial races. This aspect did not really endear the officers to the political class, which represented the true diversity of India and felt that an army led by an elite band of officers could not be trusted.

There was also this feeling that as the independence movement gathered steam, large numbers of Indian officers should have resigned their commission and joined the movement. However, leaders like Motilal Nehru, Jawaharlal Nehru's father, thought otherwise. In an anecdote narrated by noted US strategic affairs commentator of those times, Selig Harrison, in his article 'Thimayya', highlights this dilemma. The article describes an encounter at Allahabad in 1926 where Thimayya as a young subaltern was asked by Motilal Nehru during the intermission at a play: 'How does it feel in a British uniform?' A cool Thimayya replied laconically, 'Hot!'[79] Thereafter, in an intellectually stimulating discussion, he asked Motilal Nehru whether he should resign his commission and join the freedom movement to prove that he was no less of a nationalist. It was then that Motilal Nehru advised Thimayya to stay on and desist from doing anything foolish as free India would need a professional military. He also suggested that it would be best for all the Kings Commissioned officers to stay on, study the use of force and continue to serve the Crown. Similarly when Lieutenant Prem Bhagat, the Indian Army's first recipient of Victoria Cross in WW II, approached Gandhiji with a similar dilemma, he was advised by Gandhiji to stay on as independent India would need the services of committed and intensely patriotic officers to build a modern army within a democratic political framework.

This lack of social cohesion and separation from mainstream Indian society, and the inability to share a common vision of India, would be the primary reason for not only the fragile civil–military relations in the years ahead, but also the detached relationship between the armed forces and Indian society at large.[80] It would take years for the typical Indian Army officer to shake off his colonial mindset and really understand the country he was defending so heroically. General Krishnaswamy Sundarji, arguably one of India's finest soldier-scholars in the post-Independence era, was a WW II emergency commissioned officer, not one of the archetypal Sandhurst or IMA products. His view of senior army leadership at Independence is one of the most honest descriptions I have come across and is at some variance with the popular discourse of the time which tended to eulogize the KCIOs:

> Cariappa (and Thimayya) had become brigadiers just before the end of the war (WW II) and the rest remained at colonel or below almost till the end of the war, and so got their ranks pretty rapidly after independence with very little experience in each of the successive ranks. There was understandably a certain degree of tentativeness about their self-confidence and added to this was the subconscious feeling of being a second class citizen, engendered by the British. Officers today in similar ranks are professionally much more capable

> than people of that time; however on the positive side the old timers were less career conscious in their professional approach than the latter day lot![81]

Similarly, the widespread feeling that the British-trained officers and the Viceroy's Commissioned officers (junior commissioned officers) formed the rock-solid edifice of the Indian Army was also contestable as the cheerful, hardy and selfless Indian soldier of the time also merits equal recognition. Driven more by the need to uphold the honour and pride of his clan, village, province or regiment, rather than any great loyalty to the Crown, the Indian soldier's toughness in battle was much acclaimed. The ability to withstand combat stress in conditions he had seldom been exposed to could be attributed as much to the harsh conditions of his rural upbringing, as it was to the disciplined and scientific training regimen of the Crown. What else can explain the performance of the Kumaonis during the amphibious assault at Kangaw – many of these hardy hill soldiers had never seen the sea before embarking for the operation!

6

THE INDIAN NAVY

India's maritime heritage goes well beyond in the past than some of us might comprehend. With the Himalayas in the north, Indians for centuries have depended on sea routes for trade and communication with the rest of the world.

– Admiral Arun Prakash[1]

May the oceans continue to be auspicious to the plains of Hindustan until the sea-blindness affecting the subcontinent is reduced to enable India to quicken her faltering maritime stride into the twenty-first century and not remain becalmed in the Ocean of Destiny.

– Vice Admiral Mihir Roy[2]

Early History

India's maritime legacy can be traced back to the Indus Valley Civilization where signs of maritime trade linkages with other civilizations have been found at excavation sites at Harappa.[3] While clear signs of India's sea-bound forays into the Arabian Sea and towards South-East Asia emerged from the southern parts of the country in the first century AD,[4] any serious maritime expansion and conquest commenced only with the mighty Chola Empire, under its dynamic kings Rajaraja I and Rajendra I.[5] Between the later part of the tenth century AD and the beginning of the twelfth century AD, these rulers of the mighty Chola Empire extended their influence to Sri Lanka, Maldives and most parts of South-East Asia. This was done by a combination of maritime conquest, trade and cultural links, what could well be termed in modern parlance as a combination of hard and soft power. It is because of this holistic application of maritime power that Indian influence is still prevalent in many parts of South-East Asia in the garb of art forms and archeological monuments that have a distinct south Indian flavour. Indian sea power declined after the thirteenth century with the arrival of Muslim invaders from the north and was completely eclipsed by European sea power in the late sixteenth century with the arrival on the Kerala coast of the Portuguese led by Vasco da Gama.[6] Some spirited resistance though was offered by the Zamorin (Hindu rulers) of Calicut for well over ninety years in the sixteenth century.[7]

The Zamorin of Malabar ruled over a multi-religious population comprising Muslim seafaring people and Hindus around the Malabar Coast. Located in what is today large portions of the northern and central Kerala coast, their empire extended from about 60 km north of the town of Calicut (Kozhikode today), to the port of Quilon, almost 350 km to the south. The Kunjali Marakkars were a seafaring warrior clan who sailed along the Malabar Coast and commanded the Zamorin's naval fleet at a time when the Portuguese showed great interest in establishing a foothold there. Repeatedly fighting off Portuguese raids through the sixteenth century, the Marakkars can rightfully claim to have been the first organized naval defence force in late medieval India. Their resistance was finally broken down when their own rulers conspired with the Portuguese to defeat Kunhali Marrakar in a combined sea–land battle in 1604.[8]

Maratha Resurgence at Sea

As one drives along the west coast from Gujarat down to Kerala, it is impossible not to notice the number of coastal fortifications along the way. What is also clearly evident is that the number of fortifications on the Maharashtra and Konkan coast far outnumber those along the Gujarat, Karnataka and Kerala coasts. Some of these like Devgarh and Alibaug are typically Maratha in architecture and design, while others like Murud and Janjira have distinct Mughal features. The Maratha opposition to both the Mughal and British Empires was led by the Maratha warrior and guerilla king Shivaji, who not only developed a strong army but also had the vision to build a navy. It is remarkable that he visualized the imminent decline of Mughal power and the possibilities of his empire being threatened by European colonialists from the sea and kept track of Portuguese and Dutch forays on the west coast. With a keen eye for picking the right kind of leaders to support his vision of a pan-Indian Maratha Empire in the second half of the seventeenth century, he chose Tukoji Angre as his Sarkhel (Admiral in the Marathi language) and protect the seas on the Maratha coast (west coast of India) from predatory European fleets.

With his doctrine resting on a sound precept of *Jalamaiva yasya, balamaiva tasya* (whoever is powerful on sea is all-powerful),[9] Tukoji built a fleet of 200 ships and after Shivaji's death in 1680 chose to be an independent satrap with allegiance to the Maratha empire. Tukoji's son, Kanhoji, followed in his father's footsteps and even after Shivaji's death, dominated the seas around Maharashtra and Konkan from a fortress at Alibaug, a few hours south of what is today Mumbai. Kanhoji established his maritime prowess in early seventeenth century by defeating a strong Arab pirate fleet operating out of Muscat, which was looting merchant ships bound for the Konkan coast.[10] For almost thirty years till his death in 1729, Kanhoji built a powerful 300-ship flotilla with significant firepower and conducted numerous raids against Portuguese and British ships, interdicting merchant ships and men-of-war as they sailed from Surat on the Gujarat coast to Calicut on the Kerala coast. In 1721, he defeated a joint attempt by the Portuguese and the British to breach his fortress at Alibaug.[11] Like Tipu Sultan and Maharaja Ranjit Singh, Kanhoji Angre also employed Frenchmen to teach his sailors aspects of modern seamanship and firepower drills, all of which paid rich dividends in ensuring that the British East India Company remained unsuccessful in its attempts to dominate India's west coast for a long time.

Unfortunately, like in so many instances in the history of British colonial expansion in India, they managed to divide the opposition by allying with one faction to first defeat the stronger element, and then progressivelly fragmenting the remainder of the opposition. In this case, after the death of Kanhoji Angre in 1729, the British bided their time and allied with the Peshwa rulers of Pune to defeat Kanhoji Angre's son, Tulaji, at Vijaydurg in 1756. Thus ended the last vestiges of maritime resistance to British colonial expansion. Kanhoji Angre's legacy is well preserved at Alibaug and free India's first establishment in Bombay, the Western Naval Command's headquarters, was called INS *Angre* in honour of India's own Maratha admiral of the western seas. Although modern Indian fiction writers largely ignored war as a theme, Manohar Malgaonkar, a retired lieutenant colonel from the Maratha Light Infantry and a popular writer in the 1960s and 1970s, did write an eminently readable biography on the life and times of Kanhoji Angre titled *Sea Hawk.*

British Legacy

Although the first fleet for the protection of the East India Company's trade routes from pirates and Maratha sea power was set up at Surat in 1612, the real expression of British maritime might in the subcontinent was the Bombay Marine. After defeating the remnants of Maratha, French, Dutch and Portuguese sea power, the Bombay Marine set about dominating the west coast of India from Gujarat in the north to Calicut in the south. After nearly 150 years of unchallenged existence,the Bombay Marine was renamed the Indian Navy in 1830, Her Majesty's Indian Navy in 1858, Her Majesty's Indian Marine in 1877, Royal Indian Marine in 1877 and finally, the Royal Indian Navy in 1934.[12] These frequent changes reflected the constant tussle between various stakeholders of British colonial leadership for control of the primary means of transportation for the British from their homeland to their colonies. This, in turn, also controlled the distribution of wealth amongst the various beneficiaries including the Crown, the royalty and hundreds of merchants. Compared to the British Indian Army, which depended on Indian soldiers to do the bulk of their war fighting, the Royal Marine mainly had a complement of British sailors and officers.

While the officers were drawn from the Royal Navy and the East India Company, the sailors comprised mercenaries, employees of the Company and convicts working for their freedom. Records from a few towns along the Konkan coast of Maharashtra indicate that once the Marathas had been defeated at sea, the East India Company started recruiting locals and employed them on ships that sailed only along the coast of India, and not on any long voyages to England. These Konkani sailors can rightfully claim to be the first Indian sailors of the Royal Navy. After the First War of Independence in 1857, a complement of the Royal Marine was positioned at Calcutta and formed the eastern wing of the Royal Indian Marine (RIM). By the end of the nineteenth century, it had fifty ships on its inventory.

The Choppy Waters of WW I

Though the Indian Army bore the brunt of the horrors of WW I, and some Indian pilots did blaze a trail of glory across the skies of France, the RIM also contributed to the war effort in its own small way.[13] The main roles of the RIM were minesweeping, patrolling the waters of Iraq, Egypt and East Africa and ferrying troops and war supplies to the same region. The relative global mastery of the Royal Navy ensured that the Royal Indian Marine hardly suffered any attrition and did not get involved in any significant naval battles during the war. The severe limitations of the Royal Indian Marine came to the fore in the abortive Mesopotamian campaign of 1915–16, where the British were defeated at Kut[14] with the Royal Marine unable to either support the campaign with adequate troop inductions or firepower.

The aftermath of the war brought with it the miseries of downsizing, retrenchment and widespread unemployment in the villages of the Konkan coast as the Royal Indian Marine was designated a non-combatant service with only survey and patrolling tasks.[15] In response to widespread protests from leaders of India's independence movement and efforts by Lord Jellicoe, the admiral of the fleet, to realistically assess the naval defence requirements of the Indian empire, the Royal Indian Marine was once again designated as a combatant service in 1925.[16] Local recruitment was resumed and Sub-Lieutenant D.N. Mukherji joined as the first Indian officer in the engineering branch.[17]

Growing Up

The inter-war years were interesting ones for the Royal Indian Marine as it attempted to keep pace with the growth of the Indian Army; its growth was similar to that of the Indian Air Force with its niggardly complement of barely two flights of Wapiti aircraft (also called What a Pity) by knowledgeable aviators of the time. Despite the attempts by Lord Jellicoe and Lord Rawlinson, minister of defence in the Indian government[18] to amalgamte the RIM into the Royal Navy in the 1920s, it would take almost a decade more to achieve.The simple fact was that the British were supreme at sea and without even the remotest possibilities of any threat emerging to their trade routes between India and Great Britain. All that was to change by the mid-1930s when Nazi Germany embarked on a massive naval modernization.Though the focus of attention was on the Atlantic and North Sea fleets, some attention was now paid to the Royal Indian Marine. It was rechristened the Royal Indian Navy in 1934 and inaugurated with its headquarters at Bombay under a Flag Officer Commanding Royal Indian Navy (FOCRIN).[19]

A look at the maritime situation at the time will clearly reveal the reasons for continued neglect of the Royal Indian Navy even while there was significant German and Japanese naval build-up. The British appreciated that the main threats to their naval supremacy from Germany and Japan would emerge in the Atlantic and the Pacific respectively. To counter this they went about strengthening their fleet in Singapore and shoring up their Atlantic fleet. It was felt that the Indian Ocean, Arabian Sea and Bay of Bengal were well beyond the ranges of either the German or the Japanese fleet; hence the need for convoys between Britain and India and India and China to be protected came up only when they rounded the Cape of Good Hope, or passed by the Strait of Malacca. This, the British felt, would be taken on by the Atlantic and Pacific fleets – no need was thus felt to significantly beef up the Royal Indian Navy beyond converting a few merchant ships to men-of-war as minesweepers and armed escorts. The Royal Indian Navy was all of eight warships[20] and 1,300 personnel at the outbreak of WW II. Its headquarters at Bombay comprised a Flag Officer Commanding Royal Indian Navy (FOCRIN) of the rank of a rear admiral and around fifteen officers.[21] Little did it realize that the turn of events over the next few years, dictated largely by massive defeats for Britain in Singapore and Malaya, would result in a speedy build-up of the Royal Indian Navy as all attempts were made by the Crown to ensure that its colonies supported the war effort.

A Professional Service Emerges: WW II

As the Royal Navy built its Atlantic and Pacific fleets around large battleships and cruisers like the HMS *Repulse* and HMS *Prince of Wales*, the Royal Indian Navy's (RIN) force structure was limited to one that revolved around a fleet of minesweeper torpedo boats and landing craft.[22] As the war progressed, its role expanded from protection of trade routes around India and coastal defence, to supporting the land campaign by providing landing craft for seaborne assault and induction of troops in the Persian Gulf and the Arakan Coast during the Burma offensive in 1944–45.[23] Amongst the significant operations conducted by the RIN was the fighting against the Italian Navy off the coast of Somaliland, assisting in the evacuation of Allied forces in 1940 and helping in the subsequent recapture of Massawa in 1941 following the Allied offensive from the north.[24] The two major gallantry awards won by the RIN during action in the Persian Gulf – both Distinguished Service Crosses – were awarded to Lieutenant N. Krishnan and Engineer Lieutenant D. Shankar for their bravery during action on ships that were on their way to join the RIN in the Persian Gulf.[25]

Second-in-command of a small tug as part of an assault landing operation off the Iranian coast in August 1941, Krishnan boarded an enemy tug that was firing indiscriminately at Allied landing craft and disabled the firing party single-handedly before the rest of his team boarded the tug to capture it.[26] Lieutenant Shankar boarded a blazing Italian warship to capture the crew at considerable risk to his life.[27] RIN ships also carried out regular escort duties to large convoys as they sailed through the U-boat-infested waters of the Mediterranean and the Atlantic. This report from Lieutenant G.R.W.F. Horner, the commanding officer of HMIS *Kumaon*, was filed after multiple depth charges were dropped against a German U-boat that was shadowing convoy MKS 9 in the Mediterranean on 13 March 1945. The report not only reflected an analysis of the operation, but also the integrity of conservative assessment of damage to the submarine:

> The attack cannot be assessed as a conclusive kill but I am of the opinion that at least the submarine was badly damaged, especially as she was forced to the surface, and seen there myself.[28]

The war in Asia, particularly during the dark days preceding the fall of Singapore in February 1942, was marked by repeated attacks on the RIN by aircraft-carrier-based Japanese dive bombers as they attacked convoys sailing from the Dutch East Indies (modern Indonesia) to the fortress of Singapore.[29] As the Japanese juggernaut steamed into the Indian Ocean, the RIN could do little to prevent the fall of the Andaman and Nicobar Islands in June 1942 and prevent raids by Japanese submarines along the Malabar Coast of western India. Numerous ships of the RIN were sunk by Japanese submarines and the losses galvanized the speedy re-equipping of the RIN with large-scale recruitment taking place during the 1942–44 period.

Action in the Atlantic and Burma

Seeing the hammering that the RIN was taking at the hands of the Japanese, the Royal Navy commissioned a number of warships for the RIN. Amongst them were six anti-aircraft sloops and two minesweepers, all of which were initially deployed with the Atlantic fleet and then progressively transferred to the Mediterranean and Cape fleets as they made their way to India. Along the way some of these ships participated in the Allied landings at Sicily in July 1943 before joining what was called the ML (Motor Launch) Flotillas as part of the coastal forces in the Burma theatre.[30] These flotillas initially comprised coastal defence craft such as motor launches, submarine chasers, motor gunboats and motor torpedo boats.[31] These were later supplemented with anti-aircraft sloops and minesweepers as the war progressed.

During 1943–45 the RIN took part in continuous operations along the Arakan Coast of Burma carrying out anti-shipping sweeps, small raids on enemy shipping and installations with commandoes and infantry on board and offensive bombardment. It was on one of these raids that Lieutenant S. M. Ahsan was awarded the Distinguished Service Cross.[32] He later rose to become the fourth chief of naval staff of the Pakistan Navy. Equipped only with light anti-aircraft guns, ships of the RIN were extremely vulnerable to Japanese Zero fighters and flying boats, and their crew did a magnificent job by successfully engaging such aircraft with machine guns, and even shooting down quite a few of them.

As the tide turned in Burma and Slim's 14th Army pushed the Japanese out of India, numerous operations were conducted by RIN landing craft as they attempted to cut off the retreating Japanese as they made their way northwards through Burma into Malaya. The assault on Akyab in December 1944 was a classic joint battle with elements of the Indian Army (74th and 53rd Indian Brigades), the Indian Air Force and the Royal Indian Navy taking part in the operation. The icing on the cake for the RIN was the capture of Rangoon in May 1945. Code-named Operation Dracula, the operation involved a huge flotilla, which set sail on 16 April 1945 from Mandapam in Tamil Nadu and after a brief halt at Colombo made its way northwards across the choppy Bay of Bengal during what is considered the beginning of the pre-monsoon season. Joining an enormous landing force at Akyab with a large number of assault craft and other small craft amounting to over thirty ships, this was the largest display of force by the fledgling RIN during the Burma campaign.[33] As the assault force sailed up the Rangoon river with Jat, Garhwali and Punjabi soldiers, one can't help reflecting: if the Indian Army, Indian Air Force and the Royal Indian Navy had not participated in strength in the Burma campaign, would the war in Burma have ended as it did? Surprisingly, the role of the Royal Indian Navy hardly finds a mention in Field Marshal Slim's book *Defeat Into Victory* except in a few places. So much for jointness in those difficult times. However, Lieutenant General Sir Philip Christison, general officer commanding, XV Indian Corps, had this to say about the RIN after the fall of Rangoon:

> The Arakan Campaign is now virtually over. The work of all officers and ratings of the R.I.N has maintained its high standards and the spirit of cooperation and comradeship has been maintained in the face of all difficulties. The operations in which we have recently been engaged in narrow chaungs (channels) lined by mangrove swamps and often overlooked by Jap held hills, with swift currents and large rise and fall of tides has called for great skill, seamanship and courage. These qualities have enabled us to carry out operations never before attempted by any British forces. I am extremely grateful to all of them for what they have done, and all ranks of XV Indian Corps are very proud of their comrades. We will remember fighting besides them.[34]

Just as the Indian Army expanded exponentially during the war, so did the Royal Indian Navy. By the end of the war it had over 25,000 personnel[35] including over 100 Indian and Anglo-Indian officers[36], with a few from the RINVR (Royal Indian Naval Volunteer Reserve). The senior-most Indian officer was Lieutenant Commander D.N. Mukherji, who later rose to the rank of captain and retired in 1950. It had on its inventory seven sloops, four frigates, four corvettes, fourteen minesweepers, sixteen trawlers, two depot ships, thirty auxillary vessels, 150 landing craft, 200 harbour craft and several motor launches.[37] While the officers of the Royal Indian Navy did not experience the big naval battles of the Atlantic or the Pacific, nor did they participate in epic naval encounters like in the Coral Sea or the Midway, they came away from WW II with sufficient battle experience. However, from the rank structure of Indian officers at the end of WW II, it was quite clear that it would be some time before Indians would be ready to assume leadership of the Indian Navy.

Run-up to Independence

Just as Field Marshal Auchinleck was committed to leaving a fine British legacy with the Indian Army with his singular understanding of the aspirations of a battle-hardened Indian Army, Admiral John Godfrey, FOCRIN from 1943 to 1946, pushed for the establishment of an independent navy and recommended sweeping changes to the force structure of the RIN despite stiff resistance from the British Chiefs of Staff Committee.[38]

The principal task for the post-war RIN as per the committee that was constituted to look at planning requirements for India's armed forces bears a striking resemblance to the vision and mission statement of today's Indian Navy and reflects the collective maritime wisdom of Great Britain, arguably the greatest sea power the world had ever seen till the emergence of the United States in the post-WW II era. It read:

> The principal responsibility of India's Navy after the war will be the safety of Indian and Empire shipping in the ports of India and their approaches. India will also take her share in the protection of this shipping on the trade routes within the Indian Ocean. It will be an important task of India's Navy to provide facilities for the combined

> operational training of the Army formations maintained in the country and to provide a share of the escorts, assault shipping and craft required to land these troops on a hostile shore, should this prove necessary. In addition, the Navy, in conjunction with the air force must be prepared to take its share in intercepting and attacking any foreign invading force which may attempt a landing on the shores of India.[39]

Prophetic words indeed as almost all of the Indian Navy's current roles – sea denial, protection of sea lines of communications (SLOCs), out of area contingency operations and maritime air operations with navy–air force synergy – are part of the current lexicon of naval operations.

The Royal Indian Navy Revolt

Staying with post-war happenings, widespread retrenchment and downsizing of the RIN during the post-war years saw a breakdown in junior leadership and erosion of the camaraderie and fighting spirit that had evolved during WW II. An arbitrary decision to reduce the number of sailors from 27,650 to 11,000[40] caused great angst. Added to this was the exposure of the Indian sailors and officers stationed at Bombay, Karachi, Madras and Calcutta to the growing influence of the independence movement. All this and more resulted in the naval revolt of 1946.[41] The Royal Indian Navy revolt, as the leaders of India's independence called it, started on 18 February 1946, when 1,100 naval ratings of a shore-based signals training establishment, HMIS *Talwar*, struck work at Bombay at dawn. The catalyst for the simmering discontent in the training school was attributed to the persistent derogatory behaviour of the commanding officer.[42] At Karachi the HMIS *Hindustan* along with one more ship and three shore establishments, went on a lightning strike protesting against low pay and poor living conditions. There was even a short firefight between the *Hindustan* and shore-based guns. The strikes spread like wildfire to military establishments in Madras, Vishakhapatnam, Calcutta, Delhi, Cochin, Jamnagar, the Andamans, Bahrain and Aden. Seventy-eight naval ships and twenty shore naval establishments, involving 20,000 navy ratings, were affected.[43] Though the naval revolt was speedily put down and did not result in too many casualties – among the mutineers, one rating was killed and six wounded; one RIN officer was killed and one wounded; two British other ranks were wounded in Bombay and eight ratings were killed and thirty-three were wounded including British soldiers[44] – it later inspired stray incidents of violence and protest in the Indian Army and Royal Indian Air Force in 1946. Interestingly, it was Sardar Vallabhbhai Patel, one of the tall leaders of the Congress party and independent India's first home minister, who is said to have advised the agitating seamen to return to work and leave the protests to the civilians who were at the forefront of the non-violent freedom struggle. He explained to the agitating seamen a simple principle that endured after independence – politics and agitation was the prerogative of politicians. Soldiers, sailors and airmen obeyed.[45]

In May 1946, three armymen of the Royal Indian Army Service Corps went on trial in Colaba, Mumbai, for refusing to obey orders.[46] In an insightful deposition to an RIN inquiry commission on 29 May 1946, Commander A.W. Gush, officer commanding, RIN base, Karachi, listed out the main reasons for the revolt as being poor recruitment and promotion policies for Indian ratings and lack of big ships that prevented the enforcement of standard disciplinary procedures as men were scattered in small ships with poor living conditions.[47]This only added to the growing scepticism amongst British military leaders that it was about time to leave India! From an independence movement perspective, the revolters had struck a telling blow – for many they were freedom fighters and not mutineers. The revolt was also an attempt by disillusioned naval personnel to emulate the exploits of the INA. In a passionate speech at Bombay on 26 February 1946, Jawaharlal Nehru put the RIN revolt in correct perspective:

> The Indian soldier of today is different from the Indian soldier of the last war. He has seen many theatres of war and his contact with soldiers of free countries has opened his eyes to the forces of freedom operating in other countries. The present unrest among the defence services has a direct bearing on the Indian body politic.[48]

This contribution of the striking sailors to the independence movement was recognized by the Government of India in 1972 and all 476 sailors who were penalized in various ways after the revolt were eligible for the grant of a freedom fighter's pension.[49]

Flying the Indian Ensign

No one typifies the doughty post-Independence Indian naval officer better than Admiral Jayant Nadkarni, chief of naval staff from 1987 to 1990. Leaving home at the tender age of fourteen to join the merchant navy in 1946, young Nadkarni joined the training ship *Dufferin* to begin a nearly five-decade-long association with the Indian seas. Witness to the RIN revolt, he recollects that some ships off the Mumbai harbour which had been taken over by the protesting Indian sailors had even trained their guns in defiance on the iconic Taj Mahal hotel. So apprehensive were the British that they even brought in an aircraft carrier (HMS *Glory*) and a cruiser (HMS *Glasgow*) to Mumbai as a show of force. Admiral Nadkarni remembers having been taken in a group to see the *Glasgow*. He also fondly remembers having been part of a group of cadets who were taken to Ballard Pier to witness the commissioning of India's first warship, the INS *Delhi*, by Prime Minister Nehru.

Volunteering with sixteen other cadets to join the RIN, Jayant Nadkarni and fifteen other cadets set sail for the UK in March 1949 on the HMS *Ranchi*, with some officers and sailors who were selected as crew members of the three R-class destroyers (*Rajput*, *Ranjit* and *Rana*), which were to be the next acquisitions for the RIN from Britain. After four-and-a-half years of rigorous training on various ships and at various shore establishments including the Royal Naval College at Dartmouth, Nadkarni returned to India in 1953 on the Indian Navy's latest acquisition INS *Ganga* after participating in the queen's coronation review. Training was tough with no trips back home to see the family, he recollects, and the sixteen Indians had for company a motley bunch of aspiring naval officers from other dominions like Canada and Pakistan. The exposure too was excellent with Nadkarni getting an opportunity to train on the HMS *Indefatigable*, an aircraft carrier, and HMS *Bleasdale*, a Hunt-class destroyer.[50] By the time Nadkarni returned to India, the Royal Indian Navy had become the Indian Navy after India became a republic on 26 January 1950.

Numbers mean a lot even if there is not much to take home! At Independence, a Defence Service Partition Committee[51] was constituted with senior Indian and Pakistani naval officers on it to divide all RIN assets between India and Pakistan in a ratio of 2:1. While India retained thirty-three ships including WW II vintage sloops, minesweepers and motor launches, these were complemented with more recent vessels like frigates and corvettes. How recent would be a matter of opinion as Vice Admiral Pradeep Chauhan, an erudite seaman-cum-scholar, would term India's fleet of 1947 as barely being able to steam away from the Bombay harbour.[52] Pakistan, on the other hand, retained sixteen vessels of the same variety.[53] By September 1948, the RIN had added on a large cruiser, HMIS *Delhi,* with Commander Katari (later the first Indian chief of naval staff) as the first Indian commanding officer. It was inducted into the Indian Navy with much fanfare on 13 September 1948 and escorted into Bombay harbour by HMIS *Krishna* with Admiral Hall, the FOCRIN, on board and in the presence of Prime Minister Nehru.[54] In a departure from his earlier disdain for building military capability[55] and chastened in no small measure by the events of the last one year (the ongoing war with Pakistan), Prime Minister Nehru emphasized the need for building deterrent military capability. Speaking on the occasion and displaying glimpses of his dilemma he said:

> It may seem curious that the Indian people who have always stood for peace should rejoice and take pride in the possession of a unit of war such as HMIS *Delhi*. But on a deeper view, it is not curious at all, for it is not enough to have the desire for peace. We must also have the determination and means to keep peace.[56]

By 1949, the RIN had acquired greater punch with the commissioning of three more R-class destroyers and one landing craft and the stage was set for it to dominate the Arabian Sea and the Bay of Bengal for years to come. Interestingly, the finances for these purchases were adjusted against the large Indian credit that remained with Britain after Independence and also was a clever way of decommissioning the hundreds of ships that remained after WW II.[57] International navies too came calling at Indian ports, prominent amongst them being a complement of three naval warships of the US Navy, which came on a five-day goodwill vist to Bombay in August 1948 on the eve of one year of India's Independence.[58]

After all the downsizing and retrenchment of the RIN, the Indian and Pakistani navies were left with resources that were totally inadequate for coastal defence leave alone protection of SLOCs. One could say that considering the small coastline that Pakistan had compared to India and its islands of Andaman and Nicobar and Lakshadweep, Pakistan had no cause for complaint. However, Jinnah argued that Pakistan needed a larger navy to protect trade from East to West Pakistan from predatory Indian warships – something Mountbatten ignored. An interesting titbit about the role of the RIN and the Indian National Army (INA) in ensuring that Andaman and Nicobar islands was handed over to India emerges in Rear Admiral Satyindra Singh's book. Despite strong objections from the British Ministry of Defence that the Andaman and Nicobar Islands should remain with Britain as an island outpost that overlooks the Straight of Malacca, much like Diego Garcia straddles the key sea lanes in the Indian Ocean, two issues swung the issue in India's favour. First, Subhas Chandra Bose had designs of setting up a provisional Indian government in exile when the INA landed in the islands with the Japanese in March 1942 and the fact that prisoners of India's independence movement were housed at the cellular jail created an emotional bond with the mainland. Second, it was asserted by the Indian naval officers that the island chain was important for India's maritime security. Both the desire of Britain to hold on to the Andamans and the Indian resolve indicated the strategic potential of the island chain. Whether India has converted that potential into capability over the almost seven decades since Independence is a moot point considering the slow pace at which it is being developed as a bulwark against great power encroachment into the Bay of Bengal. Anyway, that is an issue for maritime strategists to dwell on and not for a mere military historian to pontificate!

The final issue to dwell upon is technology-related and its impact on the manning of the Indian Navy after Independence. The navy in those days was the most technology- and maintenance-intensive service by a long way. Along with the hundreds of years of dominance by British sea power, it resulted in great reluctance by British officers and ratings to transfer expertise to their Indian comrades at sea. This resulted in the Indian Navy having to retain British expertise the longest. As late

Naik Darwan Singh Negi, Garhwal Rifles, Victoria Cross (VC), WW I, 23 November 1914.

Sepoy Khudadad Khan, the first Indian to win the VC in WW I, 31 October 1914.

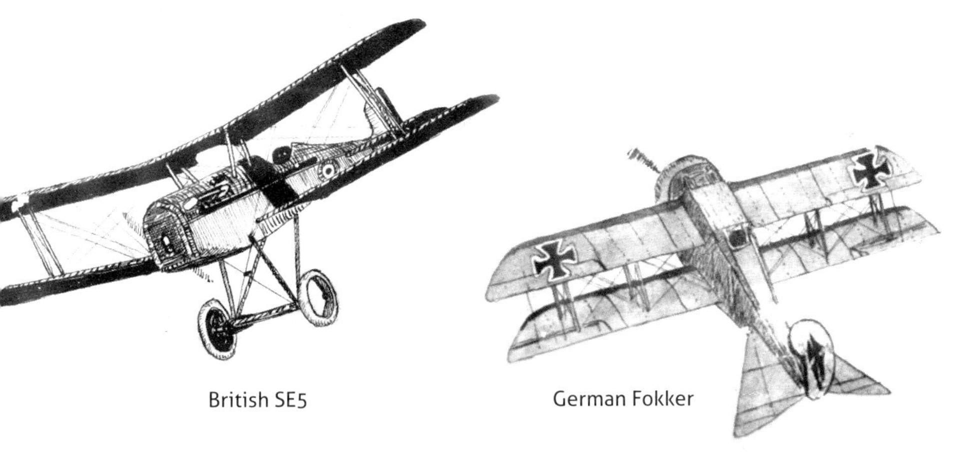

British SE5

German Fokker

Lieutenant Indra Lal Roy, Distinguished Flying Cross (DFC). He also sketched brilliantly, two samples of which are shown above.

Lieutenant Welingkar, Military Cross. He was the second Indian pilot to be killed in WW I.

Indian soldiers with Colonel Bartoli of the French army, Pas-de-Calais, Northern France, 1915.

Indian troops practise a drill with gas masks prior to the second battle of Ypres, April-May 1915.

Commander D.N. Mukherji, the first Indian naval officer.

Field Marshal Auchinleck – Friend of India.

Second Lieutenant Bhagat, the first Indian to be awarded the VC in WW II.

(Above) Battalion Commanders of the All Indian 51 Infantry Brigade. (L to R) Lieutenant Colonels Thorat and Sen, Brigadier Hutton (Brigade Commander) and Lieutenant Colonel Thimayya.

(Left) IAF Squadron Commanders in Burma (from L to R) Niranjan Prasad, Prithipal Singh, Mehar Singh, Arjan Singh, Majithia and Hem Chaudhuri.

IAF's two early DFCs, Aspy Engineer and the legendary K.K. (Jumbo) Majumdar.

Flight Lieutenant Nur Khan, later Chief of Pakistan Air Force.

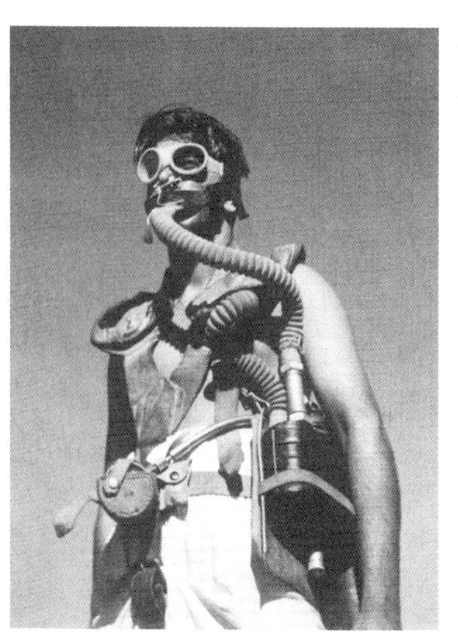
An Indian diver kitted for action.

A Royal Indian Navy ack–ack crew in action.

A Royal Indian Navy ship in the Bay of Bengal.

Havildar (later Lieutenant Colonel) Chanan Singh Dhillon of 41 Field Park Regiment, British 8th Army, commanding a Muster Parade (above), and refereeing a wrestling bout (below) at a prisoners of war camp at Limberg (near Frankfurt).

A Sikh soldier guarding Japanese prisoners of war in Burma.

A Rajput Regime
sniper cleaning his rif

Tamil gunners of 5th India Field Battalion in Burma, April 1942.

Squadron Leader Arjan Singh, DFC, 1 Squadron, in Imphal, May 1944.

Flight Lieutenant Rajaram, DFC, flight commander, with aircrew and technicians of 1 Squadron, Imphal, 1944.

Hurricanes of 6 Squadron, IAF, Cox's Bazaar, Burma theatre.

Indian, American and British troops, north Assam, 1943.

Netaji Subhas Chandra Bose reviewing a mechanized unit of the INA in Singapore.

INA parade in Singapore, July 1943.

as 1950, the RIN still had a complement of sixty-nine British officers, significantly more than what the RIAF had. The Indian Navy has always looked at itself in the post-Independence era as the Cinderella service; and not without reason in a land-centric strategic mindset for much of the twentieth century. An indicator of this lopsided perspective is reienforced by the defence budget of 1950, which saw the Navy garner only 4.7 per cent of the defence budget as against 8.93 per cent for the IAF and 72.62 per cent for the Indian Army.[59] As this peek into the historical legacy of the Indian Navy concludes, I have intentionally left out the glamorous naval aviators and the silent submariners, as I will briefly track their evolution in subsequent chapters. What of the broader contours of India's naval strategy? It was only too obvious that given the deep doctrinal influence of the Royal Navy, the Indian Navy would be modelled around British concepts of maritime strategy: sea denial, sea control and protection of commerce would emerge as key missions in the years ahead.[60]

Shano Varuna is the Sanskrit motto of the Indian Navy, which translated into English means *'May the Lord of the Ocean be auspicious unto us'*.[61]

Calm seas, light swells – full power ahead!

7

THE INDIAN AIR FORCE

No part of the British Empire has given more convincing proof of its determination to play its full part in the Battle for Freedom (WW II) than India. Not only in Libya, Abyssinia, and the Far East have her sons fought with matchless brilliance and courage, but also in another element – in the skies above Britain and over India and Burma – they have shown themselves true partners in the great brotherhood of the RAF. Today India has her own Air Force. Never before have so many castes, creeds and races been united in one single endeavour as they are in the IAF.

– Acting Air Marshal Sir Patrick Playfair, KBE, CB, CVO, MC

From Queen Mary's Book for India, 1942[1]

Early Years: WW I

Compared to the modern Indian Army and the Indian Navy whose legacies stretch back in history to Shivaji's hardy Maratha warriors, the Indian Air Force seemed to be a young upstart considering that military aviation came of age only in the second decade of the twentieth century. As WW I gathered momentum and the aerial war over Europe took its toll on Allied pilots, five Indians applied for a commission into the Royal Flying Corps (RFC) between November 1916 and April 1917. Of these, Lieutenants Srikrishna Welingkar, Eroll Chunder Sen, Indra Lal Roy and Hardit Singh

Malik saw action as front-line combat pilots on the western front. Welingkar and Indra Lal Roy perished in aerial combat, while Sen was shot down behind enemy lines and captured by the Germans – he was repatriated after the war. Hardit Malik served till the end of the war before voluntarily opting for a discharge after the armistice to pursue a civilian career.[2] Malik went on to join the Indian Civil Service in 1919–20, and after a distinguished career as a civil servant, he was appointed as India's first high commissioner to Canada after Independence. This was followed by a stint as India's ambassador to France, where he successfully negotiated the transfer of the French colony of Pondicherry (now Puducherry) to India.

The image of the WW I combat pilot was often romanticized and unrealistic. The average life expectancy of a pilot was just eleven days as pilot safety was not the first concern and pilots were not allowed to carry parachutes.[3] Excerpts from listings in the National Archives in the UK about the first Indian ace fighter pilot, Lieutenant Indra Lal Roy, Distinguished Flying Cross (DFC), are highlighted below:

> On 19 June 1918 Roy was posted to No. 40 Squadron in France. During his period of service with the squadron, he shot down nine German planes in less than 14 days. His brief and spectacular flying career ended when he was killed in action during a dogfight with a German Fokker aeroplane on 22 July, at the age of only 19. Roy was awarded the Distinguished Flying Cross. He was the first Indian to receive this honour. The citation in the *London Gazette* on 21 September 1918 praised Roy as 'a very gallant and determined officer' whose 'remarkable skill and daring' had enabled him on occasion to shoot down 'two (enemy) machines in one patrol'.[4]

Roy's life in combat was above the average – just over a month! Roy was not just a fighter ace; he loved sketching and has left behind a small collection of exquisite drawings of British and German fighters of his era, including some that depicted dogfights. The collection is placed at the entrance to the main gallery of the Air Force Museum at Palam, New Delhi.

TRIBAL CONTROL

Another interesting feature of the early years of air power in India saw it being first employed during 1916–19 against belligerent tribal armies of the Emir of Afghanistan, who had called for a 'jihad' against 'British infidels' and started harassing British garrisons located on the border in the North-West Frontier Province. Slow-moving and obsolete aircraft like BE2C executed diverse roles that are very similar to the roles that are being performed today in Af-Pak by US-led coalition and Pakistani air power. These mainly comprised armed reconnaissance missions and offensive strikes in support of ground operations. Called 'air policing' in those days, this attempt to retain control on the periphery of British colonies like Ireland, Palestine, India, South-West Arabia and Africa saw aerial bombing being used as a psychological and propagandist means of maintaining imperial peace.[5] Though the Indian Air Force had not yet come into being, 1916 saw a flight of BE2C aircraft initially deployed at Nowshera and later at Risalpur[6] as a whole squadron (31 Squadron, Royal Flying Corps) in what is now north-west Pakistan. Its task was to monitor the movement of tribal lashkars (large body of warriors) and allow some lead time for the vastly outnumbered British garrisons in the region to plan their operations.[7] The role of accurate direction of artillery fire was also taken on by 31 Squadron, as was direct bombing of tribal positions in what could be called close air support and interdiction operations.[8] At its peak during the 1920s, the Royal Flying Corps had a complement of eight squadrons in the region made up of four army cooperation squadrons and two bomber squadrons.[9]

During the period March–May 1925, these squadrons flew more than 2,000 hours and dropped more than 150 tons of bombs on the Afridi and Mahsud tribes[10] as part of the punitive military action against them. This aerial campaign turned out to be the first of its kind against non-state actors – the United States would embark on a similar punitive aerial campaign in almost the same area against the Al Qaeda nearly seventy-six years later. In the final analysis, the first deployment of combat air power in the subcontinent ensured a psychological edge, which proved critical for the ultimate success of the British Indian Army in its battles in the NWFP, and though Indian pilots were not part of the initial deployment in NWFP, the success and experience of this concept in the inter-war years sparked a renewed interest in air power as an effective coercive tool of the Raj. Summing up the experience of early aviators over the NWFP is a paragraph from an article in *Air Power Review* by Lieutenant Colonel Andrew Roe, a British Army officer with a PhD from Kings College:

> Few stationed on the frontier rarely met, or even saw, the aircrew that supported them so valiantly on a daily basis. Except for an occasional glimpse of a gauntleted arm, most only recall aircraft slowly circling overhead or diving head-on towards a tribal target with a rattle of machine-gun fire followed by the 'crumph' of a bomb as the explosion echoed off the surrounding hills. Hardly any stopped to think of the hardships and dangers faced by the aircrew on a daily basis, which were often comparable to those operating on the ground. For many airmen, the frontier was a highlight of their careers and lives, never to be repeated, but never to be forgotten.[11]

Despite five Indian officers having served with the RFC during WW I, resistance from the RAF to have Indian commissioned officers in the Royal Air Force, or allow the formation of an Indian Air Force on the lines of the Indian Army continued for long. Despite the Skeen Committee having recommended the formation of an Indian Air Force as early as April 1927, it was not until 1932 that the Indian Air Force became a separate air force under a legislative Act.[12] In the meantime, however, flying training of the first batch of six Indian officers commenced at the RAF College at Cranwell from September 1930 – five of them qualified to be pilots, while one became a logistics officer. Sensibly, the British also trained twenty-two technicians, also called 'Hawai Sepoys'.[13] These pilots and technicians can rightly claim to be the founding pioneers of independent India's air force. Air Vice Marshal Harjinder Singh, one of the first batch of hawai sepoys, recalls the reaction of the British adjutant of Air Force Station Lahore when he expressed a desire to join the RAF:

> You are not even allowed to go near those aeroplanes, leave aside fly them. To be a pilot in the RAF, you must have English blood flowing in your veins.[14]

Though the Indian Air Force was formally raised on 8 October 1932, its first squadron, No. 1 Squadron, was formed on 1 April 1933 at Drigh Road, Karachi[15] with just one flight of four Wapiti aircraft. However it was deployed in the NWFP only in 1936. After adding on a single aircraft and a flight of manpower it moved to Peshawar in April the same year. By then the RAF had gained sufficient experience in counter-insurgency operations in mountainous terrain against belligerent Pathan tribesmen. Operating alongside 20 Squadron of the RAF, the first IAF squadron was initially commanded by a British officer seconded from the RAF. It soon got into the thick of action moving to Kohat in June 1937, which was closer to the tribal areas. For almost five long years, the squadron cut its teeth in Waziristan and operated in close coordination with other RAF squadrons and the Bannu Brigade.[16] 'C' Flight of No. 1 Squadron was formed in 1938 and commanded by none other than Flight Lieutenant Jumbo Majumdar, the IAF's most accomplished pilot of the time. It soon broke all records by consistently flying over 400 hours a month.[17] Operating with the Tochi Scouts, a regiment comprising hardy Pathans who carried out ground reconnaissance and then returned to brief pilots on likely target locations, this period also heralded the birth of air–land operations in the IAF. Also in the flight was the fearless Mehar Singh, who later won accolades for his exploits in Burma and Kashmir. On reaching its full strength only in 1939,[18] Squadron Leader Subroto Mukherji was the first Indian to command the squadron in March 1939 with a largely Indian complement of pilots and technicians.[19]

Even though the early history of the IAF is synonymous with that of No. 1 Squadron, its exploits in NWFP finds no mention in the well-researched piece on air operations in the north-west frontier that I have quoted earlier, which was published by the highly respected RAF *Air Power Review* in its autumn/winter issue in 2011. An objective look at the state of the IAF prior to commencement of WW II reveals that the British were in no hurry to give wings to the fledgling IAF – just one squadron of obsolete Wapiti aircraft and a handful of pilots. It is the dark war clouds in Europe which provided the necessary impetus for further growth of this force.

On the eve of the WW II, the air forces (RAF plus the fledgling IAF) in India were only suited to the limited role of tribal operations on India's frontiers in operations that were interestingly termed as 'watch and ward' with roles that were deterrent rather than damaging. Apart from Kohat, there were only two flying bases with runways of barely 1,100 yards on the frontier – Miranshah and Peshawar – with Lahore and Ambala in the hinterland.[20] In a wonderful piece written in the IAF journal of August 1944, Flight Lieutenant Arthur Hughes succinctly highlights the roles of the two IAF squadrons in the NWFP:

> Work on the frontier by the I.A.F. comes under two headings – first, air action, against tribesmen, such as proscription bombing, and secondly, cooperation with scouts and other armed forces. The first is done only on the instruction of the political authorities and is sanctioned by the Governor of the N.W.F. Province. The second includes reconnaissance (tactical, artillery and photographic), supply dropping and communication.[21]

Very early on in its fledgling existence of barely a few decades, air power, it seems, had become a tool for both political signalling and war fighting. Hughes goes on to highlight the extraordinarily responsive liaison and coordination between the Tochi Scouts and the IAF whenever close air support was asked for – it took an average of three-and-a-half minutes for an aircraft to get airborne after a demand for air support came in from ground forces.[22] Remarkable indeed! Operations in the NWFP also got Squadron Leader A.M. Engineer a DFC, along with four others being recognized with Mention-in-Despatches. Recounting his experiences in the NWFP during the eightieth anniversary celebrations of No. 1 Squadron in February 2014, Marshal of the Air Force Arjan Singh spoke of bombing with discrimination and 'hard intelligence' from the Tochi Scouts so that collateral damage was minimized. The squadron's experience of close air support and cooperation with troops on the ground would stand it in good stead in the years ahead in the Burma campaign.[23]

Word War II

By December 1939, twenty-three more pilots had enrolled for flying training at RAF, Cranwell.[24] Of these, sixteen remained in service at the start of WW II along with 144 airmen[25] and one squadron (No. 1 Squadron) of Wapiti aircraft. While three from the lot of pre-WW II pilots, Subroto Mukerjee, Aspy Merwan Engineer and Arjan Singh, served with distinction through WW II and made it to the post of chief of the air staff, the top slot in the IAF, K.K. Majumdar (affectionately called Jumbo) was undoubtedly the star of the initial lot of pilots. History, they say, has an uncanny knack of repeating itself and so it was in the case of pilot shortages in the RAF at the beginning of WW II – similar to the situation faced by the RFC during WW I. This led to the recruitment of Indians holding a civil pilot's licence as part of the Indian Air Force Volunteer Reserve (IAFVR) force. Air Chief Marshal P. C. Lal was amongst the initial lot of navigators and pilots and writes with great humour on the circumstances that led to his volunteering for this reserve force:

> The psychology of my response to the invitation to join the Air Force was 'the prospect of being paid to do that for which my poor father spent money on me' – another version of 'I do what I like and like what I do'.[26]

Since volunteers with civil licences were hard to find after the initial lot were recruited, the IAFVR force was opened to youth between the ages of eighteen to twenty-two with a high school certificate called matriculation in those days.[27] Over 100 such aircrew from the IAFVR joined the force and initially served in units called Coastal Defence Flights. Six such flights were formed at Karachi, Bombay, Cochin, Madras, Calcutta and Vizag.[28] As the war progressed, all these flights would form the nucleus of the remaining eight front-line combat squadrons of the IAF in the NWFP and Burma. By the end of the war, more than 1,000 pilots and 25,000 men would be trained and 600 pilots posted to the nine IAF squadrons, which saw action on the Burma front.[29] Though the exact number of IAFVR pilots who stayed on to serve the Indian Air Force in the years after WW II is sketchy, many of them like Air Chief Marshal Lal, Air Marshal Rajaram, Air Chief Marshal Moolgavkar and Air Chief Marshal Latif went on to occupy higher posts with distinction in the years that followed.

One of the veterans of the Indian Air Force with lucid memories of his training days as an IAF Volunteer Reserve pilot was Air Chief Marshal Moolgavkar. When I met him at his Pune residence over a cup of tea in February 2013, we ruminated over his early days as an aviator in 1940 – he was commissioned on 30 November 1940 and pitchforked into battle with No. 1 Squadron at Peshawar.[30] He was also among the first lot of pilots from No. 1 Squadron to move along with Jumbo Majumdar when the squadron was first inducted into the Burma theatre in early 1942. (Air Chief Marshal Moolgavkar passed away after a prolonged illness on 10 April 2015.)[31]

Over Burma and Europe

Like the Indian Army, the Indian Air Force truly came of age during the Burma campaign. It was involved right through the campaign; from the gloomy days of early 1942, to the time when Assam was being threatened in 1943 by the Japanese advance across the Chindwin River April, and finally to the stirring campaign of Slim's 14th Army that turned 'defeat into victory' for the Allies in 1944. The stirring exploits of the IAF in the defence of Kohima and Imphal have gone down in aviation history as amongst the most effective counter-attacking aerial campaigns in siege conditions.

After almost six years in the NWFP, No. 1 Squadron, re-equipped with the slow-moving Lysander aircraft. Modified to carry 500 lb bombs, it moved to the Burma theatre in February 1942 with twelve aircraft to counter the rapidly advancing Japanese. Operating from a forward airfield called Toungoo and carrying out daring missions under their young squadron commander, 'Jumbo' Majumdar, it was at the time the only IAF squadron in the area. A daredevil aviator with stirring leadership qualities, Jumbo led a series of successful offensive strikes against numerous Japanese airfields with and without any fighter escorts against the vastly superior Japanese Zero fighters. However, as the Allies wilted against the Japanese onslaught, Jumbo's squadron first moved to north Burma (Lashio) to carry out aerial reconnaissance of the critical logistics link between Burma and China in support of Chiang-Kai shek's Chinese 5th Army, before finally withdrawing back to India in mid-1942 and converting on to Hurricane fighter bombers.[32] For his exploits in

Burma, 'Jumbo' was complimented by Lord Wavell when he visited the squadron in Lashio and soon after was the first Indian pilot to be awarded the Distinguished Flying Cross in WW II for his leadership and daring individual prowess.[33] Speaking during his visit to the squadron on 26 February 1942, Wavell remarked:

> I have come to Lashio to personally congratulate No 1 Squadron of the IAF. You have made history within this short time. I need not tell you that the RAF has acknowledged your bravery and skill with respect and the AOC-in-C Burma has nothing but praise for you. I am also aware of your ambition to expand your air force to ten squadrons. I promise you all help to fulfill this ambition.[34]

From 1942 to 1945, nine squadrons of the Indian Air Force (1, 2, 3, 4, 6, 7, 8, 9 and 10 Squadrons) flying a variety of aircraft including Lysanders, Vultee Vengeance dive-bombers, Hurricanes and Spitfires flew over 16,000 sorties and 24,000 hours in support of various battles of the Burma campaign.[35] As IAF pilots proved themselves in battle, a number of these squadrons were equipped with the latest Spitfire and Hurricane fighters. Some squadrons like No. 8 Squadron had one flight of Indian pilots with another flight manned by pilots from Britain and other Commonwealth countries like Australia, New Zealand and Canada. Amongst the various missions that were flown were daring counter-air missions against Japanese airfields in Burma by innovatively strapping on 500 lb and 250 lb bombs on the most unlikely of aircraft,[36] the slow-moving Lysander; interdiction missions against Japanese logistic lines and visual reconnaissance by the faster Hurricanes and Spitfires; and close air support missions by Hurricanes and Vultee Vengeance fighter-bombers against advancing Japanese columns.

In what is arguably one of the best narratives of the IAF's exploits in the Burma campaign, Air Chief Marshal Lal in his book *My Years with the IAF* is very generous in his praise for his contemporaries. He wrote about Arjan Singh, who preceded him as chief of the air staff and later became the first marshal of the IAF:

> The first person to actually see the Japanese in the northern part of Imphal was Sqn Ldr Arjan Singh. He had been out on a sortie

attacking the Japanese elsewhere and he was coming back to base ... he saw on a hill top overlooking his airfield a number of men in a strange uniform ... So he went close to have a look and he recognized them as Japanese troops. They were on the top to have a look ... He immediately called out his entire squadron on his own initiative ... He was the first to attack the Japanese who had actually arrived on the outskirts of Imphal. He and his boys were the heroes of Imphal.[37]

Lal himself, though, was no bystander in Burma, flying the Vultee Vengeance dive-bomber with No. 7 Squadron for a year before going on to command it in 1944. He converted the squadron to the Hurricane in early 1945 with the aircraft being specially modified for the fighter-bomber and reconnaissance roles.[38] His squadron stayed in Burma till victory was achieved with the fall of Rangoon in May 1945. Both Arjan Singh and Lal were awarded DFCs for their inspiring leadership of their respective squadrons. Another IAF squadron that operated in the shadow of No. 1 Squadron during the Burma campaign, but performed equally brilliantly, was No. 6 Squadron led by the indomitable Squadron Leader Mehar Singh. Equipped with Hurricane fighters and comprising a bunch of free-spirited pilots and an elephant as its mascot for much of its time in Burma, the squadron carried out reconnaissance, strafing and bombing missions on the Arakan front. Moving from Trichinopoly in Tamil Nadu where he raised the squadron to Cox's Bazaar on the East Bengal coast on 1 November 1943, Mehar Singh and his boys flew over 1,500 hours till the end of the war supporting the 5th and 7th Indian Divisions in their offensive and defensive operations. Mehar Singh was the only Indian pilot to be awarded a Distinguished Service Order (DSO) during WW II for his leadership of No. 6 Squadron in the Burma campaign. Viscount William Slim of Burma in his inspirational memoirs of the Burma campaign, *Defeat into Victory,* fondly recalls the performance of No. 6 Squadron led by Mehar Singh. The squadron, flying Hurricanes in the reconnaissance and interdiction roles, were employed in the Arakan region as the Eyes of the 14th Army. He writes:

I was impressed by the conduct of a reconnaissance squadron of the Indian Air Force (it was none other than No. 6 Squadron commanded by Squadron Leader Mehar Singh). Flying in pairs, the Indian pilots in outmoded Hurricanes went out, time and again, in the face of overwhelming fighter superiority.[39]

An interesting fact about air operations in the Indian region during WW II that has not found much mention in the existing historical discourse is the concept of Maritime Air Operations, which the RAF executed from the Arakan Sea off the coast of Burma to the Car Nicobar islands right in the middle of the Andaman Sea. Mainly comprising reconnaissance missions by Catalina flying boats and Liberator bomber aircraft, these operations in early 1943 were necessitated by the aggressive interest shown by the Japanese, which resulted in their subsequent capture of the Andaman and Nicobar Islands.[40]

While the main contribution of the IAF in WW II was in the Burma campaign, the exploits of a few Indian pilots and navigators who flew with the RAF in Europe and Africa cannot be forgotten. Twenty-four young Indian pilots went to England in 1940 to fly with the RAF; most of them would take part in air operations after the Battle of Britain in Fighter, Bomber and Coastal Command.[41] Amongst them was a Sikh officer, Squadron Leader Mohinder Singh Pujji. Flying Hurricanes, he shot down two Luftwaffe fighters and damaged three others in aerial battles over Europe and North Africa, before going on to join No. 6 Squadron of the IAF in the Burma theatre under Mehar Singh. Pujji was probably among the very few Indian pilots, if not the only one, to have fought in three theatres – Europe, Africa and Burma. He survived the war along with fifteen others despite having been shot down twice, and remained one of the oldest surviving Indian pilots who had served with the RAF in WW II till he passed away in 2010 at the ripe age of ninety-two in the picturesque English county of Kent.[42]

Not satisfied with his exploits in Burma and bored with a staff assignment after his hectic Burma tenure, Jumbo Majumdar bulldozed his way past the leadership in India and got himself posted to No. 28 RAF Fighter Reconnaissance Squadron on the eve of the Normandy landings in June 1944. Staying with the squadron in France till September 1944, he flew more than sixty-five operational missions in about 100 days on Mustang and Typhoon aircraft, winning the respect of his squadron mates and the gratitude of the RAF in the form of a Bar to DFC.[43]

Of particular significance was his high-speed reconnaissance mission across the Falaise Gap in July 1944, which provided key photographs that helped Field Marshal Montgomery plan the crucial Battle of Falaise where Field Marshal Von Kluge's Normandy Army was comprehensively defeated by a combined Allied assault.[44]

Unfortunately, this daredevil aviator would perish doing what he loved best – pushing the flying envelope in a Hurricane IIC. In a flying display at No. 1 RTC Walton, Lahore, on 17 February 1945, Majumdar would try one slow roll too many in his Hurricane fighter at a height of 500 feet, and spun into the ground attempting a third roll in front of an awe-struck crowd that included a few Chinese officers.[45] Majumdar and Mehar Singh emerged from WW II as the IAF's 'daredevil aviators', while Arjan Singh and Lal would hone their leadership skills over the skies of Burma and emerge as military leaders of high pedigree in the years that followed. In March 1945, apart from personally pinning the DFC on Arjan Singh in Imphal, Lord Mountbatten, the Supreme Commander of the Allied Forces in Asia, added on the title 'Royal' to the Indian Air Force on the decree of King George VI. The IAF thereon came to be known as the Royal Indian Air Force (RIAF) till India was declared a Republic on 26 January 1950.[46]

The IAF lost a total of sixty pilots and won a total of three DSOs,[47] twenty-three Distinguished Flying Crosses (DFC), one Bar to a DFC[48] and three Air Force Crosses, with all but one being won in the Burma theatre. The gallantry displayed by Indian pilots like Jumbo Majumdar, Arjan Singh, Lal and Mehar Singh ensured that by the end of the war Indian fighter pilots were considered as good as aviators from the other Allied air forces including the Americans, Englishmen and a sprinkling of Australians, New Zealanders, South Africans and Canadians. Such was the legacy left behind by the pioneers of the IAF.

An analysis of the air–land battle fought in the Burma campaign with stellar performances by squadrons of the Indian Air Force–cannot but be compared with the exploits of Air Marshal Tedder's Desert Air Force and its contribution to the victory of Montgomery's 8th Army over Rommel's Afrika Korps. Both air campaigns were 'in the nick of time' campaigns that blunted the enemy's advantage by exploiting the critical characteristics of air power like reach, surprise, offensive action and psychological shock. Both campaigns exploited the entire range of what was called tactical air operations, driving home the importance of reconnaissance, deep interdiction and close air support in influencing the course of the land battle. While Tedder's air–land battle campaign of WW II would be used as a standard template for the development of Western air–land doctrines in the years ahead, the IAF's air-land battle campaign in the jungles of Burma and their experiences of mountain and valley warfare in NWFP were never built on as doctrinal development and have remained as historical narratives. None of the stalwarts with years of experience in Burma or Waziristan wrote SOPs on air operations in jungle and mountainous terrain, or even if they did, they were never archived for future use. Not analysing campaigns and building on experiences gained has remained a weak area with both the IA and IAF over the last eight decades.

The Burma campaign also highlighted a fact that bombers and fighters are not necessarily the only primary weapons that an air force can wield. The movement of large bodies of troops and their maintenance by air opened a new technique of war in regions where the difficulties of transport by conventional means precludes the deployment of such forces in satisfactory numbers.[49] Though there were very few Indian pilots in the RAF and USAF (US Air Force) transport squadrons that operated from airfields in eastern India in support of the Burma and China operations, seeing the impact of these operations had a significant influence on future IAF commanders like Arjan Singh, Lal and Mehar Singh who were operating in that theatre. Many illustrious fighter pilots like Mehar Singh and K.L. Bhatia would go on to spearhead the IAF's transport fleet in the years after Independence. Apart from expanding in thirteen years from a force of four aircraft to 160 aircraft and gaining vital battle experience in joint operations, the development of airfields, infrastructure, maintenance philosophy, communications and air defence systems in the north-eastern region of India to support allied operations gave Indian officers the much needed exposure to build a modern air force. Air Chief Marshal Lal in particular would draw on his experience in WW II to shape the contours of the modern IAF prior to the 1971 war with Pakistan.

Run-up to Independence

The end of the war saw a number of officers from the IAFVR rejoining civil life as civil pilots, while a few opted for permanent commission. Many of these pilots would later be involved in independent India's first airlift operation as civilian pilots during the initial days of the first India–Pakistan conflict of 1947–48. In the run-up to Independence, all RAF squadrons left India and the RIAF resembled a garrison air force. The basic structure of the RIAF was decided by the Armed Forces Nationalization Committee in which Wing Commander Mehar Singh was the air force member. Also discussed during the deliberations of the committee was the fact that unlike the Royal Indian Navy and the Indian Army, the RIAF was a nationalized service from the day of its creation. RAF personnel had, during their normal overseas tour, served in units of the RIAF but no non-Indian has ever been commissioned or recruited into the service.[50] As the sun set on the British Empire in the subcontinent, the Royal Indian Air Force was not immune to the wind of freedom that was blowing across the country. Following on the naval revolt, there were reports of unrest at air force stations in Pune, Madras, Karachi, Allahabad and Delhi.[51]

Partition in 1947 saw the Royal Indian Air Force left with six squadrons of fighter aircraft and half a squadron of transport aircraft,[52] comprising Tempest and Spitfire fighters, Harvard trainers and half a squadron of DC-3 Dakotas, with Pakistan getting all the main bases and training establishments of Kohat, Risalpur, Peshawar, Miranshah and Lahore.

The Royal Indian Air Force became the Indian Air Force on 26 January 1950 when India became a republic. Unlike the Indian Army, which saw an Indian general take over as chief of the army staff in 1949, the IAF continued with a British chief of the air staff (CAS) till 1954. It is to the credit of Air Marshal Thomas Elmhirst, the IAF's first C-in-C, that he impressed upon Prime Minister Nehru that the IAF must be an independent service.[53] He is also vehemently said to have pushed the narrative that the IAF must not be seen 'merely as an adjunct of the Army'.[54] In 2011, I steered a project titled *Air House – 23 Akbar Road*, a historical narrative on the occupants of the official residence of the CAS. During the period of research, my team and I managed to get glimpses of the life and times of the three British C-in-Cs and their commitment to the IAF. While Air Marshal Thomas Elmhirst was a highly respected professional who laid the foundations of the modern IAF, Air Marshal Ronald Ivelaw Chapman, a dashing fighter pilot, endeared himself to the rank and file of the IAF by moving around on his inspection visits in a Spitfire.[55] Air Marshal Gibbs, a dour and professional airman, finally passed on the baton to Air Marshal Subroto Mukerjee, free India's first C-in-C of the Indian Air Force, on 1 April 1954. An era had ended and the IAF forged into the blue Indian skies on its own. The growth of the IAF in the 1950s was, however, adversely affected by the recommendations of a British operations research expert, Prof. Blackett, who was seconded to the Indian government by the British and heavily influenced Nehru's approach to developing air power capability. Blackett reckoned that India primarily needed only a tactical air force with air defence capability to ward off enemy attacks and not any significant bombing or offensive capability.[56] The effect of this was a limited fighter acquisition policy that stunted the growth of the IAF till the nation was jolted into action after the military defeat at the hands of the Chinese in 1962.

Attitudes

Unlike the Indian Army, whose DNA was shaped by multiple regional catalysts, an indelible British imprint and a historical legacy that stretched over almost 250 years, the IAF had no such burden to carry and traditions to uphold. Unlike the RIN, which was dominated by British officers, the RIAF was a small force mainly comprising Indian pilots and technicians who, though trained by the British, retained the typically independent and irreverent streak that is a global characteristic of aviators in general, and pilots in particular. Pilots like Mehar Singh made it a point to retain their rustic 'Indianness' and yet surpass their British colleagues with their daring and flying skill. There was a fierce desire to prove that Indian pilots and technicians were second to none; a desire to attain social and professional equality and to reject colonial snobbery and racism, and to be fiercely secular, progressive and modern in their outlook. There were British pilots on attachment in the RIAF squadrons, but command of most of the RIAF squadrons at the time of Independence was with Indians. Arguably, this trait more than anything else allowed the IAF to grow out of the shadow of the RAF at a pace faster than the Indian Army managed to throw off the legacy of the British Army. Had there been a larger number of senior Indian officers of the IAF at the time of Independence, it is highly likely that the baton of C-in-C would have been passed on earlier to an Indian officer. Nothing exemplifies the spirit of freedom more than this entry by a young flying officer who recorded events in the Operational Record Book of No. 8 Squadron in August 1947:

> The division of forces created quite a stir in the unit and lots of airmen and officers who had voted for Pakistan left the unit and lots were posted in from Pakistan. Now there is not one Muslim officer in this unit. The 8 Squadron airmen and officers hoisted the national flag at midnight with shouts and cheer ... The celebrations continued unabated for three days. It was obvious that something great had happened to their country.[57]

However, that is not to take anything away from the sound foundation that was laid by the RAF – a base that ensured steady growth and progress in the years that followed. *Nabha Sparsham Deeptam* is the motto of the Indian Air Force, which literally means 'Touch the sky with glory'. It has grown from strength to strength over the last few decades and is now the fourth largest air force in the world. History keeping, though, still remains a weak area despite a cautionary note from the departing British director of the Combined Inter-Services Historical Cell. In a reply to one of the sketchy squadron histories that was sent to him, he wrote:

> Unit Histories do much to raise and sustain 'espirit de corps' and morale. They have their part in the larger history of the armed forces and in the case of Indian squadrons, they should form a worthy background to India's future national forces.[58]

PART III

Teething Years

The First India–Pakistan War
1947–48

8

HOLDING ON TO KASHMIR

We shall meet each other frequently as the best of friends and in the same spirit of good comradeship that we have had the good fortune to enjoy all these years.

– General Cariappa, speaking at a farewell function for Pakistani officers in 1947[1]

Lieutenant Colonel Dewan Ranjit Rai, commanding officer (CO) of the first battalion of the Sikh Regiment (1 Sikh as it is commonly called) was a happy man as he surveyed the Gurgaon landscape from his battalion headquarters on a crisp autumn evening in late-September 1947. Lieutenant General Dudley Russell, the General Officer Commanding-in-Chief (GOC-in-C), Delhi and Punjab Area had just finished his inspection of the unit and remarked to one of his staff officers, Major S.K. Sinha (later retired as lieutenant general and vice chief of the army staff), that he was impressed with the unit and was glad that he had selected it along with its dynamic CO,[2] for the task of protecting Delhi during the troubled days of Partition. Sinha recalls:

> One could not but be struck by the confidence and bearing of the Colonel and little did I then realize that this visit would influence in selecting this battalion for a crucial assignment.[3]

Gurgaon during those days was the back of beyond and lay on the south-western approaches to the capital city of Delhi, a far cry from the bustling suburban metropolis that it is today. Lieutenant Colonel Rai was happy for one other reason – he had been selected as independent India's first military attaché to Washington and the family was all excited heading westwards. Little did they realize that fate had other things in store for the dashing infantry officer.

The speed and decisiveness with which the British decided to leave India in 1947 was in contrast to the century-long period they took to gain control of the huge land mass of the Indian subcontinent in the eighteenth and nineteenth centuries. Reeling from the financial burden of World War II and realizing that the winds of self-determination were gathering speed in Asia and blowing across British colonies from Malaya to India, a tactical retreat from Asia after having stripped large parts of the continent of much of its natural resources and wealth was the best that could be orchestrated by Clement Attlee and his Labour government without losing much face. Battle-hardened British military leaders like Auchinleck, who had led and fought alongside Indian officers and men and then occupied centre stage in turbulent post-war India offered sage advice to the political leadership on the futility of hanging on to India. Writing to Wavell, the viceroy of India in August 1945, Auchinleck pondered:

> I am continually being impressed in the present rapidly changing state of India with the urgent need of facing facts and for discarding the habit prevalent for some time past in British official circles in India of pretending that things are as they were ten or even five years ago.[4]

What of Wavell, the penultimate viceroy of India and the first military man to be entrusted the job by the Crown? Overshadowed by the flamboyant Mountbatten in the dying years of the Raj, the conservative and stodgy Wavell quietly paved the way for the creation of Pakistan as part of Britain's strategy to check the advance of the Soviet Union towards the warm waters of the Indian Ocean and the oil-rich regions of the Persian Gulf. In his correspondence and interaction with both Churchill and Attlee, he argued that a Jinnah-led Muslim state in the north-western part of the subcontinent would be far more malleable in terms of providing military bases and launch pads from where the Russians could be watched over as compared to an undivided Congress-led India. He rightly assessed that Nehru had great aspirations for India and was more than likely to chart an anti-colonial and independent foreign policy. Wavell was bang on target – Britain had played the Great Game well – right till the end.[5]

From the time the decision was taken to hand over political power to popular leaders of the independence movement, it took the British barely six months to put in place mechanisms and procedures for the partition of India into India and Pakistan. Guidelines were quickly drawn for the division of the armed forces and amalgamating the 550-odd princely states into the Unions of India and Pakistan.[6] It is paradoxical that the leaders of India's largely non-violent independence movement including stalwarts like Gandhi and Nehru had to oversee one of the most violent transfers of power in the twentieth century. The widespread carnage and horror of sectarian violence between Hindus and Muslims was something that no one, including the British, had really anticipated.

Geopolitical Landscape

It was during the early days of October 1947 when Major Onkar Singh Kalkat, an Indian and Hindu officer from the Bannu Brigade of the Pakistan Army in the North-West Frontier Province, was rummaging through some files in the absence of his brigade commander, Brigadier Murray, when he came across plans that were marked 'Operation Gulmarg – Secret' dealing with the tribal operation to seize Kashmir in early October 1947. Kalkat had not yet transferred to the Indian Army as he was waiting for his family to relocate to India before putting in his transfer papers. When suspected by his Pakistani colleagues of getting wind of the plans, he was taken to Lahore under close surveillance, but managed to escape from his captors. On reaching Delhi, he apprised his seniors at Army Headquarters, Delhi, of the audacious plans of Colonel Akbar Khan, the architect of the tribal invasion. Trashing his claims as 'flights of fantasy', the British and Indian leadership of the Indian Army, however, did take him to Nehru. The prime minister of India immediately found his story plausible and went into a rage when he was told a few days later that raiders were seen to be massing opposite Domel in the Muzaffarabad sector. When alarm bells were sounded by Major General

Rajinder Singh, the C-in-C of the beleaguered and rather ineffective and communally divided Kashmir State Forces, it is believed that Nehru was furious with the army leadership[7] and questioned the integrity of General Rob Lockhart, the first C-in-C of the Indian Army.

In all fairness to both sides, General Frank Messervy, the C-in-C of the Pakistan Army, was in the knowledge of the impending invasion of Kashmir by the tribals and had shared details of the same with both Lord Mountbatten and General Lockhart. In fact, it is also believed that at the time of Partition itself in August 1947, the British governor of NWFP, George Cunningham, had written to General Lockhart about tribals preparing to attack Kashmir. The letter was shared with the other two British service chiefs[8] and possibly with Governor General Mountbatten, but not with the Indian political and military leadership. Other less reliable sources from the Kashmiri media (*Kashmir Sentinel*)[9] indicate that Mountbatten forwarded the letter to Nehru, who later admitted in parliament that it had been accidentally destroyed. However, since the state of Jammu and Kashmir had not yet ceded to India, both Mountbatten and Lockhart chose to withhold subsequent and detailed information on the attack. Little did they realize that the tribals were going to unleash violence of staggering proportions when they captured the border towns of Baramulla, Uri and Rajouri. This was but one among many instances of the two-timing nature of British political and military advice to the fledgling Indian government during the crisis-ridden period of 1947–48.

While ruling India, Great Britain had always kept a careful watch on its frontiers.[10] Hence, it is strange that at the time of partition Lord Mountbatten and his transition team conveniently chose to ignore rumblings on India's future north-western frontier. While there is no conclusive evidence to point at a deliberate attempt by the British to ensure that Kashmir fell into Pakistani hands, it is my belief that the British realized that they had an obligation to ensure a balance of power and retain some influence in the subcontinent before they finally left.

Preoccupied with the horrors of Partition, managing refugee camps and orchestrating communal peace across the vast breadth of the nation, it is only fair to say that there was very little strategic geopolitical vision for the new nation state that emerged from within Nehru's government.

Major General D.K. Palit, one of India's more erudite soldier-scholars, recounts in a biography that he wrote of Major General Jick Rudra titled *General Rudra: His Service in Three Armies and Two World Wars:*

> Shortly after Independence, General Lockhart as the Army chief took a strategic plan to the prime minister, asking for a Government directive on the defence policy. He came back to Jick's office shell-shocked. When asked what happened, he replied, 'The PM took one look at my paper and blew his top. Rubbish! Total rubbish! We don't need a defence plan. Our policy is *ahimsa* (non-violence). We foresee no military threats. Scrap the army! The police are good enough to meet our security needs.'[11]

While this approach was cause for concern, it is possible that General Lockhart caught the PM on one of his 'off days'. The impending accession of Kashmir troubled Nehru immensely as the Government of India knew that plans were afoot to coerce Maharaja Hari Singh into ceding to Pakistan and his tentativeness on matters military led him to repose excessive trust in Mountbatten, who chaired the Defence Committee of the Indian cabinet. It was this committee which took all strategic military decisions during the ensuing conflict.

After identical telegrams offering a Standstill Agreement were sent by the Maharaja of Kashmir to both India and Pakistan on 12 August 1947, he vacillated for personal profit and did not follow up with India, who sought certain clarifications.[12] Pakistan on the other hand agreed to a Standstill Agreement, but showed no signs of stopping its preparations to launch a tribal insurrection in the Kashmir Valley as the maharaja procrastinated. Being a Kashmiri himself and wanting to avoid bloodshed in the vale, Nehru and his home minister, Sardar Patel, took some time to close ranks on a common Kashmir strategy only sometime in September 1947 and started pressurizing the maharaja to join the Indian Union.[13] While it would be fair to say that India was strategically surprised by the tribal invasion, orchestrated in full measure by the Pakistani state as a proxy actor, not enough lessons were learned and it would continue to be surprised in the years ahead by all its adversaries. Staying with the approach of independent India's tallest leaders towards matters of the armed forces and national security, Narendra Singh Sarila writes candidly about Mahatma Gandhi in his book, *The Untold Story of India's Partition:*

> The Mahatma, who galvanized and united the heterogeneous Indian people in the 1920s with his mystical appeal that amazed the world, was of little help to his countrymen as they faced aggression not from the British police, but from jihadi forces.[14]

As a final stroke to this landscape, a word about how Kashmir looked like geographically is critical as this had a predominant role in how the conflict panned out. Robert D. Kaplan in a recent book titled *The Revenge of Geography* attempts to reiterate an age-old proposition that it is mainly geography and not just economics or politics that shapes strategic and geopolitical outcomes. The conflict over Kashmir in 1947 only reinforces his argument.[15] Military operations in 1947–48 were concentrated in three distinct areas, each of which had their own geopolitical significance. The Kashmir Valley, with Srinagar as the summer capital of the princely state of Kashmir, constituted the 'heart of the state'. Control of the Valley with its docile people and immense economic potential for tourism made it a prime target for the raiders. To the north and north-east of the Valley lay the high-altitude areas of Baltistan, Gilgit, Skardu and Ladakh. These areas, protected as they were by the mighty Himalayan ranges like the Zanskar, Ladakh and Karakoram, were always seen as a bulwark against invaders from the north. The British always kept a close watch on this area as it was seen as a potential gateway for Russian entry into the area. To the south of Srinagar, ringed by the Pir Panjal and Kishtwar ranges, was the fertile plain of Jammu province with Rajouri and Poonch being the prominent towns other than the winter capital of Jammu. This area was the 'rice bowl' of the region and, more importantly, there were no geographical obstacles between the province of Jammu and the plains of Punjab. Jammu was literally a 'northern gateway' to India.

Demographically, the Northern Area of Gilgit and Baltistan had a majority of Shia Muslims, while Ladakh was predominantly Buddhist; the Kashmir Valley was inhabited largely by peace-loving Sunni Muslims who followed a moderate Sufi way of life. A fair number of Hindus and Sikhs lived among them in peace and harmony; finally, the Jammu and Poonch areas had equal numbers of Hindus and Muslim and a sizeable Sikh population.[16] Unlike the Muslims of the Valley, though, this region mainly comprised aggressive Punjabi Muslims and Pathans.[17] Significantly, the region had been a fertile ground for recruitment into the Indian Army during the period between the two world wars and there was much resentment amongst the Poonchi Muslims after many of them were demobilized during the downsizing of the Indian Army after WW II. Here again, Auchinleck was on target when he predicted the trajectory of many such groups in a letter to Wavell on 26 July 1945. He wrote:

> When demobilization begins in right earnest, we shall be unleashing on the villages a force which might be of great value, if handled properly, but which, if it is frustrated, may definitely be harmful. The mass of the men to be demobilized, however, will not have high standards of academic education but will be generally anxious to improve conditions in their villages. If they are frustrated by passive obstruction on the part of minor officials, or by mere inefficiency in administration, they might prove to be a real source of danger.[18]

Overall, the state had a significant Muslim majority; and the culture in the Valley was a predominantly Sufi one[19] with secular and mild overtones. This is one of the main reasons why Hindu Dogra rulers had lorded over the region for over a century without having resorted to religious persecution as a means of retaining control over the majority Muslim population. However, as the winds of Partition swept across the subcontinent, the Maharaja of Kashmir alienated himself from the majority Muslim population from as early as mid-1946 by employing his predominantly Hindu Dogra forces to stifle the voices of dissent emerging from educated and secular Muslims like Sheikh Abdullah[20]and radical elements of the Muslim League.[21] This resulted in the aggressive Punjabi Muslims of the Jammu and Poonch regions asserting themselves by organizing armed resistance against Maharaja Hari Singh.[22] The situation was further exacerbated when Sardar Ibrahim, a young lawyer, emerged as a radical political alternative and approached the Pakistan Army for help in orchestrating a popular rebellion.[23] Fed up with uncertainty and led by the fiery Ibrahim, a large number of Poonch Muslims rose in rebellion and formed their own Azad Kashmir government in August 1947.[24]

The Gilgit province at the geographical 'roof of India' emerged as an area of concern for Britain. Wavell had expected it to declare its allegiance to Pakistan despite Britain handing it back to the Maharaja of Kashmir after administering it directly for decades. The province had access to the Sinkiang province of China and was closest to the Soviet Union via the Wakhan corridor, which connected Afghanistan to the northern regions of Gilgit. Having assessed the geopolitical conditions rightly, it is possible that Wavell urged Mountbatten to turn a blind eye when the province was overrun by British-officer-led troops of the Gilgit Scouts soon after India and Pakistan were granted Independence as there was no way that the Maharaja of Kashmir or Indian troops could speedily intervene. Barring a fierce defence at Skardu before it fell to the raiders in mid-1948, Gilgit would remain the only part of the erstwhile princely state which was not contested for recapture by Indian surface forces in the year-long battle that would unfold in the lap of the intimidating Himalayan ranges.

Partition and Plotting

As millions of Hindus and Muslims made their choice of either throwing their lot with a secular and pluralistic India, or Pakistan, opportunistic and rabid religious fringe groups within the two newborn countries orchestrated communal violence and ethnic cleansing that has few parallels – commonly called by historians as the 'human tragedy of the partition of India'.[25] Millions of hapless men, women and children, swayed by religious and political rhetoric, packed their bags and set out on westward or eastward journeys from their homes depending on whether they were Hindus or Muslims. Marching on foot, riding rickety bullock carts, squeezed in overcrowded buses and trains, and even perched precariously atop trains, they were waylaid by armed brigands and thugs and massacred in hundreds of thousands. With both the Indian and Pakistani armies located in remote and detached cantonments and completely unfamiliar with peacekeeping and stability operations, massacres and ethnic cleansing went on unabated for almost six months till the traumatic relocation was complete.

Though the Indian Army had set up a force for protection of civilians and monitoring the flow of refugees in Punjab under a British general, Lieutenant General Dudley Russell, its strength was far too limited to be effective. Because of a similar ethnic cleansing and communal violence taking place in Bengal and the fear of unrest in Hyderabad and other parts of southern India, resident army formations had to remain deployed in those areas stretching the already thin resources available in the crisis-ridden states of Punjab and Uttar Pradesh, which also saw the maximum exchange of refugees. There was also another joint force created under the Partition Council, which was called the Punjab Boundary Force and comprised units from both the emerging Indian and Pakistan armies.[26] Tasked to control communal violence during the transition, it did a splendid job up to a point – after which it was caught up in the political wrangling between the two countries and was disbanded.

The Indian segment retained the formation sign of the 4th Division and was placed under Major General K.S. Thimayya with a mandate to control communal violence in East Punjab from Lahore and Jalandhar.[27] Harvard aircraft of the Royal Indian Air Force operating from Palam[28] were deployed to carry out visual reconnaissance of the main routes of refugee flow and report the presence of violent mobs so that troops could be rushed to the spot. It was amidst this cauldron of uncertainty that the blueprint of another tragedy was unfolding right under the nose of the British and Indian leadership in Lutyens's Delhi in the spring of 1947 when Partition was deemed imminent. It was here that a group of hard-core Islamist Muslim officers led by Colonel Akbar Khan in collusion with the future leadership of Pakistan regularly met at Jinnah's residence at Aurangzeb Road[29] and put together an audacious plan to seize the princely state of Jammu and Kashmir through armed action – the objective being to coerce the Hindu maharaja of the Muslim-majority state of Kashmir, Hari Singh, to cede to Pakistan. The plan in itself was pretty simple – train and push into the Kashmir Valley tens of thousands of warlike Pathan tribesmen from the constantly-at-war NWFP. Complemented by restive Poonch Muslims, who would spread across the Jammu province, the tribals had an added incentive of looting the prosperous towns of Srinagar, Rajouri and Poonch. The

Poonchi Muslims, on the other hand, were politically aware and were expected to play a major role in any post-war dispensation that came up in a Pakistan-dominated Kashmir. It is interesting to know that prior to Partition, these very mercenary tribesmen from the NWFP had been bribed by the British with sixteen crore of rupees annually as legal gratuity to maintain peace on the frontiers.[30] The new Pakistani regime could not afford such largesse and found it best to direct them towards the prosperous Kashmir Valley.

The next step of the plan was to see whether this tribal aggression would coerce a dithering and militarily weak maharaja into throwing his lot with Pakistan. Finally, only if required, would the Pakistan military step in to accelerate the task of severing Kashmir from India. The plan itself was audacious and considered operationally viable by the overconfident group of conspirators called the Liberation Committee led by Prime Minister Liaqat Ali Khan with Akbar Khan as the military member. They considered the likes of Nehru and Gandhi incapable of responding to this incursion with force and envisaged wresting major parts of Kashmir in three months. Following the swift operation, the Liberation Committee was confident of forcing the accession of Kashmir to Pakistan.[31] Little did Pakistan realize that these actions would change the geopolitical landscape of the subcontinent forever and sow the seeds of unending violence in the beautiful state of Jammu and Kashmir and convert it into a proxy battleground to fulfil what it would repeatedly term as an unfinished agenda of Partition.

The Forces

At this juncture, a quick overview of India and Pakistan's army and air forces would be necessary for the reader to understand how the operational contours of the India–Pakistan war of 1947–48 unfolded. Some of the key lessons of the conflict will also emerge from the force levels, equipment and indigenous leadership within the two opposing forces. After Partition, the Indian Army had a combatant strength of approximately 2,60,000 troops comprising eleven infantry regiments (not including six regiments of the Gorkhas), fourteen cavalry regiments, approximately eighteen artillery regiments and sixty-one engineer units.[32]

It also had the usual supporting element of signal regiments and allied units from the Supply and Ordnance Corps.

The Royal Indian Air Force (RIAF) had a total of six fighter squadrons, each equipped with eight to twelve Tempest fighters and four to six WW II vintage Harvard trainer aircraft for reconnaissance and limited fire support duties, twenty Spitfire aircraft with internal canons and machine guns at a training establishment at Ambala, and approximately half a squadron of Dakota transport aircraft with seven aircraft.[33] A couple of lumbering Oxford reconnaissance aircraft with the army made up the numbers. The Tempest was the main strike aircraft with its flexibility of carrying up to eight rockets with a high explosive warhead or two 500/1,000 pound bombs in addition to its twin internal Bofors 20mm guns for strafing. The aircraft had provision for external fuel tanks and had excellent range and endurance characteristics that allowed it to fly sorties of over two hours with full armament load.

The Pakistani army, on the other hand was much smaller, but was able to concentrate quickly in a small geographical area to support the tribal action at critical times. It was allotted eight regiments of infantry, seven cavalry regiments and nine artillery regiments.[34] A brigade comprised three or four battalions, an artillery regiment and its complement of supporting arms like an engineer regiment or an engineer company depending on whether the brigade was assigned an offensive or defensive role. The main artillery gun of the Indian and Pakistani armies in their early days was the 25-pounder towed gun (also called a howitzer) with a range of approximately 10.5 km. A brigade was also assigned with a squadron of armour depending on the terrain and its role. The Indian Army's main offensive element was its armoured regiment, equipped as it was with WW II vintage Stuart and Sherman tanks. Adding to the mobility were the Daimler Ferret Scout cars, which provided some protection for reconnaissance elements. The equipment and weapons hardly inspired confidence, but the men who operated them were raring to prove themselves! A typical infantry battalion on both sides had about 800 men and comprised three rifle companies and one headquarters company. It had a mortar and heavy machine gun platoon. The main infantry weapons on either side were the WW II vintage .303 bolt-action rifles, Sten carbines, Bren machine guns, and 2", 3" and 4.2" mortars.

The early years of the PAF were difficult ones for the fledgling service. Though it inherited a number of airbases and training establishments and had a denser concentration of airfields across the country as compared to the IAF, thanks to the British focus on aerial policing in the NWFP, these were outweighed by a number of systemic deficiencies. Among these was the sheer asymmetry in forces at Independence. It comprised two fighter squadrons with sixteen Tempest fighters and the other half of a squadron of Dakotas with what the PAF calls 'one or two aircraft',[35] and hardly had the potential to influence any form of conflict. The other disadvantage was that the number of qualified pilots who chose to cross over to the PAF was proportionally lower as compared to those who remained with the IAF. This was because of the pan-Indian composition of the pre-Independence RIAF and the lower number of Punjabi Muslim and Pathan officers who joined the air force. This resulted in the PAF having to rely on a number of volunteer British officers to man their two Tempest squadrons. This meant that PAF had fewer indigenous pilots who could be called upon to take part in direct action against the Indian forces as the British officers manning both the armies and air forces were directed not to assist the Indian or Pakistani forces in battle against each other. It is a different matter altogether that some British officers were more sympathetic to the Pakistani cause and believed that it was important to rein in India before it threatened the existence of Pakistan.

9

SURPRISE AND RIPOSTE

The first weeks were a desperate struggle to hold Srinagar whilst we marched troops to Jammu via Pathankot and built a road to Jammu. Our aim was clear. We had to gain time whilst we organized ourselves in India and flew in more troops and material into Kashmir.[1]

– Lieutenant General E.A. Vas

Infiltration and Reaction

By the time the Indian government got it its act together, Operation Gulmarg was well under way with thousands of tribals gathering in training camps and forming Lashkars (Persian name for organized tribal armies) in selected locations opposite the Poonch–Rajouri and Srinagar areas. These Lashkars were commanded by a tribal sirdar or malik to retain their non-state profile and complemented by a few regular officers and junior commissioned officers (JCOs) of the Pakistani army.[2] A total of approximately twenty Lashkars of a thousand men each were created, ten each for the Srinagar and Poonch–Rajouri sectors. While the northern Lashkars comprised mainly seasoned Afridi and Mahsud warriors from the NWFP,[3] the southern Lashkars comprised tribals and battle-hardened Poonchi Muslims, many with prior battle experience in WW II. These Muslim warriors were demobilized from the Indian Army after WW II and angered by the maharaja's refusal to absorb them into the state forces of J&K. Frustrated at being denied a secure livelihood, they went back to their agrarian life, waiting for an opportunity to get back at the Hindu ruler of J&K.[4] The fury of this force would come to the fore in the bloody battles of Poonch, Rajouri, Jhangar and Haji Pir, where the Indian Army would face stiffer resistance as compared to the Srinagar sector.

The training period included extensive indoctrination of the tribals and Poonchi Muslims, calling for a jihad against the Hindu ruler of Kashmir as revenge for the persecution of Muslims in the state by Hindu Dogra troops.[5] Backing these Lashkars was a regular infantry division of the Pakistan Army and an infantry brigade to back the tribal thrusts depending on how operations progressed.[6]

The fairly calibrated primary objectives of the plan were to seize the Kashmir Valley, capture the vital towns of Rajouri and Poonch with the aim of dominating the approaches to Jammu, and lastly, to capture Gilgit and Skardu as a possible gateway to further advance towards Leh and other parts of Ladakh. The secondary objectives were to clear the entire area of the minority Hindu population and reward the tribals by allowing them to plunder, loot and ravage the prosperous state just as Nadir Shah and other invaders had done in the past. The Pakistan Army was expected to move in once the tribals had achieved their initial objectives to protect what Pakistan called the legitimate aspirations of the Kashmiri people, the majority of whom would be Muslims.

Operation Gulmarg at no stage anticipated a spirited riposte as it was felt that the state forces of Jammu and Kashmir would capitulate within hours, and the Indian Army would be too preoccupied with managing the refugee and communal crisis to intervene in time. In an extremely biased rendition of events, a clearly pro-Pakistan Alistair Lamb completely discounts and ignores the role of the Pakistan Army in the operations. He also assesses the total strength of raiders[7] on all fronts including the Skardu–Leh sectors to be a meagre 7,000; a ludicrous figure indeed considering the number of areas they attacked. Lamb's clean chit to the Pakistan Army was contradicted in August 1948 by none other than Zafarullah Khan, the foreign minister of Pakistan, when he admitted in the UN that three regular brigades of the Pakistan Army were supporting the raiders[8] after they had been pushed back by the Indian Army on all fronts.

The complete lack of situational awareness on the part of the J&K state forces is clearly brought out by Lieutenant General L. P. Sen in his eminently readable operational recollections of military events of the conflict in his book *Slender Was the Thread.* While skirmishes between the J&K state forces and Poonchi Muslims and other Pakistani tribals in the Jammu sector were reported right after Independence in August 1947,[9] these were primarily seen by the Government of India and the Maharaja of Kashmir as only an extension of the ongoing Hindu–Muslim riots in Punjab and the rest of the country. This strategic oversight allowed Colonel Akbar Khan to concentrate his forces in the area opposite Srinagar, making it appear more as a show of solidarity for their Muslim brethren, rather than any planned invasion. Despite a cautionary note from the HQs of the J&K state forces to Lieutenant Colonel Narain Singh, the Hindu commanding officer of the mixed battalion at Muzaffarabad, to send his Poonchi Muslim troops to rear formations at Srinagar and replace them with Hindu Dogra troops, he ignored the advice, believing that their loyalty to the regiment was stronger than their religious affiliation. He was soon proven to be wrong.[10]

The raiders finally struck on 22 October 1947 and hordes poured into the Srinagar Valley in trucks and tractors along the main road that ran from Muzaffarabad to Srinagar via the picturesque towns of Domel, Uri and Baramulla. Opposing them along the way were a few companies of the Kashmir Brigade of the state forces of J&K, which were loosely strung along the Muzaffarabad–Srinagar road. Despite fierce opposition from Dogra (Hindu) soldiers of the state forces, the raiders overwhelmed the defences, abetted in no small measure by the defection of large numbers of Muslim troops of the J&K state forces.[11] However Sen has also this to say about a large segment of Muslim loyalists:

> One might form the impression from these incidents in Jammu and in Muzaffarabad area that Muslims of the state had risen against the Government and wished to join Pakistan. Nothing could be farther from the truth. Thousands upon thousands of Muslims in the Government, the State Forces and in the National Conference, the political party led by Sheikh Abdullah, braved death in stemming the invasion.[12]

As the positions of the state forces were overrun, their withdrawal towards Uri and Baramulla was slow as they had to escort thousands of Hindu refugees towards Srinagar. Thousands more were massacred at Uri as Brigadier Rajinder Singh, the officiating chief of staff, rallied his troops to offer a spirited response around the town on the same evening.[13] Outnumbered and overwhelmed, the state forces blew up the only bridge on the River Jhelum that connected the motorable road the next day, and withdrew to defensive positions east of Uri[14] as they continued to hold up the invaders from making a run for Baramulla and Srinagar. While this action did not stop the invaders, it certainly slowed them down, allowing vital time for the maharaja to negotiate, and for the Government of India to rush its negotiating team to Srinagar for an 'on the spot assessment of the situation'. The spirited and gallant action by the state forces led by Brigadier Rajinder Singh practically ended with the death in action of their brave commander on 24 October although they managed to stall the advance to Baramulla till 26 October. For his brave rearguard action and inspiring leadership, Rajinder Singh was awarded the Maha Vir Chakra, India's second highest gallantry award. He was the first military hero of the Indo-Pak war of 1947–48.

With very little protection, the prosperous town of Baramulla with a sizeable Hindu population bore the brunt of the raiders' greed, lust and religious bigotry. Women, children and even a British officer and nun were not spared as the tribals halted their advance, ransacking the town over the next two days for booty and pleasure as the white of the late autumn frost turned crimson with the blood of the hapless citizens of Baramulla. It is quite evident that whatever little formal military sense was there was thrown out of the window as tribal instincts took over and the raiders stayed at Baramulla for longer than planned. This singular lack of tactical acumen and operational focus saved Srinagar from falling to the invaders.

Government of India Reacts

The first direct Indian involvement was on 25 October when an Indian Air Force Dakota of 12 Squadron was hastily flown in from Agra to Delhi, where a quick crew change saw Wing Commander H.K. Dewan of Air Headquarters captaining the aircraft with V.P. Menon, the

Government of India's chief negotiator for amalgamating the various princely states into the Indian Union, and Colonel Manekshaw (later, a field marshal and chief of army staff) on board to see for themselves how grim the situation in Srinagar was. Grim it certainly was as Menon assessed that if the raiders continued at the rate at which they were advancing, they would be in Srinagar in a couple of days.[15] Menon and Manekshaw rushed back to Delhi with the maharaja's prime minister and urged the government to authorize immediate military assistance. Overruling a number of apprehensions and so-called operational risks expressed by the two British service chiefs, General Lockhart and Air Marshal Elmhirst, foremost amongst them being the vulnerability of any air-landed forces at an unsanitized and unprotected airfield (Srinagar), Nehru took what is probably the most decisive military decision of his entire political career – ordering an Indian brigade to be immediately flown in to Srinagar. He supplemented this order with another one that called for formations to be prepared to march north for the defence of Jammu and the garrisons of Poonch and Rajouri. Concurrently, Sardar Patel, the tough and uncompromising home minister and his chief troubleshooter, V. P. Menon, secured the accession of the State of Jammu and Kashmir on 26 October 1947. While there has been ample criticism of the procrastination of the Government of India in reacting to this crisis, due credit has to go to Nehru and Sardar Patel for acting as they did in the given circumstances. Some of the critical issues involved are analysed in the next chapter.

Recovery

The airborne eyes of the Indian Air Force at the time were four Harvard and one Oxford propeller-driven aircraft, which were mainly used in the visual and photo-reconnaissance role with hand-held cameras. They were only later fitted with integral cameras.[16] It is widely believed that the lone Oxford aircraft operating from Amritsar airfield provided the first reconnaissance inputs on 26 October, which indicated that the raiders were still approaching Baramulla and that Srinagar airfield was available for an air-landed operation.[17]

Lieutenant Colonel Dewan Ranjit Rai had just finished overseeing some training with his hardy Sikh troops and was headed for his office to tackle some of the routine administrative chores in a peace station when he received a call from the General Officer Commanding, Delhi and Punjab Area, Lieutenant General Dudley Russell – the call would change the lives of the Rai family, which was looking forward to their posting to Washington in the coming months. The orders for Rai and his band of intrepid Sikh warriors of 1 Sikh Regiment were crystal clear – it was to gather themselves as a fighting unit as quickly as possible and proceed to Palam airfield (Delhi) for a move to Srinagar. At Srinagar, they were to hold the airfield till reinforcements arrived, and, if possible, prevent the raiders from bypassing the airfield and heading directly for Srinagar town. Major S.K. Sinha, who was posted at Army Headquarters and entrusted with setting up the Rear Airfield Maintenance Organization at Palam, was a close friend of the Rai family. He had this to say about the colonel as 1 Sikh was preparing to depart Palam:

> At the airfield, Rai caught a few winks – with my experience of war, I was convinced that calmness and self-confidence during stress and strain are important assets of a good commander.[18]

Wing Commander Bhatia, commanding officer of 12 Squadron, the only transport squadron of the Royal Indian Air Force (RIAF)[19] was neck-deep in marshalling his depleted resources of Dakotas and aircrew to meet various commitments. A veteran of WW II with extensive combat experience on the Burma front, where he flew Blenheim bombers and Vultee Vengeance fighters with the RAF and the RIAF, Bhatia was given command of the squadron considering his seniority and diverse flying experience. Soon after Independence, the squadron had to meet the requirements of humanitarian relief flights, undertaking VIP commitments as the political leadership flew across the length and breadth of the country in an attempt to control the ongoing communal riots. It also provided logistic support to a fighter squadron that was being deployed in Gujarat to coerce the Nawab of Junagadh into joining the Indian Union. This deployment would support a military intervention, should the nawab threaten to cede to Pakistan.[20] It was in this melée that he was asked to position three Daks, as the Dakotas were affectionately called, at Palam on the evening of 26 October 1947. Complementing the RIAF Dakotas at Willingdon airport were about six or seven civil Dakotas. Thus began one of the RIAF's most successful demonstrations of air transport operations over a period of twelve months – comparable in many ways with the Berlin airlift that was undertaken with significantly larger resources in terms of aircraft and pilots available.

Taking off at the crack of dawn on 27 October 1947 (5 a.m.) and braving some ground fire as they descended into Srinagar, the three-aircraft formation led by Bhatia inducted the advance element of 1 Sikh into Srinagar airfield on a bright autumn morning. They were followed by the civil Dakotas as all the aircraft would carry out a total of twenty-eight sorties on that day to complete the induction of 1 Sikh and a battery of mortars by last light. On landing and hearing that the raiders were almost at the gates of Baramulla, Rai sent a company forward at dusk to reinforce defensive positions slightly east of Baramulla. As the raiders regrouped after overcoming stiff resistance from the Dogra troops of the J&K state forces and prepared for the final assault on Srinagar, he led the next two companies forward the next morning when he came to know that the raiders were over 4,000 strong. Sensing that their offensive foray forward was not sustainable and that the defensive positions around Baramulla were untenable, 1 Sikh commenced a timely withdrawal to a tactical high ground near Pattan, 17 miles from Srinagar – a move that may well have saved Srinagar as it put doubts in the minds of the raiders about the actual strength of the defenders.

With confirmed reports that the enemy had reached the outskirts of Baramulla on 27 October, the next morning saw fighters from the RIAF joining action with 1 Sikh around Baramulla. Two Spitfires got airborne from the Advanced Flying School, Ambala, and strafed enemy gun positions that were tying down Colonel Rai and his men as they attempted to gain a sense of the opposition.[21] Operating on the fringes of their radius of action, they subsequently landed at Srinagar and remained there for some time, repeatedly carrying out strafing attacks under close control of 1 Sikh till the threat to Srinagar receded. An interesting story here is how the Spitfires refuelled at Srinagar. Amidst all the chaos as the Dakotas streamed in from Delhi and landed at Srinagar, they were requested to part with some fuel in return for IOU (I owe you) chits, which they were told would be honoured by government authorities at a later stage. It is this fuel that sustained the Spitfires and permitted them to operate from Srinagar airfield till refuelling facilities were provided. As for the IOU chits – they were soon forgotten!

Tragically, Rai's vehicle was caught in a machine gun crossfire; he and his platoon commander were killed as they were withdrawing with the trailing elements of 1 Sikh and remnants of the state forces.[22] The action was as bold as the commander who led it; unfortunately it resulted in his death and a terrible loss to 1 Sikh and elements of 161 Brigade, which had started inducting into Srinagar. Lieutenant Colonel Rai was posthumously awarded the Maha Vir Chakra for his heroic exploits, daring initiative in the face of uncertainty and exemplary leadership. A lesser-known saga of bravery revolves around the exploits of two of Rai's company commanders, Major Harwant Singh and Major Sampuran Bachan Singh. The latter was promoted to lieutenant colonel and took over command of the battalion after its gallant CO fell. A Military Cross winner from the Italian campaign of WW II, it was Harwant's suggestion to fall back to Pattan that contributed greatly to baulking the raiders.[23] A sprightly ninety-four at the time of editing this chapter in October 2014, he has no regrets at not being decorated for his leadership of the 'paltan'[24] till a new CO took over. It is only in hindsight that one realizes that in the absence of hard intelligence about the enemy's disposition at Baramulla, lying in wait at Pattan instead of giving battle on the outskirts of Baramulla was a better option in the face of a numerically superior enemy. Ultimately, it was this action that was instrumental in confusing the enemy.[25]

By now it was clear that the need of the hour was to get an accurate sense of the enemy disposition, strength and direction of movement towards Srinagar. Operating from Jammu and Amritsar by end-October 1947, 7 Squadron of the RIAF, also called 'The Battleaxes', was the first squadron to undertake this task by carrying out visual reconnaissance sorties along the Domel–Baramulla–Pattan road using the Tempest aircraft. Air Marshal Randhir Singh, now a sprightly ninety-three year-old with crystal-clear recollections of the time, was the first one to carry out the reconnaissance – he recounts how the squadron moved from Agra to Jammu and Amritsar and operated into the Valley from there.[26] Tempests also continued to strafe the advancing enemy as they spread out into the Valley and attempted to neutralize 1 Sikh, which was fighting a brilliant defensive battle. On 29 October, two Tempest fighter aircraft from 7 Squadron at Jammu made repeated strafing runs against tribal convoys on the Domel–Baramulla–Pattan road. Flight Lieutenants Roshan Suri, Randhir Singh and J. J. Bouche reported seeing up to seventy-seven buses and vehicles with tribals and went on to wreak havoc amongst them. These actions allowed Army HQ some breathing time to further strengthen 161 Brigade and plan the defence of Srinagar with some accurate intelligence. But more about that later as we still stay with the defensive battle around Srinagar.

After the initial skirmishes around Baramulla and Pattan and the casualties suffered by 1 Sikh, it was clear that additional forces would be required to save Srinagar. After a hasty staff visit to Srinagar on 29 October by Colonel L.P. Sen from Military Intelligence and a thorough staff check by Brigadier Thapar, the director of military operations, the mood turned sombre in Delhi. Added to this was an input to Pandit Nehru from an independent source that the situation was near normal in Srinagar. Confusion prevailed and the PM was furious[27] when Army HQ sought clearance for additional forces to be airlifted to Srinagar. However, to his credit, Nehru calmed down when even the British C-in-C General Lockhart concurred with the military assessment. Finally, the green signal was given to reinforce 161 Brigade, which had by 30 October deployed around Srinagar in battle-ready formations.

Gallantry

By 31 October, 161 Brigade had almost four battalions with slightly over 3,000 personnel comprising a combination of 1 Sikh, 2 Punjab, 1 Kumaon, 4 Kumaon and a battery (six guns) of artillery around Srinagar. They were deployed at tactically sound positions to defend the airfield and prevent the raiders from bypassing it and making a direct run for Srinagar.[28] This was also the time when an ad hoc command structure came up for the defence of Kashmir. A recently promoted brigadier, L.P. Sen, was appointed the brigade commander of 161 Brigade with Colonel Harbaksh Singh as his deputy and placed under J&K Force, which was commanded by Major General Kulwant Singh. By late evening on 2 November, Sen was concerned about reports that the raiders had realized that expecting a free run along the highway to Srinagar was a pipe dream and had changed their tactics. Consequently, when faced with stiff opposition at Pattan, they had split themselves into two attacking elements – one following the highway, and the other moving cross-country to the south, threatening the airfield from Badgam. The next morning, he sent out a large offensive patrol in the direction of the raiders with three companies of the 4 Kumaon Regiment, of which one of the company commanders was Major Somnath Sharma.

Major Somnath Sharma, a high-pedigree soldier with loads of operational experience with Slim's XIV Army in Burma, was an alumnus of the Royal Indian Military College (RIMC) and passed out from the Indian Military Academy in 1942. At the young age of twenty-one he was Mentioned-in-Despatches for his gallantry and outstanding efficiency as the 'DA & QMG' at a brigade headquarter in Burma.[29] On one occasion during the battle in Burma, Somnath's orderly, Bahadur, was badly injured and was carried to safety under fire by Somnath himself despite being ordered by his commanding officer, to leave him behind as they were slowing the pace of the column. In 1947, he was the adjutant of 4 Kumaon Regiment when the regiment was ordered into action. Despite his hand being in plaster, he insisted on accompanying his battalion into action. Major Sharma's company was ambushed in the town of Badgam by raiders firing from houses and appearing from all around, supported by heavy machine gun and mortar support.[30] It is during this battle that he called for air support on wireless and two Spitfires were on the scene in minutes during the late evening, strafing the tribals[31] with the help of a scruffy little map given to them by the brigade commander till their ammunition ran out.

Outnumbered heavily, Major Sharma's Kumaon company suffered heavy casualties on 3 November 1948 and his last wireless transmission indicated that his position was under heavy fire till a blast indicated that a mortar shell had landed close by and probably killed him. Like Colonel Rai, Major Somnath Sharma too died leading his troops in the thick of battle. Along with him perished Subedar P. S. Mehta and twenty others. His last message to the brigade headquarters was: 'The enemy is only 50 yards from us. We are heavily outnumbered. We are under devastating fire. I shall not withdraw one inch but will fight to the last man and last round.' The fierce resistance put up by the Kumaonis also resulted in serious injuries being inflicted on the main leader of the tribals, who had to be evacuated rearwards to Baramulla. The impact of this battle and significant losses suffered as a result of the aerial attack by the two Spitfires resulted in the raiders again overestimating the strength of the Indian opposition and abandoning their advance. Srinagar airfield had been saved in a second joint battle. This again allowed Brigadier Sen to build up forces for a final decisive battle that was to be fought a few days later. Major Somnath Sharma was posthumously and deservedly decorated with free India's first Param Vir Chakra.

A word here about the continuing airlift into Srinagar by 12 Squadron and other Dakotas requisitioned from civil airlines. While the three or four Dakotas from 12 Squadron continued to fly round the clock till 161 Brigade (3,500 troops) was fully inducted into Srinagar by 6 November[32] with four battalions (1 Sikh, 1 Kumaon, 4 Kumaon and 2 Punjab), some supporting artillery and other logistic elements, the contribution of the civilian pilots and their machines needs to be acknowledged repeatedly. Having requisitioned all the available Dakotas from 12 Squadron for the airlift (not more than four to five aircraft were available at any time), the Government of India requisitioned all civil Dakotas to supplement the IAF ones. The bravery of the civilian pilots has largely gone unnoticed with many of them having served in the IAF as part of the Civilian Volunteer Reserve Force and then having demobilized after the war (refer to the IAF chapter) to take up a career in the fledgling civil aviation sector. However, none of the civilian pilots who took part in the airlift have chronicled or written about their experiences during this most decisive air mobility operation. Paying tribute to these intrepid aviators who rose to the call of duty, Sen writes:

> Despite all dangers and normally unacceptable hazards, the pilots of the civil airline companies cheerfully undertook flights into the Kashmir Valley with aircraft loaded with troops, ammunition and stores. They judged their loads visually and they were lavish in their load acceptance. In almost every case, the aircraft were loaded to a point, which would have confounded the manufacturers. The courage and devotion to duty displayed by the civilian pilots and their crews played a decisive part in saving Kashmir from the ravages that threatened it.[33]

Shalateng is a small hamlet about 15 miles west of Srinagar astride the Baramulla–Srinagar highway, and it is at this hamlet on 7 November that one of the finest tactical set-piece battles turned the tide in favour of 161 Brigade and pushed the raiders back to Baramulla and beyond. Brigadier Sen's deputy, Colonel Harbaksh Singh aggressively sent two battalions (1 Sikh and 1 Kumaon) forward to meet the raiders frontally at Shalateng and, in an outflanking manoeuvre that completely surprised the raiders, had a small force of Daimler Ferret armoured cars from 7 Cavalry Regiment led by Lieutenant Noel David come in from behind and decimate the opposition in a vicious crossfire.[34] Surprised and sandwiched, the raiders turned and bolted. Once a clear demarcation between Indian troops and the retreating raiders was available, Tempests from Amritsar/Jammu and Spitfires from Srinagar caused mayhem amongst the retreating vehicles with raiders in them. Amongst the key pilots with recollections of the Battle of Shalateng is Air Marshal Randhir Singh. He firmly recounted the havoc which his Tempest's 20mm cannon created amongst the tribals as he strafed them while they were in retreat.[35] He would go on to fly almost 200 hours during the entire conflict, which was about the maximum flying that any fighter pilot would do during the period. The Battle of Shalateng will go down in history as the final battle that saved Srinagar. Never again over the next one year would Srinagar be threatened.

Pursuit

When 161 Brigade entered Baramulla on 8 November, they were met with an eerie and deathly silence and clear signs of a massacre having taken place. Even the battle-hardened veterans of WW II were shocked at the brutality of the raiders as they had vandalized what had been a prosperous town. As they retreated, the tribals had torched all that could be set fire to – houses, fields, godowns, and the sky was crimson as Sen and his troops entered Baramulla. In his own words, Sen narrates:

> The sight that greeted us in Baramulla is one that no period of time can erase from the memory. It was completely deserted, as silent as a tomb with not even a whimpering pie dog. Everywhere one looked,

> whether it was a house or a shop or a shed, there were signs of pillage, arson or wanton destruction. There were unmistakable signs that the patients in the hospitals had been slaughtered in their beds or dragged out to meet the same fate in the compounds.[36]

From all the narratives that exist on the ravaging of Baramulla, it was as though Nadir Shah, Timur Lane and Ahmed Shah Abdali,[37] three invaders from the past, were back in Baramulla. Witnessing this brutality, the Indian troops were more than determined to push forward and evict the raiders completely from Kashmir. Forging ahead with aerially inducted reinforcements and much needed armour support in the form of one troop of 7 Cavalry with WW II vintage armoured cars, 161 Brigade reached Uri on 13 November. They had advanced almost 100 km on foot from Srinagar over less than two weeks, fighting their way through semi-mountainous terrain. It was no mean feat by any standards and by any logical tactical reasoning; their next objectives would be Domel, and possibly even Muzaffarabad.

During this phase of operations it was mainly 7 Squadron of the Royal Indian Air Force with Tempest fighters operating from Jammu, and a handful of Spitfires from Srinagar, which provided excellent close air support during the battles of Pattan, Badgam and Shalateng, apart from interdicting enemy columns on the road axis of Muzaffarabad–Domel–Uri–Baramulla–Pattan. To give the reader an idea of air operations, the aircraft would get airborne from Jammu; fly almost 300 km over the Pir Panjal range before getting down into the Kashmir Valley and operate over the battle area. Often braving bad weather, they would take on either immediate targets based on the requirements of the ground troops, or carry out search-and-strike missions over the road axis as mentioned above. The two squadrons together flew approximately fifty to sixty sorties or 100 to 120 hours in the Srinagar sector during this critical phase of battle between 28 October and 13 November 1947.[38] By 14 November, the rout was complete and the raiders were in complete disarray as they retreated. Colonel Akbar Khan, who had assumed the name of General Tariq during the operation, was witness to the collapse of his plan at Uri and lamented on seeing barely a dozen raiders and nothing but 'disappearing tail lights of departing vehicles'.[39] Two more Tempest squadrons of the RIAF, Nos 8 and 10 Squadrons, would join battle in December as multiple fronts opened up.

THE INITIAL FOG OF WAR

It is at this point that one gets to closely examine the fog of war that existed during the initial stages of battle. The tactical imperatives in the Valley rarely matched the operational perspectives at J&K state forces headquarters at Jammu and the politico-strategic compulsions at Delhi. As the brigade commander with some additional resources and a string of victories under his belt, 'Bogey' Sen, as he was affectionately called from his WW II days, felt that the time was ripe to push the raiders back into Pakistan. He was overruled by Lockhart and Elmhirst, the British army and air force C-in-Cs, who were overcautious in their assessment and felt that 161 Brigade had overstretched itself and that there was inadequate air support to prosecute an offensive battle with winter around the corner. Elmhirst also restrained the RIAF from attacking the bridges around Domel and Muzaffarabad as Messervy, the British C-in-C, wanted them intact. However, it was a politico-strategic and logistic compulsion that forced Brigadier Sen to halt his advance at Uri and divert a large force to head south and relieve the beleaguered garrison of Poonch.

Fully aware of the ongoing horrors of Partition and briefed by his staff on the massacre of both Hindus and Muslims at Baramulla, Uri and Rajouri by the advancing raiders, the deteriorating situation around Poonch forced Nehru to overrule both his British C-in-Cs and his Indian operational commanders by ordering 'an immediate relief of Poonch by all possible means'. In retrospect, it was the right decision for an advance to Domel would have surely meant the fall of Poonch and a great psychological victory for the raiders. The second front had to be opened in the third week of November! Apart from diverting part of Bogey Sen's 161 Brigade to get to Poonch from the north before the tribals got there, Major General Kulwant Singh, the GOC of JAK Force, ordered the elite 50 Para Brigade to advance on Poonch from the south. D.R. Mankekar, a correspondent then with

The Times of India, and later a successful writer, reported that it was fuel shortage that initially stopped Bogey Sen's brigade at Uri and allowed Nehru time to re-orchestrate his strategy. He reflects:

> Here was one of the great 'ifs' of the war. If the Indian Army had not run out of petrol at that critical moment and pursued the raiders, it would have reached Muzaffarabad, the border town of the state of Jammu and Kashmir; and then the western part of the state, now Pak-occupied, would have been ours for the asking.[40]

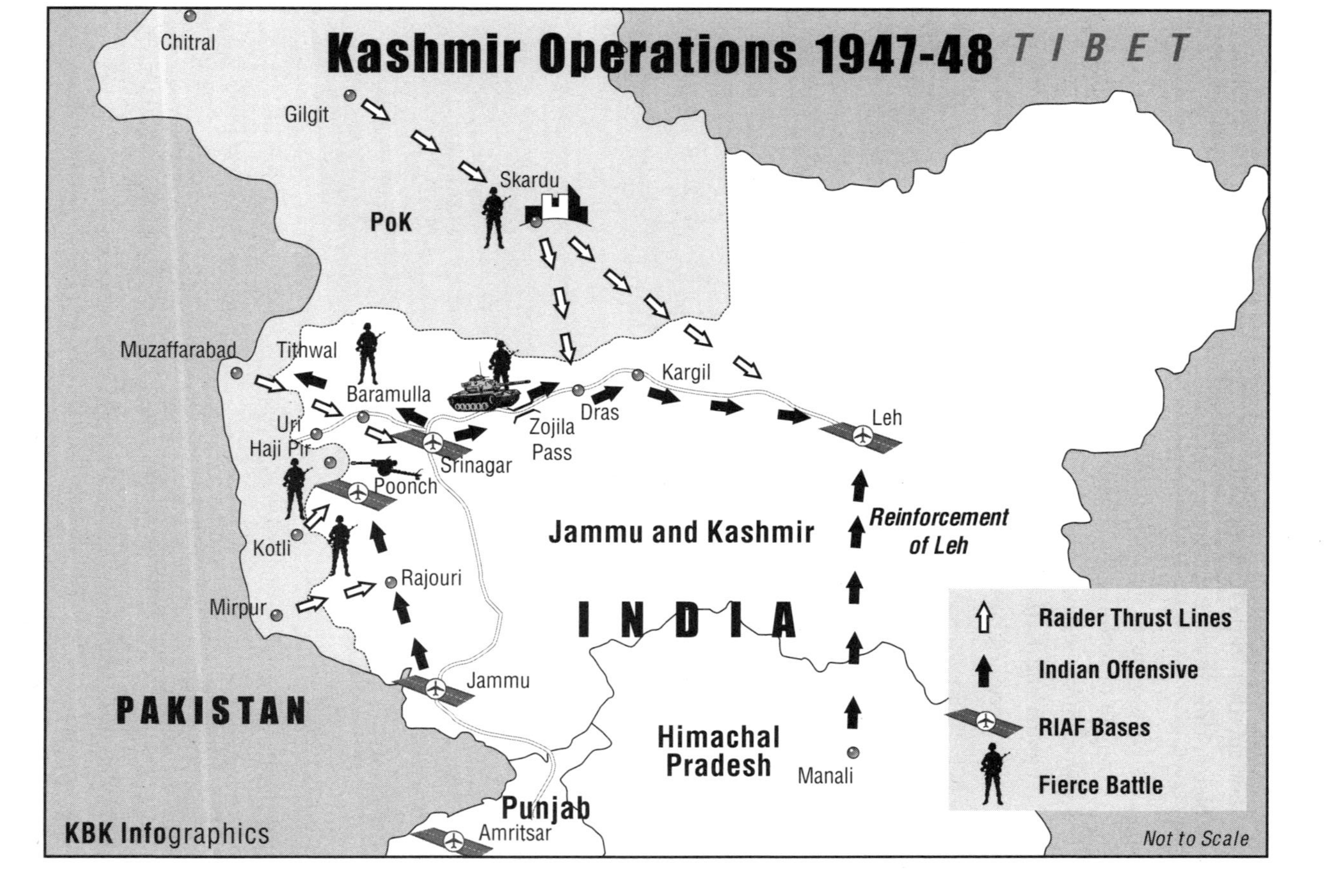

Kashmir Operations 1947-48
TIBET
Chitral
Gilgit
Skardu
PoK
Muzaffarabad
Tithwal
Baramulla
Uri
Haji Pir
Poonch
Srinagar
Zojila
Pass
Dras
Kargil
Leh
Kotli
Rajouri
Mirpur
Jammu
Jammu and Kashmir
Reinforcement
of Leh
INDIA
PAKISTAN
Himachal
Pradesh
Manali
Punjab
Amritsar
Raider Thrust Lines
Indian Offensive
RIAF Bases
Fierce Battle
KBK Infographics
Not to Scale

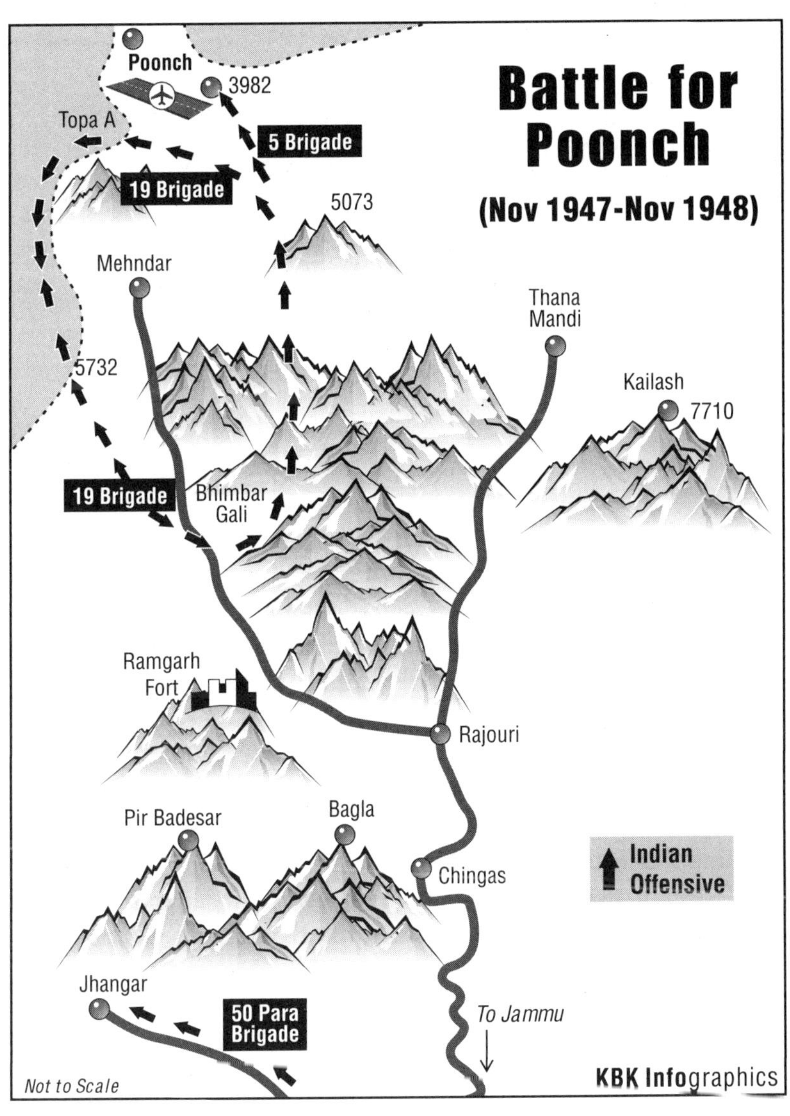
Battle for Poonch
(Nov 1947-Nov 1948)
Poonch
3982
Topa A
5 Brigade
19 Brigade
5073
Mehndar
Thana
Mandi
5732
Kailash
7710
19 Brigade
Bhimbar
Gali
Ramgarh
Fort
Rajouri
Pir Badesar
Bagla
Chingas
Indian
Offensive
Jhangar
50 Para
Brigade
To Jammu
Not to Scale
KBK Infographics

10

THE WAR DRAGS ON

In early May, with the Spring Offensive approaching, Mountbatten asked Bucher (the British C-in-C of the Indian Army) to instill in the government the notion that India was militarily impotent in order to reduce the risk of an all-out war after his departure from India in June.[1]

The Poonch Saga of Valour

The second thrust line of the raiders of Operation Gulmarg was in the Rajouri and Poonch sector. This area lies to the south of the Kashmir Valley and is separated from it by the Pir Panjal range. This range rises up to 15,000 feet and includes a number of traversable passes like the 8,000-ft-high Haji Pir Pass, which offered significant military potential. Control of these passes and this area was essential for dominating the roads that linked Jammu with Srinagar through Udhampur and the Banihal Pass and also those that ran westwards into Pakistan. Having concentrated opposite Mirpur and Kotli, and emboldened by the initial success in the Baramulla sector, eight to ten Lashkars crossed over and overran the town of Rajouri by the beginning of November, laying it to waste, and advanced towards the strategically important town of Poonch. With a population of almost 50,000 including almost 40,000 Hindus, many of whom were prosperous traders and state government officials, with the rest being Poonchi Muslims,[2] the town was a lucrative target. From an Indian perspective, Poonch had to be held at all costs!

With the diversion of a two-battalion-sized force from Uri began the heroic defence of Poonch, a relatively unsung saga of bravery, innovation and grit on the part of common people. Much like the Berlin Blockade of 1948–49, the major difference was that Berlin was not subjected to attacks and shelling in the manner that Poonch was. Climbing and clawing their way past the raiders at Haji Pir Pass, and traversing across two destroyed bridges on the Battar Nullah, a tributary of the River Poonch, Lieutenant Colonel Pritham Singh and his 1 Kumaon Regiment fought their way into Poonch by 22 November and commenced setting up defences for the winter, while the remainder of 161 Brigade headed back for Uri after suffering heavy losses en route and hearing that the raiders had regrouped there.[3]

Due to the failure of the link-up with a relief force coming from the south in the form of the elite 50 Parachute Brigade, which encountered stiff resistance on the road from Jammu at places like Naushera and Jhangar, Poonch was literally blockaded by the raiders from all directions. Thus, the first major challenge for Brigadier Pritham Singh (he was promoted overnight to the rank of brigadier and assumed command of the Poonch Garrison) was to build an airstrip that would facilitate the sustenance of the town via an air bridge. Pritham achieved this monumental task by mid-December 1947 with the help of over 6,000 citizens of Poonch.[4] The next challenge was to impress upon the IAF that the only way of sustaining the town through the long winter, or till the link-up force that was coming from the south opened the road link to Jammu, was by ensuring a steady stream of aerial replenishment.

Magnificent Flyboys

Air Commodore Mehar Singh, DSO, or Baba Mehar Singh as he was called because of his thick beard, had gathered a reputation from WW II as being one of the boldest aviators of his times. Promoted to the rank of air commodore in November 1947 after having flown all types of aircraft in the IAF inventory, he was assigned command of the 1 Operational Group in Jammu and Kashmir.[5] Leading from the front, he carried out a trial landing on 8 December at Poonch airstrip in a Harvard trainer with Air Vice Marshal Subroto Mukerjee, the senior-most Indian officer in the RIAF, on board as his co-pilot. He then took on the onerous responsibility of being the first one to land a fully loaded Dakota at Poonch along with Flying Officer Pushong as captain of the aircraft a few days later on the 750-yard-long makeshift airstrip[6] that had been prepared by Pritham Singh and his men. Carrying 6,000 lb of freight, which mainly included food and rations for the garrison, they set standards for the rest of 12 Squadron to emulate for the next one year as it maintained an air bridge to Poonch. To give you an idea of the monumental airlift, the operational record book of 12 Squadron indicates that between 10 and 20 December, almost 4,30,000 lb of load including light artillery guns were flown into Poonch.[7] So committed was the squadron to sustaining Poonch that it undertook night operations to deliver 25-pounder artillery guns that were badly needed by the defenders to counter enemy bombardment from the surrounding hills.[8] These guns were the only ones that had the necessary loft angle and range to target the raiders in their vantage positions around Poonch.

Mehar Singh also spearheaded night bombing by Dakotas of 12 Squadron in the hills around Poonch as gallant crew fused the bombs and then rolled them down from the rear. The greatest impact of these bombing missions was seen on 14 December 1947 when five Dakotas dropped a large number of 250-lb bombs on enemy positions around Poonch. This caused great confusion amongst the raiders and demoralized them and hampered their night raids around Poonch. Lieutenant General Eric Vas, a distinguished soldier with loads of combat experience and leadership, was a young major with the J&K division during the 1947–48 operations. His account of the war in the Poonch sector includes magnanimous appreciation for the Royal Indian Air Force as it assisted in sustaining Poonch for almost a year. He writes:

> Poonch, cut off from the rest of JAK FORCE, continued to fight back at the enemy encircling the stronghold from all sides. To a great measure, the credit for their ability to do so goes to the audacious and untiring efforts of the Indian Air Force who kept flying in valuable stores and manpower into Poonch.[9]

Garrison Happenings

Reinforced by a major part of a Gorkha battalion and some artillery by late January 1948, Pritham Singh had gained the confidence to send out patrols to engage the enemy on adjoining hill slopes supported by light mortars and artillery. The summer months saw a stalemate with the raiders unable to break through the defensive cordon around Poonch and the Indian Army unable to break the siege. While an initial link-up was made in June with a third battalion fighting its way from the south and being welcomed by thousands of citizens, the actual siege of Poonch was lifted only in November when two brigade-sized forces cleared all the areas around Poonch, particularly from the south. The best tribute to the defenders of Poonch came from a young and articulate major from the Corps of Signals, Maurice Cohen, who was at the forefront of setting up communications in the Poonch and Uri sector. In one of the initial first-hand accounts of the conflict published in 1955 titled *Thunder over Kashmir*, he writes with passion:

> Prime Minister Nehru's main concern was the safety of the people there. But from a military point of view the fall of Poonch would have been disastrous. Nor would it have been creditable for the Indian Army if it were to abandon 45,000 men, women and children to their fate at this critical juncture.[10]

I cannot but help staying with Maurice Cohen's book for the simple reason that when I found the book in the station library at Air Force Station, Pune, it had not been borrowed for over twenty-five years – what a wonderfully engaging book it turned out to be! I was quite amazed to read of an operation called 'Operation Grain' where Brigadier Pritham Singh used to periodically send out large patrols to engage the raiders in the surrounding hills and in the ensuing confusion bring back large quantities of grain from the local granaries along with fresh vegetables and a variety of produce from the fields. There were also periods during the harvesting season when large numbers of civilians under strong military escort from the Poonch Brigade would spend hours harvesting the ready-to-pick grain and take it back to the town. Their safety would be ensured by the escort force, which would aggressively patrol the hills around during the period. As a result of this, despite being given the option of an airlift to safe refugee camps, the citizens of Poonch chose to stay back in their homes despite the risk. So high was their morale and confidence that they knew they would be safe in the hands of the Poonch Brigade.[11] I end the initial saga of Poonch by describing a casualty evacuation operation from a small town called Potha after the first link-up (south-east of Poonch) by a young flying officer Dennis Barty from 12 Squadron. Cohen writes:

> When salutes and greetings were over, the job of evacuating the casualties was taken in hand. An airstrip was hastily constructed. About 350 yards long, it was just enough for an Auster or Fairy Moth (small aircraft). We radioed for the plane and within a short time one was seen circling overhead. When eventually he did land we were disappointed that he could take away one casualty at a time. Soon afterwards a Dakota was seen circling overhead, but since our men knew that it needed about 1,000 yards for landing, they did not take notice of it. After a short while it was seen to be circling lower and lower as though it was about to land. Somebody said, 'No it cannot be so, he will kill himself.' Then it descended almost vertically and made a perfect landing though it just grazed the rough raised ground at the far end where it frantically braked and turned round. Everyone rushed to congratulate the pilot, Flying Officer D. Barty. Despite knowing that he could have been court-martialled for taking such a risk, he said nonchalantly, 'I could not go away without landing, when I knew you lads seemed to be in an unpleasant position.' All the casualties and refugees were emplaned and alas as he got airborne, it appeared that the plane was headed straight for the hill. Then, suddenly, the plane seeming to jerk upwards and miss the trees on top of the hill by inches. A week later, Major General Atma Singh, the GOC of the Jammu Division said at the Poonch Officers Mess, 'I shall get this pilot the worst rocket that can be given for taking the risk without orders – At the same time I shall recommend him for the highest award I can.'[12]

True to his word Atma Singh ensured that young Barty would get his Vir Chakra!

The Poonch Brigade, comprising a little over two regular Indian Army battalions and some two battalions of state forces and volunteer militia, governed the town with the help of local citizens during the siege. This really was the first example of military-civic liaison in troubled areas; the Indian Army would be called on repeatedly in the years ahead to help restore equilibrium in strife-torn regions, particularly in remote frontier locations of the north-east and the state of J&K. I will return later in the chapter to the bloody initial battles fought by 50 Parachute Brigade under the redoubtable Brigadier Mohd Usman and the final assault by two brigades of the Indian Army (19 and 5 Brigade) in late autumn 1948 on the enemy around Poonch that led to a complete link-up between Jammu–Rajouri and Poonch.

Battle for the Roof of India

To its north and north-west, the central Kashmir Valley is separated from the Gilgit and Baltistan region, also called the Northern Autonomous Region in recent years by Pakistan, by the Burzil Mountains, a part of the Nanga Parbat range of the Great Himalayas. Across these mountains through the Burzil Pass at a height of 4,000 metres ran the ancient caravan route between Srinagar and Gilgit, the largest town of the region. Originally this westernmost part of the Ladakh province was under Dogra rule till the early part of the twentieth century; it was thereafter leased to the British by Maharaja Hari Singh and was seen as a defensive high-altitude buffer between British India and the Russian Empire as the 'Great Game' unfolded in the region. After Partition, it was assumed that the territory would be considered as a province of the princely state of Kashmir till accession to either India or Pakistan. To the east and north-east of the Kashmir Valley lay the main province of Ladakh, separated from the rest of Kashmir by the Great Himalayan and Nun Kun ranges.[13] These ranges are traversable through the Zojila Pass and the Baralacha Pass, which connected Ladakh to the Kashmir Valley and the state of Himachal Pradesh respectively. All these passes would play a critical role in the conduct of the 'Battle for the Roof of India' as I would like to term the series of skirmishes and pitched battles that took place in these regions in 1947–48.

Emboldened by the initial success in the south and egged on by extremist propaganda that talked about massacre of Muslims by Dogra troops of the state forces,[14] tribal laskhars played a prominent role in orchestrating a coup in Gilgit on 31 October 1947. Reinforced by large sections of the Gilgit Scouts, a regiment with a local Shia Muslim majority and a part of the J&K state forces, the force was led by a British officer named Major Brown. This was but one of many instances in which British officers of the Pakistan Army were believed to have actively assisted the raiders, and later, the regular Pakistan Army during the subsequent stages of the conflict.[15] The distribution of tribal Lashkars along the front by Colonel Akbar Khan was a tactical success as he had anticipated that the best chances for local support from jagirdars or local leaders was in the isolated northern areas where religious propaganda had good chances of succeeding in the predominantly Shia Muslim areas of Gilgit and Skardu. After the fall of Gilgit in early November 1947, it was quite easy for the raiders to build up a force of 3,000 to 4,000 troops comprising personnel from the Gilgit Scouts, Chitral Guards, tribal Lashkars and locally recruited fighters to launch two operations.[16] The first was a frontal assault on Skardu and the second was an ambitious late-winter run to Dras, Kargil and Leh.

Skardu, the second largest town in Baltistan, was defended by a small force of the Gilgit Scouts and reinforced from Leh by a small force of the Kashmir Infantry led by Major Sher Jung Thapa.[17] For over six months from February to August 1948, the garrison gallantly fought back repeated attempts by the raiders to breach the defences at the Skardu Fort where Thapa had organized his defences. A request to pull back to Kargil was denied – it would have been suicidal to attempt a trek of almost 300 km with women and children. A request for aerial replenishment akin to what was being done at Poonch was not found feasible by Air Commodore Mehar Singh for various reasons, amongst them being uncertain weather conditions across the Burzil Mountains and the apprehension that Dakotas may not be able to sustain operations from the Skardu airstrip, which was located at a height of 9,500 feet.[18] One of the big 'ifs' of the war revolves around this decision, but even if the Dakotas had managed to land there, the RIAF with its depleted Dakota squadron would have found it impossible to support both Skardu and Poonch from the air. However, Tempest fighter-bombers attempted to drop supplies in canisters with little success as many of them landed outside the fort[19] and any attempt to retrieve them was met with vicious crossfire from raiders positioned at vantage points around the fort.

February 1948 also saw the regular employment of Tempest fighter-bombers of 8 Squadron of the RIAF during the battles in the Uri, Poonch and Skardu sectors. This was soon after the commencement of defensive operations by the Skardu garrison against the raiders from Gilgit and villages around Skardu, which emerged as fertile recruiting grounds for the raiders. Flight Lieutenant Mickey Blake of 8 Squadron, RIAF, whom Air Chief Moolgavkar recollects as an 'excellent pilot, quite a daredevil and a popular flight commander of the squadron', has this to say about his first sortie over Skardu area:

> On 9 Feb 48 we had to climb to 26,000 feet because of cloud and we were blown off-course by strong easterly jet streams. However, we hit the River Indus and I was able to pin point where we were. We followed the River Indus in a westerly direction and hit Skardu and then Rondu where we hit our target with rockets. However, when we tried to strafe the area, our cannons failed to fire. I hope we gave the b******s a fright. We flew alongside Mt K2, the second highest mountain, on our way to Rondu.[21]

Having flown a little in areas like that ensconced in the comfortable cockpit of a Mirage-2000, wrapped in my high-altitude clothing with woollen inners and fleece-lined jackets, I can only marvel at the guts and seat-of-the-pants flying skill of pilots like Baba Mehar Singh, Mickey Blake, and Flying Officer Barty. Pilots those days wore plain chamois leather gloves and had to keep their fingers from going numb by constantly flexing them so that they could press the trigger. Their teeth chattered as they maintained radio contact and navigated across mountains and valleys by relying on vintage maps and what pilots call 'a seat of the pant' understanding of terrain. Oxygen masks were rudimentary contraptions and pilots had to literally suck the oxygen out to stay focused. Putting in rocket and bomb attacks at those altitudes stretched the machines to the edge of their flying envelopes and the aircraft 'screamed, juddered and protested' as pilots pulled out from attacks at dangerously low heights. It must truly have been exhilarating stuff!

Intelligence reports coming out of Skardu in early March 1948 indicated that a large group of more than 500 raiders and 200 porters had bypassed Skardu and were making their way towards Dras, Kargil and Leh.[22] Anticipating the threat to Leh a good fifteen days earlier, Brigadier Sen's 161 Brigade, still the largest formation in the Valley, had to come up with a winter solution to reinforce the Leh garrison before it fell to the advancing raiders. A sense of topography, distance and time is important to understand the travails of foot-soldiering in high-altitude regions like Baltistan and Ladakh, particularly during the winter months when tracks and passes are snowbound and cross-country movement is virtually impossible.

The Ladakh Valley itself is at a base height of around 10,000 feet. Settlements are sprinkled at heights between 12,000 and 15,000 feet and mountain heights vary from 17,000 to 25,000 feet. Srinagar to Leh via Zojila Pass is about 360 km and Skardu to Leh is a similar distance. Therefore, in tactical terms, it was a race to Leh between the raiders and the Indian Army. Forty intrepid Lahaulis (Lahaul is a hilly province of Himachal Pradesh and is accessible to the rest of the state via the 14,000-foot-high Rohtang Pass) led by Captain Prithi Chand and his cousin Captain Kushal Chand from 2 Dogra Regiment, which had come in to reinforce 161 Brigade, set out from Srinagar in mid-February 1948 to try and breach the 16,000-foot-high Zojila Pass. Facing trying winter conditions; it was a feat that had never been attempted before. Acclimatizing en route, beating drums to trigger avalances and create paths, and losing radio contact for more than ten days, the column successfully traversed the treacherous pass and reached Leh by 8 March 1948.[23] They were joined by retreating Kashmir Infantry troops of the Kargil garrison and together with the Leh garrison of a few troops, managed to organize defences ahead of the town to foil repeated attempts by the raiders as they advanced past Dras and Kargil to assault Leh in the beginning of May. Despite the organized defences, the situation turned precarious by the third week of May and the only way that Leh could be saved was by reinforcing it from the air.

Air Bridge to Leh and Defence of Ladakh

Major General Thimayya, one of India's most celebrated post-Independence generals, was part of the Indian trio that commanded their battalions during WW II in Burma as part of the 51 Brigade, and the first Indian to command a brigade in Burma during the closing stages of WW II. It was this illustrious warrior who was in operational command of all forces in the Srinagar and Leh sectors. With Leh under immediate threat, it was left to his persuasive skills to get Air Commodore Mehar Singh to attempt a landing at Leh, which is at an altitude of 11,500 ft. I reckon that seeing the fate of Skardu and probably rankled by his earlier decision not to attempt a landing there, Baba Mehar Singh took upon himself the challenge of attempting a landing at Leh after hearing about Captain Prithi Chand's frantic calls for reinforcements. Finally, on 24 May 1948, Mehar Singh, with Thimayya on board, landed at Leh in what was a red-letter day for military aviation in India. This feat opened the air bridge to Leh and despite spells of bad weather Mehar Singh himself repeatedly led missions of four and six aircraft into Leh for the next two weeks inducting a company of 2/4 Gorkha Rifles.[24] He was one of the four RIAF pilots to be decorated with the Maha Vir Chakra for his daring feats of transport flying and inspirational leadership.

The combination of Lahaulis from 2 Dogra Regiment, Gorkhas from 2/4 and 2/8 Gorkha Rifles and 12 Squadron of the IAF saved Leh – a truly joint operation. They were joined a few months later by the remainder of 2/8 Gorkha Rifles. One company of the battalion under Major Hari Chand had opened the treacherous 325-km route from Manali to Leh through Rohtang Pass, the Lahaul and Spiti Valley of Himachal Pradesh, and the formidable Baralacha Pass, linking up with Leh garrison in late July 1948. The war diary of the regiment indicates that in late May 1948, two officers, four GOs (what we now call JCOs or junior commissioned officers) and 150 GORs or other ranks, as they are now called, set off across three 15,000-feet high passes with only civilian guides on a 'two month route march across hostile terrain' with only a prayer on their lips.[25] It was only after they were some way through their epic journey did the air bridge to Leh open. Their mandate was to 'raise, train and equip a militia force and reinforce the garrison at Leh under Lieutenant Colonel Harischandra Sakharam Parab, CO of 2/8 GR, who was designated as Governor-Leh.'[26] For his leadership during the long and hazardous trek and subsequent acts of bravery in numerous guerilla actions behind enemy lines in the Leh–Kargil and Dras sectors, Major Hari Chand was awarded the Maha Vir Chakra.[27]

Having staved off the threat to Leh, Thimayya's focus would now shift to ensuring that both Kargil and Dras were cleared of the raiders as he tried his best to save Skardu. It is at this time – as summer set in – that Thimayya realized how short he was on troops to carry out operations in the Kashmir Valley and the Leh, Kargil, Dras and Skardu sectors. Attempts to send reinforcements to Skardu from Srinagar via Kargil in April and May were a complete failure as the force was continuously harassed and ambushed along the River Indus by tribals who were both well acclimatized and conversant with the topography of the region, unlike some of the Indian columns.[28] Gradually, the raiders came to dominate the whole area from Kargil to Zojila and it would take a Herculean effort in the months ahead to throw them back. As the raiders tightened their grip on the areas around Kargil and Dras in the summer of 1948, reports came in of the mass murder of Buddhist monks in Kargil by the Gilgit Scouts and Pakistan Frontier Rifles.[29] The lama of Ganskar Padam monastery was shot dead and the Rangdom Gompa, the second largest monastery in Ladakh, was desecrated and razed to the ground.[30]

As the weather improved, repeated air strikes on Skardu using Tempest fighter-bombers were launched from Srinagar from 20 June onwards to try and cause maximum attrition to the raiders, replenish the garrison with ammunition by dropping them in canisters,[31] and try and lift the siege. On 11 and 12 August fierce attacks were launched in the evening hours from eight till midnight, which were beaten back with significant casualties suffered on both nights by the attackers.[32] Despite the gallant resistance by the defenders, Skardu finally fell on 14 August 1948 after repeated attempts to reinforce it failed. As in most other places all the Hindus and Sikhs in the garrison were massacred, while Major Sher Jung Thapa and a few others were taken POW.

The late Air Chief Marshal Moolgavkar recalled a few interesting events from 1948 that marked his tenure as commanding officer of

1 Operational Wing at Srinagar in an interview with the author in February 2013:

> I was pulled out of Staff College, Wellington, in mid-1948 and before I knew, I was on a Harvard trainer aircraft from Delhi to Srinagar to replace Minoo Engineer as the CO of 1 Operational Wing at Srinagar. There was no briefing for me and I had to learn on the job immediately. There were detachments from three Tempest Squadrons (7, 8 and 10 Squadrons) operating from Srinagar by then and a few Spitfires. We mainly flew search-and-strike missions based on reports from the army liaison officer (ALO) and all the tactics we employed were adapted from the Burma campaign as we had no time to come up with new ones. The Tempest was the only aircraft capable of effective interdiction and the main weapons we used were 500 and 1,000 lb bombs, or 8 rockets and canons.[33]

The fall of Skardu troubled Thimayya immensely[34] and he tried his best to retake Skardu. Unfortunately, the difficult terrain, lack of acclimatization, and shortage of attacking formations in the correct ratios that were essential for mountain warfare ensured that it remained an unfulfilled dream. But that did not stop him from motivating the IAF to launch ferocious aerial strikes on Skardu, one of which had six Tempest aircraft attacking the Skardu Fort and blowing up an ammunition dump. Moolgavkar was part of the formation, which also included another future air marshal, Minoo Engineer. In her biography of Moolgavkar, Jyoti Rai, his daughter and an accomplished historian herself, wrote of the attack:

> HM found it difficult to lead every mission and he particularly recalled the attack on Skardu on 24 October, 1948. Air Vice Marshal Aspy Engineer (Minoo Engineer's elder brother and a future IAF chief) and Major Gen Thimayya were reviewing the attack in a Dakota. HM led six Tempest IIs, went in for a 25 degree dive attack, firing all eight R/Ps (Rocket Projectiles) together in one salvo and then pulled out safely. Afterwards, the pilots flying General 'Timmy' as Thimayya was affectionately called reported that he became very

excited at seeing the attack on Skardu, and shouted 'maro the sallas' – literally translated meaning 'hit the scoundrels'.[35]

Moolgavkar chuckled when he spoke about an incident in November 1948 when RIAF Tempest fighters on a bombing-and-strafing mission in the Northern Area spotted a Pakistani Dakota as they were returning after strafing Chilas airfield, about 260 km west of Skardu. Left with a few rounds, one of the Tempests chased the Dakota, shot at it and forced it to head back into Pakistan. Unconfirmed reports indicated that the Dakota was badly damaged and put out of action. His recollections were quite remarkable at the age of over 90 as I stumbled on a report of the Dakota incident in *The Hindu* newspaper during my numerous archival forays to the Nehru Memorial Museum and Library.[36] This incident alarmed the Pakistanis who threatened to send fighter escorts with their Dakotas to ensure that they could keep the snowbound regions of Gilgit supplied from the air. Alarmed at the turn of events that could lead to aerial encounters between Pakistani and Indian fighters and a larger escalation of the air war, the British stepped up attempts to push both countries to the negotiating table and maintain status quo in Gilgit. For their repeated offensive forays in the Kashmir Valley, Skardu operations and leadership of 1 Operation Wing at Srinagar, Wing Commanders Minoo Engineer and Moolgavkar were deservingly amongst those awarded the Maha Vir Chakra.

Spring Battles in the Vale

A history of the 1947–48 conflict with Pakistan would not be complete without a quick overview of the battles fought during the spring–summer offensive from April 1948 onwards by Thimayya's Srinagar Division in the Tithwal, Uri and Domel sectors, and the bruising battles fought by the Jammu Division to regain the heights around Poonch, Jhangar, Mendhar and Naushera. As the conflict spread across three sectors, it became an operational necessity to restructure the command in the J&K sector as it was getting extremely difficult for a single commander to coordinate operations across such a wide front – literally from Skardu in the north to Naushera in the south. By March 1948, J&K state force was converted into a J&K corps under the command of Lieutenant General Cariappa.

Before the conflict ended, Lieutenant General Srinagesh would take over as the corps commander with Cariappa moving up as army commander of the newly formed Western Army Command.[37] The J&K Corps was divided into the Srinagar Division (later 19 Division) commanded by Major General Thimayya, and the Jammu Division (later 26 Division), commanded by Major General Atma Singh. Air Commodore Mehar Singh continued to command 1 Operational Group of the RIAF from Jammu, while Wing Commander Moolgavkar commanded the main operational wing at Srinagar, which had by then inducted detachments of three Tempest fighter-bomber squadrons and a flight of Spitfires.[38]

The spring offensive in the Kashmir Valley was Thimayya's idea and a trifle ambitious considering that his division was shedding forces to protect Leh. With only one division and hardly any reserves, he wanted to pursue the raiders till the Jhelum and recapture all the territory that was lost. Facing him were not only the tribal Lashkars and elements of the Pakistan Army, but also an entire Pakistan Army division, which had been cleared for action without its British officers as Frank Messervy, the British C-in-C realized that the Indian Army had to be stopped east of the Jhelum. Lord Mountbatten and his team of British C-in-Cs had firmed up a line of penetration that ran from Uri, Poonch, Rajouri and Naushera beyond which they felt that India would be in an unfair position to dominate the whole area.[39] Thimayya advanced towards Domel with three brigades. Sen and his battle-hardened 161 Brigade met with the toughest resistance at Chakoti in the form of a Pakistan Army brigade of the 7 Division on the main axis of Baramulla–Uri–Domel. A newly promoted Brigadier Harbaksh Singh and his 163 Brigade made significant progress to the north in the Tithwal sector and captured Tithwal, while Brigadier Nair and his 77 Para Brigade attempted to outflank enemy positions at Chakoti and come to Sen's assistance[40] but did not have sufficient firepower and reserves to do so. While the three brigades were poised to move ahead and threaten the Jhelum defences of Pakistan, they could have done so only if they had been backed by at least two to three reserve brigades, a move that was blocked by General Bucher. Despite fervent appeals from Thimayya and his brigade commanders, in particular Sen, the commander of the by-now over-stretched 161 Brigade, Bucher stood firm.

Having to commit more troops and offensive air support than anticipated to the high-altitude battle that was raging in the Zojila, Kargil and Dras sectors, Thimayya realized that he did not have the luxury of reserve troops as was the case when the British Army threw the Japanese back from Kohima in WW II. The Srinagar Division advanced as far as they did only because of the quality of leadership provided by Thimayya and his inspirational brigade commanders. The limited but ready offensive air support that was provided by Spitfires and Tempest fighter-bombers of Nos 7, 8 and 10 Squadrons along with their daring band of pilots complemented the tremendous fighting spirit of the Indian troops. Ultimately logistics and numbers stalled the offensive, much to the relief of Bucher and Gracey, the C-in-Cs of the Indian and Pakistani armies.

The situation in the south was as tough for the Indian Army as it was in the Kargil and Dras sectors, primarily because of the requirement of fighting in the hills and mountains to clear all the heights that were occupied by the raiders and the Pakistani army. Before the spring offensive was launched in the Kashmir Valley, the stranglehold established by the raiders and the Pakistan Army around Poonch had to be broken and the threat to Jammu had to be seen off. This entailed a series of bruising battles in the Jhangar–Naushera–Rajouri and Poonch areas, part of the second thrust line of Operation Gulmarg. The challenge in this sector was not only to relieve the siege of Poonch, but also ensure that the Srinagar–Jammu road was kept open. This was only possible if the many heights overlooking the highway, which were overrun by the raiders, were recaptured by the Indian Army. The summer of 1948 saw a significant escalation in this sector as Pakistan threw in greater artillery firepower in the form of 25-pounder guns, 4.2" mortars and 3.7mm howitzers against Poonch and other positions held by the Indian Army.[41]

Of the many tough battles fought in this sector, I have chosen two battles that involved one of the finest field commanders who fought in this area – Brigadier Mohammed Usman, Commander of 50 Para Brigade.[42] Part of the last batch of Indian officers who were trained at Sandhurst, Usman's batchmates there included Sam Manekshaw and

Mohammed Musa. While the former would go on to become India's chief of army Staff during the 1971 war with Pakistan, Musa was at the helm of the Pakistan Army during the 1965 India–Pakistan war. Interestingly, Usman was the second-in-command of 16/10 Baluch Regiment in the Burma campaign when it was commanded by L.P. Sen as part of the 51st All Indian Brigade. Little did they realize that they would be commanding brigades on either side of the Pir Panjal ranges a few years later during the 1947–48 conflict.

Taking over command of the brigade in January 1948 from an ailing Brigadier Paranjpe after choosing to stay in the Indian Army, much to the disappointment of Jinnah, Usman found himself in a precarious situation of holding the town of Naushera despite being surrounded by thousands of tribals who were in control of Jhangar, Kotli and Rajouri. The only way that any progress could be made to relieve Rajouri and clear the way to Poonch was if Naushera and Jhangar were to be captured. Naushera is dominated by a height called Kot, approaches to which were occupied by a force of over 2,000 raiders. In response to General Cariappa's request for Kot as a gift in February 1948, Usman and his brigade fought their way to the top in a bruising infantry battle that left the enemy with over 200 dead and many more injured. By doing so, Usman's brigade was to inflict severe casualties on surprised attacking raiders a few days later, when an attempt was made to breach the defences around Naushera.[43]

In a predominantly army-centric battle, the exploits of 7 Squadron of the RIAF, first under Squadron Leader Noronha, and then Squadron Leader Masillamani, cannot be forgotten. Getting airborne from Amritsar, Tempests from the squadron pounded enemy troop concentrations and gun positions around Naushehra and Jhangar repeatedly, causing significant attrition to the enemy.[44] Thus, by early March, Usman was ready to move forward from Naushehra and take Jhangar back from the enemy along with 19 Brigade, which was commanded by another outstanding soldier with Spartan habits, a spiritual outlook and an indomitable spirit, Brigadier Yadunath Singh.[45] The Battle of Jhangar, also called Operation Vijay, lasted three days and can be counted as one of the fiercest battles in the Jammu sector – two fine brigades of the Indian Army against an equal number of entrenched and widely dispersed tribals, who were supported by regular Pakistan Army artillery. In his battle order to the brigade, Usman invoked Macaulay:

> Death Cometh soon or late and how can man die better then facing fearful odds for the ashes of his fathers and the temples of his gods ... So forward my friends, fearless we go to Jhangar, India expects everyone to do his duty.[46]

A well-read man, Usman was combining the flair of inspirational English poetry and the words of his prime minister, Jawaharlal Nehru. After the battle, 50 Para Brigade was tasked with holding Jhangar while two other brigades (19 and 5) from Atma Singh's newly formed 26 Division moved forward to Rajouri. Tragically, the 'Lion of Naushera', as Usman came to be known, was killed on 3 July in an artillery battle as he was walking around his gun positions. He was the senior-most officer of the Indian army to be killed in battle in the 1947–48 war and was honoured with a Maha Vir Chakra. He is buried in the heart of what is now the Jamia Millia University in Delhi and remains an inspiration to many students who throng the memorial service that India's Parachute Regiment conducts every year to honour this gallant paratrooper.

In October and November 1948, the Poonch garrison came under renewed fire from a combined force of raiders and units of the Pakistan Army supported by Pakistani army artillery units. With the airstrip under constant fire, aerial resupply was getting increasingly difficult and Atma Singh, GOC of the Jammu Division, wanted Brigadier Umrao Singh, the former commander of the Poonch Brigade, to fly into Poonch and assess the situation. In a daring display of airmanship, Flying Officer Newby of 10 Squadron, RIAF, with Brigadier Umrao in a Harvard trainer aircraft escorted by two Tempest fighters, flew into Poonch braving intense small arms and ack-ack fire.[47] Two days later, in a similar operation, Umrao flew out after he had taken stock of the situation. For their exploits in battles around Naushehra, Jhangar and Poonch and later in support of Thimayya's summer offensive, the two COs of 7 Squadron, Noronha and Massilamani were awarded the Maha Vir Chakra and Vir Chakra respectively,[48] while Squadron Leader Z.A. Shah, the CO of 10 Squadron, was awarded the Vir Chakra. Shah and Idris Hasan Latif, who was commanding another Tempest squadron that was not involved in the J&K conflict, were among the senior Muslim officers from the RIAF who chose to stay on with the IAF. Latif would go on to become a future IAF chief. The cavalier Mickey Blake too was awarded the Vir Chakra, being one among eight Anglo-Indians from the RIAF to be decorated for gallantry. Writing in a light-hearted manner in the squadron diary of 7 Squadron, Shah quipped:

> The squadron has had its share of enemy MMGs, LMGs, bunkers and unavoidably, a large number of mules – poor buggers![49]

Autumn Ending

As the Chinar leaves lay strewn across the bloody vale and the apple and saffron crops were laid waste by the war, the conflict stumbled along towards an impasse as the Pakistan Army openly joined the fray in the Srinagar, Rajouri and Poonch sectors. After repeated attempts by the Indian Army's 77 Para Brigade's infantry assaults to retake Zojila Pass failed in August–September 1948, Thimayya planned an audacious operation, which involved the stealthy movement of Stuart light tanks from the 7th Light Cavalry Regiment from Jammu to Srinagar in mid-October 1948. The American-built Stuart tanks were sturdy machines that were produced in large numbers during WW II and saw action with the Indian divisions in Burma. They did not have heavy armour protection like the Sherman and Centurion tanks, but had a 37mm gun along with a couple of machine guns

From Srinagar, these tanks were dismantled and transported as water carriers to Baltal, about 80 km from Srinagar. They were admirably assisted by two companies of 'Thambi' engineers of the Madras Engineering Group (MEG) under Major Thangaraju, who not only paved the way for the movement of the tanks from Jammu to Srinagar across weak wooden bridges, but also created tank-friendly tracks from Baltal all the way up to Zojila Pass, braving enemy fire as they laid the last few yards of the road.[50] While the track was being laid, the tank unit under the command of Lieutenant Colonel Rajinder Singh Sparrow acclimatized for a few days – proving the engines at high altitude before surprising the enemy in freezing conditions.

On 1 November 1948, Zojila Pass was cleared of bewildered Pakistani raiders as they were surprised by a combined arms assault by tanks and fighter aircraft over the next two weeks. Kargil and Dras would be recaptured by the Indian Army after ferocious hand-to-hand fighting.[51] With the raiders retreating to Skardu by end-November 1948.[52] *The Hindu* reported that RIAF aircraft gave close support to moving columns strafing the enemy dug-in gun positions and mortar positions on mountain slopes on either side of the defile.[53] Tempest fighter aircraft operating from Srinagar were guided on to their targets in the Zojila and Dras areas by Dakotas which acted innovatively as an air control team whenever the weather permitted. Though the number of sorties were few, the fighter attacks with rockets and bombs, along with strafing runs with cannons, caused significant psychological degradation of enemy morale and caused the raiders to collapse and retreat.[54] The criticality of the operation can be gauged by the fact that between Kargil and Leh, a distance of almost 300 km, there was just one position manned by a platoon from the Leh garrison guarding a vital bridge at Khalatse (also called Kalsi), about 80 km from Leh. Had this bridge fallen, it would have been a clear run for the raiders to Leh.

Largely forgotten over the years has also been what could be considered as the first sustained special operations campaign by Indian commandos in the Skardu sector in September 1948. Akin to operations by the famed Long Range Penetration Groups in the Burma campaign, Major Hari Chand of the Manali–Leh trek fame and his band of carefully selected Gorkha and Ladakhi troops, carried out a series of daring raids along the Indus and Shyok Valleys. They killed a number of raiders, destroyed a large howitzer that was being transported for the attack on Leh and disrupted the long lines of communications and supply lines that the raiders, had created from Skardu during their multiple offensives on Leh, Kargil and Dras.[55] This had a tremendous psychological impact on the raiders and by the time they retreated along the Indus in November, they were a bedraggled and defeated force.

Further south, some of the bloodiest battles were being fought in the Naushera and Poonch sectors by two brigades (19 and 5 Brigade) of the Jammu Division (commanded by Major General Atma Singh) as they desperately attempted to force their way from the south to make the still elusive 'Poonch Link Up' happen. The Pakistan Army had assigned almost a brigade worth of regular troops in the sector to support the two Azad Kashmir brigades and enjoyed a slight numerical superiority over Indian forces till one more Indian brigade was pushed into action in late October 1948.[56] There was near parity in artillery and the only advantage that the Indian Army had was in terms of the quality of its troops and a squadron of tanks to push through when the road links were cleared. Systematically clearing all the heights around Poonch proved to be the hardest task, as the enemy was well entrenched and could be evicted only after a frontal assault and hand-to-hand fighting. The Battle of Topa Ridge and the simultaneous assault by 5 Brigade and the Poonch Brigade on two other vital heights on 21 November were the last battles for Poonch. Maurice Cohen, the young signals officer with 19 Brigade, writes:

> Every Commanding Officer in the two brigades was summoned to a conference, to receive the last and final briefing. Brigadier Yadunath Singh standing with his feet astride facing north, pointed towards Topa Ridge, the last enemy stronghold still in our way. Raising his voice and speaking more vehemently than he had ever been known to do before, he said – 'Gentlemen, you see those two features in front of you; they must be captured at any cost and it will be done, even if all of us have to give our lives to do so ... they are the orders of our government, the Government of India – our own country. The land link will be pushed through. The population will be relieved. That is all.'[57]

An ascetic commander with Spartan habits, Yadunath was one of the heroes of the final days of the war. On 21 November 1948, the battles were won and Yadunath met Pritham Singh on the outskirts of Poonch. The year-long siege was over! This pretty much sums up the initial saga of Poonch and to this day, 21 November is celebrated by the Poonch Brigade with much fanfare with the residents of what has now become a bustling town of nearly 3,00,000.

11

GUNS FALL SILENT

For Pakistan, the possession of Kashmir was crucial to her ideology ... To India ... its integration was vital because it demonstrated that even a Muslim-majority state province could thrive within a predominantly Hindu state, thus validating the concept of a secular, democratic state.[1]

– Sumit Ganguly

Tame Ceasefire?

As a white blanket of snow heralded the onset of winter and the bare chinar trees and walnut groves sadly watched over the war, the times did not augur well for the Indian Army as operations slowed down. Further making the going tough for both Thimayya and Atma Singh was the fact that after due clearance from the Pakistan Army C-in-C, General Frank Messervy, their divisions were now frontally engaged by a division each of the regular Pakistan Army (9 Frontier Division and 7 Pak Division).[2] Much to the frustration of their aggressive brigade commanders like Harbaksh Singh and Yadunath Singh, they were ordered to wait for the spring of 1949 to build up forces for any further offensive towards Mirpur, Kotli, and Muzaffarabad and into the northern regions of J&K. This was not to be as Mountbatten pushed Nehru and the Pakistani political leadership to accept a UN-brokered ceasefire on 31 December 1948 that left large parts of the Northern Region, Kashmir Valley and Jammu province in Pakistani hands. The military angle of this nudge was that had the Indian Army supported by an increasingly confident Royal Indian Air Force chosen to conduct their spring offensive along the Indus towards Gilgit and Skardu, the strategically important region might no longer remain a buffer that could be exploited by the British in the Great Game – a possibility which they optimistically thought could be sustained for decades to come.

By August 1948, the situation had become quite precarious for Pakistan and it was at this time that Indian war correspondents reported that interrogation of regular Pakistani troops of the Punjab Regiment revealed that many high-ranking British officers were leading the raiders under direct command.[3] This was in direct contravention of the orders from Lord Mountbatten, which barred the participation of British officers from either side in the conflict. Concurrently, the Government of India was under tremendous pressure from Lord Mountbatten and the British C-in-Cs to limit military options and settle for international mediation under the auspices of the United Nations.

As referred to earlier, but in a different context, the situation as it prevailed in late 1948 gave Pakistan the strategic depth it needed, something that even Akbar Khan referred to in his book *Raiders from Kashmir*.[4] Anticipating a ceasefire by the year-end, Pakistan commenced one last attempt to push Indian forces back in two sectors of interest, Poonch–Naushera and Kargil–Dras, by mobilizing additional troops and tribals in Mirpur, Koth and Muzaffarabad.[5] In Karachi, a press communiqué called for all releases from the armed forces to be stopped and the re-enlistment of reservists.[6] War correspondents reported the massing of two brigades of Gilgit Scouts, Chitralis and Baltis in the Skardu area and a call for jihad in the Northern Area with conscription being mooted for all able-bodied men between the ages of eighteen and thirty-five.

This uncertainty was eminently suited to the end state that the British were looking at: impressing upon India the need to exercise restraint and not escalate the war with Pakistan on multiple fronts. The senior Indian military leadership, however, wanted to build up forces during the winter of 1948 and push for total victory even if it meant having to open another front in Punjab. They felt that they owed it to the officers and men who had laid down their lives in battle.

Pressurised by the UN to settle for a ceasefire for almost a year after it had surprisingly moved the Security Council to intervene in the conflict in early 1948, the Indian government settled for a UN-sponsored ceasefire on 1 January 1949. However, the much anticipated plebiscite in Kashmir never happened; that tale has been much narrated by distinguished political commentators across the world and will not be discussed in this chapter.[7] There were too many geographical preconditions that favoured Pakistan and, by not being assertive enough about retaining control over areas like the Haji Pir Pass, Gilgit and Skardu, India ceded operational advantage in the region to Pakistan. It would prove ominous in the years ahead, particularly when China started evincing keen interest in Ladakh. The Indian press by and large was accommodative and accepted the ceasefire as a fait accompli – they preferred to highlight the inability of the raiders and the Pakistan Army to press home their initial advantage, rather than question India on its inability to throw the invaders completely out of Kashmir. In an operational assessment made as early as in August 1948, the *Bombay Chronicle* commented:

> Today the invaders are exactly where they were eight months ago. They are being held at Chakoti in the West, Tithwal in the North West beyond River Kishenganga, at Gurez in the North and Zojila Pass in the North East. Only one sixth of Kashmir is held by the enemy including Muzaffarabad, Poonch Jagir, Bhimbar and Mirpur.[8]

However, the international press seemed to buy Pakistan's story better as the accessibility to the areas of conflict was easier from the Pakistani side. A typically biased and factually incorrect report from *The New York Times* by Robert Trumbull seemed to suggest that Pakistan had gained the upper hand in the conflict by capturing and occupying three-fourths of the state and dominating half the population, establishing a government and collecting taxes.[9]

And what of the Kashmiri people and how they felt about the war raging around them? Sheikh Abdullah in a speech made on the eve of the first anniversary of India's freedom was effusive in his praise for the sacrifice and gallantry of the Indian Army. However, the aspirations of freedom for the Kashmiri people had not vanished. He said:

> The attainment of our dream of independence might have received a setback or its realization delayed owing to the grim war that had been forced upon us from Pakistan. Blood which heroic sons of India have shed on the battlefields of Kashmir in defence of the people cannot go in vain and is bound to blossom forth as a symbol of comradeship between the peoples of Kashmir and India. Let us stand by the pledge that India has given us and we have given India forever.[10]

Sheikh Abdullah was to change tack as the ceasefire was implemented by once again expressing aspirations for independence and asking for guarantees from India, Pakistan, the UK, the US and the UN.[11] Though he retracted this statement after pressure from the Indian government, this flip-flop approach was to continue for years to come as he continued to search for an elusive solution for the Kashmiri people.

Early Lessons

A military historian's favourite questions are: 'What if?', or 'Why not?' His favourite cliché invariably is: 'In hindsight, if X, Y or Z had been done, the tide of battle would have turned.' However, the historian has the luxury of analysing, praising and critiquing the actions of various protagonists in a conflict from the relative comfort of his research and archival environment. As long as he realizes that and remains respectful and not disdainful of decisions that were taken in the heat of battle, he is on the right track. This is one of the many traits of John Keegan, the eminent British military historian that I have tried to emulate. If Wavell had not applied his military mind and first alerted Churchill and then Prime Minister Attlee to the dangers of leaving the north-western regions of the Indian subcontinent in the hands of a Congress-led undivided India, the idea of a Pakistan may never have been encouraged by Britain's post-war political leadership. Alive to the possibilities of Soviet expansion into Central Asia and towards the warm waters of the Indian Ocean and the petroleum-rich Persian Gulf, Wavell covertly encouraged the germination of the 'Pakistan seed' within Jinnah's mind. The reason being that Pakistan would be more amenable to staying within the Commonwealth and provide bases to Britain so that it could monitor and stay in touch with Soviet expansionism and counter a possible collusive strategy between a resurgent Soviet Union and an emerging China.

That politics and religion dictated the 1947–48 conflict between India and Pakistan is beyond doubt. The fledgling Indian government of the time has often been accused of procrastinating when it came to taking critical military decisions that could have prevented the conflict from escalating and spreading across three fronts. A mere look at what was happening in the rest of the country – Partition riots, Hyderabad and much more; the hybrid British–Indian composition of military leadership; lack of military expertise within the government; and an inherent disbelief that religious differences and fundamentalist ideologies could turn comrades into enemies in a matter of months were amongst the many reasons why Nehru's government responded as it did. What happened in Kashmir went against the grain of India's dream of building a secular, liberal and multicultural democracy.

The mechanics of Pakistan's proxy war and asymmetric tactics against India emerged during the 1947–48 conflict. Closer analysis of the conflict would reveal that the concept of jihad in J&K germinated in the indoctrination given to the raiders and elements of the Pakistani army in the run-up to the invasion by Akbar Khan and his band of religious zealots. That India chose to largely ignore such strategies till the proxy war waged by Pakistan assumed dangerous proportions in the early 1990s, could be a reflection of our initial conviction that idealism and secularism would overcome 'realpolitik' and divisive politics in India and its neighbourhood as democracy evolved in the region.

Despite his brilliant intellect and understanding of history, Nehru's ambivalent attitude towards the military comes out clearly in his correspondence with his daughter Indira Gandhi in his book *Glimpses of World History*. His disdain and circumspection towards the reality of force application as an unavoidable tool of statecraft is quite surprising considering that his view of world history was shaped during his studies and early days in England. Despite his tentativeness with matters military when forced to face the grim realities of an impending war and its impact on what was dear to him (Kashmir), many of his early military decisions were spot on. Given the precarious situation at Poonch, his decision to divert a part of the buoyant 161 Brigade southwards, much to the consternation of some of his military commanders, was instrumental in saving Poonch. Similarly, his decision to overrule his British C-in-Cs and allow the use of air power, albeit with some restrictions, against the raiders within Kashmir proved to be a significant force multiplier. Critics may, however, add that it was because of these restrictions that the RIAF could not bomb the bridges at Domel and Muzaffarabad to cut off the retreating raiders.

Jinnah on the other hand was unable to overrule his British C-in-Cs and commit the Pakistani army and the much smaller Pakistan Air Force into the conflict at an early stage. This was primarily because of Jinnah's lack of interest in matters military and the absence of adequate indigenous leadership at all levels. In an interview with Stephen Cohen, General Gracey, Pakistan's second commander-in-chief, once remarked that Jinnah and other Pakistani politicians were 'completely abysmally ignorant of what was going on in the military'.[12] It was only when the situation in the Mirpur, Kotli, Domel and Muzaffarabad sectors become critical that the Pakistan 7 and 9 Divisions were committed to the operation. Similar was the case with the employment of the Pakistan Frontier Rifles in the Ladakh sector. Geography too was against the Indian Army – Abbottabad, the hub of raider activity to Chakoti from where operations were finally launched in the Uri sector, was just 40 miles from the battle front, while Pathankot to Srinagar via the Banihal Pass was 300 miles.

What if Nehru had not ordered the airlift of 1 Sikh into Srinagar at the time he did? For sure, the raiders would have ransacked Srinagar and spread out into the Valley. Reacting to this, the Indian Army would have concentrated in Jammu and advanced towards Poonch, where they would have been given a tough fight by the raiders and elements of the Pakistan Army which would have reached Poonch and the Kashmir Valley by then. The suave Mountbatten then would have stepped in and counselled Nehru on the futility of further conflict, and barring the areas around Jammu, the rest of Kashmir may have amalgamated into Pakistan. What then of Ladakh is again a big 'if'. Could it have been defended had the Valley fallen to the raiders leaving only an axis of advance for the Indian Army from Manali and Rohtang Pass? Probably not! Would the British have allowed Ladakh to become a province of

Pakistan? I would not hazard a guess as to what status would have been assigned to Ladakh.

Post-Independence Ethos

The 1947–48 war with Pakistan showcased a remarkably refreshing emerging ethos of the Indian armed forces – an ethos that transcended its colonial legacy and showcased its secular, multicultural and multi-ethnic flavour. A Sikh regiment was the first to be rushed in to defend a Muslim-majority province. Lieutenant David, who charged in from the rear in his Daimler armoured car of 7 Cavalry and caused mayhem amongst the tribals at Shalateng, was a Christian. Major Maurice Cohen, the young Signals officer who took part in the various battles that were fought in the Poonch sector, was a Jew. Brigadier Usman and Squadron Leader Zafar Shah were Muslims who chose to stay in India despite direct approaches from Jinnah. Mehar Singh was a fiery Sikh; Mickey Blake, the dashing flight commander of one of the Tempest squadrons who made all those daring forays over Skardu, was among the many Anglo-Indians who were decorated for their exploits in combat; Minoo Engineer, the Officer Commanding of 1 Wing (Srinagar), was a Parsi; and best of all, the engineer regiment that built the track to Zojila in freezing temperature was a company from the Madras Engineering Regiment under the command of Major Thangaraju. Many of these 'Thambis' (most south Indians in the armed forces are affectionately called Thambi, which means 'little brother') had never seen snow in their lives! This is not to forget all the other ethnic communities who fought side by side – Kumaonis, Gorkhas, Jats, Ladakhis, Dogras, Marathas, Mahars, Rajputs, Coorgs, and many more. It truly was a spectacular show of unity in diversity. Lieutenant General Satish Nambiar, a veteran of the 1971 India–Pakistan war and one of independent India's most respected soldier-scholars, recollects that a fierce nationalistic and anti-colonial spirit had permeated the ranks of officer cadets at the Indian Military Academy in the mid-1950s. Much of it, he recollects, was inspired by the exploits of India's armed forces in its first post-Independence conflict in Jammu and Kashmir.[13]

The Learning Curve

India was militarily surprised by a smaller and focused adversary with a clear aim – sever J&K using jihad as a prop and unrestricted warfare as a tool. Though India's military response was delayed in every sector because of distance and lack of adequate air mobility assets, its professional soldiers and airmen were better organized, better led and committed to a larger common cause, which was well communicated to them by brilliant field commanders. The raiders were poorly led in the Kashmir Valley and driven by motives other than 'jihad'; this led to delays wherever they had the opportunities to loot and plunder the rich Kashmir countryside. However, the southern element of the raider force comprising Poonchi, Rajputana and Punjabi Muslims had more battle experience and proved more than a handful for the Indian Army. When the Pakistani army joined battle openly in mid-1948, attrition warfare with sustained artillery support became the norm. This made the going hard for Indian troops, who were hoping to make speedy gains in the Tithwal–Muzaffarabad sector where Thimayya had anticipated significant progress.

That the Pakistan Army was lacking in operational leadership too comes out clearly in an interview with B.R. Nanda in 1997 where Lord Mountbatten clearly highlighted that 'Pakistani generals at independence were not as able as the Indians'.[14] In early 1948 General Frank Messervy, the first British C-in-C of the Pakistan Army, reportedly remarked to one of his visiting friends that he had disapproved of the timid manner in which the Pakistan Army had supported the raiders: 'All it required was a battalion in plain clothes – a battalion less two companies at Srinagar and two companies at Banihal Pass and that would have been the end of the story.'[15] Messervy too had underestimated the quality of both the leadership and the fighting abilities of independent India's armed forces. Thimayya, Atma Singh, Pritham Singh, Usman, Mehar Singh, Ranjan Dutt and Moolgavkar epitomized the ethos of 'leading from the front', while 1 Sikh of Srinagar fame and the 'Thambis' of the Madras Engineering Group demonstrated the courage and adaptability of troops from a secular India.

Many have wondered why 161 Brigade was not reinforced speedily despite its commander crying hoarse on the issue. If within a week, an entire brigade and more could be airlifted by 12 Squadron and civil Dakotas. Seeing the success of the brigade in driving the invaders back, it seems strange that another brigade was not flown in with the same urgency to drive home the advantage and sustain the momentum of advance. One suspects that the two British C-in-Cs and Mountbatten were surprised at the decisiveness of the Indian commanders and deliberately stalled any requests for reinforcements from Brigadier Sen as it could have altered the operational end state that the British had in mind.

Operationally and logistically, the numbers just did not support the battle plan and had it not been for the aggressiveness of Thimayya and his field commanders in the Srinagar and Leh sectors, India may have managed to retain even less of J&K than what they ultimately got after the rather untimely ceasefire. In the Jammu sector too, after an initial period when the raiders had a numerical advantage, the Indian Army built up forces and managed to hold a powerful combination of raiders and the Pakistan Army at bay. While the build-up of forces in J&K was slow and the command and control structure left much to be desired, the moment the two divisions (Srinagar and Jammu) were formed under Major Generals Thimayya and Atma Singh, the corps commander should have orchestrated the overall battle from Srinagar, rather than rely on directions from Western Command.[16] Schooled in the Montgomery style of attrition warfare and the Slim style of pursuit warfare, Indian field commanders like Thimayya displayed a refreshing attempt to bring in manoeuvre warfare and a combined arms approach to the battlefield.

If India had not accepted the UN-brokered ceasefire, it would have built up forces methodically through the winter as Lieutenant General Cariappa had by then taken complete charge of military operations. Nehru would have seen through the fog of war and Mountbatten, who after initially sympathizing with India, had started gravitating towards Pakistan as Indian military successes through 1948 pushed Pakistan on the back foot. His assertive military commanders like Thimayya and Atma Singh would have impressed on him the need to go for the jugular and push the Pakistanis completely out of Kashmir. While this may not have been possible as the Pakistan Army would have fully joined in the fight, large tracts of territory in the Skardu region, Domel, Tithwal and

Poonch areas could have been reclaimed by the Indian Army during a spring offensive in 1949, following which India might have accepted the ceasefire after getting assurances of further withdrawal from occupied territories. Importantly, Shaksgam Valley may never have been ceded to China. All senior commanders of the time felt that had India stalled the ceasefire and built up forces for a spring offensive in 1949, the map of Jammu and Kashmir would have been significantly different today. Another proverbial 'if' which is often discussed is that if the Pakistani politico-military establishment had chosen not to push in the tribal raiders and attempted to force a popular people's insurrection, how long would Maharaja Hari Singh have held on to the Standstill Agreement and vacillated between his choices. Would India instead have forced the military option? A highly unlikely possibility considering the amount of pressure it would have faced from Mountbatten and British military commanders. Who knows whether a concurrent plebiscite in Hyderabad and J&K might have come about after protracted negotiations!

It was not to be as India and its people were fed up of strife and conflict, and Nehru and the Congress party were impatient to get the world's most populous democracy on its feet. One last point that could have changed the course of the war was when Nehru lost his trust in General Rob Lockhart and asked for him to be replaced with General Bucher as the Army C-in-C in December 1947. With the conflict at a critical stage, he was well within his right to demand that an Indian general take complete charge of operations – Cariappa and a few others were reasonably placed to assume command. That Nehru did not do so was reflective of his lack of confidence and trust in his Indian officers; something that was to translate over the years into a fragile politico-military relationship.

As far as air power was concerned, Air Marshal Thomas Elmhirst, the first C-in-C of the Indian Air Force, had this to say in his typically understated and rather condescending style in one of his observations after the war:

> So started a frontier war that went on for months. Sad as it was for two new nations, for the Indian Air Force it gave an immediate objective. Pilots came under fire and had to fire their guns and

> rockets; leadership or failure showed itself. Regrettably as it all was in principle, in fact nothing could have been better for morale and training of the new little Air Force three or four months old.[17]

In a collation of international analysis of one year of India's freedom published in the venerable *Bombay Chronicle*, Robert Trumbull of *The New York Times* in a piece titled 'First Year of Freedom – India through Western Eyes' assessed:

> Many had thought that India would be Balkanised, but it has managed to remain one nation. India resembles a crazy quilt of different patchworks stitched as one[18]

The *New Statesman* and *Nation* from London reported:

> Free India in one year has completely undone the archaic establishment by which their former British masters divided and ruled the empire.

Reporting on the continuing conflict in Kashmir, the London *Tribune* correctly assessed that the Kashmir conflict would drag on for years – maybe decades – as the stakes for both India and Pakistan were too great.

Though statistics do not always tell the actual story, their importance for the modern researcher cannot be downplayed. As per official Indian records,[19] the Indian Army lost a total of 1,103 soldiers killed in action including seventy-six officers, while the Jammu and Kashmir state forces, which bore the brunt of the raiders' initial assault, lost over 1,900 men. The RIAF lost thirty-two officers and men, the bulk of them being pilots. The enemy (Pakistani army and raiders) had casualties of over 6,000 killed and many more wounded. Small as the casualties may seem as compared to the horrific loss of life during the preceding Partition and the just concluded WW II, they do not reflect the intensity of combat over almost fourteen months in hostile terrain and harsh weather. In recognition of their valour, officers and men of the Indian Army won five Param Vir Chakras, forty-seven Maha Vir Chakras and 284 Vir Chakras, while the RIAF was decorated with four Maha Vir Chakras and twenty-eight Vir Chakras.[20] Maybe, Air Commodore Mehar Singh deserved the Param Vir Chakra for his sustained risk-taking against overwhelming odds in the Poonch and Leh operations.

The last lesson from this war which would have a bearing on future conflicts involving India was the fact that India as a country would always prefer restraint and caution when it came to using force as an instrument of statecraft. It would always prefer negotiations and diplomacy instead, revealing that as a nation it was more comfortable with articulating deterrence rather than pursuing coercion as a security strategy. This singularly meant that it would employ its defence forces in a primarily defensive role, thereby exposing it to significant initial attrition before offering a befitting riposte. It is to the credit of India's military leadership that it has respected this political strategy, albeit, at times, paying a heavy human price for it. The brave words of Major Somnath Sharma – 'I shall not withdraw an inch but will fight to the last man and the last round' – would ring true in many battles and encounters that India's armed forces would fight in the years ahead to protect Indian democracy and sovereignty.

12

LIBERATING HYDERABAD

How can I stop you from committing suicide if you want to?

– Sardar Patel to Qasim Rizvi in December 1947.[1]

The Recalcitrant Maharajas

One of the primary methods used by the British to retain their hold over their Indian empire for almost two centuries was by deft and devious parcelling of major portions of the huge Indian subcontinent into areas that could be directly governed by them, and those over which they ensured proxy control. This proxy control was exercised by what the world commonly knew as the princely states of India ruled by exotic maharajas. Owing allegiance to the British Raj in return for handsome privy purses and opulent living, most of these maharajas were oblivious to nationalistic aspirations and milked the land and their oppressed people to increase their personal wealth and that of the British Empire. At the time of Independence, India and Pakistan had to amalgamate nearly 556 princely states into their respective countries. While most princely states accepted the 'fate of geography' and acceded to India or Pakistan without a whimper, six states created problems for India: Jammu and Kashmir, Junagadh, Travancore, Bhopal, Jodhpur and Hyderabad. While Kashmir has been dealt with in the previous chapter and will come up repeatedly in the book, it was the large and prosperous state of Hyderabad which would give a political migraine to India's inexperienced leadership as it vacillated for almost a year before finally ordering military action to take control of the large state.

While Bhopal and Jodhpur acceded without much coercion, a quick look at how the Travancore and Junagadh problems of accession were resolved reveals the complexities of state-sponsored coercion by an Indian government that desperately wanted to steer a path of inclusive and amicable accession. It soon realized the necessity of coercion as a tool of statecraft thanks to its no-nonsense home minister, Sardar Vallabhbhai Patel, and his hatchet man in the Ministry of Home Affairs, V.P. Menon, who was put in charge of the accession of princely states into the Indian Union.

Oblivious to Reality: Travancore and Junagadh

At the time of Independence, the state of Travancore encompassed much of what is the modern state of Kerala and parts of Tamil Nadu. It was a relatively prosperous and literate province ruled by an enlightened maharaja and assisted by a powerful and brilliant dewan (chief minister), Sir C.P. Ramaswamy Iyengar.[2] Displaying complete strategic naivety, the dewan thought that he could create an independent state on India's southern flank and bank on sea lines of communication in the Arabian Sea to counter any kind of Indian blockade and sustain the economy. Fortunately for India, but unfortunately for the dewan, a deadly attack on him by socialists in the state[3] made him realize the futility of confrontation with India and he advised the maharaja to join India.

Junagadh, which was a princely state occupying a part of what is the Saurashtra region of the modern state of Gujarat, was a harder nut to crack. Ruled by a Muslim ruler with a predominantly Hindu population, it was surrounded on three sides by Indian states with a coastline hugging the Arabian Sea.[4] More importantly, it was also close to the birthplace of India's home minister, Sardar Vallabhbhai Patel, the man entrusted with reining in the recalcitrant maharajas.[5] Encouraged by Jinnah from Pakistan, the petulant dog-loving Nawab of Junagadh declared the accession of his state to Pakistan on 14 August 1947 and invited the extreme displeasure of Sardar Patel as other states around Junagadh had signed the instruments of accession with India.

Responding to reports of violence and incursion by troops of Junagadh against its neighbouring states of Mangrol and Babariawad, the Government of India promptly ordered a hastily put together military force to invade Junagadh in October 1947 and teach the nawab a lesson.

To execute Exercise Peace, as the operation to liberate Junagadh was called, the military force put together by India was a large one comprising a brigade at Rajkot, and an amphibious task force with a battalion of the Kumaon Regiment being landed at Jafrabad in the region of Kathiawar as a show of force under the overall command of Brigadier Gurdial Singh.[6] Amphibious exercises were also carried out on beaches at Mangrol and Porbandar. There was also a squadron of Tempest fighter aircraft (No. 8 Squadron) of the RIAF under the command of Squadron Leader Padam Singh Gill on readiness at an airfield at Jamnagar in the princely state of Nawanagar.[7] As a coercive exercise, the squadron even carried out practice rocket firing at an island (Panera) off the Nawanagar coast,[8] which was the largest princely state bordering Junagadh that was available to the Indian armed forces as a launch pad for military action in case the need arose. The joint force was completed by a Royal Indian Navy task force comprising three frigates, three minesweepers and three landing craft under the command of Commander R.D. Katari.[9] This operation was actually the first joint operation launched by independent India's armed forces and the first time a RIN task force had sailed for a mission that was not in furtherance of the British Empire's operational or strategic objectives. Seeing the large force ranged against him, the Nawab of Junagadh, Sir Mahabatkhan Rasulkhanji, fled to Pakistan with his entourage of dogs and wives, leaving his dewan, Sir Shah Nawaz Bhutto, to throw in the towel in late October 1947 as Indian ground forces entered Junagadh and IAF Tempests carried out a number of high-speed runs over the state capital. This paved the way for a referendum on 20 February 1948 in which 91 per cent of the population voted for accession to India.[10] Bhutto was, however, commended by Jinnah for his attempt to force the secession of Junagadh to Pakistan.[11] At the end of it all John Keay writes about the Nawab of Junagadh and his flight to Pakistan:

> A show of strength duly sent him winging his way to Karachi with just four wagging companions and a like number of wives. To this

day maps printed in Pakistan record the fact with a little patch of green in the middle of Indian Gujarat. Less remembered is the role played in this affair by Shah Nawaz Bhutto, the chief minister of Gujarat in 1947. Having encouraged the prince to accede to Pakistan, it was this Bhutto who, after his employer's flight, cleared the way for Indian intervention. Twenty four years later Shah Nawaz's son, Zulfiqar Ali Bhutto, would play a similar ambivalent role in respect of East Bengal/Bangladesh.[12]

Indecisiveness over Hyderabad

As the 'idea and shape of India' emerged slowly out of the cocoon of the various British-ruled provinces and princely states in 1948, apart from J&K, Hyderabad remained a thorn in India's hinterland. The state of Hyderabad was one of the oldest princely states in the Deccan and had been ruled by the Asaf Jahi dynasty since 1724, after it broke away from the declining Mughal Empire. Centred at Hyderabad, the Nizam ruled over a large state with a majority Hindu population in the west and north-western areas bordering the Maratha Empire and in the south and south-east areas bordering the Madras Presidency. The Muslim population grew around the capital of Hyderabad and provided the much needed physical security for the Nizam from the oppressed and restive majority population. From time to time the Maratha and the Mysore Empires nibbled into the Nizam's kingdom, but every time the Nizam skilfully manoeuvred his way through the crisis, aligning at different times with the French and the British to regain control over his large territory by paying huge levies and tributes. Finally, as the British gained control over the entire Deccan Plateau after defeating the Marathas in the mid-eighteenth century, the Nizam of Hyderabad became their most loyal vassal in the region and a virtual cash cow for the British Raj.

The close relationship with the British allowed the Asaf Jahi dynasty to establish trade and cultural links with Europe and it is little surprise that the last Nizam of Hyderabad, Sir Mir Osman Ali Khan Siddiqui Asaf Jah VII, emerged as amongst the richest men in the world at the time of Independence. Indians, particularly those who lived in Hyderabad, have always wondered where the Nizam accumulated such wealth. The answer lay in his ability to retain control over the rural population, extract huge taxes, exploit the fertile cotton and sugar cane belts of the region and send the produce to Great Britain and Europe in return for exotic riches and unimaginable wealth. Such control would not have been possible had it not been for the existence of Arab and Pathan militia[13] in the Nawab's army – recruited in the early nineteenth century – not only to beef up the Nizam's security forces, but also to support the ulema (holy men) in forcible conversions and spreading the Islamic faith amongst a predominantly Hindu populace. This aggression was in stark contrast to the rather benign approach of the Nawab of Junagadh, who did not force Islam on his subjects beyond a point.

As this militia integrated with the local population, they were organized into a twentieth-century militia called Razakars under a hard-line Islamist cleric named Qasim Rizvi,[14] the leader of a political party called Ittehad-ul-Muslimeen devoted to the cause of Islamic supremacy in the region.[15] It was this militia that perpetrated communal violence in the state and created a combustible security situation warranting immediate intervention by India. Unfortunately, it was allowed to fester as a wound for some months as a result of multiple pressure points on the Indian government.

First was the escalating religious violence between Muslim fundamentalists (Razakars) and a restless Hindu-majority population led by communists and a sprinkling of Andhra Hindu Mahasabha activists. This created a 'fog of communal violence' in large areas of the state away from the capital of Hyderabad, which needed to be first penetrated and analysed by the Indian state before deciding on any action. Second was a purely materialistic phenomenon of Britain wanting to 'milk its richest cow' for a while longer – allowing much of the wealth of the Nizam to be spirited away overseas while advising the Indian government to exercise caution in dealing with the Nizam. Third was that since India had chosen to internationalize the J&K conflict, it was not long before international pressure piled on India to resolve the Hyderabad crisis peacefully. Fourth was an intelligence failure that overhyped the military capability of the Razakar-led Nizam's army. News filtering out of Hyderabad talked about large purchases of arms and aeroplanes from abroad and it is quite surprising that in all the military briefings made to the political executive, while it was understandable that the British military leadership advised excessive caution to suit their own objectives, none of the senior Indian officers offered contrarian opinions and suggested immediate military action. Fifth and last was the growing realization by the majority (87 per cent) Hindu population that it was time to reclaim much of the land from an oppressive minority ruler (13 per cent of population held over 90 per cent of the land and occupied over 97 per cent of state government posts).

With so many pressure points the Government of India was initially at a loss how to peacefully resolve the issue and offered a Standstill Agreement to the Nizam in September 1947. The agreement offered significant autonomy to the Nizam, emboldening the radical elements within the Nizam's government to reject the agreement and push for complete independence. Thus, the political indecisiveness in Delhi reinforced the hands of the Nizam and his band of Razakars, ripening an already fragile and adversarial situation between the Muslims and the Hindus in the state. The situation worsened much through the first half of 1948 with stray but fairly authentic reports of killings on either side coming from British army personnel posted in Hyderabad.

Finally, the intransigence of the Nizam and increasing brutality of the Razakars, coupled with growing public opinion and pressure from the communists and the Andhra Hindu Mahasabha, forced the Indian government to seriously contemplate military action in the summer of 1948. Western reporters too wrote on the absurdity of the Nizam seeking to establish independence, the organized fanaticism of Qasim Rizvi's storm troopers, and regular gun-running from Pakistan. Robert Trumbull of *The New York Times* feared a communal backlash after military action,[16] a prediction that was to come true much to the discomfort of the secular Indian government.

Planning Military Action

One of the most interesting facets of the use of military force to coerce the Nizam of Hyderabad to accede to the India Union is the term *Hyderabad Police Action*. How and why this term was coined by the Government of India is interesting to reflect on as it has been a matter of much debate whenever the strategic community has discussed the action. While some believe that the term *police action* reveals much about the apologetic and rather diffident nature of Indian strategic thought on force application at the time of Independence, others believe that it provided early signs of the restraint and maturity that India's political leadership would display whenever its hands were forced to employ the military against its own people. Even though Jawaharlal Nehru clearly called it a *military action and not war* in one of his pronouncements at Madras[17] prior to the actual commencement of operations, he assumed that by downplaying a full-fledged military operation and calling it a mere *police action,* India would be seen as a mature and restrained power. Little did he realize that it would also reveal strategic contradictions about India's reluctance to accept that force application and demonstration of coercive power and intent were critical ingredients of statecraft, which could coexist with expressions of faith in collective international security mechanisms and altruism as effective tenets of international relations in a troubled neighbourhood.

During the reign of the British Raj, Secunderabad, a satellite town of Hyderabad, emerged as a major cantonment of the Indian Army in the Deccan. At the time of India's Independence, the senior-most British commander in Hyderabad was Major General C.E. Pert, the general officer commanding of a division located there. His advice to the C-in-C, General Bucher, was alarming and indicated that he feared that the Razakars were belligerent enough to target various stores and depots and even attack some formations.[18] He was advised to secure all Indian assets and stand by for further instructions. In all fairness, the division was a depleted one and devoid of any major infantry fighting capability and may not have been able to overcome the Nizam's army and the Razakars. However, for an officer of General Pert's stature, his appreciation of the enemy's capability was poor and alarmist.

To be fair to the British, the British GOC-in-C of Southern Command, Lieutenant General Goddard, was blunt in his assessment and, while retaining objectivity and impartiality in his prognosis, obliquely suggested immediate military action as early as February 1948. He wrote in his impressive style:

> An ageing, headstrong, ill-advised and anachronous ruler is at the head, or nominally at the head of an autocratic and worn-out administration, on which the various political agitations and trends are exercising an ever-increasing weakening influence. Behind this crumbling administrative façade stands the Itehad-ul-Muslimeen, fanatical, unrealistic and devoid of men skilled in public affairs. Engaged in a tussle with the Ittehadists are the Communists, who are in semi-open revolt in the eastern districts of the state, and the Satyagraha movement.[19]

While planning for a likely military solution started in February, actual military action commenced only in early September 1948 after a series of skirmishes between the Razakars and Indian Army units had taken place along the western and southern borders from July onwards. Indian units were repeatedly ambushed during routine patrols with some casualties and finally, after a skirmish, when an Indian armoured squadron of the Poona Horse was fired upon by armoured cars of 1 Hyderabad Lancers,[20] it was clear that the Nizam was losing control in Hyderabad. Running out of options, the Government of India realized the time was ripe for full-fledged military action – not a mere *police action* as the Historical Section of the Government of India has repeatedly stated. On 17 August 1948, the *Bombay Chronicle*, a widely respected newspaper, reported widespread attacks and looting by Razakars in Berar on the border between Hyderabad and what is present-day Maharashtra in the Nanded district.[21] On the same day the Razakar chief, Qasim Rizvi raised his battle cry at a public meeting at a town named Biloli by playing the communal card:

> The Sovereignty enjoyed by the Nizam cannot be taken away by any power on earth. We Muslims of Hyderabad are today faced with difficult problems which will decide our fate. We should neither be discouraged nor disheartened on account of the measures adopted by the Indian Union to demoralise us. We should face our enemies with courage and determination.[22]

As the ante was upped on all fronts, the communists, representing the voice of oppressed peasants, hit key railway stations in the area around the southern Vijaywada and engaged in fairly fierce skirmishes with the

Hyderabad state forces.[23] Pathans and Arabs of Kasim Rizvi's Razakar force were reported to have kidnapped women and stripped them and then made them walk naked in the streets in Bidar and Raichur.[24] As the clouds of war loomed on the horizon, gunrunning from Pakistan was stepped up as clandestine flights landed at Warangal and Bidar aerodromes, bringing in arms and ammunition for the Razakars. [25]

Soon after, the Nizam sought UN intervention on 19 August 1948 alleging threat of invasion and blockade by India, expecting that Syria, one of the Security Council members, would sponsor the resolution.[26] The process fizzled out and the stage was set for an armed confrontation between the Nizam and the Indian Union. On 10 September, all westerners including forty American missionaries were evacuated from Hyderabad by RAF and BOAC aircraft. The next day, US president Harry Truman turned down a desperate appeal from the Nizam to intervene in the matter and most British officers from the Nizam's army resigned.[27] The writing was on the wall and yet the Nizam did not see reason, blinded by his own geopolitical naivety and intimidated by Kasim Rizvi, who had actually become the de facto ruler of Hyderabad.

Multi-Pronged Offensive

One of the largest princely states of the British Raj, Hyderabad had a border of 644 km with India prior to accession. This made it a formidable task for a stretched Indian Army to plug the entire border with Hyderabad, grappling as it was to pump in more troops to support Thimayya's summer offensive in J&K and push back raiders, particularly from the Leh and Poonch sectors. Largely planned under the supervision of Brigadier J. N. Chaudhuri when he was chief of general staff at Army HQ, New Delhi, Operation Polo, as the action was code-named, was finally executed by an all-Indian team of Southern Army Command under Lieutenant General Maharaj Shri Rajendra Sinhji, a freshly promoted major general J.N. Chaudhuri (later to be COAS), the GOC of 1 Armoured Division, and Major General Ajit Anil 'Jock' Rudra, who was GOC of the Madras Area.

Lieutenant General Rajendra Sinhji was commissioned into 2 Royal Lancers and was a squadron commander in the same regiment in 1941 in North Africa where he was awarded a DSO for his exploits in leading his squadron in a fighting withdrawal in the face of superior German armour.[28] Major General Chaudhuri was one of the youngest generals in the Indian Army having been commissioned only in 1928. After seeing major action as a staff officer with the 5th Indian Division in Sudan, Eritrea and the western desert during the early years of WW II, his major exploits were reserved for the Burma campaign. Commanding 16 Cavalry, an armoured regiment, he moved the unit in a gruelling 3,000-mile induction into the Burma theatre in 1944, forming the advance guard in the march to Rangoon.[29] He was the third Indian brigadier after Cariappa and Thimayya in the pre-Independence British Indian Army. Major General Rudra was one of the earliest Kings Commissioned officers, and the oldest Indian general in the Indian Army. Blooded in battle as an enlisted soldier in WW I, he saw action in France and Belgium in the Battle of Somme and Flanders. 'Jock' as he was popularly known rose to be a sergeant before being selected for commissioning into 4/15 Punjab Regiment as an officer in 1919 in reward for his splendid performance in the Great War. During WW II, he excelled as the 2 I/C of his battalion with Slim's 14th Army in the Burma campaign.

The air element comprised a 'Polo Air Task Force' under the command of Air Commodore Subroto Mukerjee as AOC Caterpillar Air Task Force. He was later to be the first Indian chief of the air staff in 1954. Subroto Mukerjee was the first Indian commanding officer of 1 Squadron RIAF and cut his teeth as a fighter pilot and leader in the NWFP against rebellious Afridi and Mahsud tribesmen. His mandate for the use of air power in the operation was to provide photo reconnaissance and close air support to advancing Indian army columns, particularly the armoured division, with two fighter squadrons of Tempest fighter-bombers (3 and 4 Squadrons) at Pune.

At 1:45 p.m. on 12 September 1948,[30] the Indian Army commenced a five pronged thrust along the frontier with four provinces of the Union of India: Central Province, Bombay, Mysore and Madras. Symbolically, on the same day in 1727, the Marathas under Peshwa Balaji Rao defeated the Nizam of Hyderabad in the first battle he fought after declaring his independence from them.[31] The major thrust was from the west where the Sholapur–Hyderabad highway presented the best opportunity for Major General Chaudhuri's 1 Armoured Division to steamroll past stubborn state forces and Razakars at Bidar and capture Hyderabad. A subsidiary thrust by additional troops assigned to 1 Armoured Division was to commence from the north-west with the aim of capturing Aurangabad and Jalna, two important towns in the north-western areas. A north-eastern thrust was planned from Adilabad, a southern thrust from Kurnool and a major south-eastern thrust from Bezwada. Both the southern thrusts were entrusted to infantry and armoured formations from Rudra's Madras Area.[32]

RACE TO HYDERABAD

What of the opposition to the well-trained and battle-inoculated Indian force of almost two-and-a-half divisions including an armoured division? The state forces of the Nizam were poorly trained and had no battle experience. Their equipment was old and rusty and did not support the numbers of a 30,000-strong standing army, an armed police force of approximately 35,000, besides 8,000 irregulars and a large force of Razakars.[33] The strength of Razakars widely varied since it was a militia and ranged from a modest 30,000 as reported by Western commentators to a figure of 70,000 active and armed men and women, as indicated in the white paper. Contrary to initial reports, the Nizam had no air force[34] and most of his armoured cars were off-road. Indicating a sense of urgency in response to the wildly exaggerated strength of the Nizam's forces, and anticipating concurrent and prolonged operations in Hyderabad and J&K, the Union of India adopted proactive measures by summoning reserve officers from Travancore, Madras, Cochin and Coorg.[35]

In the final analysis the main threat to the advancing forces was to come from the Razakars in the Bidar and Bezwada region. Loosely organized into platoon- and battalion-sized formations and adept at hit-and-run tactics like the raiders in Kashmir, the Razakars proved to be sticky and fierce opponents, though it was only a matter of time before they capitulated in the face of superior firepower.

The operational rationale for a multi-pronged offensive was quite clear: force the Nizam to disperse his forces and dilute his fighting potential to such an extent that 1 Armoured Division could exploit the

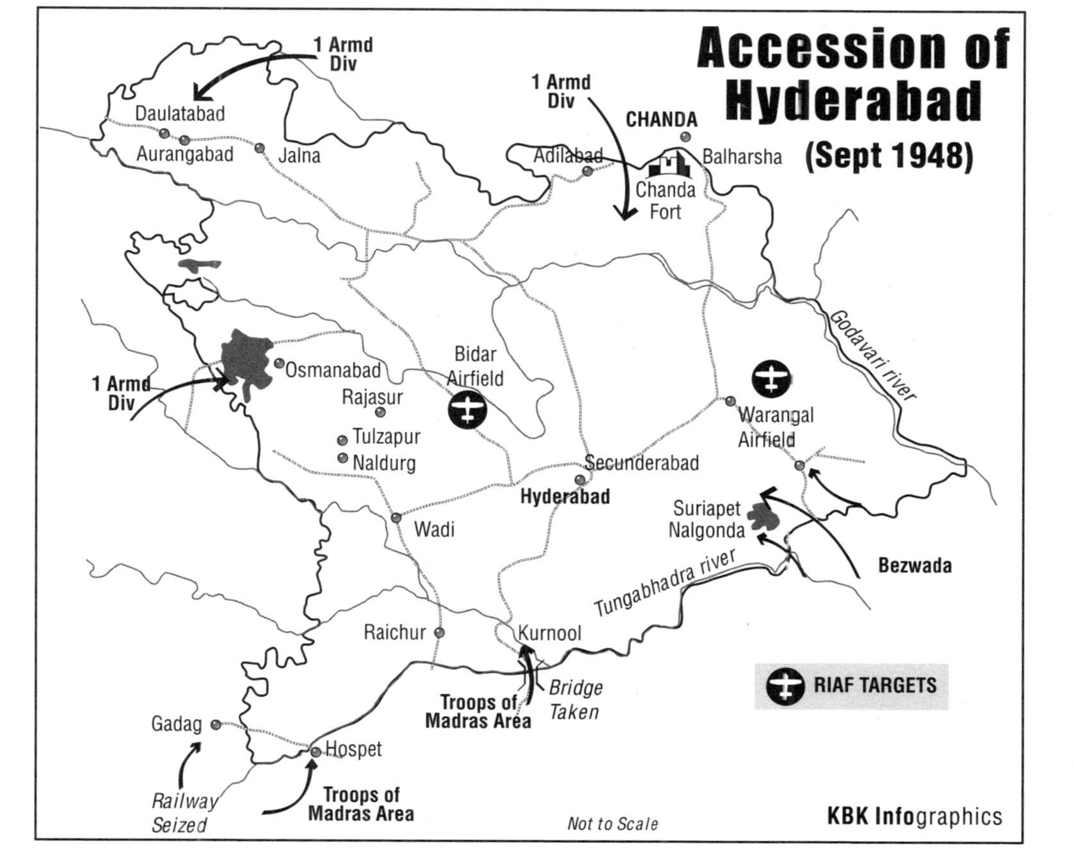
Accession of Hyderabad
(Sept 1948)
1 Armd Div
Daulatabad
Aurangabad
Jalna
1 Armd Div
CHANDA
Adilabad
Balharsha
Chanda Fort
1 Armd Div
Osmanabad
Rajasur
Tulzapur
Naldurg
Bidar Airfield
Secunderabad
Hyderabad
Wadi
Warangal Airfield
Godavari river
Suriapet
Nalgonda
Bezwada
Tungabhadra river
Raichur
Kurnool
Bridge Taken
Troops of Madras Area
Gadag
Hospet
Railway Seized
Troops of Madras Area
RIAF TARGETS
Not to Scale
KBK Infographics

Sholapur–Hyderabad highway and race to Hyderabad. The RIAF was to attack all the Nizam's airfields from where gunrunning from Pakistan was taking place, particularly those at Warangal and Bidar. Additionally, Tempest aircraft operating from Pune were to provide close air support to 1 Armoured Division and cause psychological degradation to the morale of the state forces, strafing them and even dropping leaflets – all of which were carried out professionally.

The southern forces of almost a division strength on two thrust lines were to ensure that the important road and railway bridges at Hospet and Kurnool were captured intact and prevent any escape of the Nizam's forces southwards. The south-eastern thrust in the prosperous and fertile Telangana region was important as this region saw numerous skirmishes between the Razakars and the Kisan Dal (communist militia) prior to commencement of hostilities. This region was nearly 100 per cent Hindu and it was feared that a major genocide against them could be perpetrated in the absence of a military force in the region. After three days of sporadic fighting mainly in the form of skirmishes and tough encounters with the Razakars, Chaudhuri's 1 Armoured Division supported by RIAF Tempests operating from Pune smashed past defences at Rajasur, Zahirabad, Bidar and Homnabad from the west and Aurangabad in the north-west, while General Rudra's formations forged ahead in the Suriapet salient of the Bezwada sector. By the early morning of 17 September, 1 Armoured Division was poised to take Hyderabad and by 5 p.m. on the same day, the Nizam surrendered.[36]

Aftermath

The altruism of Jawaharlal Nehru, his abhorrence of violence and empathy towards the people of Hyderabad was clearly evident in his statement on Hyderabad to parliament on 7 September. He urged the Nizam

> ... for the last time to disband the Razakars and to facilitate return of Indian troops to Secunderabad.[37]

However, in its earnest attempts at inclusiveness, the Government of India was widely criticized for being too patient and generous with the

Nizam after he had violated all the tenets of the Standstill Agreement, which was mainly signed to give him some manoeuvring space to fall in line with other princely states. With sinister communal forces at work, the Razakars engaged in widespread pogroms and atrocities on the Hindus and sowed the seeds for retaliation in the coming months. No amount of exhorting the people to steer clear of communal retaliation would prevent a Hindu backlash; something that was widely anticipated and did happen. Considering what had happened during the Partition riots and the massacre of Hindus by the raiders in Kashmir in retaliation for the perceived atrocities on Muslims by the Maharaja of Kashmir's Dogra forces, it was naive to imagine that the Hindus of Hyderabad state would amalgamate the Muslims with open arms. After the fall of Hyderabad, communal tension ran high with widespread violence rocking the state,[38] 'substantiating Nehru's concerns over the fragility of communal relations in India'.[39] The Indian government's failure to prevent this backlash was mainly because it was administratively ill-prepared, and expecting the Indian Army to maintain communal peace across the state was a tall order considering the size of the state.

While historians like Srinath Raghavan argue that the Hyderabad police action demonstrated the limited effectiveness of force application to preserve internal stability,[40] what emerged finally was the inevitability of force application to overcome radical extremism of the kind displayed by the Razakars. Had this force been applied at a time when the Razakars were not fully organized, the Government of India might have been able to limit the extent of communal violence that preceded and succeeded the military action.

13

SEIZING GOA

Portugal and her NATO allies should no longer be in any doubt about India's firm policy towards Goa. India has tried all possible means, short of war, to settle the problem of Goa. But Portugal seems determined to perpetuate colonialism in this area which is an integral part of India.

– Jawaharlal Nehru[1]

Goa's Portuguese Legacy

Goa nestles on the south-west coast of India and is among the many beautiful coastal states of the country with its pristine beaches washed by the multicultural waters of the Arabian Sea – waters that have actually shaped the destiny of modern India. Vasco da Gama was the first seafaring European explorer to set foot on Indian soil in 1498, coming ashore at Calicut, a trading hub of the Zamorin rulers in what is now the state of Kerala. Realizing the trading potential with the region, rich as it was with spices and the finest cotton muslin, the Portuguese went about ruthlessly establishing both trading and military outposts along the Kerala and Konkan coast. They were followed by the Dutch, French and the British – all realizing that India of the sixteenth century resembled a fat, rich and lazy cow waiting to be milked by all and sundry. The struggle for dominating the west coast of India peaked in the seventeenth century with the British managing to extract significant trading rights from the Mughal emperor Jahangir at Surat in modern Gujarat and other parts of India.

The Portuguese seized Goa from the Sultan of Bijapur and fought off attempts by Prince Sambhaji, the son of the legendary Maratha warrior Shivaji, and the subsequent Peshwa rulers till the mid-eighteenth century[2] to liberate it from their clutches. Fortunately for them, the Marathas were too preoccupied with fighting the Nizam of Hyderabad, and subsequently the British, to devote too much attention to Goa. At the same time, as the British asserted their naval supremacy, the Portuguese had to hand over most of their conquests on the west coast of India, including Bombay, to the British East India Company by the end of the seventeenth century.[3] The exceptions were Goa, Daman and Diu; these were to remain with them even after the British left India in 1947. Daman and Diu were separated by some distance from Goa; Daman lying 250 km to the north of Bombay to be precise and Diu, a small island with fortifications, located off the Gujarat coast close to the princely state of Kathiawar.

The Portuguese ruled Goa with an iron hand for over 400 years with the Catholic Church embarking on a ruthless conversion programme, even going to the extent of condoning large-scale extermination of local males and granting incentives for Portuguese nationals to set up home in Goa. So intense was the commitment of the church in nineteenth century Goa that it resembled an inquisition.[4] The mere fact that almost 28 per cent of the population was Catholic at the time of India's Independence reflected the domination of the church over the years. Defeated by the Dutch and the British in most of their colonial battles in Asia, Goa in India and the two African colonies of Angola and Mozambique remained the only colonial possessions of a fading European power in the twentieth century.

Procrastination in Free India

Serious students of modern Indian history have always wondered at the turn of events that resulted in the inability of one of the most inspired and effective independence movements to evict an insignificant and militarily weak colonial power for almost fifteen years after having forced the world's mightiest colonial power to leave India's shores. While the initial impetus to the freedom struggle in Goa came in 1946 from Dr Ram Manohar Lohia, a Congressman turned socialist; the movement fizzled out once he left the Congress party in 1948.[5] The reason for this neglect was geopolitics in the literal sense. With Kashmir and Hyderabad holding centre stage in the whole process of the unification of India along with the amalgamation of all the princely states into the Union, it is likely that smaller provinces like Pondicherry and Goa, which were still under colonial rule by France and Portugal respectively, were considered expendable for some time by the ruling Congress government for a few reasons.

Three reasons for the lethargic response of the Government of India to local aspirations for Goan freedom from Portuguese rule seem plausible. First was that the government expected that with the British leaving and seeing its willingness to use force to defend its sovereignty and coerce the recalcitrant maharajas, it would only be a matter of time before the Portuguese[6] left Goa. Second, the military action in Kashmir and Hyderabad was contradictory to the Congress party's professed abhorrence for violence as a means to settle political and territorial differences. Once the guns fell silent in Kashmir and Hyderabad, Nehru went on a diplomatic offensive for the next decade, championing peaceful resolution of conflicts and was highly critical of the unfolding 'cold war', even playing 'peacemaker' in Korea by having Major General Thimayya lead the UN forces there. In the bargain, he effectively put paid to any immediate chances of using force to evict the Portuguese from Goa. A third reason for the 'go slow' on Goa could be attributed to the political reality of the opposition parties like the Communist Party of India (CPI) and other parties like the Praja Socialist Party (PSP) attempting to take up cudgels on behalf of the nationalist movement in Goa and pressurizing the government to initiate military action to liberate Goa.[7] In the bargain, politics scored over nationalistic aspirations and resulted in more than a decade of procrastination on Goa by the Government of India. John Keay in his expansive book *India: A History from the Earliest Civilizations to the Boom of the Twenty-First Century* says this about India's apathy towards Goa:

> The conservation of Portuguese rule over Goa's church-ridden congregation could have been of antiquarian interest and no more

menacing to the Indian republic than was the Vatican to the Italian republic.[8]

Had the ruling Congress party been at the forefront of the Goan nationalist movement, military intervention may have come about earlier. From a Portuguese perspective, the reluctance to leave Goa was due to a misplaced sense of territorial propriety on the part of the Portuguese government under the fascist dictator Salazar, and a delusion that NATO (the North Atlantic Treaty Organization) and the US would come to its rescue should India use military force to evict them from Goa.[9]

BUILDING PRESSURE

As the 1950s passed by relatively peacefully for India, it became clear that the escalating cold war and emerging colonial conflicts in Africa meant that hoping for any kind of international pressure on Portugal to leave India was remote as Portugal was a member of NATO and the Western alliance in the global fight against communism.[10] The USSR had little to benefit from any overt support to India over Goa, preferring instead to support the anti-colonial struggle against the Portuguese in Angola and Mozambique. Thus, it was clear that any pressure to liberate Goa had to come from within India. Nehru made a number of peaceful overtures to the Portuguese government, urging them to pay heed to the nationalistic aspirations of the Goan people, but to no avail. On 15 August 1955, a large group of over 3,000 Goan freedom fighters or satyagrahis led by the communists attempted to march on the capital Panjim in a show of solidarity with the Goan freedom movement. The march was brutally opposed by the Portuguese security forces, which killed and injured many peaceful marchers; the number of casualties suffered by the peaceful protesters was put at twenty-two killed and 225 wounded as stated by Gaitonde,[11] and reported by the renowned political scientist Arthur Rubinoff in his authoritatively researched monograph.[12]

Surprised by the extensive international criticism of the satyagraha (peaceful protest) even from countries like Switzerland, Nehru's Congress government did not endorse or support the opposition-led movement stating that the violence it had perpetrated was against the principles of conflict resolution eschewed by India. It was clear that narrow and opportunistic politics and a premature need for global importance was scoring over nationalism – a characteristic that was to emerge frequently in the years ahead when it came to the application of force in statecraft. At this juncture, had the ruling government ignored international opinion and mobilized its armed forces as it had done when Kashmir was threatened, or when the Razakars in Hyderabad had stepped up genocide against the majority Hindu population, Portugal may have been sufficiently coerced to leave Goa without a fight. Unfortunately, this did not happen and Goa kept simmering with discontent for another six years.

As the political opposition to the Congress became stronger, so did the pitch for the liberation of Goa. The late 1950s saw significant international criticism of India's policy of non-alignment and lack of support for militant liberation movements in Africa,[13] particularly from within the developing world. Making matters worse for India's international stature was the failure of the Panchsheel Agreement with China and the increasing prospects of conflict with its powerful northern neighbour. Facing domestic flak over numerous developmental and security concerns, and faced for the first time with serious electoral challenges, Nehru had no choice but to silence his critics and take decisive action over Goa in the winter of 1961. In the bargain, Nehru renewed his commitment and passion to the developing world on eradicating colonialism in Asia and Africa.[14] This was despite numerous shrill voices emanating from the West, cautioning Nehru against abandoning his policy of resolving conflict through diplomacy and dialogue, rather than force.[15] The US, led by its stridently anti-India Secretary of State John Foster Dulles,[16] obliquely cautioned India not to resort to force in Goa, but stopped short of any official pronouncements supporting continued Portuguese occupation.

What of Portugal's untenable desire to hold on to Goa in times of expanding anti-colonial feelings across the developing world? Portugal rightly assessed that Goa's relative obscurity in the prevailing Indian political landscape had resulted in a lukewarm support from the Government of India for the indigenous liberation movement. However, when the movement gained momentum in the mid-1950s, it underestimated its strength. As a member of NATO, Portugal thought that it would have the military support of other NATO members, particularly the US and Britain, should India attack it.[17] Finally, its own diminishing status as a significant European power forced it to hang on to all its colonies as a demonstration of its fading power.

Decisiveness or Compulsion

Though the decision to use military force to evict the Portuguese from Goa, Daman and Diu was taken in late November/early December 1961, the armed forces had been alerted of the possibility of military action to liberate Goa in mid-1961. Lieutenant General Chaudhuri, the GOC-in-C, Southern Army Command, had already made an operational assessment in October 1961 and had his operational plans ready by November.[18] Squadron diaries and the operational record book of the Indian Air Force's Armament Training Wing at Jamnagar reveal that the quantum of operational flying had increased since June 1961 with special emphasis on armament delivery at the Sarmat air-to-ground range near Jamnagar.[19] IAF Canberra bombers from Pune airbase had started carrying out stray reconnaissance sorties over Goa, while the Indian Navy started exercising off the coast of Karwar in the vicinity of the small island of Anjadiv, one of the two islands still in the possession of the Portuguese. Anjadiv was one of the first conquests of the Portuguese when Vasco da Gama captured it in 1505 during his second voyage to India.[20] This was in response to reports that the Portuguese gun positions on the island had started harassing Indian shipping that passed by.

The final catalyst that prodded India to use force was an international conference on Portuguese colonialism hosted by India in New Delhi towards the end of October 1961. Castigated at that conference by African countries like Angola and Mozambique for not leading the colonial struggle against the Portuguese, V.K. Krishna Menon, India's defence minister, asserted that 'at no time has India abjured the use of violence in international affairs'.[21] Frustrated at his inability to convince Portugal to give up Goa peacefully, Nehru finally gave the go-ahead in early December for Operation Vijay to be launched to liberate Goa. There was, however, an element of political opportunism too in the build-up to the military action. Faced with a tough electoral battle in the North

Bombay constituency in early 1962 against one of modern India's socialist giants, J.B. Kripalani, Krishna Menon needed a face-saver: the annexation of Goa just turned out to be that.[22]

The broad military plan was to launch a division-sized force with limited armour and artillery supported by fighters and bombers operating from the airfields of Pune and Belgaum[23] against Goa, and a smaller force of approximately two battalions supported by fighters operating from Jamnagar airfield against the fortified island of Diu. The territory of Daman was lightly defended and it was expected to surrender as soon as hostilities commenced. Hence, only a battalion with light artillery support and some air effort from Bombay was allocated for the attack on Daman.[24] The advance into Goa was planned on two main axes from the north and the east with a small diversionary attack from Karwar in the south. These axes were planned keeping in mind the availability of roads and the ease with which the numerous river crossings could be executed by the infantry and the mechanized formations as they advanced towards Panjim.

In Diu, the operations were to be commenced with a boat assault across the creek to capture the fort, followed by the capture of the airfield and the rest of the island. INS *Delhi*, the Indian Navy's flagship and cruiser, would provide fire support along with fighter support provided by Vampire aircraft based at Jamnagar. Additionally, the Indian Navy was tasked to carry out a blockade of Goa by preventing any ship from entering the three harbours on the Goa coast except ships with essential supplies. The operation was scheduled to commence on the night of 15/16 December 1961 and was expected to last a maximum of three days. Rattled by the large-scale movement of troops from all parts of India to the two launch pads of Pune and Belgaum and the increased naval and air activity, the Portuguese government frantically attempted to garner Western and NATO support to stall the operation. Particularly disconcerting for them was the positioning of the crack 50 Parachute Brigade at Pune and the availability of a large naval fleet at India's disposal on the west coast. Responding to increased Western efforts to resolve the crisis, the Government of India postponed the operation by two days without diluting any of its demands, which mainly revolved around an unconditional vacation of Goa, Daman and Diu by the Portuguese government and cessation of colonial rule.

The Commanders

While Lieutenant General J. N. Chaudhuri, the flamboyant, imposing and battle-hardened veteran of WW II and the Hyderabad military action, was the overall force commander as the GOC-in-C of Southern Command, the main field commander who executed the operation was Major General K.P. Candeth, another outstanding soldier with loads of combat experience. Like Somnath Sharma, the hero of the Badgam battle, who laid down his life fighting to save Srinagar airfield from the raiders in 1947, Candeth was an alumnus of the Prince of Wales Royal Indian Military College (later called Rashtriya Indian Military College or RIMC for short). Commissioned into the Regiment of Artillery in 1936, he saw action during WW II in West Asia and then gained vital battle experience in the mountains quelling rebellious tribesmen in the North- West Frontier Province.[25] Supporting him in the operation were two outstanding officers from the Indian Air Force and Indian Navy, Air Vice Marshal Erlic W. Pinto and Rear Admiral B.S. Soman. Erlic Pinto orchestrated air operations from four bases with an aggregate of almost four squadrons of Hunter, Canberra and Vampire, Mystere and Toofani aircraft. He continued to be in the limelight in the 1962 India–China war as AOC-in-C, Western Air Command, before tragically perishing in a helicopter crash near Poonch in 1963. Rear Admiral Soman was an accomplished WW II seaman, having joined the Royal Indian Marine in 1931, and saw extensive action in the Red Sea, and even commanded the minesweeper HMS *Khyber* during the later stages of the war.[26] He had at his disposal the entire Indian fleet including the aircraft carrier, INS *Vikrant*, two cruisers including INS *Delhi* and six frigates, two of which, INS *Betwa* and INS *Beas*, were in the thick of action subsequently.

Opposing the formidable Indian forces in Goa were a combination of regular Portuguese army personnel numbering about 5,000, a naval sloop, the *Albuquerque*, three patrol boats and a sprinkling of police and volunteer paramilitary forces. Daman and Diu were defended by approximately two companies of regulars at each place. The overall command of the Portuguese forces rested with Manuel Antonio Vassalo E Silva, the Governor General of Goa since 1958.[27] Faced with an imminent attack by India, he was ordered by Salazar to fight to the last man, a ridiculous expectation given the asymmetry of forces and the ragtag army at his disposal for the defence of Goa.

The Short Battle

As large waves of IAF Canberra bombers from Poona airbase bombarded Dabolim airfield at the crack of dawn on 18 December 1961, and Hunters from the Sambra airfield destroyed the vital communications hub at Bambolim,[28] 50 Para Brigade under Brigadier Sagat Singh commenced operations from the north-east racing towards Panjim with little opposition. Sagat would later emerge as one of the principal field commanders in the 1971 war with Pakistan in the eastern theatre. Two brigades, 63 and 48 Infantry Brigades, under Brigadiers Dhillon and Gurbux Singh made up the eastern force and commenced operations simultaneously, aiming for a pincer attack on Panjim. Barring an unfortunate skirmish in which two officers and a few men from the 7 Cavalry Regiment lost their lives while trying to negotiate the release of fifty to sixty nationalist prisoners[29] who were held hostage at the Aguada Fort (now a five-star hotel resort), there was minimum attrition on both sides as the large Indian force of a division and an armoured regiment steamrolled past the hapless and inexperienced defenders, who surrendered in droves rather than put up a fight.

By noon on 19 December, Panjim and Mapuca, the two primary objectives, were captured as Chaudhuri made his way to Panjim along with Air Marshal Pinto and an intelligence officer, B.N. Mullick, later to come into prominence during the intelligence bungling prior to the 1962 India–China conflict.

The Goa sector saw fairly intensive naval operations too with the Indian Navy mounting an independent amphibious operation to take over the island of Anjadiv despite having no real capability beyond a few training drills carried out in the past.[30] After softening defences with naval gunfire support from the cruiser INS *Mysore*, an assault force from the frigate went ashore on 18 December morning on normal

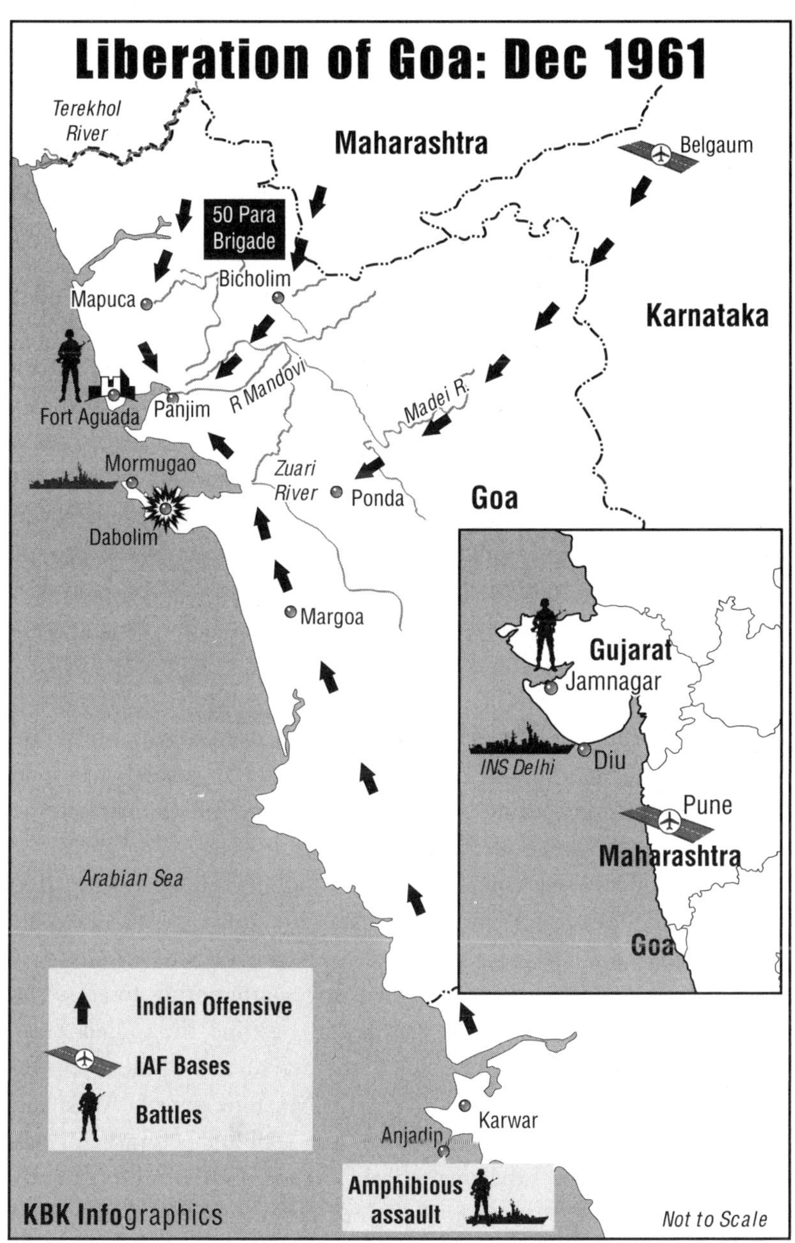
Liberation of Goa: Dec 1961
Terekhol River
Maharashtra
Belgaum
50 Para Brigade
Bicholim
Mapuca
Karnataka
Fort Aguada
Panjim
R Mandovi
Madei R.
Mormugao
Zuari River
Ponda
Goa
Dabolim
Margoa
Gujarat
Jamnagar
INS Delhi
Diu
Pune
Maharashtra
Goa
Arabian Sea
Indian Offensive
IAF Bases
Battles
Karwar
Anjadip
Amphibious assault
KBK Infographics
Not to Scale

boats, but was met with stiff resistance from machine gun positions and took some casualties. The force had to be reinforced and finally captured the island on the afternoon of 19 December.[31] After a short naval battle off Mormugoa harbour with two Indian Navy frigates, the INS *Beas* and INS *Betwa*, the lone Portuguese warship *Afonso de Albuquerque* was badly damaged and captured. Thus ended a badly lopsided battle for Goa!

The battle for Daman was short and swift and commenced at the same time as the battles for Goa and Diu. With concurrent battles being fought at all three places there was immense confusion within the Portuguese ranks considering that the IAF had rendered the main communications hub at Bambolin totally useless. This left the dispersed Portuguese forces without any higher directions for battle and totally reliant on local resources and commanders, who in any case were hardly battleworthy. The Indians had underestimated the enemy strength as they later realized that pitted against a Maratha Light Infantry Battalion was a force of approximately 500 soldiers including twenty-three officers. However, the superior training and operational plan of the Indian Army, coupled with the psychological impact and degradation of defences caused by effective IAF Mystere fighter strikes which even injured the governor of Daman, ensured that the defences were easily overrun with minimum casualties by the morning of 19 December.[32] The IAF carried out a total of fourteen missions during the two days and clearly demonstrated the growing inter-service cooperation in Operation Vijay.

From an operational point of view the toughest and most interesting battle during Operation Vijay was the battle to capture the island of Diu. Dominated by a citadel, which had numerous vantage points from where accurate fire could be directed against forces attempting to cross the creek that separated it from the Kathiawar coastline; the Indian Army grossly underestimated the strength of the defenders and the firepower they had in terms of Light and Medium Machine guns (LMGs and MMGs). Ignoring the earlier advice of the IAF and the Indian Navy to delay the crossing of the creek till the defences had been sufficiently softened up by IAF fighter strikes from Jamnagar airfield and naval gunfire from INS *Delhi*, 20 Rajput Regiment courageously attempted to carry out an assault crossing of the creek from two directions in the early hours of 18 December. Simultaneously, a company of 4 Madras Regiment attempted to capture a village opposite the citadel called Goga to provide a firm base from which subsequent attacks could be launched across the creek. All three attacks were initially repulsed by withering LMG and MMG fire with a number of boats capsizing and a fair number of casualties. This was when the IAF and the Indian Navy stepped in with some telling air strikes and accurate naval gunfire support through the morning and afternoon of 18 December. Wing Commander Mickey Blake, the chief instructor of ATW, who was in charge of operations from Jamnagar, had at his disposal a wide range of attacking options, which included Toofani fighter jets of No. 4 Squadron and Vampire trainer jets of ATW.[33] As early as 7 December, he had taken up the CO of the Rajput Regiment in a Vampire trainer to pinpoint targets and advised him to attempt the creek crossing only after the first wave of fighter strikes had been completed.[34] This advice was not heeded as the army felt that it would be preferable to launch an attack under the cover of darkness – a fair assessment at that except that whether day or night, the attack was expected and the LMGs and MMGs did not distinguish between night and day. After the Toofani jets and Vampires had plastered the Diu defences and crippled the runway, the Portuguese resistance withered and by late night, the Rajputs had taken Diu. A total of thirty-five sorties had been flown in support of the Diu assault. It was an excellent example of what air power could do in shaping the environment and battle space before a ground assault.

Admiral Nadkarni was the navigation officer of INS *Delhi* and, in an interview, he recounted the effective naval gunfire that was directed on the hapless defenders from a distance of less than 2 miles. The massive 6-inch guns of the INS *Delhi* proved to be the last straw for the defenders and the *Delhi* crew were the first ones to see the white flags being waved from the fort and conveyed the same to the ground troops.[35]

The Indian armed forces lost twenty-two men in the entire Goa, Daman and Diu operation including two officers with another fifty-four being wounded, the majority of them in the Diu and Anjadiv operations. The Portuguese lost thirty men, had another fifty-seven wounded and, more humiliatingly, had over 3,000 taken prisoners.[36] In a nutshell, a division- plus-sized ground assault force supported by a large naval and air element had defeated a poorly led, inadequately equipped and overconfident Portuguese force, which really had no idea what they were up against.

Some Strategic and War-fighting Lessons

At the strategic level, India lost an opportunity to use calibrated, state-sponsored coercion to evict the Portuguese from India in the 1950s. Instead, it had to resort to force application as a strategy despite professing abhorrence for such tools of statecraft. During the relatively quiet period of the 1950s had Nehru authorized the movement of army formations to locations around Goa, had he authorized periodic harassment of Portuguese shipping and a naval blockade of sorts, and had he authorized leaflet dropping and frequent buzzing of the airfield at Dabolim by IAF fighters and bombers – it is more than likely that the Portuguese would have folded up without a fight. But for that, Nehru would have had to shed his altruistic and liberal coat that he had so assiduously built over the years. Had Sardar Vallabhbhai Patel, India's first home minister and architect of the firm amalgamation of princely states, been alive, there would have certainly been a coercive strategy to evict the Portuguese in the early 1950s itself. The Goa crisis was the first serious challenge to Indian statecraft after the Kashmir and Hyderabad conflicts. Albeit a trifle diffident, the action was better late than never.

Intelligence gathering about Portuguese force levels was terribly inaccurate. Eleven years down the line after the Hyderabad operations, there seemed to have been very little improvement in synergies between military intelligence and civilian intelligence agencies that were responsible for piecing together all the HUMINT (human intelligence) and converting it into operational intelligence. There were ridiculous inputs about the presence of Portuguese fighter jets in Goa and the possibility of Pakistan supporting Portugal militarily in the conflict.

At the operational level, while there was reasonable synergy between the three services, two operations that had the largest number of casualties yielded some lessons for the future. First was the attempt by the Indian Navy to capture Anjadiv on its own. A small amphibious force comprising trained army units of even a platoon or company strength may have done the job in a more professional manner. In a scathing critique of the operation, Major General D.K. Palit, then a brigadier and director of military operations, recounts how he had identified a platoon of Gorkhas from the 4th Battalion of the 9th Gorkha Rifles and had them positioned at Bombay. To his surprise the GOC-in-C, Lieutenant General Chaudhuri had no intentions of sharing any glory with the Indian Navy and decided that if the army had to assault Anjadiv, it would do so on its own despite having no such assault expertise.[37] Bravely, the navy attempted it, but succeeded against amateurish opposition only after suffering heavy casualties of seven dead including two officers, and seventeen wounded. Second was the manner in which Diu was assaulted by 20 Rajput Regiment and 4 Madras Regiment. Had the defences at Diu been softened up by the Indian Navy and the Indian Air Force, the ground operation would have been a cakewalk. Underestimating the potential of the other two services would be a characteristic that would continue to plague the Indian Army in the years ahead. In a scathing critique of the manner in which the GOC-in-C of Southern Command, Chaudhuri, and other senior commanders overplayed the preparation for the operation, thereby diverting attention from the more serious China border situation, Palit recounts:

> Yet, in its consequences, Operation Vijay eventually took on greater significance: the easy conquest was taken too seriously in many quarters. The euphoria of success inflated a passing interlude of secondary military consequence into a famous victory.[38]

Brian Cloughley, an Australian colonel who spent two years as the deputy head as the UN Military Observer Group (UNMOG) in India and Pakistan, made these observations on India's reaction to its Goa victory:

> Unfortunately for the army and Indian prestige, the invasion of the tiny Portuguese enclave of Goa had been greeted with euphoric

> approval by an Indian public which considered it to be a great feat in arms, which it patently was not.[39]

In the final analysis, Operation Vijay was a reasonably well-planned and well-executed military operation against a significantly weaker adversary after almost thirteen years of peaceful existence. Though the Indian armed forces gained valuable battle experience, little did they realize that barely a year later they would be pitted against an enemy who would prove to be of a different mettle in a completely different environment.

PART IV

Across Borders

India–China War of 1962

14

UNRAVELLING THE FRONTIER WITH CHINA

Pandit Nain Singh Rawat hailed from the Johar Valley of Kumaon and spent much of his time in the 1870s mapping and documenting Tibet. The work of Nain Singh brought to light many details of a mysterious Tibet including the fact that the Tsangpo river in Tibet and the Brahmaputra in Assam were one and the same.[1]

How Complicated Was the Issue?

The India–China conflict of 1962 did not owe its origin merely to the jostling for Himalayan space between two emerging Asian powers. Nor was it only a result of the fallout of the 'Great Game' – orchestrated by Britain to protect its northern frontiers from perceived Russian ambitions of territorial expansion towards the warmer waters of the Arabian Sea. Control and influence over Tibet – considered by many strategic commentators to be the main bone of contention between India and China – did act as a trigger for the flare-up, particularly after the Dalai Lama sought refuge in India in 1959. However, a closer look at the history of the region encompassing Ladakh and Tibet reveals a complex and myriad interplay of geostrategic events. These mainly comprised attempts by various players over almost two centuries (early-nineteenth to mid-twentieth) to dominate a high-altitude wasteland that provided strategic depth to a declining power like Britain, and offered the same pay-offs to the two emerging Asian powers of the twentieth century, China and India.

Additionally, it also appeared that the 1950s saw a concerted attempt by a resurgent China to identify with the non-Han people of all the contested territories, comprising communities that resided in the regions around the Tibetan Plateau. The Chinese shrewdly offered a racial argument to what was primarily a geopolitical problem. India, on the other hand, had embraced a multicultural and multi-ethnic way of life, aspiring to amalgamate many tribes and communities in Ladakh and the north-eastern parts of the country. It felt that China's argument of racial affinity was not tenable when it came to coveting Indian territories.

A number of British geographers, explorers, diplomats and soldiers like Forsyth, Agnew, Cunningham, Johnson, Ardgah, McCartney, McDonald and Younghusband have, at various times between 1850 and 1914, offered compelling arguments to support their view of where the boundaries between Kashmir, Tibet and Sinkiang province of China ought to have been.[2] Despite forays by Indian explorers like Pandit Nain Singh, who first accompanied Forsyth on his expedition to Kashgar and Yarkand in 1873 and then forged out on his own eastwards from Leh to Tawang via Lhasa, the region did not attract the attention of independent India's military or political leadership.[3] For his exploration of nearly 2,250 km, which he measured by the length of his fixed strides and recorded secretly on prayer wheels;[4] and contribution to unravelling the mysteries of Kashgar, Yarkand and Tibet, Pandit Nain Singh was awarded the Patron's Gold Medal by the Royal Geographical Society. No other Indian would receive this award for over 125 years.[5] By the late-nineteenth century, so fascinated were the British with Tibet that they encouraged feisty Indian explorers to venture into Tibet from Sikkim. One such explorer was Sarat Chandra Das, who ran a school in Darjeeling whose covert role was to 'train interpreters, geographers and explorers who may be useful if at any future time Tibet is opened to the British'.[6] Between 1877 and 1882, Das made two trips into southern Tibet through Sikkim and finally reached Lhasa in mid-1882, purportedly to study the Tibetan scriptures. He returned to Darjeeling in December that year and wrote about his journeys in a book titled *A Journey to Lhasa and Central Tibet*.[7] Das was probably among the last of the adventurous Indians to venture into Tibet in the nineteenth century.

After they became nation states, few cartographers or explorers of eminence from India and China ventured into the icy wasteland in the 1950s even after it emerged as a geopolitically combustible region. An exception though was a 400 km exploratory trek through Tibet in 1949 by Major Zorawar Chand Bakshi in the guise of a Tibetan monk. He was awarded the McGregor Memorial Medal for military reconnaissance, the first Indian to be so awarded.[8] Bakshi would go on to become one of the Indian Army's most accomplished and decorated commanders in the years ahead.

For want of a better argument, the Indian government accepted the British position as a fait accompli, sticking to it rather adamantly during almost a decade of negotiations with China till it entered the psyche of the Indian people as a matter of national pride. This more than anything else galvanized public opinion within India to contest any use of force by China to redraw these boundaries. China on the other hand relied on scanty historical data for its claim on Aksai Chin taken from two narratives ordered by the Qing dynasty in 1782 and 1820.[9] Except for travellers' reports provided by Chinese caravans traversing from Turkestan and Sinkiang to Tibet, no cartographic exploration of the region was carried out by the Manchus of the Qing dynasty as their power waned in the region in the mid- to late-nineteenth century. Despite the plethora of accurate maps drawn by the British, communist China followed a different approach to accepting colonial boundaries.

Mao's China expected Nehru to enter negotiations considering India's own bitter experiences with the British and understand some of its geopolitical aspirations and apprehensions in the region. When India did not respond, China reacted like any powerful authoritarian state with a clear understanding of the benefits of using military force to prove a point and teach a weaker adversary 'a lesson', as Mao put it. Was it as simple as that? Obviously not! That is why a detailed historical-geopolitical-military study is an absolute imperative in any serious analysis of the conflict.

Current Geography

For most part, the India–China border of today runs across 4,250 km[10] of rugged, inhospitable and sparsely inhabited mountainous terrain, most of it contested; hence it is not an internationally recognized boundary despite being sanctified by custom and tradition and is called the Line of Actual Control or LAC. Experts have divided the contested portions of the border into three regions, most of which are located at altitudes of 10,000 ft or more. The Eastern Sector runs for over 1,200 km along the states of Arunachal Pradesh and Sikkim, with the main flashpoint being the control of Tawang, a monastery town with deep linkages with the heart of Tibet. Further east, Walong, a prominent trading outpost on a traditional trade route from Tibet and close to the trijunction of India, Burma and Tibet also emerged as a hot spot. China considers the integration of Tawang with the Tibetan Autonomous Region (TAR) as the final closure of a monumental task that Mao embarked on in 1950 when he took control of Tibet.

Running westwards along the LAC for almost 500 km from Arunachal Pradesh is the Bhutan–Tibet border with the trijunction of the Bhutan, Tibet and Arunachal emerging as a contested area along the Thagla ridge and Namka Chu watershed. The western extremities of the Eastern Sector are marked by the Sikkim–Tibet border with topographically hostile terrain that offers little potential for integrating it with TAR due to the absence of sustainable communication links from Tibet. Except for the passes at Nathu La and Chola, and an access through a narrow strip of valley called the Chumbi Valley at the trijunction of Tibet, Sikkim and Bhutan, there is little potential from the Tibetan side of expanding any sustainable military operations into Indian territory through Sikkim as compared to the possibilities offered in Arunachal Pradesh. The closer ethnic affinity of the people residing in Sikkim with those of neighbouring Nepal meant that compared to Tibet, this region did not offer much strategic potential to China. In fact, the north Sikkim plateau overlooks the Tibetan Plateau from an altitude of over 15,000 feet and offers significant strategic value to the Indian military. Despite the difficulties of sustaining military operations in Sikkim, China would continue to confront India there in the years preceding the merger of Sikkim in the Union of India in 1975. The fierce firefights at Nathu La and an adjoining pass called Chola in 1967 bear testimony to the continued sparring in the area.

The Central Sector runs for around 650 km from Taklakot, close to the India-Nepal-Tibet trijunction, to a few kilometres south of the disputed area of Chumar[11] and Demchok adjoining the Spiti Valley of Himachal Pradesh (these two posts, which form part of the combustible Western Sector of the border, have seen numerous face-offs in 2013–14). The Central Sector has remained a relatively peaceful border, once again due to the relative insignificance of the area for China and the calming presence of Nepal as a third country in the area. Over the years, Mt Kailas and the holy lake of Mansarovar, considered by all Hindus as the abode of the powerful deity Shiva and his consort Parvati, have emerged as a moneyspinner for the Tibetan Tourism Authority and acts as a spiritually de-escalating influence in the region. Hundreds of relatively prosperous and adventurous Indian pilgrims and trekkers subscribe to the rigorous twenty-one-day trek paying almost $2,000 for a round trip, which also takes them on a three-day parikrama or holy walk around Mt Kailas. Opening up this pilgrimage has also significantly contributed to reducing tension in the sector. Recent times have seen China allowing access to Indian pilgrims through Nathu La in Sikkim, which cuts down the travel time from over two weeks to barely three to four days. However, some potential flashpoints in this sector do remain in the region around the Barahoti Pass.

Running almost 1,600 km, the longest and most tension-prone sector from an Indian standpoint remains the Western Sector comprising almost the entire Ladakh–Tibet boundary including Aksai Chin, and the Shaksgam Valley of Kashmir bordering Xinjiang province. While the entire Aksai Chin region was occupied by China prior to the 1962 conflict, the Shaksgam Valley is the extreme north-eastern region of the disputed Pakistan-Occupied Kashmir and borders the Xinjiang province of China, considered by many to be the soft underbelly of China with its ethnic unrest and emergence of Islamic extremism. This region was temporarily ceded to China by Pakistan in 1963, and marked the beginning of a close strategic relationship between the two.[12] Even though the current LAC in Ladakh largely runs along the last positions which Chinese troops had occupied prior to the 1962 war, there are many areas in the Western Sector that China still contests and covets, mainly due to their proximity or ability to threaten the lines of communication that run between Tibet and Xinjiang. Amongst these small enclaves is the Depsang Plain near the Indian airfield of Daulat Beg Oldi (DBO), the Chang Chenmo area leading to the Kongka La and Lanak La, and Demchok/Chumar at the south-eastern tip of the sector.

A recent development in the region, which adds to China's apprehensions of expanding Indian influence in the area, is the current state of the military equation between India and Pakistan around the Siachen Glacier, which India dominates. Ladakh continues to simmer as India has still not reconciled to the loss of Aksai Chin, while China continues to feel threatened by India in Ladakh and Arunachal Pradesh. Current Chinese insecurity is a little strange, and reveals a misplaced paranoia about Indian capability and power-projection ambitions despite knowing very well that it would be decades before India overcomes geography in the region and matches China's ongoing capability build-up in Tibet!

Early Posturing in Ladakh and Tibet

A good time to start tracking the history of Ladakh and Tibet from an Indian perspective would be from the period of the Sikh Empire of Maharaja Ranjit Singh, the last Indian satrap to challenge and contest the advancing British Empire in India. After Ranjit Singh died in 1839, his successors, much like those of the Maratha strongman in the eighteenth century, Shivaji, failed to sustain the empire in the face of a coordinated assault by the British. General Zorawar Singh, one of Maharaja Ranjit Singh's ablest generals, was placed under the command of the Dogra governor of Jammu, Gulab Singh, and conducted numerous high-altitude campaigns between 1825 and 1841, bringing the entire region of Baltistan and Ladakh under the Sikh Empire. His unlimited appetite for adventure, conquest and territorial expansion made him look eastwards at Tibet.[13]

Tibet for most of the preceding few centuries had alternated between indirect rule and suzerainty by the Chinese Empires of the Tang and Qing dynasties, temporary conquest by Mongol invaders, and relative autonomy during short intervening periods. A conglomeration of tribes under the spiritual leadership of the Dalai Lama was thinly spread across the vast Tibetan Plateau. Though some like the Khampas of eastern Tibet possessed significant military prowess, Tibet was tempting for invaders from the north and west as a region of conquest. However, most invaders soon realized that Tibet did not have much to offer in terms of riches. When coupled with the inhospitable terrain and climate, it became difficult for outsiders to sustain any kind of formal rule. Amongst all the invaders into Tibet, the Chinese emperors of the Tang and Qing dynasty were most persistent in attempting to subjugate the various Tibetan tribes, but cultural differences between a Confucian China and the animistic and monastic Tibetans acted as a significant barrier.

Like numerous brilliant military campaigners before him, Napoleon being among them, Zorawar underestimated the importance of logistics and reserves as he traversed the vast Tibetan plateau in search of victory. Apart from underestimating the guile of the Tibetan guerrillas after having defeated the main Tibetan army in the spring of 1841 and captured significant territory in south-western Tibet, Zorawar Singh was unable to consolidate his military victory. Defeated by the weather and a Chinese–Tibetan force in December 1841, he was killed in battle along with approximately 5,000 Dogra and Sikh warriors.[14] His grave lies under a heap of stones near Taklakot in western Tibet, very close to the India–Nepal–Tibet border outpost of Lipulekh in the Central Sector. The story does not end there. After defeating Zorawar Singh, the Chinese–Tibetan force laid siege to Leh in early 1842, only to be defeated at Chushul by Dogra reinforcements, which had been sent to protect Ladakh and avenge the death of Zorawar Singh. Here, at Chushul, was signed a treaty between the Dogras, Tibetans and Chinese that read:

> On this auspicious occasion, the second day of the month Asuj in the year 1899 we – the officers of Lhasa, viz. firstly, Kalon Sukanwala, and secondly, Bakshi Sapju, commander of the forces of the Empire of China, on the one hand, and Dewan Hari Chand and Wazir Ratnu, on behalf of Raja Gulab Singh, on the other – agree together and swear before God that the friendship between Raja Gulab Singh and the Emperor of China and Lama Guru Sahib Lassawala will be kept and observed till eternity; for the traffic in shawl, pasham, and tea.

We will observe our pledge to God, Gayatri, and Pasi. Wazir Mian Khusal Chu is witness.[15]

Clearly, there was tremendous interest in the region, both geopolitical and economic. Having overcome the last vestiges of Sikh resistance in 1848 after the Second Anglo-Sikh War,[16] the British realized the difficulty of directly governing the areas north of the Punjab and cleverly handed over the governance of Jammu and Kashmir to a powerful Dogra clan headed by Gulab Singh,[17] which had earlier owed allegiance to the Sikh Empire and formed a critical element of its military and governing ability. It is this ambitious and adventurous clan, which ruled over the princely state of what is now Jammu and Kashmir for almost a century. Realizing the potential of territorial expansion towards Baltistan in the north and towards Ladakh and Tibet in the north-east with some economic gains, their focus was primarily on controlling the wool trade between Tibet and Turkestan. However, as early as 1846 and before the final defeat of the Sikhs, the British signed the Lahore Treaty with the Sikh ruler, Maharaja Duleep Singh, which gave them virtual control over Ladakh as a protectorate of the East India Company.[18]

Thus, it was not the British, but the Dogras, who first commenced the initial closing-in with the Manchus of the Qing dynasty, the Tibetan lamas and the Russian Empire. What the Dogras did not do, however, was to mark and demarcate geographical boundaries in the region. Instead, they relied on the formidable Himalayas, the Karakorams and the Kunlun mountains to act as natural barriers and frontiers, which they assumed would be respected by all in the years to come. The wily British changed this by attempting to create boundaries that catered to the requirements of the Empire. Opportunistic and clever as they were, the British realized well in time that these areas offered immense potential to provide strategic depth to their Indian Empire against possible expansionist ambitions of both the Russian Empire and possible Chinese resurgence. They proceeded assiduously to build on the initial inroads made by the Dogras, dispatching numerous expeditions in various directions to map the area.

From Leh, they went east into Tibet, north towards the forbidding Karakoram ranges, and beyond to the Kunlun mountains. Towards the west, they explored the trading routes from Baltistan to Yarkand and Turkestan, areas which would later be known as the Sinkiang autonomous region of China. Of particular interest to the British in the western regions of this high altitude was to track the progress of the Russian Empire as it attempted to expand south-eastwards after the Tsar's armies captured Tashkent and Samarkand in 1865.[19]

Between 1870 and 1875 a large British expedition led by Douglas Forsyth, the commissioner for Punjab and an expert on Central Asia, ventured beyond the Karakoram range towards the forbidding Kunlun range. He travelled to Yarkand and Kashgar in Turkestan to explore the possibilities of establishing good relations with Yakub Beg, the Muslim ruler who had driven the Chinese out of Turkestan. In this expedition were four Indian surveyors, Nain Singh, Kishen Singh, Kalian Singh and Abdul Salam.[20] So deep were these British forays that almost a century later, the Chinese premier Zhou Enlai irritatingly remarked during border talks with his Indian counterpart Nehru:

> British imperialism seeking a short-cut for invading the heart of Sinkiang, laid covetous eyes on the relatively flat Aksai Chin in the eighteen sixties and dispatched military intelligence agents to infiltrate into the area for unlawful surveys. In compliance with the will of British imperialism, these agents worked out an assessment of boundary lines for truncating Sinkiang.[21]

China was no match for the British when it came to meticulous recording of cartographic details of Tibet and Aksai Chin and knew that India possessed these records. They realized that the only way to try and negotiate with India was to push anti-colonial, current national security concerns and geopolitical arguments.

The Crown Dominates the Frontiers

One of the finest academically researched books on the origins of the boundary crisis, both in Ladakh and the Eastern Sector, has been written by Alistair Lamb, better known in India for his pro-Pakistan narration of the India–Pakistan conflict of 1947–48. In a Chatham House essay written for the Royal Institute for International Affairs in 1964 titled

'The China-India Border: The Origins of the Disputed Boundaries' he highlights the difference between frontiers and boundaries as propounded by Sir Henry McMahon at a Royal Societies of Arts function in 1935:

> A frontier is a wide tract of border land which, perhaps by virtue of its ruggedness or other difficulty, served as a buffer between two states. A boundary, he continued, was a clearly defined line, expressed either as a verbal description (delimited), or as a series of physical marks on the ground (demarcated).[22]

In another superbly researched book by a team of academics from the Institute of International Studies, University of California, Berkeley, titled *Himalayan Battleground: Sino-Indian Rivalry in Ladakh*, the rigid Chinese claim over Aksai Chin has been rightly contested by the authors based on historical evidence over four centuries that points at the region being a classic frontier and buffer zone, which was used primarily as a transit corridor between Tibet, Yarkand and the Dogra province of Ladakh.[23] They argue that the ambiguity of ownership made it a region coveted by both India and China.

As long as the regions of Ladakh including Aksai Chin and the areas north of Assam, later called NEFA (North-East Frontier Agency) by the British, were treated as frontiers, there were not many problems barring an invasion here and an occupation there. Claims of ownership by the Tibetans, Chinese, Dogras, Ahoms of Assam or the British were part and parcel of the Great Game. This is how the regions existed through much of the nineteenth and early part of the twentieth centuries. However, the moment the British started attempting to draw boundaries based on the watershed principle, or along the orientation of a mountain chain like the Karakoram and Kunlun mountains in Ladakh, and along the Himalayas in the east, there arose problems galore when it came to ratifying them with all stakeholders. The reason for this was that there were just too many mountain ranges with varying orientations for comfort. Adding to the misery of surveyors was the presence of glaciers, riverine valleys and plains, few of which followed the orientation of the mountain ranges.

An early conservative approach was followed by Moorcroft after his travels in Ladakh when he suggested in 1821 that the Karakoram

Pass was ideal as the north-western limits of the British Empire[24] and beyond that were frontiers (Aksai Chin) that could be claimed by China. The proposition considered the existence of traditional trading routes between Tibet and the provinces of Yarkand and Turkestan, both being areas that had alternated between freedom and dominance by imperial China of the Qing and Manchu dynasties, as well as the Mongols who asserted themselves in Tibet during the eighteenth century. He traced the boundary southwards from the Karakoram Pass somewhat along the LAC as it exists today. However, the more ambitious Johnson and Ardgah looked at the Kunlun range[25] as a better boundary between China and British India in terms of being closer to the creeping advance of the Russian Empire towards Kashgar and Yarkand. Such was the heady arrogance and strategic vision of the tough British explorers of the frontier regions.[26] Approved by Lord Curzon, the aggressive viceroy of India from 1899 to 1905, this line joined the Karakoram Pass and the Kunlun ranges before running south and enveloped the entire Aksai Chin region to become the de facto limit of the British Empire.[27]

The Ahoms of Burma had ruled Assam for much of the thirteenth to eighteenth centuries and also exercised nominal control over the areas to the north of the plains of Assam. These areas comprised the frontier and tribal areas immediately to the south of the eastern Himalayan ranges. Some of these like Tawang and Walong lay across high but traversable passes like Bum La and Hathung La along traditional trade routes from Tibet. The Buddhist monastery at Tawang had close spiritual affiliations with the Dalai Lama in Lhasa and was much visited by pilgrims and monks from Tibet. It was only after the Anglo-Burmese War of 1826 that the British took interest in this frontier, which comprised the Kameng, Lohit and Walong provinces after the Ahoms ceded control of the area to them. Worried about the proximity of the Yunan and Sichuan provinces of China to the region and the undue influence of Tibet, the astute British wanted to take control and seal their frontiers in the region, much like they were concurrently attempting in Ladakh.

Two connected events in the second half of the eighteenth century accelerated British interest in the region. The first was the conquest of Tashkent and Samarkand by the Russian Empire, while the second was the declining power of China's Manchu rulers of the Qing dynasty. The latter automatically translated into a declining Manchu influence on China's peripheral areas of interest – Tibet and Turkestan – and the rise of local warlords like Yakub Beg in Turkestan and others in Tibet owing allegiance to the Dalai Lama. Worried that the advancing Russians would attempt to poach on Turkestan and Tibet, the British realized that it was time to flex their muscles and establish a presence in those regions. This, in short, was what the Great Game was all about.

Without going into too many details about the various expeditions launched by the British in the areas around Ladakh, be it towards the Kunlun ranges to the north-east in what was even then known as Aksai Chin or towards Kashgar and Turkestan, the clear aim was to quickly convert this frontier into a delineated and demarcated boundary between the British Empire and Tibet to the east, and China to the north and north-west. In the east, the British were more aggressive as they realized that the Chinese influence from the Sichuan province was quite marked not only in eastern Tibet, but also in frontier areas north of the Assam valley. The Francis Younghusband expedition of 1903–04 was an aggressive attempt by the British to advance on Lhasa through the tough tribal areas north of the princely frontier state of Sikkim, and secure trade and territorial concessions from both Tibet and China. The expedition was not only a military success but also paved the way for the creation of the McMahon Line, which attempted to draw clear boundaries between British India and Tibet based on watersheds and clearly demarcated mountain ridges of the Himalayan ranges.[28] The highlight of the mission was a clear statement of intent by the viceroy, Lord Curzon, and his unstinting support for the expedition as he saw it as a timely foray to check any Russian ambitions in Tibet.[29]

When the Manchu rulers of the Qing dynasty were overthrown by China's revolutionary movement led by Sun Yat-sen in 1911, Tibet virtually became an independent state with hardly any remnants of Chinese presence in Lhasa and other areas except for normal trading links across poorly demarcated frontiers. The thirteenth Dalai Lama assumed the exalted mantle of religious leadership and was the power centre till his death in 1933. This period is considered by Tibetans as a 'golden period' in their history when they were virtually regarded the world over as an independent nation. Precipitated by some amount of friction between

British administrators and Tibetan monks, and increased religious interaction between the Lhasa and Tawang monasteries, it was in 1914 that the British initiated the Simla Conference with Tibet and China to push through their version of the Indo-Tibetan boundaries. While British India and Tibet ratified the agreement, the Chinese representative, Ivan Chen, merely initialled the agreement without ratifying it. This clearly indicated that the wily Chinese were ambiguously and dexterously playing the waiting game from a position of weakness. The main areas of contention as far as the Chinese were concerned revolved around ownership of Tawang in the east, and Aksai Chin in the west, which lay between the Karakoram and the Kunlun ranges.

The British claimed much of Aksai Chin from a position of strength based on exploratory propriety and cartographic initiative. The Chinese, on the other hand, claimed it as an area through which only Tibetans and Chinese passed through on the traditional trade route connecting the provinces of Kashgar and Turkestan with western Tibet. In the east, Tibet maintained that the areas around Tawang were both ethnically and religiously closely linked with Lhasa, and merited inclusion in Tibet. This claim suited China after it had annexed Tibet in 1950. Both these disputes were to be the main triggers of the India–China conflict of 1962.

15

SPARRING AND PROBING

There is little point in attempting a profound facetiousness and writing off China as a riddle wrapped in an enigma. Failure of intelligence, no less than failure of nerve can manifest itself in seeing Han expansionism.[1]

– General K.S. Thimayya

The Dragon Awakens, the Elephant Argues

A lot has already been written in this book on India's attempts to resolve its internal and external disputes under an initial and overarching template of extensive internal debate, negotiations, diplomacy and an overwhelming desire to be seen as a responsible and restrained nation state. The decisions to use force in Kashmir, Hyderabad or Goa were couched in a moralistic fait accompli of 'we tried our best, but ultimately had to use force against recalcitrant adversaries who underestimated our resolve to preserve the fabric of our fledgling democracy'. Somehow, the use of force to resolve disputes was seen as morally incorrect by the 'Gandhian and Nehruvian school of diplomacy'; strengthened as it was by a vindication of the success of India's non-violent ousting of the British Empire from the subcontinent.

Communist China on the other hand emerged from years of bloody military violence against the Japanese and the Kuomintang. Mao was quick to understand the inevitability of emerging post–WW II concepts of statecraft like deterrence, coercion and compellance, while Nehru bravely stuck to his liberal and altruistic belief that modern nation states were designed to negotiate and coexist. It is in the backdrop of those halcyon days of international relations in the Cold War era that India and China engaged in almost a decade of protracted negotiations over Aksai Chin and Tibet.

The years 1950–54 saw India and China approaching their frontier strategies in a starkly contrasting manner. China militarily occupied Tibet in October 1950 by systematically crushing all opposition. Soon after, it commenced building a strategic highway running through Aksai Chin linking Tibet with the south-western province of Sinkiang (now called Xinjiang). While India attempted to play down the likelihood of any confrontation with China over border differences and highlighted the Panchsheel agreement as a template for India–China relations,[2] Sardar Vallabhbhai Patel, India's nationalistic home minister, did warn Prime Minister Nehru of his apprehensions regarding India's China policy. He advocated a capability-building strategy, rather than a conciliatory one as a hedge against Chinese adventurism. In a prophetic letter written to Nehru in 1950, a few months before his death, Patel wrote:

> I have been anxiously thinking over the problem of Tibet and I thought I should share with you what is passing through my mind. I have carefully gone through the correspondence between the External Affairs Ministry and our Ambassador in Peking and through him the Chinese Government. I have tried to peruse this correspondence as favourably to our ambassador and the Chinese Government as possible, but I regret to say that neither of them comes out well as a result of this study.[3]

He goes on in the same letter to specifically highlight the strategic ramifications of China's occupation of Tibet:

> In the background of this, we have to consider what new situation faces us as a result of the disappearance of Tibet, as we know it and the expansion of China almost up to our gates. Throughout history, we have seldom been worried about our northern frontier. The Himalayas have been regarded as an impenetrable barrier against any threat from the North. We had a friendly Tibet which gave us no trouble ... China is no longer divided. It is united and strong.[4]

Though Patel was a political disciple of Mahatma Gandhi, he was a tough and practical statesman who fitted into the mould of a realist and nationalist when it came to relations between nation states. His understanding of an emerging Chinese mistrust with regards to India's position in the international order was highly accurate and perceptive. No amount of posturing by Nehru and India in the years ahead with respect to championing non-alignment would change this opinion. He wrote on this issue:

> It is impossible to imagine any sensible person believing in the so-called threat to China from Anglo-American machinations in Tibet. Therefore if the Chinese put faith in this, they must have distrusted us so completely as to have taken us as tools or stooges of Anglo-American diplomacy or strategy. This feeling, if genuinely entertained by the Chinese in spite of your direct approaches to them, indicates that, even though we regard ourselves as friends of China, the Chinese do not regard us as their friends. With the Chinese mentality of 'whoever is not with them being against them', this is a significant pointer of which we have to take due note.[5]

Despite these early warnings, Nehru did not pay heed and continued to bank on his international stature and perceived leadership of the developing world as being enough to stave off any hostility from China. China's strategy was clear. Mao with his increasing disdain for Nehru as the 1950s went by assumed control of China's strategy to 'teach India a lesson', while the consummate Zhou Enlai, China's prime minister, was entrusted with keeping India guessing about China's actual intentions with deft but argumentative diplomacy. To be fair to Zhou Enlai, he genuinely attempted at times to impress upon Nehru that it would be in India's interest to meet China halfway and understand its strategic fears about Aksai Chin in return for China's acceptance of the McMahon Line in the east. India and Nehru stuck to their guns that Aksai Chin was an intrinsic part of Ladakh and that the McMahon Line was inviolable in the east. India did not realize till 1957 that Nehru had met his match in Zhou Enlai; right or wrong was not the issue, there was no going back for China on its claim on Aksai Chin.[6]

Wing Commander Subroto Mukerjee (fourth from right) and Mrs Sharada Mukerjee (second from right) at a social function after WW II.

, 1947–48

Jawaharlal Nehru discussing military plans in the Poonch/Rajouri sector with Brigadier Usman (centre) as Sheikh Abdullah (right) looks on.

›ainting of the Battle of Badgam (3 November 1947) and ·ortrait of Major Somnath Sharma, who was posthumously ·arded independent India's first Param Vir Chakra (PVC).

Gunners of Patiala State Forces in support of 1 Sikh at Pattan, October 1947.

Wing Commanders K.L. Bhatia (left), hero of the Srinagar airlift, and Moolgavkar (right), orchestrator of air operations in Srinagar, were awarded the Vir Chakra and Maha Vir Chakra respectively for their exploits.

Dakotas of 12 Squadron evacuating civilians from the besieged Poonch.

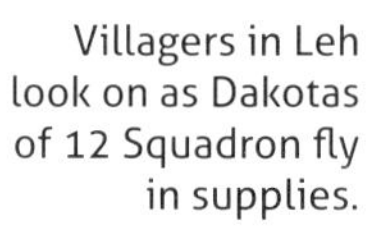

Villagers in Leh look on as Dakotas of 12 Squadron fly in supplies.

Major Thangaraju of the Madras Sappers opening the Zojila Pass, 1948.

Air Commodore Mehar Singh (third from left), Major General Kulwant Singh (fourth from left), Wing Commander M.M. Engineer (fifth from left) and officers of 12 Squadron.

Pilots of 8 Squadron with their flight commander, Mickey Blake, Vir Chakra (fourth from left).

Hiding a Harvard aircraft from enemy shelling in a Poonch courtyard, mid-1948.

Hyderabad 1948

Arms haul from retreating Razakars.

Mir Osman Ali Khan Bahadur, the Nizam of Hyderabad.

Sherman tanks of 1 Armoured Division en route to Hyderabad.

Major General E.L. Edroos (right) surrendering to Major General Chaudhuri in Hyderabad on 16 September 1948.

ombay Sappers laying a bridge across the Mandovi
uring Operation Vijay, December 1961.

Portuguese prisoners of war being repatriated to Portugal in December 1961.

1962 war

The Younghusban Route into Tibet via Jelepla in Sikkim.

Gorkhas at Pangong Tso in October 1962.

A mule patrol of Ladakh Scouts around Daulat Beg Oldi (DBO).

5 Jat Regiment during their valiant withdrawal from DBO along the frozen Shyok river.

Gorkha survivors from the Sirjap outposts along Pangong Tso.

IAF Packets on a forward dropping mission in eastern Ladakh.

IL-14s and other IAF transport aircraft at Chushu before Phase II of the war, late October 1962.

An IAF helicopter at a forward helipad in Tawang sector.

Armoured vehicles being offloaded from an An-12 at Chushul, November 1962.

A painting of 13 Kumaon at Rezangla, where Major Shaitan Singh (portrait) was posthumously awarded a Param Vir Chakra.

Reconnaissance, Indian Statecraft and Chinese Intransigence

It is widely believed that since India's Intelligence Bureau (IB) was rather strangely and naively entrusted with border management in Ladakh by the Nehru government, military intelligence was completely absent in the area. It was not so. Following on Zorawar Bakshi's forays into Tibet in 1949, Captain Rajendra Nath of the recently formed 11 Gorkha Rifles was a young officer in the Intelligence Directorate at Army HQ in 1952 and volunteered to lead the first clandestine mission into Aksai Chin after China's occupation of Tibet. The eighteen-member team was well organized with rations, mules and yaks, interpreters, and traversed two 18,000-foot passes before descending into the Changanchemo Valley. After hitting the 18,300-foot-high Lanak La they returned without encountering any Chinese troops and only heard of their infrequent patrols from local herders and grazers. Sadly, his report did not attract much attention and was not followed up at regular intervals with similar forays.[7]

The year 1957 was a defining one in India–China relations. The unveiling of the Tibet–Sinkiang Highway through Aksai Chin completely spooked India and took away the possibility of any equitable and negotiated settlement. Not only was it a blatant display of aggressive strategic posturing and admirable high-altitude infrastructure engineering, but also a very accurate analysis of India's possible reaction based on its scanty deployment of armed forces in Ladakh and near absence of any operational infrastructure worth the name. Apart from a display of an indignant 'you stabbed me in the back' and 'how could you do this to us – your partners in the fight against colonialism' kind of statements, India could do very little in terms of physically contesting the road construction through the territory it claimed. The second successful clandestine mission in 1958 to investigate reports of the highway building was orchestrated by General Thimayya, the chief of army staff at the time. Two separate patrols, one under an IB officer, and the second under an enterprising sapper (engineers) officer, found clear evidence of Chinese intrusions into Aksai Chin. While the IB officer, Karam Singh, returned safely, the young sapper officer, Lieutenant Iyengar, was apprehended by the Chinese and interrogated for almost two months before being released.[8] Consequently, the absence of an adventurous spirit that was displayed by the British and Indian explorers like Pandit Nain Singh and Sarat Chandra Das while exploring the frontiers resulted in India failing to establish innovative border management mechanisms.

It was quite obvious that the sheer physical distance, terrain impediments and weather acted as critical barriers for the Intelligence Bureau. It, however, continued to oversee border management with meagre resources, and it is only in 1957 and beyond after the discovery of the Tibet–Sinkiang Highway that the army first suggested that it take over the entire defence of Ladakh[9] and set up posts in the area. Other than absolute strategic naivety and disdain with regards to the role and capabilities of India's armed forces, there can be no other reason for keeping the Indian Army and Indian Air Force out of the area for so long. If aircraft like the Tempest fighters could actively participate in the battles of Zojila and Skardu in the 1947–48 conflict with Pakistan, it is mystifying why ten years later aircraft like the Canberra bomber, or Toofani and Mystere fighter jets were not deployed for regular photo and visual reconnaissance in the Ladakh and Aksai Chin region. Of course, though Srinagar by then was an established airbase, fighter operations were not permitted from there under the 1948 UN-sponsored ceasefire resolution over J&K between India and Pakistan. Had the Government of India been decisive enough, it could have overruled that clause citing national security imperatives with respect to China, and it is highly likely that China's road construction would have been discovered much earlier. More than anything, it would have displayed some intent on the part of India. Instead, it was only in 1960 that the long-range Canberra bomber-cum-reconnaissance aircraft of 106 Squadron flew a few missions to try and investigate the extent of China's build-up in Aksai Chin.

Mao's role in the 1962 conflict with India was underplayed for years and the Chinese perspective was kept under wraps for long. It was only in the 1990s that a series of good writing from China emerged, revealing Mao's impatience and irritation with Nehru's growing influence in the developing world and India's unwillingness to let go of Aksai Chin. Along the way, he also made some fundamental errors by wrongly assessing that after granting asylum to the Dalai Lama, India wanted to seize Tibet from China.[10] Mao is also said to have been particularly infuriated when he heard of some covert support from India to the Khampa rebellion in eastern Tibet in 1959.[11]

The Gloves Come Off

After the Dalai Lama fled to India via Tawang in March 1959 and was given shelter by India, China was convinced of India's role in stirring ferment in Tibet. Covert US operations from Sikkim in support of Tibetan Khampa rebels added fuel to the fire with China convinced that such operations could not have been launched without tacit support from the Indian state.[12] It then commenced aggressive patrolling, citing Indian forays into Aksai Chin and along the McMahon Line in NEFA as having forced its hand. The first armed incident of significant importance was reported at Longju on the NEFA border where India had set up a post right on the McMahon line and just south of the Tibetan village of Migyitun. Longju was conveniently placed on the Tsari river and allowed good visibility into Tibet. However, according to the Chinese, India had transgressed 2 miles north of the McMahon Line and the Chinese asked India to vacate the post. This face-off in August 1959 resulted in a small but fierce firefight between the PLA and the Indian Army. This can well be considered as the first serious encounter with 'gloves off' as a prelude to the 1962 war and Garver clearly places the blame on China for triggering this encounter.[13]

The Longju incident was soon followed in October of the same year by another fierce encounter in the Chang Chenmo Valley of the central Ladakh sector where an Indian paramilitary and Intelligence Bureau patrol led by Inspector Karam Singh, who had made earlier forays into the region, was en route to Lanak La to set up a post there. This pass was claimed by India as being the eastern extremity of the border in Aksai Chin. Without any real intelligence of the Chinese disposition in the area, the force was ambushed by a larger force near Kongka La, some 20 km short of Lanak La. In the ensuing firefight, nine Indian soldiers were killed and eleven personnel including Karam Singh were taken prisoner, with many suffering serious injuries.[14] The Chinese are believed to have lost fewer soldiers as they attacked from a tactically advantageous position.[15] The prisoners were returned in November after a fierce protest from India, but not before being tortured extensively.

The diplomatic fallout of these two clashes in 1959 was an offer from China for both countries to fall back by 20 km in Ladakh and to attempt not to violate the McMahon line in the east. Except for the reinforcement of the Tawang garrison by a small force comprising a battalion of the Gorkhas under Lieutenant Colonel Eric Vas, the first regular Indian Army battalion to be deployed in the region replacing the Assam Rifles, which was a paramilitary force, there was a temporary lull in hostilities till mid-1961. While China grappled with the Khampa rebellion in eastern Tibet, India was preoccupied in its efforts to dislodge the Portuguese from Goa. Concurrently, Nehru met with Zhou Enlai on numerous occasions, trying to resolve the various boundary issues without any success. Why these diplomatic parleys were unsuccessful is well documented[16] and does not merit much attention here barring a few 'realist' deductions as understood by the author over five decades later. Some of these are highlighted below:

- The two encounters at Longju and Kongka La in 1959, the inability of India to gather international support to condemn the building of the highway through Aksai Chin, and the ruthless suppression of the Khampa rebellion despite covert CIA support, convinced Mao that he was in a position to dictate terms to India from a position of strength. This, without doubt, was a correct and realistic assessment from China's point of view.
- India, on the other hand, was clearly unable to back its large territorial claims in Aksai Chin and the defence of the McMahon line with actionable intelligence and adequate military capability. Instead, a delusionary and distinctly leftist influence on the political leadership led it to believe that China was neither interested nor capable of contesting any forward posturing by the Indian Army in Ladakh and NEFA. That the military leadership failed to effectively contest this strategic misconception was a reflection of its indecisiveness and tentativeness with regards to higher defence strategy.

The Forward Policy

Pushed into a corner by China and faced with an election in a couple of years, Nehru had no other option but to harden his stance vis-à-vis China without the wherewithal to convert it into any tangible strategic game plan. The inexperienced and strategically naive political opposition within India too played its part in allowing the situation to deteriorate by badgering Nehru and accusing him of cowing down to Chinese bullying. They demanded, without realizing the skewed military balance between the two countries, that 'not an inch of Indian territory must be bartered with the Chinese'. Not one mainstream political party other than the communists suggested a negotiated settlement with China, albeit from a position of slight weakness. With the pressure building and in the absence of any let-up in Chinese incursions and military build-up, Nehru had to come up with some security policy to combat China. The *Forward Policy* was a result of this relentless pressure on the Indian government, both from the Chinese as well as the domestic constituents comprising the opposition parties, media and the public at large.

After the farcical resignation episode of India's chief of army staff, General Thimayya, in March 1960 following a bitter feud with the defence minister, and his subsequent retirement,[17] the appointment of Lieutenant General B.M. Kaul as the chief of general staff saw the Forward Policy gaining momentum through the summer of 1961 and spring of 1962.[18] This translated into over sixty posts being established in Ladakh and NEFA – many of them being within territory claimed by China and 'behind enemy lines' in Ladakh. In NEFA, however, some of these posts were extremely close to the McMahon Line despite the agreement after the 1959 clashes that both countries would withdraw 20 km from their last positions. Particularly irksome for the Chinese was Indian posturing in the Namka Chu Valley of NEFA, and the forays by Indian patrols into the Chip Chap Valley and Galwan Valley of Ladakh. While the former would be a flashpoint in October 1962, the latter would result in serious conflagrations in Ladakh.

From a military and operational perspective, the Forward Policy was a poorly conceived and politically driven military posture with almost no coercive potential against a much stronger adversary. How the Indian

Army went along with Nehru and Krishna Menon, the mercurial and acerbic defence minister, is a story by itself.[19] Crystallized into a policy directive in October 1961 and incrementally implemented right through the winter of 1961, it envisaged creation of small static enclaves of troop positions of a maximum of a platoon strength in no-man's-land very close to where the Chinese were occupying similar positions, but in much larger strength. The strategy was tactically unsound and though field commanders like Lieutenant General Daulat Singh, the commander of the Western Army Command, and Lieutenant General Umrao Singh, the top field commander in the east, expressed serious apprehensions about sustaining such a policy, they fell in line once the chief insisted on implementing the directive.[20] Instead of coercing or deterring the Chinese, it provoked them into responding with brute force and strength. While the 'nuts and bolts' of the policy will be discussed in the next chapter, the Forward Policy was the final catalyst which catapulted the situation from one of posturing to application of force – a clear disaster for Indian statecraft.

In the absence of roads and railway lines in areas where troops had to be deployed, the Indian Air Force played a pivotal role in translating the Forward Policy into an operational deployment in both NEFA and Ladakh. Tezpur, Gauhati and Jorhat in the east were the main hubs from where loads were flown by IAF Dakotas and Packets to build up and sustain the garrisons at Khinzemane, Tawang, Sela and Bomdila. The loads were either dropped at dropping zones close to the garrisons, or off-loaded at Tezpur and transported by road and mules thereafter. By mid-1961, Chandigarh, Srinagar and Pathankot airfields became hubs[21] from where the Forward Policy in Ladakh was supported. Even with airfields at Leh and airstrips at Kargil, Fukche, Daulat Beg Oldi and Chushul, numerous forward posts like the ones at Galwan Valley, Shyok Valley, Sirjap-Spangur (around Lake Pangang Tso), Khurnak Fort and Demchok[22] had to be sustained by airdropping of stores and ammunition at dropping zones. It is extremely surprising that there is no record of the IAF leadership at any time cautioning the government that such an arrangement of supporting the Forward Policy exclusively by air was fraught with danger and unsustainable in the long run.[23] Squadron Leader Baldev Raj Gulati (retd) was a young flying officer navigator flying Super Constellations, a four-engine propeller aircraft that could carry eighty-five fully equipped troops. He clearly recollects after cross-checking from his logbook that from 3 October onwards, he flew in hundreds of raw recruits from the airfields of Halwara and Adampur (airbases close to the Punjab towns of Ludhiana and Jalandhar respectively) to Tezpur. After barely a week of training, these young recruits were sent to the eastern front when it was realized that IV Corps needed to be bolstered significantly if they were to put up any kind of fight and after the western army commander, Lieutenant General Daulat Singh, clearly indicated that he had no troops to spare from his kitty. Gulati reckons that approximately 3,000 (over two battalions worth) such raw recruits were inducted into the eastern war zone between 3 October and 21 November. They would prove to be fodder for the well-equipped PLA (People's Liberation Army) troops when inducted into battle in Phase 2 of the conflict.[24]

Convening a Central Military Commission meeting in late 1961, Mao compared India's Forward Policy to a strategic move across the centre line in a game of chess. He remarked:

> Their (India's) continually pushing forward is like crossing the Chu Han boundary. What should we do? We can also set out a few pawns on our side of the river. If they don't then cross over, that's great. If they do cross, we'll eat them up.[25]

This was the signal for the PLA to abandon the agreement of 1959 and recommence their aggressive patrolling. In a chapter from a monograph brought out by the US Army War College on the PLA in 2003, Larry Wortzel argues that Mao likened India's Forward Policy to *can shi zheng ce*, or a 'nibbling policy', and asked his border troops to secure China's claim over Aksai Chin by weaving an interlocking pattern around Indian troops without seeking a fight unless provoked and fired upon.[26]As the crisis hurtled towards conflict, if one were to dissect Chinese pre-war strategy, it could be summarized as below:

> Act first with definite and time-bound strategic goals; reach a position of physical strength; then negotiate and play diplomatic hard ball leaving enough bait for a weaker adversary to bite and finally act again, this time decisively.

16

OMINOUS SIGNS

The PRC has a long history of using military force to maintain domestic stability, to guard its territorial integrity and to obstruct interference from great powers into its immediate neighbourhood. China's changing attitude to the use of force has affected stability in Asia in important ways.[1]

– JONATHAN HOLSTAG

MILITARY BALANCE ON THE FRONTIER

Except for war on the Korean Peninsula and continued anti-colonial conflict in Asia and Africa, the world at large was at peace in the 1950s, recovering from the catastrophe of WW II. As the Cold War emerged as the new global security challenge, countries like India and China were searching for a place in the comity of nations in divergent fashion. While India spoke the language of peace and friendship among developing nations and concentrated rather myopically on the security threat only from Pakistan, Chinese authoritarianism, expansionism and revisionist ambitions saw it build military power as a hedge against perceived and continued Anglo-American hegemony in Asia. It is this divergent approach which ultimately resulted in the inability of India to effectively respond militarily to China's 1962 assault along the two fronts of Ladakh and what is today called Arunachal Pradesh, but in those days was called the North-East Frontier Agency or NEFA. Some commentators and historians have called the 1962 war a set of skirmishes and even downplayed the impact of the military defeat, but when you look at the fine print of forces ranged against each other towards the second phase of the conflict in November 1962, there were two undermanned Indian divisions in the east including complements of the paramilitary forces in the form of Assam Rifles, pitted against approximately five divisions of the PLA with some armour and significant artillery support – battle-tested, equipped and acclimatized for high-altitude operations after having been in Tibet and Aksai Chin for almost twelve years.[2]

As referred to in the earlier chapter, the Indian government continued to assign the Intelligence Bureau with the defence of the Ladakh–Tibet frontier including areas of Aksai Chin till 1959.[3] The NEFA border too was defended during the same period by stray posts of the Assam Rifles, a paramilitary force raised for the defence of NEFA; the regular Indian Army came in only in 1959. So convinced was Nehru of the potential of his 1954 Panchsheel Agreement to maintain peace and tranquillity along the Indo-Tibetan border and forge a close relationship with China that he chose to ignore Sardar Patel's letter warning him of China's hegemonic ambitions in the region. The only Indian Army brigade in the region after it was entrusted with the defence of Ladakh was 121 Brigade, which was located at Kargil, primarily to stave off any Pakistani incursions from the Gilgit and Skardu sectors after the experience of the 1947–48 conflict. This brigade was assigned the additional task of defensive operations in the entire Ladakh sector.[4] Nehru even ignored the cautionary advice of his army chief, General K.S. Thimayya,[5] to beef up military capability in Ladakh along the Indo-Tibetan border despite knowing that 'Timmy' had first-hand knowledge of Chinese military capability after his stint as head of the UN Neutral Nations Repatriation Committee in Korea. During his stint there he had acquired a fair understanding of emerging Chinese strategic thought while interacting with many US commanders who had fought the Chinese during the Korean War. It is unfortunate that 'Timmy' fell out with his defence minister and resigned from his post as COAS in 1959, only to withdraw his resignation a few days later and retire honourably in March 1960.[6]

B.G. Verghese, a highly respected journalist and strategic commentator recollects that Timmy had recommended the name of Lieutenant General S.P.P. Thorat to the government as his successor, but the

Nehru–Krishna Menon combine were said to be uncomfortable with the prospect of an aggressive Maratha taking charge of the Indian Army and influencing their China strategy.[7] They instead appointed a milder and more acceptable General P. N. Thapar, who was not considered much of a strategist, as the army chief.[8] Menon and his aggressive and politically well-connected chief of general staff, Lieutenant General B.M. Kaul, then enforced the Forward Policy on an ill-prepared Indian Army. To be fair to the Indian Army, a number of field commanders like Lieutenant General Umrao Singh, the GOC of 33 Corps in charge of the NEFA region,[9] and Lieutenant General Daulat Singh, the GOC-in-C of Western Army Command, did express their dismay at the operationally unviable policy, but they were overruled by Delhi. In the absence of an army chief who could take a strong stand based on a military appreciation of the difficulties of executing a flawed strategy, a plan that was drawn up in the comfortable environs of Delhi was forced down the throat of protesting field commanders.

What does it take to put together a viable defensive line in high-altitude terrain? Dominating ground, adequate integral firepower, mutual cross-cover with adjoining defensive positions, location in areas that are covered by artillery support from the rear, and, most importantly, a robust logistic network and secure communication lines that facilitate recycling of troops. Replenishment of ammunition and other material are essentials that cannot be ignored. In case the terrain and force ratios do not support a defensive line right on the frontiers, a defensive deployment in depth that relies on channelizing the enemy into killing grounds is the next best option. All these tenets of defensive deployment in the mountains were ignored when the Indian Army was deployed in section- and platoon-sized pockets (10 to 40 troops) as they were in the Daulat Beg Oldi complex, Chip Chap Valley, Galwan Valley, and Sirjap complex on the north bank of the Pangang Tso in the Chushul sector of Ladakh.[10] A similar deployment was made in the Namka Chu Valley, the Lohit Valley and other locations in the east and west Kameng sectors of NEFA. Sinha and Athale, two very accomplished defence ministry historians, put the total number of posts set up in Ladakh across the 480 km stretch from Daulat Beg Oldi in the north to Demchok as having increased from twenty-seven to thirty-six between end-1961 and

September 1962. The number of posts in the eastern sector was put at thirty-four in July 1962. Leave alone heavy artillery support, the heaviest weapons that these posts had were light machine guns (LMGs), with only a few having some mortars. The posts were separated from each other by anywhere from 3 km to 10 km.[11] This meant that not only was there no mutual cross-cover, there were very few withdrawal options in the face of an enemy assault in the absence of roads, tracks or helipads. Pushing formations right on the McMahon Line in the Eastern Sector, and behind known enemy positions in Ladakh as a conduit for aggressive posturing and patrolling was a toothless strategy devoid of any punch and sustainability, particularly in the face of an enemy that was known to use overwhelming force by employing what was called 'human wave tactics' and attacks from multiple directions.

After the military situation started deteriorating in 1959, the entire Ladakh sector including the 85,000 sq. km of Aksai Chin and the 1,600-km-long LAC was reinforced in March–April 1960 by an undermanned 114 brigade, commanded by Brigadier T.N. Raina,[12] who later became the COAS. It initially comprised two J&K paramilitary infantry battalions and one regular infantry battalion as against a projected requirement of four regular infantry battalions. It was reinforced with another battalion and two batteries of light artillery when hostilities seemed imminent. An additional brigade with just two battalions (70 Brigade) was rushed in later for the second phase of the battle along with a troop of light AMX tanks and two infantry battalions to reinforce 114 Brigade,[13] which was badly depleted after the initial Chinese assault. Another depleted brigade was kept in reserve at Leh (163 Brigade).Ranged against this force were almost two divisions of the PLA with their full complement of artillery,[14] including an additional division for the second phase of the conflict. In terms of overall ratios, though the PLA maintained a 3:1 advantage, this would not have ensured the kind of success achieved by them had the Indian Army appreciated the key axis of attack by the Chinese and defended their areas with at least battalion-strength positions in well-prepared defences with supporting artillery and air support. For such well-prepared defences in the mountains, it is accepted that the attacker has to have significant superiority for success. That the Chinese were able to overrun Indian positions despite stiff infantry resistance was mainly due to dispersed defensive locations without any kind of mutual fire support and almost non-existent artillery support (114 Brigade had just eight towable field guns/howitzers).[15]

The troop disposition in the east was no better in terms of both tactical deployment and numerical strength. Serious reservations were expressed by both the corps commander of 33 Corps, the corps entrusted with the defence of NEFA, Lieutenant General Umrao Singh, and the brigade commander of 7 Infantry Brigade, Brigadier J.P. Dalvi, about the vulnerability of a forward deployment right on the McMahon Line in the Tawang sector. Yet, Army HQ insisted that 7 Brigade with its four battalions deploy along and around the Namka Chu. Part of the Indian Army's battle-tested 4th Division, the broad task of the brigade was to eject a Chinese division off the Thagla Ridge, amongst other places, and secure the McMahon Line. How on earth a brigade was to throw a division out was not clearly spelt out. Of course, there was no intelligence about enemy dispositions!

Further east, the entire Lohit Forward Division sector of NEFA with a frontage of approximately 150 km was defended by a mere battalion of the Indian Army, complemented by a platoon of paramilitary forces (Assam Rifles). These forces were concentrated at the trijunction of India-Burma and Tibet and strung out in pockets over a distance of 10–20 km with virtually no mutual cover and sustained support from the air by the Indian Air Force.[16] Ranged against them in mid-October 1962 were almost two Chinese regiments[17] with artillery and logistics support. The dragon clearly held the upper hand as the autumn of 1962 turned ominous for India's rather naive politico-military leadership.

The Air Situation

In the skies, the Indian Air Force (IAF) was qualitatively superior to the People's Liberation Army Air Force (PLAAF) in terms of all aircraft (fighters, transport and helicopters) that could be employed effectively both in Ladakh and NEFA. Its pilots were considerably more skilled than their PLAAF adversaries as a result of stringent training patterns that still had the RAF stamp on it.[18] A number of senior pilots in middle-level leadership appointments like flight commanders and commanding officers had seen action in the 1947–48 war against Pakistan. However, to be fair to the PLAAF, its fighter pilots too had seen action over the Korean Peninsula in the mid-1950s with some success. Even in terms of transport and helicopter support to army operations, the balance was in favour of India – this would go on to play a significant role in supporting the Forward Policy and providing casualty evacuation in hostile battle conditions as the conflict progressed. *Unsung and Unheard: The IAF in the 1962 Conflict with China* is a well-researched book by an IAF stalwart, Air Marshal Bharat Kumar (retd), which highlights the exploits of the IAF during the conflict.[19] The title of the book pretty much sums up how the IAF was seen to have contributed to the conflict. Why offensive air power was not used despite the clear superiority of the IAF and the availability of bases and aircraft that had the radius of action to operate in the areas of operation is a question that has perplexed many till now. Tezpur, Chabua and Jorhat in the east, and Adampur and Ambala in the west were airfields which were ready for operations. Had the situation demanded, Srinagar airbase could have been activated for fighter operations after overruling the UN restrictions that had been placed after the 1948 UN-brokered ceasefire following the first India–Pakistan war over Kashmir. The reasons for not exploiting the IAF have stirred a widespread debate[20] and have been widely criticized as a strategic blunder.

For now let us merely take a look at the availability of aircraft for operational exploitation on both sides and the early attempts by the IAF to provide some inputs regarding the Chinese build-up, particularly in Aksai Chin. The first comprehensive aerial reconnaissance mission in the region was undertaken by Canberra fighter-bomber-reconnaissance aircraft of No. 106 Squadron as late as on 14 December 1959,[21] nearly two years after it came to be known to the Indian government that China had built a road through Aksai Chin. Routing via Daulat Beg Oldi and braving bad weather, the single aircraft mission brought back clear pictures of the Tibet–Xinjiang highway, which were seen with great interest by the PM himself. Surprisingly, no mention of any significant military build-up towards the west was made and it could be conjectured that either bad weather prevented it or the aircrew were not briefed to look for any other target systems in the absence of any hard intelligence. In a telephonic conversation with ninety-two-year-old Air Marshal Randhir Singh, who was commanding 106 Squadron during the tumultuous period of 1959–62, he revealed to the author that he and his flight commander, Squadron Leader Nath, carried out a number of intrusive missions into Aksai Chin and across the McMahon Line in NEFA, bringing back valuable information about troop deployments and the build-up of forces. Sadly, not much of the information was taken seriously by the powers that be.[22] Air Marshal Raghavendran, who retired as the vice chief of the IAF in 1988, was at the time on the operational staff of Operational Command, which later became Western Air Command. He recollects in his book that Squadron Leader Jaggi Nath, a close friend of his and 'the bravest of the brave Canberra pilots',[23] brought back highly incriminatory photographs of thousands of Chinese troops, fortifications and vehicles in the open. While the Chinese protested at these intrusive missions, India continued to vehemently deny these instead of placing the photographic evidence before the Chinese, or even releasing it to the international media to highlight China's expansionist designs.[24]

After the clashes at Kongka La and Longju in 1959 and the subsequent ceasefire, there was a strange disconnect between the ground and air situation. While the Indian Army was asked to continue to establish posts in disputed territory as a means of outflanking Chinese positions, the IAF was restricted from flying fighter and recce missions within 15 miles of the disputed border till December 1961. Even when there were clear signs of a Chinese military build-up, there were no attempts to coerce the Chinese with fighter reconnaissance sorties. It had become too late to reverse the policy paralysis which had crept into the Indian government with regards to its ability to call China's bluff with the ill-fated Forward Policy.

With over twenty-two combat squadrons and around 500 aircraft available, the IAF in mid-1962 comprised the relatively modern Hunter Mk-56 fighter-bomber aircraft and Gnat interceptor aircraft, older but still potent French-built ground attack aircraft like the Mystere and Toofani, Canberra bomber-reconnaissance jets, and the venerable Vampire trainer-cum-ground-attack jet.[25] Of these, a total of approximately two squadrons each of Toofani and Vampire jets and a detachment of Canberra aircraft were spread amongst the airfields of Tezpur, Chabua and Bagdogra and would have been available for operations in the NEFA sector.[26] Approximately fifteen combat squadrons including the Hunter Mk-56 were available in northern

India at the airfields of Agra, Palam, Adampur, Ambala and Halwara.[27] The remainder of the squadrons were deployed at Pune and Kalaikunda. The IAF deployment clearly indicated a Pakistan-centric deployment, and no major changes barring a few detachments were made even after the conflict started. Air Marshal Vinod Patney, the Indian Air Force's most highly decorated airman, and among its cerebral and operationally proficient commanders, was posted to a Toofani squadron (29 Squadron) at Tezpur during the 1962 conflict. He recollects being quite familiar with the valleys of NEFA where they would regularly train for close air support (CAS) and interdiction missions. He recollects that joint structures for CAS with 33 Corps were in place in the form of a tactical air centre (TAC) with forward air controllers. While he agrees that effective CAS may have been a difficult proposition once the forces were engaged in a close-contact battle, particularly in the narrow valleys of Namka Chu and Tawang, he maintains that the IAF could have created havoc among the massed Chinese troop concentrations and logistics lines on the Tibetan side north of the Thagla Ridge. This, he added was because the terrain on that side was devoid of the dense vegetation that marked the Indian side of the McMahon Line.[28] He reiterated that the terrain in Ladakh was ideal for both CAS and interdiction and that the relatively modern IAF Hunters could have provided effective CAS with the Canberra bombers chipping in with interdiction missions. He also added that the older Toofanis and Mysteres with external tanks fitted could also have provided offensive air support from airfields like Adampur, Ambala and Halwara.[29]

Ranged against a professionally well-trained IAF fighter force, the offensive element of the PLAAF was a numerically superior force of obsolete platforms like the MiG-15/17, MiG-19 and medium-range IL-28 bombers, most of which were deployed against Taiwan. In the absence of any sound operational assessment of the PLAAF by the IAF,[30] the Government of India relied on inputs from the IB to calibrate its decision whether or not to use offensive air power against China. Contrary to IB reports, which indicated that the PLAAF had acquired the MiG-21, considered at that time to be amongst the most sophisticated fighters in the world, Wing Commander Asher Lee, a British air power analyst, reported in 1963 that this was grossly incorrect.[31] The IB also went on to caution the Government of India that the use of offensive air power may result in the PLAAF attacking Indian cities like Calcutta and the danger of India not being able to occupy the 'moral high ground' in case of a protracted conflict. No cognizance was taken of the fact that PLAAF aircraft could reach targets in India only if they operated from airfields in Tibet with the high altitudes imposing severe restrictions on their weapon-carrying capacity.[32] On the other hand, IAF fighters would have had the advantage of operating with full weapon loads from airfields in the plains of Assam and Punjab. The IAF leadership was completely left out of the decision-making loop and, except for being asked for one rather tepid operational assessment, Nehru and Krishna Menon decided to go with the defensive assessment of Blackett (see Chapter 7).[33] Reluctance to use offensive air power would cost India dearly as the war progressed.

As it turned out to be, the helicopter and transport aircrew of the IAF turned out to be the heroes of the 1962 war. Even with modern aircraft and state-of-the-art avionics and navigation aids, the weather and terrain in the Ladakh and Arunachal sectors still pose tremendous operational challenges to the IAF. Imagine the challenges in 1962! The IAF's transport fleet had acquitted itself superbly in the 1947–48 conflict with Pakistan, particularly in the sustenance of the Poonch garrison and the relief of Leh. In the years that followed, this capability was sustained as the Leh and Kargil garrisons had to be supported in the winter months by air. However, air activity in NEFA was restricted as there was not much requirement for air maintenance till the Forward Policy came into being. When the crisis snowballed in September 1962, the IAF had ten squadrons of operational transport aircraft divided almost equally between the Western and Eastern Sectors with a number of detachments operating in the east to support the Forward Policy in NEFA. Of the 200-plus aircraft, the mainstays were still the evergreen Dakota (2 ton payload) and the recently acquired C-119 G Packet aircraft (6 ton payload), few of which were modified with a jet pack to support high-altitude operations in 1961.[34] Complementing these war-horses was a squadron of the newly acquired An-12 (10 to 12 ton payload), two squadrons of DH-3C Otter light transport aircraft, which were used for operations from remote airstrips like Walong in NEFA and in narrow valleys. A few Super Constellation aircraft were available for VIP, communication and troop-carrying duties. All these aircraft would perform well beyond expectations during the conflict. The PLAAF transport aircraft fleet was reasonably large and known to have extensively supported the Chinese invasion of Tibet in 1950–52.[35] However, according to British intelligence and American reports, it numbered only around 200 usable aircraft in 1962, comprising a mix of ageing Soviet platforms like the An-2 and IL-12/14/18. Unlike India, China rightly realized that the only way of sustaining operations in Ladakh, Aksai Chin and Tibet was by creating a network of roads, tracks and railway lines, and not relying on air maintenance. This was to prove decisive in the long run.

While China hardly had any helicopters worth mentioning, the IAF had built up a fairly diverse mix of helicopters to support operations in jungle and high-altitude terrain. The fifty-odd helicopters comprised Russian built Mi-4s, which were inducted between 1961 and 1962, and the older American Bell 47G-3, and S-55s.[36] While 107 Helicopter Unit (HU) with Mi-4s was the sole unit in Ladakh, 105 and 110 HUs supported the Tawang and Walong Sectors in the east.[37] Aircrew proficiency was high and the rotary wing fleet took on the onerous responsibility of sustaining the number of forward picquets in NEFA and Ladakh in the absence of roads and tracks. They were, as one young company commander mentioned, 'angels from the sky'. Their exploits would unfold as the defensive battle in both sectors turned into fragmented retreats. The helicopter boys of the IAF would fly tirelessly through the war as they carried out hundreds of casualty evacuation missions and even searched for stragglers as they retreated through the jungles of Bhutan.

Sparring and Probing

As a military historian I have always wondered how the Indian armed forces, with all their battle experience of the preceding decades, allowed themselves to be caught in a state of virtual stupor when the final assault came. Many questions come rushing to my mind. Where was the intelligence regarding the gradual build-up of forces in Tibet and Aksai Chin? Did the Indian Army not realize what the preponderance of artillery resources meant in terms of the psychological shock it could create amongst its widely dispersed platoon- and company-sized localities, many of which were surrounded by Chinese positions? Why was the IAF leadership diffident about its own offensive capability, and why did it not confidently push to interdict the enemy as it built up forces in Tibet? Many distinguished soldiers and airmen have attempted to answer these questions and many more will try and do the same with the detached and dispassionate countenance of a modern-day military historian.

As diplomatic attempts to resolve the crisis faded in 1962, the Government of India continued with its ill-fated policy of pushing forward towards the McMahon Line in the east and into north-eastern Ladakh. It believed, rather naively, that China's military build-up was mere coercion and that its bluff could be called. Nothing was further from the truth if China's operational discourse of the time is to be believed.

In an objective and well-researched chapter written in a book published in 2005 by the Stanford University Press, *New Approaches to the Study of Chinese Foreign Policy,* written by Robert S. Ross and Alastair Iain Johnston, John Garver has rightly identified three events of 1962 that marked the end of diplomacy and the beginning of serious military action from a Chinese perspective. The first was a meeting at Geneva between the Indian defence minister, V.K. Krishna Menon, and Marshal Chen Yi, China's foreign minister and one of its most distinguished generals. While Krishna Menon's disdain for the military had become common knowledge, his condescending brushing off of Chen Yi when the latter asked as to what India was doing about the border problem convinced Marshal Chen that India was itching for a fight. Chen thereafter convinced Premier Zhou Enlai, the main interlocutor in the border talks with India, that Chairman Mao must be apprised about the deteriorating situation and India's stand. Irritated with India's granting asylum to the Dalai Lama and his huge entourage of almost 1,00,000 refugees,[38] and frustrated with not being able to make any diplomatic headway on Aksai Chin, it is widely believed that Mao took the decision to go to war some time in late July 1962. What he also did was to lay down a set of restrictive Rules of Engagement (ROE), which he believed would still give India a long rope and realize the folly of going to war.[39]

The second incident was an ambitious and successful attempt by a hardy Indian Army platoon from 1/8 Gorkha Regiment to advance down the Galwan Valley of Ladakh in July 1962 and outflank the Chinese position at the head of the valley and isolate it from the important Chinese post of Samzungling.[40] This operation was supported and maintained by IAF helicopters for over two months despite the Gorkha platoon being surrounded by a Chinese battalion (nine platoons). The Gorkhas were audaciously replaced by two platoons of 5 Jat Regiment in another helicopter lift in early October.[41] Both the Jat platoons were subsequently wiped out during the initial assault on 20 October.

In September 1962, the third incident that is said to have precipitated the final Chinese assault was a face-off below the Thagla Ridge in the Tawang sector of NEFA at an unviable post, the Dhola Post, on the south bank of the Namka Chu. Manned since June that year by a platoon of poorly equipped Assam Rifles despite objections from China paramilitary was surrounded by over 1,000 Chinese troops in mid-September as a demonstration of their willingness to use force to evict a small Indian force from what they considered as disputed territory.[42] In response, a poorly stocked and undermanned Indian brigade (7 Brigade under Brigadier J.P. Dalvi) was moved to occupy loosely strung out, underprepared and tactically untenable positions along the Namka Chu. Thagla Ridge was located to the north of the watershed and was publicly declared by the Government of India as the de facto northern limit of the McMahon Line as against the Chinese claim that the boundary lay along the Namka Chu. Seeing that the Chinese had occupied the ridge in strength the Indian Army was asked to launch Operation Leghorn to evict them from the ridge. Despite stiff opposition to the idea that the Namka Chu rivulet be the forward line of defence and launch pad for an offensive on the Thagla ridge from Umrao Singh, the GOC of 33 Corps, New Delhi insisted that he move a brigade forward.[43] Umrao, who wanted his defences to be concentrated around Tawang, reluctantly ordered 7 Brigade to march on foot to the Namka Chu. Led by 9 Punjab Regiment, this move finally convinced the Chinese that war was inevitable.

Speaking to his top commanders on 6 October 1962, Mao is reported to have said confidently and rather contemptuously when he referred to Nehru:

> We fought a war with old Chiang. We fought a war with Japan and with America. With none of these did we fear. And in each case, we won. Now the Indians want to fight a war with us. Naturally we don't have fear. Since Nehru sticks his head out and insists on us fighting

> him, for us not to fight him would not be friendly enough. Courtesy emphasizes reciprocity.[44]

In a subsequent meeting with his top political and military leadership that reflected a surprisingly participative and inclusive style of decision making, Mao said:

> If we fight, what should be our method? What should the war look like? Please everyone contribute your thoughts on these policy issues.[45]

Unfortunately, no such operational brainstorming took place on the Indian side with Nehru and Krishna Menon deciding military strategy with Kaul acting as their hatchet man. This broadly summed up the operational scenario in mid-October with the Chinese rapidly building up a division to overrun an undermanned and tired 7 Brigade.

Shock and Despair: The Initial Assault

Collapse in the East

While India insists that the initial Chinese move from the Thagla Ridge towards the Namka Chu forced India to move north of the Namka Chu and occupy defensive positions,[46] Chinese claims point at an Indian offensive that precipitated the outbreak of preliminary hostilities on 9 and 10 October.[47] The bottom line was that after a smaller Indian force of approximately 50–60 troops from 9 Punjab were bested in an intense firefight by over 1,000 Chinese troops in early October 1962 as they attempted to outflank Chinese positions by trying to dominate a few heights around Thagla Ridge,[48] the Chinese realized that despite the excellent performance of the Indian troops in this battle, they held both the tactical and numerical advantage. This convinced them that the time was ripe to achieve their initial operational objective – the capture of Tawang and annihilation of India's forward defences before more defences sprang up.

Despite reports now that the Chinese had built up almost two divisions opposite the Tawang sector and that it would be prudent to pull back the Namka Chu forces to Tawang, there was complete paralysis between 11 and 20 October as Umrao was replaced by Kaul as corps commander of a newly designated 4 Corps. The last straw was when Lieutenant General

Kaul, the corps commander, was evacuated to Delhi on 17 October after suffering a bout of high-altitude sickness. He was replaced overnight as corps commander by a battle-hardened Lieutenant General Harbaksh Singh, but it was too late to change the ground situation in the face of a rapid Chinese build-up opposite most defensive positions. Seeing that Indian forces were holding firm at over four positions along the Namka Chu, hell broke loose on 20 October as all positions of 7 Brigade were subjected to a relentless artillery barrage by a combination of 82 mm and 120 mm mortars, and 75 mm recoilless guns[49] before the infantry assault as part of China's 'self-defensive counter-attack'.[50] This was possible because all Indian posts had been accurately registered[51] by the Chinese during the preceding days. In response, 7 Brigade had just one troop (four guns) of 4.2" mortars and three 75 mm field guns, which had been hastily airdropped with barely 200 rounds of ammunition to equip a recently inducted 17 Para Field Regiment.[52] Two of the four battalions of 7 Brigade (2 Rajput and 1/9 Gorkha) were decimated within hours of the attack. Contrary to widespread reports, 7 Brigade did not just fold up – both the Rajputs and Gorkhas fought heroically before being overwhelmed by vastly superior forces.[53]

When a battalion loses four officers, seven JCOs and 266 men in fighting within a few hours, when eighty-one are wounded and 171 are taken prisoner in close-quarter fighting,[54] you cannot say 'why didn't the battalion fight to the last man and last round' – that is sheer ignorance of battle. I have gone through the unit histories of some of the battalions that formed part of 7 Brigade – they fought well and followed orders. It is just that the situation overwhelmed them! The other two battalions of the brigade (4 Grenadiers and 9 Punjab) too suffered heavy casualties, but managed to initially withdraw southwards to reinforce Tawang following an inexplicable hesitation on the part of the opposing Chinese commander to press home with his attack.[55] However, when Chinese forces managed to outflank them and sped towards Tawang, these battalions were forced to head westwards into Bhutan, effectively keeping them out of the battle.[56] With winter having set in, these units suffered heavy casualties along the way. Brigadier Dalvi and over 200 personnel of the brigade had to suffer the ignominy of being POWs. Within a span of twelve hours, the Chinese had crashed through India's forward defences and were poised to capture Zimithang and Tawang.[57]

By 22 October Chinese forces had advanced along two axes from the Namka Chu area towards Tawang with a division leading and another in reserve. Unlike the speedy capitulation of the Namka Chu defences, the Chinese faced stiff resistance on the third axis that they had opened through Bumla Pass. Subedar Joginder Singh of the battle-hardened 1 Sikh Regiment was commanding a platoon well ahead of Tawang on the approach from Bumla Pass, which was defended by just a section of Assam Rifles. It was only a matter of time before the post was overwhelmed and Subedar Joginder's platoon soon came under fire from an entire Chinese brigade. Fortuitously, Joginder had some artillery support and held off the attack for over eight hours, inflicting heavy casualties on the enemy – the Chinese lost over 300 troops in this action before overwhelming the Sikh platoon. Subedar Joginder Singh would live to tell his story and go on to be awarded the only Param Vir Chakra on the Eastern Front – such was the ferocity of his rearguard action ahead of Tawang.[58]

Realizing that the defence of Tawang was untenable, Major General Niranjan Prasad, the GOC of 4 Division, suggested that all forces withdraw to Bomdila for a rearguard stand; he was overruled and asked to prepare defences at Sela to stop the Chinese advance midway between Tawang and Bomdila. Tawang was vacated on 23 October and fell to the Chinese the next day. The Chinese halted their offensive on 25 October and offered a ceasefire and withdrawal to 20 km from the LAC. This was rejected by India purely due to political compulsions.[59] The disaster at Tawang resulted in the removal of Krishna Menon[60] and widespread leadership changes at the operational level.

While the main battle in Kameng revolved around Tawang, the Chinese launched a subsidiary thrust on 22 October in the Walong sector, which lay close to the trijunction of India, Burma and China. In response to repeated incursions into the Lohit Valley by Chinese patrols, the lone Assam Rifles platoon was reinforced in March 1962 by a battle-tested 6 Kumaon Regiment, and in early October 1962, by 4 Sikh Regiment.[61] After tasting spectacular success in the Tawang sector, the Chinese were in for a nasty riposte in this area during the first phase of the battle till 27 October as the Kumaonis and Sikhs were positioned at tactically well-thought-out positions. Though most positions had to finally withdraw in the face of withering MMG and mortar assaults, the Kumaonis took a heavy toll on the advancing Chinese by creating killing grounds as they withdrew. Rattled by this response, the Chinese rapidly built up their forces to over a division for the second phase of the operation.

The Aviators Pitch In

While the IAF's transport aircraft fleet tried its best to sustain 4 Division in its defensive build-up by tirelessly flying supply drop missions, the nature of the terrain with narrow valley floors and steep slopes, proximity of the two opposing forces and difficult weather conditions made it impossible to ensure that all the dropped supplies reached the units.[62] Air Marshal Bharat Kumar describes these dropping zones with great clarity:

> The dropping zone selected for Operation Leghorn besides Lumpu was Tsangdhar. The latter was just southeast of the tri-junction formed by India-Bhutan-Tibet border, and south of the Thagla ridge. The dropping zone was a small, flat but sloping piece of ground, the only one available on the narrow southern slope of the Namka Chu Valley running from west to east. The dropping zone was perched on a steep slope at a height of 14,500 feet with a 16,000–17,000 ft ridge to the south and an almost vertical drop of about 3,000 to 4,000 ft to the north into the narrow deep gorge of Namka Chu and our defensive positions.[63]

Another challenge, however, was faced by the newly formed 110 Helicopter Unit (HU) at Tezpur. Partially equipped with the recently acquired Mi-4 from the USSR, it was entrusted in late October with the difficult task of lifting light field artillery pieces and landing them at different locations on hastily prepared helipads in the Namka Chu area to support the impending offensive on the Thagla Ridge.[64] After one aborted attempt, the exercise was abandoned as being too risky. In early October, Mi-4s also started carrying out visual and photo reconnaissance missions in the Tawang sector and reported heavy troop build-up across the Thagla Ridge. These inputs seem to have been ignored! Between 20 and 23 October, Mi-4s of 110 HU, and Bell-47s and Sikorsky S-55s of 105 HU carried out numerous casualty evacuation sorties by day and night from Tsangdhar and Lumpu helipads as the Indian forces were overwhelmed by the advancing Chinese. They followed this up with numerous evacuation sorties from Tawang prior to its imminent capitulation.

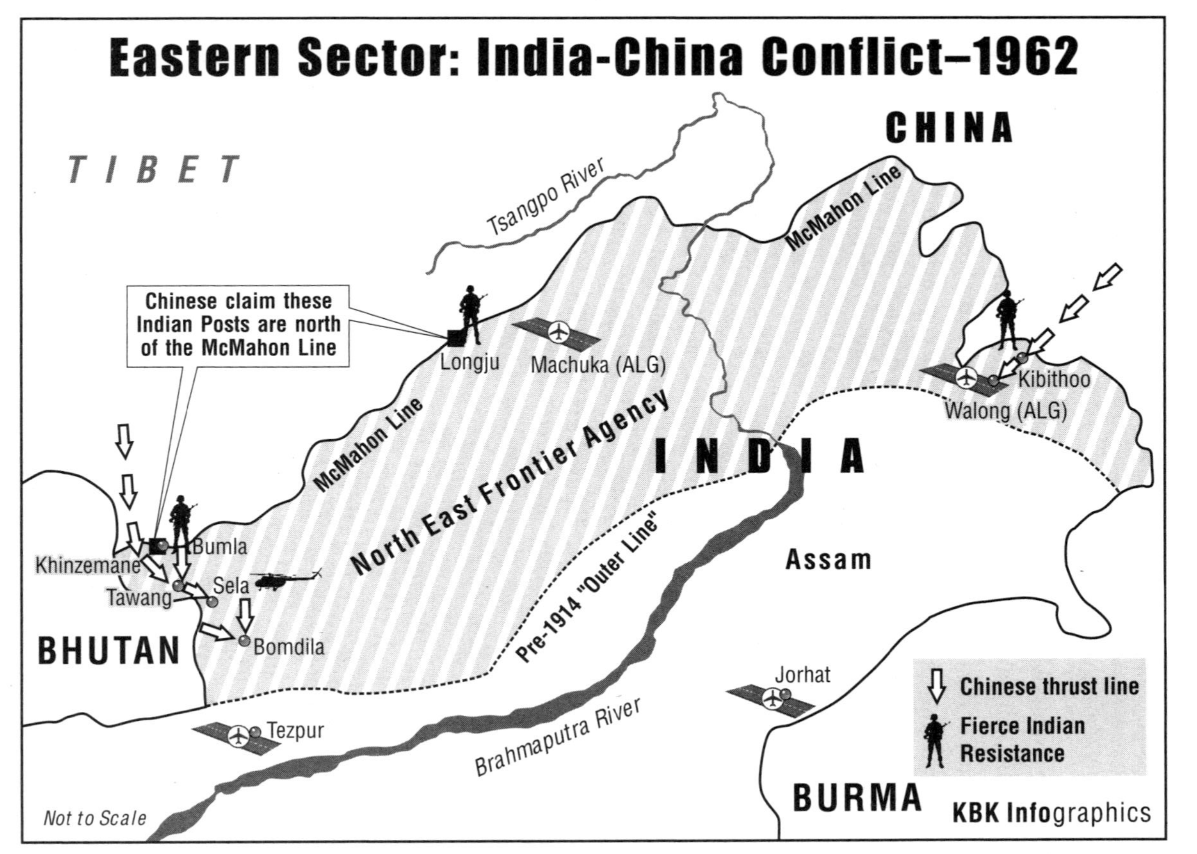
Eastern Sector: India-China Conflict–1962
TIBET
CHINA
Tsangpo River
McMahon Line
McMahon Line
Chinese claim these Indian Posts are north of the McMahon Line
Longju
Machuka (ALG)
Kibithoo
Walong (ALG)
North East Frontier Agency
INDIA
Bumla
Khinzemane
Sela
Tawang
Bomdila
BHUTAN
Pre-1914 "Outer Line"
Assam
Jorhat
Tezpur
Brahmaputra River
Chinese thrust line
Fierce Indian Resistance
BURMA
KBK Infographics
Not to Scale

Squadron Leader Arnold Williams of 105 HU was continuously involved in flying risky casevac missions from early October till 20 October when there were continuous skirmishes below the Thagla Ridge. He even undertook a daring night evacuation of a critically wounded soldier from Tsangdhar helipad despite not having any night-flying capability and using only torchlight to aid him. Tsangdhar helipad and dropping zone was the closest to 7 Brigade's location and on the morning of 20 October, one Bell-47 helicopter of 105 HU was taken by surprise when it landed there for a scheduled sortie, little knowing that the Chinese had already overrun the area. Its crew comprising Squadron Leader Sehgal and an army major from the Signal Corps were killed and the helicopter was badly damaged. Another helicopter with Williams as captain which had come to search for Sehgal when he lost radio contact was also shot at; the pilots crash-landed and escaped to safety through the jungles to fly another day.[65] Williams went on to carry out numerous search and casevac missions in the subsequent weeks and was awarded a Vir Chakra at the end of the war.

Further east, in the Walong sector too, the IAF flew tirelessly in support of the forward deployment of Assam Rifles, 6 Kumaon and 4 Sikh. Luckily for the Indian Army, Walong had an active ALG (Advanced Landing Ground) of around 3,000 to 4,000 feet from which Dakotas and DH-3C Otters operated. This was how 4 Sikh was airlifted into Walong in early October so that 6 Kumaon could move up to areas like Kibithoo closer to the McMahon Line. A few other ALGs in the area at Machuka, Tuting, Along and Teju were also used to build and sustain forces. However, this was not enough. A detachment of Mi-4s from 110 HU were positioned at Walong and during the height of hostilities lifted almost 16,000 pounds of load daily for the forward locations of Kibithoo and other posts. Better stocked than the battalions at Namka Chu, 6 Kumaon, 4 Sikh and the Assam Rifles were able to acquit themselves better during the first phase of the NEFA battle in the face of a numerically superior enemy.[66]

Ladakh Erupts

From a situation of near parity in 1960, the Chinese had gradually built up forces in eastern Ladakh by September 1962 to reach a 3:1 superiority in both infantry and artillery resources. There were also reports that the Chinese had inducted tanks and cavalry to exploit some of the open spaces on the Ladakh plateau.[67] The cat-and-mouse game in Ladakh had gone on for too long and as Chinese troops of the 54th Division rolled down the slopes of the Thagla Ridge in NEFA, the guns opened up in all the sectors of Ladakh on 20 October 1962. The initial areas of interest for China in Ladakh were chosen carefully and comprised the general area around Daulat Beg Oldi airfield, the Chang Chenmo and Galwan valleys, the Spangur gap between the Pangong Tso and Spangur lakes that would lead to Chushul airfield complex, and Demchok further south. Looking at the line of advance, it was clear that the Chinese wanted greater strategic depth for the Aksai Chin highway than what was available. From the operations conducted in the first phase it was clear that the Chinese had two major objectives.

The first was to annihilate all the forward posts that India had established, and once that was achieved, to make inroads towards Daulat Beg Oldi airfield and the Spangur Gap so as to threaten Chushul airfield. Of the two objectives, it was clear from the build-up of forces that Chushul was the primary one. A relatively lightweight J&K militia battalion along with the 5 Jat Regiment was spread across 320 km from Daulat Beg Oldi in the north through the Chip Chap and Galwan valleys, to Chushul in the south.[68] Along with a company of 1/8 Gorkha Rifles, which occupied precarious posts on the north bank of the Pangang Tso lake called the Sirijap complex, they bore the brunt of the initial Chinese assault. While the J&K militia battalion was wiped out along with the Galwan post of 5 Jats by almost a regiment of Chinese troops within hours of the initial assault, a company of 5 Jat at Daulat Beg Oldi fought valiantly in a continuous rearguard action for eighteen days as it withdrew across the frozen Shyok river, ably supported by Bell-47 and Mi-4 helicopters of 107 HU. More than 100 troops were evacuated to a forward base hospital in what can easily be considered as one of the most difficult high-altitude casualty evacuation operations ever conducted,[69] an operation that would only be rivalled twenty-two years later when the Indian Army made inroads into the Siachen Glacier. Many of these troops would be fit for action in the second phase of the conflict.

Compared to the air effort in the eastern sector, which was fraught with danger in terms of the fickle weather and suboptimal dropping zones, the situation in Ladakh was a little better despite the higher altitudes of operation. With airfields at Leh, Daulat Beg Oldi, Fukche, Thoise and Chushul acting as feeder nodes to induct and sustain troops, the 'rate of flow' of men and material was quite good during 1961–62. However, the Government of India frittered away these advantages by increasing the number of forward posts and stretching the air effort to such an extent that the moment resources from the Western Sector were diverted to the east, the build-up in Ladakh suffered. Without taking anything away from the workhorse of the IAF, the C-119G Packet, the venerable Dakota and the IL-14, all of which performed magnificently, the single biggest 'air factor' in the west was the newly inducted An-12 with its payload of 9 tons. The An-12 squadron (44 Squadron) was not aware that the Chinese had commenced their attack in the Daulat Beg Oldi sector at 11 p.m. on 19 October and on the morning of 20 October when Squadron Leader Chandan Singh, while attempting to land at Daulat Beg Oldi, was hit by ground fire and had to return to Chandigarh with nineteen hits on his aircraft.[70] He was soon back in the thick of action and was decorated with the Vir Chakra for his courage in that and many other missions through the conflict. Other aircraft including Packets, however, continued on their dropping missions in the area as Indian posts were overwhelmed one by one. On 21 October, it was one of the Packet aircraft on a forward dropping mission that reported a long trail of Indian troops (5 Jat Regiment) trudging across the Shyok river and directed the Mi-4s of 107 HU to commence their stupendous casevac operation. With fighting in the southern sector of Demchok not as intense as elsewhere, by the end of the first phase on 27 October, Chinese troops had achieved their objectives and paused for the final push towards Chushul airfield as Mao offered a ceasefire to India. The shrill cacophony of domestic politics and a lack of realization on the part of both the military and the strategic establishment that there was no way that India could claw back into the conflict meant that there was no way that India could accept a ceasefire on China's terms.

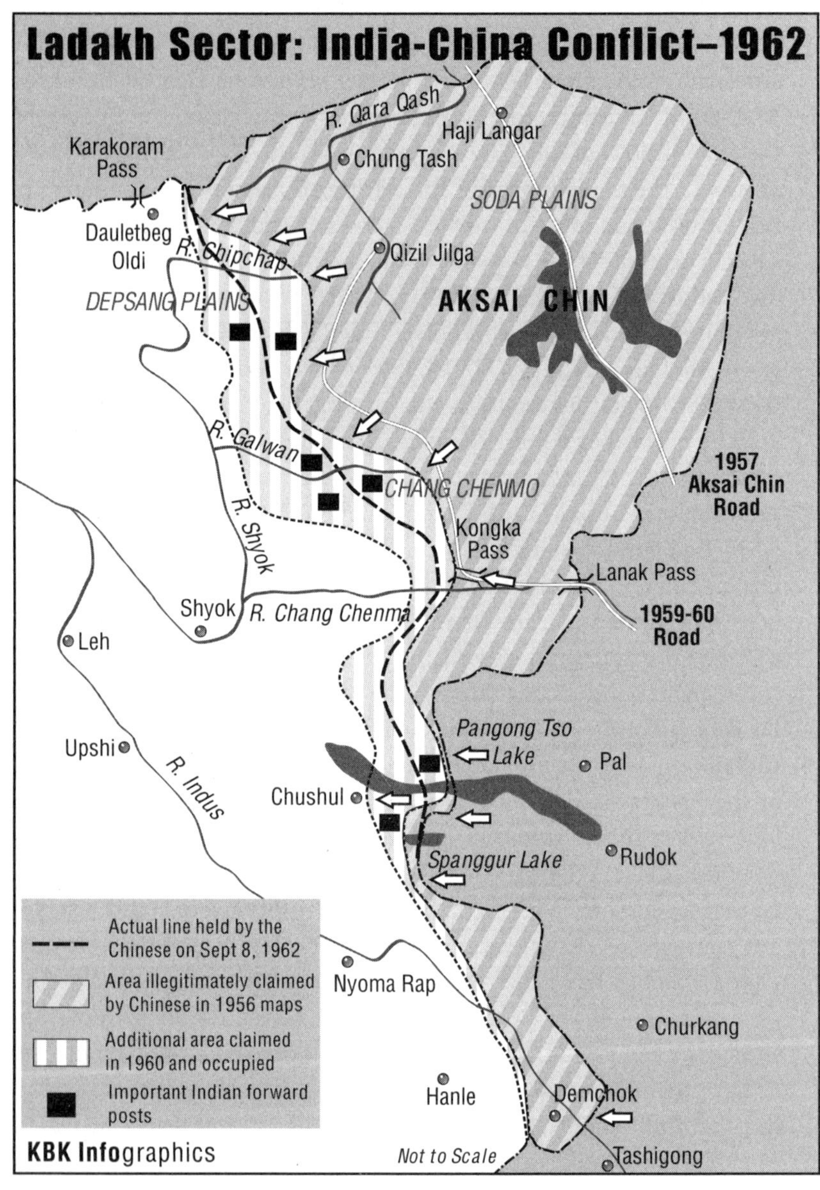
Ladakh Sector: India-China Conflict–1962
R. Qara Qash
Haji Langar
Karakoram Pass
Chung Tash
SODA PLAINS
Dauletbeg Oldi
R. Chipchap
Qizil Jilga
DEPSANG PLAINS
AKSAI CHIN
R. Galwan
CHANG CHENMO
R. Shyok
1957 Aksai Chin Road
Kongka Pass
Lanak Pass
Shyok
R. Chang Chenma
1959-60 Road
Leh
Pangong Tso Lake
Pal
Upshi
R. Indus
Chushul
Spanggur Lake
Rudok
Actual line held by the Chinese on Sept 8, 1962
Area illegitimately claimed by Chinese in 1956 maps
Additional area claimed in 1960 and occupied
Important Indian forward posts
Nyoma Rap
Churkang
Hanle
Demchok
KBK Infographics
Not to Scale
Tashigong

17

DEFEAT

Both sides bear onus for the 1962 war, China for misconstruing India's Tibetan policies, and India for pursuing a confrontationist policy on the border.[1]

– John Garver

Collapse of Sela

The Namka Chu debacle, collapse of Tawang and disintegration of all the forward posts in Ladakh sent the Indian political leadership into a state of shock – the situation was akin to trying to prop up a pack of falling cards. V.K. Krishna Menon was relieved of the charge of the Ministry of Defence, and Army HQ took complete charge of operations, using the lull in the battle to rush troops and new commanders to reinforce and direct the battles at Sela, Bomdila and Dirang garrisons. Approximately three battalions of infantry and some supporting artillery had managed to retreat from Tawang, and despite being demoralized and exhausted, were placed at vital areas ahead of the Sela defences. Under the command of Brigadier Hoshiar Singh, a war hero from the 1947–48 conflict, 62 Brigade was at the vanguard of the defensive battle, supported by 65, 48 and 67 Infantry Brigades, which were spread out between Sela, Dirang Dzong, Bomdila and Rupa.[2] A hastily put together artillery brigade and a squadron of tanks were rushed in to support the Bomdila garrison. All these forces were under a reorganized and beefed up 4 Division under the command of Major General A.S. Pathania, who had replaced

Niranjan Prasad even though Niranjan was hardly responsible for what had happened till then. In the absence of Corps Commander B.M. Kaul, who was recovering from the ill effects of high-altitude sickness and stress in Delhi, Lieutenant General Harbaksh Singh assumed temporary command of IV Corps at Tezpur. Squadron Leader Gulati clearly remembers having flown Kaul to Delhi as 7 Brigade was facing the heat at Namka Chu and recalls that he displayed no signs of high-altitude sickness or urgency to get to Delhi as he stopped at Dum Dum airport at Calcutta to meet a senior officer from Eastern Command HQ before heading for Delhi. Gulati reminisces, 'Kaul had seen the writing on the wall and had left the battle scene before it got too late.' He was right too as Kaul is said to have remarked when he witnessed the firefight between 9 Punjab and the Chinese on 10 October, 'Oh my God, you are right, they mean business.'[3] Kaul could have gone into the history books as a courageous general had he taken the decision to ask 7 Brigade to withdraw to Tawang instead of ordering them to hold fast along the south bank of the Namka Chu while he himself fled the battlefield. Gulati adds cynically, 'Kaul was met at Palam by his wife and daughter and whisked away, not to the hospital, but to his residence at Akbar Road, where he spent the entire period of convalescence[4] before returning to Tezpur for the second phase of the battle despite Harbaksh Singh having done a fair job as his replacement.'

Having built up its forces to three divisions,[5] the PLA realized that there was immense potential to outflank the defences at Sela and go for the jugular in terms of attacking the divisional headquarters at Dirang Zong and the rear objective of Bomdila to threaten Tezpur at the earliest. It employed two divisions for these outflanking manoeuvres and kept one division in reserve should the Sela garrison regroup. This was not to be and the division remained largely unused. Brigadier Hoshiar Singh fought the tactical battle at Sela well with his covering battalions causing significant attrition and repeatedly beating back Chinese attacks on 17 November, the day when the second phase of the battle commenced. One of the three battalions that had withdrawn from Tawang, namely, 4 Garhwal Rifles, covered itself with glory during the defence of Sela under the inspirational leadership of Lieutenant Colonel B.M. Bhattacharjea.

That the officers led from the front is reflected by the fact that the CO and two second lieutenants were decorated with the Maha Vir Chakra (MVC) and Vir Chakra (VrC) respectively along with Rifleman Jaswant Singh, who was posthumously decorated with an MVC, and five others with the VrC.[6] However, on the night of 17 November, even while his forces were offering stiff resistance to stall the Chinese advance, 62 Brigade was ordered by the divisional commander, Major General Pathania, to fall back to Dirang and Bomdila, where it was hoped that the final battle order would be given. Hoshiar had no intention of withdrawing from Sela and had motivated his troops to fight to the last man and last bullet, but with only less than a brigade left after the initial battle, he had little choice but to follow orders.

In hindsight, the Chinese had thought out their tactics well and even if the Sela garrison had held out, it would have been bypassed from both the east and west and isolated. As it happened, the Sela garrison withdrew right into Chinese forces and suffered heavy attrition with hundreds killed during the retreat, including Brigade Commander Hoshiar Singh, who died in a fierce firefight. He was the senior-most Indian officer to lay down his life during the India–China conflict. After the collapse of Sela, the bruised Indian Army only offered token resistance at Dirang Zong and Bomdila as 11 Division of the PLA comprising 32 and 33 Regiments of the PLA advanced by 19 November to Chakoo, barely 120 km from the strategically important town of Tezpur in the plains of north Assam. According to authentic Chinese reports analysed by Major General Datta, the PLA was surprised at the lack of resistance at Dirang Zong and Bomdila by what turned out to be reasonably strong Indian Army formations including artillery and tanks.[7] Brigadier Gurbux Singh, the brigade commander of 48 Brigade, which was tasked with the defence of Bomdila, attributes its collapse to the pulling out of forces by the divisional commander to occupy company-sized defensive positions at dispersed locations around the fortress instead of holding it in strength. While one or two positions managed to catch the Chinese by surprise and cause heavy casualties, the rest of the positions were either overwhelmed or bypassed. This marked the end of the sad saga of the disintegration of a well-stocked and well-prepared garrison at Bomdila.

The IAF's transport fleet played a very significant role in the airlift of troops at short notice from the western theatre to the east as Super Constellations and An-12s of 44 Squadron and 12 USAF C-130s[8] swung into action during 28 October to 16 November. The C-130s were sent to India along with ammunition on 2 November in response to a panicky request from the Government of India for all kinds of military assistance that included supersonic fighter aircraft. Airdropping now shifted southwards around Sela Pass during the build-up phase, but the sheer ferocity and speed of the Chinese advance surprised the IAF too because on 17 and 18 November, when pre-planned dropping missions got airborne for Sela and Bomdila, the aircrew found the route full of retreating Indian troops and vehicles converging on to Bomdila from both Sela and Walong. By the afternoon of 20 November the Sela-Bomdila rout was complete, the battle was over and the Chinese declared a ceasefire the same night. Tezpur, the largest town in the area, wore a deserted look as it was believed that the Chinese would have to merely roll down the hills to occupy it. The late B.G. Verghese, one of India's most accomplished journalists and newspaper editors, was one of the two Indian correspondents who stayed on at Tezpur. He recollects with some humour and eloquence:

> The Indian Press had ingloriously departed the previous day, preferring safety to real news coverage. Only two Indians remained in Tezpur, Prem Prakash of Visnews and Reuters, and I, together with nine American and British correspondents. Along with us, wandering around like lost souls, were some 10–15 patients who had been released from the local mental hospital. That was the most eerie night I have ever spent. Tezpur was a ghost town. We patrolled it by moonlight on the alert for any tell-tale sounds. Some stray dogs and alley cats were our only other companions. Around midnight, a transistor with one of our colleagues crackled to life as Peking Radio announced a unilateral ceasefire. Relieved and weary we repaired to our billet at the abandoned Planter's Club whose canned provisions of baked beans, tuna fish and beer (all on the house) had sustained us.[9]

Stubborn Resistance in Walong

After utter confusion regarding which brigade would reinforce Walong sector and where the main fight must be offered,[10] 11 Independent Infantry Brigade under Brigadier N.C. Rawlley finally took charge of the area by early November with three-and-a-half battalions including a fresh one (3/3 Gorkhas). One more battalion (4 Dogra Regiment) would be inducted on 14 November, way too late to have any impact on the battle.[11] Smarting from the initial resistance of the Kumaonis and Sikhs in the first phase, PLA forces continued to probe and engage them during the period of the ceasefire, and their offensive in the second phase commenced on 14 November with over a division against Rawlley's brigade. Despite launching an offensive, both 6 Kumaon and 4 Sikh wilted under the pressure of a division attacking them and the 3/3 Gorkha Regiment, and one company of the Dogra Regiment failed to offer much resistance having been inducted into that area by air a few days earlier without any acclimatization. There was not much that could be done except to resist fiercely, counter-attack wherever possible, which the Kumaonis and Sikhs did with élan and courage, and to fall back when the opposition came with overwhelming fire support and numerical superiority. Of all the units in the sector, 6 Kumaon, which had been pushed forward the most to the areas around Tri-junction and Kibithoo, suffered the maximum casualty as they fought almost to the last man and last bullet as many locations never got orders to withdraw. Rawlley acknowledged their contribution by saying:

> 6th Kumaon at Tri-junction fought and fought and fought till there was nothing left. After this there was eerie silence.[12]

One of the few battalions along with 4 Garhwal which fought unflaggingly through both phases of the conflict, 6 Kumaon won five Vir Chakras for their determined resistance in the Walong sector. Not enough credit has been given to the DH-3C Otter Fleet from 59 Squadron, which operated from Chabua airfield and the ALG at Teju. Had it not been for these aircraft, capable of operating from short strips like those available at Walong, Machuka and Teju, 11 Brigade could not have been inducted so speedily;[13] nor would 6 Kumaon and 4 Sikh been able to retain their fighting potential at forward locations for as long as they did. Not only did the squadron bring in troops, ammunition and supplies into forward ALGs for further supply forward, they also dropped stores around Kibithoo and the trijunction. The aircrew of 59 Squadron were the unsung heroes of Walong.

Resistance at Chushul and Valour at Rezangla

While the main focus of the PLA in Phase I of their Ladakh battle was in the north around Daulat Beg Oldi, Chip Chap and Galwan valleys and the areas around Pangang Tso lake and the Spangur gap, Chushul was the main objective in Phase II. This was so because it offered the greatest potential to be able to threaten Leh, the capital of Ladakh, primarily because of the existing road connectivity between Chushul and Leh. India recognized this threat and frenetic attempts were made to reinforce the defences at Chushul and Leh in the last week of October and early November. Apart from reinforcing 114 Brigade at Chushul, a divisional headquarter (3 Himalayan Division) was raised at Leh and two additional brigades were rushed in to man defences at Leh and Dungti, some 78 km south of Chushul towards Demchok. Thus, the approaches to Leh from the east and south-east were well covered and with the kind of total forces of approximately two divisions that the PLA was intending to bring in, there is no way that Leh appeared to be a military objective considering the preponderance of forces that would be required for the long haul into Leh (Chushul to Leh is about 200 km and Dungti to Chushul is about 70 km). Leh, Chushul and Thoise airfields witnessed hectic activity as An-12s, Packets and Dakotas of the IAF flew tirelessly to supplement the motor companies that plied along the Srinagar–Leh Highway bringing in troops that were positioned along the India–Pakistan Line of Control.

Major General S.V. Thapliyal, who has written the most exhaustive account of the battles in Ladakh and himself commanded a division in Ladakh, knows too well the importance of air transport and air logistics operations in that area. He writes:

> The IAF transport fleet rose to the occasion and flew much beyond its normal capability. The IAF achieved a major feat when An-12s lifted a troop of AMX-13 Tanks to Chushul on 25 October.[14]

On 18 November began the decisive battle for Chushul, and before the heroics of 13 Kumaon are narrated it is only appropriate to spare a thought for 5 Jat Regiment which had, barely two weeks before the battle of Chushul, completed a gruelling withdrawal from the Daulat Beg Oldi sector across the frozen Shyok river to Chushul. This depleted battalion would once again bear the brunt of the Chinese offensive as it was spread over a distance of 30 km without any mutual cover between the company locations. The Gorkhas too fought bravely in this sector. Deployment of 1/8 Gorkha was primarily in two areas – north of Pangang Tso lake in what was called the Sirijap complex, and in the Spangur gap at two locations, prominent among them being an imposing hill feature that would be called Gurung Hill.[15] While the Sirijap complex was overrun in no time despite the heroic resistance led by the company commander of 1/8 Gorkha Rifles, Major Dhan Singh Thapa, with the entire company killed or taken prisoner, the other two companies fought well against a numerically superior enemy with excellent artillery support from 13 Field Regiment. They managed to withdraw to Chushul despite being outflanked by the Chinese, but suffering heavy casualties.

The battle for Chushul followed a predictable pattern of forward locations and covering positions being overrun by a numerically superior force with preponderance of firepower in the form of artillery support. However, the presence of adequate artillery and tanks at the main defences around Chushul covered retreating Indian troops and made the PLA reflect on whether it would be a worthwhile proposition to fight a battle of attrition at Chushul or declare a ceasefire having achieved most of their strategic objectives on both fronts. Having occupied all the critical heights overlooking Chushul airfield, a traditional and conservative Mao wisely chose the latter, declaring a unilateral ceasefire on 20 November.

The Indian Army acquitted itself well in Ladakh and nothing embodies that better than the epic defence of Rezangla, a hill feature overlooking the initial approaches to Chushul, which was defended by a company of 124 men of 13 Kumaon Regiment under Major Shaitan Singh.[16] Beating off repeated infantry assaults, which were preceded by withering rocket and artillery fire, the Kumaonis literally fought to the last man and last bullet with only ten survivors. Cut off completely from the battalion and brigade headquarters as the hastily laid overland field telephone lines were cut during the initial mortar and artillery assault, Shaitan Singh fought on despite being grievously wounded in his arm till he was mowed down by blistering machine gun fire. For his leadership, bravery and raw courage in the face of insurmountable odds, he was awarded the Param Vir Chakra (posthumous), while eight others were awarded Vir Chakras. It remains till today among the most decorated units in battle. On a sombre note, Colonel N.N. Bhatia (retd), who was commissioned into the same regiment, writes about the battles in Ladakh:

> The hardy Chinese troops deployed for action in the high altitudes were from the Tibetan Autonomous Region. Our men from the plains had hardly any high altitude acclimatisation. 13 Kumaon reached Chushul two weeks before the war. Construction of defences in rocky frozen terrain without proper mechanised digging tools was indeed a herculean task.[17]

Standing on the harsh windswept Chushul plains and laying a wreath at the Rezangla memorial in late October 2015 was a surreal, poignant and humbling experience for me. Turning around from the memorial, one is confronted by the three massive hill features of Rezangla, Maggar Hill and Gurung Hill and a huge stretch of black alluvial-like soil that made up the erstwhile improvised landing strip of Chushul. Fully clothed in high-altitude gear, I wondered what superhuman spirit drove the Kumaonis, the Jats and the Gorkhas to resist in the manner they did. What was it that inspired Chandan Singh and the other An-12 pilots to land on a landing strip that was within range of Chinese artillery, albeit during the ceasefire period? Finally, I did spare a thought for the Chinese soldiers, who despite their numerical superiority, had to cope with an equally daunting situation wherein they faced a ferocious enemy who was willing to fight to the very end. The opaqueness of contemporary Chinese military history has prevented us from learning more about what the Chinese thought of their adversaries in eastern Ladakh. I am certain the story of the battle for Chushul inspires India's young soldiers and transport pilots even today.

A less known fact is that soon after the battle of Rezangla and other battles around Chushul were over, 7 Squadron of the IAF was alerted on 26 November 1962 to launch a four-aircraft armed reconnaissance mission in the Chushul area with its latest Hunter fighter aircraft. Commanded by Wing Commander Katre, who was the first IAF pilot to land a Hunter at Leh and later went on to become a highly respected chief of air staff, the mission was directed to investigate reports that the Chinese had violated the LAC in the Chushul area. They were however asked to exercise restraint and not resort to any firing. For Flying Officer Murdeshwar, however, the sortie was an exhilarating experience as he streaked across the icy Shyok river at over 400 knots in a fully loaded Hunter jet. Naturally, the Chinese lodged a complaint![18]

Strategic and Military Lessons

In his brilliant book *The Causes of War*, Geoffrey Blainey, the renowned Australian military historian, highlights the little nuances of fact and fiction associated with the conflict. He writes scathingly:

> In 1962 the most populous nations on the globe, India and China, fought a border war which illustrated the sheer fantasy that so often preceded and accelerated the outbreak of war. In the west it was widely believed that India was the target of Chinese aggression and therefore India's leaders were unlikely to have entered with confidence in a war in which they so soon had to concede defeat. So irrational was their confidence that they decided on the eve of the war to evict Chinese troops from a stretch of border where the Indians were outnumbered by more than five to one, where the Indian guns were inferior, where the Indian supply route was a tortuous pack trail and where the height of the mountains made the breathing difficult and the cold intense for the reinforcements who marched in cotton uniform.[19]

Enough has been written about the inability of India's higher political leadership to orchestrate diplomacy and military power in the face of a rigid and powerful adversary who displayed the deftness to cloak his military strategy with ambiguity and diplomatic dexterity. While Nehru- and Krishna Menon-bashing became fashionable amongst a certain constituency of commentators, including military officers who served during the crisis and held them directly responsible for the military defeat, the quasi-official history of the conflict clearly attempts to shield them to the extent possible and deflect the blame on both tactical and operational lapses on the part of the military. I have been sceptical about both these analyses, as well as the memoirs of generals like B.M. Kaul, Niranjan Prasad or Brigadier J.P. Dalvi. The truth, however, was that the politico-diplomatic and military-intelligence structures failed to pull their weight when the country needed them most. That would be the focus of my analysis of the conflict with a stress on matters military. It has also been widely felt within the strategic community in India that the lessons learned from the defeat in 1962 will never be meaningful unless the Henderson-Brooks Report is declassified.[20] This too is an argument that does not hold ground in the light of the reality that even when all the lessons of high-altitude warfare from 1947–48 were readily available, they were not implemented in the years preceding the 1962 war. In reality, however, all the lessons from 1962 have come out in some form or the other and the Henderson-Brooks report will have nothing much to offer other than a stinging criticism of tactical and operational military leadership in isolation as that was the extent of its mandate.

The Broad Picture

Notwithstanding what commentators have written about the success of Indian foreign policy in the 1950s, particularly in orchestrating the growth of the non-aligned movement and attempting to take on the role of the leadership of the developing world, India's China policy was delusionary and condescending. Despite cautionary notes from Sardar Vallabhbhai Patel as early as 1950, the Government of India misread China's regional ambitions, expecting that altruistic, mutually respectful and idealistic agreements like the Panchsheel would drive India–China relations. China, on the other hand, embraced a foreign policy aimed at recovering its lost glory during the colonial era through realism, restoration of historical boundaries and legacies, and development of comprehensive national power. The primary tools it used to achieve these objectives against India were ambiguity and decisive military force under an overarching nationalist plank.

Stagnation of the Indian Military

The 1950s were a period of all-round stagnation for the Indian armed forces, brought on by over a decade of relative peace and the blunting of much of the operational expertise gathered during WW II and the Indo-Pak war of 1947–48. There was stagnation in capability build-up, slumber in the development of broad military strategy and doctrine, and uncertainty regarding alliances and partnerships. Parliament too played its part by constantly questioning the defence budget and the need for strong-standing armed forces. Pakistan remained an obsession with Krishna Menon and Indian commanders and except for stray cautionary notes about China's build-up in Aksai Chin, the focus even in Ladakh lay centred on the Leh–Kargil–Dras sector as these were the areas that had to be defended against any likely Pakistani aggression. In essence, the military was not seen as a critical tool of statecraft; it was not seen as a vital element of national power; it was merely seen by a fiercely anti-colonial political leadership as a necessity of the modern times that needed to be tolerated. Much national effort was frittered away in developing paramilitary forces under the Ministry of Home Affairs – not so much for internal security as advertised, but more as a hedge against the armed forces. A disconnect between the armed forces, the political establishment, and society at large meant that lingering fears of a military coup under a strong military leader remained a troubling thought in the minds of political leaders. The situation in Pakistan, where General Ayub Khan grabbed power in 1958 after an earlier attempt in 1949 led by Major General Akbar Khan of Kashmir notoriety was foiled, did create some sense of insecurity within the Government of India about the possibility of a misadventure by the Indian military. This insecurity accentuated the distance between civil structures and the military, particularly when a charismatic Thimayya took over as COAS in 1957. His acrimonious departure gave Nehru and Menon the opportunity to appoint an army chief of their choice who would not 'rock the boat'.

Though institutions like the National Defence Academy and Defence Services Staff College (DSSC) were opened with much fanfare, these institutions were slow in moulding themselves to the requirements of modern warfare. The DSSC, for instance, was stuck in the British mould of producing officers and gentleman; it functioned more like a finishing school for mid-career officers, rather than a place to study military history, strategy or statecraft. Discussion during the period hardly revolved around China – model discussions concentrated on Pakistan – and there was little academic seriousness or intellectual debate. On the other hand, some of the more enduring legacies left behind by the British were either ignored or forgotten. Most senior commanders from brigade commanders upwards, and even a few senior battalion commanders, had seen action in WW II and the 1947–48 conflict with Pakistan and it is amazing how they forgot some of the basic tenets of warfare like 'Hardening of Troops for War'. I laid my hands on a small pamphlet of 1944 vintage bearing the same title and marvelled at the simple medico-mental flavour of the booklet.[21] Hardening of the body to resist exposure, hardening of the body to resist fatigue and staleness, and advanced training for long-distance pack marching were among the issues in the pamphlet.[22] Many of these basic principles were abandoned in the panic-stricken methodologies adopted for induction of India's military into high-altitude theatres of battle.

Strategic Leadership

Volumes have been written on the relationship of the Nehru–Krishna Menon duo with their military commanders. Nehru did display some decent military situational awareness under extreme pressure in 1947: he had to take a call on whether to allow his advancing forces to continue westwards to the India–Pakistan border, or rush to protect Poonch. He rightly chose the latter despite some objection from his military commanders. However, his socialist background and liberal leanings, and inherent dislike for matters military ensured that the military remained at the periphery of Indian strategic discourse till it was too late. Generals like Thimayya and S.P.P. Thorat attempted to infuse some military urgency into the system, particularly with respect to countering the emerging Chinese threat, but failed in the face of a disinterested political executive and an increasingly powerful civilian bureaucracy, which was entrusted with the mandate of acting as an interface between the military and political executive. This power play introduced a third player into the system – the pliant general who understood what it would take to climb the steep pyramid of senior military leadership. The unfolding of the Forward Policy was a result of this hackneyed relationship. Much has been written about this too and my take on it is very simple: A seemingly bold, but operationally untenable and unsustainable policy; orchestrated by an ill-informed and overconfident political leadership based on poor intelligence regarding the adversary and his intentions; supported by a weak military leadership that had forgotten about national interests and how to say 'No'.

I have often wondered why the senior IAF leadership too never put its foot down when asked to sustain and support the forward deployments by air beyond a point, leave alone in war. Everyone just said, 'Ours is not to question why.'

Operational Leadership

Notwithstanding the lack of actionable military intelligence before the raiders struck Kashmir, every success in the 1947–48 conflict resulted not only from inspirational leadership and individual or collective acts of gallantry but also from following them up with boots on ground and firepower. Many tactical victories could also be attributed to limited but effective employment of the limited air power resources. Whether it was Zojila, or the Srinagar battle, or the battles around Poonch, the progressive numerical superiority and firepower of the Indian Army with good offensive air support from the IAF allowed Indian field commanders like Thimayya, Usman, Atma Singh and Harbaksh Singh to be aggressive and innovative. This ensured that India had started gaining an upper hand in most of the sectors by the time the ceasefire was negotiated. The Indian Army had no such luxury in 1962 and field commanders in the thick of action like Hoshiar Singh, Dalvi, Raina or Rawlley could hardly afford to be innovative in the face of overwhelming superiority of numbers and firepower with the PLA. A complete absence of any offensive air support only made matters worse.

Much is written about the spectacular manner in which two Chinese divisions overran the vanguard of the Sela defences and then bypassed the garrison itself, going straight for the divisional headquarters at Dirang and the last anticipated line of resistance at Bomdila. This they did with most of their reserve division unemployed in battle till the end. Numbers held the key and except for Chushul garrison in the west and Walong sector in the east, most other sectors folded up because of poor divisional leadership. To blame the leadership at the brigade and battalion levels, as the Henderson-Brooks Report is said to have done, is largely unfair and harsh as units like 1 Sikh, 4 Garhwal and 6 Kumaon covered themselves with glory in NEFA.

But yes! The higher army leadership is certainly to blame for not being gutsy enough to dictate operational plans and decide on where battle was to be given to a superior enemy, if at all battle was unavoidable. Umrao Singh wanted to have his first defensive line at Tawang and Harbaksh wanted to fight his Walong sector battle at Hayuliang. They were overruled by Delhi which wanted the forward battle to be fought on the McMahon Line even if it meant committing fratricide, as it turned out to be. Even if right-wing politicians in parliament were pressurizing Nehru to stand up to the Chinese by evicting them from Indian territory, the COAS should have been asked to testify about our unpreparedness to take on the PLA. Maybe that would have precipitated a negotiated settlement, albeit with some concessions – an unthinkable proposition in those days. Constant rotation and change of corps commanders, divisional commanders and brigade commanders, particularly in NEFA, was detrimental to morale, and severely affected the army's fighting potential. Barely weeks before the conflict, Lieutenant General Umrao Singh, GOC of 33 Corps, was divested of the responsibility of the NEFA sector, seemingly because of differing with the execution of the Forward Policy. A new corps (IV Corps) under Kaul was entrusted with the initial battle in NEFA. Kaul himself displayed unnecessary bravado by trekking for days at the front line at altitudes of above 10,000 feet without proper acclimatization. Not surprisingly, he was supposedly taken ill with pulmonary oedema on 18 October before the main battle began and evacuated to Delhi, from where he insisted on directing the defensive battle.

Realizing the grave situation, Harbaksh Singh was flown in to take command of IV Corps as an interim measure and infuse some order into the chaotic defensive battle. Instead of continuing with this arrangement, Kaul insisted on returning to command the corps in November 1962 and did very little to prevent the rout that followed. Continuity in Ladakh, however, despite initial reverses, had a salutary effect on the morale of the troops, who displayed great grit in Phase II of the battle in the Chushul sector under the command of Brigadier Raina.

Speculating about leadership is a dicey proposition, but I will risk it nevertheless. Had Harbaksh Singh or Manekshaw, two plain-talking veterans from WW II, been assigned to command IV Corps in Tezpur instead of Kaul, it is highly probable that as late as early October, they would have realized the futility of attempting to string together a defensive line along the Namka Chu and right along the McMahon Line. In all likelihood Tawang and Walong would have been defended in strength and the Indian Army may have been in a position to fight a better defensive battle, particularly if the IAF had entered the fray with clear bomb lines and FLOTS available as the PLA advanced towards Tawang and Walong.

Dalvi's Dilemma

Moving back to the Tawang sector, it is totally unfair to single out Brigadier Dalvi, as many commentators have done over the years, for the disintegration of India's forward defences around Namka Chu. In an emotionally charged piece written in 2013 by his son Michael Dalvi, an accomplished first-class cricketer in the 1960s and 1970s, and forwarded to me on email, a loyal son defended his father:

> They told me, briefly, that the Army had lost contact with my father, and his forward HQ, sometime around noon on the 20th of October. That was the day the Chinese had attacked, and what was to come to be known as the beginning of the 'Battle of the Namka Chu'. Chu, in the local language, means River. Apparently, his HQ had been overrun & that he, along with some troops, and certainly some of his immediate staff officers were trying to link-up with another of his Battalions. Alas, that was in the pre-GPS era!!
>
> They explained that the last visual sighting of the Brigade Commander had been in the early afternoon of the 20th. The terrain was mountainous, deeply forested & hostile. Rations and provisions were scarce, if not non-existent. Most ominously, it was confirmed that the Chinese troops had reached positions, way behind his last known location! In short the message was 'lost, presumed killed in

> action'. That is Army parlance for a battlefield death. To establish our territorial claims along the McMahon Line, Prime Minister Nehru had embarked on an ill-advised policy fraught with danger – the 'forward policy' which entailed the establishment of forward posts, & a demarcation & unilateral interpretation of the McMahon line. But, if this was the eventual goal, why had we deployed an understaffed brigade? The planning was warped and Intelligence Agencies had no clue. The Army was shouting from the rooftops that they were facing 2 or more heavily trained Mountain Divisions. And why did we not upgrade the WWI rifles? Did the mandarins in Delhi really believe that the WWI vintage Lee Enfield .303, (10 shot bolt – action rifles) could rival the semi-automatic – AK 47? What about big guns? Ammunitions? Infrastructure? Roads? Accommodation? Front line fortifications? Supply routes. 'An army marches on its stomach'!! Rations food?? The mandarins in Delhi failed to even provide basic tools to dig trenches with!! Our soldiers were literally using their bare hands to dig themselves in? Somebody should have paid for this unforgiveable neglect with their jobs rather than our brave soldiers with their lives.[23]

Nearly fifty-one years later, writing in the United Service Institution of India journal, Major General Sandhu puts the issue of leadership and the fighting abilities of the Indian Army's Namka Chu and Tawang forces in the correct perspective. He writes:

> If one was to ascribe a single reason for the debacle on the Namka Chu and fall of Tawang, it would be – a faulty battle plan with poor generalship, made worse by political interference. The troops fought valiantly against overwhelming odds. The casualties suffered by 7 Infantry Brigade are testimony to that. Let no one fault the Indian soldier for gallantry, even in hindsight.[24]

Where Was Offensive Air Power?

One of the biggest blunders of the 1962 war was the reluctance of India's strategic establishment to use its superior aerial reconnaissance and offensive air power assets to blunt the spectacular forward run of the PLA in both NEFA and Ladakh. While Marshal of the Air Force Arjan Singh has clearly indicated in his book that he was not entirely privy to the reasons why air power was not used in the 1962 war and that the squadrons were ready to go into action, it is quite clear that both Air HQ and the Government of India were fuzzy about what the IAF could or could not do. The Indian Air Force had a dedicated reconnaissance squadron in the form of 106 Squadron equipped with fairly new British-built Canberra bomber-cum-reconnaissance aircraft. Tasked with a few sporadic missions in both the eastern sector and in Ladakh, the squadron could have done much more and acted as the eyes of the Indian government and complemented the IB's scanty intelligence inputs. It could also have assisted with building an intelligence picture and mosaic of the disposition and gradual build-up of PLA forces in Tibet and tracked their move forward in both sectors. Not only would it have provided military commanders with what they were likely to come up against, but it also could have provided Nehru with a reality check of whether he needed to temper his bravado of 'wanting to throw the Chinese out of Indian territory', sensitize the raucous opposition of what India was up against and accept China's proposal for a composite dialogue based on post-colonial realities.

Air Headquarters did not also contest the exaggerated capability of the PLAAF as conveyed to Prime Minister Nehru by the US ambassador, John Kenneth Galbraith, and chose to go along with the typically restrained political interpretation of the time that air power would be unnecessarily escalatory. With joint army–air force structures in place at the corps level, and forward air controllers with the brigades, it is clear that the IAF brass was timid and diffident about forcefully articulating to both the army and the political leadership that in an asymmetric situation on the ground, offensive air power could play a stabilizing role, if not a decisive one. If offensive air power had been used in the east, particularly on the Chinese side of the McMahon Line across the Thagla Ridge while the PLA was concentrating its forces, significant attrition could have been caused. Similarly, if the Indian Army had maintained its fortress strategy at Sela and Bomdila without retreating chaotically, Indian fighter-bomber aircraft could have caused significant attrition on PLA forces as they attempted to either lay siege to these positions or bypass them. It would be foolish to surmise that air power would have been a game changer; however, it would certainly have been a face-saver and India's armed forces may have possibly come out of the conflict in both sectors bruised, but not beaten and humiliated.

Chinese Operational Art

The most comprehensive analysis of Chinese operational art in the 1962 conflict emerged out of the US Army War College in 2003 as part of a monograph titled *The Lessons of History: The Chinese People's Liberation Army at 75.*[25] While much of the criticism of Indian strategy has relied mainly on Neville Maxwell's highly jaundiced book *India's China War* and hardly looked at the huge volume of fairly critical and objective work that has emerged from within India's strategic space, it is the analysis of Chinese strategy that is illuminating. The four major points that merit attention are the Chinese compulsion to prove that they were a force to reckon with after their lukewarm performance in the Korean War; the validation of their border strategy of 'counter-attack in self defence through rapid concentration at decisive points with massive artillery support'; adherence to the basic principles of war; and lastly, strong political leadership as a prerequisite for military victory.[26] It was indeed surprising that having read comprehensive pamphlets on Japanese tactics and operational art during the Burma campaign of WW II,[27] none of the Indian Army's senior leadership insisted that either Military Intelligence or the Intelligence Bureau put together similar pamphlets about Chinese tactics in battle in English and Hindi so that a large cross section of troops were familiar with what to expect from the adversary.

The Chinese were also ruthless in their treatment of prisoners, not in terms of physical abuse, but in their attempt to brainwash and indoctrinate them with anti-Indian and communist ideology. One of the many Indian prisoners who held their heads high during the period of captivity and withstood Chinese interrogation was Major J.S. Rathore (retd), who was then a lance naik. He recollects that though he was not tortured, he was frequently spoken to on how Britain and the US were responsible for the war. He also recollects Chinese attempts to orchestrate social gatherings like a Barakhana (a semi-formal feast in the Indian armed forces) on 26 January (India's Republic Day), a move which was resisted by him and earned him the ire of his captors.[28] Squadron Leader Gulati (retd), a veteran navigator of the IAF, flew many of the prisoners from Tezpur to Panagarh airfield near Calcutta in April 1963, where they were kept in isolation and interrogated for nearly seventeen days. He poignantly recollects that almost 1,600 of the 3,000-odd POWs were branded as 'affected' and quietly eased out of the mainstream armed forces,[29] while others like Rathore were found to have been 'outstanding' during their period of incarceration and sent back to their units with honour.[30]

In the final analysis, the 1962 war with China was a chastening experience for both India's political and military establishments. The psychological impact of the defeat on India far exceeded the physical losses if one looks at the actual casualties as per the claims of both India and China.[31] The conflict threw up many lessons – sadly the closed discourse has prevented India from exorcising the ghosts of 1962. Many of them still float around the Line of Actual Control and in the minds of those who participated in the conflict. Even after fifty years and numerous confidence building measures (CBMs), India's border with China remains unsettled and unresolved; something which unsettles the peoples of both countries even today.

Author's Note

In a laudable attempt at moving ahead and leaving behind the painful memories of a defeat, there are constituencies within India's current nationalistic political establishment that seek to highlight to a young nation the many heroic tactical battles fought by the Indian Army, rather than stick to a beaten discourse of only the failure of higher leadership. Almost two years after this chapter was completed, an article in *The Economic Times*, a respected Indian newspaper, reported:

> To ensure that the bravery of the Indian Army during the war is not undermined, the RSS wants those battles to be highlighted where the soldiers showed exemplary courage in the face of extreme odds. The India-China war need not be just a shameful episode for India. We can tell the children about one of the most embarrassing episodes of our history by highlighting the gallantry of our troops. The war could be used to instil pride and also serve as a crucial lesson in diplomacy.[32]

The Second Round: India–Pakistan Conflict of 1965

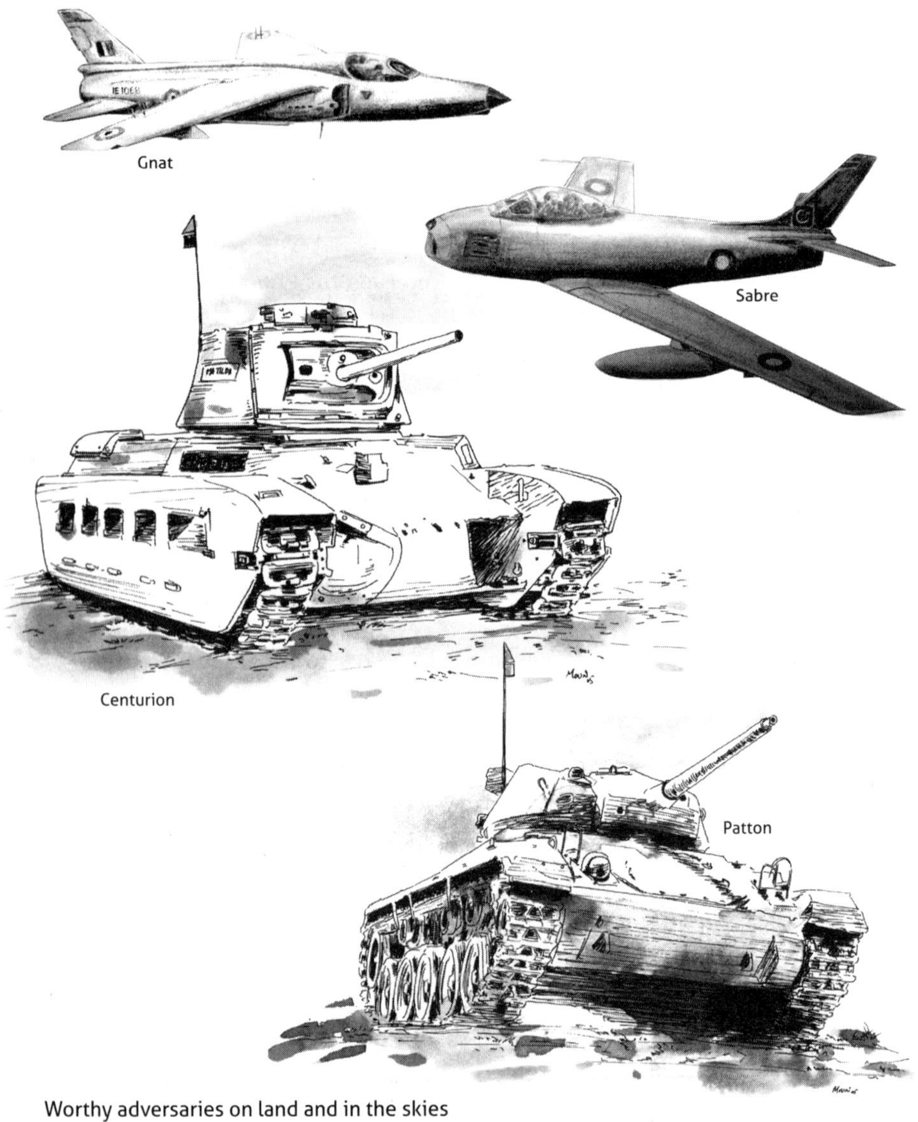

Worthy adversaries on land and in the skies
Sketches by Group Captain Deb Gohain (retd)

18

OPENING MOVES: KUTCH TO KASHMIR IN 1965

If Pakistan has any ideas of annexing any part of our territories by force, she should think afresh. I want to state categorically that force will be met with force and aggression against us will never be allowed to succeed.[1]

– Prime Minister Lal Bahadur Shastri

Opening Moves

The post-1962 period saw hectic geopolitical activity in the subcontinent accompanied by political uncertainty in India following the death of its charismatic prime minister, Jawaharlal Nehru. Shell-shocked by what he termed as 'the Chinese betrayal' in 1962, and, more importantly, the perceived decline of India's international standing in the developing world, Nehru's health declined rapidly all through 1963 till his demise on 27 May 1964. Pakistan on the other hand, ruled as it was by a fading, but ambitious military dictator, Field Marshal Ayub Khan, was making its moves to erode India's standing in the region and reduce the military and strategic differential that existed between the two countries. Egged on by his young, brilliant and equally ambitious foreign minister, Zulfikar Ali Bhutto, Ayub Khan made two defining moves, which suddenly pitchforked Pakistan into the limelight. One of the first anti-India hedging moves by Ayub Khan in 1954, spurred on to a large extent by the anti-India US Secretary of State, John Foster Dulles, was to enter into a direct military pact with the US under the Mutual Defence Assistance Agreement. Soon after, it joined the South-East Asia Treaty Organization (SEATO) and the Baghdad Pact, later called CENTO (Central Treaty Organization).[2] With this alliance, Pakistan emerged as a South Asian bulwark against the Soviet Union and the Warsaw Pact.[3] This ensured the speedy modernization of Pakistan's armed forces with US equipment, much to the consternation of India, which had failed in its attempt to procure military hardware from US in the years following the 1962 debacle.

The second smart move by Pakistan was in March 1963 when Pakistan entered into a wide-ranging strategic pact with China that centred on marginalizing India's growing power in the region.[4] The key highlights of the pact involved the ceding of a large portion of Pakistan-Occupied Kashmir, the Shaksgam Valley, to China. Located immediately to the south of the troubled Xinjiang province, the Shaksgam Valley was of no value to Pakistan considering its distance from the Punjab heartland. However, it offered greater depth to China, which remained paranoid about retaining control over its periphery after the Tibetan crisis. In return, China assured Pakistan of military support in the form of hardware and assistance in building an indigenous military industrial complex, apart from unsubstantiated assurances that China would open a second front should India threaten the national security of Pakistan.

Notwithstanding concerted attempts by India's new defence minister, Y.B. Chavan, to rebuild India's military capability, the political turmoil in India after Nehru's death and its distinctly weakened and demoralized armed forces emboldened Pakistan's attempts to push for a military solution to the Kashmir problem. Not making matters easy for India was the falling out of Sheikh Abdullah, the pro-India leader of the National Conference, which swept to power in the first elections in J&K in 1950, and Nehru over the manner in which Kashmiri aspirations were being addressed by India in the mid-1950s. This resulted in the imprisonment of Sheikh Abdullah by the Indian government for a number of years on charges of treason.[5] The ensuing deterioration of the law and order situation in J&K was fuelled partly by his continued arrest, and partly by the corruption and poor governance of the state government led by

Bakshi Ghulam Mohammad, Sheikh Abdullah's rival within the National Conference party.[6] In such an environment, one can hardly fault Ayub Khan for the timing of Pakistan's second attempt in two decades to wrest Kashmir from India. The time was ripe to unfold Operation Gibraltar, as the plan to subvert and seize Kashmir as it entered the chilly spring of 1965 came to be known. Summer saw an increase in the number of infiltrations and ceasefire violations from across the Line of Control and a pattern emerging on the contours of the likely 'takeover of Kashmir Strategy' by Pakistan.[7]

However, Operation Gibraltar will have to wait a while as we shift focus southwards to the harsh, untamed and beautiful salt pans and marshlands of Kutch. This remote frontier district of the state of Gujarat, which borders the Pakistani province of Sind, was to turn into a battleground in the early months of 1965 and act as a pointer for further conflict between India and Pakistan across a wide front. Little did the endangered flamingos and wild asses[8] of Kutch realize that their peaceful habitat was going to be shattered by two squabbling and warring nations.

Marshy Imbroglio

The Rann of Kutch is a large peninsula-shaped hybrid-marshland-cum salt pan located in the north-eastern part of Kutch, which gets partially submerged during the few monsoon months. For a major part of the year, however, it remains a marshy area interspersed with hard and dry salt pans and a permanently riverine creek, the Sir Creek, the middle of which marks the current border. Like many poorly defined and demarcated frontier areas in the subcontinent, the Rann of Kutch emerged as a contested area in the mid-1950s. Both India and Pakistan coveted the Rann[9] despite clear evidence being available in pre-Independence records that the Maharaja of Kutch had laid claims to it based on irefutable historical evidence. That the British remained quiet and did not oppose the claim, offered some legitimacy during the 1968 UN Tribunal deliberations, which largely went in favour of India. This, more than anything else, vindicated India's stand that Pakistan had been the first aggressor in 1965 and was only looking at exploiting cartographical ambiguities to lay claim on what was sovereign Indian territory.[10]

Pakistan's opening gambit that surprised India was as much a testimony to its operational ingenuity and initiative, as it was to the gross inadequacy of India's intelligence-gathering ability in Sind. Both the IB, which was mandated to gather external intelligence, and Military Intelligence failed to monitor Pakistan's troop movements and other military developments like construction of tracks and roads as being anything other than routine. This resulted in a delayed build-up of Indian forces to counter even a brigade-sized thrust by Pakistan. Pakistan on its part moved swiftly and exploited the decisiveness of a military regime which had no bureaucratic and procedural compulsions of putting an operational military plan through various processes before being approved.

Based on an operational appreciation by the Pakistan Army, Ayub decided to test India's military preparedness in an area which was considerably distant from Kashmir, where plans were finalized to launch Operation Gibraltar later in the year. He decisively moved an entire infantry brigade with armour and artillery to the remote Rann area in early April 1965 to grab some territory before the monsoons set in.[11] He would soon boost that force to almost a division as the skirmish flared up.

Operation Desert Hawk

From the manner in which the Pakistan Army had re-equipped and remodelled itself with US assistance for almost a decade prior to the onset of hostilities,[12] it was keen to test its equipment on the battlefield against an opponent whose modernization process had just begun. Specifically, along with new equipment, Pakistan had refined its artillery and air force tactics significantly,[13] and speedily wanted to validate in a restricted and limited battle environment. Though Lubna Abid Ali, a Pakistani historian, argues that the military operation was launched by Pakistan to rectify a historical injustice and restore Pakistan's territorial integrity,[14] the timing of the operation points otherwise. It was a classic probing military operation executed with some skill.

While the strategic objective of Operation Desert Hawk, as Pakistan named this limited operation, was to analyse the politico-military reaction from the new Indian government and the ensuing international reaction to Pakistani military adventurism, the military objectives were pretty focused. From the fairly large force levels that were finally employed – two brigades of the Indian Army against a division including two armoured regiments of the Pakistan Army along with supporting artillery[15] – three main military objectives emerge from a Pakistani perspective. The first was an evaluation of India's military preparedness, the second was an opportunity to test the Patton tank in manoeuvre warfare along with the infantry and with artillery support, and lastly, to grab any territory and hold it.

The provocation for the skirmish has a two-sided explanation. While the Indian Army tentatively moved its posts forward towards a small border hamlet called Kanjarkot to oppose what it believed was Pakistani encroachment into Indian territory north of the 24th Parallel,[16] the Pakistani side claimed that their armed action was to evict Indian troops from a new post called Sardar Post.[17] This, they claimed, was in Pakistani territory as per historical legacies that had seen agreements signed by the Maharaja of Kutch ceding that territory to Sindhi cattle grazers in the nineteenth century. The bottom line was that the legacy of the British leaving poorly demarcated borders in remote areas had created problems for India once again where a 'show of force' was resorted to for asserting territorial claims. While the initial setting up of posts by the Indian Army in March 1965 could not be contested by the Indus Rangers (a Pakistani paramilitary force in that region), Pakistan moved swiftly and moved the remainder elements of a whole division (8 Division) under Major General Tikka Khan into the area by 7 April. Tikka Khan was to gain notoriety six years later as the 'Butcher of East Pakistan'.

Though the Indian Army would ultimately deploy two brigades in the region (31 Brigade and a depleted 50 Para Brigade) and reorganize it as Kilo Force under Major General P.O. Dunne,[18] these were undermanned and did not have the mobility and wherewithal to counter the swift initial assault by a brigade-sized force with a squadron of Patton tanks against a company location at Sardar Post.[19] The next few days saw isolated but fierce fighting at the battalion level with the Pakistani army faring better in most initial exchanges due to its numerical superiority and employment of armour in the form of the much feared Patton tanks. Realizing that the Indian posts at Sardar Post and Vigokot were effectively mined and well defended, Tikka Khan bypassed them and made a run for the small town of Dharamsala about 30-odd kilometres inside Indian territory.[20] This forced Dunne to withdraw most of his 31 Brigade to defend Dharamsala. Employment of armour certainly took the Indians by surprise though a terrain analysis, had it been thoroughly done, would have indicated that the terrain on the Pakistan side was favourable for the employment of armour and maintenance of logistics lines as the major town of Badin was barely 30 km from the border. Compared to that the closest Indian town of Bhuj was almost 180 km from the border.[21]

An aerial reconnaissance sortie carried out by a Vampire jet of the IAF operating from Jamnagar confirmed the presence of Patton tanks and caused some consternation in Delhi, leading to a threat from Lal Bahadur Shastri, the Indian prime minister, that should Pakistan not pull back, India would be forced to contemplate widespread and immediate military action. This was something that Pakistan did not want before it had all its forces in place for its main operational plans in J&K. The situation, however, also allowed India to gather adequate international support and pin the tag of aggressor on Pakistan. In fact, on learning that a Vampire had been launched from Jamnagar airbase, the Pakistani air force chief, Air Marshal Asghar Khan is said to have called his counterpart in India, Air Marshal Arjan Singh (both of them were squadron commanders on the same side in the Burma campaign of WW II) and suggested that the two air forces stay out of this skirmish.[22] While much has been made of this exchange, it would be naive to imagine that had it not happened, India would have decisively used air power in Kutch given the rather defensive strategic mindset prevailing in Delhi.

The power equations that existed within the Pakistan military would establish that there was not much difference between inter-service relations in India and Pakistan. Just as General J.N. Chaudhuri, India's army chief, was pretty clear that that he was 'first among equals' when it came to the pecking order vis-à-vis his counterparts in the IAF and the Indian Navy, General Musa, the Pakistan Army chief, and Field Marshal Ayub Khan had pretty much the same attitude towards the PAF chief, Air Marshal Asghar Khan. Sajad Haider, one of the PAF's most illustrious fighter pilots with extensive combat experience in both the

1965 and 1971 wars with India, reckons that they were wary of Asghar's 'intrepid and strategic mind' and did not find it necessary to keep him updated with the plans for Operation Desert Hawk.[23] As a result, the closest PAF airbase at Mauripur (close to Karachi) with F-86 Sabres was too far away from the Rann of Kutch to provide meaningful air support. It was just as well because Haider adds that Pakistan thought that the IAF had activated the Bhuj airfield, while the IAF thought that the PAF would use the airfields at Hyderabad (Sind), Nawabshah or Sukkur.[24] Five decades later, it is clear that both air forces were operating in an intelligence vacuum and lost the opportunity to make an impression in Kutch. However, the PAF did leverage the existing conflict situation to hone its air–land operations by ensuring that Sabres from Mauripur flew simulated close air support missions in the 8 Division areas of operations on a daily basis under FAC control as a fighter pilot was attached to the army formation to create some synergy.[25]

Having held its own during the initial exchanges and proved its tactics and equipment, units of the Pakistani army stood their ground as hectic international diplomacy took over to limit the fallout of the skirmishes. From most accounts it appeared that India was in no mood to expand the conflict beyond mere diplomatic sabre-rattling, while Pakistan was under pressure to cease hostilities. Finally, under immense pressure from Harold Wilson, the British prime minister, Pakistan agreed to pull back and agree to a ceasefire and truce with India over the Rann on 6 June 1965.[26] The salient aspects of the ceasefire agreement included a territorial restoration of status quo on the Gujarat–West Pakistan border as on 1 January 1965, troop withdrawal within seven days and constitution of an international tribunal within two months should the two countries fail to reach a negotiated settlement.[27]

A word here about another localized military confrontation during the same time around the icy heights of Kargil in Ladakh is in order as it indicates how India was again at the receiving end during brokered negotiations after a localized conflict. Frustrated at the constant Pakistani shelling of the Srinagar–Leh highway from heights overlooking the town of Kargil, called Pt 13620 and Black Rock, Indian forces captured the heights in mid-May 1965 after a tough assault, only to give them back after the composite ceasefire of June.[28] Air Chief Marshal P. C. Lal, the

IAF's chief of air staff from 16 July 1969 to 15 January 1973, visited the area in 1972 and narrates the difficulty of combat at those rarefied heights in his memoirs. When he asked one of the officers who had participated in the 1965 assault what his experiences were and what was the most difficult part, the response was:

> Thirst! The bare stones are cold at night in these heights, 'stone cold'. The entire operation had to be done in the cover of darkness. The soldiers would have to be at the required height the previous morning, in the early hours and then lie still under the shadow, or in the shelter, of suitable boulders, hoping and praying not to be detected. Movement and liquid intake had to be minimised. When they reached the top and took it after tough hand-to-hand fighting, they were too exhausted by the time the battle and tension were over to feel any elation or triumph.[29]

Reactions in India and Pakistan after the Kutch skirmish were similar with the general perception in Pakistan being that Ayub Khan had lost a golden opportunity to give India a bloody nose with Tikka Khan's 8 Division poised for a further advance into the Rann after bypassing most of the Indian border posts. On the Indian side, the opposition led by Atal Behari Vajpayee of the Jana Sangh, a right-wing nationalist party, urged the government to offer a fitting riposte and not accept a truce. The bottom line was that with barely two brigades, hardly any armour, and unwillingness on the part of the government to use air power, the Southern Army Command of the Indian Army was in no position to deliver that riposte. Added to the unpreparedness was the fact that the IAF did not have any meaningful air assets in the region other than those at Jamnagar, which was a training base equipped with Vampire jets and a few other training aircraft.[30] A few strikes by IAF fighter aircraft from Jamnagar could have played havoc into Pakistani armour and demonstrated some intent on the part of India. But it was not to be so as Pakistan walked smugly away after validating what it had set out to do prior to commencement of the skirmish. The success of Operation Desert Hawk and the return of heights in Kargil created a false sense of euphoria within Pakistan's strategic establishment, emboldening it to invigorate the subversion and infiltration campaign in Kashmir, which had commenced in early 1965 even before the winter snows had melted.[31]

Military Balance

With India rebuilding itself militarily under Prime Minister Shastri and a fairly proactive defence minister Y.B. Chavan, albeit at a slower pace than Pakistan, its defence budget increased significantly from 2.1 per cent of GDP in 1961–62 to 4.0 per cent in 1963–64.[32] According to Sumit Ganguly, 1964–65 provided a strategic 'window of opportunity'[33] for Pakistan to strike before the gap in military capability widened in India's favour once all its acquisition and expansion plans fructified. Pakistan reckoned that it would not be long before India reached its government-cleared force levels of a one-million-strong army and a forty-five-squadron air force. At the turn of 1965 Sumit Ganguly put the Indian Army at 8,70,000 strong with sixteen infantry divisions. Four additional mountain divisions were in the process of being raised for deployment on the China front. Of these, ten divisions, some of which were undermanned,[34] were ranged against Pakistan, which had all of its seven divisions ranged against India[35] barring a few brigades on its north-west frontier. India's advantage in armour along its western front was less marked. There was near parity with both sides having an armoured division and approximately three regiments (an armoured brigade equivalent)[36] ranged against each other with Pakistan having a marginal numerical advantage. More significantly, Pakistan enjoyed a qualitative advantage in armour with the Patton tank said to be superior to the Centurion and Sherman tanks, which equipped India's armoured divisions.

From 1955 onwards the US supplied Pakistan with military hardware under the Military Assistance Programme (MAP). Included in this were 400 M-48 Patton tanks and 200 M-24 Chaffee tanks. However, the Centurion would go on to acquit itself well against the Patton tank in all the tank battles fought in the 1965 war, particularly in the battle of Khem Karan and Assal Uttar. The Patton tank was believed to have night- fighting capability and other advanced systems. However, it is believed that these were not well exploited by the Pakistani army as the war progressed. The basic infantryman's weapon in the Indian Army was undergoing a transition with the .303 rifle being replaced by the Belgian-made 7.62 mm self-loading rifle (SLR). Many battalions were still equipped with the .303 when the war broke out. The Pakistan Army on the other hand was completely equipped with the 7.62 mm SLR.

In terms of artillery too the Pakistanis outgunned their Indian opponents. Saddled with WW II vintage equipment like the towed 25 pounder, 3.7" Howitzers, 5.5" and 7.2" guns with a maximum range of 12 to 15 km, the Indian Army would be severely handicapped during artillery engagements. The Pakistan Army on the other hand benefited immensely from the MAP with the acquisition of self-propelled Howitzers (105 mm), jeep-mounted 103 mm recoilless anti-tank guns and heavy artillery (155 mm).[37] Supported by these guns, which had a maximum range of 25 to 27 km (155 mm), the basic Pak infantry company had widened its effective frontage to 1,000 yards[38] from an earlier 600 to 700 yards. This would prove particularly decisive during the Chhamb offensive operations as the Indian defences were softened prior to the armoured assault, and again during defensive operations against Indian armoured thrusts in the Sialkot and Khem Karan sectors.

In the air too the Pakistan Air Force (PAF) enjoyed a marginal qualitative superiority over the Indian Air Force (IAF) though it was outnumbered by a fair margin. The metamorphosis of the PAF into a lean and potent force with diverse capabilities began in the mid-1950s with the arrival of the F-86 Sabre jets and the Canberra bombers. Learning from the USAF experience in Korea and the initial years of the Vietnam War, PAF pilots picked up the finer nuances of air combat and air–land operations at a time when the IAF was in the midst of a wide-ranging expansion itself. The main difference being that the PAF benefited from putting all its eggs in the US basket, while India looked to Russia (MiG-21s), UK (Hunters, Gnats, Canberras) and France (Mysteres) for its expansion. Consequently, there was fair standardization of technology, tactics and procedures in the PAF as against an absence of the same in the IAF. Acquired in 1960 from the US under the MAP were 12 F-104 Starfighter supersonic interceptors armed with Sidewinder air-to-air missiles and a six-barrelled 20 mm Vulcan cannon. Though only one squadron (9 Squadron PAF) was formed with fourteen aircraft, it proved to be quite a deterrent and was believed to be far superior to both the

MiG-21 and Gnat air defence fighters of the IAF. The mainstay of the PAF, however, was the F-86 Sabre jet, a multi-role fighter, which was as effective in ground attack missions as it was in providing top cover as an air defence platform when armed with Sidewinders. Over 120 of them were procured from the US under the MAP, of which twenty-four were equipped with Sidewinders before hostilities erupted in 1965.[39] The C-130 Hercules was a superb medium-lift transport aircraft which was used for special forces' operations – the stealthy manner in which almost 200 paratroopers were dropped around three Indian airbases without any attrition caused to any of the aircraft used in the mission is testimony to its capability. Ironically, the IAF would go on to buy an advanced version of the same aircraft nearly forty-five years later.

Though the earliest description of the air battle between the PAF and IAF in the 1965 war titled *Battle for Pakistan* was written by John Fricker in 1979, it was ridiculously biased in favour of the PAF. Nearly twenty-six years later, two enthusiastic Indian aviation enthusiasts, P.V.S. Jagan Mohan and Samir Chopra, went on to write a highly readable and objective narrative of the air war, *The India-Pakistan Air War of 1965.* I have chosen to rely on this book to get a realistic view of the numbers on either side. The IAF had a total of 460 combat aircraft including eight squadrons (132 aircraft) of old and slow Vampire trainer-cum-close air support jets, acquired in 1948, and three squadrons (56 aircraft) of Ouragans of similar vintage, acquired from France in the early 1950s. This meant that the IAF had only about 270 combat-worthy aircraft. The workhorse of the ground attack fleet were the eighty-odd Mystere jets, while the sleek and manoeuvrable Hunter jet doubled up as a multi-role aircraft assisting the Gnats in air defence missions.[40] Though the IAF had inducted the first squadron of MiG-21s into 28 Squadron in mid-1963 after almost a year of hectic negotiations with the Soviet Union, the numbers available were too few to make any significant impact on its operational capability as war clouds loomed on the horizon.

The versatile Canberra was the only bomber aircraft operated by both IAF and PAF. It would come into its own during the various night raids conducted by both sides when day attrition climbed during the initial days of the war. While the IAF had approximately sixty of these aircraft with one squadron exclusively configured for the reconnaissance role, PAF had thirty-two aircraft of the modified US version.[41] This numerical superiority was to play an important role during the war as IAF Canberras carried out many deep-night strikes as the war progressed and caused a fair amount of disruption. Thus if you look at an objective force comparison between the IAF and PAF, one arrives at approximately 270 combat-worthy IAF aircraft against about 170 PAF combat aircraft. Air Vice Marshal Tiwary offers another perspective by indicating that the IAF had a large deployment of squadrons on the eastern front leaving it with only around 290 aircraft in the west against his researched strength of Pakistani aircraft of 203.[42] This resulted in a ratio of 1.5:1 in favour of the IAF. Though Prasad and Thapliyal, two official historians from the Ministry of Defence, Government of India, have quoted the Marshal of the Air Force, Arjan Singh, the Chief of Air Staff at the time, as mentioning that the IAF was in awe of the PAF, interviews with other veterans of the conflict reveal no such fear or admiration beyond a realization that the Sabre and Starfighter would be formidable adversaries.[43] A few young Indian pilots like Flying Officers McMahon, Rajkumar and Bhatia (all retired as Air Marshals) had flown the Sabre jet in the US and brought back some valuable inputs regarding US tactics and training patterns as a large number of Pakistani pilots had been trained in the US. However, there were no institutional initiatives to brainstorm or evolve central fighter and bomber tactics against the existing PAF capabilities. This was to prove ominous in some of the aerial battles in the months ahead.[44] However, as the war progressed, the IAF evolved effective tactics at the squadron level to counter both the Sabre and the Starfighter.

If there was a force multiplier for the PAF during its period of transition, it was in the form of its longest-serving chief (1957–65), Air Marshal Asghar Khan. Asghar Khan was a visionary airman who had cut his teeth exactly in a similar manner as many of the IAF's stalwarts like Mehar Singh and Arjan Singh had in the cauldron of WW II. His understanding of air power and willingness to push for an important role for the PAF in joint operations paid rich dividends. He initially had the ear of Field Marshal Ayub Khan and ensured that whatever he asked for the PAF in terms of budgetary support and creation of forward bases as a means of blunting India's numerical superiority was agreed to. The setting up of an aerobatic team and the Fighter Leaders' School in 1958,[45] followed by an aggressive air defence posture that saw an IAF Canberra being shot down over Pakistani territory in 1959 during an intrusive reconnaissance mission, saw the PAF at its aggressive best.

Though the two navies were not to see much action on the western seaboard of the subcontinent, the Indian Navy had its aircraft carrier, INS *Vikrant,* undergoing a refit and thereby lost its decisive edge over the Pakistani navy, though quantitatively it had almost three times the number of warships with the INS *Mysore* packing a mighty punch with its huge guns. The absence of the *Vikrant* and the unwillingness of the government to escalate the conflict remained the main reasons why the Indian Navy did not prosecute any major offensive operation during the 1965 conflict. Though the Sea Hawk fighters on the aircraft carrier were available for offensive strikes, integrating them into the IAF plan proved to be a problem area. The presence of a Tench Class submarine with the Pakistan Navy, the PNS *Ghazi,* did not deter the Indian Navy, as it periodically did carry out anti-submarine warfare (ASW) exercises with British submarines on the east coast.

SUBVERSION IN J&K

The inability of Pakistan to sever J&K from the Indian Union in 1948 had turned into a national obsession for Pakistan and its armed forces. It had also become a focal point in the development of an India-centric national security strategy and a rallying point for Islamists in their jihad against India. Having grabbed large chunks of territory in J&K from India in 1948 in what was an audacious plan, particularly the one which succeeded in capturing the Northern Area, Gilgit and Skardu, it was only natural that Pakistan would look for an opportune moment to occupy the rest of the state and fulfil the dreams of its founding fathers. Audacious military plans are generally the work of a small core group of strategists and soldiers. Just as Akbar Khan was the architect of the 1947–48 infiltration with tacit support from Jinnah, Operation Gibraltar, the 1965 plan for subversion, infiltration and occupation was supported and inspired by Bhutto.[46] It was then operationally stitched together by Major General Akhtar Hussein Malik, the General Officer Commanding of Pakistan's 12 Division. Air Marshal Asghar Khan, the Commander-in-Chief of the

Pakistan Air Force, describes Malik as a 'bold and imaginative officer'.[47] He was also the architect of Operation Grand Slam, the swift armoured thrust into the Chhamb and Akhnur districts of Jammu that was aimed at isolating J&K from the rest of India and thereby completing the plan to 'sandwich' J&K[48] and amalgamate it into Pakistan.

Operation Gibraltar was crafted with certain geopolitical and military assumptions, many of which would later emerge as untenable and overambitious. History has repeatedly demonstrated that the only way in which a numerically inferior force or a smaller nation can defeat a more powerful adversary is by surprising the enemy in time and space with speed and sustained offensive action. Added to this, if the local population where this military action is proposed can be subverted, the attacker has the right recipe for a high probability of success. While the geopolitical conditions have been brought out earlier in the chapter, what were the operational conditions which allowed an experienced soldier-turned-president, Ayub Khan, to finally give the green signal to launch this military adventure against India in 1965?

First, the success of Operation Desert Hawk convinced Ayub Khan of the tactical, operational and technological superiority of the Pakistan Army. With Air Chief Marshal Asghar Khan assuring the president before handing over command of the PAF to Air Marshal Nur Khan that the Pakistan Air Force with its recently acquired F-86 and F-104 Starfighter jets was far superior to the IAF, Ayub Khan could hedge his bets should India decide to counter Operation Gibraltar with a riposte in Punjab. Second, the intelligence from J&K indicated that the local population was restive and highly vulnerable to subversion, and when the time came, would rise in rebellion and fight against the Indian Army alongside the mujahids and regulars of the Pakistan Army. Lastly, though Major General Malik appreciated that the Indian Army would be better prepared to counter the infiltration campaign as compared to 1947, he was confident that his own mujahid battalions would be better trained and equipped than the ragtag force which assaulted the Kashmir Valley back in 1947. When coupled with the prevailing geopolitical instability in India resulting from Nehru's untimely death, the relatively stable military regime in Pakistan felt that it was an ideal time to strike in Kashmir.

19

OPERATIONS GIBRALTAR AND GRAND SLAM

The basic tactical concept of the Pakistan Army did not vary fundamentally from our own. In its application, however, there was an unmistakable evidence of the dominant influence of American and Chinese techniques of warfare. This selective grafting of tactical doctrine did not, however, pay the expected dividends for want of imaginative implementation.[1]

– Lieutenant General Harbaksh Singh, India's Western Army Commander during the war

Multi-Pronged Assault

Operation Gibraltar's infiltration plan comprised eight thrust lines along the ceasefire line starting from the Kargil sector in the north and extended along the river Kishenganga all the way southwards till Poonch. Learning from their 1947–48 experience, Pakistan chose not to open a large front in the Kargil sector beyond attempting to cut the Leh–Srinagar Highway as it was well defended by the Indian Army and there was little possibility of subverting the local population in Ladakh, which comprised a majority of Buddhists and a sprinkling of Shia Muslims. With Pakistan having been carved out of India, the search for a historical legacy inevitably turned to the numerous Islamic warrior-kings who invaded India from the eleventh century onwards. All the thrust lines and forces were named after these Muslim invaders and all the mujahid battalions were indoctrinated with stories of the valour of these warriors. The forces were named Tariq, Qasim, Khalid, Salauddin, Ghaznavi, Murtuza, Nusrat and Babar.[2] It is interesting to understand this strategy, coupled as it was with a political directive by Ayub Khan to his military commanders about India's ability to withstand an offensive. One of the paragraphs in that directive read:

> As a general rule Hindu morale would not stand more than a couple of hard blows delivered at the right time and place. Such opportunities should therefore be sought and exploited.[3]

While Western commentators like Brian Cloughley, an accomplished Australian military historian, called these comments as 'crass',[4] it reveals a lot of the prevailing mindsets in the subcontinent, particularly in the stereotyping of clans and races and their martial abilities. Clearly, the 'martial race' theory as propounded by the British in their reorganization of the Indian Army in late-nineteenth century had identified Punjabi Muslims, Baluchis and Pathans as excellent fighting material and this is what remained as a mindset within the Pakistan Army.

The plan of infiltration was to launch all thrusts almost simultaneously with mujahid battalions, and wherever there was potential for success, it would be further exploited by regular forces. According to Harbaksh Singh it was 'brilliant in conception'[5] and expected to garner local support and trigger a mass uprising against the state that would be impossible to handle by the state administration and the Indian Army. My own analysis points at an intelligence and analysis failure by Pakistan, which relied excessively on inputs from a few Islamist radicals within the Kashmir Valley who promised more than they could deliver in terms of being able to whip up anti-India sentiment amongst the local population.

What Ayub also did not reckon with was the Indian Army's commander of the Western Command, Harbaksh Singh. A WW II veteran who had been incarcerated by the Japanese as a POW after the fall of Singapore in 1942, Harbaksh commanded the famous 1 Sikh Regiment and then a brigade in the 1947–48 conflict in J&K. His brigade notched up numerous successes in the Tithwal sector during Thimayya's ambitious summer offensive of 1948. In October 1962, he was rushed to NEFA as corps commander of the beleaguered IV Corps after Phase I of the offensive by the Chinese to replace an ailing Kaul. Harbaksh was known to be a no-nonsense and aggressive commander with high expectations from his subordinate commanders. With so much prior knowledge of the area, there was no way in which Harbaksh was going to allow 1947 to be repeated all over again. It is quite evident that Pakistani intelligence did not anticipate the tough and immediate response from units of the Indian Army's Western Command located along the ceasefire line. His aggressive intent was evident from as early as May 1965 when he ordered 121 Infantry Brigade group, which was holding the ceasefire line in the Kargil sector, to evict Pak intruders from two prominent heights (Pt 13620 and Black Rocks). These heights were overlooking the Srinagar–Leh Highway and had the potential to act as observation points that could direct artillery fire on to the highway. Accordingly, 4 Rajput Regiment launched a daring infantry night assault on 17 May with light artillery support from 85 Light Regiment. They were led by two brave officers, Major Randhawa and Captain Ranbir Kang, who displayed leadership qualities of the highest order under fire. Major Randhawa, who was killed in the operation, was awarded the first Maha Vir Chakra of the extended conflict, while Kang was awarded the Vir Chakra.[6] This 121 Brigade would be repeatedly tested in the decades ahead.

Infiltration by the mujahid battalions and regulars of the Pakistan Army into the Kashmir Valley commenced on 5 August 1965, covered by heavy artillery fire and stray engagements between regular units of the two armies. As the mujahids initially fanned out into the Valley along seven or eight thrust lines, the main ones being in Gurez, Kupwara, Uri, Poonch, Mendhar, Naushera and Akhnur,[7] they were surprised by the singular lack of support from the local population. Many of them were captured by the Indian Army and the state police and divulged the elaborate subversion plans. It was revealed that the saboteurs were a mix of Razakars and mujahids, and according to one captured mujahid, belonged to what he called the 'Gibraltar Forces'.[8] This force was said to have numbered approximately 4,000 to 5,000 and been divided into approximately eight forces of five companies each. These companies of 110–120 were divided into infiltrating groups of 50 to 60 with regular

Operation Gibraltar
PAKISTAN
PoK
Cease-fire line
Skardu
Black Rock
Pt 13620
Keran
Gurais
Gurez-Kanzalwan
Kargil
Muzaffarabad
Tithwal
Bandipura
Baramula
121 Brigade
Murree
Rampur
Srinagar
Uri
Haji Pir
Gulmarg
Badgam
Jammu & Kashmir
12 Div
68 Brigade & 1 Para
Poonch
15 Corps
Anantnag
Rawalpindi
Patandri
Mendhar
Banihal
Mirpur
Chingas
Naushera
INDIA
Pak Infitratiion
Indian Offensive
Fierce Battles
IAF Mi 4s
Jhelum
Chhamb
Akhnur
Udhampur
Jammu
Jaurian
Sialkot
KBK Infographics
Not to Scale

junior commissioned officers (JCOs) and a few soldiers embedded in the group to provide leadership. They carried with them leaflets and pamphlets to incite the local population along with transistor radios pre-tuned to Radio Pakistan. The force commenced training in May 1965 under the supervision of HQs 12 Division in Murree, familiarizing themselves for six weeks in infiltration, sabotage techniques and the use of weapons like LMGs, rifles, Sten carbines, detonators and fuses.[9]

By 12 August, more than 1,200 infiltrators had been captured by a combination of the Indian Army and state police forces. Many of the infiltrators were in their early twenties and demonstrated a zealously calm countenance when captured, demonstrating that they had undergone extensive religious indoctrination prior to the operation. By 21 August the infiltration was crushed and the last remnants of Khaled Force, the most stubborn force, retreated into Pakistan after suffering heavy casualties.[10] An overconfident Major General Akhtar Malik, the mastermind of Operation Gibraltar, had not done his homework well! He had met his match in the form of the strapping 6-foot Sikh warrior, Lieutenant General Harbaksh Singh. Having operated extensively in the Kashmir Valley during the 1947–48 conflict, Harbaksh knew the terrain like the back of his hand and had regular forces waiting at almost all entry points.

After conducting mopping-up operations for a few days, Harbaksh decided to complete some unfinished business from 1948. Encouraged by the success of his counter-infiltration campaign and somewhat frustrated with the lack of aggressiveness of the corps commander of XV Corps, Lieutenant General Katoch, who was directing the battle in J&K, Harbaksh pushed for two major offensives to seal J&K from further infiltration. He first turned his attention to the Kishenganga–Tithwal sector area wherein, as a brigade commander in 1948, he had notched up significant successes, but could not consolidate those gains in terms of territorial gains. Three battalions comprising 2 Rajput, 3/8 Gorkhas and 1 Sikh captured four significant heights in the sector which overlooked the Muzaffarabad–Kel Road, a key road in POK that linked the western areas with the northern areas. After a series of tough battles extending for almost a month, this operation finally got over on 20 September with the capture of two heights overlooking the vital Mirpur bridge over the River Kishenganga.

The second offensive was concentrated in the strategic bulge between Uri and Poonch with a final objective to capture Haji Pir Pass and a few heights around it.[11] Interestingly, these were captured with significant casualties to own forces in 1948 and then handed back on a platter to Pakistan after the ceasefire agreement of 1948. These heights occupied a special place in the hearts of many soldiers and officers of the Indian Army who had seen action there and Harbaksh was determined to wrest them back. Troops of 68 Infantry Brigade and 1 Para (a total of five infantry battalions with adequate artillery support) from 19 Division commenced operations to capture Haji Pir Pass and other surrounding heights in the strategically located bulge between Uri and Poonch. Haji Pir Pass and seven more posts in the bulge were finally captured between 28 and 31 August after fierce fighting.[12] The valour of Major Ranjit Singh Dayal, a company commander with 1 Para Battalion during the final assault on Haji Pir Pass was specially acclaimed by Harbaksh in his book[13]. Dayal was decorated with the Maha Vir Chakra for his bold and imaginative leadership. Also decorated with the Maha Vir Chakra in these operations were Lieutenant Colonel Sampuran Singh, CO of 19 Punjab, the brigade commander of 68 Infantry Brigade, Brigadier Zorawar Chand Bakshi and the divisional commander of 19 Infantry Division, Major General S.S. Kalan.[14]

One of India's most accomplished paratroopers and counter-insurgency experts, Lieutenant General Mathew Thomas, missed the action in 1965 as he was commanding 2 Para Battalion in the north-eastern state of Tripura as part of 61 Brigade based at Agartala. He, however, recollects that during the initial operations to capture Haji Pir Pass, Sank, one of the adjoining heights, was an initial objective for 1 Para Battalion and when the first attack failed, the CO told his brigade commander, Zorawar Bakshi, that he would be able to launch a second assault only with better artillery support. With none available, it called for tremendous courage on the part of Major Ranjit Singh Dayal, one of the company commanders, to lead the attack with existing resources. Hailing from a humble Sikh family, Dayal's father was a subedar major from the pre-Independence era and the young daredevil paratrooper was always willing to push the boundaries of human endurance. The capture of Sank raised the morale of 1 Para Battalion significantly and paved the way for the subsequent fall of Haji Pir Pass on 28 August.[15] Kargil sector too saw the Indian Army quickly capturing some Pakistani posts overlooking the Leh–Srinagar Highway in a daring night operation on 15 August.[16]

Since India had honoured the 1949 UN Security Council resolution on Kashmir in terms of not placing fighter aircraft at Srinagar, the IAF could not intercept some of the clandestine missions launched by PAF C-130 aircraft to resupply and support the raiders in the Valley.[17] These resupply dropping missions, many of which were executed by night, were fairly accurate, but failed to stem the rout. Despite war not being officially declared between India and Pakistan, the IAF innovatively modified Mi-4 helicopters in the gunship role and also employed Alouette light helicopters for casualty evacuation in support of the counter-infiltration operations after Harbaksh suggested to the air chief that he badly needed helicopters to act as a force multiplier in the Valley. The willingness of Harbaksh to use all resources at his disposal to thwart the widespread infiltration campaign, and immediate support from the IAF, were essential if India was to decisively put down the multi-pronged Pakistan backed subversion in Kashmir. Responding with alacrity to a call from him, the IAF put together a helicopter task force at Srinagar comprising ten to twelve Mi-4 utility helicopters that were fitted with machine guns and modified to carry 25 lb bombs. The ability to shift small-sized forces from one sector to the other along with casualty evacuation capability in the Valley was a significant morale enhancer. Surprising the infiltrators in areas that were not accessible by ground forces, the Mi-4s caused a fair amount of psychological degradation rather than direct destruction and demonstrated good coercive intent on the part of the India's armed forces.[18]

The narration of events from an Indian perspective would not be complete without a word about 'behind the enemy lines operations' by Meghdoot Force, a special unit from the Rajputana Rifles and Rajput Regiment. Led by Major (later Lieutenant Colonel) Megh Singh, a WW II veteran with experience in covert operations in Burma, and supported to the hilt by Harbaksh Singh who himself had experience of operations behind enemy lines in Malaya during the war. The unit caused a fair amount of mayhem and confusion by blowing up bridges behind enemy lines and bringing on harassing fire on surprised infiltrators from the rear. The force was to shift south into the Chhamb sector as the conflict expanded.[19]

Tough, unyielding and a demanding commander, Harbaksh Singh had ensured by mid-September that all the infiltrators had been pushed back and the much awaited 'Liberation of Kashmir' was nothing but a pipe dream for Pakistan. In the final analysis, Operation Gibraltar ended with a whimper and a resounding victory for India. It was a chastening defeat for Ayub Khan and his rabidly anti-India foreign minister, Bhutto. For India, it was a much needed morale booster after the reverses in Kutch. Operation Gibraltar in many ways was Harbaksh's finest hour – what it also did was to give him immense confidence to tackle subsequent battles on the western front with an aggressive mindset.

The Guns Boom in Chhamb

The failure of Operation Gibraltar to achieve any of its strategic or operational objectives was a severe jolt to Ayub Khan. He had to think of a face-saving gambit to distract Harbaksh's forces in Kashmir and maintain Pakistan's offensive momentum. As Kashmir was the main plank on which Ayub and Bhutto had sold the war with India to the people of Pakistan, it was time to open another front in Kashmir as a last-ditch attempt to cut it off from Punjab.

If Operation Gibraltar had gone as per plan, the final nail in India's coffin would have been Operation Grand Slam, a surgical and swift artillery-supported armour-led thrust into the Chhamb–Akhnur bulge culminating in the capture of the vital town of Akhnur. This would have cut the arterial Pathankot–Jammu Highway and isolated J&K from the rest of the country.[20] In the prevailing circumstances, Ayub Khan decided to launch this operation anyway. It was time for high stakes and desperate measures considering that Pakistan had lost a number of passes and heights to Indian forces towards the end of August in the Tithwal, Uri and Kargil sectors.

What is not widely known is that Major General Akhtar Malik,

General Officer Commanding 12 Division, the architect of both Operation Gibraltar and Operation Grand Slam, had cleverly woven in an artillery plan to support the southern thrust lines of the infiltration. The plan was to concurrently cause heavy attrition to the lone artillery regiment that supported India's 191 Infantry Brigade, which was also supported by only a single squadron of light AMX-13 tanks. As the unsuspecting batteries of the Indian Army's 14 Field Regiment celebrated Independence Day on 15 August, they were struck at multiple locations by well-directed and concentrated fire from Akhtar Malik's artillery brigade and the regiment was crippled with the loss of 6 to 8 guns and huge ammunition stockpiles. Worse still, the brigade commander, Brigadier Masters, was killed during one of the bombardments.[21] Though Harbaksh Singh speedily replaced the loss with a battery of medium guns and placed Brigadier Manmohan Singh, who was commanding a brigade in the adjoining division in command of 191 Brigade, the damage had been done. Pakistan had scored a significant preliminary success thanks to its superior artillery before the battle had even begun.

On 1 September 1965, well before the crack of dawn, the hamlets around the Indian border town of Chhamb awoke to the rumbling of Patton tanks and a thundering artillery barrage from 105 and 155 mm guns. Pakistan's 12 Division had launched Operation Grand Slam with almost three brigades supported by two regiments of armour leading the assault with an entire artillery brigade comprising all elements including a large number of field and medium artillery guns, gun-locating regiments and an air defence regiment in support.[22] By late morning, 11 a.m. to be precise, faced with the ominous prospect of being overrun by the enemy, Brigadier Manmohan Singh, the Indian brigade commander, asked for air support to check the enemy's advance. Why he waited almost five hours after sunrise to do so remains a mystery that can only be explained as a decision dilemma caused by the 'fog of war'. It would be a further six hours before the first IAF aircraft would appear over the tactical battle area (TBA).

Though Professor Sumit Ganguly argues that India subscribed to the strategy of 'defence and deterrence through punishment and retaliation',[23] this was seen only as rhetoric and not through effective posturing on ground and in the air, particularly after India was given a wake-up call after the Rann of Kutch incident. Punishment was never a strategy that was discussed within the strategic establishment with any seriousness given India's reluctance to be seen as a country that was ready to use military power as a tool of statecraft. That India thought that any conflict in Kashmir would remain as it was in 1947–48 – a localized conflict – was strategic naivety of the highest order. That India did not expect Pakistan to launch an offensive when it finally did and be ready for it, particularly in the air, was a failure of intelligence and lapses in operational leadership.

Where was the requirement for the brigade commander to wait for a clearance from Delhi for air strikes? Should this joint appreciation not have been done in the preceding weeks by the Western Army and Air Commands and prior clearance been obtained from Delhi to launch air strikes should Pakistan attempt to expand the conflict? At 5 p.m., by the time the oldest operational aircraft in the IAF's inventory, the Vampire, was launched to stall the Pakistani armoured offensive, the two forces were in close contact on the ground – not the best situation for close air support. Flying into the setting sun without any air defence escorts, by the time sorties were flown, the effectiveness of the IAF strikes was muted. While the offensive had slowed down after quite a few Pakistani Patton and Chaffee tanks were knocked out by the Vampires, the Indian Army too lost some troops and tanks to 'friendly fire' – 3 Mahar Regiment and 20 Lancers in particular suffered. Equally demoralizing was the loss of four Vampires to ground fire and enemy air defence fighters in the form of the formidable F-86 Sabre jets, which were waiting over the tactical battle area.[24]

Two main thoughts came to my mind when I sat down to analyse the first significant air action by the IAF in the 1965 War. First was that the response was too late – the first sorties should have been launched at dawn before the Pakistani armour had come in close contact with the few tanks of 191 Brigade. This would have allowed a clear and early demarcation of the Forward Line of Own Troops (FLOT) so that there was minimal possibility of fratricide. This would have also surprised the PAF, which might not have been able to send Sabres to the area in time. Since the attacks would have come from the east and the rising sun, it would have made it more difficult for the attacking aircraft to be picked up by both ground-based ack-ack guns and air defence aircraft. Second was the rationale to first send in the slowest and most vulnerable aircraft into a fairly dense air defence environment. More about the air battle over Chhamb later as it is time to get back to the action on the ground as 12 Division of the Pakistan Army attempted to gain a foothold across the Munawar Tawi river.

Rearguard Action

After bearing the brunt of the Pakistani artillery bombardment and armoured thrust, and suffering some losses to friendly fire as IAF Vampire jets bombarded enemy positions on the evening of 1 September, 3 Mahar Regiment acquitted itself admirably under adverse conditions. Commanded aggressively by Lieutenant Colonel G.S. Sangha, who even requisitioned machine guns from battle casualty AMX tanks of 20 Lancers as his battalion withdrew, the unit continued to harass the enemy during the night. For his grit and bravery in a defensive battle under trying conditions, Sangha was awarded the Maha Vir Chakra.

As all three battalions of 191 Brigade and the lone squadron of AMX tanks withdrew, first to Jaurian by early morning on 2 September and then across the Munawar Tawi to Akhnur by the same evening, they caused significant attrition to the advancing Pakistani forces. Inexplicably, as it seemed at the time, the Pakistani offensive slowed down on 2 September as Akhtar prepared to cross the Munawar Tawi. This provided a breather for India to quickly reorganize its defensive line around Akhnur with 191 Brigade and a fresh 28 Brigade. While another newly inducted brigade in the area, 41 Brigade, created a forward defensive line around Jaurian, another tactically sound position at Troti heights overlooking the Munawar Tawi river was created. All the brigades were placed under command of 10th Division of XV Corps in a hastily put together reorganization of forces.

By the time the squadron (typically 12 to 14 tanks) of 20 Lancers withdrew across the Munawar Tawi under the nose of a whole regiment of enemy Patton tanks, they were left with only three tanks with the rest having been destroyed by the advancing Pakistani forces. A few Indian tanks were also said to have been knocked out by IAF Vampires the previous evening. The squadron commander, Major Bhaskar Roy, was also awarded the Maha Vir Chakra.

While the Pakistani offensive caught their opponents by surprise, there were differences within its senior leadership over the depth to which the offensive was sustainable. While General Musa, the Pakistan Army chief, and the headquarters staff at Rawalpindi wanted to go for the jugular and capture Akhnur at the earliest so as to threaten the Pathankot–Jammu highway, Major General Akhtar Malik, the GOC of 12 Division, seemingly felt that this plan was not sustainable as the Indian Army would regroup and cut off his force. He preferred to consolidate around Jaurian before advancing to Akhnur. Surprisingly, he was replaced by Major General Yahya Khan on 2 September. Yahya was the GOC of 7 Division, another formation that was moving north from the Lahore area to reinforce 12 Division. This change in command caused some confusion and delay amongst Pakistani ranks; many commentators have attributed this to Pakistan's failure to drive home the advantage they had gained on the opening day. When one of Yahya Khan's brigade commanders, Brigadier Janjua, pressed for a clearance to go for the jugular and take Akhnur, he was reportedly cautioned by Yahya so: 'Dig deep Ifti, my boy! Dig deep! Chaudhuri is no fool! He will counter attack!'[25]

Though that counter-attack never materialized, the delay of one day was enough for India to rush in enough reinforcements and armour to fight a decent defensive battle in the area from 3 to 6 September with almost a division-sized force. As a result, the Pakistanis just did not have the numbers to fight a meaningful offensive battle in the plains. Another reason for the delay caused to the Pakistani advance was the counter-attack launched by 41 Brigade on 4 September on the insistence of Lieutenant General Harbaksh Singh.[26] Wilting under a fierce artillery and armour assault on its integral artillery regiment on 3 September, 41 Brigade asked to withdraw to Akhnur, barely a day after occupying defences. Instead, Harbaksh Singh asked them to launch a counter-attack on 4 September and then redeploy. It was at his insistence that the forward defensive line rallied around Jaurian and blunted the Pakistani offensive, while the main divisional defences were strengthened at Akhnur. By the time the Pakistanis attacked the forward defences around Akhnur on 6 September, they ran out of firepower and were decisively beaten back. This rearguard action allowed Harbaksh sufficient time to launch his offensive in the Lahore and Sialkot sectors to deflect the immense pressure building up in Chhamb. By late evening on 6 September, Pakistan had seen the writing on the wall and started moving much of their armour and artillery out of the Chhamb sector towards the Sialkot sector, where an Indian offensive was under way, leaving just about enough forces in Chhamb to blunt any Indian counter-attack.

The IAF over Chhamb

Pathankot airfield is located at the northern tip of Punjab adjoining the Jammu region. It was developed as a forward airbase to support operations in one of the most vulnerable areas from an Indian perspective in a likely India–Pakistan conflict. The Chhamb–Akhnur–Jammu sector along with Jhangar, Poonch and Uri sectors were identified as operationally important, and aircraft from Pathankot could be over these areas in minutes, should the need arise. As Operation Gibraltar unfolded in Kashmir, Pathankot buzzed with activity as it prepared for the eventuality of a full-blown conflict. As on 1 September, the base had two Mystere squadrons and a large detachment of Vampire jet trainers. What their role was going to be was not clearly spelt out. Once the decision to employ offensive air power was taken by the Government of India at 4:30 p.m. on 1 September, the first fighters in the air were three waves of Vampire jets from 45 and 220 Squadrons in a four-aircraft formation armed with rockets in anti-armour role. They were over the target area in a jiffy and what they saw on the ground was a close-contact battle between Pakistani Patton tanks, Indian AMX tanks and troops of 3 Mahar Regiment. Despite the difficulty in segregating targets the Vampires tried their best to discriminate between friend and foe and fired their rockets. What they did not realize was that PAF Sabre jets would be over the area in a flash to intercept the second and third waves of Vampire jets. Though four Vampires were shot down in minutes by the vastly superior Sabres and fierce ack-ack fire, the exploits of Mysteres of 31 Squadron of the IAF operating from Pathankot under the command of Wing Commander William Goodman cannot be forgotten as it flew numerous close air support missions over Chhamb, and ably assisted the rearguard action by 191 Brigade by slowing down the Pak advance. IAF strikes accounted for 12 to 13 Patton and Chaffee tanks, two artillery guns and a large number of soft-skinned vehicles. Unfortunately three Indian AMX tanks, ammunition-carrying vehicles and some troop concentrations were also hit during the close-contact air-land battle.[27]

The IAF hit back fiercely in the air too on 3 September after inducting the highly manoeuvrable Gnat fighters of 23 Squadron into Pathankot. The squadron was to provide air defence cover to the town and escort the Mystere close air support missions over Chhamb and Jaurian. With an aggressive squadron commander in the form of Wing Commander Raghavendran (later Air Marshal and Vice Chief of Air Staff), and an accomplished air combat tactician, Squadron Leader Johnny Greene, who was posted at Ambala and attached to the squadron, 23 Squadron was the pioneer unit that developed low-level air combat tactics in the IAF.[28] Air Vice Marshal Milind Shankar was a young flying officer in the squadron and recounts how Johnny Greene, a UK-trained fighter combat leader and the detachment commander at Pathankot was asked by the station commander of Pathankot, Group Captain Roshan Suri, to give a pep talk to all aircrew at Pathankot on 2 September:

> The station was silent when 23 Sqn landed from Adampur. Johnny Greene was asked to speak to all aircrew on air combat; a much needed pep talk as he described the mechanics and dangers of air combat. He talked about basic things like fear and how to overcome it with skill and courage. He also spoke to us on split-second decision making, situational and combat awareness.[29] He spoke about the need to conquer our needless fear of the adversary and to go up there and shoot well and shoot straight. 'It is as simple as that,' he said. Johnny Greene inspired a bunch of eager Gnat pilots from 23 Squadron (The Panthers) to go into combat from the next day onwards with a clear sense of purpose. He was the only air defence pilot of the IAF to be awarded a Vir Chakra in 1965 for inspirational leadership without shooting down an enemy aircraft during the course of the war;[30] it is a different matter altogether that he did get into a few situations

where he was in a position to shoot down a Sabre, but the Gnat's notoriously unpredictable gun let him down.

I had the privilege of listening to Johnny Greene speak on air combat and leadership twenty years later when he was an air marshal and the senior air staff officer at Central Air Command. It was probably the most inspiring talk I have ever heard in my entire career and left an indelible impression on me about matters right and wrong, be it in air combat, leadership or within the larger canvas of life in general. It is a pity there was no YouTube or Facebook in those days – the talk would have garnered thousands of 'likes' in no time.

A better day for the Indian Air Force was 3 September 1965. Some even call it a red-letter day as 23 Squadron bagged the first aerial combat kill for the IAF since Independence. Flying as low-level escorts to a large formation of Mysteres, four Gnats engaged an equal number of Sabres and Starfighters in an aerial duel over Chhamb in which Flight Lieutenant Trevor Keelor shot down a Sabre. The next day, another 'young gun', Flight Lieutenant Pathania, bagged another Sabre. Both were awarded the Vir Chakra and the entry of the Gnats coincided with the scaling down of the Pakistani offensive in Chhamb around 6 or 7 September as the Indian Army opened up the Lahore front.

The personal war diary of a young Gnat pilot from 23 Squadron, Manna Murdeshwar, tells the tale of the IAF response between 1 and 6 September:

> **2 Sept, '65**: Sqn Ldr Johnny Greene, Self [then a flight lieutenant], Flt Lt AJS Sandhu and Flt Lt Trevor Keelor were nominated by HQ WAC to move to Pathankot – ostensibly for ORP duties at that airfield. When the 4 of us landed at sunset, we were greeted by grim faces and learnt about the downing of 4 Vamps by the PAF Sabres. We were surprised to find that 'our 4' aircraft & pilots on landing at Halwara, had been rerouted to Pathankot and were awaiting our arrival.
>
> **3 Sept, '65**: Our first Gnat ops sortie was also the first air battle post Korean War. On that day, we escorted 4 Mysteres to the C-J sector to initiate a Sabre kill. We planned for the Mysteres to be at

> 20G to entice the Sabres, while we, in the Gnats, were to remain at low level [under PAF radar] and await the arrival of the Sabres. Once they were sighted, the Mysteres were asked to return to base and we climbed up to engage the Sabres. At heights, in the combat that ensued, Trevor allegedly shot down one Sabre which was hailed as our first 'Victory.' The PAF later disputed this 'kill.' An unfortunate result of the air battle, was that one of our team members, apparently not proficient in close combat, got lost, and landed at Pasrur, in Pakistan.
>
> **4 Sept, '65**: Johnny, self, AJ and Pat enroute to C-J sector, encountered 4 Sabres strafing our troops. All of us rolled over and each managed to get behind a Sabre. Johnny was the first to get behind one, but had a high 'angle off', so was unable to fire. I was in a good 400 yds line astern position with the 'diamonds pipping' the Sabre, but my guns, frustratingly, stopped after a single round of fire! AJ too had some problem, which I can't presently recall. Pat however, managed to get a kill before his guns also jammed.[31]

Albeit with significant hiccups, the battle of Chhamb was the first air–land battle fought by India in the modern era against an adversary with better tactical and communication procedures; many of the Pakistani tank crews and fighter pilots had trained in the US under the Military Assistance Programme (MAP) and were reasonably proficient in directing close air support aircraft onto targets in the tactical battle Area. In a defensive battle, particularly in the plains, the most effective way of employing air power is not in the contact battle, but by ensuring that the attacker is not able to build his force ratios to sustain his offensive. This is done by interdicting his follow-on forces and reserves, and is possible only if a joint appreciation has been done prior to the battle. None of this was done and by calling in air power at the last moment without proficiency in forward air controlling, nothing better could have been expected. It was an eye-opener for both the IAF and the Indian Army as they did well in the years ahead to build on this experience.

The PAF too was guilty of continuing to assume a defensive posture over Chhamb and failed to carry out interdiction missions against Indian reinforcements that were being inducted for the relief of Chhamb, Jaurian and Akhnur. Had the PAF combined an interdiction and an air campaign as a counter against IAF airfields on 1 September, the Indians would have been hard-pressed to coordinate a suitable response. Pakistani tentativeness was clearly evident! As the fighting petered out in Chhamb, both India and Pakistan were readying themselves for what would be fairly intense air–land battles further to the south in the Lahore and Sialkot sectors.

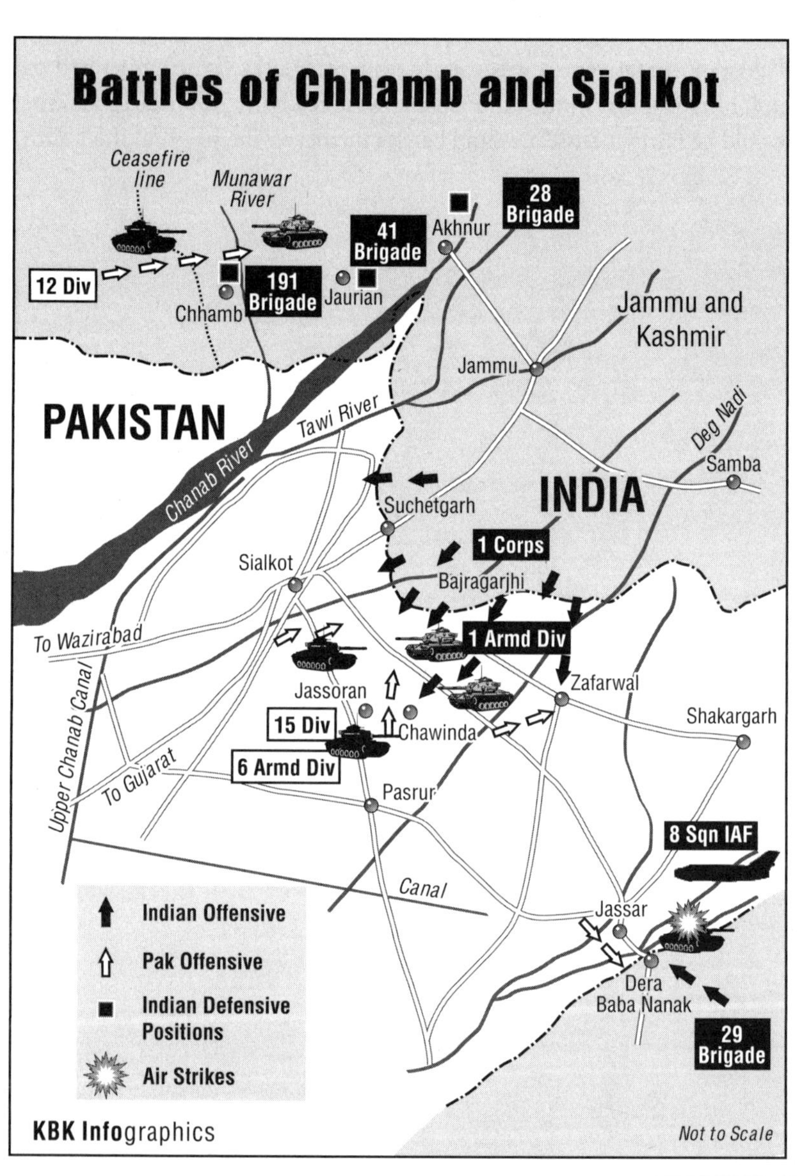
Battles of Chhamb and Sialkot
Ceasefire line
Munawar River
28 Brigade
41 Brigade
Akhnur
12 Div
191 Brigade
Jaurian
Chhamb
Jammu and Kashmir
Jammu
PAKISTAN
Tawi River
Deg Nadi
Chanab River
Samba
INDIA
Suchetgarh
1 Corps
Sialkot
Bajragarjhi
To Wazirabad
1 Armd Div
Upper Chanab Canal
Jassoran
Zafarwal
15 Div
Chawinda
Shakargarh
To Gujarat
6 Armd Div
Pasrur
8 Sqn IAF
Canal
Indian Offensive
Pak Offensive
Indian Defensive Positions
Air Strikes
Jassar
Dera Baba Nanak
29 Brigade
KBK Infographics
Not to Scale

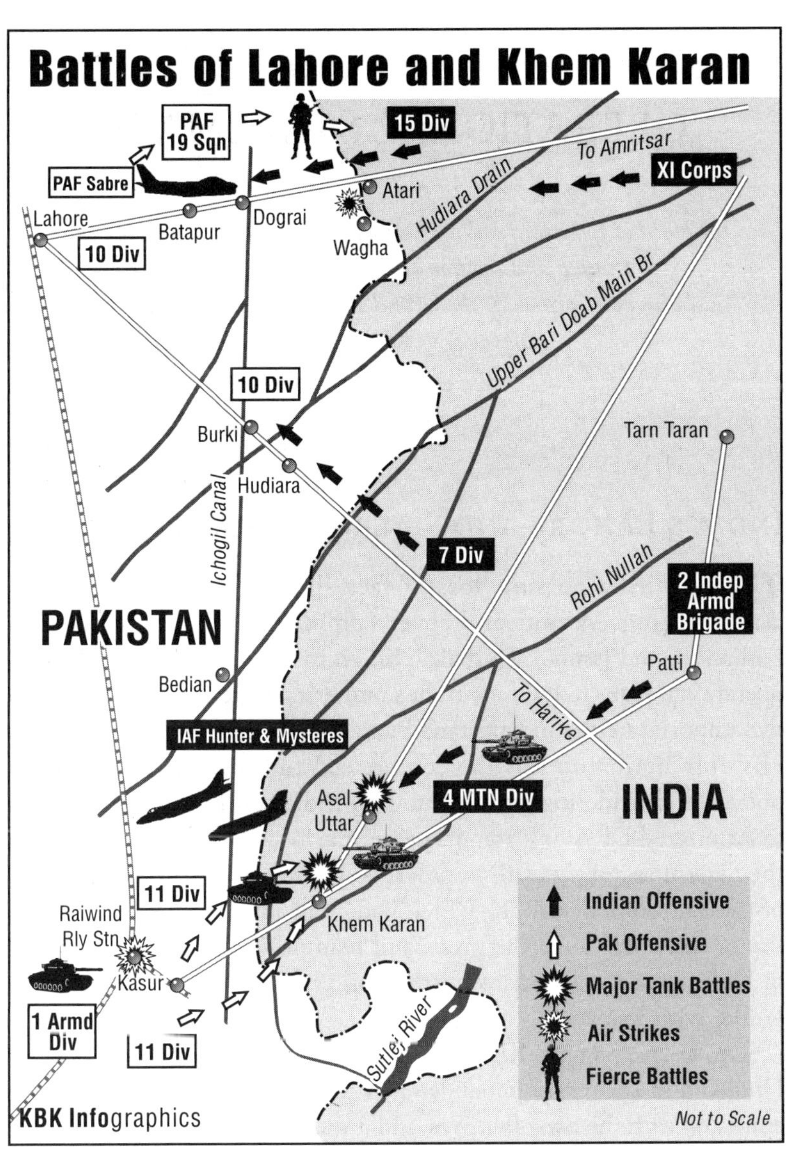
Battles of Lahore and Khem Karan
PAF 19 Sqn
15 Div
PAF Sabre
To Amritsar
XI Corps
Atari
Hudiara Drain
Lahore
Batapur
Dograi
Wagha
10 Div
Upper Bari Doab Main Br
10 Div
Burki
Tarn Taran
Hudiara
Ichogil Canal
7 Div
Rohi Nullah
2 Indep Armd Brigade
PAKISTAN
Patti
Bedian
To Harike
IAF Hunter & Mysteres
Asal Uttar
4 MTN Div
INDIA
11 Div
Raiwind Rly Stn
Khem Karan
Kasur
1 Armd Div
11 Div
Sutlej River
Indian Offensive
Pak Offensive
Major Tank Battles
Air Strikes
Fierce Battles
KBK Infographics
Not to Scale

20

OPERATIONAL STALEMATE

The blood of Pakistani and Indian soldiers stained the wheat-lands of Punjab and the stony ridges of Kashmir; vultures hung over corpses on the Grand Trunk Road, the immortal highway of Kipling's Kim.[1]

– John Frazer

India's Lahore and Sialkot Ripostes

Faced with a possible loss of face should Pakistan succeed in capturing Akhnur and sever communication links between Pathankot and Jammu, Harbaksh Singh came up with two ambitious operational plans to leverage India's numerical superiority and threaten two important cities in Pakistan's Punjab province, Lahore and Sialkot. His only limitation was the compressed time frame to launch the operation considering that the move of India's only armoured division (1 Armoured Division) from its peacetime location to its launch pad in the Sialkot sector was still in progress. This has to be seen in the light of the cantonment culture, which had crept into the Indian Army in the 1950s, and was in the process of being reviewed by the Ministry of Defence so that offensive formations could be located closer to the border with Pakistan.

Two corps, namely, XI Corps commanded by Lieutenant General Dhillon and I Corps commanded by Lieutenant General Dunne, were entrusted with the two offensives, and it was decided to open the Lahore front with XI Corps a day or two before the Sialkot offensive for two reasons. The first was that by advancing towards Lahore, XI Corps of the Indian Army hoped to draw major elements of the Pakistani armour and artillery away from Chhamb, and the second was because it would take a few more days before India's recently raised I Corps along with its integral 1 Armoured Division was ready to be inducted into the Sialkot sector. As it turned out, this arrangement worked fine for India because it stretched the Pakistan Army over a wide frontage of almost 200 km. Harbaksh Singh has been particularly critical of India's inability to launch both offensives simultaneously, but in all fairness it must be said that considering that 1 Corps was a newly raised corps with two of its four divisions unfamiliar with the Punjab terrain, it did not do too badly as the campaign unfolded.

Threatening Lahore

Pakistan's defences in the Lahore sector were based along a major canal, the Ichogil Canal, which runs almost parallel to the international boundary for almost 90 km. The northern limit of this sector was at a tri-junction of the Ichogil Canal, the Ravi and another canal system called the MLRC, while the southern limit was around Kasur and the Sutlej river where some of the fiercest armoured battles would be fought inside Indian territory during Pakistani counter-attacks. Defending the Ichogil Canal were two divisions of the Pakistan Army comprising 10 and 11 Infantry Divisions. While 10 Infantry Division mainly occupied well-prepared defences behind the canal around Lahore with some aggressive deployment ahead of the canal, 11 Division occupied defences to the south of Lahore in the area around Kasur. Importantly, Indian intelligence missed out on the presence of Pak 1 Armoured Division lurking behind 11 Division, waiting for an opportunity to exploit any initial inroads made by it. This deployment at Kasur was light on infantry and heavy with armour and motorized infantry. It offered good potential for a Pakistani offensive into Indian territory around Khem Karan with a view to outflank India's ongoing offensives to the north, and threaten Amritsar with a right hook from the south. However, as per classical defensive deployment in the plains along a linear obstacle that demanded a three-division deployment, Pakistan was stretched to the limit as it had similar commitments all along the international border.

India's main objectives of the offensive were for XI Corps to threaten Lahore from two directions (east and south-east) and conduct a diversionary thrust further south to keep 11 Division occupied. India's attacking forces in all sectors were infantry-heavy with only limited armour and mobility on each thrust line. It hoped to surprise the enemy with multiple thrust lines and an artillery assault that would, it was hoped, lead to the establishment of multiple crossing points on the Ichogil Canal. The entire 15 Infantry Division was to race down the Grand Trunk Road in a symbolic bid to assault the Ichogil Canal and establish multiple bridgeheads through which follow-on forces could be inducted for the proposed advance to Lahore. Similarly, 7 Infantry Division was to make inroads along another axis to the south while 4 Mountain Division was to advance along the Khem Karan–Kasur Road at the southern extremes of the sector. An independent armoured brigade (2 Independent Armoured Brigade) was kept as a reserve to be deployed at a place and time of India's choosing. Normally, such formations are inducted into battle only when a clear breach is made in enemy defences, and used as a final sucker punch. Little did India realize on 6 September that this formation would come in handy a few days later at a critical juncture of a defensive battle at Khem Karan against elements of the much talked about 1 Armoured Division of Pakistan.

From 6 to 10 September, the two armies fought a series of bruising battles of attrition for control of the Ichogil Canal and areas surrounding it. While the Indian Army tried its best to establish a foothold across the canal and consolidate its gains before attacking Lahore, the Pakistan Army launched a series of counter-attacks led by its superior armour and mobile artillery, not forgetting some telling attacks through the afternoon on the Indian Army's advancing 15 Division by PAF Sabre jets of 19 Squadron. Leading the six-aircraft Sabre mission was Sajad Haider, the squadron commander of 9 Squadron, PAF, who had detached two of the six Sabres to provide top cover should the IAF decide to interfere with his ground-attack mission.[2] Why the IAF did not mount combat air patrols over what was the main thrust line is completely inexplicable and only points at suboptimal army–air force coordination.[3] This is more so because on the previous day (5 September), the war diary of the defence minister indicates that he had discussed the Lahore offensive with the two chiefs.[4] While some formations of 15 Division made spectacular initial progress, there was very little coordination and orchestration of follow-on forces to consolidate the gains made. In fact, what it resulted in was the inability of these infantry-heavy formations to withstand any counter-attacks by armour or from the air.

Pak Seizes Initiative in the Air – IAF Responds Well

India's reactive mindset and lack of air–land synergy was clearly evident from the fact that the three-pronged Lahore offensive of 6 September was not backed by a simultaneous air offensive against Pak bases. Nor were there any combat air patrols airborne. Had such missions been launched on the morning of 6 September, it would have declared India's offensive intent very clearly and also deterred the strikes on IAF bases that were to follow in the evening. In their indictment of India's air–land strategy, Jagan Mohan and Chopra write:

> The only briefing that the air force received in relation to the ground offensive was to hit targets of opportunity. The intelligence provided was poor, occasionally, targets were not found after reaching the designated areas. Whatever the reason behind the inaction, the IAF lost out on a critical opportunity to hit hard at the PAF's offensive capability, with little risk of attrition and to influence the outcome of the war.[5]

Instead of launching widespread aerial counter-attacks on PAF airbases on the morning of 6 September in tandem with the early-morning Lahore offensive, the IAF instead launched sporadic raids by Canberra bombers, Mysteres and Hunters against opportunity Pakistan Army targets in the Chander, Chhamb and Kasur sectors, all of which were intercepted and led to needless waste of effort.[6] The all-too familiar 'no clearance from Delhi' as counter attacks from air would unnecessarily escalate the situation left the IAF vulnerable to attack. One wonders that even at this stage was India's political leadership hopeful of calibrating the conflict? Air Marshal Asghar Khan, former Commander-in-Chief of the PAF ruminates in his book:

> If they had intended to attack us first their best time was the early hours in the morning of the 6th. Since they had launched a pre-arranged attack, the omission of the Air Force was deliberate. Our decision to launch the air offensive was taken at about 3 p.m. The attack was to be launched at the Indian airfields simultaneously a few minutes after sunset.[7]

Pakistan seized the initiative in the air on the evening of 6 September with a coordinated strike from Sargodha, Mauripur and Peshawar against four Indian airfields, Adampur, Halwara, Pathankot and Jamnagar. While near-simultaneous strikes were planned, only the Pathankot strike managed to surprise the Indians as the other strikes were delayed and met with opposition over the target airfields.[8] While the strikes on Pathankot, Adampur and Halwara were carried out by Sabres, B-57 Canberra bombers from Mauripur hit Jamnagar. Pathankot was hit badly, losing ten aircraft on the ground comprising nine fighters including two new MiG-21 fighters and a transport aircraft. The Pathankot story would have been different had the station commander at Pathankot, Group Captain Roshan Suri, heeded the advice of Wing Commander Raghavendran, the squadron commander of 23 Squadron, the Gnat squadron that had come in from Halwara to mount a combat air patrol over the airfield that evening.[9]

Manna Murdeshwar's diary entry for 6 September reads:

> **6 Sept '65:** Escorted Mysteres which were tasked to destroy the Pak tanks and attack the retreating Pak troops. A number of Pak tanks were destroyed and their advance was halted. While the 4 Mysteres were returning to base, one of them, flown by Flt Lt 'Dinky' Jatar, had a problem and therefore had to restrict its max speed to 250 kph. I informed the Mystere leader (Sqn Ldr Trilochan Singh) to proceed to base and said that I would escort the lone Mystere. My No. 2 also stated he was low on fuel and I agreed to his request to return to base.
>
> Both 'Dinky' and I returned with our fuel gauges reading zero – and to ensure that we immediately touched down safely, we landed on either end of the R/W [runway]– his was direct from the north and I from the south. Just when I was entering my blast

> pen, at the end of the R/W, six Sabres pulled up and before the first bullets strafed my Gnat, I managed to jump out!! That day we also lost a few Mysteres and a Packet aircraft parked at the dispersal area.

The story at Jamnagar from a naval aviator's perspective is worth telling too. Vice Admiral Vinod Pasricha (retd), one of the Indian Navy's most distinguished aviators, was a young lieutenant in 1965 and posted with the Indian Naval Air Squadron (INAS) 300, also called the White Tigers. Disappointed that INS *Vikrant* was undergoing a refit, the squadron nevertheless continued to hone their skills by proceeding to Jamnagar on 1 September for an air-to-ground firing practice detachment. Following the Chhamb offensive by Pakistan, the squadron was also tasked to man the Operational Ready Platform (ORP) at Jamnagar as a precautionary air defence measure, albeit without any radar cover. On the evening of 6 September, there were two Sea Hawks on the ORP with pilots strapped in and ready for take-off. A gut feeling told Commander R.V. Singh, the commanding officer of the squadron, that there would be some action that evening. While in those days, the IAF would cease day flying at sunset, the Indian Navy permitted its fighters to operate for half an hour or so after sunset the period commonly called dusk. R.V. Singh himself was one of the two pilots on ORP and asked the tower for permission to take off at dusk, but was denied permission and had to reluctantly get out of the cockpit and wind up for the day. A few minutes later, the PAF Canberras struck Jamnagar and made repeated passes over the airfield. That was not all. The Sea Hawks had planned a six-aircraft strike on the only PAF radar in the area at Badin near Karachi the next day, but due to reasons of command and control, they were summarily asked to leave Jamnagar and head for Goa, their home base. Lack of coordination between the IAF and the Indian Navy resulted in the squandering of vital offensive air power assets in the Kutch Sector.[10]

Alerted by the 5 p.m. Pathankot raid and aided by the delays in the other raids, Group Captain G.K. John, the aggressive and proactive station commander at Halwara (the IAF base near the industrial town of Ludhiana in Punjab) got four Hunters (two each from 7 and 27 Squadron) airborne in anticipation of a raid[11] on his base even as three other Hunters from his base were returning to base after a ground-attack mission over Tarn Taran. Engaged over the TBA by three Sabres, which were actually headed for Adampur, one of the Hunters flew into the ground as he attempted to shake a Sabre off his tail. Low on fuel after this unplanned engagement, the Sabres aborted their strike on Adampur. As the first formation of Hunters landed just before 6 p.m., three Sabres arrived over Halwara and got embroiled with the four Hunters and some classic dogfights were seen over the skies of Punjab. Hunters of No 7 and 27 Squadron shot down three Sabres (though the PAF claimed that one of the Sabres got back) and lost two of their own (Pingale and Ghandhi); more importantly they ensured that none of the Sabres managed to inflict much damage on the two airfields.[12] Three of the four pilots involved in the aerial dogfight that evening, Flight Lieutenants Ghandhi and Rathore and Flying Officer Neb, were awarded Vir Chakras. Flight Lieutenant Pingale would go on to get his on 16 September after he shot down a Sabre in a high-altitude aerial engagement near Amritsar. Though the PAF had initially seized the initiative, it had not reckoned with the fact that it was not only the Gnat, but the Hunter fighter-bomber too that was proving to be more than a match for the Sabre in aerial combat. This, more than anything else, resulted in no more day raids over IAF airfields for the rest of the war. As alluded to earlier in the chapter, six B-57 bombers from Mauripur raided Jamnagar after dusk and in poor weather, inflicting limited damage on a few Vampires on the ground. B-57s also attacked Adampur where they completely destroyed a MiG-21 at the ORP and damaged a second. Halwara too was attacked at night. The IAF was clearly rattled by these strikes and as Air Marshal Asghar Khan writes: 'We had got in the first punch and given the Indian Air Force a bloody nose.'[13]

While Asghar Khan was certainly a bold and imaginative commander, he conveniently forgets in his book that one of his 'brain child' operations was the botched-up Special Forces airborne assault operations by C-130s around designated IAF airfields. In a bold but unsustainable action, three C-130s dropped sixty paratroopers each of the elite Special Services Group (SSG) around the airfields of Pathankot, Adampur and Halwara, hoping to either seize the airfields or cause maximum destruction. To the PAF's credit, the operation was carried out stealthily and though the C-130s safely dropped their paratroopers, they could not drop them with the kind of precision that is available today. To complete the story, of the 180 paratroopers, twenty were killed, 132 were captured and only twenty made it back to Pakistan.[14]

The IAF riposte to the PAF strikes came early next morning at dawn on 7 September when large formations of Mysteres from 1 and 8 Squadrons attacked the PAF's main Sargodha airbase and a satellite base nearby called Chhota Sargodha. These were followed minutes later by Hunters from 27 Squadron. While the Mysteres managed to destroy a few aircraft on the ground including a B-57 bomber and an F-104 Starfighter, the highlight of the mission was a valiant dogfight waged by Squadron Leader 'Tubby' Devayya against the superior F-104 Starfighter. It was only years later that Devayya would be posthumously awarded a Maha Vir Chakra for shooting down Flight Lieutenant Amjad Hussain of the PAF close to Sargodha. The IAF Hunter strikes from 27 Squadron and 7 Squadron were relatively ineffective as PAF interceptors were alert by then and forced the Hunters to shed their load prematurely and engage in aerial dogfights with Sabres, one of which claimed two Hunters, with another going down because of fuel starvation. It is during these Hunter missions that Squadron Leader Mohammed Alam, a Sabre pilot, claimed five Hunters over Sargodha within a flash of thirty seconds. Sensationalized by John Fricker in his article 'Thirty Seconds over Sargodha',[15] the story would generate immense heat over the years as Indian and Pakistani pilots would exchange notes at staff colleges in the UK and the US, arriving at a plausible claim of two Hunters for Alam. The next Mystere strike by 1 Squadron of the IAF over Sargodha around noon was the most successful one and got the squadron two Vir Chakras for Squadron Leader Handa and Flight Lieutenant Kahai respectively. At the end of the second full day of the air war, though the IAF initially claimed fifteen PAF aircraft on the ground, realistic estimates indicate 8 to 10 aircraft lost on the ground and 6 to 7 fighters shot down in aerial combat. The IAF had lost 6 to 7 aircraft to aerial combat and almost twenty aircraft on ground during airfield attacks. The day ended with more strikes on other PAF airfields as a realization dawned within

Pakistan's strategic establishment that India had the stomach for a fight and would now go the whole hog with air power thrown in.

In an interestingly candid email exchange with the author on 15 January 2014, Air Marshal Philip Rajkumar shared his perspective on both joint and air operations:

> Hi Arjun,
>
> As I was in the 1 Sqn crew room at Adampur those days I will attempt to answer your questions. The main question we kept asking ourselves from 01 Sep to 05 Sep was 'When the hell do we get to see some action?' We used to wait hungrily for news from our friends in Pathankot who were in the thick of it from day one. We did night flying to become fully ops during those four nights. When I got airborne in the dark at 0530 am on 07 Sep it was my third night take off in a Mystere! And it was at max AUW with full fuel and 2x1000 lbs bombs.
>
> On 06 Sep we were told that the Army had opened the Lahore front. As young Fg Offrs we were utterly perplexed and dismayed that we were wasting time sitting in the crew room when our army was advancing towards Lahore. We had two Hunter Sqns 17 &27 at Halwara, three Mystere Sqns1, 8 &32 at Adampur and two Mystere Sqns 3 & 31 at Pathankot. There was enough air power available to make a decisive difference.1 Sqn carried out a search and strike mission over Gujranwala rly stn at dawn on 06 Sep. After that we sat on the ground. At 1.30pm we heard FM Ayub Khan broadcast to his nation that the Indians had attacked the sacred soil of Pakistan in the Lahore sector. We waited till PAF Sabres raided Pathankot and Halwara. Adampur was lucky because at about the same time as the Pathankot raid I saw a flight of three or four Sabres on the western horizon as I was peeing into one of those funnel urinals at the rear of our crew room. I immediately ran inside and alerted everyone and the air raid siren was sounded. The aircraft could not have been more than 5–6 Km away as I could clearly identify them as Sabres having seen and flown them at Nellis AFB, USA the previous September.
>
> From Jagan's research we now know that the formation leader was Sqn Ldr Alam who gained notoriety by claiming

> five Hunters in 30 secs over Sargodha the next morning. Unlike Rafiqui over Halwara, who fought well, Alam developed cold feet and did not attack his designated target. At about 6.30 pm a PAF B-57 raided Adampur and destroyed a MiG 21. The next morning we attacked Sargodha but with modest results. *In 33 sorties on 07 September we clearly shot down one F-104 in the air (Devayya's), claimed a Sabre, and destroyed one Sabre on the ground (Handa's) and lost two Mysteres and three Hunters. A poor exchange ratio by any yard stick.* The only good that came out of these strikes was that the PAF never again attempted a counter air strike against our bases in the western sector. Hopefully our spirited response was the cause.[16]

Contrary to tall claims thus far, the PAF realized that it could not sustain the kind of attrition it had met with after the encounter of 7 September. Both air forces were at low key; licking their wounds and deciding which way to progress the air war. The bottom line was that the IAF was larger; its Hunters and Gnats were matching the Sabres and the F-104s; and there was no way in which the PAF could win a war of attrition against the IAF. With IAF MiG-21s also carrying out combat air patrols over Lahore and Kasur, the knockout punch never came – the IAF was clawing its way back into the fight.

Valour at Dograi and Dera Baba Nanak

Of all the brigade-level battles fought around the Ichogil Canal, the Battle of Dograi merits attention from an Indian perspective. Of the three battalions of 54 Infantry Brigade which fought in the battle, it was a single battalion (3 Jat under a dynamic battalion commander, Lieutenant Colonel Desmond Hayde) that came out with its head held high during the continuous fighting over almost two-and-a-half weeks. It was the first unit to go into battle on 6 September and among the last to stop firing on 23 September.[17] Dograi is a small hamlet across the Ichogil Canal, 8 km from the international border and 14 km from the outskirts of Lahore. With this as an initial objective, 3 Jat under Hayde was the first to cross the international border in the wee hours of the morning of 6 September. Under the cover of an early morning mist, the battalion outflanked a company of the Pakistan Rangers and raced towards the canal, surprising the scanty forward deployment of the Pakistan Army and sending the defenders scurrying back towards Lahore. By midday 3 Jat had secured the bridge over the canal leading to Dograi despite six Sabres of the PAF having caused havoc amongst the advancing brigade. With all Pakistani troops in the area having withdrawn to the west of the canal, there was a clear Forward Line of Own Troops (FLOT) for the PAF to exploit. The Indian brigade with one armoured regiment was an easy target for PAF Sabres as they ripped into 54 Brigade, which hardly had any ack-ack guns or aerial cover from the IAF.

Despite suffering heavy losses, 3 Jat did not waver and looked back for support from its parent brigade. The support was not forthcoming as the other two battalions of the brigade had been slowed down significantly by the air strikes and artillery fire from across the canal. It was only a matter of time before the defenders would recoup and launch a counter-attack; this time with armour and artillery. The two companies of 3 Jat, which had made the crossing and captured the hamlet of Dograi, now came under withering fire and had to withdraw to the safety of the east bank of the canal. A golden opportunity to secure at least one crossing was lost because of poor communications, no follow-on support, no air cover and poor higher leadership, which failed to take the correct decisions under fire. For the next ten days, 15 Division would fight an attrition battle to stay inside Pakistani territory and wait for an opportunity to capture Dograi again. When that opportunity came on 23 September, 3 Jat was again the lead battalion during the recapture of Dograi after a bloody battle. By the time ceasefire was declared the battalion had lost over fifty personnel, but inflicted much heavier losses on the enemy – they captured an enemy battalion commander along with three officers and 100 men in the final assault. This was the finest hour for the Indian Army in the 15 Division sector thrust towards Lahore. It remained the best bargaining chip that India had during the ceasefire negotiations and one of the numerous decisive victories achieved by it at the tactical level. It was a pure infantryman's battle with all grit, guts and glory! Lieutenant Colonel Hayde, the CO, and Major Tyagi, one of the company commanders who perished in battle, were awarded Maha Vir Chakras. While the performance of the rest of the division was severely criticized by the commander of the Western Army Command, Lieutenant General Harbaksh Singh,[18] 3 Jat Regiment stood tall with the CO providing inspirational leadership through the battle.

The Air–Land Battle at Dera Baba Nanak

A question which a lot of Indian Army officers ask even today is where the IAF was on 6 September when XI Corps launched its assault across the Ichogil Canal? Why were IAF fighters not over the crossing area at first light when 3 Jat was making inroads across the canal? If the Gnats could shoot down Sabres over Chhamb, why did they not prevent Sabres from having a field day over 3 Jat and 54 Brigade as they attempted to secure a foothold on the western bank of the Ichogil Canal? From all reports, apart from the extensive damage to vehicles and equipment, the psychological impact of the Sabre strikes was instrumental in blunting 5 Jat's offensive and allowing Pakistani forces to recoup. The simple and highly plausible answer from most air force officers was: 'We were ready and waiting with fully armed aircraft, but the call for close air support from the army never came. How could you expect us to just get airborne and loiter over the tactical battle area?'

There are no easy answers for this as around the same time 8 Squadron with their Mysteres operating from Adampur airfield outside Jalandhar was playing havoc with Pakistani armour in response to a call for close air support from the brigade commander of 29 Infantry Brigade on the evening of 6 September. The brigade was tasked with offensive operations in the Dera Baba Nanak sector as part of operations in the northern limits of the Lahore sector.[19] Air Marshal Vinod Patney was a young flight lieutenant at the time, raring to go into action as many of his contemporaries were. He remarked in an interview with me: 'I was flying Toofanis as a flying officer in the Eastern Sector from Tezpur in 1962 and we were ready and capable of hitting the Chinese as they formed up prior to their assault. It was frustrating to sit and twiddle one's thumbs as the action unfolded. There was no way we were staying away from the action this time around.'[20] When queried why they did not provide close air support to the 3 Jat-led main Lahore thrust along the Grand Trunk Road, he bluntly remarked, 'No one asked for it. Did we not react immediately at Dera Baba Nanak.'[21] A telling comment indeed!

The Dera Baba Nanak area marked the northern edge of the Lahore sector and the southern boundary of the Sialkot sector. Since 1 Corps was still forming up for India's offensive in the Sialkot sector, Harbaksh Singh was keen that a suitable offensive action between the two sectors be launched, albeit with limited resources to keep the Pakistanis guessing about where the main assault was going to take place. However, he did not reckon with the spirited riposte offered by Pakistani armour in response to the Indian attempt to secure a foothold across the River Ravi by capturing the bridge at Dera Baba Nanak intact. Harbaksh was a demanding commander and his expectations of an infantry brigade with limited armour to be able to make inroads across the Ravi against a brigade-defended locality were unreasonable. However, when his brigade flattered to deceive after initial success on 6 September, and almost wilted in the face of a fierce counter-attack that evening, he had to step in and negate a request from the brigade commander, Brigadier Pritham Singh, to withdraw.[22]

This was where the IAF came into the picture late in the evening on 6 September as four Mysteres of 8 Squadron under the call sign of Black Formation streaked towards the Dera Baba Nanak bridge across which 10–12 Patton tanks were firing and advancing on Indian positions on the east bank of the Ravi. Picking up the dust kicked up by the tanks from miles, Patney recollects that the four Mysteres played havoc amongst the Pattons, making two passes and emptying their entire load of SNEB rockets.[23] For this mission and numerous other close air support missions and interdiction missions during the war, all members of Black Formation, Squadron Leader 'Dinky' Jatar and Flight Lieutenants Patney, Chopra and Bhatia, were awarded the Vir Chakra – they were part of the hard-working 'ground attack' boys who in jest always felt that the glamorous 'air defence' fighter jocks in their Gnats and Hunters cornered much of the glory in the air. Thanks to Jagan Mohan and Samir Chopra in their book, this aerial action over Dera Baba Nanak is recorded for posterity.[24] What a shame that the official history of the war hardly mentions this engagement![25]

Armoured Battles at Khem Karan and Assal Uttar

As 15 and 7 Divisions were fighting battles of attrition around Lahore, the Kasur sector saw one of the fiercest tank battles after WW II in Khem Karan and Assal Uttar on Indian territory. The battles comprised a rearguard action by 4 Mountain Division and 2 Independent Armoured Brigade to thwart a bold thrust by 11 Division of the Pakistan Army along with elements of the crack Patton-tank-heavy 1 Armoured Division. The Pakistani plan, which aimed to cut off India's 15 and 7 Divisions and threaten Amritsar in a quid pro quo outflanking operational trade-off, was reminiscent of the armoured battles in North Africa between Montgomery's 8th Army and Rommel's Afrika Korps, the only difference being that the terrains were completely different.

It was all along envisaged by India that action along the southern flank of the Lahore sector in the Kasur sector was going to be a holding action and a diversionary thrust by the Indian Army so that the main thrust lines in the centre could make speedy inroads and capture maximum territory. However, a comedy of errors and poor intelligence on both sides led to miscalculations about where the adversary's main armour was going to concentrate. While India had no clue that Pakistan was concentrating its 1 Armoured Division in the Kasur area and that they had another armoured division (6 Armoured Division) in the Sialkot area, Pakistan was not sure where India's 1 Armoured Division was going to be used – in the Lahore sector or further north in the Sialkot sector. Therefore, when India's limited offensive around Kasur was immediately blunted and its forces were pushed back well to the east of Khem Karan, a small village in India, the danger of losing a large chunk of territory galvanized the Indian forces into action.

The battle of Khem Karan and Assal Uttar can be divided into two phases. The first phase lasted from 6 to 8 September, when infantry of the 'Red Eagles' 4 Mountain Division surprised Pak defences. As was the case in most initial encounters across the Punjab front, the forces failed to withstand a counter-attack because of a distinct lack of situational awareness, inadequate artillery, air and armoured support, and poor leadership in the 'fog of war'. Here too three of the six battalions of the Indian division wilted under a 'combined arms' assault by the Pakistan Army's 11 Division, 1 Armoured Division and some Sabres of the PAF.

By last light on 7 September, the situation was desperate and the reason why Pakistan's 1 Armoured Division paused a while instead of pushing past Khem Karan cannot be attributed to anything but a lack of situational awareness as the Indian corps commander had not yet committed his reserve armoured brigade into the defensive battle in support of the beleaguered 4 Mountain Division. Less known also is the impact of crippling air strikes on 8 September by IAF Hunters of 7, 20 and 27 Squadrons on an ammunition-laden train at Raiwind marshalling yard on the progress of Pakistan Army's 1 Armoured Division operations. After destroying the train, the same Hunter formations destroyed a large number of vehicles and a few tanks around Kasur that were moving up to reinforce the advancing Pakistani armoured brigades. This was followed on 9 September by equally crippling strikes by Mysteres from 31 Squadron led by the CO, Wing Commander William Goodman, on a tank-transporting train, destroying and damaging more than twenty tanks.[26] These debilitating interdiction strikes on critical forces that were on the verge of being inducted into the tactical battle area would shape the thinking of the IAF in the years ahead in terms of looking at battlefield interdiction as an air power mission with greater impact than close air support.

Left with limited ammunition and depleted by the loss of a large number of tanks to IAF air strikes, the leading elements of Pakistani 1 Armoured Division, which had raced beyond Khem Karan, had to fall back to Khem Karan and wait for further orders. This permitted Major General Gurbaksh Singh, the beleaguered Indian commander, to reorganize his defences around a town called Assal Uttar, some 15–20 km north-east of Khem Karan. It also allowed the corps commander, Lieutenant General Dhillon, to induct his corps reserve in the form of 2 Independent Armoured Brigade equipped with Centurion tanks to push back the advancing Pakistani armoured assault. However, none of the Indian commanders anticipated what was to follow!

Counter-attack at Assal Uttar

The second phase of the battle from 9 to 11 September revolved around a surprisingly cautious tactical battle plan by Major General Nasir Ahmed, the GOC of Pakistan's 1 Armoured Division, and a bold defensive response from the Indian side. While Nasir adopted a conservative three-pronged assault on the Indian defences, Gurbaksh, along with his artillery commander, Brigadier Sandhu, and Brigadier Theogaraj, commander of the freshly inducted 2 Independent Armoured Brigade, worked on a plan to lure two of the three Pak armoured brigades into a tactical trap around the village of Assal Uttar (literally translated into English as 'actual reply') about 10 km north-east of Khem Karan. Occupying tactically well-chosen positions and after having flooded large areas of land through which Pakistani armour had to advance by breaching a canal, the Indians created a horseshoe-shaped killing ground with well-hidden tanks and anti-tank teams. The area thus created proved to be a virtual graveyard for Nasir's Patton and Chaffee tanks.[27]

Supported by a well-directed artillery fire plan and well-positioned jeep-mounted tank-busting teams with recoilless anti-tank weapons, also called RCLs, and for once covered by artillery, 2 Independent Armoured Brigade quickly neutralized the 2:1 numerical superiority. Tank hunting teams systematically picked out Pakistani tanks as they got bogged down by the soggy ground and converged towards the killing ground. One such team was led by Havildar Abdul Hamid of 4 Grenadiers, who in a matter of minutes destroyed three Patton tanks and added one more to his tally on 10 September before being located and targeted by the rest of the advancing tanks. Killed in action, Abdul Hamid was awarded the Param Vir Chakra for his conspicuous act of gallantry – he could have chosen to withdraw after knocking out three tanks, but chose to fight to the end. He was one of the two PVC awardees in the conflict. Ably supported by 2 Independent Armoured Brigade, Gurbaksh's quietly methodical leadership under trying circumstances and operational acumen to recoil gave the enemy a bloody nose with the available resources. They were responsible for holding the enemy at Khem Karan and preventing any further loss of territory.[28]

Having failed in its attempt to make serious inroads beyond Khem Karan, Pakistan pulled out more than one armoured brigade from this sector and switched it to the Sialkot sector on 11 September when India's 1 Armoured Division finally made its move. As a result of this and like in the Lahore sector, the ongoing battles in the Khem Karan sector were devoid of any teeth and ended up as mere attrition battles with India trying to recapture Khem Karan without the necessary numerical superiority, while Pakistan dug in to retain their territorial gain in the sector. The PAF was quite active in supporting this rearguard battle by the Pakistan Army that resulted in their retaining Khem Karan. Many an Indian infantry attack was blunted by accurate strafing by Sabres under effective FAC control. The see-saw battle of attrition continued till the ceasefire, with the IAF continuing to try and assist in pushing the Pakistan Army out of Khem Karan by targeting its launch pad of Kasur. A four-Hunter aircraft strike from 20 Squadron against army positions in Kasur led by Flight Lieutenant Nanda Cariappa, the son of the first Indian COAS, met with heavy ack-ack fire in the target area. Badly hit, Nanda ejected in enemy territory. The story goes that when Ayub Khan came to know of the incident, he offered to intervene and accord special treatment to a 'special friend's' son as he and Field Marshal K. M. Cariappa were close friends from pre-Partition days. In the finest tradition of the IAF, Nanda refused any special privileges and was among the last IAF POWs to be repatriated.[29] With the shift in focus to the Sialkot sector, it is time to look at some of the big battles there, Phillaur and Chawinda being the biggest of them all. However, before that, it is also important to see in some detail how two emerging modern air forces fought the battle in the air.

Air Battles of Attrition

Except for the innovative use of Mi-4 helicopters in J&K to assist X Corps in fighting the proxy insurgency launched by Pakistan in August 1965, the IAF was not dovetailed into the ground plan as J.N. Chaudhuri, the COAS, and Harbaksh Singh, the commander of Western Army Command, were themselves engaged in a highly personality-oriented process of ascertaining threat perceptions and likely military responses. Much older to the air chief, Air Marshal Arjan Singh, General Chaudhuri was an imposing personality who dominated the whole military planning process in the period after the Chinese debacle of 1962. It is in this context that one has to see how the IAF responded to a situation in which it was always asked to react to the situation, and not lead the way into battle or even shape the battlefield. Even after the initial air battles over Chhamb, and the close air support and interdiction missions flown from Pathankot against the advancing Pakistani armour, there was little coordination between the Indian Army and the IAF in terms of prioritizing air effort in specific areas.

The IAF's Canberra fleet of bombers comprising 5, 35 and 16 Squadrons along with the JBCU[30] (Jet Bomber Conversion Unit) matched the fighter boys for their daring and more! Their night raids on Sargodha, Peshawar, Badin (the most elusive PAF radar that had been effective) and Sakesar kept the Pakistanis on tenterhooks. Wing Commander P.P. Singh led a six-aircraft mission 600 km deep into enemy territory to strike the PAFs bomber force at Peshawar on 13 September. While there is no questioning the daring raid and its psychological impact on the PAF, the results did not do justice as the PAF's whole bomber force was lined up in the open and could have been destroyed completely had the force reallocated targets after the lead Canberra had dropped flares to illuminate the target area and spotted so many aircraft lined up.[31] Jagan Mohan and Chopra attribute this miss to bad luck as a single 4,000 lb bomb is said to have exploded in soft soil close to the tarmac. Additionally, there was no intelligence available to the aircrew that indicated that the whole force would be lined up in the open. Squadron Leader Pete Wilson was part of a daring Canberra strike on 21 September against the radar installation at Badin and had a direct hit on the radar dome, destroying it completely. Even their night interdiction missions at Kasur caused a fair amount of damage to the Pakistan Army in the Khem Karan sector, and complemented the day strikes by Mysteres and Hunters.[32] Wing Commander P.P. Singh, Wing Commander Nath and Squadron Leader Gautam from the Canberra fleet bagged three of the five Maha Vir Chakras, while Wing Commander Goodman and Squadron Leader Devayya, both Mystere pilots, bagged the other two.[33]

TANK BATTLES IN THE SIALKOT SECTOR

India had planned two simultaneous counterpunches to Pakistan's Chhamb offensive in the Lahore and Sialkot sectors. Though it was an ambitious and tactically sound plan, it could not be backed up by speedy deployment of forces and necessary numerical superiority to force a decisive victory in the plains.[34] While XI Corps under Dhillon was essentially a defensive or 'holding corps',[35] I Corps under Lieutenant General P.O. Dunne was India's strike corps in the making. It revolved around three infantry divisions and one armoured division and was formed barely months before hostilities erupted. Except for the armoured division and one infantry division, all other forces had to move up from peacetime locations in the hinterland once the decision was taken to offer a befitting riposte to the Chhamb offensive. As a result, instead of going in along with XI Corps on 6 September, the Sialkot offensive had to be delayed till the wee hours of 8 September morning. This delay of almost forty-eight hours would play a crucial role in the days ahead as India's 1 Armoured Division attempted to make serious inroads into Pak territory. India's offensive force comprised three infantry divisions (26 Infantry Division, 6 Mountain Division and 14 Infantry Division) and the lone armoured division (1 Armoured Division). Except for 26 Division, all other formations were undermanned. For example, an ideal composition of the armoured division should have been two armoured brigades with four tank regiments in each brigade, one infantry brigade with significant mobility in the form of armoured personnel carriers or APCs, an artillery brigade and other supporting elements like an engineer regiment. This was not the case with 1 Armoured Division, which was short on both armour and artillery.[36] In this case, 6 Mountain Division had only two brigades, while 14 Infantry Division was reinforced only days before being inducted into battle. More importantly, the corps had neither trained, nor war-gamed their contingencies together, and this was to prove crucial after the initial successes.

Opposing I Corps in the Sialkot and Shakargarh sectors, as appreciated by Harbaksh Singh, was a strong force comprising 15 Infantry Division and 6 Armoured Division, which was commanded by a WW II stalwart, Major General Ibrar Hussain. Most crucially, an entire artillery brigade was in support.[37] Also to be appreciated is that this force could be reinforced both from the north and from the south depending on the progress of the battles raging there.[38] As it turned out, both India and Pakistan switched forces from the Lahore sector to the Sialkot sector when both armies realized that a stalemate had developed around Lahore and Khem Karan.

Most military historians and analysts are unanimous about one feature of the battles in the Sialkot sector; the largest tank battles after the ones at Kursk during WW II were fought here at Phillaur and Chawinda as both countries hammered at each other for control over a few hundred square kilometres of Pakistani territory. Sialkot (almost 80 km from the border) was always going to be a 'town' too far for India's strike corps considering the strength of forces opposing it. Almost 400 tanks clashed in suboptimal manoeuvre terrain marked by obstacles and sugar cane fields. After making heavy weather for two days from 8 to 10 September as the Indian Army's 26 and 6 Divisions made slow progress in establishing a foothold across the international board, 1 Armoured Division entered the fray and attempted to exploit the limited space and break through towards Phillaur and Chawinda as initial objectives. On 11 September, even though India claimed initial success at Phillaur and managed to destroy a large number of Patton tanks (1 Armoured Division claimed sixty, but only thirty were verified as kills) in what were bruising tank battles of fire and attrition, progress on ground was slow. Harbaksh Singh describes the battle of Phillaur thus: 'The Battle of Phillora will always rank high in the annals of Armour Warfare – a glowing tribute to skilful junior leadership and astonishingly accurate gunnery.'[39]

The reason for this glowing tribute was the particularly stellar performance of 1 Armoured Brigade comprising 16 Cavalry, 4 Horse, 17 Poona Horse and 2 Lancers. Led from the front by Brigadier K.K. Singh, who was later awarded the Maha Vir Chakra for his leadership in the battle of Phillaur and would go on to command I Corps in 1971, two of the commanding officers of his tank regiments, Lieutenant Colonels M.M.S. Bakshi of 4 Horse and Ardeshir B. Tarapore of 17 Horse, performed admirably, knocking out a number of Pattons themselves. Bakshi was awarded a Maha Vir Chakra for his gallantry, while Tarapore would go on to blaze a trail of glory in the battle of Chawinda. Having secured Phillaur, I Corps made the same mistake as the Pakistanis did at Khem Karan; they paused to regroup for two days before attempting to take Chawinda.

A word here about the Pakistan perspective on operations in the sector from 8 to 11 September is only fair. It is widely believed that the real hero of the Pak resistance to Major General Sparrow's 1 Armoured Division was 25 Cavalry, a Patton regiment led by Lieutenant Colonel Nissar Ahmad Khan. He responded to a desperate 'do something' from his brigade commander with a brilliantly fought 'offensive-defensive' battle that kept 1 Armoured Brigade of the Indian Army busy for over two days. He was later awarded the Sitara-e-Jurat, Pakistan's third highest gallantry award.[40]

By then, Chawinda had been significantly reinforced by elements of Pakistan's 1 Armoured Division from the Kasur–Khem Karan area after the brilliant rearguard action by Nissar's 25 Cavalry. This ensured that Sparrow, the Indian GOC of 1 Armoured Division, had no choice but to pause and allow 14 Infantry Division to catch up and try to shape the battlefield between Phillaur and Chawinda before he moved forward. This is where the absence of APCs (armoured personnel carriers) with 14 Infantry Division hampered mobility and allowed the Pakistanis to regroup. A Pakistani assessment of the Indian pause in operations is more critical. Major (retd) Agha Humayun Amin, a noted military historian, has written an extensive chapter on 'The Battle of Chawinda' in his book *The Pakistan Army till 1965*. He writes:

> The Indians fought well but in the overall strategic context, the capture of Phillora was of little consequence. Had the Indians shown similar resolution and modified their plans at the brigade and divisional level on the 8th of September, by 11th September they would have been leisurely holding the east bank of MRL. The Pakistani position on the night of 11/12 September was serious but luckily Pakistan possessed an extremely resolute man in the person of Major General Abrar Hussain (an MBE of Second World War). Abrar remained calm and unperturbed and luckily the Indian higher commanders opposite him failed to understand that by remaining inactive on 11th and 12th September they were losing their last

> opportunity to inflict a decisive defeat on Pakistan at a time when fresh tank regiments from the 1st Pakistani Armoured Division had not yet reinforced 6 Armoured Division.[41]

As it turned out, 14 Division ran into tough opposition to the south and by the time the whole corps gathered itself for an assault on Chawinda, the Sialkot battle turned into a corps versus corps battle with near parity in all respects. The much talked about strike corps offensive had fizzled out; the element of surprise had been lost; holding battles were being fought in adjoining sectors with very little prospects of any significant territorial gain; and Chawinda was a do-or die-situation for Pakistan. The battle seesawed for over six days with huge division-sized forces jostling for control of a few villages and tactically vital crossroads and other vital ground. The pattern of battle was predictable and involved armour-led thrusts with infantry following, counter-attacks and periods of lull in the battle during which both sides licked their wounds. Both sides took stock of their losses and waited for a moment of operational brilliance or folly that never came. This was the battle in which numerous commanding officers lost their lives, foremost amongst them being one of the heroes of the battle of Phillaur, Lieutenant Colonel A.B. Tarapore, the commanding officer of 17 Poona Horse. He went down with his guns firing despite being wounded and refusing to abandon his crippled Centurion tank. For his sustained heroism, he was awarded the Param Vir Chakra. By 19 September, I Corps had given up hopes of capturing Chawinda, leaving Harbaksh, the Western Army Commander, despondent and ruing all the lost chances in battle. He was characteristically unsparing of command failures in a post-mortem of the battle when he said: 'Following in the wake of our deplorable performance in the first attempt on Chawinda by 1 Armd Div, the fiasco in the Chawinda-Badiana-Zafarwal complex added to our string of disappointing failures.'[42]

A keen student of the ground battle himself, Air Marshal Asghar Khan was similarly critical of the mindset of the Pakistan Army leadership during these battles. He adds:

> Partly because of shortage of infantry but largely because of unimaginative and timid leadership, we were forced to use our armour

> in an ant-tank role. The battle in the Sialkot-Chawinda area became a slogging match between tank formations. Tank casualties were heavy on both sides and it soon became evident that a stalemate had been reached which only superior generalship could remove.[43]

Though the tank-to-tank battles resulted in constantly changing the forward line of troops, which created hesitancy on the part of both air forces to be forthcoming in providing close air support, the Sialkot sector too saw some extensive interdiction and close air support missions by both the PAF and the IAF. However, compared to the Khem Karan, Kasur and Lahore sectors, the air effort towards supporting the Sialkot battle was surprisingly low. Both air forces had suffered heavy attrition by then and were reluctant to commit air effort in the absence of clearly demarcated targets arising out of the extremely close-contact armoured battles being fought.

The most effective air strike by the IAF in this battle was carried out on 11 September at Phillaur and Chawinda by Mysteres from Pathankot where eighteen tanks were reportedly destroyed.[44] The Sialkot battle also saw 1 Armoured Division shoot down a Sabre and damage a few other aircraft with accurate anti-aircraft fire. This too acted as a dampener for continued PAF support at the battle of Chawinda. As a safer measure, both the IAF and PAF resorted to night bombing even over the tactical battle area using Canberra bombers. These caused a harassing effect rather than any significant damage. When ceasefire was finally declared, India had captured around 500 sq. km of real estate in the sector. Both countries had paid a heavy price in the sector. India claims to have destroyed 144 tanks against own losses of seventy (twenty-nine destroyed and forty-one damaged).[45] General Mohammed Musa, the Pakistani army chief, though, had different thoughts to offer when he said that India had bigger wounds to lick in the battle of Chawinda thanks to the superb performance of the PAF in knocking out Indian tanks.[46]

Dogfight Over Chawinda

An aerial dogfight involving two or more fighter aircraft is a thrilling spectacle if witnessed from the ground; for the aerial gladiators, however, it is a matter of life and death with split-second decision making and situational awareness holding the keys to survival and victory. By 19 September, the IAF had recovered from the initial setbacks and started asserting itself in aerial battles with PAF Sabres. Not only had many IAF Gnat and Hunter pilots selectively deciphered Pakistani tactics, they had also started imposing their numerical superiority and started wearing down the PAF, which had started preserving its dwindling air resources after the first week of the war. One such dogfight involved four Gnats from the IAF's 9 Squadron, also called the Wolfpacks, and four Sabres from the PAF's 17 Squadron.[47]

The four Gnats were flown by Flight Lieutenant Denzil Keelor as leader with Flying Officer Rai as his No. 2, Flight Lieutenant Vinay Kapila as subsection leader and No. 3, and Flight Lieutenant Mayadev as his No. 4. Escorting four Mysteres of 1 Squadron who were on a tank-hunting and busting mission, they spotted two Sabres (there were two more around, reported to have joined the fight according to some) loitering over the tactical battle area. As roughly depicted in the diagram on the next page, and based on a detailed conversation with Mayadev, the two pairs of Gnats were flying on both flanks of the Mysteres and it was the left pair that spotted the Sabres first. As Kapila and Mayadev peeled off for the attack, they were spotted by the Sabres, who executed what was known in those days as a defensive split in which the lead aircraft continues turning loosely in the same initial direction while the second aircraft momentarily tightens his turn and then pulls up to pose a dilemma to the attacking pair whether they should split too and convert the fight into two separate one-versus-ones, or continue to fight as a pair. The danger in doing the latter was that the defender who had split could now manoeuvre offensively and get behind the second attacker. This was a standard PAF tactic and the IAF was still hazy about how to counter it. This was surprising because Sajad Haider confirmed in his email to Jagan Mohan that the PAF had been practising this manoeuvre since 1957. It is even more perplexing why the IAF pilots who had trained in the US on the Sabre did not insist that the IAF understand these tactics and evolve standard operating procedures (SOPs). These then could have been widely disseminated to all fighter and bomber squadrons so that they could be reasonably prepared to counter them.

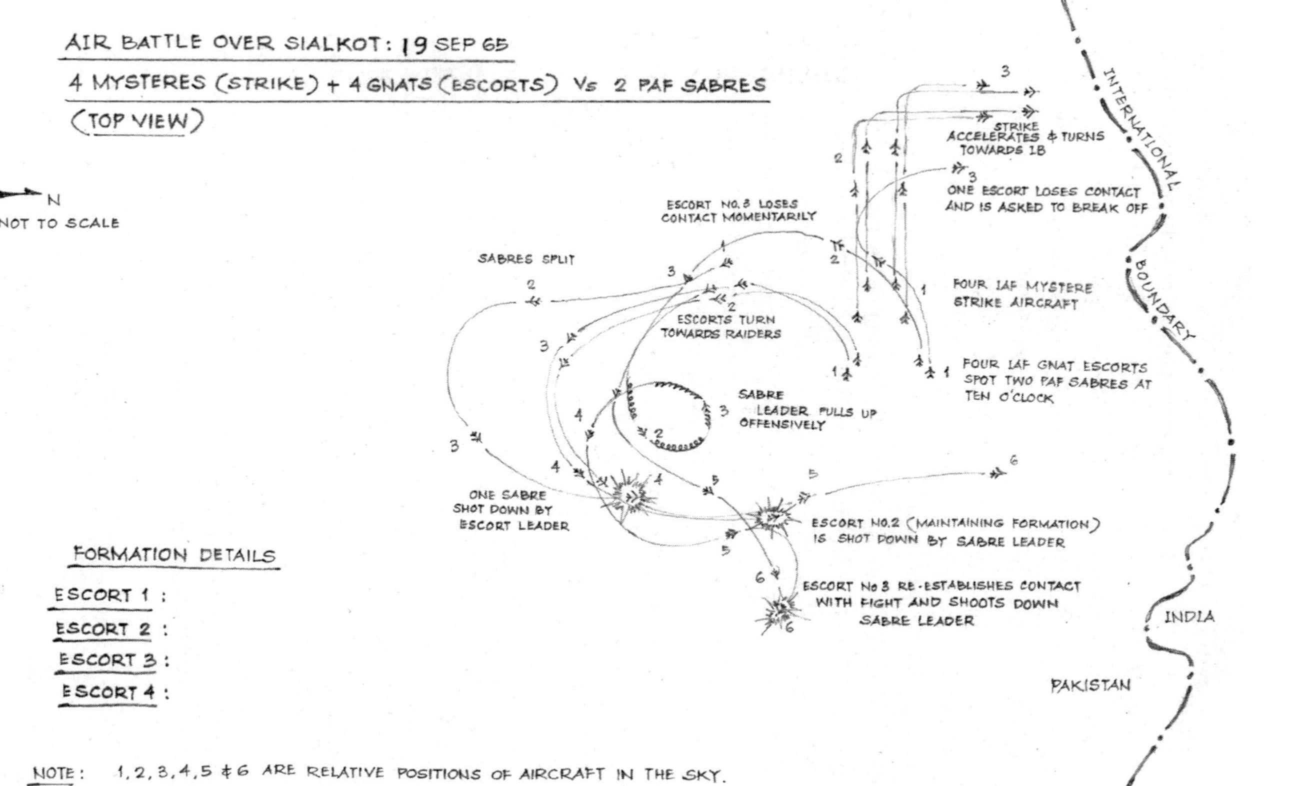
AIR BATTLE OVER SIALKOT: 19 SEP 65
4 MYSTERES (STRIKE) + 4 GNATS (ESCORTS) Vs 2 PAF SABRES
(TOP VIEW)
N
NOT TO SCALE
INTERNATIONAL BOUNDARY
INDIA
PAKISTAN
STRIKE ACCELERATES & TURNS TOWARDS IB
ONE ESCORT LOSES CONTACT AND IS ASKED TO BREAK OFF
ESCORT NO.3 LOSES CONTACT MOMENTARILY
SABRES SPLIT
FOUR IAF MYSTERE STRIKE AIRCRAFT
ESCORTS TURN TOWARDS RAIDERS
FOUR IAF GNAT ESCORTS SPOT TWO PAF SABRES AT TEN O'CLOCK
SABRE LEADER PULLS UP OFFENSIVELY
ONE SABRE SHOT DOWN BY ESCORT LEADER
ESCORT NO.2 (MAINTAINING FORMATION) IS SHOT DOWN BY SABRE LEADER
ESCORT NO 3 RE-ESTABLISHES CONTACT WITH FIGHT AND SHOOTS DOWN SABRE LEADER
FORMATION DETAILS
ESCORT 1 :
ESCORT 2 :
ESCORT 3 :
ESCORT 4 :
NOTE: 1, 2, 3, 4, 5 & 6 ARE RELATIVE POSITIONS OF AIRCRAFT IN THE SKY.
POSITION OF STRIKE AND ONE ESCORT DISCONTINUED AFTER '3' AS THE AIRCRAFT ARE OUT OF BATTLE.

In this aerial encounter, while Kapila got behind the lead Sabre with Mayadev covering his tail, the second Sabre, after executing a split, managed to sneak in behind Mayadev and shoot him down before the second pair of Gnats led by Denzil Keelor could come to his assistance. It is a different matter, however, that soon after Mayadev was shot down, Denzil Keelor did shoot down the second Sabre too. For the record, it was two Sabres shot down for the loss of one Gnat – and two Vir Chakras for Kapila and Keelor. The exchange ratio, Mayadev felt, could have been better had the IAF exploited their numerical superiority better and flown more aggressively. Luckily for Mayadev, he survived to tell his tale as he ejected over enemy territory and was taken POW and returned along with others in January 1966.[48] More than describing the combat over Chawinda, the diagram represents how fighter pilots of the time would come back from a mission and try to recapitulate what happened in the air on a blackboard in what was a called a 'combat debrief'. Such a debrief system would continue in the IAF till sophisticated aircraft like the Mirage-2000 and Su-30 were inducted in the 1980s and 1990s. Needless to say, combat debriefs have always been bruising encounters in aircrew briefing rooms across the world as fighter pilots debate the correctness or otherwise of split-second decisions and manoeuvres executed at speeds of up to 1,000 km/hour.

For many young combat pilots of the IAF, the years preceding the 1965 war saw them fly as many as five combat aircraft in three years. The absence of a centralized combat and tactics development establishment and minimal interaction with more developed Western air forces meant that their learning curve was slower than their Pakistani counterparts, who had benefitted immensely from their training at United States Air Force combat schools. While the IAF did set up a combat school after the 1965 war, it continued to remain isolated from innovative Western aerial tactics till the 1980s.[49] The last two weeks of the war saw a lot of night missions being flown by Canberras from both air forces and continuous close air support and interdiction missions in support of the various ground battles, but no more classical large-scale aerial engagements were seen in the western sector till the guns fell silent.

21

STRATEGIC REVIVAL

With the rigour of Newtonian physics, every action in Indo-Pakistan civil and military relations has an equal and opposite reaction.[1]

– SHUJA NAWAZ

THE DESERT AND EASTERN FRONTS

There can be no better name for these two fronts than the 'reluctant fronts' as both India and Pakistan had their hands full in the J&K and Punjab sectors. Beyond mere posturing, both countries did not have the resources and numbers to derive benefit from any sustained military action on these fronts. During the early decades after Independence, the Sind province of Pakistan and India's border areas of Gujarat and Rajasthan comprised mainly of underdeveloped desert and semi-desert terrain that was fit only for armour and mechanized warfare. With most of the armour facing off in Punjab, both armies were left with little to manoeuvre and India's limited offensive in Rajasthan was more a response to Pakistan's Kutch foray rather than a serious 'third front'.

The action in the desert revolved around the road and railway line that ran from Barmer in Rajasthan to the town of Hyderabad in Sind. While the Indian Army's 11 Infantry Division was commanded by Major General N.C. Rawlley of Walong fame, Pakistan's 8 Division was responsible for defences in the area. Both divisions had limited armour (approximately two squadrons each), which resulted in the limited ability of forces to move only on prepared roads and tracks. While Indian forces made some advance beyond Gadra Road village towards Sakarbu in Pakistani territory, the Pakistanis almost overran an Indian post at Munna Bao, attempting to capture it till the end and hold on to it as bargaining territory after the ceasefire. While the PAF was very active with their Sabres and Canberras, using them effectively to blunt the Indian advance, the IAF had no resources worth the name in Jodhpur to provide close air support, and had to rely on Canberra bombers from Jamnagar to carry out interdiction missions. The advance of 11 Division advance was limited to a few miles into Pak territory – no sizable gains worth highlighting were made by either side.[2]

The two main opposing airbases in the southern sector were Jamnagar in Gujarat and Mauripur near Karachi in Sind. Jodhpur on the Indian side was a large training base and the IAF did not consider it necessary to locate any strike or air defence aircraft there since it was not anticipated that any large-scale ground offensive would be planned in the area. While Jamnagar had a large force of Canberra bombers and Vampires, Mauripur airbase (now PAF base Masroor) had a squadron of Canberra bombers and a squadron of Sabres. Both were used extensively in countering India's offensive in Gadra Road; particularly impactful here too were strafing missions by the Sabres. To put things in the correct perspective, strafing missions demand close coordination between a forward air controller on the ground and the pilot. This is possible only if there is compatible communication between the two and a clear understanding of issues like FLOT, aircraft performance, presence of enemy air defence guns, etc. As in other sectors, this was the qualitative difference between PAF and the IAF when it came to carrying out close air support. In retrospect, the IAF could have relocated some fighter assets from the east to Jodhpur and added some teeth to Rawlley's operations?

A tragic incident involving the shooting down of an eight-seater Beechcraft twin-engine executive jet with the chief minister of the Indian state of Gujarat on board by Sabres of the PAF has attracted attention in recent years; particularly in forums that are actively involved in the India–Pakistan peace process.[3] From a military perspective, the Indian jet was shot down in Indian territory near the coastal town of Dwarka on 19 September 1965. The jet was piloted by Jehangir Engineer, a retired

IAF officer and one of the four Engineer brothers of the IAF, one of whom was Aspy Engineer, who was the previous COAS. With the war raging across the western front and knowing the risks of flying without adequate radar and air defence cover, it is surprising how the sortie was undertaken at all. From a PAF perspective, the two countries were at war and having scrambled two Sabre jets from Mauripur under control of the highly effective Badin air defence GCI radar, which was later destroyed by IAF Canberras, it is only an ethical issue that remained when Flying Officer Q. A. Hussain, the Sabre pilot, was faced with a situation and an order to shoot down a civilian aircraft. He has gone on record almost forty-five years later, deeply regretting the incident.[4] Such are the tragedies brought on by war!

The eastern front was more an aimless aerial battle with ill-defined military and strategic objectives. Eastern Command of the Indian Army under Lieutenant General Manekshaw was tied down with the China front and combating insurgency in Nagaland. India's operational appreciation on opening a fourth front with Pakistan was based on two critical factors. First was the China factor that looked at a possible intervention by China should India aim to attack East Pakistan. The second factor was lack of popular Bengali support for any Indian military action in East Pakistan and no tangible gains from an advance into monsoon-affected terrain. It is not widely known that a series of aggressive but ill-directed IAF Canberra and Hunter strikes on the night of 6 September and the early hours of 7 September against PAF airfields like Chittagong, Kurmitola and other bases precipitated a ferocious response from No 14 Squadron, PAF, against Kalaikunda, Central Air Command's pivotal base in West Bengal. Shockingly, the IAF had such poor intelligence about the location of the only Sabre squadron in East Pakistan that it attacked every base in East Pakistan except Tejgaon, the airbase outside Dacca (now Dhaka) where 14 Squadron, PAF, had a detachment of twelve Sabres.[5]

In the absence of any combat air patrol to oppose enemy strikes, and aircraft being parked in the open at air force station Kalaikunda, the IAF lost eight aircraft (four Canberras and four Vampires) to two Sabre strikes on 7 September. However, the IAF's moment of glory in the east unfolded over Kalaikunda in an aerial battle the same morning as a young IAF ace with 14 Squadron of the IAF, Flight Lieutenant Alfred Cooke, in a Hunter, shot down two Sabres of 14 Squadron PAF. In an epic dogfight witnessed by hundreds of awe-struck students that pitted the two 'fourteens' over the Indian Institute of Technology, Kharagpur, Cooke and his No. 2, Flying Officer Mamgain,weaved trails across the sky as they turned and yo-yoed with the four Sabres, getting the better of them. Two Sabres were clearly shot down by Cooke and a third probably limped back to Tezgaon with serious battle damage. Cooke would go on to immigrate to Australia in 1968 and returned to his squadron forty-seven years later to present his Vir Chakra to the squadron at an emotionally charged function at Ambala in September 2015. The air war in the east meandered for another two weeks without any major successes on either side. What it did provide was some battle inoculation for both air forces!

Naval Dilemma

What of the Indian and Pakistan navies? After the initial fanfare with which both navies equipped themselves in the 1950s with refurbished British cruisers, destroyers and frigates, much to the delight of the languishing British economy, the focus shifted away from the maritime domain as India grappled with a triumphant China and a militarily resurgent Pakistan. The acquisition of eight new frigates[6] and an aircraft carrier, the INS *Vikrant* (earlier the HMS *Hercules*), along with its complement of Sea Hawks and Alizes, by India between 1958 and 1961 spurred Pakistan to acquire a suitable deterrent in the form of the first submarine in the subcontinent, the PNS *Ghazi*. A Tench Class diesel submarine in service with the US Navy since 1944, it was inducted with much fanfare in 1963. Armed with twenty-eight torpedoes, it was a significant deterrent against the much larger Indian Navy during the conflict.[7] At the strategic level, both the Indian and Pakistani navies grappled with the stepmotherly treatment meted out by the land-centric and army-dominated military leadership of the two countries. Both Field Marshal Ayub Khan and General J.N. Chaudhuri did not factor in their respective navies in any battle plans that were discussed before the 1965 war. Ayub Khan in particular was rather disdainful of the navy and condescending about the PAF, an issue much discussed by Air Marshal Asghar Khan in his interesting little book.[8]

Though much larger in size and packing a greater punch as compared to the Pakistan Navy, much of the Indian Navy's numerical advantage was offset by a large number of ships that were under refit during the time. Adding to India's woes was the fact that its 'game changer', the aircraft carrier INS *Vikrant*, too was undergoing a refit. This put paid to any prospects of exercising sea control in the Arabian Sea and threatening the key Pakistani port of Karachi. Having to defend a coastline of over 5,500 km and contend with a possible threat to the Andaman and Nicobar Islands from Indonesia, a close ally of Pakistan at the time,[9] Vice Admiral Soman, India's chief of naval staff, had no clear directives from the Government of India regarding the employment of the navy besides that it was to 'defend territorial waters and the island territories of India and not venture beyond a distance of 200 miles from Bombay and north of Porbandar along the west coast of India'. It is believed that when he met the defence minister and the prime minister, they categorically told him that they did not envisage an offensive role for the Indian Navy despite his asserting that even without the aircraft carrier, the Indian Navy had the wherewithal to blockade Karachi.[10] The Pakistan Navy too had no clarity from Ayub Khan, and much of the initiative exercised by the Pakistan Navy can be attributed to their fleet commander.

As the two navies waited for orders to engage in battle, a look at how they matched up would be in order. With the INS *Vikrant* out of the fray and being almost evenly matched as far as cruisers and destroyers were concerned, India's main advantage lay in the punch and firepower of its frigates. Pakistan, on the other hand, had a major game changer in the form of *Ghazi*.[11] As events in Kutch unfolded, the Indian fleet under Rear Admiral Samson was given orders after much coaxing to sail for the Kathiawar coast. However, it was apparent that as the war progressed, both India and Pakistan had no stomach for a full-fledged naval battle. While the Sea Hawks and Alizes were moved around between Jamnagar and Bombay,[12] the Indian fleet was mainly involved in anti-submarine action to keep the PNS *Ghazi* at bay.

The Pakistan Navy, however, did launch an ineffective attack on the Indian port of Dwarka[13] on 7 September with its cruiser PNS *Babar*, five destroyers and a frigate[14] disguised as merchant ships. Even though the Indian Navy frigate, INS *Talwar*, which was on station at Okha, a few miles south of Dwarka, was alerted of a possible attack after intercepting heavy communication traffic between the Pakistan Navy ships, it did not give battle because of instructions which prevented it from heading north towards Dwarka. According to Air Marshal Asghar Khan, Admiral Ahsan was responsible for the capture of hundreds of Indian fishing boats around the Chittagong coast of East Pakistan.[15] However, these claims are highly dubious and not backed by much documented evidence even in newspaper reports of the time. Towards the end of the war, Indian Navy frigates are said to have engaged PNS *Ghazi* and may have damaged it.[16] No confirmation is available from Pakistan to this claim. As a contrary claim, the Pakistan Navy claimed that the submarine fired torpedoes at an Indian frigate, INS *Brahmaputra* and sank it. These claims were rubbished by India soon after the war when foreign naval attaches were invited on board the INS *Brahmaputra* in Bombay.[17] In a rather emotional pitch, Admiral S.N. Kohli in his book *We Dared* wrote about the frustration of the Indian Navy having to fight with one hand tied behind its back.[18] He goes on to add:

> The Pakistani naval raid left the officers and the men of the Indian Navy infuriated and somewhat humiliated. I vowed to myself that if ever there was another round involving naval forces and if I was in any kind of position of responsibility, I would go to the farthest extremes to teach the enemy a lesson.[19]

Peace at a Cost

Strategic Revival

With the failure of Operation Gibraltar, Ayub Khan realized early in the war that his war objectives were not going to be met. He very astutely despatched Bhutto and Air Marshal Asghar Khan to make a dash to China and some Islamic countries like Indonesia and Turkey to ascertain the extent of help that would be forthcoming in case of a crunch. India, on the other hand, concentrated on fighting the war, led by their deceptively resolute prime minister, Lal Bahadur Shastri, and a gutsy defence minister, Y.B. Chavan. India did not engage in much diplomacy during the early days of the war except in managing pressure from the UN Security Council, which was urging it to declare a unilateral ceasefire from as early as 11 September onwards. U Thant, the Secretary General of the UN, visited both Pakistan and India soon after they went to war and acted as a key interlocutor, cajoling both warring nations to finally declare a much anticipated ceasefire on 23 September.

Both nations agreed to pull back by 26 February 1966 to positions on ground prior to that which were held as on 5 August 1965. While India had captured approximately 700 sq. km of Pak territory in the Sialkot and central Lahore sector, apart from the Haji Pir Pass and key heights in the Kishenganga bulge of the Tithwal sector, Pakistan had managed to seize around 400 sq. km of Indian territory, primarily in the area south-east of Lahore, around Khem Karan and in the Chhamb area. Despite being given the flexibility by the defence minister to extend operations for a few more days, Chaudhuri, India's COAS, endorsed the decision to accept the ceasefire as he felt that the stalemate on the ground did not support the possibilities of making any major gains.[20] The argument that the Pakistan Army was desperately short of ammunition and had stocks that would last only for a few days[21] – however true this may have been at the time – could not be substantiated due to poor intelligence, and was not reason enough for India to prolong the conflict, according to Chaudhuri. Arjan Singh, India's air chief, however, recollects having advised the defence minister against accepting the ceasefire as the IAF was gaining ascendancy in the air.[22]

Over the years, many Indian military analysts and commentators have felt that the Indian government squandered an excellent opportunity in 1965 to hold on to Haji Pir Pass and the Tithwal heights. They argue that India should have only agreed to a ceasefire if the pre-August 1965 positions only related to those areas across the international border that were in opposing hands. Since Haji Pir Pass and the Tithwal heights were in territory claimed by India (POK), these should not have been part of the ceasefire negotiations, they argue. The Indian negotiators, I suspect, would have considered this option, but dropped it as it would have been a non-starter from the word go and would have jeopardized any chances of a ceasefire. Having deployed the bulk of its forces in the sectors where a stalemate existed, India may not have been able to sustain a renewed offensive in Kashmir. Unfortunately, the focus had shifted to the plains because of the obsession of both countries with Punjab!

At the end of it all, the armour from both sides started withdrawing on 24 September after both countries had suffered heavily during the conflict.[23] The formal ceasefire agreement known as the Tashkent Agreement was signed on 10 January 1966 by Prime Minister Lal Bahadur Shastri and President Ayub Khan. Sadly, Prime Minister Shastri passed away in Tashkent on 11 January 1966 after a massive heart attack and did not live to see the implementation of the agreement.

Some Ground Covered – Lessons Learnt

One of the significant takeaways from the 1965 conflict is the change in the manner in which military analysts looked at the India–Pakistan military balance with respect to the calibre of military leadership and fighting abilities of the two countries. Chastened after they received a bloody nose in J&K and the Lahore and Sialkot sectors, and surprised by the stiff resistance offered by India in Chhamb and the fightback by the IAF's fighter and bomber pilots after a reactive initial response, Pakistan's strategic establishment no longer looked down on India's military. As Stephen Cohen again puts it very interestingly: 'There is a more realistic assessment of India as a military foe; no longer do Pakistani officers boast that one Muslim is worth five or ten Hindus.'[24]

Strategic Lessons

At the strategic level, India emerged from the conflict as a responsible and restrained power which had brushed aside transgressions in Kutch, and resorted to military force only in the face of serious provocations in Kashmir. Its political leadership under Lal Bahadur Shastri, with Y.B. Chavan at the helm of the defence ministry, was stable and not given to any flights of fancy with regard to India's actual preparedness and ability to take the war into Pakistan. However, to be objective, it is clear that the Indian government was excessively cautious during the early days of the war and procrastinated on many decisions, including the use of the air force and navy, by still subscribing to the rather diffident Nehruvian policy of 'minimum use of force to further state policy'.

Just look at the military situation that panned out in the Rann of Kutch in the early summer of 1965. In a tremendously risky military operation, Ayub Khan decided to test India's willingness to go to war by sending in almost a division worth of infantry supported by more than a regiment of tanks without any air support in terrain that had no natural cover at all. Notwithstanding their obsolescence, the Indian Air Force station at Jamnagar had Vampire jet trainers based there with decent ground attack capability – they could fire guns, rockets and bombs with deadly accuracy. With the Rann well within their radius of action, air strikes on Pakistani Patton tanks were well within the realm of possibility and legitimacy. All that was required was for the IAF to position a forward air controller amidst one of the defended localities from where he could direct fire. The IAF could also have called upon Canberra bombers from Pune or Hunters and Mysteres from elsewhere to move to Jamnagar and carry out strikes on Pakistani positions. All that was required was an understanding that Pakistan's intrusion was an act of war and that air power could be used as an effective tool of deterrence! Instead, India chose to bank on the good offices of Harold Wilson, the British prime minister, to broker a ceasefire and allowed Ayub Khan to validate his operational concepts and prepare for the ensuing confrontation in Kashmir and Chhamb. If India had responded fiercely with air power also thrown in, Ayub might have thought twice before launching Operation Gibraltar and Operation Grand Slam. Military decisiveness on India's part in Kutch may well have prevented the expansion of conflict, thereby expanding and validating its doctrine of deterrence.

Pakistan, on the other hand, emerged as a state that was willing to resort to military brinkmanship as a tool of state policy. Taken in by his wily but impatient foreign minister, Bhutto, and elements of the Pakistan Army who wanted to finish what they started in 1947,[25] Ayub Khan underestimated India's resolve in every domain – be it diplomatic, political or military. Ayub's biggest mistake, however, was his inability to orchestrate the insurrection in Kashmir. Bhutto also misled Ayub into believing that Marshal Chen Yi, the Chinese defence minister, had assured him of China's intervention in the conflict should Pakistan be pushed into a corner militarily by India. In reality, Chen Yi had given no such assurance and beyond some sabre rattling in Sikkim towards the third week of September, China had no intention of getting embroiled in a conflict where it would directly be seen as an aggressor.

Operational Takeaways

Operation Gibraltar was a disaster as far as Pakistan was concerned. It was not backed by adequate intelligence regarding the extent of popular support for the rebellion, and turned out to be a damp squib despite the ambitious plan and multiple thrust lines. Comfortable in the mountains of Kashmir, where he had cut his teeth as a battalion and brigade commander, Harbaksh Singh was in his element orchestrating the tough battles at Kargil, Haji Pir Pass and Tithwal as the Western Army Commander. Had Chhamb been better protected, he could have driven home the advantage further in these areas. It was, however, not to be as his attention was diverted to the other sectors of Chhamb, Lahore and Sialkot. In one of the most objective books written on the history of the Pakistan Army, *Crossed Swords,* Shuja Nawaz argues that middle-level Indian commanders had supposedly anticipated Pakistan's Chhamb offensive to the smallest details as early as 1956 and even developed scenarios for deployment of Pakistani armour in the Infantry School at Mhow. However, the Indian Army's senior leadership was not interested![26] The conduct of these battles at the operational level do not make for very happy reading on both sides; the fog of war took its toll on divisional and corps commanders and very few brilliant operational moves were made. To be fair to the generals, the terrain in Punjab and near-parity in forces left little room for imaginative generalship. While caution may have been a bonus at the political level, it proved to be the undoing at Chawinda for the Indians and at Khem Karan for the Pakistanis.

When the IAF rushed into action over Chhamb on the evening of 1 September, the chief of air staff, while agreeing without hesitation to go to the army's support, pointed out that in attacks launched without adequate preparation, losses must be accepted and that pilots may make mistakes between friend and foe.[27] There was visible lack of synergy between the army and air force notwithstanding assertions from senior air force leadership that 'the IAF was more or less ready for ground support and waiting for a signal the whole day'.[28] In actuality, IAF squadrons may have been armed and ready to go into battle, provided they had some kind of situational awareness, which it was the army's job to provide them with. This was completely absent, and beyond knowing that there was a battle raging in Chhamb, the station commander at air force station Pathankot had no idea of the disposition and movement of enemy forces, and issues like FLOT and the extent of PAF activity in the region. Even if the brigade commander was busy in the tactical battle, why couldn't the divisional commander or the corps commander coordinate air support through the existing mechanisms?

There also seemed to be a lack of understanding within India's strategic establishment that air power could have been used as an offensive tool to complement the XI Corps offensive in the Lahore sector in the early-morning hours of 6 September. By attacking the airfields from where the PAF could get its fighters airborne to support the defensive operations in Lahore, the IAF may well have facilitated 15 Division's advance towards Lahore. Instead, the IAF held back inexplicably, only to be hit in strength by the PAF that evening.

In an offensive battle, however, particularly in the plains, the most effective way of employing air power is not only to continuously remain in contact battle, but to ensure that the defender is not able to build his force ratios to sustain his defensive operations. This is done by interdicting his follow-on forces and reserves, and is possible only if a joint appreciation has been done prior to the battle. Since General Musa had not shared his plans with Air Vice Marshal Nur Khan, who had strangely replaced Asghar Khan as the chief of air staff barely months before the war, the PAF had no plans for interdicting any forces that India was bringing in to reinforce the Chhamb brigade. It thus lost a golden opportunity to deplete the Indian Army's combat potential and revealed deep cracks in army–air force synergy. The IAF, on the other hand, ventured relatively deep into enemy territory with its Mysteres and Hunters on 'search and strike' interdiction missions against railway sidings, trains and armoured concentrations, albeit with limited success, given the complete absence of intelligence. Punching a hole in the myth that the PAF outperformed the IAF in the execution of close air support missions, one of the major reasons for the inability of the Pakistan Army to drive home the advantage in Chhamb – apart from the tough response from Harbaksh Singh – was poor army–air force coordination. It was a poor understanding on the part of Ayub and Musa about the effectiveness of air power that allowed India to recoil. Had Ayub allowed the PAF the freedom to conduct interdiction and airfield strike missions along with the army offensive, India would have been completely surprised. Instead, by deploying the PAF only over the tactical battle area and in air defence roles, the IAF gained vital time to relocate its forces at forward bases in the few days before the PAF commenced its counter-campaign in air on 6 September.

Though Pakistan moved its armour from one sector to another with relative freedom throughout the war, a few decisive strikes by Hunters, Mysteres and Canberras in the Khem Karan sector showed that though the IAF did not have sufficient intelligence to interdict these movements, when they did get an opportunity to do so, they struck decisively. A few well-directed strikes severely impeded the combat potential of 1 Armoured Division of Pakistan as it moved from Kasur in the Lahore sector to the Sialkot sector between 11 and 13 September. The much hyped Patton tanks and Sabre jets performed suboptimally and it was as early as 18 September 1965 that Romesh Thapar, a noted Indian journalist and commentator, wrote about it as well as the battle resilience of the two armies in the *Economic and Political Weekly*:

> The experts claim that the Pakistan Army is either over-mechanised (muscle-bound!) or it doesn't know how best to exploit its undoubted advantage in armour and the fire-power superiority provided by its self-propelled guns. Much the same kind of theorising can be done about the failure of the Sabre jets ... even in combat with the Bangalore manufactured Gnats. While the progress of the battles has pushed much of this discussion into the realm of history, the question of the 'staying power' of the two armies remains very relevant.[29]

In terms of operational focus, both air forces were trying out modern concepts of air power for the first time and the lessons learned by the USAF in Korea seem to have been passed down when the Sabres and Starfighters were inducted into the PAF. PAF counter-operations in air were initially effective against IAF bases only because of poor aircraft dispersal procedures – more than half of the IAF's losses were on the ground. After a few initial setbacks, Air

Marshal Arjan Singh, Chief of Air Staff of the IAF, remained cool and inspirational throughout the war. He was, however, handicapped and tied down by India's reactive strategy. A positive takeaway for the IAF was the emergence of good squadron- level leadership and combat skills. Squadrons like 23 Squadron (Gnats), 1, 31 and 8 Squadrons (Mysteres) and 7, 20, 27 and 14 Squadrons (Hunters) matched the PAF with some excellent tactical innovations. The IAF's Canberra bomber squadrons too acquitted themselves better than their PAF counterparts with their daring strikes deep inside Pakistani territory.

The IAF lost thirty-six aircraft on the ground with a further seventeen damaged; it lost seventeen aircraft in aerial combat and eleven to ground fire. The PAF lost far fewer aircraft (IAF figures indicate ten, while PAF claims no more than three) on the ground to IAF strikes. However, their losses in the air during combat and to ground fire were greater than the Indian losses at eighteen and twenty-five respectively. In sortie generation rates too, the IAF fared better than their adversaries. The IAF flew a total of 3,927 sorties as against 2015 flown by the PAF.[30] Considering the 1:1.5 ratio in strength, the IAF fared better. In the overall context then, if one discounts the losses suffered by the IAF on the ground and factors in the higher number of sorties flown, the attrition rate suffered by the IAF was significantly lower than the PAF figure.[31] These figures are official Indian ones and have naturally been contested by analysts from Pakistan, but it is not something to lose sleep over! Among the other positives for the IAF was that it was able to operationally try out a Russian fighter aircraft (MiG-21) for the first time even though it was not able to impact operations in any way after being touted as the IAF's much awaited counter to the PAF's F-104 Starfighter.

Leadership

Much has been written about the lack of inter-services synergy during the build-up to the war, precipitated in no small measure by the overbearing personality of General J.N. Chaudhuri, the COAS. His frequent differences of opinion with Lieutenant General Harbaksh Singh, the commander of the Western Army Command, severely hampered decision making at critical times before and during the war and even though Marshal of the Air Force Arjan Singh (then air marshal and chief of air staff) has never openly criticized his much older Indian Army counterpart, his successor, Air Chief Marshal P.C. Lal, is quite critical of his overbearing fellow Bengali. He writes about Chaudhuri: 'Gen Chaudhuri looked upon the Air Force as rather young and inexperienced – fit for his avuncular interest but not to be taken too seriously.'[32]

Going on to highlight the lack of joint operational planning before the 1965 war, Lal, who was the Vice Chief of Air Staff during the 1965 war, adds:[33]

> Chaudhuri later said that the Chad Bet incursion in Kutch had given him a clear indication of Pak's intention in Kashmir. If so, he did little to alert the other two service chiefs about the danger ahead. He only discussed the issue with the Prime Minister and Defence Minister. Sometime later the Air Chief was informed through informal meetings from which the Naval Chief was excluded. To ensure this, the general applied the 'need to know' yardstick so thoroughly that the Chiefs of Staff Committee and the joint intelligence and planning staff were completely bypassed. He ignored the basic concepts of higher defence organisation and displayed what may be called the 'Supremo Syndrome'.

To be fair to Chaudhuri, however, the fog of war, overall national strategy of restraint and lack of adequate actionable intelligence severely hampered his naturally flamboyant style of leadership, and it is only fair to give him adequate credit for reviving the Indian Army's elan and reputation after the debacle of 1962.

His Pakistani counterpart, General Mohammed Musa, was shackled by the duo of Ayub Khan and Bhutto and did not inspire much; nor did most of his corps commanders. The army–air force synergy was only marginally better in Pakistan with Air Marshals Asghar Khan and Nur Khan being kept out of the decision-making loop till the last moment. Though Air Marshal Nur Khan was an able deputy to Asghar Khan for years, it is perplexing that he replaced Asghar Khan as the chief of the PAF at a time when war clouds were looming on the horizon. The only reason for this change could have been power politics in Pakistan that saw the combination of Ayub Khan, Musa and Bhutto becoming increasingly apprehensive about Asghar Khan's aggressive articulation of war-fighting strategies and criticism at being left out of the various operational planning processes that were under way for the Kutch and Kashmir operations. Asghar's absence was sorely felt by the PAF when the IAF got its act together. In the realm of aerial strategy, the PAF was confused whether its primary aim was to take the air battle into enemy territory and destroy the IAF's combat potential with a series of swift and surgical strikes on IAF bases, or whether it was to defend Pakistan's skies and prevent the IAF from denting the Pakistan Army's combat capability. As it turned out, after an initial spell of intense offensive action, the PAF chose the latter option and went into what the IAF has called since as 'combat preservation mode'.

Brilliant and tough as he was, Harbaksh Singh managed to orchestrate the anti-infiltration campaign in J&K, direct the defensive battle in Chhamb, and inspire the revival of 4 Mountain Division at Assal Uttar. He was the aggressive face of the Indian Army! Of Harbaksh's operational commanders, Major General Gurbaksh Singh, divisional commander of 4 Mountain Division, stood tall as one of the few field commanders who managed to stay cool under battle stress and counter-attack during the battle of Assal Uttar. There were too many *ifs* during the war for any military historian to take home any lasting lessons. If the Indian Army had defended Chhamb in greater strength and called for air support in the morning, would they have been able to beat back the initial Pak offensive? Had the IAF been allowed to adopt a more proactive operational strategy and had there been greater inter-service synergy, would India then have taken the initiative and launched their twin assaults in Lahore and Sialkot a few days earlier and achieved better surprise? Was Lahore a city too far and what would have happened if its main thrust was only in the Sialkot sector? Would Pakistan then have gone in for an offensive in Khem Karan or switched its 1 Armoured Division to Sialkot to support 6 Armoured Division.

At unit, regimental and squadron level both the Indians and the Pakistanis fought equally well! Desmond Hayde leading 3 Jat and Tarapore leading the Poona Horse were as good and inspirational as Nissar Ahmad Khan of 25 Cavalry. Rafique, Haider and Alam in their Sabres were matched by Keelor, Patney, Ghandhi, Rathore, Gautam and Cooke in their Gnats, Mysteres, Canberras and Hunters. India and Pakistan had fought the first major war after WW II involving skirmishes, bruising mountain battles, intense air battles and pitched infantry and tank battles with near parity in military capability.

The only major operational question asked of the Indian Navy despite the restrictions imposed by the government would be why a routine maintenance[34] of INS *Vikrant* could not have been postponed considering the simmering tension, thereby ensuring that the Navy's punch remained intact. Notwithstanding the indignation expressed by the Indian Navy's senior leadership of the time at being shackled so, Vice Admiral Pasricha was candid enough to admit that the navy was hardly in 'ship shape' and would have been hard-pressed to either enforce a blockade of Karachi or carry out a coordinated attack on it.[35] When one adds the neglect of the navy during the post-1962 years, it is only natural that the service feels sore about the war even today.

Though Ramachandra Guha succinctly says: 'In truth, the war must be considered a draw,'[36] the overall result has to be seen in the context of how military victories are benchmarked in modern warfare. Victory through annihilation of the enemy was restricted to the Middle Ages and ended after the two great wars of the twentieth century, WW I and WW II. Since then, the genre of conventional conflict has mainly seen limited wars in which results are analysed after considering the protagonists' strategic objectives. Looking at the result from that prism, despite a few tactical losses for the Indian Army and the IAF, India took the honours at the operational and strategic levels as none of Pakistan's initial objectives were met – its frustration would show in the years ahead! After years of propounding the myth of victory, fifty years after the conflict, even Pakistani historians like Akbar S. Zaidi and others admit that the existing discourse in Pakistan has been distorted.[37] Though many in the Indian Army believe that its ethos of *Naam, Namak aur Nishan* owes its origin to the legacy of a colonial past, there are others who assert that a fresh, secular and multicultural ethos emerged after the 1947–48 and 1965 conflicts with Pakistan. Geoffrey Blainey's wisdom on why wars begin and end hold true for the India–Pakistan war of 1965. In a pithy two-liner he captures the essence of the strategic mindset of the two countries:

'Wars usually end when the fighting nations agree on their relative strength, and wars usually begin when fighting nations disagree on their relative strength.'[38]

The Liberation of Bangladesh, 1971

22

SOUTH ASIA IN TURMOIL

India wants to avoid a war at all costs but it is not a one-sided affair, you cannot shake hands with a clenched fist.[1]

– INDIRA GANDHI

TURMOIL

War, it seemed, had taken its toll on both Indian and Pakistani leadership. The aftermath of the 1965 conflict saw two prominent casualties – the death of India's prime minister, Lal Bahadur Shastri, in early 1966, and the handing over of power by Field Marshal Ayub Khan as president of Pakistan in 1969 to his army chief, General Yahya Khan. The two events would have a significant impact on the manner in which the geopolitical landscape unfolded in the subcontinent as both India and Pakistan hurtled towards another war. Political power in India passed on to Indira Gandhi, the feisty daughter of Pandit Jawaharlal Nehru, India's first elected prime minister. A sharp and ambitious lady tutored in history and statecraft by her illustrious father for over three decades in diverse environments, Indira Gandhi surprised her political opponents with her ability to manoeuvre in the minefield of post-Independence Indian politics. Installed as a 'proxy' PM after Shastri's death by the 'old guard' of the Congress party, she started asserting herself over the party after a rather insipid performance by the Congress in the 1967 general elections. In a series of decisive moves she deftly outmanoeuvred all her opponents to establish a vice-like grip over the Congress party and the country by winning a landslide victory in the general elections of March 1971. To a large extent, this victory empowered Indira Gandhi to act decisively in the months ahead.

As Field Marshal Ayub Khan faded into the sunset of his career amidst widespread dissent and unrest, he appointed one of his cronies, General Yahya Khan, his undistinguished army chief, as his successor on 25 March 1969. Sensing the mood of the nation, Yahya Khan immediately declared martial law to restore law and order in both West and East Pakistan. Then in an attempt to gain political legitimacy and make the transition to democracy, and influenced in no small measure by Zulfikar Ali Bhutto, his wily foreign minister, Yahya Khan surprisingly announced general elections in early 1970. He did so, convinced that Bhutto's PPP (Pakistan People's Party), the major political force in West Pakistan, would come to power. He had, however, not reckoned with the possibility of a political party from the more populous East Pakistan getting an absolute majority in the National Assembly.

East Pakistan had always been given stepmotherly treatment by the Punjabi-, Pathan- and Mohajir-dominated[2] West Pakistan. However, the largely peaceful Bengalis of East Pakistan bore this stoically for almost two decades after choosing to join Pakistan in 1947, largely because of poor representation in the overall political structure. A crisp overview of the December 1970 elections and how the East Pakistani Muslims looked upon their West Pakistani counterparts as 'predatory ruling classes' is rendered by Ramachandra Guha in his book *India after Gandhi*.[3] The emergence of Sheikh Mujibur Rahman in the aftermath of the 1965 war led to the rallying of all East Pakistanis behind one powerful political entity, the Awami League.[4] In a surprisingly free and fair election in December 1970, the Awami League captured 167 out of 311 seats and staked its claim to form the government. While this startled Yahya Khan and the people of West Pakistan, it infuriated Bhutto, who had been scheming all these years to capture political power from the Pakistan Army. After months of negotiations in which Bhutto and Yahya attempted to reach a settlement with Sheikh Mujib (as Mujibur was popularly known) on power sharing, the talks broke down in March 1971. Consequently, Bhutto pushed Yahya to impose martial law in East Pakistan; Sheikh Mujib was arrested on 23 March and spirited away to West Pakistan, where he was placed under house arrest. The stage was thus set for a human tragedy that has very few parallels in modern history.[5]

The Crackdown

A most recent and exceptionally well-researched book titled *Blood Telegram: India's Secret War in East Pakistan* by Prof. Gary J. Bass from Princeton University provides an updated and objective perspective of Operation Searchlight, as the crackdown by Yahya Khan came to be known. In a brave and desperate telegram to the White House on 6 April 1971, Archer Blood, the US consul general in Dacca, the capital of erstwhile East Pakistan, reported mass killings of the majority Bengali population that had been unleashed by General Yahya Khan on 26 March 1971. The telegram with the heading 'Dissent from US policy towards East Pakistan' said it all. Signed by twenty officials from the consulate and other US development agencies, the telegram highlighted 'the suppression of democracy', 'bending over backwards to accommodate the West Pak dominated government', and 'our dissent with current policy and fervent hope that our true and lasting interests here can be defined and our policies redirected in order to salvage our nation's position as a moral leader of the free world'.[6] Days before, a secret CIA memorandum downplayed the crackdown by calling it merely a 'campaign'. The report also correctly assessed that the Pakistan Army had overestimated their ability to destroy the Awami League and disarm the over 13,000 strong East Bengal Rifles.[7]

A brave and committed diplomat with years of experience in the subcontinent, no Westerner had a better ringside view than Archer Blood of the traumatic events of 1971 that led to the birth of Bangladesh. Always at odds with the powerful and mercurial national security advisor, Henry Kissinger, and President Richard Nixon over the indifference of the US towards human rights violations in East Pakistan, Blood and his team at the US consulate displayed rare courage and empathy in pressing for US intervention before the situation got out of hand.

In a scathing indictment of the opportunistic appeasement of the military regime of Yahya Khan in the early 1970s by Nixon, Gary J. Bass dismantles the smug aura of success that has generally been attached to the Kissinger–Nixon era of US foreign policy. Digging deep into recently declassified official documents and oral transcripts from Delhi, Dacca and Washington, Bass is unsparing of the apathy of the White House towards the unfolding brutality unleashed on millions of Bengalis by Major General Tikka Khan, later known as the Butcher of Bangladesh.

The prime driver of US policy towards East Pakistan and the main reason for ignoring the horrors of the widespread killings was Nixon's obsession with creating history by restoring languishing ties with China. Pakistan was an important pawn in this endeavour as Kissinger used Yahya Khan and Bhutto as key interlocutors with the Chinese for what ultimately turned out to be a path-breaking visit by Nixon to China in 1972. As the crisis spiralled out of control, the decisive humanitarian and military intervention by India in December 1971 did not change the duo's approach towards India. They consistently refused to recognize India's predominant status in the region despite advice from stalwarts such as Kenneth Keating, the US ambassador in Delhi, and Edward Kennedy, the influential Democrat from Massachusetts. Instead, Kissinger and Nixon attempted all along to crudely convince the Indians not to intervene through back-channel meetings and enticements of increased aid.[8]

Beginning with the massacre of Bengali intellectuals and academics at the University of Dacca on 26 March 1971, Blood looked on helplessly as US equipment including Chaffee tanks and Sabre jets were used against civilians. The most he could do along with his staff was to shield many Bengali families for days together from marauding Pakistani troops and Razakar mobs. Bass writes objectively on India's growing concern over the influx of millions of refugees into north-east India and the nationwide outcry of public and political opinion against the atrocities committed by the Pakistan Army. He too suggests that India could have militarily intervened in East Pakistan as early as April–May 1971. Seeing an opportunity to cut Pakistan to size and genuinely concerned with the plight of the oppressed Bengali population of East Pakistan, Indira Gandhi was keen to launch a military action into East Pakistan immediately. However, a cautious and conservative Indian Army chief, General Manekshaw, was not comfortable with sustaining a two-front operation during the summer and monsoon months, rightly preferring a campaign in the cooler winter months. It was this decision that led to the growth of the Mukti Bahini as a potent guerrilla force and the face of Bengali resistance till India finally intervened with its lightning campaign to liberate East Pakistan in December 1971.[9]

In the midst of the carnage, however, there were examples of compassion and courage among a few Pakistani officers who had the courage to question Yahya Khan's crackdown. Air Commodore Zafar Masud, a distinguished PAF fighter pilot and commander of the Sargodha fighter base in 1965, was one of them. The senior-most PAF officer in East Pakistan from April 1970 onwards, Masud appealed to Yahya Khan in a briefing to desist from embarking on what he called was a 'mismatched war' with India and refused to endorse the use of Sabre jets against civilian population in Dacca when the crackdown was ordered.[10] Seeing the futility of his resistance, he honourably resigned from his post, and the only reason why Yahya and Bhutto desisted from incarcerating or eliminating him was his immense popularity within the PAF.

India Prepares, Pakistan Stumbles

Offering a macro perspective of the various regional, situational and structural factors of the time, most of which directly or indirectly led to the conflict, Sumit Ganguly highlights some very important issues for the military historian to take note of. These are the unresolved historical legacies of Partition; ideological and religious schisms, particularly over Kashmir, exacerbated by the situational instability caused by the refugee crisis; and finally triggered by an increasingly assertive India.[11] Ganguly also highlights the sophistication with which India orchestrated the final lap of diplomacy – aligning it along the way with the more hawkish pronouncements emanating from India's fledgling strategic community led by K. Subrahmanyam. Subrahmanyam would emerge as India's foremost strategic thinker in the decades that followed the 1971 war.[12]

A key departure from earlier times was the clarity with which Mrs Gandhi made up her mind to use force to further India's strategic objectives. This resulted in even the normally accurate and conservative CIA to overestimate her war objectives. In a secret memo issued on 7 December 1971 it listed out her war objectives as 'liberation of

Bangladesh, the incorporation into India of the southern area of Azad (Pakistan-held) Kashmir and the destruction of Pakistan's armoured and air force strength so that Pakistan can never again threaten India'.[13] She even queried her army chief, General Manekshaw, in April 1971 whether it was possible to launch an attack into Bangladesh immediately. This she did after being thoroughly and rightly briefed by India's intelligence agencies that the humanitarian crisis had the potential to assume humungous proportions in the months ahead. She is reported to have been a trifle disappointed that General Manekshaw had a watertight case for asking for time till December to build up his forces, rather than rushing headlong into conflict weeks before the onset of monsoon. Complementing the army chief's cautious view by advising restraint till all diplomatic options were exhausted was Indira Gandhi's affable foreign minister, Swaran Singh.[14] That Indira Gandhi listened to them was indeed quite creditable considering that she was quite a dominating personality.

The lessons of 1962 and 1965 loomed on the horizon as Manekshaw wanted to have his forces better trained, better equipped and ready for battle. Lieutenant General B.T. Pandit, now an alert and articulate octogenarian, and among the few officers from the Corps of Engineers to have commanded a front-line corps after Independence, recounts his experience at the Military Operations (MO) Directorate in early 1971 as a major:

> Early in March, I was called to the ops room and found General Manekshaw, the vice chief of army staff, the director of military intelligence and my boss, the director of military operations, engaged in animated discussion. My boss, who was at the lectern, told me as soon as I came in: 'Tell the Chief.' Manekshaw cryptically asked, 'KK tells me that it will take three months to do the logistic stocking; are you sure?' I said 'Yes Sir.' 'Have you consulted Eastern Command and spoken to Sethna? (Sethna was the brigadier general staff at HQ, Eastern Command). I said 'Yes, sir.' The chief probed further, 'Have you spoken to Jakes (Lt General Jacob was the chief of staff of Eastern Command, and a trusted lieutenant of Manekshaw)? I said, 'No, sir, but I would assume that he would have been told.' Manekshaw was relentless and probed, 'Is that the best you can do?' I stuck to my guns.

> 'That bloody takes me to the middle of the monsoon. What if I want to cut it short to a month?' I said 'Sir, you will be able to go in only from Calcutta.' I was clear that we would not be able to envelope East Pakistan from all directions, as Manekshaw had planned.[15]

Supporting Manekshaw in a remarkable show of solidarity, Admiral Nanda, the naval chief, and Air Chief Marshal Lal, the air chief, went about readying their forces for battle with remarkable vigour and professionalism. Some military analysts and historians feel that Manekshaw was excessively cautious and influenced heavily by the fear of failure.[16] As a result, they say, India missed a golden opportunity to stop the un-calibrated massacres in East Pakistan, as also stem the flow of refugees into India. Others like John Gill, a South Asia expert at the National Defense University, Washington, and the author of a definitive monograph on the war, add that Manekshaw was waiting for the winter so that any kind of Chinese intervention could be ruled out.[17] His scepticism of the Chinese was understandable for he had been given the unenviable responsibility of commanding the Indian Army's Eastern Army Command in the years following the 1962 debacle. He had done a great deal to restore the fighting spirit and elan of the units in his command and had no intention of frittering away those gains.

In Pakistan, however, the politico-military establishment was in a mess. While its armed forces were at the peak of their professional competence around the 1965 war, buoyed as they were then by an exposure to the latest US military hardware, training and tactics, the post-1965 era saw a gradual increase in the involvement of the military in political affairs. This gradual peripheral distraction gathered momentum around the time when General Yahya Khan replaced Field Marshal Ayub Khan as president and promptly declared martial law. Adding to their woes was the defiance from East Pakistan and the rise of the ambitious Bhutto, who was scheming to exploit the precipitous situation. In the absence of a stable politico-diplomatic-military interface, there was no way in which Pakistan could extricate itself from the quagmire it had created for itself in Bangladesh.

From July to November 1971, Indira Gandhi and her foreign minister, Sardar Swaran Singh, assisted by a few other astute negotiators, globetrotted across the Western world, attempting to build a consensus to force a UN resolution condemning the Pakistani atrocities in Bangladesh. Realizing that Nixon's planned historic visit to China in 1972 would have a negative impact on Indo-US relations despite Kissinger's assertions to the contrary,[18] India wasted no time in sealing its own Friendship Treaty with the Soviet Union in August 1971. Prof. Arun Mohanty at New Delhi's Jawaharlal Nehru University succinctly sums up the essence of the treaty as 'to neutralize the emerging Washington-Beijing-Islamabad axis and defend their geopolitical interests'.[19] The treaty effectively paved the way for accelerated Soviet military assistance and diplomatic support in the build-up to the conflict. There was no procrastination in seeking Soviet help as India realized that any UN resolution on East Pakistan would be vetoed by both US and China and that it was important to solicit Soviet help to block any kind of international censure should India get embroiled in a conflict with Pakistan. After a successful visit to the Soviet Union in September, Prime Minister Gandhi failed to make any headway in her talks with President Nixon on the last lap of her visit to the West in early November.[20] She returned to India knowing that India had no option but to go to war. It is only after her return that the Indian Army commenced its full-fledged probing attacks into East Pakistan along with the Mukti Bahini.

Building Asymmetry: The Military Balance

In 1965, an overconfident Pakistan was rudely surprised by India's response despite seizing the initial advantage. The chastening experience of the strategic defeat and the ignominy of the loss of large swathes of territory to India highlighted the inherent advantage of geographical size, strategic depth and quantitative edge that India would always have. Having already displayed tremendous resilience and fighting spirit in 1947–48, the Indian soldiers and airmen proved beyond doubt in 1965 that man-to-man they were as good as, if not better, than the more 'martial' Pakistani Pathan or Punjabi.

India's military force structure strategy vis-à-vis Pakistan prior to the 1971 war was simple: build asymmetry by widening the quantitative gap and narrowing the technical gap between the two armed forces. This it did by adopting a four-pronged strategy involving upgrading existing platforms like the Hunter and MiG-21 fighter aircraft; complementing old but reliable platforms like the Centurion tanks with the T-55 and Vijayanta tanks; acquiring new systems like the 130 mm artillery guns, Sukhoi-7 fighter-bomber aircraft, Foxtrot class submarines and OSA fast attack craft from the Soviet Union; and lastly, galvanizing the indigenous military industrial complex to support capability building. Organizations like Hindustan Aeronautics Limited (HAL), heavy vehicle factory and the ordnance factories pitched in to accelerate India's defence preparedness. Aiding this indigenous drive was the growing Indo-Soviet strategic bonhomie, which resulted in an accelerated weapons and technology transfer programme. This was further cemented by the Indo-Soviet Friendship Treaty of August 1971.

One story, though, merits attention. Though the MiG-21 was inducted into the IAF before the 1965 war, its main shortcoming was the poor performance of the K-13 air-to-air missile in comparison with the Sidewinder missiles possessed by the PAF. The absence of an internal gun to aid in close combat made matters worse and something had to be done before the war to exploit the large numbers of MiG-21s that formed the backbone of the IAF's air defence fleet. When HAL expressed its inability to fit external guns at short notice, Air Marshal Malse, the Air Officer Maintenance, took on this task and had a fair number of aircraft from the MiG-21 fleet, mainly from the squadrons in the western sector, fitted with the external Gondola Pack (GP) with the 23 mm GSh gun that had a rate of fire of over 3,000 rounds per minute. The fitment was done at the IAF's Kanpur Base Repair Depot in a record time of three months. Lal had chosen his key advisors well!

What of Pakistan's attempts to keep pace with its larger neighbour who was making sure that the uncertainty of 1965 would never be repeated? In many ways the period from 1966 and 1971 was strategically 'too hot' for its military establishment to handle. Softened by the trappings of power and led by a 'fading' strongman, there were too many political distractions for Ayub Khan to monitor the military closely and ensure that the professionalism that he had infused in the military in the previous decade was sustained into the 1970s. Aggravating the situation was the slowdown in the US Military Assistance Programme, absence of an indigenous defence industry, and the requirement to cater for increased military presence in East Pakistan owing to the resurgent Bengali nationalism. Recognizing that he needed to convince the Americans to refurbish his ageing military equipment, Yahya threatened to go to the Russians in mid-1970. Much to the consternation of the Indians, Kissinger convinced President Nixon to release some symbolic aid in the form of B-57 bombers and M-48 Patton tanks to keep Pakistan in the US fold.[21] The Jordanians too would pitch in as the war commenced with ten F-104 Starfighters, which were flown in to Karachi in early December with their complement of Pakistani instructor pilots on deputation to the Royal Jordanian Air Force.

In more specific terms, the Indian Army realized that its main deficiencies in the 1965 war were quality of armoured fighting vehicles, lack of long-range artillery guns and inadequate mobility. In 1969 some of the oldest battalions from various infantry regiments were equipped with Czech armoured personnel carriers (APCs) called Topaz and attached to the armoured division and the independent armoured brigades. This provided much needed mobility and safety that allowed the infantryman to keep pace with his own tanks as against the earlier concept of 'lorried brigades'. Unfortunately, 1 Armoured Division, India's only armoured division, was not used in the conflict at all, and the decision not to equip the armoured brigades that were integral to the divisions which were earmarked for the initial offensives with the Topaz was highly questionable. As it turned out, the battle of Shakargarh saw little employment of the Topaz by India in what turned out to be the only major tank-versus-tank battle of the 1971 war.

Much has been written over the years about the overwhelming advantage enjoyed by the Indian Army in the eastern theatre. A closer look at numbers reveals that the asymmetry conformed to more or less a ratio of 3:1, which was generally a globally accepted norm for victory during offensive operations in the plains. The Indian Army's Eastern Command under Lieutenant General J.S. Aurora deployed a little over three corps around East Pakistan comprising around nine infantry/mountain divisions and three regiments of armour. Added to this were approximately two divisions of 'fighting fit' Mukti Bahini regulars at dispersed locations, both within Bangladesh and on the borders. Ranged against this force were a little over three and a half divisions and almost two regiments of armour of the Pakistan Army, albeit hastily organized and reinforced from the West.[22] If there was a significant advantage enjoyed by the Indians, it was in the area of covert and guerrilla operations with the strength of the Mukti Bahini being significantly higher than the 35,000 Razakar and Mujahid force organized by Lieutenant General Niazi, the overall commander of Pak forces in the east.[23] Complementing the Mukti Bahini in covert operations was the Special Frontier Force, which caused much havoc behind enemy lines in the Chittagong sector.

As expected, there was near parity in the western theatre, and though India enjoyed a nominal advantage in terms of infantry divisions, it must be borne in mind that three of India's eleven divisions were deployed in a defensive posture in J&K against only seven POK brigades (equivalent of about one and a half divisions) of the Pakistan Army. This left Western Command of the Indian Army under Lieutenant General K.P. Candeth with not much to play around in the area extending southwards from Chhamb to Anupgarh, a distance of about 600 km.

South of Anupgarh and extending through the desert sector of Rajasthan to Kutch was a large expanse of almost 1,800 km of desert and semi-desert terrain, an area which had tactically and operationally not gained much importance since the 1965 war. It was, however, defended by a little over two infantry divisions with just one armoured regiment to provide any kind of punch. India's Southern Army Command under Lieutenant General G.G. Bewoor was entrusted with operations in this area. Facing it was one division of the Pakistan Army with approximately two regiments of armour, and another division waiting in depth as part of an Army HQ reserve, parts of which were used when the situation turned grave.[24]

Pakistan continued to have a quantitative edge in terms of armour, with two armoured divisions and two independent armoured brigades against India's one armoured division and three independent armoured brigades. The qualitative edge which Pak armour had enjoyed in 1965, though, had disappeared with India having inducted the Soviet T-55 and the indigenous Vijayanta tanks with better firepower. Just as it did in 1965 in the battle of Assal Uttar, the robust and reliable British Centurion tank would outgun the Patton tank even in 1971. What was it that allowed the older Centurion to match the technologically more advanced Patton?

Two issues caught my attention while browsing through an unpublished monograph written by Brigadier R.R. Palsokar (retd) on the exploits of 16 Independent Armoured Brigade, the brigade that would go on to cover itself with glory in the battle of Basantar. The primary reason was the superior training and fierce competitiveness among the Centurion crews during the build-up to the war. Their approach to ranging techniques and field firing allowed them to operate inside the decision cycle of the Pattons. At a distance of 1,000–1,200 yards, a well-trained Centurion crew would take about 30–40 seconds from target identification to destruction.[25] The Patton crews, on the other hand, struggled to master the sophisticated technology at their disposal, particularly the ranging and targeting systems. The second reason for the superiority of the Centurions was their complete integration with artillery crews and the engineer regiments that allowed them to breach minefields and operate with close fire support.[26]

Most successful attacks by Pakistan in the 1965 conflict were preceded by withering artillery bombardment, the Chhamb offensive being a classic case. The decisive edge that Pak artillery enjoyed in that conflict was due to a significant superiority in medium-range artillery. While this edge continued in 1971, the Indian Army raised a number of medium regiments to bridge the gap. These were to play a significant role, both in the eastern and the western theatres.[27]

The relentless build-up of India's military capability was also reflected in the skewed force structure comparison between the two navies prior to the outbreak of the war. Though India flexed its naval muscle with a fully serviceable aircraft carrier with its full complement of combat aircraft and helicopters, a cruiser, seven modern frigates, four operational submarines and eight recently acquired OSA missile boats as its main offensive ships, all was not hunky-dory. Vice Admiral Pasricha recollects that INS *Vikrant* was not in the best of shape and could barely reach speeds of 18–21 knots as against its maximum speed of 24.5 knots, the optimum speed required to facilitate air operations of the Sea Hawks and Alizes, the main strike force on board. At these speeds it would have been vulnerable to submarine attacks and hence was shifted from the

Western Fleet to the safer waters of the Bay of Bengal where it lay in wait in the Andamans before being unleashed against Chittagong and Cox's Bazaar.[28]

The story of the acquisition of the OSA class missile boats is interesting, particularly when it comes from the youngest of the 25 Squadron's commanding officers of the time, thirty-five-year-old Lieutenant Commander Bahadur Kavina.[29] Kavina remembers clearly that after initially procrastinating over the purchase of these boats, the successful sinking of the *Eliat,* an Israeli destroyer, by Egyptian missile boats of the Komar class (inferior to the OSA class, but armed with the same missiles) in 1967 convinced the Indian Navy to go back to the Russians and accept their offer for eight boats. With their onboard surface-to-surface radar with a range of almost 40 km, and deadly Styx surface-to-surface missile with an effective range of just over 20 nautical miles, the boats packed a deadly punch. The crew of the OSA boats trained in complete secrecy till September 1971, surprising even the aggressive commander of the Western Fleet, Rear Admiral Kuruvilla, when Kavina claimed during a fleet briefing that they were capable of picking up targets at 40 nautical miles against the existing maximum pick-up ranges of 20 nautical miles that any of the larger ships in the fleet could provide.[30] The Indian Navy now knew it had a formidable weapon and factored it into their operational plans.

Complementing the offensive element was a large depot ship, three old frigates, four old destroyers, two Soviet Petya class anti-submarine frigates, three landing ships and four patrol craft – a sizable force as compared to 1965, but by no means sufficient to defend India's vast coastline and island territories.[31] Ranged against this force was the Pakistan Navy, which was struggling to modernize in the face of a predominantly land-centric military leadership. Its complement of an old cruiser, four obsolete destroyers and two vintage frigates was no match for India's superiority on the surface. Where the Pakistan Navy matched its Indian counterpart was in the sub-surface domain, where deterrent capability was provided by their four submarines, three of which (French Daphne class) were deployed in the Bay of Bengal and one (American Tench class) in the Arabian Sea.

Naval aviation emerged as a significant force multiplier in the 1971 war. As promised earlier in the book, this potent and proud arm of the Indian Navy has not been forgotten. Even though the Royal Navy operated Catalina flying boats from Cochin, on the west coast of India, during WW II, Lieutenant Y.N. Singh was the first Indian naval aviator in the true sense as he flew Wildcats on Royal Navy escort carriers during the closing stages of WW II and even engaged in a dogfight with Japanese Kamikaze fighters in the waters around the Andaman and Nicobar Islands.[32] While the first Royal Indian Navy's naval air station was commissioned in Cochin only in 1946, the Indian Navy's first aircraft carrier was commissioned in the UK with much fanfare and sailed for India under the command of Captain Mahendroo, a WW II veteran, in mid-1961 with its onboard complement of Sea Hawks and Alizes. While the Sea Hawks were British jet fighters and made up the Indian Naval Air Squadron (INAS 300) or the White Tigers as they were called, the Alizes were French-built turboprop aircraft with anti-submarine warfare capability and made up the second squadron on board, INAS 310.[33] After an initial period of location of INS *Vikrant*'s on board squadrons at Cochin, and at Sulur airbase near Coimbatore in the southern state of Tamil Nadu, it was felt that the naval airbase at Dabolim, Goa, would provide an appropriate home base to the fighter squadrons embarked on the carrier. From 1964 onwards INS *Hansa*, the airbase at Dabolim, was to become home to the Sea Hawks and Alizes and the Vampire jet trainers on loan from the IAF, which formed the striking power of the Indian Navy's air arm for many years to come. The free spirit of India's naval aviators is captured in wonderful prose by Vice Admiral Mihir Roy in his book *War in the Indian Ocean.* He writes about the charm and mystique of the brood of naval aviators:

> Naval Aviators are considered, even within the Navy, to be strange and unusual creatures – half airmen and half sailors! In the outside world, some people truly believe they are slightly crazy in trying to land on a 300-feet [sic] deck, which is not only moving at 20 knots but bouncing up and down even in a relatively calm sea.[34]

With the INS *Vikrant* inexplicably in the dry dock at the outbreak of the 1965 war, its complement of a flight of Sea Hawks was positioned at Jamnagar, the IAF airfield in the Kathiawar region of Gujarat. The pre-emptive strike on Jamnagar by PAF Canberras prompted the Indian Navy to withdraw its main strike aircraft to Bombay instead of launching the much prepared retaliatory strikes against Karachi, much to the dismay of its pilots.[35] The Indian Navy had thus lost a chance to showcase its prowess in the 1965 war because of poor planning, poor inter-service coordination and cautious leadership. In 1971, though, the naval chief, Admiral Nanda, had no such defensive plans. Despite INS *Vikrant* facing serious problems in one of its four boilers that severely restricted its speed to 14 knots, Nanda searched for solutions to ensure that the other three boilers were checked out thoroughly and not only was INS *Vikrant* up and steaming at over 20 knots by June 1971,[36] its entire complement of eighteen Sea Hawk and five Alize turboprop fighters with anti-submarine capability were raring to get into action.[37]

Submarines gained their reputation as 'killers in the deep' during World War II as German U-boats stalked Allied naval warships and merchant vessels in the icy cold waters of the Atlantic. The years after WW II saw the battle between submarines on one side and a combination of surface ships and aircraft on the other seesaw back and forth. The tag of 'the silent service' attached to the Indian Navy was apt as it expanded its submarine fleet in the late 1960s.[38] INS *Virbahu* at Visakhapatnam was the first home for the submarines, supposedly at the behest of the Soviets, who wanted them to be kept away from the prying eyes of the West. This was almost five years after the hectic negotiations between India and Great Britain over the sale of modern submarines had failed to reach any meaningful conclusion. Unreasonable restrictions articulated by Britain on various aspects and the growing asymmetry in the submarine force levels vis-à-vis the Pakistan Navy forced India to look to the Soviet Union to narrow the operational gap. The price of the submarines was pegged at Rs 3 crore each with credits spread over ten years.[39] The Soviet-made submarines made up the 8th Submarine Squadron and ensured that the sub-surface advantage enjoyed by the Pakistan Navy in 1965 was effectively neutralized by the time the two countries went to war in 1971. Despite the loss of one of their US-built submarines, PNS *Ghazi*, the Pakistan

Navy would go on to more than match the Indian Navy when it came to exploiting these silent killers.[40]

After a 'learning' performance in the 1965 war that saw it grow in confidence about its ability to influence the course of subcontinental conflicts, the IAF also forged ahead in terms of plugging gaps and building operational capabilities. Both the eastern and western theatres saw significant upgradation of airfields that could facilitate fighter operations. While the eastern theatre had nine operational airfields including Dum Dum at Calcutta, the airfields at Jaisalmer, Utterlai (Barmer) and Nal (Bikaner) in the desert sector were upgraded to support fighter operations south of Fazilka and Anupgarh. The greatest asymmetry was in the east where one squadron of sixteen upgraded PAF F-86 Sabre jets was pitted against almost twelve squadrons of IAF fighters and bombers with an available strength of about 160 aircraft excluding Canberra bombers, which were based in the Central Air Command base of Gorakhpur.[41] Included among these squadrons were three MiG-21 FL squadrons with ground-attack capability.

On the western borders the IAF had almost 350 fighters and bombers available for full-fledged operations considering that all squadrons had been asked to ensure a serviceability of 75 per cent at the very minimum. A distinguished fighter pilot and scholar, Air Vice Marshal A.K. Tiwary, though, puts the figure at 419.[42] These included over four squadrons of MiG-21s with the innovatively added external gun pack, upgraded Hunters, Gnats, the recently acquired Soviet Sukhoi-7s, HAL-built HF-24s, Mysteres, Canberra bombers and the obsolescent Vampire jets, which would go on to play a decisive role in the J&K sector. Facing them were 260–280 PAF fighters and bombers including a squadron of twenty-four newly acquired Mirage-IIIs from France. A squadron of ageing F-104 Starfighters was reinforced by an additional ten from the Royal Jordanian Air Force, while around seven squadrons of the battle-hardened Sabre jets including ninety upgraded Sabres from the German Air Force[43] made up the main strike element. Completing the force was one squadron of B-57 bombers; and five squadrons of the Chinese variant of the MiG-19, the F-6, gifted to Pakistan by China in 1966.[44] While the Gnats continued to dominate the Sabres, the enhanced ground-attack punch provided by the upgraded Hunters and the relatively new Sukhoi-7s gave the IAF a decisive qualitative and quantitative advantage over the PAF. Most importantly, the coercive impact of the MiG-21s in the air defence role meant that the PAF was not going to have a free run if it attacked IAF airfields and other ground targets. While in 1965 the IAF was somewhat surprised by PAF tactics, it was better prepared in 1971. There was a refreshing aggression in the manner in which IAF squadrons trained during the months prior to the war. Air Marshal Patney recollects that tactics were disseminated to squadrons after extensive trials and validation by TACDE, the IAF's combat development outfit,which comprised a selected bunch of 'hot shot' fighter jocks. Young IAF fighter pilots were subjected to rigorous lead-in training in the squadrons, and when the air war broke out, Gnats, Hunters and MiG-21s were always game to take on the Sabres in a one-versus-one fight. The enhanced range of the Hunters meant that there was no airfields in Pakistan that they could not reach. Wing Commander Parker and his boys from the IAF's 20 Squadron would go on to demonstrate this. The IAF had also trained for low-level bombing by night in moonlight conditions with a motley bunch of MiG-21 and Sukhoi-7 pilots from its recently formed Tactics and Combat Development Establishment putting together standard operating procedures for 'blind bombing' in limited moonlight conditions. This was to pay rich dividends during the initial days of the air campaign in the western sector.[45] More significantly, the Indian Army could call upon almost 30 Mi-4 and Alouette helicopters for heliborne and battlefield surveillance operations in the eastern sector. These along with the almost fifty light and medium lift transport aircraft would play a significant role in the speed with which the Indian Army would envelope Dacca, not only from all directions on the ground, but also from the third dimension – the skies. The Pakistan Army had no such support in the east, while in the west, despite having a large fleet of C-130 Hercules medium lift transport aircraft, there was no flexibility for the Pakistan Army to plan an airborne operation. They were not about to forget the disastrous experience of 1965![46]

What was significant in the steady build-up of IAF capability was the fact that its chief, P.C. Lal, had a ringside view of all the mistakes made during the 1965 war – he was the vice chief during the period. In his quiet and unassuming way, Pratap Chunder Lal went about addressing the major deficiencies using a systems approach. Building of blast pens to disperse and protect aircraft; procurement of and locating air defence radars and modern communication systems to prop up the air defence network; locating mobile observation posts (MOPs) along the border to provide early warning to airfields of incoming air strikes through radio communication; and ensuring adequate armament stocks and moving squadrons from their peacetime locations to the forward locations were among the measures initiated to ensure that the IAF was ready in all respects to fight a two-front war.[47] As against a PAF air defence network which comprised one high-level radar in the east and five radars in the west with two high-level and three low-level radars,[48] the IAF had a better organized radar network.[49] This would play a critical role in improving the interception rates of incoming strikes. Overall, except for a near parity on ground in the western sector, there was significant asymmetry on the high seas and in the air.

23

SHAPING THE EASTERN FRONT

The Mukti Bahini cadres were the 'eyes and ears' of the Indian Army during the early days of the Bangladesh Campaign. They ensured that we did not have to manoeuvre in a vacuum. That was their greatest contribution in our victory.[1]

– Lieutenant General Shamsher Mehta (Retd)

The Mukti Bahini and Covert Operations

Initially formed as the Mukti Fauj or the Mukti Bahini, or simply the 'Freedom Fighters' when translated into English, the force primarily comprised the armed organizations that fought alongside the Indian armed forces against the Pakistan Army during the Bangladesh Liberation War. It was dynamically formed by Bengali regulars and civilians after the proclamation of Bangladesh's independence on 26 March 1971. Subsequently, by mid-April 1971, the former members of the East Pakistan armed forces formed the 'Bangladesh Armed Forces' and M.A.G. Osmani assumed their command. The civilian groups continued to assist the armed forces during the war. After the war 'Mukti Bahini' became the general term to refer to all forces of former East Pakistani origin fighting against the Pakistani armed forces during the Bangladesh liberation war. Inspired in part by the revolutionary Che Guevara, the Mukti Bahini operated as a highly effective guerrilla force to keep the Pakistan Army on tenterhooks.

The 'soldier nucleus' of the Mukti Bahini comprised regular officers and men of the East Bengal Rifles (EBR) who rebelled against the Pakistan Army after the crackdown of March 1971. Led by commanders like Colonel Osmani and Major Zia-ur-Rahman (later president of Bangladesh), they operated in a diffused manner alongside local commanders like 'Tiger' Siddiqui with two primary objectives. The first was to exert pressure on the Pakistan Army from the periphery using Indian territory as firm bases; the second and more dangerous one was to chip away at the core of Pakistan's defences in the heartland by carrying out hit-and-run attacks and then melting away into the countryside.

India's role in indoctrinating, training and equipping the Mukti Bahini prior to the commencement of actual operations in December 1971 is well documented from both the intelligence and military angle. It had identified as early as 1968 that East Pakistan offered immense potential for covert action – this emerged as one of the two main tasks assigned by Prime Minister Indira Gandhi to the Research and Analysis Wing (R&AW). R&AW was hived off from the Intelligence Bureau (IB) to develop covert capability; East Pakistan was one of its first tests.[2] After influencing sections of the East Bengali intelligentsia to rise against the dominating West Pakistani leadership, Mujib's electoral success and Yahya's crackdown provided the much needed fillip for expansion of these operations. Much before the Indian Army took over the role of training the Mukti Bahini, R&AW had already commenced training small groups of volunteers and pushing them inside East Pakistan. When large elements of the East Bengal Rifles revolted and crossed over to India, the Indian Army took over the mandate of converting this guerrilla force into one, which was capable of supporting it during full-fledged operations.

Contrary to rather far-fetched claims by Niazi that the total strength of the Mukti Bahini was over 2,50,000 trained and armed fighters,[3] a more realistic figure pointed at a little over a two-division-sized force of regulars comprising remnants of the East Pakistan Rifles, East Bengal Regiment, civil police and around 50,000 irregulars and guerrillas trained by India to wage war on Niazi's formations.[4] Split into battalion groups along the three-sided border with India with specific sectors and sub-sectors assigned to each group,[5] the Mukti Bahini initially operated through the Border Security Force (BSF) sectors; they later merged effortlessly into the various Indian Army formations when they massed along the border in preparation for the final assault into East Pakistan.[6] Significant credit for raising the war-fighting potential of this force must go to Indian field commanders like Brigadier Shabeg Singh and Brigadier Sant Singh, who worked tirelessly with Mukti Bahini commanders like Major Zia-ur-Rahman to create brigade-sized forces which had the confidence of taking on fortresses at places like Kamalpur and Jessore.[7] Shahbeg would later gain notoriety for his role as the principal military commander of Sant Jarnail Singh Bhindranwale, the Sikh terrorist leader who fought the Indian Army in the early 1980s before being killed inside the Golden Temple during Operation Bluestar in 1984.

Most accounts of the growth of the Mukti Bahini do not do justice to its naval and air wings. Mukti Bahini frogmen operated with freedom in the riverine areas of Chittagong, Chalna and Khulna and played an important role in interdicting supplies coming in from the sea to support the occupation forces in the eastern part of Bangladesh. Led by Bengali sailors and submariners who defected from the Pakistan Navy, particularly from the Daphne class submarine PNS *Mangro*,[8] they specialized in mining water channels and placing limpet mines, causing incalculable damage to Pakistan's trade and shipping.[9] Lloyds of London hiked its insurance rates for the area after the frogmen sunk over 1,00,000 tons of merchant shipping from July to November 1971, and damaged another 50,000 tons.[10] The naval element of the Mukti Bahini was later called Force Alpha as it integrated with the Indian Navy as the war progressed.

Many Bengali officers and men from the Pakistan Air Force and Pakistan International Airlines (PIA) joined the Mukti Bahini and quickly made the transition to being 'land warriors'. Many of them, like Wing Commander Bashar, were sector commanders and participated in raids. However, the aspiration to form an air wing remained – it only needed some support from India in the form of an airfield and a few aircraft to fructify into a reality. It was not long before Air Chief Marshal P.C. Lal, himself a Bengali, realized the potential of such a force and gifted a few aircraft and assigned a base to 'Kilo Force', as the fledgling Bangladesh Air Force came to be known in late September

1971.[11] Operating out of Dimapur, a small airstrip in Nagaland, Kilo Force was commanded by Group Captain Khandokar, who later became the first chief of the Bangladesh Air Force. It had on its inventory a Dakota freighter aircraft, an Otter light transport aircraft and an Alouette helicopter. The Otter and Alouette were suitably modified to fire rockets and guns: they would extensively take part in ground support operations during the conflict. Group Captain Chandan Singh, a highly accomplished transport pilot of the IAF and station commander of the air force station at Jorhat in Assam, mentored the fleet with an ace IAF helicopter pilot, Flight Lieutenant Singla, attached as an instructor.[12] With his eye for talent, Lal picked Chandan Singh as his key interface man with the Indian Army's IV Corps, which would go on to blaze new trails of joint operations during the ensuing conflict.

To suggest that all was well between the Mukti Bahini and their Indian trainers would be unrealistic considering that by September 1971, the Mukti Bahini was getting restless and straining at the leash imposed by the Indian Army. There were reports of the Mukti Bahini complaining to Indira Gandhi through the R&AW about the conservative approach of the commander of the Eastern Army Command, Lieutenant General Aurora, in prosecuting the covert war. Indian Army trainers, on the other hand, were deeply sceptical about the sustained fighting ability of the Mukti Bahini when faced with regular troops of the Pakistan Army in entrenched defences. However, these remained minor pinpricks and, to their credit, the Mukti Bahini and the Indian Army leadership never lost sight of the final objective.

A story that must be told is that of the role of the Special Frontier Force (SFF) in covert operations in the marshy hill tracts of Chittagong during November 1971. A force mainly comprising Tibetan commandos raised in the aftermath of the 1962 conflict with China to conduct covert operations in Tibet, the SFF was tasked to interdict the Pakistani brigade in the Chittagong region and ensure that Pakistani forces did not open an escape route into Burma. A secondary mission was to ensure that insurgents from India's north-east were prevented from exploiting the situation and operating from camps in East Pakistan. Operating in eight teams under the leadership of Major General S. S. Uban with IAF helicopter support for insertion of troops, the force caused havoc amongst the Pakistani ranks and had degraded their fighting ability significantly by the time regular Indian forces moved into the area. The exploits of the force have not been declassified but they have been obliquely referred to in a book written by the force commander.[13]

The Players

The larger-than-life personalities of Indira Gandhi and General Manekshaw (later Field Marshal) have dominated the strategic discourse of the 1971 war. Not having commanded forces in battle in the 1947–48 conflict with Pakistan as many of his contemporaries did, and missing the action in 1962 because of falling out of favour with the defence minister and the army chief, Manekshaw had a point to prove. With his flagging career having been resuscitated after the 1962 debacle, he was given command of Eastern Army Command in 1964 to repair the damage done after the Chinese stormed into NEFA. Little did he realize that fate would keep him out of action in the 1965 war too as India did not open a second front in the east except for brief battles in the air. It is in such circumstances that when presented with an opportunity to do battle, he was determined to make it count!

Sharing centre stage with them, however, were about a dozen other key players. Among them was the earthy Jagjivan Ram, a shrewd political associate of Indira Gandhi who replaced Y.B. Chavan as the defence minister in 1970. With his predecessor having done all the hard work in rebuilding India's armed forces and somewhat restoring its pride and elan, Jagjivan Ram delegated complete responsibility to the service chiefs and established a close personal relationship with each one of them. By doing so, he won their respect for his astute and 'hands off style of functioning'. Even the Indian Army's field commanders like Major General W.A.G. Pinto were impressed with the manner in which he connected with the men, visited troops on the front line with his wife, gamely agreeing to be driven around rough terrain in the commander's jeep.[14] He was the quiet orchestrator of 1971.

Like Manekshaw, Pratap Chunder Lal had gone through a rocky decade prior to being appointed as the air chief. A victim of Defence Minister Krishna Menon's high-handedness, Lal's services were terminated in September 1962 over a disagreement with Menon on replacements for the ageing Dakota aircraft while on deputation to the Indian Airlines Corporation. Luckily for Lal, he was reinstated in December 1962 after Krishna Menon fell from grace in the wake of the 1962 debacle. After highly successful stints as air officer maintenance, vice chief of air staff during the 1965 war, and chairman of Hindustan Aeronautics Limited, he took over as chief of air staff in July 1969. By then this intellectual and 'thinking airman' had acquired a comprehensive view of what needed to be done to ensure that the IAF emerged as an equally important element of joint operations. His focus was on building of new airfields, erecting concrete shelters for aircraft and improving the air defence network. He was the transformational leader the IAF was looking for.

The Indian Navy was seething after it was kept out of action during the 1965 war for no fault of its own, and like many senior naval officers, Admiral Nanda, the chief of naval staff, was determined to make amends for the 'no show' in 1965. Baptized into the navy during WW II and having seen the famous 'revolt' of 1946 as a young officer, he gained vital operational experience on India's first warship, INS *Delhi*. Nanda's major contribution was in convincing the political establishment that maritime power would have a major role to play if India wanted to establish clear military supremacy over Pakistan. He, more than anyone else, infused self-belief in the Indian Navy and propagated an offensive mindset amongst his operational planners.[15] His insistence on creating a reasonably potent eastern fleet and unleashing INS *Vikrant* on Chittagong, Cox's Bazar and Khulna ports despite the submarine threat from the Pakistan Navy was one of the defining moments of the war.

Though intelligence gathering in the western sector remained as scanty as it was in 1965, particularly when it came to tracking the deployment of Pakistan's 1 and 6 Armoured Divisions, significant credit for the success of covert operations in Bangladesh must go to R.N. Kao, the chief of R&AW, the hush-hush outfit that was hived out of the Intelligence Bureau in 1968 specifically for the conduct of covert operations. A close confidant of Indira Gandhi, the flamboyant Kao came into his own during the period April–December 1971 as he orchestrated a psychological warfare campaign in East Pakistan and set the ball rolling for the training of the Mukti Bahini in camps which were set up secretly in the eastern parts of India. His role has to be seen in the light of Indira Gandhi's desire to commence the Bangladesh campaign in April 1971. When Manekshaw was candid enough to indicate that he was not ready, Kao stepped in to keep the East Pakistan pot boiling till the army chief was fully prepared.[16]

Two distinguished civil servants merit special attention for their enabling role as effective and approachable interfaces between the military and the political establishment. They were P.N. Haksar, the principal private secretary to the PM and D.P. Dhar, who headed the Foreign Policy Planning Committee during the run-up to the conflict. These two kept the service chiefs continuously updated on diplomatic parleys and political discussions through the chairman of the Chiefs of Staff Committee. It was teamwork of the highest order and very rarely was it to be repeated during future contingencies.[17]

The Indian Army's strategy was to exploit the inroads made by the Mukti Bahini and other covert operators, and overwhelm East Pakistan with a multidirectional offensive which would result in the capitulation of all the fortress defences put together by Niazi. Dacca was never the initial objective and it was only the spectacular advance of the Indian Army in the IV Corps sector and the success of the Tangail airdrop that resulted in Dacca emerging as a possible objective.[18] Both these operations are discussed in subsequent chapters. Concurrently, the Indian Air Force and the Indian Navy were to exert overwhelming pressure from the air and sea, which would result in a psychological capitulation of the enemy.

Much to the displeasure of Lieutenant General K.P. Candeth, the GOC-in-C, Western Army Command, his formations were to adopt a 'holding strategy' in the west considering that there was near parity of forces[19] and because both sides had created linear defences that would have required overwhelming force superiority to ensure a decisive victory. 'Hold, probe, advance and hold' was the mantra in the west as part of what later came to be known as the 'Offensive Defensive Strategy' of Manekshaw. Aggressive field commanders like Major Generals Zorawar Chand Bakshi and W.A.G. Pinto were hampered by this strategy and the latter called it 'a neither here nor there strategy'.[20]

The IAF had concentrated its forces in the east with four main objectives. First was to achieve air superiority over the East Pakistan skies by overwhelming the single Sabre squadron, either in aerial combat, or destroying them on ground. This, the IAF argued, would enable the Indian Army to progress its operations unhampered by aerial interference. Surprisingly, cratering of Tezgaon airfield at Dacca, the home base of the Sabre squadron, was not initially considered a means to achieve the first objective. This would result in a lot of unnecessary air effort being wasted on the first two days of the war before the IAF struck on the right weapon to render Dacca airfield unusable. Second was to preserve its own air assets against aerial attack with robust all-round air defence. Third was to support ground operations with responsive close air support, effective interdiction of rear echelons and supply lines that connected the various East Pakistani fortresses and enclaves. The last objective was to aid in vertical envelopment of enemy positions by special helicopter-borne (SHBO) and airborne operations. In the western sector, the strategy was a little different with air defence occupying primacy; interdiction and close air support came next; and offensive strikes against Pakistani airfields and other strategic targets came last in order of priority.[21]

The Indian Navy's objectives were equally offensive and reflected its impatience to be counted. The strategy in the east was to completely dominate the Bay of Bengal and choke the coastal approaches to East Pakistan. Other naval objectives were to cripple the Pakistan Navy in Chittagong, Cox's Bazar, Chalna and Khulna with a combination of surface and air actions from the aircraft carrier; and a last-minute plan to carry out an amphibious assault operation towards the closing stages of the conflict.[22] The defensive tasks were primarily directed towards protecting the aircraft carrier from submarine attack. On the western seaboard the role of the Western Naval Command was to dominate the Arabian Sea and attempt an economic blockade of Pakistan by attacking Karachi. Offensive forays towards the Makaran coast were planned with a combination of surface attacks and stealthy submarine patrols.[23] Defensive tasks included protecting the ports of Kandla, Okha, Dwarka and Bombay.

While 'Sam' Manekshaw dominated the formulation of joint plans, the air and naval chiefs were assertive enough. There was some strain alright, but both Lal and Nanda were low key and mature commanders who managed their relationship with 'Sam' without allowing it to affect preparations for the conflict. An interesting anecdote in July or August reveals this, albeit with a tinge of humour. Manekshaw had called for a final presentation of plans and after the air force and naval plans had been presented, he announced, 'That's it, gentleman – we seem to have everything in place.' While his fellow chiefs, Lal and Nanda, got up to leave, a hand shot up from amongst the motley bunch of senior staff officers present at the briefing. It was Air Marshal Malse, the feisty Maratha who was the Air Officer-in-charge Maintenance (AOM) at Air HQ, and one of Lal's key advisors during the 1971 war. A fighter pilot who had converted to transport aircraft midway through his career, Malse had been the vice chief before being asked by Lal to take over as AOM to streamline the maintenance branch in the IAF and prepare it for war. 'Sir, what about the army plans?' There was a stunned silence in the room and, to Manekshaw's credit, he recovered quickly and said, 'Ah, how did we forget, we will have it tomorrow at the same time.'[24]

Shaping the Eastern Battlefront

By October 1971, the Mukti Bahini was ready to test Niazi's defences along the border. Divided into eleven sectors,[25] it made regular incursions into East Pakistan, conducting harassment raids and intelligence-gathering forays. However, whenever it attempted to hold territory or frontally attack the well-entrenched Pakistan Army positions, it suffered attrition and had to fall back into Indian territory.

Early November 1971 saw an escalation in violence and military action at multiple points along the India–East Pakistan border with the Indian Army complementing the Mukti Bahini at a number of places with troops and firepower. It was as though Indira Gandhi had told her commanders to step up the military pressure during her absence from the country. Though she was on a whirlwind tour of the West seemingly to try and prevent war and occupy the moral high ground, in actuality she was shrewd enough to realize that war was inevitable and that her visits were merely to legitimize the military action that was to follow.[26]

Lieutenant General Jagjit Singh Aurora, the soft-spoken commander of the Eastern Army Command, had divided the eastern war zone into four sectors. The north-west sector comprised the Siliguri corridor and the Cooch Behar district on the Indian side, and the towns of Rangpur, Rajshahi and Bogra in East Pakistan. The area of operation was boxed between the Ganga, Teesta and Jamuna rivers and had numerous tributaries of the rivers criss-crossing the countryside. Operations in the area were assigned to XXXIII Corps of the Indian Army led by Lieutenant General M.L. Thapan, a seasoned WW II veteran and commander of 26 Division – a division that saw extensive action during the Sialkot offensive in the 1965 war with Pakistan. Comprising two homogeneous mountain divisions, one of which was undermanned, and a third division of mixed forces, it was opposed by a regular division of the Pakistan Army (16 Division), which was stretched across a frontage of almost 350 km.

The western sector was psychologically an important sector with the bustling Indian metropolis, Calcutta, barely 100 km away from the border, while Jessore and Khulna were important garrisons for the Pakistan Army. This sector was dominated by the mighty River Padma[27] and its tributaries as it rushed towards the Bay of Bengal. Offensive operations in this sector were assigned to the Indian Army's II Corps led by Lt General T. N. Raina. It was Raina's brigade that put up a stout display against the Chinese in the Chushul battle of 1962. He had two well-oiled infantry divisions (4 Mountain Division of Assal Uttar fame and 9 Infantry Division) with a regiment of tanks to take on the lone Pakistan Army division (9 Division) ranged against him.

Covering the largest area and varied terrain ranging from the mountains of the Chittagong hills, to the coastal regions of Cox's Bazar and the plains of Sylhet and Comilla, the main punch of the Indian Army rested with IV Corps with its HQ at Agartala. With three full divisions, three squadrons of armour and the entire complement of approximately eight battalions of the East Bengal Regiment, Lieutenant General Sagat Singh, the whiskey-drinking, tough and battle-tested corps commander in the Patton mould, was supremely confident of dominating the eastern approaches to Dacca and taking control of the Chittagong, Ashuganj and Sylhet sectors. His innovative combat leadership would prove to be decisive in the final result of the Bangladesh campaign. Facing him was one regular division (14 Division) and elements of two ad hoc and hastily assembled divisions of little consequence (36 and 39 Divisions). Of these, 36 Division was virtually static around Dacca and its neighbourhood fortress of Nawabganj.

The northern flank of advance was looked after by 101 Communication Zone, which was essentially an administrative formation, but innovatively reinforced with fighting units to create an undersized divisional force. Initially commanded by Major General Gurbux Singh Gill, an unfortunate accident on 6 December put him out of action. He was replaced by Major General Nagra, who commanded the formation with distinction for the rest of the war. The formation was a brainchild of Manekshaw, who himself had spent many years as the commander of the Eastern Army Command and knew the area like the back of his hand. After a couple of early battles, the formation would surprisingly deliver the coup de grâce at Dacca as one of its brigades would link up with an airborne force to race past a lone and helpless Pakistani brigade at Mymensingh. Manekshaw had rightly assessed that to overwhelm the Pakistani defences he needed to have a northern hook to his offensive. It was through this zone that he launched a psychologically decisive airborne operation that would go on to influence the final battle for Dacca.[28]

Lieutenant General A.A.K. (Tiger) Niazi, a veteran of the Burma campaign and the 1965 war with India,[29] was in command of all field forces in East Pakistan as commander, Eastern Command. An accomplished field commander with gallantry awards in all the conflicts he had participated in, he was the 'fall guy' chosen by Ayub Khan to try and orchestrate a battle he knew was already lost. Though on paper Niazi had three divisions and had hastily formed two more for the defence of the Sylhet and Comilla sectors, he committed the cardinal mistake of 'spreading his forces too thin' and adopting a 'fortress strategy' without having the firepower to cause sufficient attrition when these fortresses were attacked. His strategy was based on thinly spread forward defences, which would fall back to fortresses like Khulna, Rangpur, Mymensingh, Sylhet and Comilla. This left his defences vulnerable to being bypassed as he hardly had any armour and offensive air assets to block these bypassing manoeuvres.[30]

In the air, too, the IAF had built up its forces methodically and the only PAF air defence radar at Dacca was kept on its toes by the sheer volume of operational flying done by the IAF in the months leading up to the war. Reflecting the improved synergy between the three services, most airfields in the eastern sector had adequate offensive punch and were carefully chosen to support the ground offensive.[31] While the fighter squadrons at the airfields of Panagarh, Dum Dum and Kalaikunda were allocated forces to support II Corps operations, the north Bengal airfields of Bagdogra and Hashimara had a good mix of air defence and ground attack capability in the form of Gnats and Hunters to support XXXIII Corps and 101 Communication Zone operations. Similarly, air assets at Gauhati, Kumbhigram and Agartala in the form of fighter squadrons and helicopter units were to prove invaluable in providing support to Sagat Singh's IV Corps and operations by 101 Communication Zone. Though the forces allocated during the actual conflict were not specifically meant for a particular corps, keeping in mind the flexibility of air power and its ability to influence far-flung battles in multiple corps zones, great thought was given to basing forces to remain synchronous with the ground battle.[32]

The Indian Navy too revealed its aggressive hand early enough by complementing the meagre resources of Eastern Naval Command by transferring its sole aircraft carrier, INS *Vikrant*, along with two potent frigates, INS *Brahmaputra* and INS *Beas*, from the western fleet to its eastern fleet, much to the disappointment of the commander of the Western Naval Command, Vice Admiral S.N. Kohli.[33] The newly formed eastern fleet with its aircraft carrier, two frigates, a destroyer, a submarine, eight patrol crafts and three landing ships[34] would prove decisive in keeping the pressure on Pakistan's sea lines of communications to the vital ports of Chittagong, Khulna and Chalna. For the first time after Independence, carrier-borne fighters were also tasked to add on to the overall air effort in tandem with the IAF. Alizes and Sea Hawks from the INS *Vikrant* were dovetailed into India's aerial offensives to render the airfields of Chittagong and Cox's Bazar unusable, as well as to provide close air support whenever called upon to do so. Interdiction of coastal fortifications and shipping were also important tasks assigned to Captain Swaraj Prakash, the captain of INS *Vikrant*.

Skirmishes or War

Pakistan has always maintained that India commenced the 1971 war as early as November 1971, and this accusation has not been without good reason. However, India's post-war media blitz, marked as it was by triumphalism after a long-awaited victory, all but completely blanked many of the actual facts. All accounts of the war from Pakistan, prominent among them being the ones written by Niazi[35] and Shuja Nawaz,[36] clearly mark the beginning of the conflict with the deep forays by the Indian Army into East Pakistan in the Boyra and Belonia bulges on the western and eastern borders of East Pakistan. In what is probably the most objective and academically well-researched work on the Indo-Pak war of 1971, R. Sisson and L.E. Rose write:

> The scope of Indian military involvement increased substantially in the first three weeks of November 1971 but in most cases the Indian units would hit their objectives in East Pakistan and withdraw to Indian territory. After the night of 21 November, however, the tactics changed in one significant way. Indian forces did not withdraw. From 21 November several Indian army divisions divided into small tactical units launched simultaneous military actions on all key border regions of East Pakistan from all directions with both armour and air support...[37]

As early as September 1971, specialist counter-insurgency troops from an Indian Army Jat battalion (31 Jat) made deep forays into the Chittagong sector and ambushed a large convoy of Pakistan Army boats, inflicting heavy casualties and then melted away into the jungle and returned to their home base in Tripura.[38]

While much of this is corroborated by a number of Indian authors, the most detailed analyses are by Major General Randhir Singh in his biography of Sagat Singh, the commander of IV Corps during the Bangladesh campaign, and by Jagan and Chopra in their comprehensive account of the air war over East Pakistan.[39] Sisson and Rose, though, are wrong when it comes to their assessment of air support to the Indian ground operations. Prior to 3 December and much to the frustration of some of the Indian field commanders, the IAF first provided air cover to them on 22 November in the battle of Boyra, where three PAF Sabre jets on a close air support mission were shot down by IAF Gnats. There were also a few intrusive reconnaissance missions carried out by IAF Hunters of 37 Squadron in October and early November to collect information about deployment of PAF assets in Dacca and army deployments in the Jamalpur, Sherpur and Comilla areas.[40] In the only cartographically well-depicted account of the 1971 war, John H. Gill, a US Army colonel and faculty member at the National Defense University, has clearly marked out a number of areas in East Pakistan which were captured by the Indian Army prior to the opening of the western front by Pakistan on the evening of 3 December.[41] One of the fiercest early encounters took place in late October in Sagat Singh's IV Corps sector around the picturesque tea estate of Dhalai. Located right on the border between the Indian state of Tripura and East Pakistan and about 35 km south-east of the important town of Maulvi Bazaar, the verdant gardens saw a pitched battle for over three days between 61 Brigade of the Indian Army and 12 Frontier Force, a Pakistan Army battalion from 14 Division. After suffering a fair number of casualties following some stout resistance from the Pakistan Army battalion, the tea estate was captured by the Indian Army and used as one of the many launch pads for the subsequent offensive. 'Shaping the battlefield' was not just a term that Indian field commanders had talked about at their war colleges; they went about translating it into capture of vital ground that would allow them to send in large forces when operations would start a few days later.

24

DESTINATION DACCA

Jaggi, I am a Corps Commander. I am expected to exploit an opportunity. If an opportunity presents itself to cross the Meghna and give you an aim plus I will take it. I am giving you the West Bank and beyond; you should be happy.[1]

– Lieutenant General Sagat Singh to his Army Commander

The Early Battles in the East

The first major attacks into East Pakistan by the Indian Army along with elements of the Mukti Bahini were launched on the night of 20/21 November along multiple ingress points. Shuja Nawaz goes to the extent of indicating that twenty-three salients inside East Pakistan were attacked[2] as fierce brigade battles were fought at Boyra in the western sector, Hilli in the north-western sector, Akhaura in the eastern sector and Sylhet in the north-eastern sector. Two brigades of the Indian Army's 9th Division made significant progress towards Niazi's fortress of Jessore by capturing a large enclave that comprised the forward defensive localities of Boyra and Garibpur by the end of November.

The curtain-raiser for the air campaign also took place in this sector between Sabres of 14 Squadron, PAF, and Gnats of 22 Squadron, IAF. The Gnats were operating an air defence detachment at Dum Dum airport at Calcutta as it was a mere 80 km from the border and needed air defence protection. Corroborating what Shuja Nawaz and John

Gill write about large-scale action by the Indian Army in November, Jagan and Chopra suggest that the Indian Army had made significant inroads as early as 12 November and that PAF Sabres were called into action on 19 November to support a beleaguered 107 Brigade, which was fighting a rearguard action around Boyra against two marauding Indian brigades.[3] On 21 November, as the Pakistanis called upon the lone armoured squadron of approximately fourteen Chaffee tanks along with repeated air strikes to throw back the numerically superior Indian forces, the IAF was finally called into action, much to the relief of the Indian brigades under attack.

Controlled by a radar unit located at Barrackpore, a few miles out of Calcutta, four Gnat fighters of 22 Squadron were 'scrambled' on two occasions – once in the morning and again in the evening – to try and intercept Sabres that were attacking the Indian brigades. Much to the frustration of the Gnats and the Indian brigades, the Sabres had vanished from the area by the time the IAF fighters arrived over Boyra. After another unsuccessful attempt on the morning of 22 November, the Indians finally drew blood in the afternoon thanks to some aggressive flying by a bunch of four 'young guns'.[4]

In a classic aerial dogfight between two comparable machines, the IAF Gnats pounced on a careless bit of tactical flying on the part of the experienced PAF squadron commander who was leading his formation of four Sabres on a ground attack mission. While Wing Commander Chaudhry, the commanding officer of the squadron, managed to get back in a damaged aircraft unscathed, his two young formation members were shot down by Flight Lieutenant Roy Massey and Flying Officers Lazarus, Ganapathy and Soares. Massey, Lazarus and Ganapathy were the IAF's first Vir Chakra awardees of the conflict. This tactical engagement has been one of the most dissected aerial engagements of the 1971 war and numerous lessons were drawn from it. The encounter is rated amongst the five top air combats in the post WW II era and 22 Squadron celebrates 'Boyra Day' even today. When Lal visited the squadron soon after, he remarked, 'there was such jubilation, it appeared that the war was already won.' S. Sajad Haider, one of the PAF's most accomplished fighter pilots and the CO of 14 Squadron at Dacca before Chaudhry, is scathing in his comments about how Chaudhry conducted himself in battle.[5]

To the north-west, significant gains were made towards Thakurgaon and Dinajpur; the border defences at Hilli, though, were a tough nut to crack. It was 4 Frontier Force (FF), and a company of 13 Frontier Force along with some armour and artillery, which fought a valiant defensive battle against 202 Brigade of the Indian Army from well-fortified defences. This prolonged battle of attrition from 22 November to 7 December ended when the defences at Hilli were bypassed by another Indian brigade as the defenders withdrew to their depth defences at Bogra. After incurring some losses during the initial days of the war, the Indian Army rightly looked at bypassing fortified forward defences, rather than taking them on headlong.[6] Air Marshal B.N. Gokhale, also called Bingo, was amongst the youngest IAF pilots to take part in the 1971 operations. He recollects that his first mission on 4 December as part of a four-aircraft Hunter formation from 7 Squadron was an interdiction mission against a railway station near Hilli. This was part of the operational plan to isolate Hilli and prevent any reinforcements from coming in, or enabling the defenders to withdraw towards their depth defences at Bogra.[7]

Niazi's northern sector defences comprised a small but compactly defended border post at Kamalpur; a larger battalion defended the town of Jamalpur on the southern bank of the River Lakhya, and the brigade headquarters at Mymensingh. The stubborn but static resistance offered by 31 Baluch at Kamalpur and Jamalpur was broken down by tactically mobile and numerically superior Indian forces from 101 Communication Zone after initial attacks by the Mukti Bahini were repulsed. The Baluchis along with remnants of the Mymensingh Brigade headquarters were then ordered to fall back to Dacca. The battle for Jamalpur was particularly fierce with 1 Maratha Regiment and 13 Guards fighting a brilliant tactical battle that involved the laying of multiple ambushes as Pakistani troops retreated to Dacca. Complementing their effort were a series of air strikes by IAF Hunters as they softened up a surprisingly resilient garrison. Recounting the intricate process of creating ambush positions with mutual cover, Lieutenant General Satish Nambiar, then a major and senior company commander of 1 Maratha, recalls that among the major actions prior to the fall of Jamalpur on 11 December was the trapping of a large Pakistani convoy and causing mayhem among

Pakistani ranks with accurate machine gun fire from multiple directions. The surrender of the garrison the next morning saw the crumbling of the last vestiges of resistance to the Indian Army's northern thrust towards Dacca. Nambiar and his commanding officer, Lieutenant Colonel 'Bulbul' Brar, were among the five Vir Chakras awarded to the 'Jangi Paltan' (Warring Unit) during the race to Dacca.[8]

To the east, the fortress of Akhaura was just across the border from the Indian town of Agartala and its defences were organized in a similar manner as they were at Hilli. After a spell of spirited resistance from 27 Brigade of 14 Division, the overwhelming pressure exerted by two regular Indian Army brigades attacking from the south, and two battalions of the East Bengal Rifles, proved too much for Brigadier Saadullah. The Pakistani brigade commander withdrew to Bhairab Bazaar on the west bank of the River Meghna in the face of fierce assaults by 73 and 311 Brigades of the IV Crops led by Sagat Singh, but not before blowing up portions of a vital bridge at Ashuganj on 9 December.[9] It was during this battle that Lance Naik Albert Ekka, a young tribal soldier from Bihar, serving with the Indian Army's 14 Battalion of the Regiment of the Guards (simply called 14 Guards) won the only Param Vir Chakra in the eastern theatre while assaulting fortified Pakistani defences and gun positions at the Gangasagar railway station, some 5 km south of Akhaura.[10] His company commander, Major Ashok Tara, too would be decorated with a Vir Chakra for his leadership during the same battle – he would later be involved in a dramatic rescue operation involving one of Bangladesh's second-generation political leaders, Sheikh Hasina Wazed, a daughter of Sheikh Mujibur Rahman. Recalling the operational momentum after the fall of Akhaura where another battalion of the Regiment of Guards (4 Guards) performed magnificently, Lieutenant General Shamsher Mehta, then a major, was commanding a squadron of PT-76 amphibious tanks from 63 Cavalry Regiment and attached to 57 Division, one of the IV Corp divisions. Affectionately called 'Shammi' because he resembled a glamorous Indian film star of the 1960s, he offered a rivetting account of the operational momentum created by Sagat Singh despite the blowing up of a major bridge across the River Meghna by the Pakistan Army that any other commander might have found difficult to work around. Added to that was the challenge of crossing

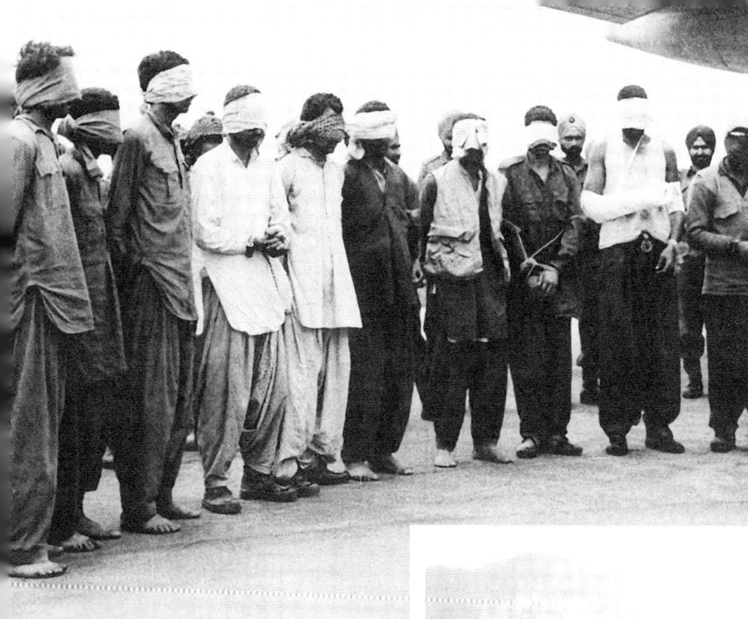

Captured Pakistani raiders during Operation Gibraltar, August 1965.

965 war

Major Ranjit Singh Dayal (fourth from left) and his team from 1 Para with Brigadier Zorawar Bakshi, Brigade Commander of 68 Infantry Brigade.

Indian medium gun in action after the capture of Haji Pir.

Sabre killers from Halwara, Flying Officer Neb (left) and Flight Lieutenant Rathore (right) with the Air Chief, Arjan Singh, September 1965.

Dr Karan Singh, Governor of J&K, flanked by Major General Sparrow (left) and Lieutenant General Dunne atop a destroyed Palton tank in Sialkot sector.

Flight Lieutenant Alfred Cooke from 14 Squadron next to the Hunter in which he shot down two PAF Sabres in a classic dogfight over Kalaikunda.

Rearming Mysteres of 1 Squadron at Adampur, September 1965.

A Gnat scramble at a forward base, September 1965.

Ground attack boys of 1 Squadron at Adampur with their commanding officer, Wing Commander O.P. Taneja (standing fifth from right).

Defence Minister Y.B. Chavan with troops of 3 Jat after the Battle of Dograi.

A canteen for arriving troops set up by the citizens of Amritsar at the city railway station.

Lal Bahadur Shastri with UN Secretary General U. Thant (centre).

Lieutenant General Harbaksh Singh (fourth from left) with veterans of 1 Sikh just after the 1965 war.

A senior Indian Army officer shares a light moment with hi Pakistani counterparts on the Ichogil Canal after the ceasefi

Training the Mukti Bahini somewhere in the Eastern theatre.

A young Mukti Bahini fighter displays his marksmanship.

Defence Minister Jagjivan Ram being driven around the frontline by Major General Pinto.

General Manekshaw with Lieutenant General K.K. Singh (right), Major General Pinto (second from left) and Brigadier Vaidya (third from left) in Shakargarh.

Ladakh Scouts after the capture of Turtuk, December 1971.

oxtrot Class submarine INS *Kalavari* entering Mumbai
gainst the backdrop of the iconic Taj Mahal Hotel.

Wing Commander Kaul (right), the commanding officer of 37 Squadron, briefing his No. 2, Flying Officer Masand, prior to a recce mission.

Air Defence Gunners in action around Amritsar, December 1971.

Lieutenant General Sagat Singh, the unstoppable commander, addressing troops before the final assault on Dacca from the east.

A destroyed Pakistani T-59 tank near Longewala.

Loading the deadly T-10 rockets on a Hunter aircraft.

29 Squadron (Scorpios) of MiG-21s saw much action in the desert sector.

IAF Packets over Tangail. Over fifty aircraft of various types were used in this airborne operation.

Indian tanks on the road to Dacca, December 1971.

Group Captain Chandan Singh (left) an
Lieutenant General Sagat Singh (right), the tw
architects of the joint operation in Banglades

(From left to right) Brigadier Kler, Major General Nagra, Lieutenant Colonel Pannu and Brigadier Sant Singh in Dacca.

INS *Vikrant* in the Bay of Bengal with her full complement of aircraft.

ce Admiral Krishnan with
ildren in Chittagong.

Lieutenant General Candeth being briefed by Major General Bakshi, 26 Infantry Division sector, December 1971.

Sheikh Hasina and her family after their release from house arrest on 16 December 1971.

Osa Class missile boats used by the Indian Navy in the attacks on Karachi.

Vice Admiral Kohli (centre) with Commander Babru Yadav, MVC, on his right and Lieutenant Commmander Kavina, VrC, on his left.

Indira Gandhi visiting a wounded soldier at a military hospital.

Indira Gandhi greeting Air Chief Marshal Lal while his fellow chiefs look on.

Sheikh Mujib reviews a parade by the Indian Army in March 1972.

the Meghna, 'a river as wide as a sea and whose far bank we never saw'.[11] Mehta says: 'Sagat needed to open a door after pushing the Pakistanis back and continue with the pursuit.'

The extreme southern sector comprised the two vital port towns of Chittagong and Cox's Bazar. The whole area was defended by two lightly configured brigades and not assigned much of a task other than defending Chittagong port and town. As two brigades of IV Corps including the Kilo Force of the Mukti Bahini advanced slowly towards Chittagong during the initial days of the war, they were complemented by Brigadier Uban's Special Frontier Force as it captured Rangamati and prevented the escape of enemy forces into Burma. The two depleted Pakistani brigades huddled in the fortress of Chittagong and hardly offered any resistance.[12]

Extremely vulnerable to attack from three sides, the north-eastern areas of East Pakistan were rather lightly defended by two brigades, one at Sylhet and the other one at Maulvi Bazaar. These forces were meagrely complemented by a ragtag grouping of Mujahids, Razakars and civil defence units. They were literally encircled by an Indian division and a well-led Echo Sector of the Mukti Bahini through a series of tactically well-thought-out operations. This ensured that as the Pakistani forces from other sectors were being effectively squeezed in towards Dacca by simultaneous pressure from the advancing Indians, the two brigades in the Sylhet sector were prevented from withdrawing southwards and reinforcing the defences around 'fortress Dacca'.[13] Instead, they were 'boxed in' at the fortress town of Sylhet and left vulnerable to a pincer encirclement by forces from Major General Krishna Rao's 8 Mountain Division as it closed in on them from the south and north-east.

Early Action by the IAF

The early days of the 'shadow war', or shaping the battlefield prior to 3 December, as India would later call it, saw Sabres from 14 Squadron of the PAF provide effective close air support to Pakistan Army's 27 Brigade at Akhaura. Since there was very little Indian radar cover in the area and the closest IAF airfields were over 130 miles away, intercepting these PAF missions proved to be difficult.[14] It was only when IAF fighters started operating from Agartala that close support for IV Corps became easily available.

The initial days of the air war saw two major objectives being achieved by the IAF. First was the effective neutralization of the lone Sabre squadron in East Pakistan by repeatedly attacking Tezgaon airfield outside Dacca till it was unusable. Commenting on the decision to launch the first long range (almost 400 km) strikes against Dacca on the morning of 4 December by IAF Hunters of 37 and 17 Squadrons from Hashimara, an airbase in northern West Bengal, Group Captain Manna Murdeshwar (then a squadron leader and a key member of the planning staff at Eastern Air Command) reflects that the IAF might have prevented some initial losses had the Hunters been escorted by air defence fighters like the MiG-21. Notwithstanding the initial IAF losses, its MiG-21s, Hunters and Gnats repeatedly engaged the Sabres in aerial dogfights, shooting down at least three of them in the first three days, with another two claimed by Indian Army ack-ack guns. The systematic degradation of Tezgaon airfield forced the Sabre squadron's pilots to abandon eleven of the sixteen aircraft by 6 December and flee to West Pakistan via Burma in a Twin Otter light aircraft. Despite the poor leadership of their squadron commander, the rest of the pilots led by their flight commander, Squadron Leader Dilawar, took on a much superior IAF with courage and bravery.[15]

Without belittling the effort of the Hunter and Sukhoi strikes over Tezgaon (Dacca) airfield, it was without doubt the innovative steep-dive bombing attacks by MiG-21s of 28 Squadron and 4 Squadron that created irreparable craters and made the runway unusable. Planned and orchestrated by the enterprising duo of Group Captain Mally Wollen (station commander at Tezpur) and Wing Commander Bishnoi (squadron commander of 28 Squadron, also at Tezpur), Flight Lieutenant Manbir Singh of 28 Squadron, now a sprightly and adventurous septuagenarian, recollects that he was amongst the first to carry out live trials of steep-dive attacks. Armed with 500 kg Russian bombs, MiG-21's attacked Kurmitola, an unused airfield close to Dacca, on 5 December, before peppering Tezgaon airfield for the next two days and three nights with similar attacks.[16] Manbir was among the 'young guns' of the IAF who represented a refreshingly aggressive approach during the war.

Why the IAF chose to attack Tezgaon airfield with rockets for the first two days of the war baffles many even today. Though the IAF suffered a fair bit of attrition during the first few days of the air campaign, both to Sabres and ground fire, it achieved almost total air superiority by 7 December, thus paving the way for unrestricted close air support (CAS), heli-borne and airborne operations thereafter.

The second objective was to provide effective close air support at some of the tough peripheral battles being fought at Hilli, Kamalpur, Akhaura and the Belonia bulge. The one significant difference this time as compared to 1965 was that every corps had a Tactical Air Centre (TAC) with trained forward air controllers (FACs) who orchestrated the close air support in response to the requirements of field commanders.[17] The overwhelming superiority of numbers meant that the IAF could not only provide air support to the forward battles being fought, but also carried out interdiction of trains, ammo dumps and defences around the fortresses of Dacca, Narayanganj and Sylhet. This was done primarily by the rocket-firing Hunters and Sukhoi-7s as they blasted logistics reinforcements and defences around the beleaguered garrisons.

A Forward Air Controller's Tale

Sealing the fate of the Sylhet garrison was the success of the first large heli-borne operation by the Indian Army on 6 and 7 December. Large and audacious it was if one considers that almost an entire battalion(4/5 Gorkha Rifles) of over 350 fierce khukri-wielding Gorkhas were lifted to within sniffing distance of the Sylhet garrison, which was manned by over 6,000 Pakistani regular and irregular troops.[18] Despite numerous half-hearted counter-attacks from the garrison, which thought that a brigade had been heli-lifted, the battalion held fast for a week till another battalion linked up with it. Courageous personal leadership under persistent fire by Lieutenant Colonel Harolikar and Major Ian Cardozo, the commanding officer and second in command respectively, saw the regiment acquit itself with tremendous grit.

An FAC provides the last-mile connectivity between attacking airborne platforms (could be fixed-wing aircraft or attack/armed helicopters) and their designated targets on the ground. The FAC could either be ground based or direct-fire from a light/scout helicopter. The FAC concept became an integral part of air–land operations in WW II where it was used effectively by Montgomery's 8th Army and Tedder's Royal Desert Air Force against Rommel's Afrika Corps and during Allied operations in Italy and the Normandy landings. The concept was further refined during the Vietnam War and adapted well by the Pakistan Army during the 1965 India–Pakistan war. One of the reasons for the relatively better performance of the PAF in close air support missions as compared to the IAF in 1965 was because of better integration of FACs.

Air Chief Marshal Lal took cognisance of this and ensured that all Indian Army corps in 1971, particularly in the eastern theatre, had well-trained FACs seconded to them well before the outbreak of hostilities. One such FAC was Flight Lieutenant S.C. Sharma, a Dakota pilot from 49 Squadron on attachment to 8 Mountain Division, commanded by Major General K.V. Krishna Rao, which was part of Sagat Singh's rampaging IV Corps. After a spell of intensive training at Tezpur to familiarize himself with fighter operations and controlling fighter aircraft during close air support, little did Sharma realize that he would be part of the first heli-borne operation conducted by the Indian armed forces on 7 December as the entire 4/5 Gorkha Regiment would be landed close to the Sylhet garrison by 105 Helicopter Unit led by Squadron Leader C. S. Sandhu and supported by a couple of armed Mi-4 helicopters led by Flight Lieutenant Singla.[19] Recounting his version of the action-packed eight days that he spent with the Gorkhas in the thick of battle, directing close air support missions and coordinating aerial resupply and Casualty Evacuation Missions (CASEVAC) with a call sign of *Hellcat Control*, Sharma recollected over the phone from Jaipur, Rajasthan:

> After a helicopter recce of the proposed landing zone to the south of the road railway bridge south of Sylhet on the morning of 7 December by Group Captain Chandan Singh, Brigadier Quinn, the brigade commander, and Lt Colonel Harolikar, the CO of 4/5 Gorkhas, it was decided that the whole battalion would be landed between p.m. and sunset in about four waves. I was in the first wave with the CO and two other officers and about 75–80 troops of 'C' Company.

> To our surprise, the Pakistanis were waiting for us at the landing zone with at least a company of well-dispersed troops. As soon as the helicopters started hovering for landing, the firing commenced.
>
> Drowned by the noise of the helicopters we were unaware of the reception waiting for us until the helicopter crew asked us to get off quickly by jumping off the hovering choppers from about 5 feet. It was only when we had jumped off with all our equipment dispersed here and there that we realized we were under fire. Quickly assuming control after asking all troops to lie still in the fading light, Lt Col. Harolikar took stock of the situation and realized that the subsequent waves were not coming in until he radioed that the landing zone was clear. Having ascertained the position of the defenders as they shouted Allah-O-Akbar to intimidate the pinned down Gorkhas, he and his company crawled stealthily across the landing zone and when they had closed in to less than 40 metres, the Gorkhas sprang up in unison shouting 'Jai Kali Maa, Ayo Gorkhali' and closed in with Pakistani troops of 31 Punjab Regiment, mowing down many with their khukris. The defenders retreated to a village 400 metres away and when all was clear, Sharma radioed via his LUP-734 portable radio set that all was clear and the remaining waves could come in. Lighting up the landing zone with merely two lights, the rest of the battalion was heli-landed through the night as 'C' company ensured no interference from the Punjabis and a Baluchi company, which had reinforced the Pakistani defences around midnight. The stage was set for a fierce battle the next morning.[20]

The Indians had not anticipated such fierce resistance at Sylhet and as Harolikar and his men fought the Sylhet brigade in a series of skirmishes, Sharma was right there at the forefront of the battle with Harolikar as part of his 'Rover Group'. For the next six days Sharma directed air strikes by Hunters and Gnats against targets in and around Sylhet and ensured a steady stream of dropped supplies and regular CASEVAC by Mi-4 helicopters of 105 HU. Harolikar is effusive in his praise of Sharma as he repeatedly directed IAF fighters on to targets in the Sylhet garrison.[21] The young IAF officer was awarded a Vir Chakra for his courage and willingness to stay with forward elements of the battalion as they closed in on Sylhet. Sharma recollects that he even ventured out on a few night ambushes as the Gorkhas harassed Pakistani troops during offensive patrols towards the Sylhet garrison. Sharma also recalls the events leading to the surrender of the entire Sylhet Garrison of over a brigade to a mere battalion of the Indian Army on 16 December. After spending another ten-odd days in the area, Sharma returned to his Dakota squadron by early January 1972. He had no idea that he would be put up for a gallantry award and it was only in March 1972 that he came to know from the papers that he had been awarded a Vir Chakra. His experience with 4/5 Gorkhas is what 'Jointmanship' is all about!

INS *Vikrant* in Action

While the IAF and the Indian Army were overcoming initial resistance, the Indian Navy with its 'mini' carrier battle group comprising the aircraft carrier, INS *Vikrant* and the frigates, INS *Brahmaputra* and INS *Beas*, was lying in wait at Port Cornwallis in the Andamans to attack Chittagong and Cox's Bazar. There was a problem, however, that worried Captain Swaraj Prakash and his C-in-C, the diminutive but battle-innoculated veteran from WW II, Vice Admiral Krishnan.

The presence of PNS *Ghazi*, an American-built Tench Class diesel submarine, in the Bay of Bengal was a direct threat to the *Vikrant*. Highlighting the complete absence of intelligence on both sides was the fact that the Pakistanis all along thought that the *Vikrant* was in the waters between Vizag and Madras, while it was actually almost 800 nautical miles away in the calm Andaman waters. Fortuitously, the sinking of the *Ghazi* outside Vizag harbour in the wee hours of the morning of 4 December paved the way for the *Vikrant*, *Brahmaputra, Beas* and the rest of the eastern fleet to set sail from the Andamans and operate with impunity in the Bay of Bengal. The sinking of the *Ghazi,* though, still remains shrouded in mystery. Was it sunk by the destroyer, INS *Rajput*, or was it the victim of a suicidal foray into an area that it had mined a few days earlier?[22] Needless to say, the impact of the sinking of the *Ghazi* was tremendous and gave INS *Vikrant* the freedom to sail all over the Bay of Bengal like a heavyweight boxer with his guard down and punching at will.

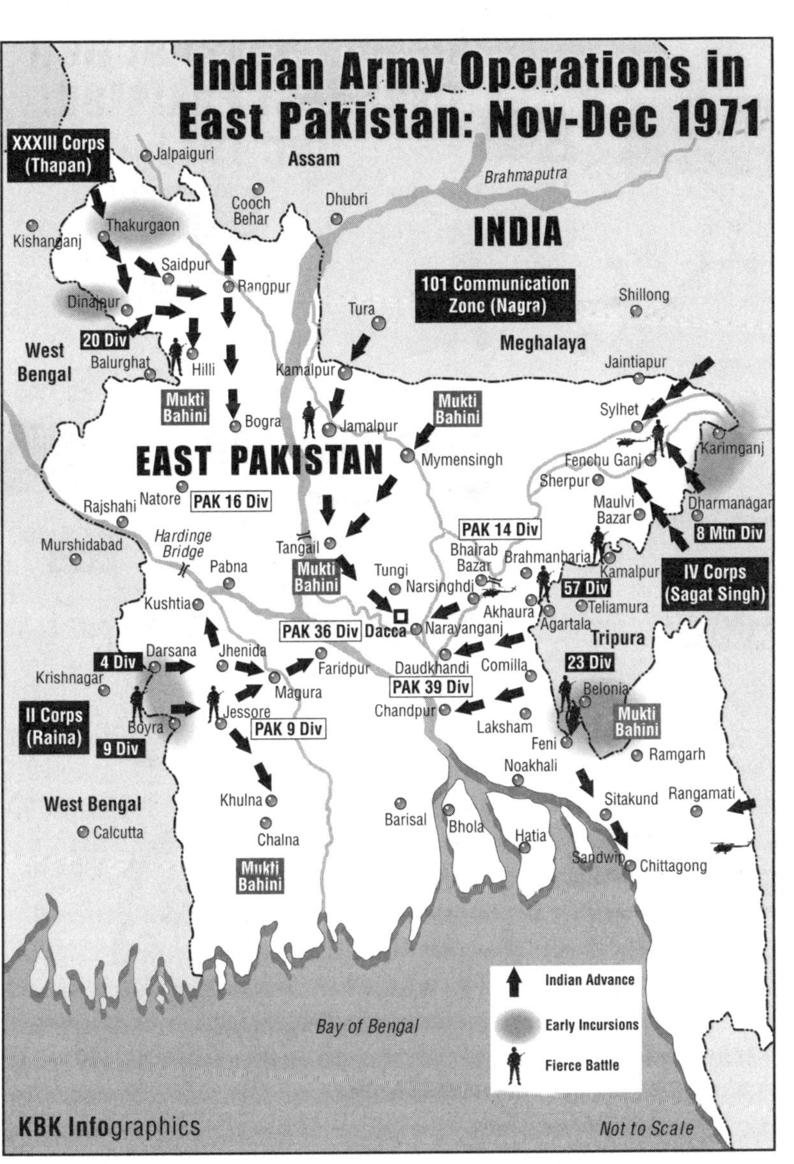
Indian Army Operations in East Pakistan: Nov-Dec 1971
XXXIII Corps (Thapan)
Jalpaiguri
Assam
Brahmaputra
Cooch Behar
Dhubri
INDIA
Kishanganj
Thakurgaon
Saidpur
Rangpur
101 Communication Zone (Nagra)
Shillong
Dinajpur
Tura
20 Div
Meghalaya
West Bengal
Balurghat
Hilli
Kamalpur
Jaintiapur
Mukti Bahini
Bogra
Jamalpur
Sylhet
Karimganj
EAST PAKISTAN
Mymensingh
Fenchu Ganj
Sherpur
Natore
PAK 16 Div
Rajshahi
Maulvi Bazar
Dharmanagar
Murshidabad
Hardinge Bridge
Tangail
PAK 14 Div
8 Mtn Div
Bhairab Bazar
Brahmanbaria
Pabna
Tungi
Narsinghdi
Kamalpur
IV Corps (Sagat Singh)
57 Div
Kushtia
Akhaura
Teliamura
Agartala
PAK 36 Div
Dacca
Narayanganj
Tripura
4 Div
Darsana
Jhenida
Faridpur
Daudkhandi
Comilla
23 Div
Krishnagar
Magura
PAK 39 Div
Belonia
II Corps (Raina)
Jessore
Chandpur
Boyra
PAK 9 Div
Laksham
9 Div
Feni
Ramgarh
Noakhali
West Bengal
Khulna
Sitakund
Rangamati
Calcutta
Barisal
Bhola
Chalna
Hatia
Sandwip
Chittagong
Indian Advance
Early Incursions
Fierce Battle
Bay of Bengal
KBK Infographics
Not to Scale

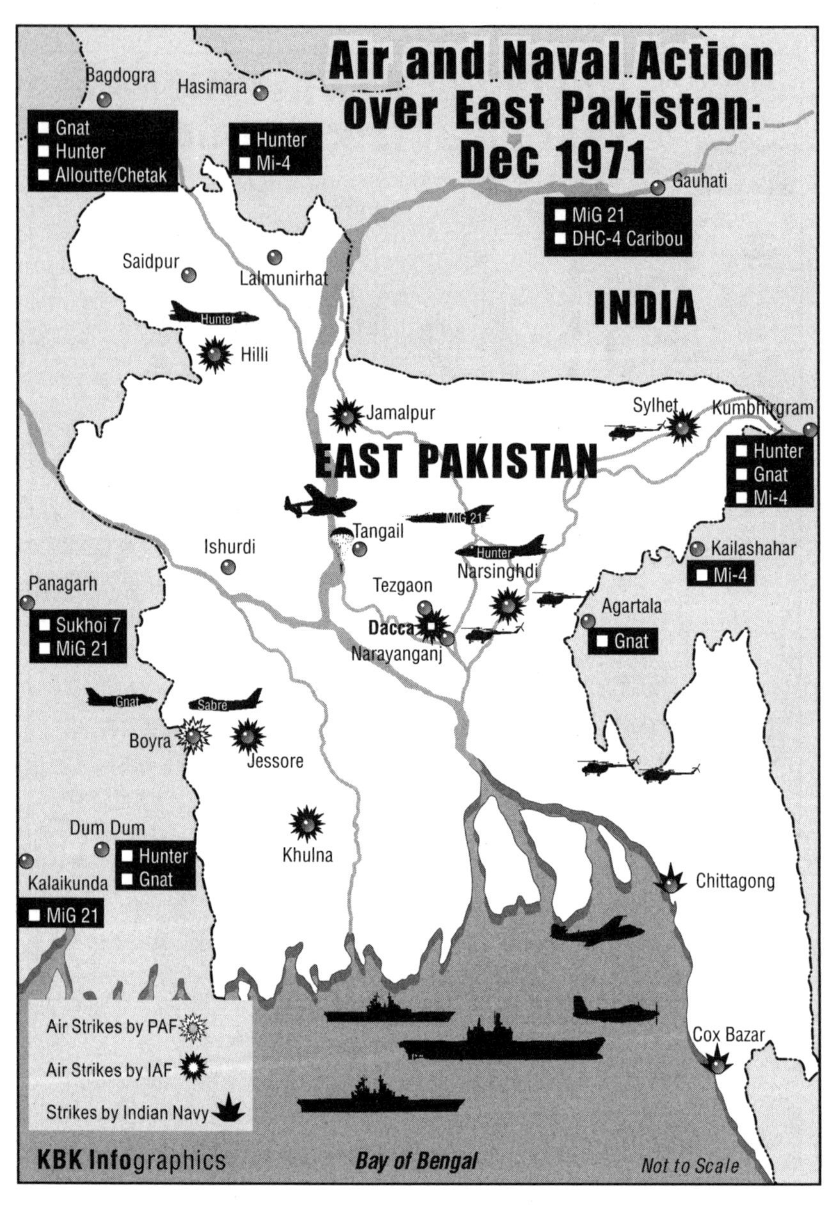

Air and Naval Action over East Pakistan: Dec 1971
Bagdogra
Gnat
Hunter
Alloutte/Chetak
Hasimara
Hunter
Mi-4
Gauhati
MiG 21
DHC-4 Caribou
INDIA
Saidpur
Lalmunirhat
Hunter
Hilli
Jamalpur
Sylhet
Kumbhirgram
Hunter
Gnat
Mi-4
EAST PAKISTAN
MiG 21
Tangail
Ishurdi
Hunter
Narsinghdi
Kailashahar
Mi-4
Panagarh
Sukhoi 7
MiG 21
Tezgaon
Dacca
Narayanganj
Agartala
Gnat
Sabre
Boyra
Jessore
Khulna
Dum Dum
Hunter
Gnat
Kalaikunda
MiG 21
Chittagong
Cox Bazar
Air Strikes by PAF
Air Strikes by IAF
Strikes by Indian Navy
KBK Infographics
Bay of Bengal
Not to Scale

The morning of 4 December saw an initial flurry of attacks by IAF Hunters of 14 Squadron on Chittagong airfield; INS *Vikrant* then took over the task of carrying out airfield attacks on Cox's Bazar airfield[23] and interdiction missions against shipping with their Sea Hawks. By doing so they indirectly supported 83 Brigade of IV Corps as it headed south to capture Chittagong. From 5 December to 14 December, not only did the inland riverine ports of Khulna and Chalna face heavy air attacks from the *Vikrant*,[24] there was also extensive destruction of port infrastructure, runway installations at Cox's Bazar and Chittagong and significant destruction of the Pakistan Navy's residual naval potential in the east in the form of patrol boats and landing craft.[25] Sea Hawks and Alizes of INAS 300 and INAS 310 with their guns, rockets and bombs sank almost eight patrol boats and an equal number of merchant ships with the INS *Brahmaputra* too joining the lopsided naval battle by sinking a few patrol boats off the coast of Chittagong.[26] The effective blockading of Chittagong and Cox's Bazar not only sealed off any escape routes for Pakistani forces but also choked the seaborne supply routes into East Pakistan. Vice Admiral Pasricha recalls operations from the flight deck of the *Vikrant* during those exciting early days of combat:

> I flew about fifteen sorties on the Sea Hawk in those seven days of operations and we mainly used 4" rockets and 250/500 lb bombs to attack surface targets. The entire complement of eighteen Sea Hawks and five Alizes were on board. With the limitations of the *Vikrant*'s maximum speed due to technical problems, launch used to be quite a tricky proposition with full weapon load. We would achieve sustainable speed after the catapult launch only by either flying level or even having to lose about 10–15 feet of height as soon as we cleared the carrier. It demanded flying skill of the highest order and was highly risky, to say the least.[27]

Never before had all three services of India's armed forces operated with such simultaneity before, although much of the joint effort in the Chittagong sector was unplanned. When I asked Vice Admiral Pasricha about the synergy in air, naval and ground operations while he was operating from the *Vikrant*, he candidly replied, 'There was none and we had no intelligence at all about PAF activity in Chittagong and Cox's Bazar. We also did not know that IAF Hunters had visited the area before us on 4 December.'[28] Despite these minor snafus (Snafu is a military acronym from WW II which means *Situation normal, all f---d up)*, the end result of the various successful operations by the three services was that it precipitated the collapse of Pakistani resistance across sectors and gave hope to aggressive generals like Sagat Singh to revise their initial operational objectives and go for the big prize, Dacca. The lack of inter-service coordination in the Chittagong sector was not a widespread malaise, however, as the Indian Army and Indian Air Force demonstrated great camaraderie in many sectors. The Sylhet battle was one such example.

Three-pronged Race to Dacca

Sagat Singh was without doubt the most aggressive operational commander on display during the 'Lightning Campaign of Bangladesh'. Endowed with an irreverent streak, he had a mind of his own and displayed front-line leadership of the highest quality. The hard-fought battles of Akhaura during the initial stages of the campaign saw him at his 'omnipresent' best as he flirted with danger and rallied his troops as they ran into tough opposition from a well-entrenched enemy. Once the enemy had been bested, Sagat Singh steamrolled past the opposition with some daring improvisations of heli-borne and river-crossing operations across water obstacles in the Sylhet and Ashuganj sectors as he outflanked the static Pakistani defences.[29]

If Sagat Singh's heli-borne operation at Sylhet was a heavyweight boxer's right hook, he followed up like any good boxer with a solid punch to Niazi's gut between 9 and 11 December when he heli-lifted more than a brigade worth of troops from Ben Gonsalves's battle-hardened 57 Division across the mighty Meghna to two landing zones at Raipura and Narsingdi, which were barely 60 km from Dacca. Not satisfied with that, he pressed on with a left hook on 12 December by heli-lifting another brigade to Narayanganj, around 40 km south-east of Dacca. Between 6 and 12 of December, a fourteen-helicopter task force from three units (105, 110 and 111 Helicopter Units of the IAF) had landed over 4,000 troops and most of their supporting equipment including ammunition and light artillery guns in three locations by flying around 350 sorties including over 100 by night.[30] The operation was summed up by Air Vice Marshal Chandan Singh, then a group captain and commander of the helicopter task force. A teetotaller and God-fearing fellow Rajput, he developed an excellent professional rapport with the flamboyant Sagat and wrote:

> The success of the heliborne operations was mainly due to the guts, determination, perseverance and courage of the pilots. However, it must be said that without the air supremacy achieved by our fighters and fighter-bombers, this colossal task could not have been carried out.[31]

Cooped up in Bhairab Bazar and anticipating an all-out assault from the rear when they came to know of the multiple heli-borne operations between 9 and 11 December, the Pakistani brigade dug in and were surprised when Sagat's heli-borne forces bypassed them and headed for Dacca. Concurrently, Shammi Mehta and his squadron of fourteen PT-76 amphibious tanks floated across the Meghna, hopping from island to island after Mehta had done a thorough recce of the river by helicopter the previous day. Mehta's squadron caught up by 13 December with 4 Guards, the leading battalion from IV Corps, and raced to the outskirts of Dacca by 14 December. When asked whether he was intimidated by the crossing during which the far bank of the river was not initially visible, Mehta replied, 'I hardly thought of it that way. We were charged up and young and when you are young, you don't analyse to paralyse. When you get older, though, you tend to think for the enemy and that slows you down.'[32]

Floating Down from the Skies

Adding to Niazi's woes was the Tangail paradrop operation by 2 Para Battalion on 11 December in the area to the north of Dacca. This was in an area that was under the operational control of 101 Communication Zone, the division-sized force under Major General G. C. Nagra. Initially planned as a brigade-sized drop by 50 Para Brigade in three separate operations of a battalion each with objectives that ranged from capture of a bridge, an airfield, and to secure a bridge at Tangail, it was reduced to a battalion drop due to various tactical reasons that are discussed later. Suffice to say, it was a cautious decision that looked at leveraging the surprise of a small force and making it look like a large force, rather than risk a large force without much strategic pay-off. Even then, the successful operation involved over fifty transport aircraft of different types along with Gnat and MiG-21 fighter escorts, which got airborne from two airfields, Dum Dum and Kalaikunda. While the bulk of the heavy drop equipment and a small complement of troops emplaned on Packet aircraft at Dum Dum, the majority of the paratroopers got on board Dakotas at Kalaikunda. Supporting this ambitious operation was another covert operation led by a young Corps of Signals officer, Captain P.K. Ghosh, who had linked up with the Mukti Bahini in mid-November in the area between Mymensingh and Tangail. His role in identifying the dropping zones, keeping them under surveillance, and directing harassing raids on convoys played a critical role in shaping the battlefield.[33] The operation was reminiscent of the many covert operations conducted by the Allies prior to Operation Market Garden, as the airborne operation to capture the areas around the bridge at Arnhem in Belgium came to be known. The operation fulfilled its objectives as it caused panic in Dacca as news trickled in that a brigade had been dropped and that it was only a matter of time before forces converged on to Dacca. One of the first interviews given by an Indian officer after the fall of Dacca was at the Intercontinental Hotel where Lieutenant Colonel K.S. Pannu, the flamboyant commanding officer of 2 Para, spoke to reporters.[34] Along with 4/5 Gorkhas, 14 Guards and 2 Para, 1 Maratha emerged as among the most decorated units of the Bangladesh campaign.

Lieutenant General Mathew Thomas, now an alert and fit eighty-six-year-old and a soldier scholar of some repute, has very fond memories of the Tangail drop for very obvious reasons. As the brigade commander of the Agra-based 50 Para Brigade of which 2 Para was an integral part, he clearly recollects the planning process for the drop. As a gung-ho brigade commander, Thomas initially suggested that the battalion drop be carried out over Kurmitola airfield, one of Dacca's subsidiary airfields approximately 20 km north of the city. Once the battalion had secured the airfield, the rest of the brigade would be air-landed and would make a run for Dacca. Looking back, he acknowledges that the plan was fraught with too many risks. Even though it was assessed that the IAF would have achieved air superiority within the first few days of the air war, there was no certainty that the landing transport aircraft would not be shot at by ack-ack and small arms fire. Losing large aircraft with paratroopers on board was too risky a proposition for Sam Manekshaw, who asked 'Jakes' (Lieutenant General Jacob, the chief of staff at Eastern Army Command) to consult with Air Marshal Dewan, the air officer commanding-in-chief of Eastern Air Command, and take a call. Finally, it was decided that a battalion drop at Tangail was the best that the IAF could support – the counsel of the older soldiers and airmen proved to be right after all! Thomas begged Lieutenant General Jacob to allow him to jump with his men, but was dismissed with a 'we need you for bigger things'.[35] When asked about the IAF support for the operation, he said that they gave it all they had but lacked the resources to provide adequate resupply. The troops were on their own, and had the link-up operation with Nagra's troops from 101 Communication Zone taken much longer, it could have been a problem.[36]

A word here about India's paratroopers – jumping out of an aircraft into unknown enemy territory and fighting your way to an objective is among the harder operations of war and that is why paratroopers across the world are considered to be a 'special breed'. The only Indian officer to have participated in a clandestine airborne operation during World War II was Lieutenant General Inder Singh Gill, who as a young second lieutenant was part of a para commando operation over Greece in 1942. Gill was awarded the Military Cross for his part in the operation that saw his commando team dropped at a wrong location and then having to fight its way through enemy-occupied territory to destroy its objective. The story did not end there as the team's planned rendezvous with a submarine went awry and the commandos had to retrace their steps into the jungles of Greece to join the Greek guerrillas till they were extricated a few months later.[37] Many in the Indian Army consider Gill as among the most professionally competent senior officers in the post-Independence era. As a major general, he was Manekshaw's right-hand man as director of military operations during the 1971 war.

With their red berets perched jauntily on their heads, India's paratroopers have done the Indian Army proud since they were reorganized after Independence. Of the two para brigades (50 and 77 Para Brigades) left behind by the British, 77 Para Brigade was disbanded in 1950, and in 1952, all three battalions of 50 Para Brigade were taken away from their parent regiments to form a new regiment called The Parachute Regiment.[38] From fixed-class battalions, these battalions gradually took in volunteers from other classes and became representative of a truly multi-ethnic regiment that demonstrated the Indian Army's resolve to break down barriers of class as established by the British. After a series of distinguished operational performances during their deployment in Korea with the UN forces (a field ambulance unit); Operation Vijay in Goa where 1 Para led the charge into Panjim, the capital of Goa; and during the 1965 war with Pakistan where 1 Para again was primarily responsible for the capture of Haji Pir Pass, the Parachute Regiment had evolved into a potent fighting force by the time India entered the 1971 war.[39] Sam Manekshaw was not going to lose an opportunity to unleash 2 Para to deliver a final blow on the tottering Pakistan Army towards the closing stages of the campaign.

Game Over

By 12 December, Sagat Singh had mustered almost a division-sized force for the final assault on Dacca from multiple directions. At the same time 2 Para, which was earlier 3 Maratha Light Infantry and comprised primarily Maratha troops, linked up with 1 Maratha Light Infantry from 95 Brigade at Poongli bridge, a few kilometres north of the drop zone. Lieutenant General Nirbhay Sharma, who became the governor of Mizoram in 2015 and was a paratrooper himself, was the adjutant of 2 Para during the drop at Tangail as a young captain. Reminiscing about some of the lighter moments of the operation during lunch at the National Defence College on 17 November 2015, he recalled that as the battalion was regrouping after the drop and had gathered most of the equipment, the subedar major of the battalion approached him and reported that the only piece of equipment missing was a well- wrapped case of rum that was to be handed over to 1 Maratha Light Infantry after the link-up had taken place. Needless to say, it was soon found – 1 Maratha had been fighting for over a week and were well rewarded with some rum thanks to the considerate paratroopers with Maratha affiliations.

By dusk on 15 December, a large force commanded by Brigadier Hardev Kler comprising 2 Para, 1 Maratha Light Infantry and other units of 101 Communication Zone contacted the defences around 20 km north of Dacca with the Romeo Force comprising the Mukti Bahini led by Brigadier Sant Singh following closely. Surrounded by five Indian Army brigades, Niazi offered to surrender at 5 a.m. on 16 December along with 93,000 troops and other government personnel – the war in the eastern theatre was over. The formal surrender was, however, conducted in the afternoon of 16 December after the fine print was orchestrated by Lieutenant General Jacob, the chief of staff of the Indian Army's Eastern Command, who flew down from Calcutta to Dacca. His role in the psychological war waged by India during the closing stages of the campaign was significant. Lieutenant General Satish Nambiar recollects that Pakistani commanders were apprehensive of immediate reprisals by the restive and angry Bengali population in Dacca and communicated that to the Indian Army's leadership. In a demonstration of the professionalism and empathy with which the Indian Army treated their defeated adversaries, Pakistani troops of the Dacca garrison were allowed to retain their personal weapons till 18 December, when a formal ceremony marked the laying down of arms.

The psychological impact of innovative operations generally gets underplayed in any post-war analysis as it seemingly takes away some sheen from the hard-core contact and aerial battles that occupy pride of place in conventional warfare. One operation that caused a disproportionate impact on the psyche of East Pakistan's leadership as they huddled in Dacca during the closing stages of the war was the strike by IAF fighters on Governor's House in Dacca on 14 December. In an operation driven by hard intelligence based on wireless intercepts, four MiG-21s and four Hunters attacked the palatial house in the vicinity of the Dacca Cricket Stadium in quick succession while Governor Malik himself was chairing a meeting with UN officials in attendance. MiG-21s from 28 Squadron followed up this attack with rocket attacks on specific buildings in Dacca University where suspected Pakistani troops and collaborators were taking shelter. Analysing the impact of these attacks, Jagan Mohan and Samir Chopra write: 'The IAF's attack, an act of visible, spectacular intimidation, was the last psychological blow to a crumbling regime.'[40]

Shammi Mehta called the bombing 'a game changer in the fall of Dacca and that he considered the IAF's bombing campaign around Dacca as a 'victory of the mind over matter'. In a few days, Flight Lieutenant Manbir Singh, one of the stalwarts of 28 Squadron, would find himself on the steps of Governor's House examining the damage his squadron had done. More importantly, he would walk away with two small brass cannons as war booty – they now occupy pride of place in 28 Squadron and 4 Squadron of the IAF, the two MiG-21 squadrons that participated in the air strikes on Governor's House.

Joint Operations: The X-Factor in the East

Was the capitulation of Dacca so simple, or was it a result of joint orchestration of forces in multiple operations that caused a psychological disintegration, rather than a physical destruction of combat capability? Group Captain Manna Murdeshwar (retd), one of the key members of the operational planning staff at Eastern Air Command, had a ringside view of the operations in the eastern theatre and recollects vividly that it needed a little over six months of continuous effort by way of visits, discussions, conferences and persuasions to build a rapport with both 101 Communication Zone and IV Corps.[41]

Operations of the IV Corps provide an ideal case study for the conduct of aggressive joint operations driven by operational commanders. Group Captain Chandan Singh, the station commander at Jorhat, an accomplished and aggressive transport pilot with extensive operational experience and a gallantry award under his belt for his exploits during the 1962 conflict with China, was the single-point contact with Sagat Singh. Between them, they juggled with the fairly large complement of helicopter resources at their disposal. With almost two squadrons worth of Mi-4s put together from 105, 110 and 111 Helicopter Units, and a few IAF and Army Aviation Alouette helicopters, Sagat and Chandan worked tirelessly to plan multiple heli-borne and heli-lift operations to outflank and surprise the enemy. Over 350 sorties were flown by the

Mi-4 and Alouettes of the IAF and the 659 Army's Air Observation Post (AOP) unit in the Sylhet and Ashuganj sectors, lifting almost three brigades with their logistics and artillery requirements in what came to be known as the 'Meghna Air Bridge Operation'.[42] This operation also marked the baptism by fire of the Indian Army's small helicopter arm as pilots like Major Sihota flew risky communication and reconnaissance sorties with their daring Corps Commander Sagat Singh and one of his equally enterprising divisional commanders, Major General Ben Gonsalves, as they put the pieces of their innovative heli-lift operation across the river together.[43] He was among the few army pilots to have been decorated with the Vir Chakra for his exploits in Bangladesh. Two bold commanders with tremendous 'out of the box' risk-taking ability, Sagat Singh and a much junior Chandan Singh, changed the contours of the 'Race to Dacca'.

Even in the case of close air support, IV Corps exploited the IAF's fighter assets to the maximum. Out of a total of approximately 1,350 close air support missions flown in the Eastern theatre, over 500 were flown in support of IV Corps.[44] Sagat Singh understood the importance of additional firepower and psychological impact of close air support and pushed both the TACs to their limits as they struggled to cope with the pouring requests from Sagat's formation commanders for continuous air support. To its credit, Eastern Air Command responded brilliantly and supported Sagat's rapid advance by even sending Gnats of 24 Squadron to operate in the ground attack role from Agartala runway on 12 December. The runway was extended by a few thousand feet so that fighters could operate from there and strike targets at Sylhet, Maulvi Bazaar, Ashuganj, Bhairab Bazar and Brahmanbaria within minutes.[45] The effort was reminiscent of Brigadier Pritham Singh and Air Commodore Mehar Singh's attempts to operationalize the Poonch airstrip in 1947–48. Shammi Mehta has fond recollections of the joint effort and questions why the Indian Army and Indian Air Force have never done a joint study on IV Corps operations that could be a case study at various institutions of higher learning in the military.[46] In a glowing tribute to IV Corps, Air Chief Marshal Lal writes:

> By bold and imaginative use of the air force available to it, 4 Corps presented a most convincing demonstration of how well the two

> services could work together. This was possible due, in large measure, to the fact that the GOC of the Corps himself (Sagat Singh) was a paratrooper, who had lived and worked in close proximity with the Air Force for many years. 4 Corps never asked the Air Force to do what it could not and whatever the Air Force was called upon to do, it did most effectively.[47]

Considering that the Indian Armed Forces had never undertaken an airborne operation before, the 2 Para drop at Tangail on 11 December to capture the bridge on the River Poongli merits attention as a timely manifestation of this newly found cooperative operational spirit between the Indian Army and the IAF that Lal refers to.[48] The pressure exerted by the Indian Navy with its persistent attacks on Chittagong and Cox's Bazar, sustained interdiction of Pakistani shipping, and a small but rather ill-fated amphibious assault by a company of Gorkhas, played a part in piling on 'joint pressure' up Niazi to surrender.[49]

Without doubt it was joint operations which played a pivotal role in the Bangladesh campaign. On display also was the quality of operational art exercised by Indian commanders like Sagat Singh, Mally Wollen, Chandan Singh and Swaraj Prakash as the battle progressed. At the tactical level, Shammi Mehta fondly recollects that informal camaraderie, pre-launch bonding and free-flowing operational communication, where rank and protocol did not matter, was the hallmark of operations in the IV Corps sector. However, what was also clear was that this synergy was 'personality driven' and not 'institutionally driven' joint operations that was on display. This particular trait of Indian operational art continues even today.

US Seventh Fleet Shows Up in the Bay of Bengal

The closing days of the eastern naval campaign saw further excitement in the maritime domain with news of the likely entrance of the powerful US Seventh Fleet into the Bay of Bengal. This was seen as likely 'arm twisting', or a typically American coercive strategy to put the brakes on what was turning out to be a highly successful Indian military campaign in the eastern theatre. In a desperate attempt to bolster Pakistan's flagging war effort and delay its imminent capitulation in the east, Nixon despatched the muscular Seventh Fleet to the Bay of Bengal. Heading there from the Gulf of Tonkin, where it was deployed, the Seventh Fleet was a mighty formation of eleven warships comprising the nuclear-powered aircraft carrier, USS *Enterprise,* and a mix of destroyers, missile frigates, amphibious assault ships and a helicopter carrier.[50] Jacob, the chief of staff of Eastern Army Command, recalls that Admiral Krishnan, the feisty and rotund flag officer commanding in chief of Eastern Naval Command, expressed his concern at this turn of events and even linked it with the possibility of the Pakistan Navy slipping in another Daphne class submarine into the Bay of Bengal to threaten INS *Vikrant*.[51]

Krishnan's fears were unfounded as the Seventh Fleet hung around the south-eastern part of the Bay of Bengal for a week or so from 12 December onwards, hoping to coerce the Indians sufficiently so as to prevent the fall of Dacca. This triggered a response from the Soviets, who alerted a task force, which was already operating in the Indian Ocean and was believed to have included a nuclear-powered submarine, to be ready for a move in the direction of the Seventh Fleet should it get threateningly close to Indian waters. Seeing that India refused to blink and somewhat reassured by the Russians that India would agree to a ceasefire soon after the fall of Dacca, the Seventh Fleet called off its coercive deployment in the Bay of Bengal.[52] In retrospect, the diversion of the fleet was a much hyped up non-event, played up even more by a raucous media. In a cable to President Nixon, the US Ambassador to India, Kenneth Keating, expressed his disapproval of the move, pretty much summing up the cowboyish nature of the entire exercise:

> UP UNTIL LAST FEW DAYS I HAVE FELT ABLE TO DEFEND U.S. POLICY ON THE BASIS OF OUR OVERRIDING CONCERN TO BRING A HALT TO HOSTILITIES. I AM NOW TROUBLED BY THE FACT THAT A NUMBER OF MY DIPLOMATIC COLLEAGUES VIEW DEPLOYMENT OF CARRIER TASK FORCE AS MILITARY ESCALATION BY U.S.[53]

25

OPENING THE WESTERN FRONT

It is this fear of losing territory that has caused us to deploy forward and has caused conflicts between India and Pakistan to turn into slugging matches rather than wars of movement. In a short war what is required is 'strike forces' with enormous fire power and mobility so as to punch a hole in the enemy defences, penetrate deep into enemy territory while the formations following through will deal with pockets of resistance.[1]

– LIEUTENANT GENERAL K.P. CANDETH

PAK REACTS PREDICTABLY

From October 1971 onwards, Candeth, the commander of the Western Army Command, was a restless and worried man after being literally forced to implement Manekshaw's 'holding strategy' on the western front. A number of his formations were allocated to the eastern theatre, resulting in a situation of near parity with Pakistan as far as infantry, armour and artillery were concerned.[2] A seasoned gunner (artillery officer) with loads of operational experience in West Asia during WW II, in NWFP in the years before independence, in Kashmir during the 1947–48 conflict, and as the field commander during Operation Vijay (liberation of Goa in 1961), Candeth was also the Deputy Chief of Army Staff during the 1965 war. He had no more than approximately ten or eleven infantry divisions to defend his vast area that stretched across Jammu and Kashmir, Punjab and northern Rajasthan with his main offensive formations, 1 Corps and 1

Armoured Division, scattered in the hinterland. He shrewdly realized that unless his strike formations were mobilized and moved speedily to their operational locations, Pakistan's slightly superior armoured formations could easily exploit his vulnerabilities and quickly make some inroads before parity was restored. Leveraging some scanty intelligence reports regarding the move of Pakistani armoured divisions into areas that could threaten Akhnur and Chhamb, Candeth mobilized 1 Corps in a swift operation that tested the efficiency of the Indian Railways and civil–military liaison networks. By 26 October, 1 Corps was occupying positions from where it could undertake both defensive and offensive operations – Pakistan had lost the initiative.

Preoccupied as he was with the spiralling insurgency in East Pakistan, and preventing a stubborn Mujib and an equally scheming Bhutto from plunging Pakistan into a crisis, Yahya Khan missed an opportunity to catch the Indians by surprise in the western theatre. Had he launched military operations in late September, or early October 1971, India may well have lost territory and yielded the initiative to Pakistan. Bangladesh, then, might never have been formed. Such are the ramifications of strategic decisions! Compared to the Indian Army, the Indian Air Force and Indian Navy were in a better position vis-à-vis their adversaries in the west. This was primarily due to the systematic build-up of airbases[3] and acquisition of reasonably potent strike aircraft, and the availability of fast-attack craft with the western naval fleet. More about their exploits later!

Since the entire western front had seen action in the 1965 war, and the ceasefire line between India and Pakistan was quite clearly defined after the Tashkent Agreement, heavily defended linear defences quickly sprang up on both sides, particularly along canals in the areas of Jammu, Punjab and Rajasthan.[4] This left little scope for any posturing or imaginative manoeuvring; both sides maintained an eyeball-to-eyeball contact along most of the international border and the ceasefire line. Frustrated by his inability to force the Americans to coerce India into withdrawing from an offensive posture in the eastern theatre, Yahya Khan did what any militarily powerful but smaller state would do against a larger adversary once it came to know that conflict was inevitable. On 3 December 1971, he opened the western front with widespread and simultaneous pre-emptive air strikes on IAF airfields. Inspired by the Israeli counter-campaign and blitzkrieg against Arab airfields in 1967, the PAF hoped to provide the necessary impetus to a quick ground offensive in limited sectors.

The First Week

The opening days of the war showed that India had learnt its lessons from 1965, both in the air and on the ground. While Candeth had all his formations in place, the wily Air Chief Marshal P.C. Lal had not only dispersed and camouflaged his aircraft well, but also positioned early-warning radars and mobile observation posts (MOFs) all along the border, which gave all his bases reasonably adequate warning of incoming air raids. The raids on IAF airfields and installations on the evening of 3 December and early in the morning of 4 December were spread across the western front. Srinagar and its satellite airbase of Avantipur in the J&K sector, Pathankot, Amritsar, Halwara, Ambala and Sirsa airfields in the Punjab sector, and Bikaner, Jaisalmer, Jodhpur and Uttarlai in the Rajasthan sector, were all attacked by fighter and bomber aircraft of the PAF.[5] However, poor planning, inadequate force levels (barely 35–40 sorties were flown in the first strike), poor execution and robust IAF air defence[6] resulted in a negligible impact on the operational potential of the IAF to respond, which it did with measured professionalism the next day. The existing IAF discourse does not give enough credit to the impact of the induction of the second lot of MiG-21s on the operational philosophy of the IAF. Returning to India from Lugovoy, Russia, in 1967 and introducing the second variant of the MiG-21 called the T-77, the training methodologies imparted by IAF fighter pilots like Pingale, Krishnaswamy, Rathore, Patney, Verma[7] among others created a trickle-down effect of professionalism in the other fleets too. Many among this lot were to form the IAF's Tactics and Combat Development Establishment (TACDE) that sought to streamline and standardize both ground attack and air defence tactics.[8] The MiG-21 proved to be a major intimidatory factor in 1971, much as the F-104 had proved in 1965.

Hoping to draw the IAF towards Sargodha in large retaliatory strikes, the PAF was surprised[9] that the IAF chose to respond by carrying out limited strikes through the day with their all-weather day/night capable fighter bombers, the Sukhoi-7 and the dependable Hunters, with the Canberra bombers, Sukhoi-7s and MiG-21s, keeping up the pressure by night. The MiG-21s and Gnats provided effective top cover to ground attack missions and ensured that the IAF managed to keep attrition down on the first few days. Here too, having seen the debilitating impact of the opening days of the 1965 air war on IAF morale, Lal had realized that it was important to keep attrition down at commencement of hostilities.

A story worth telling is about the exploits of a bunch of 'hot shot' fighter jocks from the IAF's Tactics and Combat Training Establishment (TACDE) who were asked by Lal to develop innovative tactics that would 'disrupt and distract' the enemy by night. Consequently, Sukhoi-7s and MiG-21s from TACDE trained for months before the war by practising single-aircraft low-level bombing missions in dim moonlight conditions and even pitch-dark night conditions to evolve procedures and sortie profiles that could result in accurate navigation to the target and weapon delivery with reasonable accuracy. Halwara and Hindon airfields were used to validate the concept in near blackout conditions and by the time the war began, Air Marshal Patney recounts that they were raring to hit PAF airfields.

Thirteen PAF airfields were attacked by day and night during the opening days of the war, some of them with as low a force as two aircraft, and it was quite clear that the IAF's counter-response was low key, calibrated and yet effective as the number of sorties reduced from a maximum of 140 on 4 December to seventy the next day and finally to about less than 10–20 sorties after 10 December. Though these airfield raids were not massive ones, the PAF lost a few aircraft on ground at its airfields at Shorkot, Murid and Mauripur. Airfields like Sargodha and Chander were among those hit at night in dim moonlight conditions by TACDE during the first week of the conflict, and Patney is emphatic that these sorties achieved what they had set out to do: to disrupt and distract. An innovative element of these missions was the constant communication of these pilots with a ground control code named 'Sparrow Control', which had the PAF guessing that it could be a Soviet aircraft that was guiding these night missions.10 Much like Mehar Singh and the modified Dakotas of the 12 Squadron in performing bombing missions around Poonch in 1947–48, the medium lift transport aircraft of the IAF in 1971, the An-12, was modified for the bombing role by night in a transformed IAF under Lal. Tons of bombs were rolled out from An-12s as Wing Commander Vashisht and his boys from 44 Squadron delivered telling blows on the night of 3 December and caused mayhem at a well-concealed armament and logistics depot at Changa Manga forest, about 80 km southwest of Lahore. The destruction severely affected the flow of ammunition both to the northern and southern sectors.

One of the two-aircraft day missions on 4 December was a Hunter mission from Pathankot led by Wing Commander (later Air Marshal) Cecil Parker, CO of 20 Squadron, IAF. Tasked to hit Peshawar airfield, almost 400 km away and on the extreme limits of the Hunter's radius of action (ROA), the strike was more a demonstration of intent that the IAF had come a long way from 1965. Parker and his number two, Dhillon, strafed the airfield, possibly destroyed a Sabre on the ground and then made their getaway when they were pounced upon by two Sabres doing a combat air patrol over Peshawar. Both Hunters were shot at by the pursuing Sabres, but Parker gave battle while ordering his number two to 'hit the deck' and head east. An experienced fighter jock, Parker claims to have shot down one Sabre, a claim fiercely refuted by the PAF, and got back with empty tanks as his Hunter 'flamed out' after landing. Lady Luck, Father Fortune and a cat with nine lives – all seemed to have followed the two Hunters. Parker's squadron, the Lightnings, would emerge as one of the workhorses of the IAF and represented the aggressive spirit of the IAF.

Admiral Arun Prakash, a former chief of naval staff and an erudite soldier scholar of high pedigree, was a young naval lieutenant on secondment to 20 Squadron (Lightnings) of the IAF for almost a year before the war broke out. Not only was Arun Prakash a naval aviator, he was also a 'wanderer' as he ventured out in mid-1971 for a long summer hitchhiking trip that saw him travel to Germany and France via Iran, Turkey, Greece and the Balkans.[11] The air force, it seemed, was far more lenient than the navy when it came to granting leave for such adventurous gallivanting! He returned from his jaunt well in time for his share of spoils during the war as he flew numerous interdiction and airfield strike missions. He even earned the ire of Colonel Chuck Yeager, the USAF advisor, when he destroyed Yeager's executive Beechcraft jet during a raid on Chaklala airfield. The young naval lieutenant took a particular liking to the C-130s at Chaklala during two raids and was awarded the Vir Chakra for his exploits. He recounts: 'Cecil Parker was an outstanding leader and we would follow him anywhere. We were well prepared as a squadron and had all our maps and routes ready before the outbreak of the war.'[13] The Lightnings would emerge at the end of the war as the most decorated squadron of the IAF during the conflict.[14] Not to be kept out of action during the early days of the war were the Canberra bombers who formed the main punch of the IAF's night-strike capability and carried out repeated harassing raids over numerous PAF airfields in depth like Mianwali near Peshawar, keeping the PAF constantly on its toes. Wing Commander Gautam would go on to add a Bar to his Maha Vir Chakra for his exploits while in command of 16 Squadron.

Air Chief Marshal Lal in his book highlights that the IAF concentrated on many forward airfields like Chandler, Murid, Lahore and Chak Jhumra, and a few of the lightly defended airfields in depth like Rafiqy and Risalwala.[15] Sargodha too was attacked on the evening of 4 December by four IAF Sukhois, with limited success. Lal's strategy on the western front was clear – conserve fighter resources so that they remained available for air defence of the homeland, and support the land battle. Kaiser Tufail, an outstanding PAF fighter pilot, tries to downplay the negligible impact of PAF's pre-emptive strike by writing: 'PAF's first dusk strikes were nothing more than the start of a disruptive counter-air campaign at best, aimed at overburdening the IAF in its flying effort generation capabilities.'[16]

He also suggests that some PAF planners claimed later that its pre-emptive strike was mainly aimed at provoking the IAF to retaliate impulsively as it did in 1965 by attacking well-defended airfield targets (implying Sargodha) in strength and face heavy casualties. If it was so, the strategy failed as even though the IAF retaliated, it did so in a measured manner so that its planned interdiction strategy did not suffer. The numbers too tell the story. Kaiser Tufail puts the total number of sorties flown by the PAF against IAF airfields and radar sites between the evenings of 3 and 4 December at around 150, a figure disputed as too high by the IAF, while P.V.S. Jagan Mohan puts the number of IAF's retaliation strikes on 4 December at around seventy-eight.[17] If one includes another twenty-odd sorties as air defence and supporting missions, the figure still hovers around 100 sorties (Tiwary's figures are higher). Clearly with almost 350 aircraft available in the west, the IAF clearly kept its effort in check. Lal had thought things out well.

As the air battle raged on the evening and night of 3 December, Lieutenant General K.K. Singh, the battle-hardened corps commander of 1 Corps who had recently moved on promotion from Army HQ, was waiting expectantly for his orders to launch an offensive into the Shakargarh bulge. As he gazed across the vast expanse of the Punjab plains, his thoughts inevitably went back to his baptism by fire as the brigade commander of 1 Armoured Brigade during the 1965 war as it attempted to make headway in the Sialkot sector against some determined resistance from Pakistani armour. As his forces moved into their launch pads by the night of 4 December and were ready to go across on the next morning, he wondered whether he was going to have a free run into Shakargarh. K.K. Singh had not forgotten his experiences of commanding an armoured brigade at Chawinda in 1965 and was prepared for a typical tank-vs-tank attrition battle. Having shed some of his offensive forces to bolster the defensive battle in Poonch, he turned cautious as he was apprehensive whether he would be able to decisively punch a hole in the opposing forces. Adding to his woes were the complete lack of intelligence about the location and movement of the enemy's strategic reserves in the form of 6 Armoured Division and 17 Infantry Division.[18]

In such circumstances it was Lieutenant General Sartaj Singh, the aggressive commander of 15 Corps with the largest area to worry about (Jammu and Kashmir), who would be the first to commit his formations into battle in the Chhamb and Poonch sectors. Hours after the first air raid sirens were sounded at most IAF airfields, Major General Iftikhar Janjua, the flamboyant commander of Pakistan Army's 23 Division, opened his guns – all of nine regiments – along a 30–40 km front. Soon after, he launched a well-planned attack with sufficient armour on 191 Brigade, the only brigade from 10 Division defending the area west of the Munawar Tawi river.[19] Positioned in hastily prepared defences and mentally unprepared to fight a defensive battle as the division was initially assigned an offensive role along with the division to the south (26 Division), Brigadier Jasbir Singh's men from 191 Brigade fought valiantly to blunt the initial offensive. Particularly noteworthy in blunting the advance of Pakistan's 23 Division in the critical northern part of the Chhamb–Jaurian sector was 5 Sikh Regiment under Lieutenant Colonel Prem Khanna.[20] However, after two days of bitter fighting they were asked to withdraw east of the Munawar Tawi by none other than the corps commander, Lieutenant General Sartaj Singh, who had by then taken charge of the battle.[21]

Sartaj Singh was another no-nonsense and hard-driving general in the mould of Harbaksh Singh and had won a George medal during the British era for disarming an armed soldier who had run amok in his unit. He was also one of the brigade commanders during the last-ditch defence of Bomdila in 1962. Inexplicably and much like in 1965, Pakistani forces stopped to regroup before attempting to cross the Munawar Tawi. This allowed Sartaj Singh and Major General Jaswant Singh, the beleaguered divisional commander of 10 Division, to reorganize their forces; the IAF too was more effective this time around as there was a clearly demarcated forward line of troops (FLOT) in the form of the Munawar Tawi river. Sukhois from 26 Squadron and 101 Squadron based at Adampur were particularly effective during this period and managed to destroy a large number of tanks and blunted the offensive by 7 December. A total of seventy-eight sorties were flown by the IAF in support of the Chhamb operations, comprising both close air support missions in direct support of 191 Brigade, and interdiction missions by Hunters to prevent reinforcements from getting to Pakistan 23 Division.[22] The death of Iftikhar Janjua in a helicopter crash soon after took the wind out of this offensive, and though Pakistan managed to hold on to the west bank of the Munawar Tawi till the end of the war, some of their offensive resources were diverted south to the Shakargarh sector.

Unfolding a fairly predictable battle plan without the necessary numerical superiority, the battles in the Poonch sector turned out to be ones of attrition and did not result in any tangible gains for either side. To the credit of the Indians, two brigades, 93 Brigade and 33 Brigade, fought excellent defensive battles between 3 and 6 December, foiling all attempts by Major General Akbar Khan's attempts with 12 Division to threaten Poonch[23] at the same time as Iftikhar was attempting to threaten Akhnur and Chhamb. The IAF innovatively used the slow and lumbering Harvard trainer aircraft, which could take off and land from the small Rajouri airstrip to provide close air support and target enemy guns positions in vantage positions overlooking Poonch.[24] The obsolete but manoeuvrable Vampire jets of 121 Squadron from Srinagar supported the Uri and Poonch battle with telling strikes against enemy emplacements and gun positions on hilltops and slopes.[25]

Flying Officer Anil Thapar, affectionately called 'Tarzan' by his friends, was posted to 20 Squadron and had just one sortie to go before he would have been declared 'Fully Ops' and fit to do battle when he met with a motorcycle accident that had him out of action for six months. So, off he went to do duty as a forward air controller with 161 Infantry Brigade in the Uri sector. Attached to an infantry battalion of the Rajputana Rifles (4 Rajputana Rifles), Tarzan has wonderful memories of the few months he spent with them. Not only did the strapping six-footer direct fire on Pakistani positions across the ceasefire line, he also accompanied the battalion on a number of offensive and defensive patrols. Thapar, who sought voluntary retirement as a group captain after commanding a MiG-27 squadron in the 1990s, recollects that among the innovative contraptions that the IAF put together to aid the foreword air controllers was something called a 'Satpal Light'. Named after the IAF engineering officer who modified a MiG-21 landing light to act as a bright visual aid that would help aircraft spot a forward controller location and then pick up a target in relation to that position, it was equipped with wheels to provide it with mobility and was an object of much amusement in the field.[26] It was also a reflection of an innovative and 'can do' spirit that had crept into the IAF led by P.C. Lal as war clouds loomed on the horizon.

The third battle that merits attention during the initial days of the war on the western front was the 'wringing of the Chicken's Neck' by elements of 26 Division of the Indian Army, commanded by one of its most highly decorated officers, Major General Zorawar Chand Bakshi.[27] Disappointed during the early days of the war that one of his brigades had been assigned a defensive role in another sector, Bakshi's ambitious plan to race to Sialkot had to be tempered down to a limited offensive that would capture the 'Chicken's Neck' area of some 170 sq. km. Known as the 'Dagger' before he took over command of 26 Division because the salient pointed like a dagger at India, the aggressive Bakshi called it the 'Chicken's Neck' waiting to be snapped. Bakshi commenced his attack on 5 December night by infiltrating forces behind enemy lines and used commandos to disrupt communications and set up roadblocks. Having surprised the enemy he then moved in a regular brigade to complete a rout of the enemy by 7 December with minimum casualties to own troops.[28] Sadly, Bakshi's division was thereafter engaged only in defensive operations and flank protection as Candeth clearly lost out on exploiting a brilliant commander who had not lost a single inch of own territory in all his actions, be it in the 1947–48 or 1965 wars with Pakistan. One can only conjecture what might have happened had Zorawar Bakshi spearheaded the Chhamb operations. While Zorawar Bakshi's biographer, Major General V.K. Singh, is scathing in his indictment of the rather passive role that Bakshi's 26 Division performed for the rest of the war, Lieutenant General Pandit looked at it dispassionately nearly forty-three years later and said: 'Zorawar had a task to perform – his formation had a defensive role and a significant one at that – so to say that he was under-exploited is merely a result of his tasking and not anything else.'[29]

Offensive on Karachi and More: The Indian Navy Comes of Age

After nearly twenty-five years of Independence, the Indian Navy finally managed to take its rightful place alongside its sister services, the army and the air force, as equal stakeholders in national security. Nothing exemplifies this coming of age better than the daring strikes by Indian Navy missile boats on Pakistan Navy warships and shore-based installations at Karachi harbour on the nights of 4 and 8 December. Commander Kavina (retd) recollects that when war broke out on 3 December, two OSA boats (INS *Nipat* and INS *Veer)* along with the two Petya Class frigates (INS *Kachal* and INS *Kiltan)* were lying in wait around the island of Diu, while the other two missile boats were already off the Gujarat coast around Okha. Carrying out a rendezvous and a quick briefing on the high seas on the evening of 4 December, the first strike involved three missile boats of 25 Missile Squadron led by Commander Babru Yadav comprising INS *Nipat, Veer* and *Nirghat*. The briefing to them was precise – they were cleared to fire their missiles at any contact they made with targets that were in an arc of 100 nautical miles or less from Karachi. Commencing their attack from about 150 nautical miles south of Karachi at about 6 p.m., they made their first radar contact with PNS *Khyber*, a destroyer. INS *Nirghat* sank the *Khyber* with two direct hits. Emboldened with their first success, Kavina, who was captaining INS *Nipat*, was the next to let go of his missiles on another hapless target, which turned out to be the *Venus Challenger*, a Liberian merchant freighter laden with ammunition and armament for Pakistan.[30] Kavina recollects that the size of the radar contact initially led them to believe that it was the PNS *Babar*, the Pakistan Navy flagship. As they approached closer to Karachi, *Veer* joined the action by sinking a minesweeper (PNS *Muhafiz)* as it headed to pick up survivors from the *Khyber*.[31] As they approached within 25 nautical miles of Karachi, Kavina opened up his radar and picked up the echoes from the Kiamari oil refineries and let go of his third missile, and so did the *Veer*. The strike completely demoralized the Pakistan Navy surface fleet and the oil tanks were ablaze for days together.

Staying with naval operation on the western seaboard, Vice Admiral S.N. Kohli, the aggressive C-in-C of Western Naval Command, had planned another offensive strike on Karachi on 6 December along with sea control operations along the Makaran coast, to the west of Karachi. He even aggressively positioned one of his Foxtrot Class submarines around the approaches to the Karachi and Makaran coast, hoping to bring in synergy in its operations with any subsequent offensive surface operations. This was in response to reports from Naval Intelligence that a large portion of the Pakistani fleet was lying in wait there. However, the mission had to be called off at the last moment. Four days later, an IAF reconnaissance mission of the Gwadar area on the Makaran coast bordering Iran reported no Pakistan Navy ships in the area – it was just as well that Admiral Kohli's ambitious sea control operation was called off.

Similar damage was inflicted on a Pakistan Navy tanker, the PNS *Dacca*, and the Kiamari oil installations by another audacious missile boat strike by INS *Vinash* on the night of 8 December. The simultaneous impact of IAF strikes on Karachi harbour by Hunters from Jamnagar led by Wing Commander Donald Conquest on the morning of 4 December,[32] and by Canberra bombers in the wee hours of 9 December, proved to be decisive. Wing Commander Badhwar of 35 Squadron clearly remembers that he was leading a formation of eight Canberras on a strike to Masroor airfield and decided that four of these would also attack the oil storage tanks close to Karachi harbour.

It was a remarkable coincidence that the IAF and Indian Navy strikes took place within minutes of each other without any prior coordination at all. This only indicates the lack of synergy between the IAF and the Indian Navy during the Karachi operations, although excellent reconnaissance photographs of Karachi harbour were given to the Indian Navy on 4 December by 106 Squadron flying Canberra photo reconnaissance aircraft. Commander Kavina, who was awarded the Vir Chakra for the operation, dismisses the needless debate about who hit Karachi first and says that whoever did it, did it for the Indian flag, and rightly so it was. Commander Babru Yadav, the commander of the 25 Missile Squadron, and Commander Gopal Rao, who commanded the escort frigate INS *Kiltan* during the operation, deservedly won Maha Vir Chakras for the two attacks on Karachi, while Wing Commanders Badhwar and Conquest were awarded Vir Chakras for their attacks on Karachi.[33]

An interesting vignette on the missile boat attack on Karachi comes from Admiral Nadkarni. Undergoing a course at the Naval War College in the US, the admiral recollects that the Pakistani officer doing the course with him was recalled when the war broke out and returned to complete the course on cessation of hostilities. When he returned, he told Nadkarni: 'Not fair, the Russians were manning your boats during the attack on Karachi.' Therein lay an interesting tale. All the crew of the missile boats had just returned from the Soviet Union after extensive training on the missile boats during the acquisition period. They were all fluent in Russian and Kavina confirms that they would break into Russian during the operation to confuse the Pakistanis.[34]

The sinking of the PNS *Ghazi* outside Vizag harbour had shaken the Pakistan Navy and its remainder Daphne Class submarines were out to avenge that loss on the western seaboard. INS *Khukri* and INS *Kirpan*, two of the Indian Navy's relatively new anti-submarine-warfare (ASW) frigates, were on aggressive patrol around 35 nautical miles south-west of Diu on the night of 9/10 December when three successive torpedoes from PNS *Hangor*, a Daphne Class submarine, ripped into the *Khukri*. The crippled frigate sank within minutes taking down with her Captain Mahendra Nath Mulla, eighteen officers and over 170 men. For his bravery under fire, steadfast dedication to duty and refusal to abandon his command post on the bridge, Captain Mulla was awarded the Maha Vir Chakra. While the actual story of the loss of the *Khukri* is still shrouded in mystery and remains classified, an analysis of the encounter after much discussion and reading reveals that ships of the *Khukri* type had only forward-throwing depth charges that reached a maximum of 2 nautical miles and this was woefully inadequate against submarines of the Daphne Class that had torpedoes with ranges of around 10 nautical miles. This loss provoked Admiral Kohli immensely and for the next three days, he pressed in all his ASW resources to hunt down the 'killer' sub, but to no avail. Writing in his book *Transition to Triumph,* Vice Admiral Hiranandani, one of the Indian Navy's most prolific contemporary historians, offers a balanced perspective of what could have gone wrong that night:

> The tragic loss of the KHUKRI will remain a vexed issue. If at all, a two ship Search and Attack Unit (SAU) had to be sailed to take on a submarine whose capabilities were known to be superior to those of the ships of the SAU, then the SAU should have been closely supported by all available anti-submarine air effort – Seakings, Alizes and Super Connies. On the other hand, had KHUKRI been following well established torpedo counter measure procedures like high speed, zig-zags and weave, she would never have been such an easy target. The Captain of KHUKRI took the calculated risk of overcoming the limitations of his ship's sonar by doing slow speed and using the BARC developed sonar modification to help increase his sonar's detection range. Regrettably luck was not on Khukri's side.[35]

The overall naval effort, however, was commendable and reflected a refreshingly aggressive Indian Navy. The coercive effect of the repeated missile boat attacks on Karachi and prowling Indian Foxtrot Class submarines in the waters off the Makaran coast resulted in the Pakistani surface fleet rarely venturing out of Karachi, and it was left to the Daphne Class submarines to restore some fighting spirit within the Pakistan Navy. When asked about a relative comparison between the Indian Navy's Foxtrot Class and the Pakistan Navy's Daphne Class submarines, Admiral Nadkarni was candid enough to say that the Daphne was distinctly stealthier and more capable as it was a generation ahead of the Foxtrot, but for some reason the Pakistan Navy was not aggressive enough while employing it. When asked why the Pakistan Navy chose to send the WW II vintage *Ghazi* to the east coast instead of the Daphne Class, the admiral pointed at the larger range of the *Ghazi* as it was a WW II vintage submarine that had been designed not so much for stealth as for range and endurance so that it could operate for long periods in the Atlantic.

Any narrative on naval operations during the 1971 conflict would not be complete without an undersea tale from a submariner. One of the two Foxtrot Class submarines of the western fleet to have seen action for the entire duration of the conflict was INS *Karanj,* which replaced the INS *Kursura,* which had been on watch-and-patrol duties in the Arabian Sea since mid-November.[36] Commanded by Commander Shekhawat, who went on to be the first submariner to become chief of naval staff, it prowled off the Karachi coast in its patrol area for almost two weeks from 2 December seeking action. The extremely stringent rules of engagement and visual recognition criteria for offensive action, however, made it almost impossible for her to resort to any kind of offensive action.[37]

It is also believed that Shekhawat's submarine had an unverified encounter in the northern Arabian Sea with what the crew initially believed was a Russian nuclear submarine, which could have been on its way to the Bay of Bengal as a counter to the movement of the US Seventh Fleet into the region. However, the Soviets denied the presence of any of their submarines after the war, leading to speculation that it may well have been a US Navy nuclear submarine. The actual truth has still not been unravelled.

A poem written by a naval midshipman after the 1971 war, recollecting events as he embarked on board his first warship, the INS *Tir*, reveals the excitement and pride within the Indian Navy as the war at sea progressed. I have reproduced excerpts below.

I remember that day with the POP (Passing out Parade) scheduled for next day, we had gone for a movie at Eros at Churchgate, and had taken permission to stay out a little late, only to be greeted on return at the gangway that we would be sailing quickly at the dawn of day.

I remember that day with the boats in tow at short stay.

First to Okha we did sail and thence towards the enemy's coast.

To show up his vain and empty boast.

Slipping the tow in the dark, we lay in wait, close enough to hark.

I remember that day reading only a single word I pray. All it said on the message was 'Sansar'. A code word we knew which meant open war. No more fun and no more games. From now it was only fire and flames.

I remember the day when the Missile Boats came back, storming their way. We rushed to the top and lined up around the ship. With caps in hand, cheering from the heart and waving from the hip.

Karachi was on fire, we were told. It was one big advantage we were to hold.

I remember that day on a misty morning gray when lower decks were cleared and we assembled with eyes blurred with tears for the gallant Khukri crew. Her sinking, a gain to the enemy did accrue.

I remember that day when the Navy went on a foray. My heart swelled with pride on being part of that historic ride. Delivering a crushing blow from which the enemy couldn't recover. Victory at sea was ours when we made him cower![38]

26

ATTRITION BATTLES

The Battle of Basantar was one of the great tank battles fought by the Indian Army. Like all great battles, the outcome was a close run affair. After about eight hours of bitter fighting, tanks of the Poona Horse had destroyed almost two Pakistani armoured regiments. Indeed they too paid a heavy price but stood victorious.[1]

– Lieutenant General W.A.G. Pinto

Forgotten Battles of Ladakh

As in 1965, some of the toughest battles in 1971 were fought on the icy heights overlooking Kargil, a town at an altitude of 8,780 ft located on the banks of the River Shingo and a critical stop on the Srinagar–Leh Highway.[2] Control over Pt 13620 and Black Rock, as two of the fiercely contested heights overlooking Kargil were called, was again the focus of attention in December 1971. This time, however, it was the peak of winter and with only one division entrusted with the defence of the entire Ladakh sector, it was tough going for Brigadier M.L. Whig and his 121 Brigade. As it attempted to take control of territories that were captured by them in 1965, and then saw them being returned to Pakistan after the Tashkent Agreement, the Indian Army did not anticipate that Pakistan would set up well-stocked posts there and interdict the Srinagar–Leh Highway with well-directed artillery fire.[3] The odds against which almost five battalions[4] with suboptimal winter clothing and canvas boots captured numerous heights between 13,000 and 15,000 ft in the Kargil sector over two weeks of bitter fighting will go down in the annals of Indian military history as amongst the most underrated and least written about mountain operations. Almost three decades later, in 1999, the same area would see bitter fighting in full media glare as Pakistan exploited India's vulnerability by surreptitiously occupying numerous heights in the Kargil and adjoining sectors of Batalik, Dras, Kaksar and Mushkoh.

As in 1948, when Spitfires and Tempest fighters from Srinagar had valiantly supported Thimayya's breaching of Zojila Pass, the IAF supported the Kargil and Partapur sectors with airdrops of supplies through two weeks, and interestingly, close air support and interdiction by a detachment of obsolete Vampire jets in early December 1971.[5] In a mail to the author, P.V. S. Jagan Mohan confirmed that Flight Lieutenant Sekhon (later Air Marshal) did indeed operate from Srinagar and provide vital support during the assault.[6] The exploits of a handful of obsolete Vampire jet fighters of 121 Squadron operating from Srinagar airfield as they knocked out gun positions, strafed dug-in troops and interdicted supply lines in the area was well acknowledged by the Indian Army. Sekhon won his Vir Chakra for his untiring efforts and numerous sorties of offensive and reconnaissance missions that he flew over two weeks.

In a telephonic conversation with the author on 21 July 2014, the air marshal recounted how he was in frequent contact with the dynamic corps commander of 15 Corps, Lieutenant General Sartaj Singh.[7] Sartaj, he recollected, was a daring and innovative field commander who had drawn up plans for the capture of Skardu and the entire district of Baltistan. However, the setback in Chhamb necessitated his presence there as he played an inspirational role in rallying units of 10 Division to offer a suitable riposte between 8 and 12 December. Sekhon went on to add that Sartaj was often seen in knee-deep water waving his baton as he urged his formations to ensure that Pakistan did not get a lodging on the east bank of the Munawar Tawi. Much of the air action in Uri, Poonch and the dangerous Kargil and Mushkoh Valleys of Ladakh have not been recorded and archived in the published history of the 1971 war and my inquiries from the air force station at Srinagar on the exploits of this small group of pilots during the war drew a blank. However, accounts in the war diaries of 121 Brigade acknowledge the excellent support by IAF Vampires.

From Leh, as one travels north across the Khardungla Pass, one reaches the village of Partapur, which lies almost at the confluence of the Shyok and Nubra rivers, both tributaries of the mighty Indus. North-west from Partapur along the Shyok river, one passes the small hamlet of Turtuk before hitting the ceasefire line, and onwards to Skardu, the scene of a bloody siege in 1948 before it fell to raiders from Pakistan. This area too saw bitter fighting in 1971 in freezing conditions. Defended as a sector with barely a battalion worth of troops comprising three companies of hardy Ladakh Scouts and hastily trained but well-acclimatized Nubra Guards (locals from the area), these wonderfully led troops by Colonel Udai Singh and Major Rinchen gave the Karakoram Scouts of the Pakistan Army a bloody nose, as described by General Candeth:

> Thus this sector headquarters had in 14 days advanced 22 kilometres and captured approximately 804 sq kms. I doubt whether any other army had ever battled in such appalling conditions and it speaks much for the determination, motivation and physical toughness of our troops and commanders that they were able to carry out their tasks so well.[8]

However, after capturing the heights around Kargil and Turtuk in exhausting battles, Sartaj had rather unreasonably hoped for Whig's troops to link up with the Ladakh Scouts and make a bid to capture Khapalu and Skardu, if the opportunity presented itself. This was not to be as by then the ceasefire had been declared and Whig's brigade was stretched to the very limits of human endurance. Skardu, though, had its share of action thanks to some daring strikes by three IAF Canberra bombers and a lone An-12 piloted by Wing Commander Vashisht on the last day of the war (3:45 p.m. on 17 December).[9] The Ladakh Scouts and 121 Brigade would once again be thrust into the limelight twenty-eight years later as India battled to recover lost ground. For their exploits in the Kargil and Turtok sectors, Whig and Rinchen were awarded Maha Vir Chakras.

As the war reached its climax in the second week of December, the beautiful Srinagar skyscape saw a classic dogfight between a single Gnat of the IAF flown by Flying Officer Nirmaljit Singh Sekhon and a six-aircraft Sabre formation led by Wing Commander Changezi of 26 Squadron PAF. Taking off from Srinagar runway while it was under attack by four of the Sabres, Sekhon not only ensured that the Sabres were not allowed to put in another attack, but also shot down one of them and damaged another one before being outnumbered and shot down by the fifth Sabre. Though he ejected from a crippled aircraft, the height was too low for him to survive. He remains the IAF's only Param Vir Chakra.[10]

Staying in Srinagar, a bizarre incident that reflected the rather conservative mindset that still existed at the time needs to be recounted. It caused the IAF to miss out on an opportunity to cause some damage to Pakistani troop emplacement in the Poonch, Rajouri and Tithwal sectors of Jammu and Kashmir. Air Commodore S.S. Kaushik (retd) clearly recollects that there were fairly large stocks of napalm bombs at Srinagar which the Vampires had planned to drop. He goes on to add that they were asked to cancel their napalm mission at the last moment by the station commander at Srinagar to avoid offending the religious sentiment of the Pakistani troops by 'causing death by fire'. So, off the bombs went into storage and next day, the storage area was attacked with pinpoint accuracy by PAF Sabres, causing a huge explosion and the death of a few local labourers belonging to the very community that the IAF did not want to offend. Kaushik remarked: 'That was but the first of many occasions when our armed forces would be asked to fight with one hand behind their backs in Kashmir.'

Limited Success in Shakargarh

The showpiece operation of the Indian Army was undoubtedly meant to have been the offensive launched in the Shakargarh salient by India's only offensive corps, 1 Corps, which was commanded by K.K. Singh.[11] Tasked with pre-empting any attempt by Pakistan to threaten the vital road from Pathankot to Jammu from the direction of the salient when there was another offensive expected in Chhamb, the offensive lacked adequate teeth. K.K. Singh just did not have the necessary numerical and firepower superiority, and the need to protect his flanks warranted additional caution. He engaged in much operational discussion with his army commander, Candeth, on reallocating some forces for the defence of his flanks and may have lost the opportunity to launch his offensive at the same time as Pakistan made inroads into Chhamb. While the delayed offensive in the Sialkot sector in 1965 was understandable as 1 Corps was still fetching up into their operational area from peacetime locations and there was the distraction of a concurrent offensive in the Lahore sector, there was no such compulsion in 1971.

Considering that an extensive network of linear defences had come up in the area, K.K. Singh did not have a decisive quantitative superiority in terms of infantry, armour and artillery as compared to 1 Corps of Pakistan. It was insufficient to support his rather ambitious plan of heading for Sialkot as he did not have the required 3:1 superiority that was generally considered as being essential to force a decisive result in a battle of attrition in the plains. A typical example of how divisions were depleted of vital offensive assets to cater for defensive tasks was the detaching of an armoured regiment from the integral armoured brigade, which was attached to 54 Division, for defensive flank protection. As it turned out, when his first division (39 Division) failed to make inroads in the first few days of the offensive, he had to utilize his second division (54 Division) to attempt thrusts into the Shakargarh bulge from the north. Commanded by the aggressive Major General W.A.G. Pinto, 54 Division fought a series of infantry and armour battles with just two armoured regiments and till today Pinto wonders what could have happened had he been given all his armoured regiments for offensive operations. After his retirement General Pinto has settled in his little bungalow on Alexandra Road in the sylvan surroundings of the Pune cantonment. I would walk past it every day and finally mustered up the courage to visit him and take a peek into the life and times of one of the Indian Army's finest field commanders. His still booming laugh and racy book, *Bash On Regardless*, exemplify the aggressive spirit that he exuded on the battlefield. In my second interview session with him, he handed me a sheet of paper with a remarkably clear handwritten anecdote and said, 'Young man, your narrative cannot be devoid of some humour. I have jotted down some light memories; see whether they are of any use.' It read like this:

> The Calm before the storm! We were dug in behind the Border Security Force (BSF), which was manning its Border Out Posts (BOPs) on the International Border. Patrolling had been banned on grounds of secrecy, security and surprise. While heaps of last-minute

intelligence trickled down from ground troops, Air Observation reports, IB reports, wireless intercepts, contacts with ambassadors and military attaches of friendly countries through staff channels, one particular message drew my attention and amused me immensely. It read 'Pak attack imminent, ensure highest operational preparedness.' I flashed a reply – 'Preparedness already heightened. Observation Post on the highest branch of solitary Peepul Tree. Cannot climb higher!' Bang came the rejoinder, 'Stop being facetious stop ensure strict compliance with orders. Message ends'.

Valour at Basantar

Fierce tank battles raged at Basantar, Zafarwal and the village of Shakargarh, which saw many classic encounters between tanks of the Indian Army's 16 Armoured Brigade comprising 17 Poona Horse and Hodson Horse (16 Cavalry was the third regiment that was deployed in a defensive posture), and two regiments of the Pakistan Army's 8 (Independent) Armoured Brigade comprising 13 Lancers and 31 Cavalry with 27 Cavalry in reserve.[12]

A young second lieutenant of the Indian Army's Poona Horse Regiment, Arun Khetarpal, displayed courage of the highest order by first knocking off 3–4 Patton tanks and then refusing to abandon his damaged tank since its gun was still firing. He was finally killed when his tank received a direct hit from a tank commanded by Major Khwaja Naser, a squadron commander of 13 Lancers. He was awarded the Param Vir Chakra and remains a source of inspiration even today for young officers of India's Armoured Corps, while his brigade commander, Vaidya, who later went on to become chief of army staff, was awarded a Maha Vir Chakra. More than thirty years later a poignant meeting between Arun Khetarpal's father and Brigadier Naser reveals that despite the prolonged enmity between the two countries, deep professional respect for each other exists within the two militaries.

Arun Khetarpal was not the only hero to emerge from the battle of Basantar in the Shakargarh sector. Major Hoshiar Singh, a hard-core infantryman and a company commander with 3 Grenadiers, would live to tell his tale of courage and bravery as the only surviving Param

Vir Chakra awardee from the 1971 war. Tasked to capture the 'Jarpal Complex' across the Basantar nala (stream or rivulet in Hindi) on 15/16 December as part of 54 Division's larger plan of capturing the town of Zafarwal, Hoshiar was involved in a tough battle of attrition over two days as he first captured Jarpal, and then held on to it in the face of repeated infantry and armoured assault by a determined 8 Infantry Division of Pakistan Army. It is in response to the armoured attack in the Jarpal Area by 8 Armoured Brigade that Poona Horse swung into action, only to lose Arun Khetarpal. It was not only the Indians who performed valiantly in the Basantar battle; Colonel Mohammad Akram Raja, the commanding officer of Pakistan's 35 Frontier Rifles, led a frontal attack with two companies on Hoshiar's position, only to be met with withering fire from tactically well-positioned Indian troops. Hoshiar had planned well and executed his plan brilliantly. Though wounded during the attack; he continued to motivate his troops to give it all. At the end of almost two hours of fierce fighting, Raja and almost a hundred Pak troops were killed, and many were taken prisoner. After acknowledgement of his valour and bravery by an Indian officer, Raja was awarded the Hilal-e-Jurat, Pakistan's second highest gallantry award.[13]

After the war, India did well to post Major Hoshiar Singh to the Indian Military Academy (IMA) as a company commander of Sinhgarh Company. He proved to be a tremendous inspiration for the cadets and turned the company into the champion company for much of his tenure there. I was a young schoolboy and a cadet at the Rashtriya Indian Military College and whenever we visited the IMA and went past Sinhgarh Company, we were told: 'Look, that is the PVC Company. You know who the company commander is; it is Major Hoshiar Singh!' So much for inspirational cadet tales!

Engineer regiments of the Indian Army gained prominence during the early battles of WW II where Lieutenant Prem Bhagat was the first Indian officer to be awarded the Victoria Cross. Sappers, as they are called, are among the leading elements that go in ahead of the armour during offensive operations as they strive to clear minefields under withering fire to create lanes for tanks to forge ahead. During the battle of Basantar, 9 Engineer Regiment, a Madras sapper unit, emerged as the most decorated engineer regiment of the war as it cleared innovative Pakistani minefields of varying depth using a combination of manual mine clearance and the new Russian mine trawlers mounted on a T-55 tank chassis. Lieutenant General Pandit recalls that as the CO of the regiment, he led from the front and saw his unit suffer heavy casualties during the battles of Basantar and Zafarwal. The unit suffered thirty casualties including seven officers and was also the most highly decorated engineer unit in the war with one Maha Vir Chakra, three Vir Chakras and a clutch of other awards.[14] He also graciously acknowledged: 'Pakistan fought the battle of attrition against us well. They laid innovative and unpredictable minefields and exploited our lack of cross-country and night-fighting capability.' The minefields extended to over 1,600 yards and were designed to ensure that breaching during the hours of darkness would be extremely difficult and the possibility of Indian armour being bogged down was extremely high. Handling their tank trawls skilfully and led admirably well, 9 Engineer Regiment accompanied by 5 Engineer Regiment repeatedly breached tricky and deep minefields during the night to create adequate safety lanes, thereby allowing unrestricted flow of tanks into battle.[15]

Even though Air Chief Marshal Lal in his book has indicated that the IAF provided adequate close air support over Shakargarh in the form of SU-7s from Adampur and Hunters from Pathankot with MiG-21s providing top cover, the IAF effort was more than well matched by the PAF. Recognizing the importance of the battle, the PAF dedicated three squadrons of F-86 Sabres and two squadrons of F-6s to the battle. They flew a total of 296 sorties in the area,[16] while the IAF could manage to put in approximately 230 sorties during the same period. An objective analysis of the air battle revealed that the IAF had shown a significant improvement of tactics and procedures, and with the availability of an effective tactical air centre alongside 1 Corps, it had caught up with the PAF when it came to close air support.[17] Yet, in all honesty, Air Chief Marshal Lal acknowledges in his book that though adequate air effort was available, the right kinds of targets were not identified for attack by IAF fighters.[18] The Sukhois were large aircraft that could be spotted from a great distance, and despite packing quite a punch whenever they delivered their rockets against Pakistani armour, they proved to be quite vulnerable to ack-ack guns and came out second best when engaged by PAF F-86 Sabres and F-6s in aerial combat,[19] losing three aircraft in the battle. In the final analysis, though the battle of Basantar was a victory for the Indian Army and the number of tank casualties suffered by Pakistan's 8 Division and 8 Armoured Brigade far outnumbered the Indian casualties, the PAF and the IAF played an important role in limiting the gains made by both sides.[20] It is believed that the Israeli air force studied the aerial campaign over Shakargarh prior to the 1973 war with Egypt, which saw large scale engagement of armour by aircraft from both sides. At the end of almost ten days of fighting, though the Indian Army had captured 265 sq. miles in the Shakargarh bulge, it was unrealistic to imagine that it would be held on to after post-war negotiations.

Lost Opportunities in the Desert

Barring a bit of an embarrassment in Kutch in the 1965 war, the Indian Army and IAF had little experience of offensive operations in the desert sector. Two divisions and a brigade (defending Kutch) with limited armour was all that Lieutenant General G.G. Bewoor, the bespectacled GOC-in-C of Southern Command, had to progress operations in the sector. Like Candeth, an illustrious alumnus of RIMC and a future chief, Bewoor had seen extensive action in the 1947–48 operations in J&K while commanding his Garhwal regiment during Thimayya's spring offensive. This time around he had 11 Infantry Division in the southern desert around Barmer, and 12 Infantry Division in the northern parts of the Thar Desert around Jaisalmer.[21] Providing him air cover in the region were six Hunters from the Armament Training Wing, Jamnagar, on detachment at Jaisalmer airfield. He also had fighter aircraft in the form of 10 Squadrons and 220 Squadrons with the indigenously built HF-24s at Utterlai and Jodhpur for close air support, and could even call upon Canberra bombers from Pune, if the need arose. Realizing the threat posed by PAF F-104s, Sabres and Mirage-IIIs based at Karachi, the IAF had a squadron worth of MiG-21s at Jamnagar and a detachment of six aircraft at Utterlai. A lone Pakistani division (18 Division) with some reserve forces in depth opposed the two Indian divisions over an extended frontage of almost 700 km. Surprisingly, there was no PAF squadron to directly support any offensive operation by 18 Division in the Jaisalmer sector despite having the airfield of Jacobabad available for operations. PAF support for defensive army operations in the Barmer sector, though, would be forthcoming and more effective than IAF operations in the sector as the war progressed.

Yet, on the night of 4 December, in a rash decision that spoke poorly of Pakistan's overconfident operational leadership, its 18 Division launched an armour-heavy offensive with one infantry brigade and two tank regiments towards Jaisalmer without any air cover or preliminary softening up of defences. The operation was a disaster as the armoured thrust was first held up by a company of 23 Punjab at Longewala led by Major Kuldip Singh Chandpuri and then Hunters from Jaisalmer responded early next morning at first light to an SOS from the besieged company locality and played merry hell into the two regiments of Pakistani armour. The air force station at Jaisalmer was commanded by Wing Commander M.S. Bawa, who marshalled his resources admirably during the war. By the end of the day, the IAF Hunters had flown over twenty sorties and knocked off over twenty tanks and numerous light vehicles. They were assisted in no small measure by two gallant air observation patrol (AOP) pilots in the form of Major Atma Singh and Captain Sangha in their light Krishak aircraft as there were no forward air controllers present in the area. The Indian Army and the IAF had scored a major 'joint' victory in the desert! The next day (6 December) also saw the Hunters from Jaisalmer causing havoc among the retreating tanks, and by the end of the day, they had destroyed another twenty tanks. Major Chandpuri was awarded a Maha Vir Chakra for his night-long rearguard action against a much larger force, while seven Hunter pilots, along with two air observation pilots of the Indian Army, were awarded Vir Chakras for their sharpshooting. The commander of Pakistan's 18 Division, Major General Mustafa, was ignominiously dismissed from service after the war. Among the Hunter pilots were Squadron Leaders F.J. Mehta and R.N. Bali and Flight Lieutenants Gosain, Suresh and Jagbir Singh. Surprisingly, the brigade commander who led the Pakistani offensive towards Jaisalmer was later awarded the Sitare-Jurat for his courage under fire when his tanks were subjected to a merciless pounding by the IAF Hunters.

Emboldened by this victory at Longewala, Major General Khambatta's

12 Division pressed forward and captured a large chunk of territory in Islamgarh on the way to Rahim Yar Khan, a strategic town east of the River Indus and on the railway line running from Bahawalpur to Jacobabad. Led by 13 Kumaon and supported by some aggressive artillery fire, the advance had fair momentum. But with no logistics backup and inadequate air support, and restricted by the 'hold territory' policy in the west, Bewoor baulked from advancing further. The division was also slow in blocking the withdrawal of a depleted 18 Division of Pakistan as it retreated from Longewala. One of the major chances of destroying Pak combat potential in this sector was lost!

Further south, 10 Para Commando led by Lieutenant Colonel Bhawani Singh from the princely family of Jaipur captured Chachro in a daring jeep-borne operation.[22] It was poised to link up with the main force of 11 Division as it captured Naya Chor and advanced towards Chor. However, the operation halted before the intermediate objective of Chor due to constraints of logistics and the overarching defensive mindset along the entire western front. Interdiction and airfield strikes at Utterlai airfield (the IAF airfield close to the town of Barmer in Rajasthan) by PAF fighters and Canberra bombers from Masroor airbase (Karachi) also contributed to the hold-up in the advance of 11 Division. Without taking away anything from the excellent performance of the MiG-21s in both air defence and ground attack roles (they destroyed the lone PAF radar at Badin in the sind Sector),[23] the IAF did not have the necessary force ratios. It had two HF-24 squadrons at Jodhpur and Utterlai respectively, a Hunter Squadron divided between Jamnagar and Jaisalmer, a squadron and a half of MiG-21s divided between Jamnagar and Utterlai, and a lone Canberra squadron at Pune. The squadrons between them could not generate enough sorties to achieve a favourable air situation so as to facilitate the speedy advance of the Indian divisions. Though F-104 Starfighters leased by Pakistan from Jordan and based at Masroor attacked Jamnagar and Utterlai as 11 Division advanced, they suffered heavy losses at the hands of IAF MiG-21s of 47 and 29 Squadrons, which performed quite brilliantly in the conflict. Despite losing three aircraft in aerial dogfights, the F-104s did destroy one HF-24 and damaged another as they were about to take off from Utterlai base. Kaiser Tufail rightly assesses in his blog: 'Had the IAF's counter-air campaign in the sector been more whole-hearted, Major General R.D. Anand, commander 11 Division may well have been planning his next moves from the district headquarters of Mirpur Khas.'[24]

The Indian Army's operations in the Khem Karan, Fazilka and Ferozpur sectors of southern Punjab were entrusted to Lieutenant General Rawlley's XI Corps. Located in the same area at Muktsar was India's only armoured division. Readers would recollect that Rawlley's brigade was the lone brigade that offered stubborn resistance in the face of the PLA onslaught in the Walong Sector in 1962. Facing these forces were equally strong formations on the Pakistani side comprising their 'Southern Strike Force' comprising a corps including their own 1 Armoured Division which was lying in wait for an opportune moment to strike should India choose to move its armoured division elsewhere. Beyond a few fierce infantry-heavy battles with some air power thrown in around Fazilka, Dera Baba Nanak, Ferozpur and Hussainiwalla,[25] it was attrition warfare all the way in this sector. No major gains were made by any side in the region, and the fact that none of the three armoured divisions got to see any real fighting beyond a few of their regiments being allocated out indicates the rather static, attritionist and defensive mindset of commanders on both sides. To bolster this force, Manekshaw rushed the para brigade from the eastern sector to the Fazilka sector in the last few days of the war to cater for 'the counter attack from Pakistan's 1 Armoured Brigade that never happened'. The anticipated mother of all battles between the two armoured divisions remained in the realm of fiction. According to reliable sources, a planned Pakistani offensive south of Fazilka in the Ganganagar sector never materialized as forces had to be diverted to bolster the 18 Division as it retreated towards Rahim Yar Khan.

Peace after Two Weeks of War

Barely had Governor Malik and his military advisor, Major General Rao Farman Ali, cleared the dust off their clothes and emerged from the debris of the Government House following the IAF attack on 14 December, Yahya Khan ordered the Pakistani forces in the eastern theatre to lay down their arms and surrender as 'you have now reached a stage where further resistance is no longer humanly possible'.[26] Much has been written about the surrender ceremony and the author has no intentions of revisiting the issue in detail. Suffice it to say that it was a well-orchestrated ceremony in the afternoon of 16 December that was attended by all senior commanders of India's Eastern Army Command, Naval and Air Force Command, which showcased to the world that India had arrived on the world military stage and could no longer be messed around with.[27]

The ceasefire in the west was less spectacular as Indira Gandhi was only waiting for a decisive outcome in the east before accepting any offer of an olive branch from Pakistan. She took the lead and announced a unilateral ceasefire in Parliament on 17 December. Yahya Khan immediately accepted India's offer as both countries realized that they could ill afford to continue a needless war.[28]

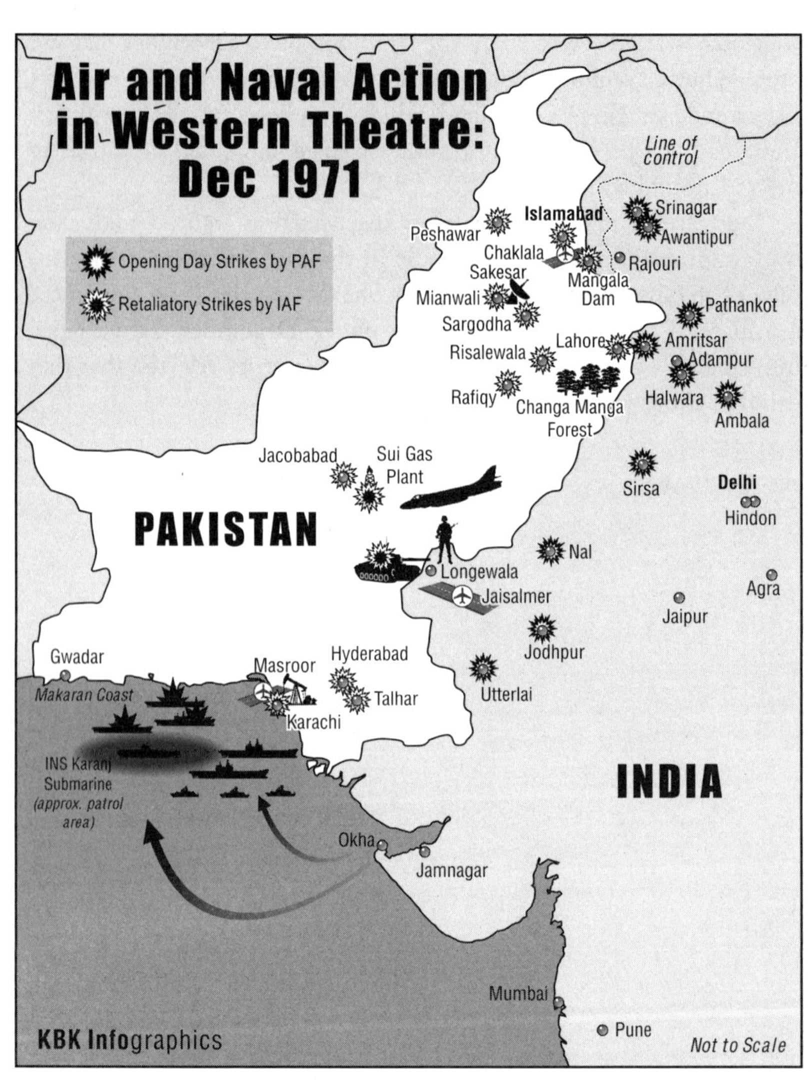

Air and Naval Action in Western Theatre: Dec 1971
Opening Day Strikes by PAF
Retaliatory Strikes by IAF
Line of control
Islamabad
Peshawar
Chaklala
Sakesar
Mianwali
Sargodha
Mangala Dam
Srinagar
Awantipur
Rajouri
Pathankot
Lahore
Amritsar
Adampur
Halwara
Ambala
Risalewala
Rafiqy
Changa Manga Forest
Jacobabad
Sui Gas Plant
Sirsa
Delhi
Hindon
PAKISTAN
Nal
Longewala
Jaisalmer
Agra
Jaipur
Jodhpur
Utterlai
Gwadar
Makaran Coast
Masroor
Hyderabad
Talhar
Karachi
INS Karanj Submarine (approx. patrol area)
INDIA
Okha
Jamnagar
Mumbai
Pune
KBK Infographics
Not to Scale

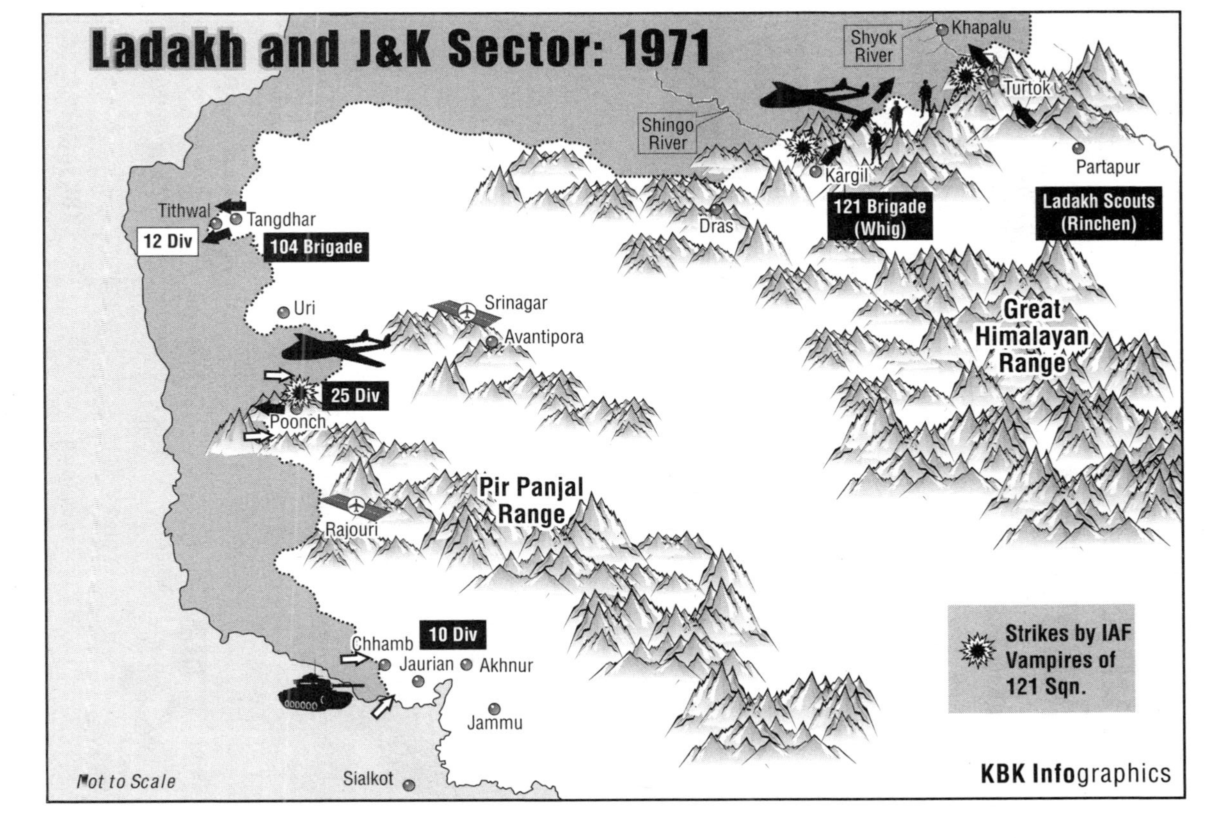
Ladakh and J&K Sector: 1971
Shyok River
Khapalu
Turtok
Shingo River
Kargil
Partapur
Tithwal
Tangdhar
12 Div
104 Brigade
Dras
121 Brigade (Whig)
Ladakh Scouts (Rinchen)
Uri
Srinagar
Avantipora
Great Himalayan Range
25 Div
Poonch
Pir Panjal Range
Rajouri
10 Div
Chhamb
Jaurian
Akhnur
Jammu
Sialkot
Strikes by IAF Vampires of 121 Sqn.
Not to Scale
KBK Infographics

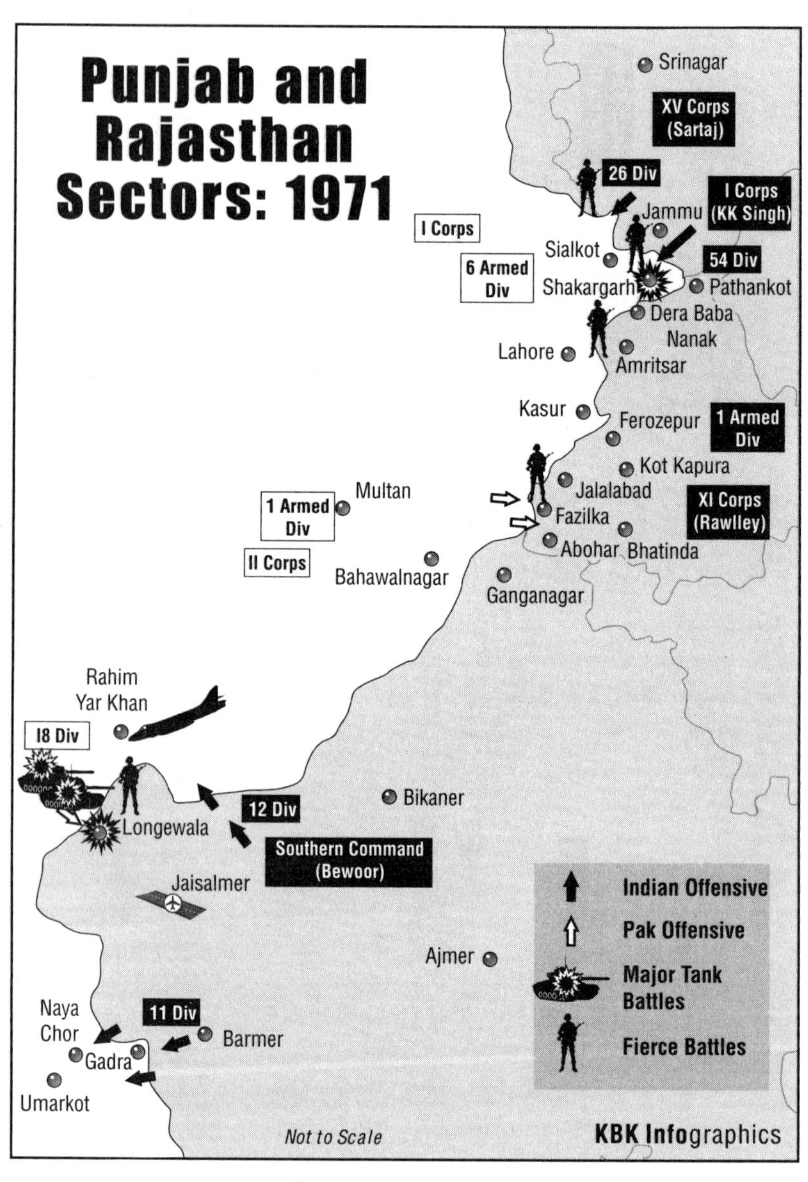
Punjab and Rajasthan Sectors: 1971
Srinagar
XV Corps (Sartaj)
26 Div
I Corps (KK Singh)
Jammu
I Corps
6 Armed Div
Sialkot
54 Div
Shakargarh
Pathankot
Dera Baba Nanak
Lahore
Amritsar
Kasur
Ferozepur
1 Armed Div
Kot Kapura
Jalalabad
Multan
1 Armed Div
XI Corps (Rawlley)
Fazilka
Abohar
Bhatinda
II Corps
Bahawalnagar
Ganganagar
Rahim Yar Khan
I8 Div
Bikaner
12 Div
Longewala
Southern Command (Bewoor)
Jaisalmer
Indian Offensive
Pak Offensive
Major Tank Battles
Fierce Battles
Ajmer
Naya Chor
11 Div
Barmer
Gadra
Umarkot
Not to Scale
KBK Infographics

27

WHAT 1971 MEANS TO INDIA AND PAKISTAN

How did we perform in December 1971? Well, we can generally say we did not do too badly. In fact, we did rather well: we won the war ... It takes a war to make our people work together. Peace breaks them up into narrow sectional pieces. We must learn to rise above sectarian interests and work for what is best for our country.[1]

– Air Chief Marshal P.C. Lal

The Dolphins Swim Again

As the guns fell silent in Dacca, the endangered South Asian dolphin, which inhabits the waters of the Meghna and the Ganga delta, surfaced again after months. The light winter mist across the Gangetic plains of the youngest country in the world, Bangladesh, concealed a tension that would remain for years. The four-day period, from 15 to 18 December 1971, saw some horrific killings, both by the Razakars and the Bengali nationalists as mobs exploited the vacuum created by the surrender. Hard-core elements of the Al-Badr, a fundamentalist Islamic group supported by Pakistan and comprising the Razakars (Pakistan Army loyalists), went on a killing spree of Bengali intellectuals on 15 December when they came to know that a surrender was imminent.

Many killers would remain at large in Bangladesh for years[2] till they were hunted down and prosecuted by the Awami League government led by Sheikh Hasina Wajed after it was returned to power in 2013.[3] Bengali anger against the Biharis and Razakars surfaced as widespread mob killings, particularly in the jute mills of Khulna, disturbed the fragile peace till public order was restored in a few months.[4]

Amidst the tension and uncertainty, there were heart-warming stories of bravery and compassion too. While Sheikh Mujib was spirited away to Pakistan and placed under house arrest in Karachi, his family was isolated under similar circumstances in a heavily fortified double-storey house in a Dacca neighbourhood. Had it not been for a brave and unarmed Indian Army major, Ashok Tara, a tense and stressed-out complement of Pakistan Army soldiers guarding the house may well have killed Sheikh Mujib's family on the morning of 17 December. Having been awarded with a Vir Chakra as a company commander with 14 Guards during the Akhaura and Gangasagar battles, Tara had to use his persuasive skills to convince the young and nervous Pakistani guards at the house that the game was up and that Niazi had surrendered the previous day. The current prime minister of Bangladesh, Sheikh Hasina Wazed, was a spirited twenty-four-year-old with a babe in arms, and remembers the event with gratitude. Major Tara, an energetic seventy-two-year-old now, was feted with a 'Friend of Bangladesh' award by her in 2012.[5]

Strategic Lessons

Many Western authors are reluctant to praise India for its strategic decisiveness and willingness to train the Mukti Bahini guerrilla fighters despite knowing that it risked a two-front war with Pakistan.[6] However, they do admit that despite its fractured polity, for once India was united across party lines as its leadership combined 'realpolitik' with genuine empathy for victims of the genocide. Indira Gandhi initially thought that given the training and significant material assistance to the Mukti Bahini, it would be able to defeat the Pakistan Army in East Pakistan on its own. She had not reckoned with the increasing brutality of the Pakistan Army and the spiralling refugee crisis. With over ten million refugees streaming into India by November 1971, there was no alternative but to go to war on the eastern front. So certain was she of this decision that one cannot but help benchmarking her decision against the seven markers which Geoffrey Blainey, the noted Australian military historian, laid out for assessing the relative strength of countries on the brink of war. These are:

> military strength and the ability to apply that strength efficiently in the chosen zone of war; predictions of how outside nations would behave in the event of the war; perceptions of internal unity and of the unity or discord of the enemy; memory or forgetfulness of the realities and sufferings of war; perceptions of prosperity and of ability to sustain economically; the personality and mental quality of the leaders who weighed the evidence; nationalism and ideology; and the personality and mental qualities of the leaders who weighed the evidence and decided for peace or war.[7]

On every count, India, Indira Gandhi and her team were well ahead of Yahya Khan, Bhutto and the fragmented Pakistani strategic leadership. Hoping for some irrational success, Pakistan struck first on the western front on 3 December 1971 and allowed India to supplement its operational superiority with the opportunity to occupy the moral high ground in the ensuing fourteen-day conflict.

The surrender of Dacca and the splitting of Pakistan remains the single most impactful strategic event of the war. Lieutenant General Shammi Mehta put the whole campaign in the east in the right perspective, albeit with a touch of drama and flair, so typical of the Armoured Corps, when he said:

> The Indian Armed Forces had in 14 days, liberated a country from where it withdrew in 90 days, picked up 93,000 prisoners, and released them one year later at an average body weight of one-and-a–half times their original weight.[8]

Though the military victory was greeted with much triumphalism by the Indian media, the Indian Army conducted itself with great dignity when it came to treating the POWs, particularly from the Pakistan Army. Just as the Sikh and Gorkha soldiers of the 8th Indian Division of the British 8th Army had protected women and innocents in the captured Italian town of Taranto during WW II, the Indian Army intervened on numerous occasions to prevent marauding and furious Bengali mobs from lynching many Pakistani soldiers. Many senior Indian officers remembered the horrors of the Japanese POW camps of WW II and the brainwashing sessions of Indian Army POWs by the Chinese after 1962. Strict orders flowed down from Army HQ to ensure compliance of the Geneva Convention. Lieutenant General Mathew Thomas recollects that his Para units in Agra had to vacate their barracks and move to tents to accommodate the Pakistan Army POWs. Despite instructions from Army HQ not to mingle with the POWs, Thomas decided one morning to go to the barracks on an inspection visit – he was warned that there were many surly POWs, particularly from Pakistan's Special Forces, and that there was possibility of some unrest should he decide to visit. As he marched through the barracks with his baton in hand, and with two escorts armed only with pickaxes, most of the POWs who had lined up beside their beds stood to attention in deference to a senior officer's arrival, but not the few bearded Pakistani Special Forces soldiers. When ticked off by Thomas, some of them reluctantly complied, but one man burst out: 'Why should I stand in attention when I am worried about my wife and children; I have not heard from them for three months.' Thomas told him that he would find out and let him know. Find out he did by calling the director of military operations in New Delhi to help him out. The family was fine and a smile returned to the face of the burly Special Forces soldier of the Pakistan Army.

The defeat further shattered the martial myth of the Punjabi- and Pathan-dominated Pakistan Army as it crumbled in the face of a secular and diverse Indian armed forces and the non-martial Bengalis. The scars of the dismembering remain a debilitating legacy, particularly within the Pakistan Army, though the PAF and the Pakistan Navy took the defeat more objectively. This is reflected in much of the writing that has emerged from Pakistan on the 1971 war in recent times.[9] The slow normalization of relations between India and Pakistan since the 1971 war can mainly be attributed to the obsession of the Pakistan Army to 'get even' with India and avenge the loss of 1971.

India emerged as the clear regional power in South Asia after the 1971 war with Pakistan by demonstrating significant national will to tackle a crisis of enormous proportions. A concurrently well-executed political diplomatic and military strategy with clear objectives for much of 1971 allowed India to explore all possible options before resorting to military action in East Pakistan. By diplomatically engaging with Russia, western Europe and the US, and sensitizing them about the ongoing human tragedy in East Pakistan and the spiralling refugee crisis in India, the Indian government succeeded in conveying to the world that it wanted a peaceful solution to the problem. However, the speed with which it commenced military operations indicated its resolve and willingness to use military force in pursuit of its national interests.

If India was outmanoeuvred strategically at any stage, it was during the Simla Conference of 1972 where a wily Bhutto managed to convince Indira Gandhi of the need to delink a Kashmir settlement from the negotiations to release the 93,000 Pakistani prisoners held by India. This, he emphasized, was essential for the survival of his democratically elected government.[10] An internationally recognized agreement over Kashmir in terms of converting the ceasefire line into a clearly delineated and demarcated boundary may have sorted out the Kashmir issue once and for all. Hussain Haqqani, an astute strategic commentator, academic and former Pakistani ambassador to the US, offers telling comments on the Simla Agreement. He writes:

> He (Bhutto) pleaded with Gandhi not to insist on including a final resolution of the Jammu and Kashmir dispute in any bilateral agreement although, from India's point of view, this would have been the ideal opportunity to impose a solution.[11]

In a moment of triumphant magnanimity, Indira Gandhi lost a golden opportunity to remove the 'Kashmir' thorn from India's flesh. It also allowed Pakistan to keep the pot boiling till it reworked its strategies to wrest Kashmir from India. Continuing at the strategic level, Indira Gandhi's understanding of 'realpolitik' meant that unlike her father, she was not unduly preoccupied with altruistic and idealistic aspirations of non-alignment; rather she embraced the concept by looking at it from a 'balance of power' perspective. The Indo-Soviet Treaty of Peace and Friendship of September 1971 must be seen in this prism.

Clear and congruent strategic objectives from both the PM and the defence minister, along with effective politico-military interfaces between the service chiefs and key interlocutors from the prime minister's office resulted in a commonality of purpose. Capacity building was given top priority and the service chiefs enjoyed a fair degree of independence when it came to designing their concept of operations. Even though the Indian Army and its talismanic chief Manekshaw retained their importance as 'first among equals' in a predominantly land-centric armed forces, Indira Gandhi and Jagjivan Ram, her portly and jovial defence minister, realized the value of air and maritime power in a two-front battle. Due credit must go to their chiefs, Air Chief Marshal P.C. Lal and Admiral S.M. Nanda, for transforming Indian air and sea power into powerful and flexible tools of military power, which had the ability to contribute significantly to a joint military campaign. This ensured that Manekshaw as chairman of the Chiefs of Staff Committee had no other choice but to create joint war-fighting capability by amalgamating air and sea power into his overall theatre battle plans in both the eastern and western theatre.

Standing Up to the US

There is little doubt that the metamorphosis and 'hardening' of Indian diplomacy took place in the run-up to the 1971 conflict. Recently declassified White House conversations of President Nixon with Kissinger reveal him as a self-serving president with little interest or empathy for the developing world in general, and South Asia in particular. Kissinger, on the other hand comes across as a brilliant, hard-driving and mercurial czar of US diplomacy – he understood the crisis, but chose to go along with Nixon on the path to restoring relations with China as that is where he felt lay the most tangible gains for US foreign policy.[12] As the crisis unfolded and the Indo-Pak war ended in a decisive victory for India, both Nixon and Kissinger were clearly irked by Indira Gandhi's assertiveness and refusal to cower before US hegemony in the region. Her refusal to get rattled by the posturing of the Seventh Fleet only increased their frustration at not being able to coerce India into ceasing military operations before its objectives were met. Hardball realpolitik coupled with a fair degree of empathy for the suffering population of East Pakistan forced Indira Gandhi to 'do the right thing' and wage what can easily be called today a 'just war'.

Operational Takeaways

What then were the major operational takeaways from the 1971 war from an Indian perspective? While much of the current discourse on the 1971 war concentrates excessively on the meticulous military planning and orchestration at the highest level, particularly at Eastern Army Command Headquarters, it is the conversion of that plan into more than just successful operational outcomes that takes pole position. This was only possible because of the initiative and innovation by field commanders like Lieutenant General Sagat Singh, Captain Swaraj Prakash, Group Captain Wollen and Group Captain Chandan Singh. Had Sagat Singh not bypassed Akhaura, Bhairab Bazar and Sylhet; had Chandan Singh not responded as he did when it came to urging the Mi-4 helicopter crews to press on regardless as they transported men, logistics, ammunition and artillery guns across the River Meghna; had Wollen not asked his MiG-21 pilots to experiment with steep-dive attacks on Tezgaon airfield; and had Swaraj Prakash and Major General Uban not kept almost half a division tied down in the Chittagong sector, Dacca may not have fallen when it did.

For the first time after Independence, India made serious attempts at shaping the battlefield in the sector of its choice, the eastern sector, before engaging in full-scale operations. Whether it was covert operations by small teams of R&AW-trained Mukti Bahini operatives initially, or large battalion-sized incursions from November onwards, the psychological impact of the Mukti Bahini can hardly be disputed. Lieutenant General Shammi Mehta puts the overall contribution of the Mukti Bahini in the right perspective by praising them effusively:

> One of the greatest contributions of the Mukti Bahini was in providing intelligence for manoeuvre. If I had to manoeuvre in a vacuum in Bangladesh, I would have ended up waging attrition warfare like in the western sector. During the initial stages of the war, we almost exactly knew where the enemy was thanks to the Mukti Bahini and later on, even if we did not, we could predict their moves thanks to the inputs given by the Mukti Bahini.[13]

In the western theatre, though, the Indian Army entered the war with a rather defensive mindset much to the chagrin of Lieutenant General Candeth, the commander of the Western Army Command. The concept of 'Offensive defence', which gained traction from Army HQ, had its merits as the war on the western front unfolded. It called for exploiting fleeting opportunities while retaining a defensive balance; dynamic generals like Pinto exploited this flexibility and tasted success in Shakargarh and Basantar with a refreshingly aggressive approach at every stage. Up north, an aggressive corps commander like Sartaj Singh managed to stabilize Chhamb and score victory after victory in northern Kashmir, Kargil and Turtok sectors. However, despite making good progress, an inspirational leader like Major General Zorawar Chand Bakshi was held back in a defensive role after making spectacular progress in the Chicken's Neck area. Holding the west was imperative for the success of India's two-front strategy.

General Shammi Mehta highlighted that in all of India's earlier wars, attrition warfare ruled the roost without much success whenever two forces bashed against each other head-on without much success, inspired by what he calls the 'hierarchical inheritance of Montgomery, the grand-dad of attrition warfare'. He points out that wherever the Indian Army tasted success in 1971, it was because of prosecuting manoeuvre warfare.[14] Dispelling the widespread notion that only armoured corps officers possessed the mindset of a manoeuvrist, General Pinto, a hard-core infantryman, looked at manoeuvre as a state of the mind and not merely a movement of forces on the ground. He went on further to highlight that proactive and reactive strategies of warfare were merely an extension of manoeuvre and attrition warfare. Pakistan, he added, were purely reactive in 1971. When asked whether he was surprised that Pakistan did not use their idle armoured division (6 Armoured Division) against his 54 Division, he chuckled and said, 'Had they done so, I would probably not be here talking to you.' He was equally critical that India's idle and sole armoured division (1 Armoured Division) was not rushed to his sector once he had made inroads. Closing the discussion on the battle of Basantar, he laughed his still infectious laugh and said, 'The offensive–defensive concept still baffles me.' In the overall context, however, it was a balanced mix of manoeuvre, aggression and offensive defence that resulted in a comprehensive military victory for India.

The next major operational takeaway from a joint perspective was that training, logistics and infrastructure requirements had been well anticipated by India in the six months prior to the war. Across the border, the Pakistan Armed forces had got lethargic and used to the trappings of political power. Their army was mainly engaged in 'mass-killing operations' in East Pakistan, and was not really prepared for war. When asked how his division trained for war, the ninety-two-year-old General Pinto said, 'We were much better prepared than the formations had been in 1965. As the divisional commander, I spent a lot of time in conceptual thinking and then testing these concepts during sand-model discussions. Though the peacetime location of my division was in Secunderabad, we made regular visits to the I Corps HQ at Mathura and onwards to our operational locations. We knew exactly what we had to do when the balloon went up. Intellectual sharpness is essential in modern warfare; the air chief, P.C. Lal, was one of those with a sharp and incisive mind,' he chuckled.

While the IAF went about building airfields, stringing across air defence networks and developing innovative tactics,[15] the PAF had slackened its usually stringent operational training. It failed to build on the operational successes during the 1965 war despite best attempts by Air Marshal Nur Khan, the PAF chief during the interim years, to keep pace with the IAF.[16] The IAF gained complete air superiority over East Pakistan in a few days and flew over 2,300 sorties of fighters, helicopters and transport aircraft.

With near parity in the western sector between the IAF and PAF, the IAF flew more than twice the number of sorties in 1971 compared to 1965.[17] Furthermore, though it was not able to achieve complete air superiority, it was able to keep down the PAF and prevent it from operating to its full potential. The PAF suffered greater attrition in the 1971 war as compared to 1965 and had to reckon with a resurgent IAF as the war progressed. Interdiction of follow-on forces and operational support requirements by the IAF proved to be quite decisive when it came to denying the Pakistan Army of reinforcements when they were needed the most. The innovative bombing of a Pak artillery brigade in Haji Pir and the largest ammunition dump in the Changa Manga forest by

An-12 transport aircraft led by the brilliant Wing Commander Vashisht contributed immensely to the IAF's deep interdiction campaign. He too was awarded the Maha Vir Chakra for his exploits in battle. Though Lal had articulated a departure from old aerial strategies, the temptation of creating an impact by *Strategic Interdiction* was too great and the IAF did carry out some effective strikes on the Kiamari oil refineries at Karachi harbour, Sui gas plant in Sind, Mangala dam and the Attock oil refinery near Rawalpindi. Even though some Indian military historians have questioned the impact of such strikes on a short war such as the one fought in 1971,[18] their offensive flavour certainly had an impact on the Pakistani mindset and demonstrated India's willingness to strike deep in order to hurt an adversary's economic potential.

The seriousness with which the Indian Navy went about operationalizing its new missile boats was reflected in the audacious manner in which they were used during the war. A holistic and integrated approach to preparing for war paid rich dividends for India. Deception was executed successfully as a mission of war by concealing the presence of the aircraft carrier INS *Vikrant* as it lay in wait in the Andamans. Another instance of effective deception by the Indian Navy was seen during the missile attacks on Karachi wherein the crew of the missile boats communicated with each other in Russian, baffling the Pakistanis. With the Indian Navy's Carrier Battle Group performing well in the Bay of Bengal, concepts of 'sea control' took seed in the Indian Navy as it sought to build significant asymmetry vis-à-vis the Pakistan Navy. Indigenization of warship design commenced in right earnest after the 1971 war and would pay rich dividends in the years to come. The Pakistan Navy, on the other hand, failed to put together an offensive naval strategy, preferring instead to rely on the deterrent capabilities of its submarine fleet.

One of the biggest strategic and operational 'ifs' of the 1971 war would have been: 'If' Manekshaw had acquiesced in Indira Gandhi's compulsions of wanting to go into East Pakistan in April 1971, would there have been a different end result? Despite many distinguished analysts having since debated Manekshaw's conservative approach, I believe there would have been a less than favourable outcome for several reasons. First and most importantly, the 'eyes and ears' of the Indian

Army, the Mukti Bahini, would not have been the 'force multiplier', as they eventually turned out to be. This would have meant that India's field commanders would have operated in an intelligence vacuum similar to the one that existed on the western front. Their ensuing progress would have been significantly slower than what actually happened, considering that there would have been no Mukti Bahini to nibble, snipe and harass the Pakistanis in the hinterland. The second reason for a different outcome would have been the absence of an 'enveloping strategy' that Manekshaw had envisaged. As discussed earlier in the book, Manekshaw's staff had candidly told him that in the option for an operation in April/May, it was only the 'western option' with an entry into East Pakistan from Bengal that could be supported logistically. This meant that only XXXIII Corps and II Corps would have been available for operations in full strength and fully stocked. As it turned out, these corps made the slowest progress during the final campaign. Considering the larger distance from the west to Dacca and the more than formidable river obstacles, whether Dacca could have been threatened in the time frame that it eventually was would be well next to impossible to predict. The last major reason for the likely stalling of an early attack was the possibility of getting bogged down by the monsoon should operational momentum be impacted by various reasons.

In the desert sector too, 'if' the commander of the Southern Army Command, Lieutenant General Bewoor, had had a backup force, he could have been more aggressive; 'if' Major General Khambatta, the divisional commander of 12 Infantry Division, had cut off Pakistan Army's 18 Division as it retreated after getting a bloody nose at Longewala despite all his logistics and terrain constraints; 'if' the IAF had been less ecstatic about its exploits at Longewala and pursued the retreating Pakistani brigade in close coordination with 12 Infantry Division; the Indian forces could have scored a major victory in the desert and even contemplated threatening the town of Rahim Yar Khan.

Coming to the psychological dimension of the Bangladesh campaign, Niazi's will to resist was broken by a combination of 'feeling enveloped' from all directions. The immense pressure exerted on him by a 'manoeuvrist' commander in the form of Sagat Singh, who used the third dimension of aerial pressure effectively in tandem with the Tangail paradrop, effectively broke his will to resist. When combined with the precision strike by IAF MiG-21s and Hunters on the Government House in Dacca, the psychological disintegration of Niazi's forces was complete and Pakistan's field commanders were convinced that it was better to surrender than be held responsible for an inevitable defeat and heavy loss of life. Commenting on the contribution of operational commanders and staff at headquarters, Shammi Mehta says:

> If there was no Sagat Singh and no Chandan Singh, there would have been no Dacca. If there was no Jacob (Lieutenant General Jacob was chief of staff at Eastern Command HQ), there would have been no spectacular surrender. One was a genius with troops and the other a genius with manipulating the mind of the enemy. It is as simple as that.[19]

Leadership

The 1971 war reaffirmed the importance of inspirational senior leadership in battle and heralded the emergence of a new fighting class amongst younger officers and men of India's armed forces, most of whom were born in the late 1930s and 1940s. Identifying talent and nurturing it for operational effect seemed to be the forte of all the three chiefs. While Manekshaw placed all the talented officers who had worked with him at Eastern Command, Defence Services Staff College and Infantry School, like Lieutenant General Aurora, Major General Jacob, Lieutenant General Sagat Singh and Major General Inder Gill, in key positions prior to the 1971 war, Lal too had his men like Malse, Wollen and Chandan Singh as his point men at key places. In Krishnan, Kohli and Swaraj Prakash, Admiral Nanda had chosen an excellent team to execute the naval campaigns on the eastern and western seaboards.

An old military adage says, 'There are no good troops or bad troops, only good or bad leaders.' What then were the leadership traits of the successful field commanders of the Indian armed forces in the 1971 war? While all the three services displayed higher leadership skills of an exceptional order, there were some stand-out performances. While initiative and momentum were exploited well by Pinto in Basantar, Sartaj in Kargil and Zorawar Bakshi in the Chicken's Neck sector, Swaraj Prakash, the captain of INS *Vikrant*, dominated the eastern seas off the East Pakistan coast just as Chandan Singh used all his experience from the 1962 conflict to orchestrate the heli-borne operations. However, it was not too difficult to single out the one operational leader who stood head and shoulders over the rest – Sagat Singh.

Sagat was a go-getter from his younger days and General Pinto remembers him as a dashing type at the Infantry School and even later as a divisional commander when he controlled the Mizo insurgency in 1966 and gave a bloody nose to the Chinese in 1967 during two successive encounters at Nathula and Chola passes. Sagat Singh not only inspired officers and troops from the Indian Army under his command but also transmitted his aggression to many IAF helicopter pilots who served in the eastern sector. Air Vice Marshal 'Harry' Ahluwalia, one of the IAF's most distinguished and operationally proficient helicopter pilots, recalls his association with Sagat when the latter was commanding 101 Communication Zone as a major general in 1966 during the early years of insurgency in the north-eastern region of the country:

> Soon after the Mizo trouble started in 1966 General Sagat, then a major general, was posted to Shillong as the GOC 101 Communication Zone area. There used to be a four-Mi-4 detachment of 110 Helicopter Unit in Kumbhigram to look after the operations in Mizoram. Actually I am one of the pioneers of the Mizo operations having taken part in them from in March 1966 when the trouble first erupted. Anyway, General Sagat used to visit Mizoram very often as that was the only operational area that he had under his HQ. He also became very friendly with us chopper guys as we would fly him around, and we would do anything for him. He once planned to attack a Mizo camp in East Pakistan. I was the detachment commander in Aizawl (I don't really have the date with me but it must have been in 1967–68). He wanted fourteen army guys to go in the chopper as he had information that the camp in Zupui (across the border with Mizoram) had some hostiles staying there. I agreed to do the job. Our plan was to drop them there and they would do what they had to do and return across the border. In those days communications were

> almost non-existent and so there was no way of informing the unit which was then in Tezpur. In any case we never told the commanding officer or the flight commander what we did on detachment. Choppers in those days had very limited experience and we would just read what the Yanks did in Vietnam and try and emulate that. I can relate many such stories to you. I did the sortie for him, and we dropped the guys where we were supposed to, but they found the camp to be deserted. General Sagat too was on board the chopper.
>
> I say this only to show that the guy was willing to take chances and I as a young flying officer, and others like me, were quite in awe of him. He had a very easy way about him and frankly we felt honoured to do what we could for him. The army guys used to tell us that the 101 Communication Zone posting was a full stop for him, but his success in Mizoram saw to it that he made it to Lieutenant General. Little wonder then that many years later he still turned to 110 HU to spearhead the airlift into East Pakistan during 1971.

What of the younger lot? They were represented by officers and men like Hoshiar Singh, Arun Khetarpal, Albert Ekka, Don Lazarus, Nirmaljit Sekhon, Arun Prakash, and Bahadur Nariman Kavina, who commanded INS *Nipat*, the missile boat during the Karachi attack. Bold and fearless, and reflecting the true diversity of independent India, they would prove to be role models for the next generation of war fighters who would be blooded in a completely new genre of warfare. The 1971 war further demolished the martial race proposition, with troops from the southern part of India and the tribal belt of central India acquitting themselves with honour in various battles, foremost amongst them being in the battles of Akhaura, Basantar and Shakargarh.[20]

Final Thoughts

Like most major decisions of war in the twentieth century, India's decisions to go to wars during the period 1947–71 were primarily political ones. Whenever these political decisions were accompanied by sound military advice, India's armed forces emerged victorious. Nehru's reluctance to send a backup brigade to Srinagar in 1948 to follow 161 Brigade as it drove the raiders back towards Domel and

Muzaffarabad occurred because he relied more on the military advice of his British C-in-C, rather than on his young Indian commanders. Had he immediately sent in a backup brigade, the final ceasefire line could have been different. Similarly, the reluctance to allow the RIAF to attack bridges at Domel and Muzaffarabad allowed the raiders to withdraw and be replaced instead by regulars of the Pakistan Army. It emerges now that there was a clear vacuum of military advice as Nehru replaced one British C-in-C with another one as the war progressed. Compare this with all the major decisions of WW II where Roosevelt and Churchill completely dominated their military commanders, but listened to them when they were offered sage military advice. The likes of Eisenhower, Marshall, Montgomery and Alan Brooke were known to mince no words when it came to placing the right military template over a political one and empowering their operational leaders to fight their battles as they deemed fit.

Indira Gandhi and Jagjivan Ram were no great strategic geniuses, nor were they endowed with a sound understanding of matters military. Where they played their cards well in 1971 was when they gave clear political objectives and adequate space and respect to the service chiefs, who in turn came up with sage advice that was well taken and woven into an overall grand strategy. In the final analysis, India's victory in the 1971 war proved that if effectively used, India's armed forces could emerge as a cutting-edge tool of statecraft. Strong political will, synergy between all stakeholders of national security and a fierce national spirit to overcome adversity against all odds cleared the fog of war and resulted in a decisive victory. The aftermath of the 1971 war was a good opportunity for introspection and thinking about how wars of the future would be fought and whether there was a need to improve 'jointmanship' at every level, be it in the politico-military domain, or between the three services.

Writing in her brilliantly researched but controversial book on some of the lesser-known happenings during the birth of Bangladesh titled *Dead Reckoning*, Oxford historian Sarmila Bose, a Bengali herself, writes:

> Flying helicopters in the dark during the war, pilots used 'dead reckoning' when one's best judgement was that by going in a particular direction for a certain time one was likely to arrive at the

> intended destination … Navigating through the conflicting memories of 1971 seemed a very similar journey. There is only partial visibility and many treacherous twists and turns with plenty of room for error. Yet by steering a firm course charted by an open mind, research based on evidence and corroboration, fairness to all sides and analysis anchored on data … one is likely to arrive, inshallah, at the best approximation of the ideal destination.[21]

With all humility and a quest for the truth with objectivity, I have tried in this book with all earnestness to uphold the principles of *Dead Reckoning* as suggested by Sarmila Bose. Not only do pilots resort to dead reckoning, even paratroopers and special forces resort to it when they find themselves over unfamiliar territory – sniffing their way to the target based on prior knowledge, a gut feeling and complete situational awareness.

Sydney Schanberg of *The New York Times* was among the few international reporters with a prolonged ringside view of the war in East Pakistan. When I approached him to offer some insights into military operations in Bangladesh, the eighty-year-old journalist replied very graciously in an email to me: 'Your project is very interesting and I can say that all my experiences with the Indian Armed Forces were very positive and impressive. Their professionalism and fairness were always in sight. Good luck with your project.'[22]

PART V

Conclusion

28

REMEMBERING KAUTILYA

Kautilya, also known as Chanakya and Vishnugupta, was a master strategist who was well-versed in the Vedas (Hindu religious texts) and adept at creating intrigues and devising political stratagems.[1]

– L.N. Rangarajan

Kautilya and India's Modern Wars

As I crossed the finish line, I wondered how Kautilya, India's master strategist of ancient times, would have assessed the manner in which India conducted itself during all its wars and conflicts after Independence. Despite India's spectacular success in 1971, he would have been largely critical, I reckoned. Nevertheless, I thought it would be worthwhile to benchmark how a fledgling modern state prosecuted war and statecraft against some of the principles and templates of war postulated by him around two thousand years ago.

For the uninitiated, Kautilya was said to be a key advisor or minister in the court of Chandragupta Maurya, the founder of the powerful Maurya Dynasty which ruled India between 322 and 185 BC. Kautilya's claim to fame rests on a series of texts that are believed to have been initiated by him on statecraft under the title *Arthashastra*. The treatise covers the entire range of strategies, policies, tenets of leadership and governance which a king must follow to ensure that his subjects get to live in a prosperous and secure nation state. Not revered in India as much as Confucius and Sun Tzu are in China, or Clausewitz and Machiavelli in the West, Kautilya is the closest that any Indian strategist has come to propounding realpolitik and understanding military organizations and war as key tools of statecraft. His work seemed to have disappeared for a long time in a patchwork conglomerate of states that India was in the Middle Ages – a fragmented polity that seemed to have reconciled to being dominated by invaders and colonists like the Mughals and the British for almost six centuries. It re-emerged in the early part of the twentieth century in the sleepy south Indian town of Mysore where Shama Sastry, a Sanskrit scholar, set about translating a parchment that was given to him by a fellow scholar.

When this patchwork called India finally did attain Independence, it did so by waging war of a different kind on its colonial masters – a war that was based on satyagraha and ahimsa, and not on structured violence that the world commonly knew as war. Interestingly, Nehru's dilemmas about the manner in which independent India would conduct statecraft seem to have deepened after he read Shama Sastry's translation of *Arthashastra*; the ruthless wielding of power and the overwhelming dominance of the state over the individual seems to have disturbed him. These dilemmas were then articulated by him in a series of essays written in the 1930s under the pseudonym of Chanakya, which clearly indicated his discomfort with the realpolitik of Kautilya.[2] Though a number of researchers have indicated that India's post-Independence obsession with idealism, liberalism and morality as the main pillars of statecraft meant that Kautilya was consigned to the periphery of strategic thinking, one of his few supporters was K.P.S. Menon, independent India's first foreign secretary. He once noted in 1947 that 'realism of Kautilya is a useful corrective to our idealism in international politics'.[3]

As a result of independent India's rather pacifist strategic orientation, war as a proactive tool of statecraft remained a peripheral tool for decades till Indira Gandhi discovered its importance in 1971. Understanding war as more than mere combat – as a complex and interconnected set of activities across layers of human interaction – Kautilya looked at hard power as exercised by the military as an important element of statecraft.[4] Its effectiveness, however, depended on the manner in which the king used it along with diplomacy and covert operations. Avoidance of war, according to Kautilya, was the ultimate test of the efficiency of a king and his army. I guess they call it deterrence these days! Let us look at a few critical principles of employment of the military as proffered by Kautilya and see whether India's military has looked at them with some seriousness. I have heard of seminars being conducted from time to time on the relevance of Kautilya in modern statecraft, but very rarely has there been any critical dissection of Indian statecraft in the Nehruvian era against Kautilyan principles of hard-nosed realpolitik. This was only natural because the liberal and altruistic flavour of modern Indian democracy did not see eye to eye with it. Many of the principles of *Arthashastra* support what we could call today enlightened autocracy. However, much of his treatise also endorses the sustenance of a disciplined democracy, the likes of which have sprung up in countries like Singapore and Switzerland. But that is straying from the military dimension of *Arthashastra*.

Important Sources

The primary source of my offering is the book *Kautilya: The Arthashastra*, edited, rearranged, translated and introduced by L.N. Rangarajan, a diplomat and scholar of the highest pedigree. It is a difficult read, but instructive and illuminating, as one grapples with the subtle nuances of statecraft in an era long gone by. Some military tenets that I felt were relevant to modern warfare as experienced by the Indian armed forces in recent times are discussed in subsequent paragraphs. Two other excellent papers on Kautilyan thought have proved to be immensely helpful. The first is a well-written dissertation on Kautilyan strategy by Wing Commander Vinay Vittal (now group captain) for his master's degree at the School for Advanced Air and Space Power Studies, United States Air Force Academy.[5] The second paper is a robust academic piece in the *Journal of Military History*, January 2003, by Professor Roger Boesche, a professor of politics and history in the US, entitled 'Kautilya's Arthashastra on War and Diplomacy in Ancient India'.[6] Both these studies do not refer to any of India's modern conflicts and address only Kautilya's thought. The following paragraphs attempt to benchmark much of what has happened in contemporary Indian military history against some of his ancient tenets.

Some Tenets

Higher Leadership

Comparing Kautilya's treatise with Machiavellian radicalism in the realm of realism as a tool of political strategy, Max Weber, the famous German political philosopher of the late nineteenth and early twentieth centuries calls Machiavelli's *The Prince* harmless.[7] Kautilya often writes on the 'responsibilities of a leader in defending his subjects from external aggression'. Unlike Roosevelt, Churchill and Mao, Nehru's approach to the role of force and the military in statecraft demonstrated ambivalence and reluctance with a touch of 'forced realism' when pushed against the wall. Writing to me on this in early 2015 as part of a critique on my book, a young and perceptive group captain very incisively wrote:

> Also, Nehru's remark about not needing any Army makes sense to me after reading his *Glimpses of World History*. Despite his breadth and depth of history, his anti-military bias shows up in his offhand remarks to Indira throughout the book. I found it very surprising that despite his intellect showing through in his analyses, he was blind to the reality of Force as a permanent catalyst for the flow of history.

While Churchill and Mao had military experience that empowered them to take decisive military action during times of crisis, Roosevelt was a keen student of military history and strategy and had a core group of trusted military officers like Eisenhower and George Marshall to help him navigate through WW II. Nehru had no such interest – his judgement about matters military in fact was clouded by his experience with India's non-violent struggle for independence to such an extent that he started believing in it as a tool for the creation of a new international order based on altruism and idealism. Rather than understanding military strategy and war fighting, he devoted much of his focus towards civil–military relations and reducing the risks of a military takeover.[8] Many of Nehru's admirers assert that he did after all use force extensively when peaceful attempts at conflict resolution failed, but all these applications were reactive rather than proactive, be it in J&K (1947–48), Hyderabad (1948) or Goa (1961). Reactive deterrence of the kind that India displayed by rolling out the Forward Policy in 1961 without adequate coercive capability became a cornerstone of India's national security posture for years to come!

Operational Preparation for War

Kautilya is emphatic when he says that an army that has marched for days and is tired and hungry before battle is half defeated already. He also refers to how when troops are directly inducted into battle without any acclimatization, it adversely impacts the way they fight. In October 1947, fresh and highly motivated troops of the Sikh and Kumaon Regiments were airlifted to Srinagar and fought off numerically superior raiders from Pakistan because they were better led, well motivated and battle-hungry as they fought for a cause. In the case of 7 Brigade at Namka Chu in 1962, Brigadier Dalvi and his men were exhausted by the time they occupied makeshift defences. Similarly, the Chhamb brigade prior to the 1971 war was geared up for offensive operations. When they were suddenly asked to fight a defensive battle instead, they floundered because they did not have enough time to prepare well-fortified defences. One of Kautilya's tenets in the build-up before war states: 'Till the enemy's weakness is known, he should be kept on friendly terms.'[9]

This is exactly what Mao Zedong and Zhou Enlai did with India for almost seven years after the Panchsheel Agreement was signed between the two countries. China used that time to build an unassailable power differential vis-à-vis India before striking at a time and point of its own choosing.

Arthashastra talks about an army that is not abandoned in war and left leaderless without reinforcements. The story of India's defeat in the Eastern Sector in 1962 is replete with examples where these principles were abandoned as the corps commander, Lieutenant General Kaul, fled the battle scene to recuperate from a mysterious illness in Delhi. In Ladakh, however, reinforcements for the defence of Leh and Chushul and decisive leadership by Lieutenant General Daulat Singh, the army commander, and Brigadier 'Tappy' Raina made the Chinese think twice before pushing forward in Phase II of the battle. They settled for a clear victory in the east and stopped short of complete victory in the west because Mao upheld some of Sun Tzu's tencts that called for an avoidance of a complete humiliation of the enemy. Chanakya also clearly said in his treatise: 'It is better to allow an army to withdraw than perish in a frontal battle. It should not be allowed to be sandwiched between a frontal enemy and an enemy in the rear.'[10]

The debacle at Namka Chu was because of the vulnerability of 7 Brigade to a frontal assault and its subsequent encirclement. The Sela garrison too faced the same contingency and came up short on strategies to counter it despite numerous accounts of individual gallantry and the presence of a battle-proven field commander in the form of Brigadier Hoshiar Singh.

Calamities

In its own subtle way, *Arthashastra* very succinctly deals with the vagaries of the seasons, weather and logistics, and their impact on military organizations and the conduct of war. Rather aptly called *calamities,* the treatise looks at almost thirty of these calamities that deal with a variety of issues related to human hygiene, environment and morale. An interesting calamity that Kautilya refers to is the *cutting of an army's supply of grain,*[11] and how if grain is brought in from under the enemy's nose, it could act as a significant morale booster. In the early spring of 1948, Brigadier Pritham Singh, the Poonch garrison commander during the almost year-long siege of the town, realized that food stocks were dwindling rapidly and that the aerial supplies were not going to be sufficient to sustain the civil population through the harsh winter. To supplement his grain stock, Pritham Singh organized audacious raids against enemy posts in the hills around Poonch with the aim of bringing back as much as wheat, rice and other staple food like potatoes and lentils. Emboldened by the success of this operation, he then encouraged villagers to farm their lands around Poonch during hours of daylight under armed escort, withdrew them into the garrison by evening, set up ambushes by night, and dared the enemy to upset this plan. This clearly rattled the enemy and lifted the morale of the nearly 40,000 civilians in Poonch when the grain was finally harvested months later.[12] Over two decades later, Manekshaw clearly took note of many of these *calamities* as he prepared for the 1971 war. He ensured that the fighting season was right by doing his staff checks correctly and resisted pressure from Indira Gandhi to commence hostilities before the onset of the monsoon.

Covert Operations

Kautilya strongly advocated what he called *covert activities* as a means of degrading the fighting potential of the adversary before he actually did battle. He said, 'Miraculous results can be achieved by practising the methods of subversion.' He advocated what he called clandestine war (*Gudayuddha*), using covert methods to achieve the objective without actually waging a battle. To engage in clandestine war, he advocated the use of agents, analysts, double agents, allies, vassal kings, tribal chiefs and supporters of the enemy.[13]

Military intelligence operations were an intrinsic element of the Crown's strategy to keep track of its frontiers, particularly in the early part of the twentieth century when the Russian Empire emerged as a strong competitor in the 'Great Game' that was being played for control of Central Asia. The other role for British Military Intelligence in India was to keep close track of the activities of the leaders of India's freedom movement. Many arrests, incarcerations and deaths were attributed to the activities of intelligence operatives of the Crown. Soon after Independence Nehru practically demolished all structures of military intelligence and handed over the conduct of covert warfare to the Intelligence Bureau (IB), a new organization that was not really geared up for any meaningful covert operations in hostile territory. Military intelligence is vital for creating a multifaceted mosaic of likely battle spaces, which then allows a military commander to assess enemy deployments and plan military operations. Penetration of enemy lines and operational areas for intelligence gathering is best done by agents with a military background, much like what British Intelligence achieved behind German lines in France during WW II. With this arm barely functional in the 1950s, India's strategic planners were virtually blind to what was happening in Aksai Chin and Tibet and had to make do with scanty IB reports.

Indira Gandhi used this form of warfare to great effect before conventional military operations commenced in East Pakistan in December 1971. Not only did she employ the R&AW for this purpose, she assigned similar covert tasks to the Indian Army as the possibilities of armed encounters during the process of intelligence gathering increased when India and Pakistan closed in to do battle. Realizing very astutely that she needed to buy time to allow her three chiefs to prepare their forces for conventional war, she needed to exert pressure on the East Pakistan military establishment. This, she hoped, would impose some check on the mass killings, reduce the flow of refugees into India, and exert constant psychological pressure on the Pakistan military. This was where the R&AW and co-opted officers from the Indian Army and Indian Air Force exploited the wave of anger amongst the East Bengalis towards their West Pakistani rulers, and used it to train the Mukti Bahini or Mukti Fauj. This covert force exerted pressure on the Pakistani military in every way for over six months (May–December 1971). The two major successes of this initiative were psychological degradation of the enemy and the building of a good intelligence picture, both of which contributed significantly to the success of the December campaign. Readers would recollect having read earlier in the book that a signals officer of the Indian Army infiltrated into the Tangail area well before the airborne operation to provide operational intelligence from the area.

Operational Flavour

Kautilya studied not only higher strategy but delved deep into operational art and even battlefield tactics, offering perspectives that have stood the test of time. His three maxims of generalship encompassed professional excellence and knowledge of strategy and tactics, individual warrior skills; and an understanding of all the wings of the military and their integration (what we call today 'jointmanship').[14] Kautilya's understanding of the importance of chariots is akin to the attributes of modern-day armoured fighting vehicles. He looked at chariots not only as offensive and manoeuvre elements that can break up the enemy and make an 'awesome noise', but also as defensive elements that can 'protect the army'. The employment of the Indian Army's 2 Independent Armoured Brigade in the battle of Assal Uttar (Khem Karan sector) in the 1965 war was a classic 'defensive' deployment of armour that was subsequently converted into offensive action. Staying in the sector and giving due credit to the enemy, Pakistan's initial success at Khem Karan was a result of Major

General Gurbaksh Singh's 4 Mountain Division being surprised by the emergence of Major General Nasir Ahmed's 1 Armoured Division behind the lead assaulting division, 11 Infantry Division. Kautilya offers his perspective: 'The conqueror may conceal a strong force behind a weak force and when the weak force has penetrated the enemy ranks, reinforce the attack with the strong one.'

Staying with the 1965 war, Kautilya writes that 'any force which has to fight facing the sun or the wind shall be attacked'. When IAF Vampire jets rushed to Chhamb on the evening of 1 September, they were flying westwards into the sun and were easy picking for the PAF Sabres waiting over the battle area.

Motivation, Inspiration and Leadership

Inspiring and motivating troops to willingly walk into the 'jaws of death' for their nation, their regiment or their leader is one of the most important tasks assigned to leadership prior to battle. Kautilya says, 'The conqueror shall collect his forces and say to them: "I am as much a servant of the state as you are; we shall share the wealth of this state. Attack these, mine enemies."'[15] India's commanders have been no less inspiring prior to many of their successful battles. Brigadier Mohammad Usman, one of India's finest battlefield commanders in the 1947–48 conflict with Pakistan and the senior-most Indian military officer to lay down his life in the line of duty during that conflict, delivered one of the most inspiring pre-battle orders prior to his brigade's successful assault on Jhangar in March 1948. The officers received the message in English, while the men received it in Hindi. It read:

> Comrades of 50 Parachute Brigade Group, Time has come when our planning and preparation for the recapture of Jhangar has to be put to test. It is not an easy task but I am confident of success – because our plan is sound and our preparations have been good. More so, because I have complete confidence in you all to do your best to recapture the ground we lost on 24 December and to retrieve the honour of our arms. The eyes of the world are on us. The hopes and aspirations of our countrymen are based upon our efforts. We must not falter – we must not fail them.[16]

> So forward friends, fearless we go to Jhangar. India expects everyone to do his duty.

Similarly, during the early days after Pakistan's surprise attack in Chhamb in 1965, the morale of IAF pilots in Pathankot was pretty low and one of the catalysts for a turnaround was an inspirational talk given by a young wing commander, Johnny Green, who urged all pilots to 'conquer your fears and seek battle with the Sabres'. By the end of the war, the Gnats came to be known as 'Sabre Slayers' and carried that reputation into the 1971 war.

While visionary higher leadership and strategic acumen were in short supply many a time during India's early wars after Independence, these were finally demonstrated in full measure in the 1971 war. There has, however, been no shortage of inspirational, operational and tactical leadership on the battlefield, in the air or on the high seas. Thimayya, Usman Somnath Sharma, Mehar Singh and others in 1948; Subedar Joginder Singh, Major Shaitan Singh and the numerous unsung transport and helicopter pilots in 1962; Lieutenant General Harbaksh Singh, Lieutenant Colonel Tarapore and the bunch of Gnat pilots in 1965; and finally, Lieutenant Generals Sagat Singh and Sartaj Singh, Group Captains Mally Wollen and Chandan Singh, Second Lieutenant Arun Khetarpal, Major Hoshiar Singh, Lance Naik Ekka, Flying Officer Sekhon, Captain Mulla and Commander Babru Yadav in 1971, all displayed heroism and leadership comparable to the best any nation had to offer at the time. Kautilya would have approved!

Writing in the *The Times of India,* Henry Kissinger, considered by many to be the doyen of twentieth-century realpolitik, argues that '... for Kautilya, power was the dominant reality. It was multidimensional, and its factors were interdependent.'[17] Emphasizing the central theme of the treatise, Kissinger goes on to add, 'The *Arthashastra* sets out, with dispassionate clarity, a vision of how to establish and guard a state while neutralizing, subverting, and (when opportune conditions have been established) conquering its neighbours. The *Arthashastra* encompasses a world of practical statecraft, not philosophical disputation.'[18] Barring the conquering bit, which is out of fashion in modern geopolitical strategy, the rest remains ever so relevant today.

When a nation and its people accept and acknowledge that force application, however undesirable it may seem, is an intrinsic element of statecraft and critical to protecting what is dear to them, military history automatically fits into the main historical discourse. As a result its study will always be continuous and important to policymakers. That is how I reckon Kautilya would have approached the study of military history. Comparing Machiavelli, Sun Tzu and Kautilya, Professor Boesche argues:

> And thus compared to Kautilya and Sun Tzu, Machiavelli's writings on warfare are tired and tedious, filled with nostalgia for long-dead legions that once gained glory. He wanted the public battlefield, the grand spectacle, fame for some and cowardice for others. Sun Tzu and Kautilya did not care a whit for glory and fame. They wanted to win at all costs and to keep casualties—on both sides—to a minimum. Said Sun Tzu, 'For to win one hundred victories in one hundred battles is not the acme of skill. To subdue the enemy without fighting is the acme of skill.' They were also prepared to win in ways Machiavelli would regard as dishonourable and disgraceful—assassination, disinformation, causing quarrels between ministers by bribes or by means of jealousy over a beautiful woman planted as a secret agent, and so on. Machiavelli—who offers no systematic discussion of even guerrilla warfare—would have been easily outmatched by generals reading either Sun Tzu or Kautilya.[19]

In the final analysis, Kautilya may not have been a genius. It is highly probable that *Arthashastra* was left incomplete by him and completed over centuries by a series of scholars from the same school of thought. What is undisputable is the fact that no one after him has been able to convert knowledge into deliverables of statecraft and strategy as he has. His legacy has been one of giving confidence to Indian kings and statesmen that intellect, knowledge and common sense, when combined, make for sustainable and long-lasting power. His treatise is the closest we have come to articulating comprehensive national power in which the military is a key element.

29

POSTSCRIPT

As I conclude, I cannot help but draw a relationship between India's post-Independence strategic culture and the importance given to the study of military history. The yearlong 1947–48 war with Pakistan gave India's fledgling strategic community an opportunity to study three operational scenarios for posterity, and derive strategic lessons, which it did not. The siege of Poonch from November 1947 to November 1948 was not only a remarkable saga of resilience, it was also the first opportunity to study civil–military relations as the Indian Army and Indian Air Force created an environment of trust and faith among the 40,000 civilians and created a template for governance in a combat environment. It was also the first time that the fledgling RIAF embarked on a sustained aerial campaign to keep Poonch supplied in the absence of a road link for almost a year. The fine print of the operation has not been narrated and preserved for posterity. As against this, look at the manner in which the West has told the story of the Berlin airlift as a saga of the triumph of democracy in the form of numerous narratives.

The second example I want to offer is that India lost a golden opportunity to record and study the origins of Pakistan's proxy war as an instrument of state policy. The tribal invasions of 1947 and 1965 were orchestrated by Pakistan's military and supported by the Pakistani political establishment, and yet, when Pakistan unleashed its proxy war in J&K in the early 1990s, India was underprepared! The reason was quite simple – the narrative of extremism and subversion was lost in the interim years as India grappled with much more and basked in the limelight of the 1971 victory.

The third set of operational lessons from 1947–48 that were lost to India's strategic planners for decades were the difficulties faced by General Thimayya as he first attempted to save Skardu and Leh, and then force the raiders to retreat along the Indus to Skardu. Years of strategic lethargy thereafter meant that the problems of high-altitude infrastructure creation and logistics supply were not factored in prior to the 1962 war as India attempted to string together a line of vulnerable defences against the Chinese as part of the ill-fated Forward Policy.

All the three themes that I have talked about are right up the street of a military historian to create interesting narratives. Sadly these stories only formed part of biographies and campaign descriptions. Many such examples are available from both the 1965 and 1971 wars. I will highlight two of them which point to an evolving strategic culture of status quo, compromise, diffidence and misplaced generosity. In 1965, despite having captured the Haji Pir Pass and some other areas in Tithwal and Kargil sectors with some difficulty after losing them in 1947–48, India vacated them without adequate pay-offs and relatively unmindful of the sacrifices involved during their recapture. In 1972, Indira Gandhi's one moment of weakness after Bhutto pleaded with her not to include the resolution of the Kashmir problem in the Simla Agreement still haunts India today. An anxiety to occupy a moral high ground, however divorced from realpolitik, has resulted in India's inability to translate military lessons into strategic ones.

From an Indian perspective, the 1971 war with Pakistan was the last full-blown multi-front war fought by the Indian armed forces. I thought it would be a good idea to take a breather here. There is a flip side though when you take a breather – you see a glass that is half-filled. Now, whether you look at it as half-filled or half-empty depends entirely on you. If you see an opportunity, or a space to be filled, it is half-filled; that is exactly where I see my narrative. My greatest worry as I called a halt to this narrative was whether I had done justice to all the three services – I for one can cross my heart and say that I have tried my 'darn best' and donned a 'purple' uniform as I wrote the book. Interestingly, purple is a colour in India's modern armed forces that depicts 'jointness' and emerges from a fusion of the army's olive green, navy's white and air force's blue. I knew I was on the right track when a young group captain who read my manuscript during the early days told me: 'As I read along, I forgot that you wore the blue uniform of the IAF.'

Over a cup of coffee with Ramachandra Guha at Koshy's, Bangalore, and with Sugata Bose at the National Defence Academy, I expressed my apprehension that writing a book on all the wars and conflicts that India has experienced since Independence, and squeezing it into one volume would be a Herculean task. I also wondered whether a young civilian military history enthusiast, or a captain in the Indian Army on a lonely post at Siachen, would really prefer reading a slimmer volume (something I have failed to achieve as 500-plus pages can hardly be called slim!) from times gone by and digest it thoroughly before moving on to wars and conflict that he or she is more familiar with. Both Guha and Bose agreed with the readership and the rationale I was looking at, and suggested that I split my work into two volumes. Ram Guha, however, cautioned that a second volume would always be more difficult to write. Getting back into the rhythm would be challenging, he said, also adding that I had to be prepared for the long haul. A point of six to eight years is what he said was a reasonable time frame for both volumes to see the light of day. My wife, Mowthika, though, was aghast at hearing about this time frame as it would mean a continuation of the many spells of complete hibernation. It has been over three years since we met at Koshy's and Ram's prediction seems to be right. All I can tell Mowthika now is: 'Hang in there for my sake; it will be worth the effort!' As I wrapped up the book between September and November 2015, I started getting the traditional pre-publication jitters that afflict first-time authors when they see a lot of good writing emerge on a subject that is similar to theirs. In my case the writing emerged from Delhi's various military think tanks on the 1965 war with Pakistan as the country dissected it threadbare fifty years later. However, I was relieved that like much of Indian military history writing so far, it remained service specific. I knew that I could rest easy!

Jai Hind! As we march ahead with blue skies and calm seas around us.

30

FURTHER READING

That men do not learn very much from the lessons of history is the most important of all the lessons that history has to teach.

– Aldous Huxley

This book merely scratches the surface of what has been a fascinating period of modern Indian history. Military history cannot be read in isolation; it has to be complemented with a reasonably sound understanding of social and political history of the time. Ramachandra Guha's *India after Gandhi* provides just the right base before embarking on a detailed study of modern India's military history. It is by far the most definitive, objective and well-researched book on India's post-Independence history.

DNA of India's Armed Forces

My favourite books on Shivaji and the rise of the Maratha Empire are three volumes of the *History of the Mahrattas* by James Grant Duff, an eminent soldier-historian who served in India for much of his life in the eighteenth century. The second is an exhaustively researched book from the heartland of the erstwhile Maratha Empire, Pune, called *Solstice at Panipat: 14 January 1761* by a dentist-turned-military history buff, Uday S. Kulkarni. Khushwant Singh's two-volume *History of the Sikhs* and a definitive work exclusively on Maharaja Ranjit Singh's empire, *The Empire of the Sikhs*, by Jyoti Rai and Patwant Singh offer deep insights into the rise of the martial Sikh community and its contribution to India's recent military history. Jyoti Rai is also the daughter and biographer of Air Chief Marshal Moolgavkar, one of the pioneers of the IAF.

Four books on the colonial legacy and early years of the Indian Army are on my list of 'must reads'. These are Philip Mason's *A Matter of Honour: An Account of the Indian Army, Its Officers and Men;* Dr Anirudh Deshpande's *The British Raj and Its Indian Armed Forces;* Daniel Marston's *The Indian Army and the End of the Raj* and Stephen P. Cohen's *The Indian Army: Its Contribution to the Development of a Nation.* Prof. Steven Wilkinson of Yale University complements the above books with a recent offering – *Army and Nation: The Military and Indian Democracy.* The book offers a deep structural insight into the reasons for the apolitical nature of India's armed forces in the post-Independence years.

The biographies of Field Marshals Wavell and Auchinleck by John Connell provide illuminating perspectives into the growth of the Indian Army in the years preceding Independence – they remain among the best military biographies of the last century. Complementing the widespread colonial narrative of India's armed forces is *His Majesty's Opponent,* an intensely nationalistic biography of Subhas Chandra Bose by his nephew, Harvard professor Sugata Bose. The growth, travails and effect of the INA on Britain's decision to leave India are brilliantly chronicled by Prof. Bose.

Of the three colonial arms of British India's armed forces, the Royal Indian Navy at the time of Independence was the smallest in terms of size and manning. Its historical legacy was tracked best in Bisheshwar Prasad (editor), *The Royal Indian Navy*, published by the Agra University Press. This book was published as part of the 'Official History of The Indian Armed Forces in the Second World War 1939–45'. Rear Admiral Satyindra Singh's *Under Two Ensigns: The Indian Navy 1945–50,* provides an Indian overview of the transition of the Indian Navy, while an Australian naval officer, James Goldrick's *No Easy Answers: The Development of the Navies of India, Pakistan, Bangladesh and Sri Lanka 1945–1996* offers a Western perspective of pre and post-colonial happenings in the Indian Navy. Vice Admiral Mihir Roy's *War in the Indian Ocean* and Vice Admiral Hiranandani's *Transition to Triumph* are comprehensive accounts of not only the early years of the growth of the

Indian Navy and its moment of glory in the 1971 war with Pakistan, but also give a crisp overview of the subsequent growth and development of India as a maritime power.

The early years of Indian military aviation provide for fascinating reading and have been best chronicled by Rana Chinna in his book *Eagle Strikes: The Royal Indian Air Force 1932–1950.* Inspiring personal perspectives on the Burma campaign and the growth of the IAF are offered by Air Chief Marshal P.C. Lal in his autobiography, *My Years with the IAF,* and by Air Commander Jasjit Singh in his biography of the Marshal of the IAF, Arjan Singh, *The Icon.* Air Vice Marshal A.K. Tiwary provides a fighter pilot's aggressive perspective on the exploits of the IAF in battle since its inception in his detailed account called *The Indian Air Force in Wars.*

The First India–Pakistan War of 1947–48

Sumit Ganguly and Chidananda Dasgupta offer compelling geopolitical perspectives with a liberal dosage of military operations in their books titled *The Origins of War in South Asia: Indo-Pak Wars since 1947* and *War and Diplomacy in Kashmir: 1947–48* respectively. Alistair Lamb highlights a well-researched but jaundiced Pakistani perspective in his books *Danger over Kashmir* and *Birth of a Tragedy: Kashmir 1947.* Lieutenant General L.P. Sen, who as a brigadier commanded 161 Brigade that saved Srinagar, vividly describes operations in the Kashmir Valley in his slim volume called *Slender Was the Thread,* while Lieutenant General Eric Vaas has penned down a detailed recollection of operations in the Jammu and Poonch sectors titled *Without Baggage: A Personal Account of the Jammu & Kashmir Operations 1947–49.* Rounding off the list are Air Marshal Bharat Kumar's *The Incredible War: Indian Air Force in Kashmir War 1947–48* and the *Official History of the 1947–48 War with Pakistan,* an offering from the Historical Division of India's Ministry of Defence. Akbar Khan, the architect of the audacious infiltration plan, has penned down his version of the conflict in *Raiders in Kashmir.* It is a fascinating insight into the emergence of early jihadi perspectives in Kashmir; the book, however, is extremely hard to source.

THE 1962 CONFLICT WITH CHINA

An understanding of the wild and uncharted northern and eastern frontiers of colonial India is essential to grapple with events that finally led to the India–China war of 1962. Though known to be an India baiter, Alistair Lamb's Chatham House essay titled *The China-India Border: The Origins of the Disputed Boundaries*, published by Oxford University Press in 1964, is a superbly researched and well-illustrated little book with excellent maps. *The India-China Boundary Problem: 1846–1947* by A. G. Noorani, an eminent Indian lawyer and historian, remains the most well-researched offering by an Indian author.

Numerous books have been written on the India–China war of 1962 from a strategic and operational perspective. Despite its distinct anti-India flavour and the markedly leftist leanings of its author, *India's China War* by Neville Maxwell remains an enduring read. John Garver is a China expert and professor at a leading US university. His chapter 'China's Decision for War with India in 1962,' in *New Approaches to the Study of Chinese Foreign Policy* by Robert S. Ross and Alastair Iain Johnston, remains the most objective Western perspective on the war. Of all the books written by Indian authors, Major General D.K. Palit's *War in the High Himalayas* is a reasonably objective and lucid offering, albeit concentrating mainly on the eastern theatre. For those who want to study the battles in Ladakh, Major General S.V. Thapliyal, who commanded a division in Ladakh, has written an excellent article in the United Services Institution of India Journal titled 'Battle of Eastern Ladakh: 1962 Sino-Indian Conflict'. Rounding off the list is an excellent monograph from the US Army War College, *The Lessons of History: The Chinese People's Liberation Army at 75,* co-authored by Laurie Burkitt, Andrew Scobell and Larry M. Wortzel.

THE 1965 INDIA–PAKISTAN WAR

Stephen P. Cohen's *The Idea of Pakistan* and Sumit Ganguly's *Conflict Unending: India Pakistan Tensions since 1947* are my picks to understanding the strategic nuances of the 1965 war. However, my favourite book remains Sumit Ganguly's first offering on India–Pakistan conflicts, *Origins of War in South Asia: Indo-Pakistan Conflicts since 1947*. Shuja Nawaz's magisterial *Crossed Swords* offers a sweeping narrative of the Pakistan Army through all its triumphs and tribulations. It is by far the best read on the modern Pakistan Army by a Pakistani, though Cohen's *The Pakistan Army*, is an equally 'must' read.

The official history of the war as chronicled by the Indian Ministry of Defence and edited by Dr S.N. Prasad and Dr U.P. Thapliyal, *The India-Pakistan War of 1965*, is a rather voluminous, conservative and chronological account of the conflict from an Indian perspective. It is embellished with excellent maps and is a 'must refer' book. Of all the accounts written by the participants of the war, two accounts stand out as interesting ones. The first one is a ringside view of action on the western front as seen by Lieutenant General Harbaksh Singh, the General Officer Commanding-in-Chief of India's Western Army Command. Titled *War Despatches* it is a hard-hitting account by a battle-hardened soldier. Unsparing of his colleagues and critical of higher military strategy, Harbaksh feels that India could have done better with greater overall aggression. General Mohammed Musa, the chief of the Pakistan Army, offers an interesting but rather apologetic recollection of events in *My Version: India-Pakistan War 1965*. Finally, two books on the air battles during 1965 make worthy reading. The first is a fascinating autobiography of a Pakistani fighter pilot, S. Sajad Haider, called *Flight of the Falcon*. The book is not only an excellent recollection of aerial battles of 1965 and 1971 as narrated by an active participant, but also one of the best books coming out of the subcontinent on the adrenalin-high career of a fighter pilot. A better researched version of the air war comes from two Indian civilian air power enthusiasts, P.V.S. Jagan Mohan and Samir Chopra. Their book, *The Air War in 1965*, is a detailed account in terms of the opposing forces, aerial strategies, and operational philosophies of both forces and a chronological progression of the air war with fairly accurate and candid analysis. Of all the analysts and commentators who are prolific on the Internet, I found the analysis of Major (retd) Agha Humayun Amin, a Pakistani analyst, to be the most interesting.

THE 1971 WAR

Srinath Raghavan (*A Global History of the Creation of Bangladesh*), J.N. Dixit (*India-Pakistan in War and Peace)*, Sumit Ganguly (*Conflict Unending*), Shuja Nawaz (*Crossed Swords*) and Sisson and Rose (*War and Secession: India, Pakistan and Bangladesh)* provide the best strategic and geopolitical perspectives of events that led to the 1971 war. P.C. Lal (*My Years with the IAF)*, Lieutenant General A.A.K Niazi (The *Betrayal of East Pakistan)* and Lieutenant General K.P. Candeth (*The Western Front: India Pakistan War of 1971)* offer a participative operational account of the two-front war. John Gill, a professor at the National Defence University, Washington DC, has written the most objective military account of the war in the form of a monograph embellished with wonderfully crafted maps titled *An Atlas of the 1971 India-Pakistan War.* The official history of the 1971 war as chronicled by the Indian Ministry of Defence was released in 2014 – see S.N. Prasad and U.P. Thapliyal (*The India-Pakistan War of 1971*). The Indian Navy opened its writing score after this war with commanders of both the Western and Eastern Naval Command penning down their highly personalised memoirs of the war. See Admiral S.N. Kohli (*We Dared*) and Vice Admiral Krishnan (*A Sailor's Story*). *Transition to Triumph* is a painstakingly researched book on the operational evolution of the Indian Navy in the 1960s and 1970s written by Vice Admiral Hiranandani. The duo of P.V.S. Jagan Mohan and Samir Chopra has written an excellent account of the rather lopsided air campaign in Bangladesh (*Eagles over Bangladesh*). The Bangladesh narrative has generally been silent on the Bengali backlash and the targeting of Pakistani sympathizers in East Pakistan during and after the conflict. Treading on delicate turf, an Oxford historian of Bengali origin, Sarmila Bose, precisely does that in her richly researched narrative, *Dead Reckoning: Memories of the 1971 Bangladesh War.* She asks uncomfortable questions based on extensive interviews. The book is a must read to understand the many horrors of war that are hidden in the shadows of victory and defeat. Of all the international journalists who covered the birth of Bangladesh, Sydney Schanberg of *The New York Times* was the best; all his articles are available in the archives of *The New York Times.*

The best collection of Internet material on the 1971 air and ground war comes from Major Agha Humayun Amin and another accomplished Pakistani fighter pilot, Kaiser Tufail, who blogs under the name of *aeronaut*. Finally, the Indian website www.bharat-rakshak.com has an excellent repository of material of all kinds on India's wars after Independence and about the Indian armed forces – it is a must visit. By no means is the suggested reading list all-encompassing. Any omissions are unintentional and solely reflect the limitations of the author.

Happy Reading!

NOTES

Chapter 1: Sighter Burst

1. Lawrence Freedman, *Strategy: A History* (New York: Oxford University Press, 2013), p. xvi.
2. Air Vice Marshal A.K. Tiwary, 'Jointmanship in the Military', *Indian Defence Review* Vol. 26, No. 2 (April–June 2011), available at http://www.indiandefencereview.com/news/jointmanship-in-the-military/ (accessed 8 February 2015).
3. Swami Vivekananda was a nineteenth-century monk and philosopher who first introduced Vedanta philosophy and yoga to the Western world.

Chapter 2: A Personal Quest

1. This thread emerged from a stimulating and rewarding exchange of ideas over email in March 2015 between the author and Prof. Rana Mitter, an eminent Oxford historian.
2. Arjun Subramaniam, 'Kargil Revisited: Air Operations in a High Altitude Conflict,' *CLAWS Journal*, Summer 2008, p. 183–95 at http://www.claws.in/images/journals_doc/464654525_ASubramanian.pdf. CLAWS is Centre for Land Warfare Studies, New Delhi.
3. Benjamin Lambeth, 'Airpower at 18,000: The Indian Air Force in the Kargil War,' a monograph published by the Carnegie Endowment for Peace, available at http://carnegieendowment.org/2012/09/20/airpower-at-18-000-indian-air-force-in-kargil-war.

Chapter 3: Whither Military History and Understanding the Military

1. From a talk delivered by the author at the Nehru Memorial Museum and Library titled 'The Neglect of Modern Indian Military History and its Impact on India's Strategic Culture' on 16 July 2015.

2. He represents the Aam Aadmi Party, having won a legislative election in Delhi during the 2013 state elections.
3. Steven Wilkinson, *Army and Nation: The Military and Indian Democracy* (Cambridge, Massachusetts: Harvard University Press, 2015), from the Kindle edition, Introduction: The Question.
4. Ibid., p. 9.
5. Tami Davis Biddle and Robert M. Citino, 'The Role of Military History in the Contemporary Academy,' A Society for Military History White Paper, 30 November 2014, available at http://www.smh-hq.org/docs/SMHWhitePaper.pdf (accessed 14 March 2015).
6. Ibid.
7. Ibid.
8. Ibid.

Chapter 4: The Indian Army: Indian or Colonial?

1. An Indian Army publicity hoarding from recent times.
2. Philip Mason, *A Matter of Honour* (London: EBD Education in arrangement with Jonathan Cape, 1988), p. 50–54. For an operational and tactical analysis of Shivaji the warrior, also see Colonel R.D. Palsokar, *Shivaji: The Great Guerrilla* (Dehradun: Natraj Publishers, 2003).
3. Patwant Singh and Jyoti Rai, *The Empire of the Sikhs* (New Delhi: Hay House India, 2008), p. 171–73.
4. For a painstakingly researched book on Maratha power after Shivaji, see Uday S. Kulkarni, *Solstice at Panipat: 14 January 1761* (Pune: Mulla Mutha Publishers, 2012).
5. James Grant Duff, *History of the Mahrattas*, Vols I, II & III (New Delhi: Low Price Publications, 1990, first published in 1863), p. 215.
6. Stephen P. Cohen, *The Indian Army: Its Contribution to the Development of a Nation* (New Delhi: Oxford University Press, 1990), p. 45.
7. Philip Mason, *A Matter of Honour* (London: EBD Education in arrangement with Jonathan Cape, 1988), p. 50
8. Bipin Chandra, *History of Modern India* (New Delhi: Orient Blackswan, 2009), p. 41.
9. Philip Mason, *A Matter of Honour* (London: EBD Education in arrangement with Jonathan Cape, 1988), p. 133–34.
10. Bipin Chandra, *History of Modern India* (New Delhi: Orient Blackswan, 2009), p. 27.

11. Khushwant Singh, *A History of the Sikhs,* Vol. I: 1469–1839 (New Delhi: Oxford University Press, 1999), p. 73–94. The book is a highly readable and extensively researched narrative of Sikh history by one of India's most popular and prolific authors and columnists.
12. Philip Mason, *A Matter of Honour* (London: EBD Education in arrangement with Jonathan Cape, 1988), p. 353–54. Also see Bipin Chandra, *History of Modern India* (New Delhi: Orient Blackswan, 2009), p. 33.
13. Patwant Singh and Jyoti Rai, *The Empire of the Sikhs* (New Delhi: Hay House India, 2008), p. 63–66. Also see Philip Mason, *A Matter of Honour* (London: EBD Education in arrangement with Jonathan Cape, 1988), p. 259.
14. Ibid., p. 63. Also see Khushwant Singh, *A History of the Sikhs,* Vol. I: 1469–1839 (New Delhi: Oxford University Press, 1999), p. 81.
15. Khushwant Singh, *A History of the Sikhs,* Vol. I: 1469–1839 (New Delhi: Oxford University Press, 1999), p. 199–200. Prior to Maharaja Ranjit Singh assuming power, the armies of the Sikh chieftains were dominated by the cavalry, and foot soldiers were generally looked down upon.
16. For a detailed review of the Lahore Treaty of 1809, see Khushwant Singh, *A History of the Sikhs,* Vol. I: 1469–1839 (New Delhi: Oxford University Press, 1999), p. 362.
17. William Dalrymple, *Return of a King* (London: Bloomsbury, 2013), p. 11.
18. 'The 12 Misls of Ranjit Singh's Era,' http://www.indianmilitaryhistory.org/index.html (accessed 25 October 2014). For a detailed description of the Battle of Chilianwalla, see K.S. Randhawa, 'When fate and destiny conspired against Sikh Victory,' *The Tribune,* Chandigarh, 13 January 2002, http://www.tribuneindia.com/2002/20020113/edit.htm#1 (accessed 15 October 2014).
19. Khushwant Singh, *A History of the Sikhs* – Vol. II: 1839–2004 (New Delhi: Oxford University Press, 2009), p. 80–81.
20. Khushwant Singh, *A History of the Sikhs* – Vol. II: 1839–2004 (New Delhi: Oxford University Press, 2009), p. 1.
21. Philip Mason, *A Matter of Honour* (London: EBD Education in arrangement with Jonathan Cape, 1988), p. 307–308.
22. Ian Cardozo, ed., *The Indian Army: A Brief History* (New Delhi: Centre for Armed Forces Historical Research, 2005), p. 66.
23. Bipin Chandra, *History of Modern India* (New Delhi: Orient Blackswan, 2009), p. 30–31.
24. Philip Mason, *A Matter of Honour* (London: EBD Education in arrangement with Jonathan Cape, 1988), p. 246–68.

25. Stephen P. Cohen, *The Indian Army: Its Contribution to the Development of a Nation* (New Delhi: Oxford University Press, 1990), p. 22–27.
26. Ibid., p. 40–41.
27. Lord Roberts, quoted in Stephen P. Cohen, *The Indian Army: Its Contribution to the Development of a Nation* (New Delhi: Oxford University Press, 1990), p. 46.
28. Bipin Chandra, *History of Modern India* (New Delhi: Orient Blackswan, 2009), p. 164.
29. Discussion with Ramachandra Guha on email, 19 November 2014.
30. Philip Mason, *A Matter of Honour* (London: EBD Education in arrangement with Jonathan Cape, 1988), p. 347–48.
31. William Dalrymple, *Return of a King* (London: Bloomsbury, 2013), p. 6–8.
32. For a detailed overview of the Anglo-Gorkha Wars see: http://en.wikipedia.org/wiki/Anglo-Nepalese_War (accessed 24 April 2013).
33. Bipin Chandra, *History of Modern India* (New Delhi: Orient Blackswan, 2009), p. 164.
34. John Gaylor, *Sons of John Company: The Indian and Pakistan Armies, 1901–1991* (Turnbridge Wells: Para Press Ltd, 1992), p. 5.
35. John Connell, *Auchinleck: A Biography of Field Marshal Sir Claude Auchinleck* (London: Cassell, 1959), p. 767.
36. Stephen P. Rosen, *India and Its Armies* (New Delhi: Oxford University Press, 1996), p. 196.
37. Michael Howard, *War in European History* (Oxford: Oxford University Press, 2009), p. 121.
38. Ibid.
39. Kaushik Roy, 'The Armed Expansion of the East India Company: 1740s-1849,' in Daniel P. Marston and Chander S. Sundaram, ed., *A Military History of India and South Asia,* (New Delhi: Pentagon, 2007), p. 2.
40. Ibid., p. 6.
41. Stephen P. Cohen, *The Indian Army: Its Contribution to the Development of a Nation* (New Delhi: Oxford University Press, 1990), p. 60.
42. John Gaylor, *Sons of John Company: The Indian and Pakistan Armies, 1901–1991* (Turnbridge Wells: Para Press Ltd, 1992), p. 4.
43. The exact figure according to Phillip Mason was 13,02,394. See Philip Mason, *A Matter of Honour* (London: EBD Education in arrangement with Jonathan Cape, 1988), p. 411.

Chapter 5: The Indian Army: Coming of Age

1. Inscription at Chetwode Hall, Indian Military Academy, Dehradun.
2. Christopher Bayly and Tim Harper, *Forgotten Armies: The Fall of British Asia, 1941–1945* (Cambridge, Massachusetts: Belknapp Press of Harvard University, 2004), p. xxxi.
3. David Omissi, *Indian Voices of the Great War* (New Delhi: Penguin/ Viking, 2014), p. 3.
4. Ian Cardozo, ed., *The Indian Army: A Brief History* (New Delhi: Centre for Armed Forces Historical Research, 2005), p. 27–28.
5. Ibid., p. 28.
6. From the Honours and Awards Gallery section at the Bombay Sappers Regimental Centre at Kirkee, Pune.
7. For an excellent article on Hodson's Horse and the exploits of the Indian Army in WW I, see the official magazine of India's Ministry of External Affairs, *India Perspectives*, Vol. 29, No. 4 (July–August 2015), p. 60–64.
8. Mandeep Singh Bajwa, 'Indian Cavalry on Western Front, 1914–1919,' *Hindustan Times*, Chandigarh, 24 August 2014, available at http://www.hindustantimes.com/punjab/chandigarh/indian-cavalry-on-western-front-1914-18/article1-1255827.aspx (accessed 17 October 2014).
9. Ian Cardozo, ed., *The Indian Army: A Brief History* (New Delhi: Centre for Armed Forces Historical Research, 2005), p. 29–30. Though Cardozo puts the number of Victoria Crosses at sixteen, a more recent brochure brought out by the Commonwealth Graves Association puts the figure at eleven.
10. Stephen P. Cohen, *The Indian Army: Its Contribution to the Development of a Nation* (New Delhi: Oxford University Press, 1990), p. 68.
11. Philip Mason, *A Matter of Honour* (London: EBD Education in arrangement with Jonathan Cape, 1988), p. 443.
12. Ibid.
13. John Gaylor, *Sons of John Company: The Indian and Pakistan Armies, 1901–1991* (Turnbridge Wells: Para Press Ltd, 1992), p. 315.
14. The Prince of Wales Royal Indian Military College was later renamed as the Rashtriya Indian Military College (RIMC) after Independence. It boasts amongst its alumni four army chiefs and one air force chief from independent India's armed forces. Major Somnath Sharma, an old boy of the school, was the first Param Vir Chakra winner in independent India.
15. John Gaylor, *Sons of John Company: The Indian and Pakistan Armies, 1901–1991* (Turnbridge Wells: Para Press Ltd, 1992), p. 22–24.

16. John Keay, *India: A History* (London: Harper Press, 2000), p. 475–77.
17. Christopher Bayly and Tim Harper, *Forgotten Armies: The Fall of British Asia, 1941–1945* (Cambridge, Massachusetts: Belknapp Press of Harvard University, 2004), p. 74.
18. Air Marshal K.C. Cariappa, *Field Marshal K.M. Cariappa* (New Delhi: Niyogi Books, 2007), p. 40–41.
19. Ian Cardozo, ed., *The Indian Army: A Brief History* (New Delhi: Centre for Armed Forces Historical Research, 2005), p. 42.
20. Daniel P. Marston, 'A Force Transformed: The Indian Army and the Second World War,' in P. Marston and Chandar S. Sundaram, ed., *A Military History of India and South Asia,* (New Delhi: Pentagon, 2007), p. 103.
21. Ibid.
22. Excerpts from GHQ letter No. 66805/E.I.B dated 17 September 1941, from the Bombay Engineering Group (Bombay Sappers) Regimental Centre, Kirkee, Pune.
23. Daniel P. Marston, 'A Force Transformed: The Indian Army and the Second World War,' in P. Marston and Chandar S. Sundaram, ed., *A Military History of India and South Asia,* (New Delhi: Pentagon, 2007), p. 108. For a more detailed analysis of the Indian Army in the North Africa Desert, see Kaushik Roy, ed., *The Indian Army in the Two World Wars* (Leiden: Brill, 2011).
24. Extracts from the unpublished memoirs of Lieutenant Colonel Chanan Singh Dhillon, courtesy his son Gurbinder Dhillon.
25. Extracted from an email written by Captain (retd) Raj Mohindra, Indian Navy, who was on the INS *Brahmaputra* in 1967. For a detailed write-up on the Taranto landings by the 8th Indian Division, see Daniel P. Marston, *The Indian Army and the End of the Raj* (Cambridge, UK: Cambridge University Press, 2014), p. 59.
26. Ian Cardozo, ed., *The Indian Army: A Brief History* (New Delhi: Centre for Armed Forces Historical Research, 2005), p. 49.
27. Christopher Bayly and Tim Harper, *Forgotten Armies: The Fall of British Asia, 1941–1945* (Cambridge, Massachusetts: Belknapp Press of Harvard University, 2004), p. 294.
28. John Connell, *Auchinleck: A Biography of Field Marshal Sir Claude Auchinleck* (London: Cassell, 1959), p. 757.
29. 'Victory over Japanese at Kohima Is Britain's Greatest Battle,' Reuters report from London in *The Indian Express*, New Delhi, 22 April 2013.
30. Raghu Karnad, *Everybody's Friend* (London: Ebook from Vintage Digital, Random House, 2013).

31. C.B. Khanduri, *Thimayya: An Amazing Life* (New Delhi: KW Publishers, 2006), p. 83.
32. D.R. Mankekar, *Leaves from a War Reporter's Diary* (New Delhi: Vikas Publishers, 1977), p. 120.
33. From the archives of Kumaon Regimental Centre, Ranikhet.
34. D.R. Mankekar, *Leaves from a War Reporter's Diary* (New Delhi: Vikas Publishers, 1977), p. 121.
35. C.B. Khanduri, *Thimayya: An Amazing Life* (New Delhi: KW Publishers, 2006), p. 97.
36. John Gaylor, *Sons of John Company: The Indian and Pakistan Armies, 1901–1991* (Turnbridge Wells: Para Press Ltd, 1992), p. 316.
37. Ian Cardozo, ed., *The Indian Army: A Brief History* (New Delhi: Centre for Armed Forces Historical Research, 2005), p. 48. Also see 'Tiger Triumphs,' India Defence Department, Director of Public Relations, London, 1946.
38. Latest figures from the Commonwealth Graves Commission brochure issued during the centenary commemoration of WW I in early 2015.
39. Address to Kashmir National Conference, Srinagar, 19 August 1945. It was featured in *The Tribune* of 20 August 1945. S. Gopal, ed., *Selected Works of Jawaharlal Nehru*, Vol. 14 (New Delhi: Orient Longman).
40. Christopher Bayly and Tim Harper, *Forgotten Armies: The Fall of British Asia, 1941–1945* (Cambridge, Massachusetts: Belknapp Press of Harvard University, 2004), p. xxxii.
41. Interview with Lieutenant General (retd) W.A.G. Pinto, 23 October 2014.
42. Lieutenant General Harbaksh Singh, *In the Line of Duty* (New Delhi: Lancer, 2000), p. 130–36.
43. Stephen P. Cohen, *The Indian Army: Its Contribution to the Development of a Nation* (New Delhi: Oxford University Press, 1990), p. 99–102 and 150–62.
44. Sugata Bose, *His Majesty's Opponent* (New Delhi: Penguin, 2011), p. 266–79.
45. Ibid., p. 265–66.
46. Ibid.
47. Raghu Karnad, *Everybody's Friend* (London: Ebook from Vintage Digital, Random House, 2013).
48. Philip Mason, *A Matter of Honour* (London: EBD Education in arrangement with Jonathan Cape, 1988), p. 516–18.
49. S. Gopal, ed., 'Letters from Nehru to V.K. Krishna Menon,' *Selected Works of Jawaharlal Nehru*, Vol. 14 (New Delhi: Orient Longman).

50. Christopher Bayly and Tim Harper, *Forgotten Armies: The Fall of British Asia, 1941–1945* (Cambridge, Massachusetts: Belknapp Press of Harvard University, 2004), p. 428. For a detailed description of the rearguard battles fought by the INA in 1944–45, see Eric A. Vas, *Subhas Chandra Bose: The Man and His Times* (New Delhi: Lancer, 2005), p. 199–200.
51. John Connell, *Auchinleck: A Biography of Field Marshal Sir Claude Auchinleck* (London: Cassell, 1959), p. 797.
52. Ibid., p. 368.
53. Interview with Lord Mountbatten by B.R. Nanda, Oral History Project, NMML, 26 July 1967.
54. John Connell, *Auchinleck: A Biography of Field Marshal Sir Claude Auchinleck* (London: Cassell, 1959), p. 802–07.
55. Ibid.
56. John Connell, *Auchinleck: A Biography of Field Marshal Sir Claude Auchinleck* (London: Cassell, 1959), p. 806. Of all the British field commanders of the twentieth century who commanded Indian officers and troops during their service careers, Field Marshal Auchinleck understood them the best. His sagacity, empathy and apolitical approach in deciding the future of the Indian Army in a post-colonial dispensation shaped the thinking of many Indian commanders like Cariappa and Thimayya. It is only fair to attribute much of the leniency shown towards the high-profile INA prisoners to the wisdom of Auchinleck.
57. S. Gopal, ed., *Selected Works of Jawaharlal Nehru*, Vol. 14, from speech at Murree on 21 August 1945. Also see, Vol. 15, p. 90, letter to Claude Auchinleck and advice from Wavell, p. 95.
58. Shuja Nawaz, *Crossed Swords: Pakistan, Its Army, and the Wars Within* (Karachi: Oxford University Press, 2008), p. 18–19.
59. Sugata Bose, *His Majesty's Opponent* (New Delhi: Penguin, 2011), p. 294.
60. Bipin Chandra, *History of Modern India* (New Delhi: Orient Blackswan, 2009), p. 325.
61. Sugata Bose, *His Majesty's Opponent* (New Delhi: Penguin, 2011), p. 295.
62. Brigadier R.R. Palsokar (retd), 'Whom We Serve,' a prize-winning essay submitted in 2013 to *Defence Watch,* a monthly journal of defence and security affairs published from Dehradun.
63. http://en.wikipedia.org/wiki/Qadam_Qadam_Badaye_Ja (accessed 2 Apr 2013).
64. Narendra Singh Sarila, *The Shadow of the Great Game* (New Delhi: HarperCollins, 2009), p. 189.
65. Daniel P. Marston and Chander S. Sundaram, ed., *A Military History of India and South Asia,* (New Delhi: Pentagon, 2007), p. 131–33.

66. Ibid.
67. Michael Howard, *War in European History* (Oxford: Oxford University Press, 2009), p. 138.
68. Ibid.
69. John Gaylor, *Sons of John Company: The Indian and Pakistan Armies, 1901–1991* (Turnbridge Wells: Para Press Ltd, 1992), p. 278–85.
70. This argument is repeatedly reinforced by Steven Wilkinson, *Army and Nation: The Military and Indian Democracy* (Cambridge, Massachusetts: Harvard University Press, 2015).
71. For a detailed analysis see Stephen P. Cohen, *The Indian Army: Its Contribution to the Development of a Nation* (New Delhi: Oxford University Press, 1990).
72. Major General V.K. Singh, *Contribution of the Armed Forces to the Freedom Movement in India* (New Delhi, KW Publishers, 2009), p. xii.
73. Christopher Bayly and Tim Harper, *Forgotten Armies: The Fall of British Asia, 1941–1945* (Cambridge, Massachusetts: Belknapp Press of Harvard University, 2004), p. xxix.
74. Ibid. p. 191
75. John Gaylor, *Sons of John Company: The Indian and Pakistan Armies, 1901–1991* (Turnbridge Wells: Para Press Ltd, 1992), p. 258.
76. Stephen P. Rosen, *India and Its Armies* (New Delhi: Oxford University Press, 1996), p. 211.
77. Narendra Singh Sarila, *The Shadow of the Great Game* (New Delhi: HarperCollins, 2009), p. 175.
78. Ibid.
79. General K.S. Thimmaya, Selig Harrison, Thimayya Papers No. 16, NMML, New Delhi.
80. Stephen P. Rosen, *India and Its Armies* (New Delhi: Oxford University Press, 1996), p. 197–98.
81. General K. Sundarji, *Of Some Consequences: A Soldier Remembers* (New Delhi: HarperCollins, 2000), p. 112.

Chapter 6: The Indian Navy

1. Admiral Arun Prakash, 'At Sea about Naval History', 7 October 2006, available at www.bharat-rakshak.com/NAVY/History/Maritime-Heritage/17-At-Sea-With-Naval-History.html (accessed 10 May 2013).
2. Vice Admiral Mihir Roy, *War in the Indian Ocean* (New Delhi: Lancer Publishers, 1995), p. xiv.
3. Ibid.

4. 'Indian Navy, A Historical Overview', available at www.bharat-rakshak.com (accessed 15 April 2013).
5. Also see Bisheshwar Prasad, ed., *The Royal Indian Navy* (Agra: Agra University Press, 1964), p. 1–3.
6. Ibid., p. 3.
7. Rear Admiral Satyindra Singh, *Under Two Ensigns: The Indian Navy 1945–50* (New Delhi, Oxford & IBH Publishing, 1986), p. 9.
8. Rajiv Theodore, 'India's First Naval Heroes – Unsung and Unwept – Kunjali Marakkars,' available at www.americanbazaar.com/2014/09/11/India's-first-naval-heroes-unsung-unwept-kunjali-marakkars/ (accessed 12 September 2014). For a detailed history of the Zamorins also see K.V. Krishna Aiyyar, *The Zamorins of Calicut* (Calicut: Norman Printing Bureau, 1938). The book was referred to from a digital library collection at calicutheritage.com/Digital_Library.aspx (accessed on 12 September 2014).
9. Ibid.
10. Rear Admiral Satyindra Singh, *Under Two Ensigns: The Indian Navy 1945–50* (New Delhi, Oxford & IBH Publishing, 1986), p. 13.
11. 'Kanhoji Angre', available at http://en.wikipedia.org/wiki/Kanhoji_Angre (accessed 10 May 2013).
12. 'The Genesis of the Indian Navy,' available at www.bharat-rakshak.com/History/Maritime-Heritage/28-Genesis.html?tmpl=co. (accessed 8 April 2013).
13. Bisheshwar Prasad, ed., *The Royal Indian Navy* (Agra: Agra University Press, 1964), p. 6.
14. James Goldrick, *No Easy Answers: The Development of the Navies of India, Pakistan, Bangladesh and Sri Lanka 1945–1996* (New Delhi: Lancer Publishers, 1997), p. 3.
15. Bisheshwar Prasad, ed., *The Royal Indian Navy* (Agra: Agra University Press, 1964), p. 6.
16. James Goldrick, *No Easy Answers: The Development of the Navies of India, Pakistan, Bangladesh and Sri Lanka 1945–1996* (New Delhi: Lancer Publishers, 1997), p. 4.
17. Bisheshwar Prasad, ed., *The Royal Indian Navy* (Agra: Agra University Press, 1964), p. 8. Also see James Goldrick, *No Easy Answers: The Development of the Navies of India, Pakistan, Bangladesh and Sri Lanka 1945–1996* (New Delhi: Lancer Publishers, 1997), p. 5.
18. Ibid.
19. Ibid., p. 8.
20. 'The Genesis of the Indian Navy,' available at www.bharat-rakshak.com/History/Maritime-Heritage/28-Genesis.html?tmpl=co. (accessed 8 April 2013).

21. Bisheshwar Prasad, ed., *The Royal Indian Navy* (Agra: Agra University Press, 1964), Appendix II, 'Composition of Naval Headquarters at Bombay as of 1941.' Rear Admiral Satyindra Singh has put the figure at 114 officers, 1,732 ratings and sixteen officers manning the Naval HQ at Bombay.
22. James Goldrick, *No Easy Answers: The Development of the Navies of India, Pakistan, Bangladesh and Sri Lanka 1945–1996* (New Delhi: Lancer Publishers, 1997), p. 5–7.
23. Bisheshwar Prasad, ed., *The Royal Indian Navy* (Agra: Agra University Press, 1964), p. 36.
24. http://en.wikipedia.org/wiki/Red_Sea_Flotilla (accessed 6 June 2013).
25. Rear Admiral Satyindra Singh, *Under Two Ensigns: The Indian Navy 1945–50* (New Delhi, Oxford & IBH Publishing, 1986), p. 25.
26. Bisheshwar Prasad, ed., *The Royal Indian Navy* (Agra: Agra University Press, 1964), p. 86
27. Rear Admiral Satyindra Singh, *Under Two Ensigns: The Indian Navy 1945–50* (New Delhi, Oxford & IBH Publishing, 1986), p. 25.
28. File no. MOD 601/10450/H, Ministry of Defence, Historical Division, New Delhi.
29. Bisheshwar Prasad, ed., *The Royal Indian Navy* (Agra: Agra University Press, 1964), p. 95
30. Ibid., p. 255
31. http://en.wikipedia.org/wiki/Coastal_Forces_of_the_Royal_Navy, also see http://en.wikipedia.org/wiki/Coastal_Forces_of_the_Royal_New_Zealand_Navy (accessed 14 May 2013).
32. Bisheshwar Prasad, ed., *The Royal Indian Navy* (Agra: Agra University Press, 1964), p. 256.
33. Ibid., p. 311–15.
34. Ibid., p. 313–314.
35. James Goldrick, *No Easy Answers: The Development of the Navies of India, Pakistan, Bangladesh and Sri Lanka 1945–1996* (New Delhi: Lancer Publishers, 1997), p. 6.
36. Bisheshwar Prasad, ed., *The Royal Indian Navy* (Agra: Agra University Press, 1964), p. 360–65.
37. Rear Admiral Satyindra Singh, *Under Two Ensigns: The Indian Navy 1945–50* (New Delhi, Oxford & IBH Publishing, 1986), p. 28.
38. James Goldrick, *No Easy Answers: The Development of the Navies of India, Pakistan, Bangladesh and Sri Lanka 1945–1996* (New Delhi: Lancer Publishers, 1997), p. 7.
39. Rear Admiral Satyindra Singh, *Under Two Ensigns: The Indian Navy 1945–50* (New Delhi, Oxford & IBH Publishing, 1986), p. 32.

40. Vice Admiral Mihir Roy, *War in the Indian Ocean* (New Delhi: Lancer Publishers, 1995), p. 46.
41. Bishwanath Bose, *RIN Mutiny, 1946: Reference and Guide for All* (New Delhi, Northern Book Centre, 1988).
42. Narendra Singh Sarila, *The Shadow of the Great Game* (New Delhi: HarperCollins, 2009), p. 172.
43. http://ajitvadakayil.blogspot.in/2013/02/the-indian-navy-mutiny-of-1946-only-war.html (accessed 15 May 2013).
44. Rear Admiral Satyindra Singh, *Under Two Ensigns: The Indian Navy 1945–50* (New Delhi, Oxford & IBH Publishing, 1986), p. 54.
45. Brigadier R.R. Palsokar (retd), 'Whom We Serve,' extracts from a prize-winning essay submitted in 2013 to *Defence Watch*, a monthly journal of defence and security affairs published out of Dehradun.
46. *Bombay Chronicle*, 29 May 1946, p. 1.
47. Ibid., 30 May 1946, p. 5.
48. S. Gopal, ed., Speech at Bombay – 26 February 1946, *The Hindu*, 27 February 1946, *Selected Works of Jawaharlal Nehru*, Vol. 15 (New Delhi: Orient Longman), p. 22–25.
49. Rear Admiral Satyindra Singh, *Under Two Ensigns: The Indian Navy 1945–50* (New Delhi, Oxford & IBH Publishing, 1986), p. 90.
50. Interview with Admiral Jayant Nadkarni on 3 December 2014. The eighty-two-year-old admiral was happy to share his experiences during the fledgling years of the Indian Navy.
51. Also see, Vice Admiral Mihir Roy, *War in the Indian Ocean* (New Delhi: Lancer Publishers, 1995), p. 54–55.
52. From a personal discussion with Vice Admiral Pradeep Chauhan on the importance of military history on 12 August 2015.
53. James Goldrick, *No Easy Answers: The Development of the Navies of India, Pakistan, Bangladesh and Sri Lanka 1945–1996* (New Delhi: Lancer Publishers, 1997), p. 12. Also see Rear Admiral Satyindra Singh, *Under Two Ensigns: The Indian Navy 1945–50* (New Delhi, Oxford & IBH Publishing, 1986), 'Division of the RIN' (behind the Contents page). The figures in his book are at slight variance to the ones mentioned above. While there is no difference between Goldrick and Satyindra Singh on the division of major vessels, there are minor variations with respect to smaller vessels like harbour defence motor launches (HDML).
54. 'Delhi becomes Flagship,' *Bombay Chronicle*, 15 September 1948, p. 7.
55. This disdain comes out clearly in Chapter 8.
56. 'India determined to protect peace,' *Bombay Chronicle*, 16 September 1948, p. 10.

57. Interview with Admiral Nadkarni.
58. 'US Warships on 5 Day Goodwill Visit to City Harbour,' *Bombay Chronicle*, 24 August 1948, p. 1.
59. Vice Admiral Mihir Roy, *War in the Indian Ocean* (New Delhi: Lancer Publishers, 1995), p. 57.
60. For a detailed reading of an Indian perspective on modern maritime strategy, see Rear Admiral Raja Menon, *Maritime Strategy and Continental Wars* (London: Frank Cass, 1998), p. 55–61.
61. In Indian mythology, Lord Varuna is the all-powerful lord of the oceans.

Chapter 7: The Indian Air Force

1. Rana Chhina, *The Eagle Strikes: The Royal Indian Air Force, 1932–1950* (New Delhi: Ambi Knowledge Resources), p. 317.
2. Somnath Sapru, *Armed Pegasus: The Early Years* (New Delhi: KW Publishers, 2011), p. 66–69.
3. http://www.bbc.co.uk/learningzone/clips/the-perils-of-being-a-first-world-war-flying-ace/7227.html (accessed 18 March, 2013).
4. http://www.nationalarchives.gov.uk/pathways/firstworldwar/people/lalroy.htm (accessed on 18 March 2013).
5. David E. Ommissi, *Air Power and Colonial Control* (Manchester: Manchester University Press, 1990), p. viii.
6. Somnath Sapru, *Armed Pegasus: The Early Years* (New Delhi: KW Publishers, 2011), p. 100–02.
7. Lieutenant Colonel Andrew Roe, 'Good God Sir, Are you Hurt? The Realities and Perils of Operating in India's Troubled North-West Frontier,' *Air Power Review*, Vol. 14, No. 3 (Autumn/Winter 2011), p. 61–82.
8. Somnath Sapru, *Armed Pegasus: The Early Years* (New Delhi: KW Publishers, 2011), p. 102–05.
9. S.C. Gupta, *History of the Indian Air Force: 1933–45* (New Delhi: Orient Longman, 1961), p. xviii. Though the book is one of the few authentic and rigorously researched official accounts of the early years of the IAF, it was extremely surprising to see that not a single senior RAF or IAF officer, serving or retired, was on the advisory committee of the book. It included eminent army generals like Lieutenant Generals K.S. Thimayya, S.P. Thorat and Dudley Russell.
10. David E. Ommissi, *Air Power and Colonial Control* (Manchester: Manchester University Press, 1990), p. 48.
11. Lieutenant Colonel Andrew Roe, 'Good God Sir, Are you Hurt? The Realities and Perils of Operating in India's Troubled North-West

Frontier,' *Air Power Review*, Vol. 14, No. 3 (Autumn/Winter 2011), p. 63.

12. http://www.bharat-rakshak.com/IAF/History/1930s/1084-Pioneers.html (accessed 18 March 2013).
13. Air Chief Marshal P.C. Lal, *My Years with the IAF* (New Delhi: Lancer, 1986), p. 12.
14. B.K. Nigam, *Challenge in the Sky* (New Delhi: R.K. Books, 1985), p. 5.
15. S.C. Gupta, *History of the Indian Air Force: 1933–45* (New Delhi: Orient Longman, 1961), p. xix.
16. The Bannu Brigade was formed as part of the Northern Army of the Indian Army in the first decade of the twentieth century and was deployed in the North Western Province. It continued there till WW II and gained significant operational experience in the Third Afghan War and the ensuing war against tribals in Waziristan. The brigade was one of the first units of the Indian Army to operate closely with units of the RAF and the newly formed IAF during operations against the Faqir of Ipi between 1936 and 1941.
17. B.K. Nigam, *Challenge in the Sky* (New Delhi: R.K. Books, 1985), p. 11.
18. Air Commodore Jasjit Singh, 'The Indian Air Force in Wars,' *Air Power Review*, Vol. 14, No. 3 (Autumn/Winter 2011), p. 84.
19. Literally translated *Hawai Sepoys as Air Warriors*; almost seventy years later, all personnel of the IAF irrespective of rank or branch were called air warriors.
20. Air Commodore G.H. Vasse, deputy SASO, Air Command, SE Asia, from a paper entitled 'The Modernisation of the Air Forces in India,' September 1939, taken from the Historical Division of the Ministry of Defence, New Delhi.
21. Rana Chhina, *The Eagle Strikes: The Royal Indian Air Force, 1932–1950* (New Delhi: Ambi Knowledge Resources), p. 49–54.
22. Ibid., p. 51.
23. During an impromptu dinner speech on 14 February 2014 at the Air Force Officers Mess, Gwalior.
24. http://www.bharat-rakshak.com/IAF/History/1930s/1021-Training-Days.html (accessed 18 March 2013).
25. Air Chief Marshal P.C. Lal, *My Years with the IAF* (New Delhi: Lancer, 1986), p. 13.
26. Ibid., p. 16.
27. S.C. Gupta, *History of the Indian Air Force: 1933–45* (New Delhi: Orient Longman, 1961), p. 36.
28. Ibid., p. 4.

29. http://www.bharat-rakshak.com/IAF/History/1965War/Chapter1.html (accessed 15 October 2013).
30. Interview with Air Chief Marshal Moolgavkar on 14 January 2013. Also see, Jyoti Rai, *Leading from the Cockpit* (New Delhi: The Society for Aerospace Studies, 2010), p. 16–20. Also see, 'IAF in the First Burma Campaign,' IAF Historical and Warrior Studies Cell, College of Air Warfare, Secunderabad (2005): p. 20–21.
31. For a well-written obituary, see Shoumit Banerjee, 'Former IAF Chief Moolgavkar Dead,' *The Hindu,* 11 April 2015, available at http://www.thehindu.com/news/national/former-iaf-chief-moolgavkar-dead/article7090057.ece (accessed 7 June 2015).
32. B.K. Nigam, *Challenge in the Sky* (New Delhi: R.K. Books, 1985), p. 15. For a most comprehensive description of the contribution of the IAF during the early days of the Burma campaign, see Rana Chhina, *The Eagle Strikes: The Royal Indian Air Force, 1932–1950* (New Delhi: Ambi Knowledge Resources), p. 56–72. Also, for a consolidated squadron-wise breakdown of flying in the Burma campaign, see Appendix D, p. 315–16.
33. I am grateful to No. 1 Squadron for allowing me full access to their wonderfully preserved museum; it remains the best squadron museum in the IAF.
34. 'IAF in the First Burma Campaign,' IAF Historical and Warrior Studies Cell, College of Air Warfare, Secunderabad (2005): p. 33.
35. Air Chief Marshal P.C. Lal, *My Years with the IAF* (New Delhi: Lancer, 1986), p. 45. Also see Rana Chhina, *The Indian Air Force Memorial Book* (New Delhi: Air Headquarters Press, 1996), p. 104.
36. Jasjit Singh, *The Icon: An Authorised Biography* (New Delhi: KW Publishers, 2009), p. 36–45.
37. Air Chief Marshal P.C. Lal, *My Years with the IAF* (New Delhi: Lancer, 1986), p. 33–36.
38. Ibid., p. 38.
39. Field Marshal Viscount Slim, *Defeat into Victory* (Dehradun: Natraj Publishers, 2014), p. 232.
40. Air Commodore G.H. Vasse, deputy SASO, Air Command, SE Asia, from a paper entitled 'The Modernisation of the Air Forces in India,' September 1939, p. 31, taken from the Historical Division of the Ministry of Defence, New Delhi.
41. 'IAFVR Pilots in UK', available at http://www.bharat-rakshak.com/IAF/Galleries/History/WW2/RAF24/ (accessed 28 December 2014). Also see B.K. Nigam, *Challenge in the Sky* (New Delhi: R.K. Books, 1985), p. 17.

42. See 'Gravesend unveils statue of fighter pilot Mahender Singh Puji,' 28 November 2014, available at http://www.bbc.com/news/uk-england-kent-30251269 (accessed 30 November 2014). Also see, Manimugdha Sharma, 'WW II pilot honoured with a statue in UK,' *The Times of India*, Pune, 30 November 2014, p. 13.
43. B.K. Nigam, *Challenge in the Sky* (New Delhi: R.K. Books, 1985), p. 18–19.
44. 'An Asian Hero,' http://asianaffairs.in/december2014/an-asian-hero.html. For an overview of the Battle of Falaise, see http://www.historylearningsite.co.uk/falaise_pocket.htm (both sites accessed on 31 January 2015).
45. 'Air Forces in India,' Air HQ, India, File no. GOI/10975/H/Air HQ (I) 017554/Air, Ministry of Defence, Historical Division, New Delhi.
46. Jasjit Singh, *The Icon: An Authorised Biography* (New Delhi: KW Publishers, 2009), p. 84.
47. Two of the DSOs were won by British officers who were commanding No. 4 and No. 10 Squadrons of the IAF in Burma, while Squadron Leader Mehar Singh was the lone Indian among the three.
48. http://www.bharat-rakshak.com/IAF/Database/Awards/awards.php?qaward=AFC (accessed 19 March 2013). S.C. Gupta puts the figure at twenty-one DFCs and one Bar to DFC, p. 190. Also see Rana Chinna, Appendix B, p. 310–11. The figures as available with the Historical Studies Cell at the IAF's College of Air Warfare are marginally at variance and indicate one DSO, twenty-one DFCs, one Bar to DFC, two OBEs, two Air Force Crosses (AFC), seven MBEs and forty-five Mention-in-Despatches (M-in-Ds). These anomalies are insignificant and can be ignored as long as one keeps in mind the overall brilliant performance by Indian aviators in WW II.
49. Air Commodore G.H. Vasse, deputy SASO, Air Command, SE Asia, from a paper entitled 'The Modernisation of the Air Forces in India,' September 1939, p. 3, taken from the Historical Division of the Ministry of Defence, New Delhi.
50. Annexure IV-A of Recommendations of Armed Forces Nationalization Committee, 'Thimayya Papers,' File No. 1, NMML, New Delhi.
51. Narendra Singh Sarila, *The Shadow of the Great Game* (New Delhi: HarperCollins, 2009), p. 173.
52. Air Commodore Jasjit Singh, 'The Indian Air Force in Wars,' *Air Power Review*, Vol. 14, No. 3 (Autumn/Winter 2011), p. 84. Air Chief Marshal Lal's figures are marginally different. He has mentioned in his book that of the ten squadrons, India was left with seven.

53. Somnath Sapru, *Armed Pegasus: The Early Years* (New Delhi: KW Publishers, 2011), p. xviii.
54. Air Chief Marshal P.C. Lal, *My Years with the IAF* (New Delhi: Lancer, 1986), p. 555.
55. Directorate of Public Relations, Air Headquarters, Air House, New Delhi, 2011.
56. Air Vice Marshal A.K. Tiwary, *Indian Air Force in Wars* (New Delhi: Lancer, 2012), p. 4–5.
57. Operational Record Book of No. 8 Squadron, January 1947–December 1954, Ministry of Defence, Historical Division, New Delhi.
58. GOI/10975/H, Historical Division, Archives, Ministry of Defence, New Delhi.

Chapter 8: Holding on to Kashmir

1. Shuja Nawaz, *Crossed Swords: Pakistan, Its Army, and the Wars Within* (Karachi: Oxford University Press, 2008), p. 21.
2. Lieutenant General S.K. Sinha, *A Soldier Recalls* (New Delhi: Lancer, 1992), p. 96.
3. Ibid.
4. John Connell, *Auchinleck: A Biography of Field Marshal Sir Claude Auchinleck* (London: Cassell, 1959), p. 790–91.
5. For an absolutely riveting narrative of Wavell's machinations to covertly ensure the partition of India, see the chapter, 'Wavell Plays the Great Game,' in Narendra Singh Sarila, *The Shadow of the Great Game* (New Delhi: HarperCollins, 2009), p. 167–98.
6. Ramachandra Guha, *India after Gandhi* (London: Pan Macmillan, 2007), p. 36.
7. 'There was enough evidence of a tribal raid,' from http://ikashmir.net/pakraid1947/evidence.html (accessed 3 April 2013). Also see *Operations in Jammu and Kashmir: 1947–48,* Ministry of Defence, GOI, published by Natraj Publishers, Dehradun.
8. C. Dasgupta, *War and Diplomacy in Kashmir: 1947–48* (New Delhi: Sage Publications, 2002), p. 52.
9. http://kashmirsentinel.org/there-was-enough-evidence-about-tribal-raid/ (accessed 3 April 2013).
10. For a detailed analysis of Indian strategic thought at the time of partition, see Jaswant Singh, *Defending India* (Bangalore: Macmillan, 1999), p. 1–60.
11. D.K. Palit, *Major General Rudra: His Service in Three Armies and Two World Wars* (New Delhi: Reliance Publishing, 1997), p. 67.

12. V.P. Malhotra, *Defence Related Treaties of India* (New Delhi: ICC India Pvt. Ltd., 2002), p. 5.
13. C. Dasgupta, *War and Diplomacy in Kashmir: 1947–48* (New Delhi: Sage Publications, 2002), p. 35–38. Also see Ramachandra Guha, *India after Gandhi* (London: Pan Macmillan, 2007), p. 59–63.
14. Narendra Singh Sarila, *The Shadow of the Great Game* (New Delhi: HarperCollins, 2009), p. 406.
15. Robert D. Kaplan, *The Revenge of Geography* (New York: Random House, 2012), p. xix–xii. The book is a masterly exposition of geography and its impact on strategic outcomes of interstate relations.
16. For a comprehensive description of the demographic distribution in Jammu and Kashmir, see Victoria Schofield, *Kashmir in Conflict: India, Pakistan and the Unending War* (New York: I.B. Tauris, 2000), p. xiii, 8.
17. Joseph Korbel, *Danger over Kashmir* (Princeton: Princeton University Press, 1966), p. 8. The book mainly articulates a Pakistani viewpoint of the whole crisis and sensationalizes the persecution of Muslims by Hindus without sufficient evidence of first-hand narratives or eyewitness accounts. The pro-Pakistan tilt interspersed with impeccable research can be attributed to geopolitics at the time the book was written (1966) considering that the US was wooing Pakistan as a front-line ally against the Soviet Union. However, for the sake of objectivity, many well-made arguments and facts have been used from the book.
18. John Connell, *Auchinleck: A Biography of Field Marshal Sir Claude Auchinleck* (London: Cassell, 1959), p. 789.
19. Sufism is a moderate form of Islam that is closest to secular in form. It spread in Kashmir in the sixteenth and seventeenth centuries.
20. Sheikh Abdullah represented the secular and moderate voice of the Kashmiri Muslim population and would go on to be the first chief minister of the state of Jammu and Kashmir after the war.
21. 'Kashmir in Charge of Blimps – High Handedness of the Kashmir State Forces,' *Bombay Chronicle*, 29 May 1946, p. 1. Also see *Bombay Chronicle*, 30 May 1946, p. 8 (accessed Nehru Memorial Museum and Library on 1 June 2013).
22. Ibid.
23. An excellent Pakistani perspective on the role of Poonch Muslims is offered by Shuja Nawaz. See Shuja Nawaz, *Crossed Swords: Pakistan, Its Army, and the Wars Within* (Karachi: Oxford University Press, 2008), p. 44.
24. John Connell, *Auchinleck: A Biography of Field Marshal Sir Claude Auchinleck* (London: Cassell, 1959), p. 930.

25. A moving account of the Partition reinforced by a treasure trove of archival sources is available in Ramachandra Guha's book, *India after Gandhi*.
26. C.B. Khanduri, *Thimayya: An Amazing Life* (New Delhi: KW Publishers, 2006), p. 105–113.
27. Ibid.
28. War Diaries of No. 7 Squadron, RIAF, Ministry of Defence, Historical Division, New Delhi.
29. Lieutenant General S.K. Sinha, *A Soldier Recalls* (New Delhi: Lancer, 1992), p. 102.
30. Papers of Lieutenant General S.P. Thorat, NMML, New Delhi.
31. Narendra Singh Sarila, *The Shadow of the Great Game* (New Delhi: HarperCollins, 2009), p. 350–51. For a jihadi perspective of the tribal invasion, a must read is Major General Akbar Khan's book *Raiders over Kashmir* (Karachi: Army Press, 1992).
32. Jaswant Singh, *Defending India* (Bangalore: Macmillan, 1999), p. 96–98.
33. After extensive research, the most authentic source of information came from the Historical Cell at the Directorate of Operations (Joint Planning), Air HQ, New Delhi. Also see the Operational Record Books of Nos 7, 8, 10 Squadrons, IAF, at the Ministry of Defence, Historical Division, New Delhi. Air Vice Marshal Tiwary puts the total strength of aircraft at sixty-eight Tempest fighters, thirteen Spitfires, thirty Dakotas with barely half a dozen serviceable and about sixty Harvard trainers. See Air Vice Marshal A.K. Tiwary, *Indian Air Force in Wars* (New Delhi: Lancer, 2012), p. 48.
34. Jaswant Singh, *Defending India* (Bangalore: Macmillan, 1999), p. 96–98.
35. History of the PAF, from http://www.paf.gov.pk/history.html (accessed 6 April 2015).

Chapter 9: Surprise And Riposte

1. Lieutenant General E.A. Vas, *Without Baggage* (Dehradun: Natraj Publishers, 1987), p. 13. This book was published by the author almost forty years after he had written it – it lay in cold storage through the officer's entire career and was published after he retired.
2. Rohit Singh, 'Operations in Jammu and Kashmir 1947–48,' *Scholar Warrior* (Autumn 2012): p. 134.
3. Joseph Korbel, *Danger over Kashmir* (Princeton: Princeton University Press, 1966), p. 73.
4. Ibid., p. 67.

5. In his fairly objective analysis of the reasons for tribal angst on the eve of Partition, Sumit Ganguly in his book *The Origins of War in South Asia: Indo-Pakistani Conflicts since 1947* liberally quotes Joseph Korbel from his book *Danger in Kashmir.*
6. Ibid.
7. Alastair Lamb, *Birth of a Tragedy: Kashmir 1947* (Oxford: Oxford University Press, 1994), p. 123.
8. Srinath Raghavan, *War and Peace in Modern India* (Ranikhet: Permanent Black, 2010), p. 135.
9. Lieutenant General L.P. Sen, *Slender Was the Thread* (New Delhi: Orient Longman, 1969), p. 34–36.
10. Ibid.
11. Rohit Singh, 'Operations in Jammu and Kashmir 1947–48,' *Scholar Warrior* (Autumn 2012): p. 136–38.
12. Lieutenant General L.P. Sen, *Slender Was the Thread* (New Delhi: Orient Longman, 1969), p. 36–38. For the sake of objectivity and a differing viewpoint on the extent of Muslim support for the tribal invasion, Alastair Lamb offers a pro-Pakistan viewpoint in his book *The Kashmir Problem*. Similarly, Colonel Akbar Khan, the brain behind Operation Gulmarg, offers a fundamentalist and inflammatory opinion justifying the tribal invasion.
13. 'Capture of Uri,' *The Hindu*, 16 November 1947, p. 1. The special correspondent of the United Press of India reported that 30,000 civilians were believed to have been massacred as the raiders first captured Uri and then retreated as they were pushed back by the Indian Army. He went on to report that when the troops of the Union of India entered Uri, they found the town completely devastated and deserted by the raiders.
14. Ibid.
15. C. Dasgupta, *War and Diplomacy in Kashmir: 1947–48* (New Delhi: Sage Publications, 2002), p. 46.
16. Air Marshal Bharat Kumar (retd), *An Incredible War* (New Delhi: KW Publishers, 2009), p. 355.
17. Ibid.
18. Lieutenant General S.K. Sinha, *A Soldier Recalls* (New Delhi: Lancer, 1992), p. 99.
19. After Independence, India's air forces were called the Royal Indian Air Force till the 'Royal' prefix was dropped when India became a Republic on 26 January 1950.
20. Air Marshal Bharat Kumar (retd), *An Incredible War* (New Delhi: KW Publishers, 2009), p. 338–39.

21. The Spitfires belonged to the Advanced Training Wing of the IAF at Air Force Station, Ambala. The wing was commanded by Group Captain Arjan Singh, later Marshal of the Air Force.
22. Lieutenant General L.P. Sen, *Slender Was the Thread* (New Delhi: Orient Longman, 1969), p. 47–49.
23. Mandeep Singh Bajwa, '1947 Gallantry awaits recognition,' *Hindustan Times*, Chandigarh, 19 June 2012, http://hindustantimes.com/punjab/chandigarh/1947-gallantry-awaits-recognition/article1-874795.aspx (accessed 17 October 2014).
24. 'Paltan' is Hindi for 'platoon'. However, it does not indicate a number of troops as platoon does, but broadly indicates which regiment a soldier belongs to.
25. Lieutenant General Harbaksh Singh, *In the Line of Duty* (New Delhi: Lancer, 2000), p. 195–96. As deputy commander of 161 Brigade, Harbaksh was the aggressive face of the operation.
26. Telephonic conversation with Air Marshal Randhir Singh on 11 October 2013.
27. Lieutenant General L.P. Sen, *Slender Was the Thread* (New Delhi: Orient Longman, 1969), p. 55–57.
28. S.N. Prasad and Dharam Pal, ed., *Operations in Jammu and Kashmir 1947–48*, an official history sponsored by India's Ministry of Defence (Dehradun: Natraj Publishers, 2005), p. 34–35.
29. From the School Chronicles of RIMC, Dehradun, the alma mater of Major Somnath Sharma.
30. Lieutenant General L.P. Sen, *Slender Was the Thread* (New Delhi: Orient Longman, 1969), p. 72–75. Also see Rohit Singh, 'Operations in Jammu and Kashmir 1947–48,' *Scholar Warrior* (Autumn 2012): p. 138
31. Air Marshal Bharat Kumar (retd), *An Incredible War* (New Delhi: KW Publishers, 2009), p. 311.
32. Air Vice Marshal A.K. Tiwary, *Indian Air Force in Wars* (New Delhi: Lancer, 2012), p. 43.
33. Lieutenant General L.P. Sen, *Slender Was the Thread* (New Delhi: Orient Longman, 1969), p. 45.
34. Ibid., p. 78–100. While Sen in his book claims to have orchestrated the Battle of Shalateng, an interesting perspective on the Battle of Shalateng is offered by Major General Kuldeep Singh Bajwa in his book *Jammu and Kashmir War, 1947–1948: Political and Military Perspective*, published by Har Anand Publishers in 2003. Bajwa claims that Harbaksh Singh and not L.P. Sen actually controlled the battle and that the appearance of 7 Cavalry from the rear echelons of the raiders' position was a

result of Lieutenant David losing his way and then finding himself in an advantageous position to surprise them. See p. 130–33. Also see Lieutenant General Harbaksh Singh, *In the Line of Duty* (New Delhi: Lancer, 2000), p. 204. Harbaksh writes in his memoir that L.P. Sen came on the scene at the Battle of Shalateng only after the raiders were in full retreat.

35. Mandeep Singh Bajwa, 'Tempests on the Attack in Kashmir,' *Hindustan Times*, Chandigarh, 26 January 2014, available at http://hindustantimes.com/punjab/chandigarh/tempests-on-the-attack-in-Kashmir/article1-1176832.aspx (accessed 17 October 2014).
36. Lieutenant General L.P. Sen, *Slender Was the Thread* (New Delhi: Orient Longman, 1969), p. 103. Also see Papers of S.P.P. Thorat, 'Report on Kashmir Massacres,' NMML, New Delhi. Conducted by Justice J.L. Kalam and Shri Bamzai, 289 Muslims were witness to a spate of massacres of Hindus in Muzaffarabad, Rajouri, Badgam, Teethwal and Handwara.
37. Mongol warlord Timur Lane invaded India in the fourteenth century, plundering and laying waste the city of Delhi before heading back to Central Asia. Nadir Shah was a Persian king who invaded India in 1738–39 and ruled for a year before reinstating Muhammad Shah as a weak Mughal emperor of India. His invasion more or less heralded the rapid decline of the mighty Mughal Empire.
38. These figures have been extrapolated from the squadron operational record books and figures given by Air Marshal Bharat Kumar in his book. See Air Marshal Bharat Kumar (retd), *An Incredible War* (New Delhi: KW Publishers, 2009), p. 311, 332.
39. Major General Akbar Khan, *Raiders over Kashmir* (Karachi: Army Press, 1992), p. 68. From Narendra Singh Sarila, *The Shadow of the Great Game* (New Delhi: HarperCollins, 2009), p. 352.
40. D.R. Mankekar, *Leaves from a War Reporter's Diary* (New Delhi: Vikas Publishers, 1977), p. 152–53.

Chapter 10: The War Drags On

1. C. Dasgupta, *War and Diplomacy in Kashmir: 1947–48* (New Delhi: Sage Publications, 2002), p. 206.
2. For a detailed official record of the siege of Poonch, see Chapter XIII, 'The Relief of Punch,' in S.N. Prasad and Dharam Pal, ed., *Operations in Jammu and Kashmir: 1947–48* (New Delhi: Ministry of Defence, Historical Division), p. 238–62.
3. Lieutenant General Harbaksh Singh, *In the Line of Duty* (New Delhi: Lancer, 2000), p. 213–17.

4. Lieutenant Colonel Maurice Cohen, *Thunder over Kashmir* (Bombay: Orient Longman, 1955), p. 19.
5. P.S. Chanana, 'The Air Warrior Who Knew No Fear,' *The Tribune*, Chandigarh, 25 May 2011.
6. Air Marshal Bharat Kumar (retd), *An Incredible War* (New Delhi: KW Publishers, 2009), p. 340. There are conflicting claims that the airstrip was actually a mere 600 yards. See Rana Chhina, *The Eagle Strikes: The Royal Indian Air Force, 1932–1950* (New Delhi: Ambi Knowledge Resources), p. 270. Also see Air Vice Marshal A.K. Tiwary, *Indian Air Force in Wars* (New Delhi: Lancer, 2012), p. 55.
7. The operational record book of the single transport squadron of the IAF (12 Squadron) between September 1947 and April 1948 reveals stupendous figures of 3,404 hours flown, three million pounds of supplies flown in or dropped, 4,000 troops transported, 10,000 refugees evacuated and over 1,000 casualties flown out. Also see Air Marshal Bharat Kumar (retd), *An Incredible War* (New Delhi: KW Publishers, 2009), p. 345.
8. Rana Chhina, *The Eagle Strikes: The Royal Indian Air Force, 1932–1950* (New Delhi: Ambi Knowledge Resources), p. 271–72.
9. Lieutenant General E.A. Vas, *Without Baggage* (Dehradun: Natraj Publishers, 1987), p. 80.
10. Lieutenant Colonel Maurice Cohen, *Thunder over Kashmir* (Bombay: Orient Longman, 1955), p. 11.
11. Ibid., p. 21. Also see Lieutenant General E.A. Vas, *Without Baggage* (Dehradun: Natraj Publishers, 1987), p. 76.
12. Ibid., p. 65.
13. Ibid.
14. Primarily offering a Pakistani perspective on the Kashmir conflict, Joseph Korbel highlights rumours of Dogra atrocities against Muslims in Kashmir as being one of the key precipitants of the tribal invasion of 1947. See Sumit Ganguly, *The Origins of War in South Asia: Indo-Pakistan Conflicts Since 1947* (New Delhi: Vision Books, 1999), p. 42.
15. Lieutenant General L.P. Sen, *Slender Was the Thread* (New Delhi: Orient Longman, 1969), p. 188–91.
16. Rohit Singh, 'Operations in Jammu and Kashmir 1947–48,' *Scholar Warrior* (Autumn 2012): p. 152.
17. Ibid., p. 148.
18. Air Chief Marshal P.C. Lal, *My Years with the IAF* (New Delhi: Lancer, 1986), p. 65.
19. Ibid.
20. Interview with Air Chief Marshal (retd) Moolgavkar.

21. From the 8 Squadron war diary, Ministry of Defence, Historical Division. Also at http://www.bharat-rakshak.com (accessed 10 January 2013).
22. Lieutenant General L.P. Sen, *Slender Was the Thread* (New Delhi: Orient Longman, 1969), p. 194.
23. 'The Relief of Leh,' at http://www.bharat-rakshak.com/IAF/History/1948War/Leh.html (accessed 12 Jan 2013).
24. Ibid.
25. War diary of 2/8 Gorkha Rifles, January 1948–December 1960, Ministry of Defence, Historical Division, New Delhi.
26. Ibid.
27. Ibid.
28. Rohit Singh, 'Operations in Jammu and Kashmir 1947–48,' *Scholar Warrior* (Autumn 2012): p. 148. For a fairly critical analysis of the Indian Army's attempts to recapture Dras and Kargil and send reinforcements to Skardu in May 1948, see S.N. Prasad and Dharam Pal, ed., *Operations in Jammu and Kashmir: 1947–48* (New Delhi: Ministry of Defence, Historical Division), p. 297–303.
29. 'Mass Murder in Ladakh Valley – Invaders Swoop Down with Fire and Sword,' *Bombay Chronicle*, 23 August 1948, p. 1.
30. Ibid.
31. C.B. Khanduri, *Thimayya: An Amazing Life* (New Delhi: KW Publishers, 2006), p. 131.
32. *Bombay Chronicle*, 17 August 1948, p. 1.
33. Interview with Air Chief Marshal Moolgavkar, 1 February 2013.
34. C.B. Khanduri, *Thimayya: An Amazing Life* (New Delhi: KW Publishers, 2006), p. 132.
35. In conversation with Jyoti Rai, 1 February 2013.
36. 'Pakistan Dakota Chased by RIAF,' *The Hindu*, API report, 11 November 1948, p. 4. From the NMML archives.
37. Ibid., 119–120.
38. Jyoti Rai, *Leading from the Cockpit* (New Delhi: The Society for Aerospace Studies, 2010), p. 71–72.
39. For a macro and strategic perspective on the reasons why the British were reluctant to allow India to recapture the whole of Kashmir, see Sumit Ganguly, *The Origins of War in South Asia: Indo-Pakistan Conflicts Since 1947* (New Delhi: Vision Books, 1999), p. 41.
40. A Pakistani perspective in Shuja Nawaz, *Crossed Swords: Pakistan, Its Army, and the Wars Within* (Karachi: Oxford University Press, 2008), p. 66.
41. 'Foreign Aid to Pak,' *Bombay Chronicle*, 17 August 1948, p. 1.

42. Rohit Singh, 'Brig Mohammed Usman, MVC, The Lion of Naushera,' *Soldier Scholar* (Autumn 2010): p. 156.
43. Ibid., p, 156–161.
44. Air Marshal Bharat Kumar (retd), *An Incredible War* (New Delhi: KW Publishers, 2009), p. 310–15.
45. Lieutenant Colonel Maurice Cohen, *Thunder over Kashmir* (Bombay: Orient Longman, 1955), p. 54–55.
46. Rohit Singh, 'Brig Mohammed Usman, MVC, The Lion of Naushera,' *Soldier Scholar* (Autumn 2010): p. 159.
47. 10 Squadron Operational Record Book (2010), Ministry of Defence, Historical Division, New Delhi.
48. Air Marshal Bharat Kumar (retd), *An Incredible War* (New Delhi: KW Publishers, 2009), p. 321.
49. 7 Squadron Operational Record Book, October 1948, Ministry of Defence, Historical Division, New Delhi.
50. From the Madras Engineering Group Archives at the Regimental Centre in Bangalore.
51. C.B. Khanduri, *Thimayya: An Amazing Life* (New Delhi: KW Publishers, 2006), p. 130–134. Also see S.N. Prasad and Dharam Pal, ed., *Operations in Jammu and Kashmir: 1947–48* (New Delhi: Ministry of Defence, Historical Division), p. 356–358.
52. 'New Offensive in Kashmir. Thrust through Zojila Pass: RIAF Support for Ground Forces,' *The Hindu*, 17 November 1948, p. 3.
53. Ibid.
54. For a description of the Dakota-aided fighter strikes, see Air Vice Marshal A.K. Tiwary, *Indian Air Force in Wars* (New Delhi: Lancer, 2012), p. 64–66.
55. Also see *Official History of the 1947–48 India-Pakistan Conflict* (New Delhi: Ministry of Defence), p. 340–42.
56. Lieutenant General E.A. Vas, *Without Baggage* (Dehradun: Natraj Publishers, 1987), p. 163–166.
57. Lieutenant Colonel Maurice Cohen, *Thunder over Kashmir* (Bombay: Orient Longman, 1955), p. 110.

Chapter 11: Guns Fall Silent

1. Sumit Ganguly, *The Origins of War in South Asia: Indo-Pakistan Conflicts since 1947* (New Delhi: Vision Books, 1999), p. 37.
2. Lieutenant General E.A. Vas, *Without Baggage* (Dehradun: Natraj Publishers, 1987), p. 111. For a review of the deployment of Pak regular

forces in the autumn of 1948, see S.N. Prasad and Dharampal, ed., *Operations in Jammu and Kashmir 1947–48*, an official history sponsored by India's Ministry of Defence (Dehradun: Natraj Publishers, 2005), p. 367.

3. 'High Ranking British Officers in Enemy Lines,' *Bombay Chronicle*, API report, 6 September 1948, p. 1. Also see *Bombay Chronicle*, 30 August 1948, p. 1.
4. Major General Akbar Khan, *Raiders over Kashmir* (Karachi: Army Press, 1992), p. 12–16. Also see Sumit Ganguly, *The Origins of War in South Asia: Indo-Pakistan Conflicts since 1947* (New Delhi: Vision Books, 1999), 39–42.
5. 'Secret Military Preparations in NWFP,' *Bombay Chronicle*, 3 September 1948, p. 1.
6. *Bombay Chronicle*, 20 September 1948, p. 7.
7. For an objective analysis of the various UN initiatives on Kashmir in 1948, see Srinath Raghavan, *War and Peace in Modern India* (Ranikhet: Permanent Black, 2010). For a perspective sympathetic to Pakistan, see Joseph Korbel, *Danger over Kashmir* (Princeton: Princeton University Press, 1966).
8. 'Invaders Plan Foiled in Kashmir: No Material Gain after 10 Months Operations in the Valley,' *Bombay Chronicle*, 25 August 1948, p. 7.
9. 'Misleading Reports in US Press,' *Bombay Chronicle*, 1 December 1948, p. 4.
10. 'Resolve to Stand by India,' *Bombay Chronicle*, 16 August 1948, p. 2.
11. Srinath Raghavan, *War and Peace in Modern India* (Ranikhet: Permanent Black, 2010), p. 147.
12. Steven Wilkinson, *Army and Nation: The Military and Indian Democracy* (Cambridge, Massachusetts: Harvard University Press, 2015), p. 204.
13. Interaction with Lieutenant General Satish Nambiar at his residence on 30 July 2015.
14. Interview with Lord Mountbatten by B.R. Nanda on 26 July 1967, NMML Oral History Project.
15. Shuja Nawaz, *Crossed Swords: Pakistan, Its Army, and the Wars Within* (Karachi: Oxford University Press, 2008), p. 52.
16. 'DEP Redesignated as Western Command,' *Bombay Chronicle*, 6 November 1948, p. 1.
17. IAF Historical Cell, Air HQ.
18. 'First Year of Freedom: India through Western Eyes,' *Bombay Chronicle*, 24 August 1948, p. 8.

19. S.N. Prasad (chief editor) and U.P. Thapliyal (general editor), *The India-Pakistan War of 1965: A History* (Dehradun and Delhi: Natraj Publishers, 2011), p. 379–80, an official history of the ministry of defence.
20. Ibid.

Chapter 12: Liberating Hyderabad

1. After signing the Standstill Agreement with the Nizam of Hyderabad, Sardar Vallabhbhai Patel met with Qasim Razvi, the militant leader of the Ittehad-ul-Muslimeen, and reacted strongly when Rizvi indicated that Hyderabad would fight tooth and nail if attacked by Indian forces. From K.M. Munshi, *The End of an Era* (Bombay: Bharatiya Vidya Bhavan, 1957), p. 72.
2. Ramachandra Guha, *India after Gandhi* (London: Pan Macmillan, 2007), p. 45.
3. Ibid., p. 46.
4. Ibid., p. 49.
5. Rajmohan Gandhi, *Patel: A Life* (New Delhi: Navajivan, 1991), p. 292.
6. Rear Admiral Satyindra Singh, *Under Two Ensigns: The Indian Navy 1945–50* (New Delhi, Oxford & IBH Publishing, 1986), p. 98
7. Ibid.
8. Operational Record Book of No. 8 Squadron RIAF, Ministry of Defence, Historical Division, New Delhi.
9. Ibid.
10. Ramachandra Guha, *India after Gandhi* (London: Pan Macmillan, 2007), p. 51.
11. Farzana Sheikh, 'Zulfikar Ali Bhutto: In Pursuit of an Asian Pakistan,' in Ramachandra Guha, ed., *Makers of Modern Asia* (Cambridge: The Belknapp Press, 2014), p. 269.
12. John Keay, *India: A History from the Earliest Civilizations to the Boom of the Twenty-first Century* (London: Harper Press, 2010), p. 512.
13. S.N. Prasad, *Operation Polo: The Police Action against Hyderabad 1948* (New Delhi: Historical Section, Ministry of Defence, 1972), p. 4.
14. Operation Polo, at en.wikipedia.org/wiki/Operation Polo.
15. S.N. Prasad, *Operation Polo: The Police Action against Hyderabad 1948* (New Delhi: Historical Section, Ministry of Defence, 1972), p. 9.
16. 'First Year of Freedom: India through Western Eyes,' *Bombay Chronicle*, 24 August 1948, p. 6.
17. 'The New Hyderabad,' *Bombay Chronicle*, 14 September 1948, p. 6.
18. S.N. Prasad, *Operation Polo: The Police Action against Hyderabad 1948* (New Delhi: Historical Section, Ministry of Defence, 1972), p. 22.

19. Ibid., p. 26.
20. Operation Polo, at en.wikipedia.org/wiki/Operation Polo.
21. 'Razakars Attack Village on Berar and Razakars loot Nanded Border,' *Bombay Chronicle*, 17 August 1948, p. 8.
22. Ibid.
23. 'Reds Attack Nizam's State Railway Stations,' *Bombay Chronicle*, 18 August 1948, p. 8.
24. 'Razakar Orgies at Gulbarga, Bidar, Raichur,' *Bombay Chronicle*, 24 August 1948, p. 7.
25. Josy Joseph, 'Hyd Nizam Said: Gandhi an old Fool,' *The Times of India*, 2 August 2013, p. 12.
26. 'Nizam to Seek UN Intervention,' *Bombay Chronicle*, 20 August 1948, p. 1.
27. *Bombay Chronicle*, 11 and 13 September 1948.
28. *Bombay Chronicle*, 14 September 1948, p. 4. Some of the finest and most objective details of the initial days of the campaign can be found in this newspaper, which established a fine legacy of military reporting in all of India's initial conflicts.
29. Ibid.
30. S.N. Prasad, *Operation Polo: The Police Action against Hyderabad 1948* (New Delhi: Historical Section, Ministry of Defence, 1972), p. 51.
31. Ibid.
32. For a detailed overview of all the forces involved, see S.N. Prasad, *Operation Polo: The Police Action against Hyderabad 1948* (New Delhi: Historical Section, Ministry of Defence, 1972), Appendix III to Appendix X, p. 126–78.
33. White Paper on Hyderabad from *Bombay Chronicle* some time in September 1948.
34. 'Where is the Nizam's Air Force,' *Bombay Chronicle*, 17 September 1948, p. 1.
35. 'Reserve Officers in South Summoned,' *Bombay Chronicle*, 17 September 1948, p. 1.
36. 'Nizam Surrenders to Indian Union,' *Bombay Chronicle*, 18 September 1948, p. 1.
37. 'Hyderabad on the Brink,' *Bombay Chronicle*, 8 September 2013, p. 8. Also see, Proceedings of the Legislative Assembly, September 1948, at NMML.
38. Srinath Raghavan, *War and Peace in Modern India* (Ranikhet: Permanent Black, 2010), p. 98–100. Also see A.G. Noorani, 'Of a Massacre Untold,' *Frontline*, Vol. 18, No. 5 (3–16 March 2001), available at www.

frontlineonnet.com/fl1805/18051130.htm (accessed 10 September 2013).

39. Ibid., p. 100.
40. Ibid.

Chapter 13: Seizing Goa

1. In a speech in the Rajya Sabha in September 1957, from *The Economic and Political Weekly*, 21 September 1957. The procrastination of the Government of India after such aggressive pronouncements by its PM reveals Nehru's reluctance to use force, even if it was against the last vestiges of colonialism in India. Excerpts of the speech are available at http://www.epw.in/system/files/pdf/1957_9/38/base_in_goa.pdf (accessed 6 November 2014).
2. Bipin Chandra, *History of Modern India* (Hyderabad: Orient Blackswan, 2009), p. 37. Also see P.D. Gaitonde, *The Liberation of Goa: A Participant's View of History* (London: Oxford University Press, 1987), p. 3.
3. Ibid., p. 57.
4. P.D. Gaitonde, *The Liberation of Goa: A Participant's View of History* (London: Oxford University Press, 1987), p. 2–3.
5. Satya Mitra Dubey, 'Dr Ram Manohar Lohia: A Rebel Socialist and Visionary,' *Mainstream*, Vol. XLIX, No. 13 (19 March 2011), available at http://www.mainstreamweekly.net/article2629.html (accessed 19 November 2014).
6. P.D. Gaitonde, *The Liberation of Goa: A Participant's View of History* (London: Oxford University Press, 1987), p. 58. Also see Arthur G. Rubinoff, *India's Use of Force in Goa* (Bombay: Popular Prakashan, 1971), p. 2.
7. P.D. Gaitonde, *The Liberation of Goa: A Participant's View of History* (London: Oxford University Press, 1987), p. 102–04.
8. John Keay, *India: A History from the Earliest Civilizations to the Boom of the Twenty-first Century* (London: Harper Press, 2010), p. 534.
9. Arthur G. Rubinoff, *India's Use of Force in Goa* (Bombay: Popular Prakashan, 1971), p. 63–64.
10. Ibid.
11. P.D. Gaitonde, *The Liberation of Goa: A Participant's View of History* (London: Oxford University Press, 1987), p. 108.
12. Arthur G. Rubinoff, *India's Use of Force in Goa* (Bombay: Popular Prakashan, 1971), p. 56.
13. P.D. Gaitonde, *The Liberation of Goa: A Participant's View of History* (London: Oxford University Press, 1987), p. 154. Also see Arthur G.

Rubinoff, *India's Use of Force in Goa* (Bombay: Popular Prakashan, 1971), p. 78–80.

14. John Keay, *India: A History from the Earliest Civilizations to the Boom of the Twenty-first Century* (London: Harper Press, 2010), p. 534.
15. Arthur G. Rubinoff, *India's Use of Force in Goa* (Bombay: Popular Prakashan, 1971), p. 57.
16. Ibid., p. 67–69.
17. Ibid., p. 102
18. P.N. Khera, *Operation Vijay: The Liberation of Goa* (New Delhi: Ministry of Defence, 1974), p. 40.
19. Group Captain Kapil Bhargava, *Operations at Diu: The One Day War*, available at www.bharat-rakshak.com/IAF/1961Goa/1013-Diu.html (accessed 28 October 2013).
20. P.N. Khera, *Operation Vijay: The Liberation of Goa* (New Delhi: Ministry of Defence, 1974), p. 9.
21. Ibid., p. 38.
22. Ramachandra Guha, 'Kripalani versus Menon,' *The Hindu*, 1 August 2004, available at http://www.thehindu.com/thehindu/mag/2004/08/01/stories/2004080100290300.htm (accessed 19 November 2014).
23. P.N. Khera, *Operation Vijay: The Liberation of Goa* (New Delhi: Ministry of Defence, 1974), p. 57.
24. For a detailed break-up of forces and threat assessment, see P.N. Khera, *Operation Vijay: The Liberation of Goa* (New Delhi: Ministry of Defence, 1974), p. 46 and Appendix 1 at p. 145, which highlights the essentials of an appreciation by Lieutenant General J.N. Chaudhuri submitted to the Government of India on 10 November 1961.
25. http://en.wikipedia.org/wiki/Kunhiraman_Palat_Candeth. Also see an obituary: 'K.P. Candeth Dead,' *The Hindu*, 20 May 2003, available at http://hindu.com/2003/05/20/stories/2003052002461300.htm
26. http://en.wikipedia.org/wiki/Bhaskar_Sadashiv_Soman (accessed 10 December 2013).
27. http://en.wikipedia.org/wiki/1961_Indian_annexation_of_Goa (accessed 10 December 2013).
28. P.N. Khera, *Operation Vijay: The Liberation of Goa* (New Delhi: Ministry of Defence, 1974), p. 129. Also see http://www.rediff.com/news/special/goa-liberation-fifty-years-on/20111219.htm (accessed 11 December 2013).
29. Ibid., p. 70–73.
30. Interview with Admiral Nadkarni.
31. P.N. Khera, *Operation Vijay: The Liberation of Goa* (New Delhi: Ministry of Defence, 1974), p. 117.

32. Ibid., p. 100–02.
33. Group Captain Kapil Bhargava, 'Operations at Diu: The One Day War,' available at www.bharat-rakshak.com/IAF/History/1961Goa/1013-Diu.html (accessed 14 December 2013).
34. Ibid.
35. Interview with Admiral Nadkarni.
36. P.N. Khera, 'Casualties during Operation Vijay', *Operation Vijay: The Liberation of Goa* (New Delhi: Ministry of Defence, 1974), p. 238.
37. Major General D.K. Palit (retd), *War in the High Himalayas: The Indian Army in Crisis, 1962* (New Delhi: Lancer, 1991), p. 143–44. Readers may wonder how Goa figured in a book about the 1962 war with China. The book has a chapter on Operation Vijay, the military operation to liberate Goa in December 1961, the same time as things were hotting up along the India–China border.
38. Ibid., p. 111.
39. Brian Cloughley, *A History of the Pakistan Army* (New Delhi: Lancer, 1999), p. 59.

Chapter 14: Unravelling the Frontier with China

1. Dr Uma Bhatt and Dr Shekhar Pathak, *On the Back of Asia* (Nainital: People's Association for Himalayan Area Research, 2007). The original in Hindi is titled *Asia ki Peeth Par*. Also see a review of the book at http://www.thehindu.com/features/magazine/walking-with-nain-singh/article4364702.ece (accessed 6 November 2014).
2. Major General D.K. Palit (retd), *War in the High Himalayas: The Indian Army in Crisis* (New Delhi: Lancer, 1991), p. 28–38. Also see Bertil Lintner, *Great Game East: India, China and the Struggle for Asia's Volatile Frontier* (New Delhi: HarperCollins, 2012), p. 10–12.
3. Extracted from Proceedings of the Royal Geographical Society, Vol. VII (1885): p. 75, available at https://google.com/maps/ms?ie=UTF8&msa=0&msid=202977559498639344429.0004a65eaf28cb9c88b92
4. Shyam G. Menon, 'Walking with Nain Singh,' *The Hindu*, 2 February 2013, at http://www.thehindu.com/features/magazine/walking-with-nain-singh/article4364702.ece (accessed 6 November 2014).
5. Harish Kapadia, 'A Trek in Tawang Tract,' *The Himalayan Journal*, No. 60 (2004), available at http://www.himalayanclub.org/journal/a-trek-in-tawang-tract/.
6. Michael Ward, 'Early Exploration of Kanchenjunga and South Tibet,' *The Alpine Journal* (2001): p. 191, at http://www.alpinejournal.org.uk/

Contents/Contents_2001_files/AJ%202001%20191- 196%20Ward%20 Kangchenjunga.pdf (accessed 21 February 2015).

7. Ibid. Also see https://archive.org/details/journeytolhasace00dass (accessed 20 February 2015). The book was published in 1902 from both New York and London and is probably the only detailed account in English of journeys in Tibet written by an Indian explorer.
8. 'Lieutenant General Zorawar Chand Bakshi PVSM, MVC, VrC, VSM, India's most decorated General,' from http://faujibyheart.blogspot.in/2011/08/lt-general-zorawar-chand-bakshi-india.html (accessed 24 October 2014).
9. For a detailed study of the Aksai Chin region from a historical perspective, see Margaret W. Fisher, Leo E. Rose and Robert A. Huttenback, *Himalayan Battleground: Sino-Indian Rivalry in Ladakh* (New York: Praeger, 1963), p. 98–128.
10. Dr P.B. Sinha and Colonel A.A. Athale, S.N. Prasad (chief editor), *History of the Conflict with China, 1962* (New Delhi: Ministry of Defence, 1992), p. 2, available at http://www.bharat-rakshak.com/LAND-FORCES/Army/History/1962War/PDF/index.html (accessed 10 November 2013).
11. Chumar is an area that has seen a face-off between Indian and Chinese troops as recently as in June 2013. China protested against the construction of bunkers and installation of surveillance cameras, an act that greatly irked them. Chinese troops went on to smash those cameras till a flag meeting was held to reduce the tension. For a detailed report on the Chumar incident see, 'China-India face off at Chumar post on June 17,' *The Times of India*, 12 July 2013, available at http://articles.timesofindia.indiatimes.com/2013-07-12/india/40536089_1_chumar-chinese-troops-dbo (accessed 9 September 2013).
12. The simplest description of the Sino-Indian border dispute with clear maps is available in Alastair Lamb, *The China-India Border: The Origins of the Disputed Territories* (London: Oxford University Press, 1964), p. 5–12. However, much in tune with his pro-Pakistan stance, he has underplayed the ceding of Pakistan-occupied Kashmir territory to China by General Ayub Khan in 1963. For a detailed review of this event and other Sino-Pak collusive border transgressions in Kashmir, see Pradeep Katoch, 'Himalayan Plunder,' Centre for Land Warfare, Article 2288, 2 January 2013, available at http://www.claws.in/index.php?action=master&task=1289&u_id=183 (accessed 9 September 2013).
13. For a detailed military review of General Zorawar's exploits, see Major General G.D. Bakshi (retd), *Footprints in the Snow* (New Delhi: Lancer, 2008).

14. https://en.wikipedia.org/wiki/Zorawar_Singh_Kahluria (accessed 7 July 2013).
15. Alfred P. Rubin, 'The Sino-Indian Border Disputes,' *The International and Comparative Law Quarterly*, Vol. 9, No. 1 (January 1960): p. 96–125.
16. Bipin Chandra, *History of Modern India* (Hyderabad: Orient Blackswan, 2009), p. 83.
17. Ibid.
18. Alastair Lamb, *The China-India Border: The Origins of the Disputed Territories* (London: Oxford University Press, 1964), p. 60. For the full text of a letter from Lord Hardinge, the British viceroy, to the Chinese authorities in Tibet after signing the Lahore Declaration, see Appendix I of the same book, p. 177–79.
19. Major General D.K. Palit (retd), *War in the High Himalayas: The Indian Army in Crisis* (New Delhi: Lancer, 1991), p. 23. Also see, Neville Maxwell, *India's China War* (London: Cape, 1970), p. 28.
20. Michael Ward, 'The Pundits beyond the Pamir: The Forsythe Mission of 1870 and 1873,' *The Alpine Journal* (2003): p. 203–04, available at www.alpinejournal.org (accessed 3 October 2013).
21. Bertil Lintner, *Great Game East: India, China and the Struggle for Asia's Volatile Frontier* (New Delhi: HarperCollins, 2012), p. 10.
22. Alastair Lamb, *The China-India Border: The Origins of the Disputed Territories* (London: Oxford University Press, 1964), p. 14.
23. Margaret W. Fisher, Leo E. Rose and Robert A. Huttenback, *Himalayan Battleground: Sino-Indian Rivalry in Ladakh* (New York: Praeger, 1963), p. 98–100.
24. Alastair Lamb, *The China-India Border: The Origins of the Disputed Territories* (London: Oxford University Press, 1964), p. 61–62.
25. Ibid., p. 107.
26. The region of Aksai Chin then fell within the British Empire if one were to consider this frontier.
27. Ibid.
28. Bertil Lintner, *Great Game East: India, China and the Struggle for Asia's Volatile Frontier* (New Delhi: HarperCollins, 2012), p. 12.
29. Sir Francis Younghusband, *India and Tibet* (London: John Murray, 1910), p. 96–97. The book is a treasure trove of historical information on Sikkim, Nepal and Tibet of the early twentieth century. It is also a saga of courage as the expedition braved the vagaries of nature to enter Tibet through the Chumbi Valley.

Chapter 15: Sparring and Probing

1. From correspondence between General Thimayya and Romesh Thapar soon after the India–China war of 1962, NMML Archives, accessed January 2013.
2. The Panchsheel Agreement between India and China was signed with much fanfare at the Bandung Conference in 1954 and laid down five tenets of peaceful coexistence between India and China. These were mutual respect for each other's territorial integrity, mutual non-aggression, mutual non-interference in each other's internal affairs, equality and mutual benefit and peaceful coexistence.
3. Claude Arpi, *1962 and the McMahon Line Saga* (Atlanta: Lancer, 2013), p. 430.
4. Ibid., p. 434.
5. Ibid.
6. Dr P.B. Sinha and Colonel A.A. Athale, S.N. Prasad (chief editor), *History of the Conflict with China, 1962* (New Delhi: Ministry of Defence, 1992), p. 52–59. Zhou Enlai was skilful and consummate in his letters to Nehru, hoping that India would realize in time that they would not be able to cope with Chinese aggression.
7. Mandeep Singh Bajwa, 'General Nath's Recce in Aksai Chin,' *Hindustan Times,* Chandigarh, 22 January 2013, available at http://www.hindustantimes.com/punjab/chandigarh/gen-nath-s-recce-in-aksai-chin/article1-997975.aspx. Mandeep Bajwa goes on to lament that Captain Nath's report remains a Top Secret document even today and cannot be published. Thus, Captain Nath lost an opportunity to receive the United Service Institution's McGregor Medal that is awarded for military reconnaissance.
8. C.B. Khanduri, *Thimayya: An Amazing Life* (New Delhi, KW Publishers, 2006), p. 222.
9. Ibid., p. 213–215.
10. John Garver, 'China's Decision for War with India in 1962,' in Robert S. Ross and Alastair Iain Johnston, ed., *New Approaches to the Study of Chinese Foreign Policy* (Stanford University Press, 2005). From a PDF extract of the chapter (p.4) taken from http://indianstrategicknowledgeonline.com/web/china%20decision%20for%201962%20war%202003.pdf (accessed 9 September 2013).
11. Ibid., p. 13.
12. Ibid., p. 10–11.
13. Ibid., p. 32.

14. R.D. Pradhan, *Debacle to Revival: Y.B. Chavan as Defence Minister, 1962–65* (New Delhi: Orient Longman, 1999), p. 2.
15. Neville Maxwell, *India's China War* (London: Cape, 1970), p. 110.
16. For a detailed analysis of India–China diplomacy during those turbulent times, also see Ramachandra Guha, *India after Gandhi* (London: Pan Macmillan, 2007), p. 301–21. For a biased China-centric view see Neville Maxwell, *India's China War* (London: Cape, 1970). For Nehru's perspective on his attempts to diplomatically resolve the boundary impasse, see S. Gopal, ed., *Selected Works of Jawaharlal Nehru*, Vol. 14 (New Delhi: Orient Longman).
17. For a detailed general review of Thimayya's resignation drama, see C.B. Khanduri, *Thimayya: An Amazing Life* (New Delhi, KW Publishers, 2006), p. 282–95. The episode reveals the deep and debilitating schisms that existed within the politico-military interface of the time because of the dominating and condescending approach of Defence Minister V.K. Krishna Menon towards senior military leadership.
18. Ibid.
19. For a detailed analysis of the Forward Policy, see Major General D.K. Palit (retd), *War in the High Himalayas: The Indian Army in Crisis* (New Delhi: Lancer, 1991), p. 90–100. Also see Major General Jagjit Singh, *While the Memory Is Fresh* (New Delhi: Lancer, 2006), p. 101–10.
20. The Indian Army's operational dissent to the Forward Policy is well chronicled by Neville Maxwell, *India's China War* (London: Cape, 1970), p. 199–205.
21. Dr P.B. Sinha and Colonel A.A. Athale, S.N. Prasad (chief editor), *History of the Conflict with China, 1962* (New Delhi: Ministry of Defence, 1992), p. 343–46.
22. Air Chief Marshal P.C. Lal, *My Years with the IAF* (New Delhi: Lancer, 1986), p. 100–106.
23. The IAF and the Indian Army had calculated that to sustain the Forward Policy in the east a monthly airlift of 2,200, tons was the bare minimum required. Despite its best efforts the IAF could manage an average of only 1,200 tons a month. If one factors in the 25–30 per cent loss due to the small size of the dropping zones and narrow valleys, the airlift was woefully inadequate. See Dr P.B. Sinha and Colonel A.A. Athale, S.N. Prasad (chief editor), *History of the Conflict with China, 1962* (New Delhi: Ministry of Defence, 1992), p. 353.
24. Interview with Squadron Leader Baldev Raj Gulati (retd) on 17 October 2014. A highly experienced navigator, Gulati remains till today a bitter man about India's defeat in 1962 and retains vivid recollections of the conflict which he shares very willingly.

25. John Garver, 'China's Decision for War with India in 1962,' in Robert S. Ross and Alastair Iain Johnston, ed., *New Approaches to the Study of Chinese Foreign Policy* (Stanford University Press, 2005), p. 35.
26. Larry M. Wortzel, 'Concentrating Forces and Audacious Action: PLA Lessons from the Sino-Indian War,' in Laurie Burkitt, Andrew Scobell and Larry Wortzel, ed., *The Lessons of History: The Chinese People's Liberation Army at 75* (US Army War College Monograph, 2003), p. 336.

CHAPTER 16: OMINOUS SIGNS

1. Jonathan Holstag, 'China's Rise and the Use of Force: A Historical and Geopolitical Perspective,' Chapter 1, *Adelphi Series*, Vol. 50, No. 416, p. 19–28, available at http://dx.doi.org/10.1080/19445571.2010.548033 (accessed 13 October 2013).
2. Larry M. Wortzel, 'Concentrating Forces and Audacious Action: PLA Lessons from the Sino-Indian War,' in Laurie Burkitt, Andrew Scobell and Larry Wortzel, ed., *The Lessons of History: The Chinese People's Liberation Army at 75* (US Army War College Monograph, 2003), p. 341.
3. For a detailed rationale of why the IB was put in charge of the defence of eastern Ladakh, see B.N. Mullick, *My Years with Nehru* (Bombay: Allied Publishers, 1973). The essence of Mullick's argument that it was sufficient to have stray patrols by IB teams in eastern Ladakh, rather than have the army deployed there in numbers, pointed at a Pakistan-centric threat analysis in Ladakh. Therefore, the army was asked to concentrate on western Ladakh (Kargil and Dras) and leave eastern Ladakh to the IB. Mullick completely overestimated the military potential of the IB!
4. Major General S.V. Thapliyal (retd), 'Battle for Eastern Ladakh: 1962 Sino-Indian Conflict,' http:// www.usiofindia.org/ Article/?pubno=5608&ano=482# (accessed on 10 August 2013).
5. C.B. Khanduri, *Thimayya: An Amazing Life* (New Delhi, KW Publishers, 2006), p. 233–38.
6. Ibid., p. 296–97.
7. B.G. Verghese, '50 Years After 1962: A Personal Memoir,' from a presentation delivered at the India International Centre, Subbu Forum, SPS Round Table on '50 Years after 1962: Recall and Review' on 6 September 2012, available at southasiamonitor.org/detail.php?type=yearsafter&nid=3844 (accessed 28 November 2014).
8. Also see Dr P.B. Sinha and Colonel A.A. Athale, S.N. Prasad (chief editor), *History of the Conflict with China, 1962* (New Delhi: Ministry of Defence, 1992), p. xxii.

9. Major General D.K. Palit (retd), *War in the High Himalayas: The Indian Army in Crisis* (New Delhi: Lancer, 1991), p. 179. Also see p. 247–55.
10. For a complete deployment in the Ladakh sector, see Major General S.V. Thapliyal, 'Battle of Eastern Ladakh: 1962 Sino-Indian Conflict' at http://www.usiofindia.org/Article/?pub=Journal&pubno=560&ano=482.
11. For a detailed tactical deployment, see Dr P.B. Sinha and Colonel A.A. Athale, S.N. Prasad (chief editor), *History of the Conflict with China, 1962* (New Delhi: Ministry of Defence, 1992), p. 67–73.
12. Major General S.V. Thapliyal, 'Battle of Eastern Ladakh: 1962 Sino-Indian Conflict' at http://www.usiofindia.org/Article/?pub=Journal&pubno=560&ano=482. Also see Major General Jagjit Singh, *While the Memory Is Fresh* (New Delhi: Lancer, 2006), p. 125–32. Jagjit Singh was the brigade major of 114 Infantry Brigade and had a ringside view of operations in the 1962 conflict.
13. Ibid.
14. Larry M. Wortzel, 'Concentrating Forces and Audacious Action: PLA Lessons from the Sino-Indian War,' in Laurie Burkitt, Andrew Scobell and Larry Wortzel, ed., *The Lessons of History: The Chinese People's Liberation Army at 75* (US Army War College Monograph, 2003), p. 339.
15. Major General Jagjit Singh, *While the Memory Is Fresh* (New Delhi: Lancer, 2006), p. 330.
16. Brigadier J.P. Dalvi, *Himalayan Blunder* (Dehradun: Natraj Publishers, 1969).
17. A PLA regiment was equivalent to an Indian Army brigade in terms of combat potential.
18. Interview with Air Marshal Vinod Patney on 2 June 2013. The air marshal was a young flying officer and posted at Tezpur during the conflict.
19. Air Marshal Bharat Kumar, *Unknown and Unsung: Indian Air Force in Sino-Indian War of 1962* (New Delhi: KW Publishers, 2013).
20. See R. Sukumaran, 'The 1962 India-China War and Kargil 1999: Restrictions on the Use of Air Power,' *Strategic Analysis*, Vol. 27, No. 3 (July–September 2003): p. 332–55. Also see Arjun Subramaniam, 'Clearing the Air,' *The Indian Express*, New Delhi, 21 October 2012, p. 2.
21. Air Marshal Bharat Kumar, *Unknown and Unsung: Indian Air Force in Sino-Indian War of 1962* (New Delhi: KW Publishers, 2013), p. 39.
22. Telephonic conversation with Air Marshal Randhir Singh in October 2014. He revealed during that interview that he was asked to assume

command of 106 Squadron after it had one aircraft shot down over Pakistan in 1959 during a clandestine intrusive mission.

23. Air Marshal S. Raghavendran, *Panther Red One* (New Delhi: KW Publishers, 2013), p. 141.
24. Ibid., p. 187.
25. Ibid., p. 83–84. Also see R. Sukumaran, 'The 1962 India-China War and Kargil 1999: Restrictions on the Use of Air Power,' *Strategic Analysis*, Vol. 27, No. 3 (July–September 2003): p. 333. Also see S.N. Prasad, ed., *History of the Conflict with China, 1962* (New Delhi: Ministry of Defence, 1992), p. 356–57.
26. A detachment of Canberra reconnaissance and bomber aircraft from Agra was moved to Tezpur and worked in close liaison with HQ 4 Corps. Also see Air Marshal Bharat Kumar, *Unknown and Unsung: Indian Air Force in Sino-Indian War of 1962* (New Delhi: KW Publishers, 2013), IAF deployment map, p. 95.
27. Ibid.
28. Interview with Air Marshal Patney on 2 June 2013.
29. Ibid.
30. An operational assessment from Air HQ sounded extreme caution with regard to close air support (CAS) in NEFA. However, it is surprising that the same report does not mention that CAS in Ladakh could be a worthwhile proposition. Also see R. Sukumaran, 'The 1962 India-China War and Kargil 1999: Restrictions on the Use of Air Power,' *Strategic Analysis*, Vol. 27, No. 3 (July–September 2003): p. 337.
31. Asher Lee, *The Russian and Chinese Air Forces, Brasseys Annual – The Armed Forces Yearbook* (London: William Clowes and Sons, 1963), p. 97–99. Also see R. Sukumaran, 'The 1962 India-China War and Kargil 1999: Restrictions on the Use of Air Power,' *Strategic Analysis*, Vol. 27, No. 3 (July–September 2003): p. 335–336.
32. Most of the twenty-odd airfields in Tibet were at altitudes of above 3,500 m, with some as high as 4,500 m.
33. Also see Air Vice Marshal A.K. Tiwary, 'No Use of Air Power in 1962,' *Indian Defence Review*, Vol. 21, No. 3 (July–September 2006), available at http://www.indiandefencereview.com/spotlights/no-use-of-combat-air-power-in-1962/ (accessed 29 November 2014).
34. Air Marshal Bharat Kumar, *Unknown and Unsung: Indian Air Force in Sino-Indian War of 1962* (New Delhi: KW Publishers, 2013), p. 103–10.
35. Ibid.
36. Ibid., p. 130–33.
37. Dr P.B. Sinha and Colonel A.A. Athale, S.N. Prasad (chief editor),

History of the Conflict with China, 1962 (New Delhi: Ministry of Defence, 1992), p. 353–55.

38. B.G. Verghese, '50 Years After 1962: A Personal Memoir,' from a presentation delivered at the India International Centre, Subbu Forum, SPS Round Table on '50 Years after 1962: Recall and Review' on 6 September 2012, available at southasiamonitor.org/detail.php?type=yearsafter&nid=3844 (accessed 28 November 2014).
39. John Garver, 'China's Decision for War with India in 1962,' in Robert S. Ross and Alastair Iain Johnston, ed., *New Approaches to the Study of Chinese Foreign Policy* (Stanford University Press, 2005).
40. Major General D.K. Palit (retd), *War in the High Himalayas: The Indian Army in Crisis* (New Delhi: Lancer, 1991), p. 178.
41. Lieutenant Colonel Gautam Sharma, *Valour and Sacrifice: Famous Regiments of the Indian Army* (New Delhi: Allied Publishers, 1990), p. 170–71.
42. For a detailed analysis of the Namka Chu battle see Major General P.J.S. Sandhu (retd), '1962 – The Battle of Namka Chu and the Fall of Tawang (A View from the Other Side of the Hill)', *USI Journal*, New Delhi (April–June 2013): p. 271–89.
43. Neville Maxwell, *India's China War* (London: Cape, 1970), p. 303–09.
44. John Garver, 'China's Decision for War with India in 1962,' in Robert S. Ross and Alastair Iain Johnston, ed., *New Approaches to the Study of Chinese Foreign Policy* (Stanford University Press, 2005), p. 48.
45. Ibid., p. 49.
46. Major General D.K. Palit (retd), *War in the High Himalayas: The Indian Army in Crisis* (New Delhi: Lancer, 1991), p. 224–25.
47. John Garver, 'China's Decision for War with India in 1962,' in Robert S. Ross and Alastair Iain Johnston, ed., *New Approaches to the Study of Chinese Foreign Policy* (Stanford University Press, 2005), p. 55.
48. Neville Maxwell, *India's China War* (London: Cape, 1970), p. 335–40.
49. Major General P.J.S. Sandhu (retd), '1962 – The Battle of Namka Chu and the Fall of Tawang (A View from the Other Side of the Hill)', *USI Journal*, New Delhi (April–June 2013): p. 283.
50. Zhou Enlai at an expanded Politburo meeting on 18 October. See John Garver, 'China's Decision for War with India in 1962,' in Robert S. Ross and Alastair Iain Johnston, ed., *New Approaches to the Study of Chinese Foreign Policy* (Stanford University Press, 2005), p. 59.
51. Registering is a military term that denotes the process of attempting to exactly ascertain the coordinates of a tactical location by firing a few artillery rounds, and then validating the accuracy with visual

confirmation, either from a vantage location on ground, or from an aerial reconnaissance platform like a helicopter.

52. See Major J.S. Rathore (retd), 'Memoirs of a Prisoner of War: Sino Indian War of 1962,' *USI Journal* (January–March 2014): p. 128–29. The officer was part of 17 Para Field Regiment who was captured during the battle of Namku Chu and remained a prisoner for over nineteen months.
53. Lieutenant Colonel Gautam Sharma, *Valour and Sacrifice: Famous Regiments of the Indian Army* (New Delhi: Allied Publishers, 1990), p. 142–43.
54. Ibid.
55. Major General P.J.S. Sandhu (retd), '1962 – The Battle of Namka Chu and the Fall of Tawang (A View from the Other Side of the Hill)', *USI Journal*, New Delhi (April–June 2013): p. 283.
56. Major General D.K. Palit (retd), *War in the High Himalayas: The Indian Army in Crisis* (New Delhi: Lancer, 1991), p. 242.
57. For a detailed and poignant defence of 7 Brigade's performance in the battle of Namka Chu, see Brigadier J.P. Dalvi, *Himalayan Blunder* (Dehradun: Natraj Publishers, 1969). Major portions of the book were written by Brigadier Dalvi during his six months as a POW after his brigade was run over by a massive Chinese assault on 20 October 1962.
58. Mandeep Singh Bajwa, 'The Hero of Battle of IB Ridge,' *Hindustan Times,* Chandigarh, 23 October 2012, available at http://www.hindustantimes.com/punjab/chandigarh/the-hero-of-battle-of-ib-ridge/article1-948985.aspx (accessed 18 October 2014).
59. An aggressive right-wing opposition with scanty knowledge of the operational situation on ground did not leave any political space for Nehru to negotiate with China after the humiliating experiences of the first few days of the war. Instead, he continued to harp on 'throwing the Chinese out'. It was clear that political wisdom and sagacity was replaced by nationalistic warmongering.
60. Air Chief Marshal P.C. Lal, *My Years with the IAF* (New Delhi: Lancer, 1986), p. 95.
61. 'Battle of Walong: 18 Oct-16 Nov 1962,' www.bharat-rakshak.com/LAND-FORCES/Army/History/1962War/Walong,html (accessed 2 September, 2013). Also see Lieutenant Colonel Gautam Sharma, *Valour and Sacrifice. Famous Regiments of the Indian Army* (New Delhi: Allied Publishers, 1990), p. 281–82 and Major General D.K. Palit (retd), *War in the High Himalayas: The Indian Army in Crisis* (New Delhi: Lancer, 1991), p. 299.
62. See note 23 in the previous chapter describing the perils of air dropping in the Eastern Sector.

63. Air Marshal Bharat Kumar, *Unknown and Unsung: Indian Air Force in Sino-Indian War of 1962* (New Delhi: KW Publishers, 2013), p. 181.
64. Ibid., p. 175.
65. Air Vice Marshal A.K. Tiwary, *Indian Air Force in Wars* (New Delhi: Lancer, 2012), p. 73–76. Tiwary offers a detailed account of the events of 20 October.
66. A passionate account of the exploits of 110 HU has been written by Air Commodore Melville Rego, who was a young engineering officer in the unit during the battle of Walong. See Air Commodore Mellvile C. Rego, 'In the Line of Fire – 110 Helicopter Unit,' http://www.bharat-rakshak.com/IAF/History/1962War/1092-Rego01.html?showall=1 (accessed 30 November 2014).
67. Major General S.V. Thapliyal (retd), 'Battle for Eastern Ladakh: 1962 Sino-Indian Conflict,' http:// www.usiofindia.org/Article/?pubno=5608&ano=482# (accessed on 10 August 2013).
68. Lieutenant Colonel Gautam Sharma, *Valour and Sacrifice: Famous Regiments of the Indian Army* (New Delhi: Allied Publishers, 1990), p. 170.
69. Air Marshal Bharat Kumar, *Unknown and Unsung: Indian Air Force in Sino-Indian War of 1962* (New Delhi: KW Publishers, 2013), p. 257.
70. Ibid., p. 245.

Chapter 17: Defeat

1. John Garver, 'China's Decision for War with India in 1962,' in Robert S. Ross and Alastair Iain Johnston, ed., *New Approaches to the Study of Chinese Foreign Policy* (Stanford University Press, 2005), p. 3.
2. Jaidev Singh Datta, *Recollections of the Sela Bodila Debacle 1962* (New Delhi: KW Publishers, 2013), p. 30–33.
3. Major General P.J.S. Sandhu (retd), '1962 – The Battle of Namka Chu and the Fall of Tawang (A View from the Other Side of the Hill)', *USI Journal*, New Delhi (April–June 2013): p. 277.
4. Interview with Squadron Leader Gulati, 17 October 2014.
5. Jaidev Singh Datta, *Recollections of the Sela Bodila Debacle 1962* (New Delhi: KW Publishers, 2013), Order of Battle – Chinese Army, p. 127–32.
6. Ibid., p. 149–65. Also see Lieutenant Colonel Gautam Sharma, *Valour and Sacrifice: Famous Regiments of the Indian Army* (New Delhi: Allied Publishers, 1990), p. 255.
7. Ibid. Taken from the chapter 'Chinese Offensive'. The main source for this material, according to the author, was from an official Chinese

book *China's War of Self Defence Counter Attack on India* published by the Academy of Military Sciences, Beijing, 1994.

8. Air Marshal Bharat Kumar, *Unknown and Unsung: Indian Air Force in Sino-Indian War of 1962* (New Delhi: KW Publishers, 2013), p. 249.
9. B.G. Verghese, '50 Years After 1962: A Personal Memoir,' from a presentation delivered at the India International Centre, Subbu Forum, SPS Round Table on '50 Years after 1962: Recall and Review' on 6 September 2012, available at southasiamonitor.org/detail.php?type=yearsafter&nid=3844 (accessed 28 November 2014).
10. Harbaksh Singh felt that offering resistance at Walong was a sure recipe for disaster and tried to convince his superiors to develop Hayuliang as the main defence, but he was overruled by Delhi. See Lieutenant General Harbaksh Singh, *In the Line of Duty* (New Delhi: Lancer, 2000), p. 312.
11. L.N. Subramaniam, 'Battle of Walong: 18 October–16 November 1962,' http://www.bharat-rakshak.com/LAND-FORCES/History/1962War/263-Walong.html (accessed 19 November 2014). Also see Dr P.B. Sinha and Colonel A.A. Athale, S.N. Prasad (chief editor), *History of the Conflict with China, 1962* (New Delhi: Ministry of Defence, 1992), p. 238–41.
12. Ibid.
13. Air Marshal Bharat Kumar, *Unknown and Unsung: Indian Air Force in Sino-Indian War of 1962* (New Delhi: KW Publishers, 2013), p. 237.
14. Major General S.V. Thapliyal (retd), 'Battle for Eastern Ladakh: 1962 Sino-Indian Conflict,' http:// www.usiofindia.org/Article/?pubno=5608&ano=482# (accessed on 10 August 2013). Also see Air Marshal Bharat Kumar, *Unknown and Unsung: Indian Air Force in Sino-Indian War of 1962* (New Delhi: KW Publishers, 2013), p. 264–66.
15. Conversation with Lieutenant General Rustam Nanavatty on 10 November 2013.
16. Lieutenant Colonel Gautam Sharma, *Valour and Sacrifice: Famous Regiments of the Indian Army* (New Delhi: Allied Publishers, 1990), p. 279–80. Also see Major General S.V. Thapliyal (retd), 'Battle for Eastern Ladakh: 1962 Sino-Indian Conflict,' http:// www.usiofindia.org/Article/?pubno=5608&ano=482# (accessed on 10 August 2013). Numerous accounts are available on this epic battle. Also see Battle Honours section at the Kumaon Regimental Centre, Ranikhet.
17. Colonel N.N. Bhatia (retd), '1962 – War in the Western Sector (Ladakh),' *USI Journal* (January–March 2014): p. 134–37.
18. Interview with Group Captain M. Murdeshwar on 15 March 2015 at Pune. The author cross-checked the reference to the sortie in his well-preserved logbook.

19. Geoffrey Blainey, *The Causes of War* (New York: The Free Press, 1988), p. 50.
20. The Henderson Brooks Report is a still a 'Top Secret' report on operational aspects of the 1962 war. It has not been declassified, supposedly because its contents may have a detrimental effect on the morale of India's armed forces. More importantly, it may also reveal the complete absence of apportioning any blame for the debacle elsewhere.
21. 'Hardening of Troops for War – February 1944,' distributed by the manager of publications, Government of India, with a caption: This document must not fall into the hands of the enemy.
22. Ibid.
23. Assorted email correspondence from friends who wanted to help and contribute to the chapter.
24. Major General P.J.S. Sandhu (retd), '1962 – The Battle of Namka Chu and the Fall of Tawang (A View from the Other Side of the Hill),' *USI Journal*, New Delhi (April–June 2013): p. 289. According to Sandhu, 832 Indian soldiers of all ranks were killed in the battles of Namka Chu and Tawang against just 115 killed on the Chinese side.
25. Laurie Burkitt, Andrew Scobell and Larry M. Wortzel, ed., *The Lessons of History: The Chinese People's Liberation Army at 75* (US Army War College, 2003), available at http://www.strategicstudiesinstitute.army.mil/pubs/display.cfm?pubID=52 (accessed on 20 October 2014).
26. Ibid, p. 327–46.
27. Directorate of Military Intelligence, *Japanese in Battle*, Part 1, Enemy Method (New Delhi: Manager Publications, Government of India, 1943).
28. Major J.S. Rathore (retd), 'Memoirs of a Prisoner of War: Sino-Indian War of 1962,' *USI Journal* (January-March 2014): p. 132–33.
29. Interview with Squadron Leader Gulati.
30. Major J.S. Rathore (retd), 'Memoirs of a Prisoner of War: Sino-Indian War of 1962,' *USI Journal* (January-March 2014): p. 133.
31. While the Ministry of Defence, Government of India, puts Indian losses at 1,383 soldiers killed, 1,696 missing, 1,047 wounded and 3,968 captured, PLA archives put the number of killed as much higher at 4,897 as against Chinese losses of only 722 killed and 1,047 wounded. However, Chinese casualties are likely to have been much higher considering the number of battles wherein there was stiff resistance from entrenched Indian troops. See Laurie Burkitt, Andrew Scobell and Larry M. Wortzel, ed., *The Lessons of History: The Chinese People's Liberation Army at 75* (US Army War College, 2003), p. 343, available at http://

www.strategicstudiesinstitute.army.mil/pubs/display.cfm?pubID=52 (accessed on 20 October 2014).

32. Bhavna Vij Arora, 'RSS Wants Students to Learn More about India-China War,' *The Economic Times*, New Delhi, 2 June 2015, p. 2.

Chapter 18: Opening Moves: Kutch to Kashmir in 1965

1. Speaking to the Indian nation on All India Radio, 13 August 1965. From Ramachandra Guha's blog at http://ramachandraguha.in/archives/the-forgotten-prime-minister-the-hindu.html (accessed 8 November 2014).
2. Stephen P. Cohen, *The Idea of Pakistan* (New Delhi: Oxford University Press, 2004), p. 102. The other members of CENTO were Turkey, Iran and the USA. Also see Mohammed Ayub Khan, 'The Pakistan-American Alliance', *Foreign Affairs* (January 1964), available at http://www.foreignaffairs.com/articles/23567/mohammed-ayub-khan/the-pakistan-american-alliance (accessed 19 November 2014).
3. Sumit Ganguly, *The Origins of War in South Asia: Indo-Pakistan Conflicts since 1947* (New Delhi: Vision Books, 1999), p. 57.
4. Key features of this treaty were defended by Bhutto in his speech to the UN Security Council on 26 March 1963. See http://www.bhutto.org/1957-1965_speech45.php
5. Sumit Ganguly, *The Origins of War in South Asia: Indo-Pakistan Conflicts since 1947* (New Delhi: Vision Books, 1999), p. 51–52.
6. Ibid.
7. Lieutenant General Harbaksh Singh, *War Despatches: Indo-Pak Conflict of 1965* (New Delhi: Lancer International, 1991), p. 22.
8. The Rann of Kutch is a desolate and beautiful region with tremendous diversity of flora and fauna. The wild asses of Kutch are an endangered species that roam the salt pans, and so are the flamingos which frequent the riverine waterways of the province.
9. For a Pakistani viewpoint on the ownership of the Rann, see Lubna Abid Ali, 'The Rann of Kutch and Its Aftermath,' *South Asian Studies: A Research Journal of South Asian Studies,* Vol. 24, No. 2 (July–December 2009): p. 251–52.
10. Report of International Arbitral Awards; The Indo-Pakistan Western Boundary (Rann of Kutch) between India and Pakistan, Vol. XVII (19 February 1968): p. 400–500.
11. For a detailed description of force levels and a chronological sequence of events, see S.N. Prasad (chief editor) and U.P. Thapliyal (general editor),

The India-Pakistan War of 1965: A History (Dehradun and Delhi: Natraj Publishers, 2011), p. 20–30. This book is an official history of the war, brought out by the Ministry of Defence, Government of India.

12. Stephen P. Cohen, *The Pakistan Army* (New Delhi: Himalayan Books, 1984), p. 64
13. Stephen P. Cohen, *The Idea of Pakistan* (New Delhi: Oxford University Press, 2004), p. 102.
14. Lubna Abid Ali, 'The Rann of Kutch and Its Aftermath,' *South Asian Studies: A Research Journal of South Asian Studies,* Vol. 24, No. 2 (July–December 2009): p. 253–55.
15. S.N. Prasad (chief editor) and U.P. Thapliyal (general editor), *The India-Pakistan War of 1965: A History* (Dehradun and Delhi: Natraj Publishers, 2011), p. 27–28.
16. 'The Preliminaries: Line-up and the Rann of Kutch,' www.bharat-rakshak.com/IAF/History/1965war/chapter2.html (accessed on 14 September 2013).
17. Lubna Abid Ali, 'The Rann of Kutch and Its Aftermath,' *South Asian Studies: A Research Journal of South Asian Studies,* Vol. 24, No. 2 (July–December 2009): p. 252.
18. Ibid. Also see S.N. Prasad (chief editor) and U.P. Thapliyal (general editor), *The India-Pakistan War of 1965: A History* (Dehradun and Delhi: Natraj Publishers, 2011), p. 27.
19. P.C. Lal, *My Years with the IAF* (New Delhi: Lancer, 1986), p. 124.
20. For a crisp account of the Kutch battle, see K.C. Praval, *India's Paratroopers* (New Delhi: Thomson Press, 1974), p. 240–48.
21. S.N. Prasad (chief editor) and U.P. Thapliyal (general editor), *The India-Pakistan War of 1965: A History* (Dehradun and Delhi: Natraj Publishers, 2011), p. 21.
22. P.V.S. Jagan Mohan and Samir Chopra, *The India-Pakistan Air War of 1965* (New Delhi: Manohar, 2009), p. 62.
23. In an email exchange between Jagan Mohan and Sajad Haider on 5 March 2015, the PAF veteran shares some illuminating perspectives on the 1965 war.
24. Ibid.
25. John Fricker, *Battle for Pakistan* (Surrey: Ian Allen Ltd, 1979), p. 42.
26. Lubna Abid Ali, 'The Rann of Kutch and Its Aftermath,' *South Asian Studies: A Research Journal of South Asian Studies,* Vol. 24, No. 2 (July–December 2009): p. 254.
27. S.N. Prasad (chief editor) and U.P. Thapliyal (general editor), *The India-Pakistan War of 1965: A History* (Dehradun and Delhi: Natraj Publishers, 2011), p. 36–37.

28. P.C. Lal, *My Years with the IAF* (New Delhi: Lancer, 1986), p. 124–25.
29. Ibid.
30. P.V.S. Jagan Mohan and Samir Chopra, *The India-Pakistan Air War of 1965* (New Delhi: Manohar, 2009), p. 36.
31. Lieutenant General Harbaksh Singh, *War Despatches: Indo-Pak Conflict of 1965* (New Delhi: Lancer International, 1991), p. 22.
32. Sumit Ganguly, *Conflict Unending: India-Pakistan Tensions since 1947* (New Delhi: Oxford University Press, 2002), p. 37.
33. Ibid., p. 31.
34. S.N. Prasad (chief editor) and U.P. Thapliyal (general editor), *The India-Pakistan War of 1965: A History* (Dehradun and Delhi: Natraj Publishers, 2011), p. 13.
35. Sumit Ganguly, *Conflict Unending: India-Pakistan Tensions since 1947* (New Delhi: Oxford University Press, 2002), p. 37.
36. While Sumit Ganguly indicates that India had two armoured divisions against Pakistan's one, a more accurate holding is provided by Brian Cloughley, *A History of the Pakistan Army* (New Delhi: Lancer, 1999), p. 67–68. The Pak advantage over India was mainly in the form of an extra armoured brigade with six armoured divisions.
37. For a detailed tabular comparison of all forces, see S.N. Prasad (chief editor) and U.P. Thapliyal (general editor), *The India-Pakistan War of 1965: A History* (Dehradun and Delhi: Natraj Publishers, 2011), p. 9–11.
38. Shuja Nawaz, *Crossed Swords: Pakistan, Its Army, and the Wars Within* (Karachi: Oxford University Press, 2008), p. 193.
39. P.V.S. Jagan Mohan and Samir Chopra, *The India-Pakistan Air War of 1965* (New Delhi: Manohar, 2009), p. 55.
40. Ibid., Appendix G, p. 358–359.
41. This version had a fighter-style tandem cockpit as against the British version with India which had the navigator lying on his belly in the nose. The US version had ejection seats for both the pilot and the navigator, while only the pilot had an ejection facility in the IAF Canberra; the navigator had to bail out.
42. Air Vice Marshal A.K. Tiwary, *Indian Air Force in Wars* (New Delhi: Lancer, 2012), table at p. 119.
43. Interview with Air Marshal Patney, 2 June 2013. Air Marshal Pingale and Air Marshal Ghandhi would confirm to the author in numerous conversations that there was no such feeling in IAF squadrons.
44. The fact was confirmed in a telephonic conversation with Wing Commander Mayadev, who as a flying officer accompanied McMahon and Bhatia to train on Sabres in the US. He recalls that in a briefing

in 9 Squadron (Gnats) prior to the sortie in which he was shot down, Mayadev had queried the formation leader on what they should do if the Sabres 'split'. When there was no clarity, he decided to stick with his leader even when he saw the Sabres in front split, with one of them then manoeuvring offensively to shoot down Mayadev.

45. 'Mitty Masud Folds His Wings,' at http://www.dawn.com/news/1065137/dawn-features-october-13-2003 (accessed 11 April 2015).
46. Farzana Sheikh, 'Zulfikar Ali Bhutto: In Pursuit of an Asian Pakistan,' in Ramachandra Guha, ed., *Makers of Modern Asia* (Cambridge: The Belknapp Press, 2014), p. 281.
47. M. Asghar Khan, *The First Round Indo-Pakistan War 1965* (Ghaziabad: Vikas Publishing House, 1979), p. 75.
48. Major General Lachhman Singh, *Missed Opportunities: Indo-Pak War 1965* (Dehradun: Natraj Publishers, 1997), p. 117, 155. For a detailed analysis of the role played by Akhtar Malik in Operation Gibraltar and Operation Grand Slam, see S.N. Prasad (chief editor) and U.P. Thapliyal (general editor), *The India-Pakistan War of 1965: A History* (Dehradun and Delhi: Natraj Publishers, 2011), p. 51–55, 123–24.

Chapter 19: Operations Gibraltar and Grand Slam

1. Lieutenant General Harbaksh Singh, *War Despatches: Indo-Pak Conflict of 1965* (New Delhi: Lancer International, 1991), p. 186.
2. S.N. Prasad (chief editor) and U.P. Thapliyal (general editor), *The India-Pakistan War of 1965: A History* (Dehradun and Delhi: Natraj Publishers, 2011).
3. Brian Cloughley, *A History of the Pakistan Army* (New Delhi: Lancer, 1999), p. 71.
4. Ibid.
5. Lieutenant General Harbaksh Singh, *War Despatches: Indo-Pak Conflict of 1965* (New Delhi: Lancer International, 1991), p. 26.
6. For a short and crisp account of the battle, see Mandeep Singh Bajwa, 'The First Kargil Battle,' *Hindustan Times*, Chandigarh, 2 July 2012, available at http://www.hindustantimes.com/punjab/chandigarh/the-first-kargil-battle/article1-882367.aspx (accessed 18 October 2014).
7. 'Pak Saboteurs begin Armed Raid', *The Sunday Standard*, New Delhi, 7 August 1965, p. 1, microfilm at Nehru Memorial Museum and Library (NMML), (accessed 16 September 2013). Also see Brian Cloughley, *A History of the Pakistan Army* (New Delhi: Lancer, 1999), p. 65.

8. 'Pakistan Guerilla Attack Crushed,' *The Indian Express*, New Delhi, 11 August 1965, p. 1 on microfilm at NMML, (accessed 16 September 2013).
9. Ibid.
10. 'Indian Troops Cross Ceasefire Line at Two Places', *The Indian Express*, New Delhi, 26 August 1965, p. 1.
11. For a detailed analysis of the Tithwal sector and Haji Pir operation see Lieutenant General Harbaksh Singh, *War Despatches: Indo-Pak Conflict of 1965* (New Delhi: Lancer International, 1991), p. 44–47. Also see S.N. Prasad (chief editor) and U.P. Thapliyal (general editor), *The India-Pakistan War of 1965: A History* (Dehradun and Delhi: Natraj Publishers, 2011), p. 70–74.
12. Lieutenant General Harbaksh Singh, *War Despatches: Indo-Pak Conflict of 1965* (New Delhi: Lancer International, 1991), p. 48–50.
13. Ibid.
14. S.N. Prasad (chief editor) and U.P. Thapliyal (general editor), *The India-Pakistan War of 1965: A History* (Dehradun and Delhi: Natraj Publishers, 2011), p. 74–77.
15. Interview with Lieutenant General Mathew Thomas (retd) at Pune on 30 January 2015.
16. S.N. Prasad (chief editor) and U.P. Thapliyal (general editor), *The India-Pakistan War of 1965: A History* (Dehradun and Delhi: Natraj Publishers, 2011), p. 67–68.
17. P.V.S. Jagan Mohan and Samir Chopra, *The India-Pakistan Air War of 1965* (New Delhi: Manohar, 2009), p. 64–66.
18. Rajesh Isser, *Purple Legacy: Indian Air Force Helicopters in Service of the Nation* (New Delhi: KW Publishers, 2012), p. 25–27. Also see S.N. Prasad (chief editor) and U.P. Thapliyal (general editor), *The India-Pakistan War of 1965: A History* (Dehradun and Delhi: Natraj Publishers, 2011), p. 77. Harbaksh Singh also acknowledges the role of helicopters in the counter-infiltration campaign in the 'Lessons Learnt' portions of his book. See Lieutenant General Harbaksh Singh, *War Despatches: Indo-Pak Conflict of 1965* (New Delhi: Lancer International, 1991), p. 197.
19. Lieutenant General Harbaksh Singh, *War Despatches: Indo-Pak Conflict of 1965* (New Delhi: Lancer International, 1991), p. 52–53.
20. Brian Cloughley, *A History of the Pakistan Army* (New Delhi: Lancer, 1999), p. 72.
21. For a detailed account of the lopsided artillery battle during the battle of Chhamb, see Brigadier Chowdhury, 'Chhamb – The Artillery Battle', *USI Journal* (April–June 2013): p. 294–302.

22. The best commentary on the Chhamb battle from a Pakistani perspective comes from Major Agha Humayun Amin (retd). See Major Agha Humayun Amin (retd), 'Grand Slam – A Battle of Lost Opportunities,' at http://www.defencejournal.com/2000/sept/grand-slam.htm (accessed 3 January 2015).
23. Sumit Ganguly, *Conflict Unending: India-Pakistan Tensions since 1947* (New Delhi: Oxford University Press, 2002), p. 38.
24. According to Shuja Nawaz, 'PAF Sabres, however, provided superb ground support in all phases of the attack.' See Shuja Nawaz, *Crossed Swords: Pakistan, Its Army, and the Wars Within* (Karachi: Oxford University Press, 2008), p. 211.
25. Ibid., p. 212.
26. Major General Lachhman Singh, *Missed Opportunities: Indo-Pak War 1965* (Dehradun: Natraj Publishers, 1997), p. 168.
27. P.V.S. Jagan Mohan and Samir Chopra, *The India-Pakistan Air War of 1965* (New Delhi: Manohar, 2009), p. 75.
28. For a detailed narrative of his years as the CO of 23 Squadron during the 1965 war, see Air Marshal S. Raghavendran (retd), *Panther Red One: The Memoirs of a Fighter Pilot* (New Delhi: KW Publishers, 2013).
29. Conversation with Air Vice Marshal Milind Shankar on 25 October 2013. He was a young pilot in 23 Squadron, which was the first Gnat squadron to draw blood in combat with the Sabres.
30. Air Marshal S. Raghavendran (retd), *Panther Red One: The Memoirs of a Fighter Pilot* (New Delhi: KW Publishers, 2013), p. 213.
31. Email exchange with Group Captain Manna Murdheshwar (retd).

Chapter 20: Operational Stalemate

1. John Frazer, 'Who can win Kashmir?' *Reader's Digest*, January 1996, from Ramachandra Guha, *India after Gandhi* (London: Pan Macmillan, 2007), p. 399.
2. Email exchange in March 2015 between P.V.S. Jagan Mohan and Sajad Haider.
3. Email exchange with Group Captain Manna Murdeshwar on Indo-Pak war of 1965 –reflections on Pathankot operation, 29 September 2014.
4. Air Vice Marshal A.K. Tiwary, *Indian Air Force in Wars* (New Delhi: Lancer, 2012), p. 117.
5. P.V.S. Jagan Mohan and Samir Chopra, *The India-Pakistan Air War of 1965* (New Delhi: Manohar, 2009), p. 95.
6. Air Vice Marshal A.K. Tiwary, *Indian Air Force in Wars* (New Delhi: Lancer, 2012), p. 17.

7. Air Marshal Asghar Khan (retd), *The First Round Indo-Pakistan War 1965* (Ghaziabad: Vikas Publishing House, 1975), p. 20.
8. Ibid., p. 21–23.
9. Air Marshal S. Raghavendran (retd), *Panther Red One: The Memoirs of a Fighter Pilot* (New Delhi: KW Publishers, 2013), p. 219–21.
10. Interview with Vice Admiral Vinod Pasricha on 4 September 2014 at Pune.
11. Interview with Air Marshal A.R. Gandhi in December 2013. Gandhi was one of the Hunter pilots of 7 Squadron involved in the dogfights over Halwara on 6 September 1965.
12. P.V.S. Jagan Mohan and Samir Chopra, *The India-Pakistan Air War of 1965* (New Delhi: Manohar, 2009), p. 108–14.
13. Air Marshal Asghar Khan (retd), *The First Round Indo-Pakistan War 1965* (Ghaziabad: Vikas Publishing House, 1975), p. 26.
14. P.V.S. Jagan Mohan and Samir Chopra, *The India-Pakistan Air War of 1965* (New Delhi: Manohar, 2009), p. 116–117.
15. John Fricker, *Battle for Pakistan* (Surrey: Ian Allen Ltd, 1979), chapter titled 'Thirty Seconds over Sargodha', p. 11–20. Air Commander 'Cinch' Sinha (retd) was in the Hunter formation and did the Staff College at Camberly with Alam where he sorted out many of the ambiguities (shared with the author in a conversation at Pune).
16. Email exchange between the author and Air Marshal Philip Rajkumar on 15 January 2014.
17. For a detailed description of the battle of Dograi, see Lieutenant General Harbaksh Singh, *War Despatches: Indo-Pak Conflict of 1965* (New Delhi: Lancer International, 1991), p. 119. For a personal account of the battle and other exploits of 3 Jat during the 1965 war, see Brigadier Desmond Hayde, *Battle of Dograi and Batapore* (Dehradun: Natraj Publishers, 2005).
18. Ibid.
19. P.V.S. Jagan Mohan and Samir Chopra, *The India-Pakistan Air War of 1965* (New Delhi: Manohar, 2009), p. 124–25.
20. Interview with Air Marshal Patney.
21. Ibid.
22. V. Ganapathy, 'Military Lessons of the 1965 Indo-Pakistan War,' *Scholar Warrior* (Autumn 2014): p. 168. The journal is published by CLAWS.
23. Interview with Air Marshal Patney and telephonic conversation with Air Marshal Bhatia.
24. For a detailed account of the aerial action over Dera Baba Nanak as narrated by Flight Lieutenant Vinod Bhatia, see P.V.S. Jagan Mohan

and Samir Chopra, *The India-Pakistan Air War of 1965* (New Delhi: Manohar, 2009), p. 125.

25. Ibid.
26. http://www.bharat-rakshak.com/IAF/Database/Awards/awards.php?qyear=1965&qaward=MVC. Also see Dara Cooper, 'September 1965 – III: The Land–Air War (Punjab Area),' available at marutfanswordpress.com (accessed 17 October 2014). This is a widely read blog by Dara Cooper, a retired IAF fighter pilot. Also see Air Vice Marshal A.K. Tiwary, *Indian Air Force in Wars* (New Delhi: Lancer, 2012), p. 135.
27. Peter Wilson Prabhakar, *Wars, Proxy Wars and Terrorism: Post Independent India* (New Delhi: Mittal Publications, 2003), p. 83–84.
28. Mandeep Singh Bajwa, 'A Quiet General Goes to War,' *Hindustan Times*, Chandigarh, 18 September 2012, available at http://www.hindustantimes.com/punjab/chandigarh/a-quiet-general-goes-to-war/931818.aspx (accessed 18 October 2014).
29. 20 Squadron IAF, *When Lightning Strikes* (New Delhi: The Society for Aerospace Studies, 2006), p. 27. The book is a commemorative volume that was released during the golden jubilee of the squadron in 2006.
30. P.V.S. Jagan Mohan and Samir Chopra, *The India-Pakistan Air War of 1965* (New Delhi: Manohar, 2009), p. 356–57.
31. Ibid., p. 243–245.
32. Ibid.
33. Ibid., p. 351.
34. Conventional post–WW II armies went by the ballpark planning figure of a 3:1 and 5:1 numerical superiority in the plains and mountains respectively, which were required to force a decisive result in a battle between evenly matched adversaries.
35. In Indian Army parlance, a holding corps is essentially an infantry-heavy defensive formation with limited armour, which is deployed along the international border. These formations have limited offensive capability and are designed to shape the battlefield for the 'strike corps' to exploit. Unfortunately, India had only one fledgling strike corps at the time.
36. S.N. Prasad (chief editor) and U.P. Thapliyal (general editor), *The India-Pakistan War of 1965: A History* (Dehradun and Delhi: Natraj Publishers, 2011), p. 188–89.
37. Lieutenant General Harbaksh Singh, *War Despatches: Indo-Pak Conflict of 1965* (New Delhi: Lancer International, 1991), p. 131.
38. For a detailed order of battle in the Sialkot sector, both from the Indian and the Pakistan perspectives, see Lieutenant General Harbaksh

Singh, *War Despatches: Indo-Pak Conflict of 1965* (New Delhi: Lancer International, 1991), p. 163–167.

39. Ibid., p. 147.
40. Agha Humayun Amin, *India-Pakistan Wars – 1947–1971: A Strategic and Operational Analysis* (Arlington: Strategicus and Tacticus, 1999), p. 170–75.
41. S.N. Prasad (chief editor) and U.P. Thapliyal (general editor), *The India-Pakistan War of 1965: A History* (Dehradun and Delhi: Natraj Publishers, 2011), p. 212.
42. Air Marshal Asghar Khan (retd), *The First Round Indo-Pakistan War 1965* (Ghaziabad: Vikas Publishing House, 1975), p. 94.
43. S.N. Prasad (chief editor) and U.P. Thapliyal (general editor), *The India-Pakistan War of 1965: A History* (Dehradun and Delhi: Natraj Publishers, 2011), p. 253.
44. Ibid., p. 216.
45. Ibid., p. 217.
46. Telephonic conversation with Wing Commander Mayadev (retd) on 3 December 2014. Mayadev was one of the formation members during the dogfight. Also see P.V.S. Jagan Mohan and Samir Chopra, *The India-Pakistan Air War of 1965* (New Delhi: Manohar, 2009), p. 268–70.
47. Telephonic conversation with Wing Commander Mayadev on 3 December 2014.
48. Ibid.
49. Attrition figures are reasonably accurate and if enthusiasts want more authentic figures, they could compare an Indian perspective in P.V.S. Jagan Mohan and Samir Chopra's book, while a Pakistani perspective is available in Asghar Khan's book. The flavour of my rendition of events primarily focuses on the rather amateurish planning of missions by both the PAF and the IAF. To be fair to both air forces, it was probably the first real aerial tussle between two 'at par' air forces without much prior combat experience in the modern 'aerial war fighting' era, which commenced over Korea in the mid-1950s.

Chapter 21: Strategic Revival

1. Shuja Nawaz, *Crossed Swords: Pakistan, Its Army, and the Wars Within* (Karachi: Oxford University Press, 2008), p. 219.
2. For a detailed chapter on the limited operations in Rajasthan/Sind sector called Operation Barrel by India, see S.N. Prasad (chief editor) and U.P. Thapliyal (general editor), *The India-Pakistan War of 1965: A History* (Dehradun and Delhi: Natraj Publishers, 2011), p. 223–38.

3. Shobhan Saxena, 'War and Grief,' *The Times of India*, 21 August 2011.
4. Ibid.
5. P.V.S. Jagan Mohan and Samir Chopra, *The India-Pakistan Air War of 1965* (New Delhi: Manohar, 2009), p. 178.
6. The frigates were the INS *Brahmaputra*, *Beas*, *Betwa*, *Khukri*, *Kuthar*, *Kripan*, *Talwar* and *Trishul*.
7. Air Marshal Asghar Khan (retd), *The First Round Indo-Pakistan War 1965* (Ghaziabad: Vikas Publishing House, 1975), p. 33.
8. Ibid., p. 4.
9. Admiral S.N. Kohli, *We Dared: Maritime Operations in the 1971 Indo-Pak War* (New Delhi: Lancer, 1989), p. 1–3. (This is from the Prologue highlighting the frustration of the Indian Navy at not being able to participate effectively in the 1965 war).
10. From a presentation delivered by Vice Admiral Anup Singh on the role of the Indian Navy in the 1965 war held at Vivekananda Foundation on 11 September 2015.
11. Ibid.
12. S.N. Prasad (chief editor) and U.P. Thapliyal (general editor), *The India-Pakistan War of 1965: A History* (Dehradun and Delhi: Natraj Publishers, 2011), p. 278–79.
13. Ibid., p. 275. Also see Air Marshal Asghar Khan (retd), *The First Round Indo-Pakistan War 1965* (Ghaziabad: Vikas Publishing House, 1975), p. 34.
14. Vice Admiral Mihir Roy, *War in the Indian Ocean* (New Delhi: Lancer Publishers, 1995), p. 84–85.
15. Air Marshal Asghar Khan (retd), *The First Round Indo-Pakistan War 1965* (Ghaziabad: Vikas Publishing House, 1975), p. 33.
16. S.N. Prasad (chief editor) and U.P. Thapliyal (general editor), *The India-Pakistan War of 1965: A History* (Dehradun and Delhi: Natraj Publishers, 2011), p. 278.
17. Vice Admiral G.M. Hiranandani, *Transition to Triumph: Indian Navy 1965–1975* (New Delhi: Lancer Publishers, 2000), p. 39–40.
18. Admiral S.N. Kohli, *We Dared: Maritime Operations in the 1971 Indo-Pak War* (New Delhi: Lancer, 1989), p. 1–2.
19. Ibid.
20. R.D. Pradhan, *Debacle to Revival: Y.B. Chavan as Defence Minister, 1962–65* (New Delhi: Orient Longman, 1999), p. 283–88. Also see Air Vice Marshal A.K. Tiwary, *Indian Air Force in Wars* (New Delhi: Lancer, 2012), p. 109.

21. Gohar Ayub Khan, 'The Kashmiris didn't back Pakistan in 1965,' *The Tribune*, 3 June 2005, at http://www.tribuneindia.com/2005/20050603/main2.htm (accessed 27 November 2014). Gohar Ayub Khan is the son of Field Marshal Ayub Khan.
22. Arjan Singh, 'I advised Shastri against ceasefire,' *The Week*, 23 August 2015, p. 42–43.
23. Key features of the ceasefire agreement are available in R.D. Pradhan, *Debacle to Revival: Y.B. Chavan as Defence Minister, 1962–65* (New Delhi: Orient Longman, 1999), p. 255–57.
24. Ibid.
25. Also see Farzana Sheikh, 'Zulfikar Ali Bhutto: In Pursuit of an Asian Pakistan,' in Ramachandra Guha, ed., *Makers of Modern Asia* (Cambridge: The Belknapp Press, 2014), p. 281.
26. Shuja Nawaz, *Crossed Swords: Pakistan, Its Army, and the Wars Within* (Karachi: Oxford University Press, 2008), p. 209–10.
27. R.D. Pradhan, *Debacle to Revival: Y.B. Chavan as Defence Minister, 1962–65* (New Delhi: Orient Longman, 1999), p. 258.
28. Air Chief Marshal P.C. Lal, *My Years with the IAF* (New Delhi: Lancer, 1986), p. 127.
29. Romesh Thapar, 'A Fight to the Finish?' *Economic and Political Weekly*, 18 September 1965, available at www.epw.in/system/files/pdf/1965_17/38/a_fight_to_the_finish.pdf (accessed 4 July 2015).
30. Air Vice Marshal A.K. Tiwary, *Indian Air Force in Wars* (New Delhi: Lancer, 2012), p. 127.
31. Attrition rate is the number of aircraft lost per 100 sorties and is arrived at by multiplying the number of aircraft lost by 100 and dividing the product by the number of sorties flown. Based on reasonably accurate statistics, Jasjit Singh, India's foremost air power historian and strategist, puts the attrition rates for the IAF and PAF at 1.50 and 1.82 respectively.
32. Air Chief Marshal P.C. Lal, *My Years with the IAF* (New Delhi: Lancer, 1986), p. 159.
33. Interview with Group Captain Manna Murdheshwar (retd). The eighty-three-year-old veteran of the 1965 war recounts that Lal was almost in tears when he addressed officers in the Base Operations Room during a visit to Pathankot in the first week of the war.
34. Admiral S.N. Kohli, *We Dared: Maritime Operations in the 1971 Indo-Pak War* (New Delhi: Lancer, 1989), p. 2.
35. Interview with Vice Admiral Pasricha.
36. Ramachandra Guha, *India after Gandhi* (London: Pan Macmillan, 2007), p. 399.

37. 'We lost terribly in 1965 war, says Pak historian,' *The Times of India*, New Delhi, 6 September 2015, p. 13.
38. Geoffrey Blainey, *The Causes of War* (New York: The Free Press, 1988), p. 122.

Chapter 22: South Asia in Turmoil

1. Indira Gandhi's press conference in New Delhi on 19 October 1971, quoted in Sydney H. Schanberg, 'Indian and Pakistani Armies Confront Each Other along Borders,' *The New York Times*, 20 October 1971, p. 6.
2. Mohajirs are an ethnic group in modern Pakistan comprising mainly Muslims who migrated from India to Pakistan in the aftermath of Partition. They are concentrated around Karachi and the Sind province of Pakistan. For an interesting article on the Mohajirs, see Nadeem Paracha, 'The Evolution of Mohajir Politics and Identity,' *Dawn*, Karachi, 20 April 2014, available at http://www.dawn.com/news/1100948 (accessed 07 March 2015).
3. Ramachandra Guha, *India after Gandhi* (London: Pan Macmillan, 2007), p. 449–450.
4. The Awami League was a Bengali-dominated political party representing the aspirations of the huge Bengali population of East Pakistan, which outnumbered the population of West Pakistan.
5. For an excellent Western perspective on the Bangladesh crisis, see Gary J. Bass, *Blood Telegram: India's Secret War in East Pakistan* (New Delhi: Random House, 2013).
6. Ibid., p. 77–78.
7. CIA report dated 12 April 1971 – declassified in June 2005 and available on the website of the Center for Indian Military History in the US State Department Documents pertaining to India and Pakistan 1971 – p. 25–26. Assembled by Ramesh Shanker at http://www.indianmilitaryhistory.org/
8. Arjun Subramaniam, 'Brave Diplomacy amidst Genocide,' *The Hindu*, 3 December 2013, http://www.thehindu.com/books/books-reviews/brave-diplomacy-amidst-genocide/article5415254.ece
9. Ibid.
10. 'Mitty Masud Folds His Wings,' an obituary in the *Dawn* newspaper of 13 October 2003, at http://www.dawn.com/news/1065137/dawn-features-october-13-2003 (accessed 11 April 2015).
11. Sumit Ganguly, *The Origins of War in South Asia: Indo-Pakistan Conflicts since 1947* (New Delhi: Vision Books, 1999), p. 84–85.

12. Ibid., p. 102–03. K. Subrahmanyam, an IAS officer with a remarkable feel for 'matters strategic', was then director of IDSA, a fledgling strategic think tank nurtured by him with adequate support from the Government of India.
13. 'CIA Memorandum,' 7 December 1971, declassified June 2005, US State Department Documents pertaining to India and Pakistan 1971, p. 219. Assembled by Ramesh Shanker at http://www.indianmilitaryhistory.org/
14. J.N. Dixit, *India-Pakistan in War and Peace* (New Delhi: Books Today, 2002), p. 182–83.
15. Interview with Lieutenant General Pandit at Pune on 19 September 2014. The general was remarkably modest and has excellent recollections of the 1971 war in which he played an active part, first as part of Military Operations (MO) Directorate and then as CO of 9 Engineer Regiment in the battle of Basantar.
16. Amongst those who felt that Manekshaw was excessively cautious is Air Marshal Vinod Patney, the IAF's most decorated officer and veteran of both the 1965 and 1971 wars. He felt that the three months from April to the onset of monsoon in early June would have been adequate to secure victory even if India had to go in through only one or two fronts in the east. More importantly, he asserts, had that been agreed to, India's demographic disaster may well have been averted. Srinath Raghavan, a promising army officer turned military historian/strategic commentator, concurs with that assessment in his book *1971: A Global History of the Creation of Bangladesh*.
17. John. H. Gill, *An Atlas of the 1971 India-Pakistan War: The Creation of Bangladesh* (Washington: NDU Press, 2003), p. 13.
18. Sumit Ganguly, *The Origins of War in South Asia: Indo-Pakistan Conflicts since 1947* (New Delhi: Vision Books, 1999), p. 104, referring to the memoirs of T.N. Kaul, India's foreign secretary at the time.
19. For an excellent commentary on the treaty four decades after it was signed, see Arun Mohanty, 'Toasting the Legacy of 1971 Indo-Soviet friendship Treaty,' 9 August 2011, http://in.rbth.com/articles/2011/08/09/toasting_legacy_of_1971_indo-soviet_friendship_treaty_12842.html (accessed 7 March 2015).
20. Gary J. Bass, *Blood Telegram: India's Secret War in East Pakistan* (New Delhi: Random House, 2013), p. 250–60. Also see Ramachandra Guha, *India after Gandhi* (London: Pan Macmillan, 2007), p. 457.
21. Declassified US State Department documents pertaining to India and Pakistan 1971, p. 10–12. Assembled by Ramesh Shanker at http://www.indianmilitaryhistory.org (accessed 27 November 2014).

22. For an Indian perspective of the force levels in the east, see Major K.C. Praval, *Indian Army after Independence* (New Delhi: Lancer, 1988), p. 401–11.
23. The most objective comparison of forces, both in the eastern and western theatres, is provided by John H. Gill, a faculty member at the National Defense University, Washington. See John. H. Gill, *An Atlas of the 1971 India-Pakistan War: The Creation of Bangladesh* (Washington: NDU Press, 2003), p. 69–90.
24. Ibid., p. 57.
25. Brigadier R.R. Palsokar, 'A History of the Black Arrow Brigade,' (unpublished monograph – cited with permission from the author).
26. Ibid.
27. S.N. Prasad and U.P. Thapliyal, ed., *The India-Pakistan War of 1971* (Dehradun: Natraj Publishers, 2014), p. 102.
28. Interview with Vice Admiral Pasricha, who was a young Sea Hawk pilot on board the *Vikrant* in 1971.
29. Interview with Commander Bahadur Kavina (retd) on 5 December 2014. Though the interview was not planned so, it happened to be on the same day, thirty-three years ago in 1971, when 25 Squadron triumphantly returned after carrying out their famous strikes on Karachi harbour that left the Pakistan Navy reeling.
30. Kavina recollects that he was hauled up for revealing the ranges at the briefing but asserts that it was time for the Indian Navy to realize the potential of the boats.
31. S.N. Prasad and U.P. Thapliyal, ed., *The India-Pakistan War of 1971* (Dehradun: Natraj Publishers, 2014), p. 372–75.
32. 'Commander Y.N. Singh, the Pioneer Naval Aviator,' at http://www.bharat-rakshak.com/NAVY/Aviation/Resources/202-Pioneer-Aviator.html (accessed on 31 January 2015).
33. The exploits of INAS 300 are best chronicled in an article written on the fiftieth anniversary celebrations of the White Tigers in the *Vayu Aerospace Journal*, available at http://www.vayuaerospace.in/images1/Indian_Navy_The_White_Tigers.pdf (accessed 31 January 2015).
34. Vice Admiral Mihir Roy, *War in the Indian Ocean* (New Delhi: Lancer Publishers, 1995), p. 95. For a detailed review of the growth of naval aviation in India see Chapter 17 (The Naval Air Arm) of G.M. Hiranandani, *Transition to Triumph: History of the Indian Navy, 1965–1975* (New Delhi: Lancer, 2000), p. 262–79.
35. Interview with Vice Admiral Pasricha (retd).
36. G.M. Hiranandani, *Transition to Triumph: History of the Indian Navy, 1965–1975* (New Delhi: Lancer, 2000), p. 120–21.

37. While Indian Naval Air Squadron (INAS 300) was equipped with the British Sea Hawks, INAS 310 was equipped with the French-built Alize anti-submarine warfare aircraft. Also see G.M. Hiranandani, *Transition to Triumph: History of the Indian Navy, 1965–1975* (New Delhi: Lancer, 2000), p. 266–70.
38. Vice Admiral Mihir Roy, *War in the Indian Ocean* (New Delhi: Lancer Publishers, 1995), p. 112. For a detailed history of the submarine arm of the Indian Navy, see G.M. Hiranandani, *Transition to Triumph: History of the Indian Navy, 1965–1975* (New Delhi: Lancer, 2000), p. 254–56.
39. Admiral S.N. Kohli, *We Dared: Maritime Operations in the 1971 Indo-Pak War* (Lancer: New Delhi, 1989), p. 116–19.
40. For a detailed overview of the evolution of the Indian Navy's submarine arm, also see http://indiannavy.nic.in/book/submarine-arm (accessed on 5 October 2014).
41. For an exact inventory of IAF aircraft, see P.V.S. Jagan Mohan and Samir Chopra, *Eagles over Bangladesh* (New Delhi: HarperCollins, 2013), Appendix A, p. 379.
42. For an Indian perspective on the comparative force ratio in the west, see Air Vice Marshal A.K. Tiwary, *Indian Air Force in Wars* (New Delhi: Lancer, 2012), p. 197.
43. For a Pakistani perspective of force levels see, S. Sajad Haider, *The Flight of the Falcon: Demolishing Myths of the Indo-Pak Wars of 1965 and 1971* (Lahore: Vanguard Books, 2009), p. 227–28.
44. A reasonably comprehensive orbit of both air forces is available at 'India Sub-Continent Database,' http://www.acig.org/artman/publish/article_326.shtml (accessed on 8 February 2014).
45. Interview with Air Marshal Vinod Patney on 5 September 2015.
46. See Chapter 19, p. 7.
47. Air Chief Marshal Lal's comparative analysis of all the measures initiated to strengthen the IAF are succinctly described in a narrative form in his book. See Air Chief Marshal P.C. Lal, *My Years with the IAF* (New Delhi: Lancer, 1986), p. 187–89 and p. 223. Though Lal argues that the combat strength of both the air forces in the western sector was almost similar, an objective analysis indicates that this was not so with the IAF having at least twenty-five frontline fighter squadrons as against about 18–19 with the PAF. Prasad and Thapliyal have indicated in their book, which is more or less the official history of the war from an Indian perspective, that the IAF had more than twenty-five squadrons of deployable fighters and bombers if one considered two squadrons that were withdrawn from the eastern sector after the first week of the war. Adding to the IAF strength were a few training flights with Vampire jets and MiG-

21s. S.N. Prasad and U.P. Thapliyal, ed., *The India-Pakistan War of 1971* (Dehradun: Natraj Publishers, 2014), p. 206–09.

48. S. Sajad Haider, *The Flight of the Falcon: Demolishing Myths of the Indo-Pak Wars of 1965 and 1971* (Lahore: Vanguard Books, 2009), p. 227.
49. S.N. Prasad and U.P. Thapliyal, ed., *The India-Pakistan War of 1971* (Dehradun: Natraj Publishers, 2014), p. 210.

Chapter 23: Shaping the Eastern Front

1. From an interview on 12 October 2014 with Lieutenant General Shamsher Mehta, a key participant in the race to Dacca.
2. B. Raman, *The Kao Boys of R&AW: Down Memory Lane* (New Delhi: Lancer, 2007), p. 9. The book not only offers an insider's view of covert operations in Bangladesh but also an overview of the growth of an organization that has led the development of covert operations in Indian statecraft.
3. Lieutenant General A.A.K. Niazi, *The Betrayal of East Pakistan* (New Delhi: Manohar, 1998), p. 69. The book is an interesting and detailed 'personal defence' of his stint as commander of the Eastern garrison in 1971, and it must be read thus, and not as an authentic history of a Pakistani perspective of the birth of Bangladesh.
4. S.N. Prasad and U.P. Thapliyal, ed., *The India-Pakistan War of 1971* (Dehradun: Natraj Publishers, 2014), p. 47–51.
5. The Mukti Bahini was divided into eleven sectors under three major formations called Z, S and K forces under the command of Majors Zia-ur-Rahman, Shafiullah and Khalid Musharraf respectively.
6. Lieutenant General A.A.K. Niazi, *The Betrayal of East Pakistan* (New Delhi: Manohar, 1998), p. 72.
7. General V.K. Singh, *Courage and Conviction: An Autobiography* (New Delhi: Aleph, 2013), p. 54–57. The book has an extremely well-written chapter on his experiences of the Bangladesh campaign as a young lieutenant. His unit was deployed in a sector in Meghalaya where there was intense Mukti Bahini activity.
8. S.N. Prasad and U.P. Thapliyal, ed., *The India-Pakistan War of 1971* (Dehradun: Natraj Publishers, 2014), p. 57.
9. Vice Admiral Mihir Roy, *War in the Indian Ocean* (New Delhi: Lancer Publishers, 1995), p. 148–150.
10. Ibid., p. 170–171.
11. P.V.S. Jagan Mohan and Samir Chopra, *Eagles over Bangladesh* (New Delhi: HarperCollins, 2013), p. 45–49.

12. Ibid.
13. The exploits of the Tibetan commandos of the SFF in the run-up to the 1971 war have been covered in the book *Phantoms of Chittagong* by Major General S.S. Uban. The website www.bharatrakshak.com also covers it briefly. Taken from www.rediff.com/news/2003/jan/08spec.htm?zcc=rl (accessed 29 January 2014).
14. Interview with Lieutenant General W.A.G. Pinto (retd).
15. From a book review of Admiral S.M. Nanda's book *The Man Who Bombed Karachi,* by Ashok Mehta, http://indiatoday.intoday.in/story/book-review-of-s-m-nandas-the-man-who-bombed-karachi-a-memoir/1/204795.html (accessed 10 February 2014).
16. For a detailed review of R&AW operations in Bangladesh and the legacy left behind by its founding director, see B. Raman, *The Kao Boys of R&AW: Down Memory Lane* (New Delhi: Lancer, 2007), p. 9–14.
17. Haksar Papers, NMML.
18. While Lieutenant General J.F.R. Jacob, the chief of staff of the Indian Army's Eastern Command, takes credit for the initial focus on Dacca as the final objective of the Indian Army's offensive, the COAS, General Manekshaw, overruled him from Army HQ by laying down more conservative military objectives. These included the capture of key towns like Jessore, Khulna and Chittagong. See J.F.R. Jacob, *Surrender at Dacca: The Birth of a Nation* (New Delhi: Manohar, 1997), p. 126–27.
19. Lieutenant General K.P. Candeth, *The Western Front: The India Pakistan War of 1971* (Dehradun: The English Book Depot, 1997), p. 18.
20. Interview with Lieutenant General W.A.G. Pinto.
21. Air Chief Marshal P.C. Lal, *My Years with the IAF* (New Delhi: Lancer, 1986), p. 174. Lal has particularly emphasized in his book that India's air strategy was different from the one prosecuted in 1965. It was discussed extensively at the annual Air Force Commanders Conference in 1969 and highlights his participative decision-making style.
22. Vice Admiral Mihir Roy, *War in the Indian Ocean* (New Delhi: Lancer Publishers, 1995), p. 214–15.
23. Admiral S.N. Kohli, *We Dared: Maritime Operations in the 1971 Indo-Pak War* (New Delhi: Lancer, 1989), p. 36.
24. From an interview with Brigadier Palsokar (retd) in January 2013. The event was narrated by Air Marshal Malse to Brig Palsokar.
25. S.N. Prasad and U.P. Thapliyal, ed., *The India-Pakistan War of 1971* (Dehradun: Natraj Publishers, 2014), p. 49–50.
26. Indira Gandhi's international forays to explain India's case are vividly described in the following books: Ramachandra Guha, *India after*

Gandhi, p. 457; Gary Bass, *The Blood Telegram*, p. xvii and p. 243–45; D.R. Mankekar, *Pakistan Cut to Size*, p. 32–34.

27. As the Ganga enters Bangladesh, it is known as the Padma. The mighty Brahmaputra becomes the Jamuna. The combined flow known as the Meghna drains into the Bay of Bengal at the eastern flank of the huge Ganga delta which extends almost 400 km from Calcutta in the west to Chittagong in the east.
28. The force comparison has been extracted from a plethora of Indian and Pakistani sources, and a lone but highly accurate Western monograph. See Major General Sukhwant Singh (retd), *India's Wars since Independence* (New Delhi: Lancer, 2009); Lieutenant General A.A.K. Niazi, *The Betrayal of East Pakistan* (New Delhi: Manohar, 1998); John. H. Gill, *An Atlas of the 1971 India-Pakistan War: The Creation of Bangladesh* (Washington: NDU Press, 2003).
29. For a detailed profile of his early career, see Lieutenant General A.A.K. Niazi, *The Betrayal of East Pakistan* (New Delhi: Manohar, 1998), p. 1–32.
30. Ibid., p. 106–08. Also see John. H. Gill, *An Atlas of the 1971 India-Pakistan War: The Creation of Bangladesh* (Washington: NDU Press, 2003), p. 17–20.
31. See map depicting 'Airfields and IAF units in the eastern sector' in P.V.S. Jagan Mohan and Samir Chopra, *Eagles over Bangladesh* (New Delhi: HarperCollins, 2013), p. v.
32. Air Chief Marshal P.C. Lal, *My Years with the IAF* (New Delhi: Lancer, 1986), p. 187–88.
33. Admiral S.N. Kohli, *We Dared: Maritime Operations in the 1971 Indo-Pak War* (New Delhi: Lancer, 1989), p. 32.
34. Vice Admiral Mihir Roy, *War in the Indian Ocean* (New Delhi: Lancer Publishers, 1995), p. 199.
35. Lieutenant General A.A.K. Niazi, *The Betrayal of East Pakistan* (New Delhi: Manohar, 1998), p. 118.
36. Shuja Nawaz, *Crossed Swords: Pakistan, Its Army, and the Wars Within* (Karachi: Oxford University Press, 2008), p. 292.
37. R. Sisson and L.E. Rose, *War and Secession: Pakistan, India and the Creation of Bangladesh* (Karachi: Oxford University Press, 1992), p. 213.
38. Mandeep Singh Bajwa, 'A Young Officer's First Taste of War,' *Hindustan Times*, Chandigarh, 20 July 2014, available at http://www.hindustantimes.com/punjab/chandigarh/a-young-officer-s-taste-of-war/article1-1242501.aspx (accessed 17 October 2014).
39. P.V.S. Jagan Mohan and Samir Chopra, *Eagles over Bangladesh* (New Delhi: HarperCollins, 2013), p. 81–83. General V.K. Singh also confirms

in his autobiography that he actively participated in offensive forays into East Pakistan in November 1971. See General V.K. Singh, *Courage and Conviction: An Autobiography* (New Delhi: Aleph, 2013), p. 58–60.

40. P.V.S. Jagan Mohan and Samir Chopra, *Eagles over Bangladesh* (New Delhi: HarperCollins, 2013), p. 70, 94. Also see *Forever Fearless*, Vol. 25 of Squadrons of the IAF, Historical and Air Warrior Studies Cell, College of Air Warfare, Secunderabad, 2013. This is a limited series and unclassified booklet for internal circulation within the IAF.
41. John. H. Gill, *An Atlas of the 1971 India-Pakistan War: The Creation of Bangladesh* (Washington: NDU Press, 2003), p. 16.

Chapter 24: Destination Dacca

1. Conversation between Lieutenant General Sagat Singh and his army commander, Lieutenant General Jagjit Singh Aurora, when Aurora came to know that Sagat was planning multiple crossings of the Meghna using helicopters to create an air bridge. See Randhir Singh, *A Talent for War: The Military Biography of Lieutenant General Sagat Singh* (New Delhi: Vij Books, 2013), p. 198–99.
2. Shuja Nawaz, *Crossed Swords: Pakistan, Its Army, and the Wars Within* (Karachi: Oxford University Press, 2008), p. 293.
3. P.V.S. Jagan Mohan and Samir Chopra, *Eagles over Bangladesh* (New Delhi: HarperCollins, 2013), p. 81–83.
4. The four Indian pilots were Flight Lieutenants Massey and Ganapathy and Flying Officers Lazarus and Soares.
5. S. Sajad Haider, *The Flight of the Falcon: Demolishing Myths of the Indo-Pak Wars of 1965 and 1971* (Lahore: Vanguard Books, 2009), p. 235–37. Chaudhry is said to have disengaged prematurely from combat (sic) instead of coming to the assistance of his two young wingmen. He is also said to have falsely claimed to have shot down a Gnat, much to the amusement of his colleagues in the squadron who, after analysing his air combat film, remarked that they 'could not even see a bird in the picture frame, leave alone an aircraft'.
6. For an excellent tactical narrative of the battle for Hilli, albeit from an Indian perspective, see Major General Sukhwant Singh (retd), *India's Wars since Independence* (New Delhi: Lancer, 2009), p. 146–47. A Pakistani version of the battle has been narrated by the brigade commander of 205 Brigade under whose command the defences at Hilli were placed. See interview with Major General (retd) Tajjamul Hussain Malik by Major Agha Amin, one of Pakistan's best modern military historians, in 'The Battle of Hilli – A Narration by Pakistan Brigade

Commander,' http://defence.pk/threads/the-battle-of-hilli-a-narration-by-pakistani-bde-commander.143866/ (accessed 9 March 2014).

7. Conversation with Air Marshal Gokhale on 18 September 2014 at Pune.
8. A detailed account of the Jamalpur battle and the link-up with 2 Para at Tangail was offered by Lieutenant General Satish Nambiar at his residence in Noida.
9. For a most detailed narrative of the battle for Akhaura and how the Indian Army's IV Corps shaped the battlefield in the area, see Randhir Singh, *A Talent for War: The Military Biography of Lieutenant General Sagat Singh* (New Delhi: Vij Books, 2013), p. 168–175.
10. For an interesting narrative with a human touch on independent India's Param Vir Chakra winners, see Rachna Bisht Rawat, *The Brave: Param Vir Chakra Stories* (New Delhi: Penguin, 2014). Lance Naik Albert Ekka's story is between pages 145 and 154.
11. Interview with Lieutenant General Shammi Mehta, 12 October 2014.
12. John. H. Gill, *An Atlas of the 1971 India-Pakistan War: The Creation of Bangladesh* (Washington: NDU Press, 2003), p. 32–33. Also see Randhir Singh, *A Talent for War: The Military Biography of Lieutenant General Sagat Singh* (New Delhi: Vij Books, 2013), p. 320.
13. Both Lieutenant General Niazi and John Gill are critical of the decision of the brigade commander of the 313 Brigade at Maulvi Bazaar to withdraw north to the Sylhet garrison rather than head south towards Ashuganj and reinforce 27 Brigade, which had fought a reasonably successful defensive battle as it withdrew from Akhaura to Ashuganj, and then finally across the Meghna to Brahmanbaria.
14. Interview with Lieutenant General Shammi Mehta, who corroborated this, on 12 October 2014.
15. The dogfight between Dilawar's formation and Wing Commander Sundaresan's formation of Hunters, also from 14 Squadron, IAF, comes to life in P.V.S. Jagan Mohan and Samir Chopra, *Eagles over Bangladesh* (New Delhi: HarperCollins, 2013), p. 147–49. For a PAF perspective, also see S. Sajad Haider, *The Flight of the Falcon: Demolishing Myths of the Indo-Pak Wars of 1965 and 1971* (Lahore: Vanguard Books, 2009), p. 238–39.
16. Interview with Air Commander (retd) Manbir Singh, VrC, on 5 January 2014, at Pune. Also see Air Chief Marshal P.C. Lal, *My Years with the IAF* (New Delhi: Lancer, 1986), p. 203.
17. P.V.S. Jagan Mohan and Samir Chopra, *Eagles over Bangladesh* (New Delhi: HarperCollins, 2013), p. 159.
18. For a detailed account of the Sylhet heli-lift operation by the CO of 4/5 Gorkha Rifles, Lieutenant Colonel A.B. Harolikar, see Brigadier A.B.

Harolikar, 'The Battle for Sylhet Nov–Dec 1971 by Maj (Retd) Mumtaz Hussaini Shah, Pakistan Army – A Rejoinder by Brig A.B. Harolikar, Indian Army,' http://bravestofthebrave.com/?p=66 (accessed 25 October 2014). Also see Randhir Singh, *A Talent for War: The Military Biography of Lieutenant General Sagat Singh* (New Delhi: Vij Books, 2013), p. 195–98. The strength of the garrison appears to have been exaggerated by the Indians and was estimated to number around 4,000.

19. Sandhu, Singla and another young Mi-4 pilot P.K. Vaid would go on to win Vir Chakras for their exploits during the numerous heli-borne missions they would fly during the war.
20. Telephonic interview with Wing Commander (retd) S.C. Sharma, VrC, on 11 and 12 January 2015.
21. Brigadier Harolikar, 'Inside a Chakravyuh in Sylhet,' http://bravestofthebrave.com/?p=14 (accessed 25 October 2014).
22. S.N. Prasad and U.P. Thapliyal, ed., *The India-Pakistan War of 1971* (Dehradun: Natraj Publishers, 2014), p. 375–77. The sinking of PNS *Ghazi* is covered in great detail.
23. P.V.S. Jagan Mohan and Samir Chopra, *Eagles over Bangladesh* (New Delhi: HarperCollins, 2013), p. 130–50. Also see S.N. Prasad and U.P. Thapliyal, ed., *The India-Pakistan War of 1971* (Dehradun: Natraj Publishers, 2014), p. 380.
24. For a crisp narration of naval action during the first week of the war, see Vice Admiral Vice Admiral Mihir Roy, *War in the Indian Ocean* (New Delhi: Lancer Publishers, 1995), p. 202–212.
25. S.N. Prasad and U.P. Thapliyal, ed., *The India-Pakistan War of 1971* (Dehradun: Natraj Publishers, 2014), p. 381–385.
26. B. Harry, 'Damage Assessment – 1971 Indo-Pak Naval War,' at http://www.ordersofbattle.darkscape.net/site/cimh/navy/kills%281971%29-2.pdf (accessed 8 February 2015).
27. Interview with Vice Admiral Vinod Pasricha on 4 October 2014.
28. Ibid.
29. A small paragraph on the entire IV Corps operations under Sagat Singh does not do justice to the actual impact it had on the ultimate fall of Dacca. See Randhir Singh, *A Talent for War: The Military Biography of Lieutenant General Sagat Singh* (New Delhi: Vij Books, 2013), p. 163 190. Chapter 7 in the book, aptly called 'The Hammer', covers the decisive second week of operations in great detail.
30. For a personal narrative of the operation from the man who orchestrated it as the IAF commander alongside Sagat Singh, see Air Vice Marshal Chandan Singh, 'The Meghna Crossing', in Major General Dhruv

Katoch and Lieutenant Colonel Quazi Sajjad Ali Zahir, ed., *Liberation: Bangladesh 1971* (New Delhi: Bloomsbury, 2015), p. 218–22.

31. Ibid.
32. Interview with Lieutenant General Shammi Mehta.
33. 'The Saga of Captain P.K. Ghosh, VrC,' from Veekays History Book, a blog maintained by Major General V.K. Singh, one of India's prolific military writers. Available at veekay-militaryhistory.blogspot.in/2013/4/the-saga-of-captain-pk-ghosh-vrc-html.
34. From an interview sourced from the archives of 2 Para Bridge.
35. Interview with Lieutenant General Mathew Thomas in Pune on 30 January 2015.
36. Ibid.
37. K.C. Praval, *India's Paratroopers: A History of the Parachute Regiment of India* (New Delhi: Thomson Press, 1974), p. 280. For an exhilarating account of the operation, see Densys Hamson, *We Fell among the Greeks* (London: Cape, 1946).
38. K.C. Praval, *India's Paratroopers: A History of the Parachute Regiment of India* (New Delhi: Thomson Press, 1974), p. 190. The initial three battalions were from the Punjab Regiment, Maratha Light Infantry and Kumaon Regiment.
39. From three battalions, the Indian Army added seven more battalions to the Parachute Regiment by the time India entered the 1971 war including two Para Commando Battalions. These seven battalions were attached to different fighting formations based on the operational need. Also see K.C. Praval, *India's Paratroopers: A History of the Parachute Regiment of India* (New Delhi: Thomson Press, 1974) for a detailed account of the evolution and growth of the Indian Army's Parachute Regiment.
40. P.V.S. Jagan Mohan and Samir Chopra, *Eagles over Bangladesh* (New Delhi: HarperCollins, 2013), p. 336.
41. Email exchange between the author and Group Captain Murdeshwar in February 2014 on his perceptions of what was right and what went wrong during the 1971 war.
42. For a detailed narrative of the Meghna Air Bridge Operation, see P.V.S. Jagan Mohan and Samir Chopra, *Eagles over Bangladesh* (New Delhi: HarperCollins, 2013), p. 215–21, and Randhir Singh, *A Talent for War: The Military Biography of Lieutenant General Sagat Singh* (New Delhi: Vij Books, 2013), p. 175–195. Lieutenant General Niazi is less charitable about the impact of the heli-borne operations. See Lieutenant General A.A.K. Niazi, *The Betrayal of East Pakistan* (New Delhi: Manohar,

1998), p. 216–17. For a recent analysis of the heli-bridge and heli-borne operations by an IAF helicopter pilot, see Air Commodore Rajesh Isser, *The Purple Legacy: Indian Air Force Helicopters in Service of the Nation* (New Delhi: KW Publishers, 2012), p. 63–79.

43. Mandeep Singh Bajwa, 'Flying to Victory: An Air OP pilot's story,' *Hindustan Times,* Chandigarh, 12 January 2014, available at http://www.hindustantimes.com/punjab/chandigarh/ flying-to-victory-an-air-op-pilot-s-story/article1.aspx (accessed 18 October 2014).
44. P.V.S. Jagan Mohan and Samir Chopra, *Eagles over Bangladesh* (New Delhi: HarperCollins, 2013), p. 383 (summary of sector-wise close air support missions).
45. Air Chief Marshal P.C. Lal, *My Years with the IAF* (New Delhi: Lancer, 1986), p. 212.
46. Interview with Lieutenant General Shammi Mehta.
47. Air Chief Marshal P.C. Lal, *My Years with the IAF* (New Delhi: Lancer, 1986), p. 214–15.
48. P.V.S. Jagan Mohan and Samir Chopra, *Eagles over Bangladesh* (New Delhi: HarperCollins, 2013), p. 291–95.
49. For a detailed overview of Operation Beaver, see Ministry of Defence publication, *Official History of the India-Pakistan 1971 War*, p. 649–52, http://www.bharat-rakshak.com/LAND-FORCES/Army/History/1971War/PDF/ (accessed on 2 January 2014).
50. S.N. Prasad and U.P. Thapliyal, ed., *The India-Pakistan War of 1971* (Dehradun: Natraj Publishers, 2014), p. 407–09.
51. Lieutenant General J.F.R. Jacob, *Surrender at Dacca: Birth of a Nation* (New Delhi: Manohar, 1977), p. 134.
52. Ibid. Also see declassified US State Department correspondence of the time.
53. Department of State telegram from New Delhi to Washington dated 15 December 1971 from declassified US State Department documents pertaining to India and Pakistan 1971, p. 383. Assembled by Ramesh Shanker, http://www.indianmilitaryhistory.org/ (accessed 26 November 2014).

Chapter 25: Opening the Western Front

1. Lieutenant General K.P. Candeth, *The Western Front: The India Pakistan War of 1971* (Dehradun: The English Book Depot, 1997), p. 173.
2. Ibid., p. 17.
3. Air Chief Marshal P.C. Lal, *My Years with the IAF* (New Delhi: Lancer, 1986), p. 239–55.

4. Popularly called Ditch-cum-Bund or DCB, these came up along rivers and canals and proved to be significant obstacles during the ensuing conflict.
5. Air Vice Marshal A.K. Tiwary, *Indian Air Force in Wars* (New Delhi: Lancer, 2012), p. 199–200.
6. Air Vice Marshal A. K. Tiwary in his book describes very succinctly the layered air defence network put up by the IAF and its role in establishing a favourable air situation in the sector. See ibid., p. 197–98.
7. From these distinguished fighter pilots of the IAF, Krishnaswamy went on to become the chief of air staff, while all others rose to the rank of air marshal.
8. Conversation with Air Marshal Pingale on 4 January 2015.
9. S. Sajad Haider, *The Flight of the Falcon: Demolishing Myths of the Indo-Pak Wars of 1965 and 1971* (Lahore: Vanguard Books, 2009).
10. Interview with Vinod Patney on 5 September 2015.
11. Admiral Arun Prakash, 'How I Crossed Swords with Chuck Yeager,' *Vayu Aerospace and Defence Review*, Vol. 1/2007, from http://www.bharat-rakshak.com/IAF/History/1971War/ArunPrakash.html (accessed 6 March 2015).
12. 20 Squadron IAF, *When Lightning Strikes* (New Delhi: The Society for Aerospace Studies, 2006), p. 29–37.
13. Telephonic conversation with Admiral Arun Prakash in September 2014.
14. The squadron bagged two MVCs, five VrCs, one Vayusena medal and three Mentioned-in-Despatches (M-in-D). See 20 Squadron IAF, *When Lightning Strikes* (New Delhi: The Society for Aerospace Studies, 2006), p. 37.
15. See Air Chief Marshal P.C. Lal, *My Years with the IAF* (New Delhi: Lancer, 1986), p. 255–60.
16. Kaiser Tufail, 'PAF on the Offensive,' at kaiser-aeronaut.blogspot.in/2011/08/paf-on-offensive-1971-war.html (accessed 5 July 2014).
17. Email exchange on 17 July 2014 with P.V.S. Jagan Mohan on the air effort dedicated by the IAF during the initial counter-campaign.
18. Interview with Lieutenant General Pandit. Pandit recollects K.K. Singh as having personally shared with him his anguish at having to maintain a 'defensive balance' in the absence of any hard intelligence about the enemy's armoured formations on 10 December.
19. Brian Cloughley, *A History of the Pakistan Army* (New Delhi: Lancer, 1999), p. 227–30.
20. The valour of 5 Sikh Regiment in the battle of Chhamb has been well chronicled by Major Raj Mehta. See Major General Raj Mehta, 'Déjà

vu at Chhamb,' *South Asia Defence and Strategic Review* (1 January 2014) at www.defstrat.com/exec/frmArticleDetails.aspx?DID=454 (accessed 26 November 2014).

21. For a detailed review of Brigadier Jasbir Singh's defensive battle, see Sukhwant Singh, *India's Wars since Independence* (New Delhi: Lancer, 2009), p. 249–51.
22. Air Chief Marshal P.C. Lal, *My Years with the IAF* (New Delhi: Lancer, 1986), p. 229–31.
23. Brian Cloughley, *A History of the Pakistan Army* (New Delhi: Lancer, 1999), p. 227. For a detailed tactical-level appreciation of operations in the Poonch and Rajouri sectors, also see Lieutenant General K.P. Candeth, *The Western Front: The India Pakistan War of 1971* (Dehradun: The English Book Depot, 1997), p. 63–71.
24. Ibid., p. 70.
25. Telephonic conversation with Air Marshal Sekhon on 22 July 2014.
26. Telephonic interview with Group Captain Anil Thapar (retd) on 12 January 2015.
27. Major General V.K. Singh, *Leadership in the Indian Army* (New Delhi: Sage Publications, 2005), p. 350–352. Major General Bakshi had won a Vir Chakra in the 1947–48 war with Pakistan; he was back in action in the 1965 war, winning a Maha Vir Chakra for his leadership of 68 Brigade in the capture of the Haji Pir Pass.
28. Ibid.
29. Interview with Lieutenant General B.T. Pandit.
30. S.N. Prasad and U.P. Thapliyal, ed., *The India-Pakistan War of 1971* (Dehradun: Natraj Publishers, 2014), p. 252–54.
31. Commander Kavina described the operation in great detail in an interview with the author on 5 December.
32. Ibid. Details of the IAF strike are on p. 230.
33. For a detailed Indian Navy perspective of the missile boat attacks on Karachi, see Admiral S.N. Kohli, *We Dared: Maritime Operations in the 1971 Indo-Pak War* (New Delhi: Lancer, 1989), p. 45–67 and 88–93. P.C. Lal offers the IAF perspective on the bombing of the fuel storage tanks at Karachi harbour. See Air Chief Marshal P.C. Lal, *My Years with the IAF* (New Delhi: Lancer, 1986), p. 290.
34. Interview with Admiral Nadkarni. Also refer interview with Commander Kavina.
35. Vice Admiral G.M. Hiranandani, *Transition to Triumph* (New Delhi: Lancer, 2000). See Preface.
36. Ibid., p. 212.

37. For a detailed account of the induction and operations of the Foxtrot Class of submarines, see P.R. Franklin, *Foxtrots of the Indian Navy* (Mumbai: Frontier India Technology Press, 2015), p. 133–43.
38. This is a poem written by Commodore S.P.R. Reddy (retd) and shared with us by Group Captain Unni Kartha (retd) on our school Yahoo group.

Chapter 26: Attrition Battles

1. Lieutenant General W.A.G. Pinto, *Bash on Regardless* (Dehradun: Natraj Publishers, 2013), p. 103.
2. Lieutenant General K.P. Candeth, *The Western Front: The India Pakistan War of 1971* (Dehradun: The English Book Depot, 1997), p. 47–53.
3. Kuldeep Singh Bajwa, 'Kargil Remembered,' *The Sunday Tribune*, 27 June 1999, http://www.tribuneindia.com/1999/99jun27/sunday/head2.htm (accessed 21 July 2014).
4. Lieutenant General K.P. Candeth, *The Western Front: The India Pakistan War of 1971* (Dehradun: The English Book Depot, 1997), p. 48. Also see John H. Gill, p. 40.
5. Air Chief Marshal P.C. Lal, *My Years with the IAF* (New Delhi: Lancer, 1986), p. 226–27.
6. Email correspondence between the author and P.V.S. Jagan Mohan on 16 July 2014.
7. Telephonic conversation with Air Marshal Sekhon on 22 July 2014.
8. Lieutenant General K.P. Candeth, *The Western Front: The India Pakistan War of 1971* (Dehradun: The English Book Depot, 1997), p. 45–46.
9. Wing Commander Vashisht dropped thirty-six bombs on Skardu with great accuracy and displayed courage and innovativeness of the highest order. See Air Chief Marshal P.C. Lal, *My Years with the IAF* (New Delhi: Lancer, 1986), p. 303. Also see S.N. Prasad and U.P. Thapliyal, ed., *The India-Pakistan War of 1971* (Dehradun: Natraj Publishers, 2014), p. 220.
10. A wonderfully crafted animation video on the Srinagar dogfight was made by Anurag Rana and is available at https://www.youtube.com/watch?v=df7FmZ5ejHw.
11. The most detailed Indian perspectives on the 'much hyped' Shakargarh offensive are available in Lieutenant General K.P. Candeth, *The Western Front: The India Pakistan War of 1971* (Dehradun: The English Book Depot, 1997), p. 97–110 and K.C. Praval, *India's Paratroopers: A History of the Parachute Regiment of India* (New Delhi: Thomson Press, 1974), p. 470–76. For a crisp Pakistani perspective, see Shuja Nawaz, *Crossed*

Swords: Pakistan, Its Army, and the Wars Within (Karachi: Oxford University Press, 2008), p. 304–05.

12. For a crisp account of the battle of the Shakargarh bulge from an Indian perspective, see Major General Ian Cardozo, ed., *The Indian Army: A Brief History* (New Delhi: Centre for Armed Forces Historical Research, 2005), p. 151–53. I was also lucky to lay my hands on an unpublished monograph on the history of India's 16 (Independent) Armoured Brigade by Brigadier Palsokar. The monograph authenticated much of the research I had already done.
13. Much of this narrative unfolds poignantly in Rachna Bisht Rawat, *The Brave: Param Vir Chakra Stories* (New Delhi: Penguin, 2014), p. 175–84.
14. Interview with Lieutenant General B.T. Pandit. Also see Lieutenant General B.T. Pandit (retd), 'Only Lucky Soldiers Get to See War,' 16 December 2011, available at www.rediff.com/news/slide-show-1-only-lucky-soldiers-get-to-see-war/20111216.htm#1 (accessed 26 November 2014).
15. From the Madras Engineering Group Archives at the Regimental Centre in Bangalore in a demi-official letter written to the author by Colonel C.S.S. Prakash on 3 May 2014.
16. Kaiser Tufail, one of the PAF's accomplished fighter pilots, writes objectively on India–Pakistan conflicts. His descriptions of the air battles over Shakargarh are quite compelling. They can be accessed at kaiser-aeronautblogspot.in/2010/04/air-support-in-shakargarh-1971-war.html (accessed on 26 November 2014).
17. Tactical air centres were employed by the IAF for the first time alongside the Indian Army's corps to act as real-time interfaces for close air support, reconnaissance and other missions in support of the land battle.
18. Air Chief Marshal P.C. Lal, *My Years with the IAF* (New Delhi: Lancer, 1986), p. 240. Attacking minefields by fighter aircraft was one of the examples given by him of wrong targeting.
19. Kaiser Tufail, kaiser-aeronautblogspot.in/2010/04/air-support-in-shakargarh-1971-war.html (accessed on 26 November 2014). For a detailed Indian perspective on losses, also see P.V.S. Jagan Mohan, 'Indian Air Force Losses in the 1971 War,' http://www.bharat-rakshak.com/IAF/History/1971War/Appendix2.html (accessed 28 July 2014). Kaiser Tufail's claims are corroborated by Jagan Mohan, thus raising the credibility of his writings on the air war of 1971.
20. Ibid.
21. Headquarters Southern Command Publication, *The Southern Cross* (Pune: Command Press, 2012), p. 62.
22. Ibid., p. 68.

23. Rajkumar and Pushpindar (2013), p. 57–72.
24. Kaiser Tufail, 'Air Support in Thar-1971,' at kaiser-aeronaut.blogspot.in/2009/10/air-war-in-thar.html.
25. For a detailed description of battles in the Fazilka, Ferozpur, Hussainiwala and Ganganagar sectors, see S.N. Prasad and U.P. Thapliyal, ed., *The India-Pakistan War of 1971* (Dehradun: Natraj Publishers, 2014), p. 172–90.
26. Major General Fazal Muqueem Khan, *Pakistan's Crisis in Leadership* (Islamabad: National Book Foundation, 1973), p. 187.
27. A detailed description of the surrender ceremony has been written by Lieutenant General Jacob, the chief of staff of Eastern Army Command. See Lieutenant General J.F.R. Jacob, *Surrender at Dacca: Birth of a Nation* (New Delhi: Manohar, 1977), p. 135–56. Also see S.N. Prasad and U.P. Thapliyal, ed., *The India-Pakistan War of 1971* (Dehradun: Natraj Publishers, 2014), p. 414–17.
28. Ibid., S.N. Prasad and U.P. Thapliyal, ed., *The India-Pakistan War of 1971* (Dehradun: Natraj Publishers, 2014).

Chapter 27: What 1971 Means to India and Pakistan

1. Air Chief Marshal P.C. Lal, *My Years with the IAF* (New Delhi: Lancer, 1986), p. 319–29.
2. Sarmila Bose, *Dead Reckoning: Memories of the 1971 Bangladesh War* (New Delhi: Hachette, 2011), p. 149, 160. Sarmila Bose writes of numerous intellectuals, doctors and professors being systematically killed by the Razakars and Al-Badr.
3. Ghulam Azam, the founder of the Al-Badr group, an auxiliary force which was set up to help the Pakistan Army identify and kill pro-independence Bengali activists, was sentenced on 15 July 2013 to ninety years in jail for crimes against humanity. See www.bbc.co.uk/news/world-asia-20970123
4. Sarmila Bose, *Dead Reckoning: Memories of the 1971 Bangladesh War* (New Delhi: Hachette, 2011), p. 159.
5. Sujan Dutta, 'Unarmed major who disarmed Pak soldiers and saved a future PM,' *The Telegraph*, 28 June 2012, available at www.telegraphindia.com/1120628/jsp/frontpage/story_15666585.jsp#VHa6hnZkm-A
6. Arjun Subramaniam, 'Brave Diplomacy amidst Genocide,' *The Hindu*, 3 December, 2013 at http://www.thehindu.com/books/books-reviews/brave-diplomacy-amidst-genocide/article5415254.ece

7. Geoffrey Blainey, *The Causes of War* (New York: The Free Press, 1988), p. 123.
8. Interview with Lieutenant General Shammi Mehta.
9. Shuja Nawaz, Hussain Haqqani, Sajad Haider, Kaiser Tufail and Agha Humayun Amin are amongst those whose writings emerge as objective and incisive.
10. Hussain Haqqani, *Pakistan: Between Mosque and Military* (Washington DC: Carnegie Endowment for International Peace, 2005), p. 98–99. The book has excellent chapters on the India–Pakistan relationship and is one of the most objective books on the Pakistan Army in the modern era.
11. Ibid., p. 98–99. Also see J.N. Dixit, *India-Pakistan in War and Peace* (New Delhi: Books Today, 2002), p. 225–31.
12. See Arjun Subramaniam, 'Brave Diplomacy amidst Genocide,' *The Hindu,* 3 December 2013, available at http://www.thehindu.com/books/books-reviews/brave-diplomacy-amidst-genocide/article5415254.ece
13. Interview with Lieutenant General Shammi Mehta.
14. Ibid.
15. Air Chief Marshal P.C. Lal, *My Years with the IAF* (New Delhi: Lancer, 1986).
16. S. Sajad Haider, *The Flight of the Falcon: Demolishing Myths of the Indo-Pak Wars of 1965 and 1971* (Lahore: Vanguard Books, 2009), p. 187–88
17. P.C. Lal puts the total number of sorties flown in the 1971 war at over 7,500 as against a total number of around 4,000 sorties flown in 1965.
18. S.N. Prasad, *Official History of the 1971 War*, Chapter X, p. 433–34.
19. Interview with Lieutenant General Shammi Mehta.
20. Major General Pinto's 54 Division was primarily a south Indian division with bulk of the troops being from the Madras Regiment and the Madras Engineering Group (MEG).
21. Sarmila Bose, *Dead Reckoning: Memories of the 1971 Bangladesh War* (New Delhi: Hachette, 2011), p. x.
22. Email to the author from Sydney Schanberg on Christmas Eve of 2014.

Chapter 28: Remembering Kautilya

1. L.N. Rangarajan, ed., *Kautilya. The Arthashastra* (New Delhi: Penguin, 1987).
2. An excellent commentary on Kautilya by Prof. Sunil Khilnani is available on a BBC 4 podcast under the series *Incarnations: India in 50 Lives.*

3. Ashok Kapur, *India's Nuclear Option: Atomic Diplomacy and Decision Making* (New York: Praeger Publishers, 1976), p. 77.
4. Vinay Vittal, 'Kautilya's Arthashastra: A Timeless Grand Strategy,' from a thesis submitted at the School of Advanced Air and Space Power Studies, Maxwell AFB, June 2011.
5. Ibid.
6. Roger Boesche, 'Kautilya's Arthashastra on War and Diplomacy in Ancient India,' *Journal of Military History*, Vol. 67 (January 2003): p. 9–38.
7. Ibid., p. 9.
8. Steven Wilkinson, *Army and Nation: The Military and Indian Democracy* (Cambridge, Massachusetts: Harvard University Press, 2015), p. 15.
9. Vinay Vittal, 'Kautilya's Arthashastra: A Timeless Grand Strategy,' from a thesis submitted at the School of Advanced Air and Space Power Studies, Maxwell AFB, June 2011.
10. L.N. Rangarajan, ed., *Kautilya: The Arthashastra* (New Delhi: Penguin, 1987), p. 640.
11. Ibid., p. 642.
12. Lieutenant Colonel Maurice Cohen, *Thunder over Kashmir* (Bombay: Orient Longman, 1955), p. 35.
13. L.N. Rangarajan, ed., *Kautilya: The Arthashastra* (New Delhi: Penguin, 1987), p. 676, from the dissertation by Vinay Vittal.
14. Rangarajan refers to them as qualifications of the chief of defence staff and puts them slightly differently. See L.N. Rangarajan, ed., *Kautilya: The Arthashastra* (New Delhi: Penguin, 1987), p. 647.
15. Ibid., p. 672.
16. Major General V.K. Singh, *Leadership in the Indian Army: Biographies of Twelve Soldiers* (New Delhi: Sage Publications, 2005), p. 171–72.
17. Ibid.
18. Henry Kissinger, 'The World According to Gita,' *The Times of India*, Pune, 21 November 2014, p. 18. The article is the lead article on the editorial page.
19. Ibid.
20. Roger Boesche, 'Kautilya's Arthashastra on War and Diplomacy in Ancient India,' *Journal of Military History*, Vol. 67 (January 2003): p. 37.

INDEX

ACKNOWLEDGEMENTS

This book is the result of one simple idea: I wanted to share an important and less-written-about facet of contemporary Indian history with more than merely the military fraternity in mind. I am grateful to all the veterans who welcomed me into their homes and shared their experiences of war, both good and bad. I am particularly grateful to the late Air Chief Marshal Moolgavkar, Admiral Nadkarni, Admiral Arun Prakash, Lieutenant General W.A.G. Pinto, Lieutenant General Mathew Thomas, Lieutenant General B.T. Pandit, Lieutenant General Satish Nambiar, Lieutenant General Shammi Mehta, Air Marshals Patney, Pingale, Rajkumar, Bhatia and Sekhon, Vice Admiral Pasricha, Group Captain Murdeshwar, Wing Commander Mayadev, Commander Kavina and many other veterans for their narratives, support and words of encouragement. There were others too from across the country who shared their experiences. My gratitude goes out to them.

Any endeavour such as this needs periodic boosters to propel it far enough; Prof. Sugata Bose, Dr Ramachandra Guha and Admiral Arun Prakash provided those. While Prof. Bose was the first one to see value in the project in late 2012, Dr Guha was the first to read the entire manuscript in 2014 and approve of its broad contours. I am indeed privileged to have spent time with these most accomplished historians. Words cannot express my gratitude to Admiral Arun Prakash for urging me to follow my passion and not get bogged down by a few career setbacks. Prof. Rana Mitter from Oxford, Brigadier Palsokar, Squadron

Leader Rana Chhina and Group Captain Ashish Singh offered insightful and incisive critiques after my first draft. These allowed me to make relevant mid-course changes. Lieutenant General Satish Nambiar, Air Marshal Patney and Air Marshal Reddy went through my final draft and offered highly constructive suggestions. I am also grateful to the Photo Division of the Ministry of Defence, the Armed Forces Films and Photo Division, archives from *The Hindu*, numerous regimental centres, squadrons and war colleges from where I managed to collect an excellent repository of photographs and records of action. Rana Chhina, P.V.S. Jagan Mohan and Air Vice Marshal Vikram Singh were extremely kind in sharing their vast repository of rare photographs and filling gaps in my narrative.

To the Indian Army for having taken me into their fold at Pune for over two years during which time the book was written, and for having respected me as a professional, I can only offer my dedication in the form of this book. I am indebted to the Indian Air Force for clearing the book. Had it not been for Air Chief Marshal Raha, the Chief of Air Staff, and Air Marshal Dhanoa, the vice chief, this book may not have seen the light of day. The National Defence College was the perfect place where I could give the finishing touches to this book and Lieutenant General Ghei, the commandant, has been most supportive of my endeavour.

Krishan Chopra, Siddhesh Inamdar and Bonita Vaz-Shimray at HarperCollins brought the narrative to life and helped me clear the minefield of publishing. The ever-cheerful warrant officer, Sahoo, the head of my office staff in Pune and Delhi, ensured that I never got hassled by routine administrative work.

I am indebted to my parents for encouraging a spirit of inquiry and challenging me to keep my passion for history alive. My wife Mowthika was a pillar of strength during these past three years of uncertainty. She handled the choppy waters with the dexterity of an experienced navigator on the high seas. My girls Shruti and Meghna jokingly called me a bipolar father during this critical period for them as teenagers. This book would not have been possible without their resilience and fortitude.

PHOTO CREDITS

I am grateful to the following organizations, units, regimental centres, fleets, squadrons and individuals for sharing photographs and helping with sketches so willingly. Their contributions added significant value to the narrative.

Ministry of Defence Photo Division and Armed Forces Film and Photo Division, special thanks to Major V.K. Singh (retd) and Mr Sreekumar

Air Force Museum and Institute of Flight Safety, Palam

Mr Gurbinder Dhillon

Squadron Leader Rana Chhina

Netaji Research Bureau

Kumaon Regimental Centre, Ranikhet

A.V.M. Vikram Singh

Parachute Regimental Centre

MEG Regimental Centre

BEG Centre

Armoured Corps Centre

Artillery Centre

Ladakh Scouts Centre

Eastern Naval Command

No. 1 Squadron, IAF

No. 4 Squadron, IAF

No. 12 Squadron, IAF

No. 14 Squadron, IAF

4 Mech Regiment (formerly 1 Sikh)

Photo archives of *The Hindu* (special thanks to N. Ravi and Pothen Jacob)

www.bharat-rakshak.com

Lieutenant General W.A.G. Pinto (retd)

P.V.S. Jagan Mohan

Group Captain Deb Gohain (retd)

Air Commodore Nagesh Kapoor

Eastern & Western Naval Command Archives

ABOUT THE AUTHOR

Air Vice Marshal **Arjun Subramaniam** is an accomplished military historian and the author of *Shooting Straight: A Military Biography of Lt Gen. Rostum K. Nanavatty* and the two-volume *India's Wars: A Military History*. Subramaniam was the President's Chair of Excellence in National Security Affairs at the National Defence College, New Delhi, from February 2021 to March 2023; a Visiting Fellow at the Harvard University Asia Center and the Changing Character of War Programme, Oxford University; and Visiting Professor, Fletcher School of Law and Diplomacy. He is currently a Visiting Faculty at Kautilya School of Public Policy, Hyderabad, and several war colleges across the three services.

HarperCollins *Publishers* India

At HarperCollins India, we believe in telling the best stories and finding the widest readership for our books in every format possible. We started publishing in 1992; a great deal has changed since then, but what has remained constant is the passion with which our authors write their books, the love with which readers receive them, and the sheer joy and excitement that we as publishers feel in being a part of the publishing process.

Over the years, we've had the pleasure of publishing some of the finest writing from the subcontinent and around the world, including several award-winning titles and some of the biggest bestsellers in India's publishing history. But nothing has meant more to us than the fact that millions of people have read the books we published, and that somewhere, a book of ours might have made a difference.

As we look to the future, we go back to that one word—a word which has been a driving force for us all these years.

Read.